ONE

Between Marx and Coca-Cola

Youth Cultures in Changing European Societies, 1960–1980

Edited by

Axel Schildt and Detlef Siegfried

Berghahn Books
New York • Oxford

Sponsored by the Fritz Thyssen Stiftung, Cologne

First published in 2006 by

Berghahn Books

www.berghahnbooks.com

Library of Congress Cataloging-in-Publication Data
Between Marx and Coca-Cola : Youth Cultures in Changing European
  Societies, 1960–1980 / edited by Axel Schildt and Detlef Siegfried.
    p. cm
  Includes bibliographical references and index.
  ISBN 10: 1-84545-009-4 (hbk.) -- 1-84545-333-6 (pbk.)
  ISBN 13: 978-1-84545-009-0 (hbk.) -- 978-1-84545-333-6 (pbk.)
  1. Youth--Europe. 2. Young consumer--Europe. 3. Youth--Europe--
  Political activity. 4. Popular culture--Europe. 5. Subculture--Europe.
  6. Social change--Europe. I. Schildt, Axel. II. Siegfried, Detlef.

HQ799.E9B47 2005
305.235'094'09045--dc22
                                                          2004055425

British Library Cataloguing in Publication Data
A catalogue record for this book is available from the British Library
Printed in the United States on acid-free paper

ISBN 10: 1-84545-009-4   ISBN 13: 978-1-84545-009-0   hardback
ISBN 10: 1-84545-333-6   ISBN 13: 978-1-84545-333-6   paperback

Contents

Acknowledgements

We would like to thank all those who contributed to the production of this volume – primarily those who presented papers, chaired sessions and participated in the discussions, at a stimulating conference in Copenhagen, May 2002. Furthermore, we very much appreciate those authors who subsequently joined this project. In particular, we are grateful to the Fritz Thyssen Stiftung, Cologne, for their generous financial support without which the conference could not have taken place nor this volume been published. We are also indebted to the Goethe-Institut and the German embassy in Copenhagen for their cooperation and hospitality. Hans Sørensen was a great help during the course of organizing the conference. Nora Helmli, Julia Kramer, Olaf Kruithoff, Birte Lotz, Peter Pritchard, Bernd Trommer, and Wayne Yung provided essential assistance during the translation and editing of the manuscript.

Axel Schildt and Detlef Siegfried
Hamburg/Copenhagen, December 2004

Youth, Consumption, and Politics in the Age of Radical Change

Axel Schildt and Detlef Siegfried

In his movie *Masculin—Féminin or: The Children of Marx and Coca-Cola*—a 1965 French-Swedish coproduction—Jean-Luc Godard depicts the complicated love affair of two "children of the 1960s," a young man with social interests and a young female pop vocalist, who regularly frequented Parisian coffee houses. The movie, blending fictional and documentary elements, dealt with the problem of navigating in a world in which politics involved individuals more than before and in which consumption on an unprecedented level opened up a myriad of opportunities to pursue one's life. The movie succeeded as a political commentary of its time and as a document of an age because, in a delightful manner, it pointedly gave a name to one of its time central spheres of tension. The paradigm "Marx" represented the renaissance of the political sphere, "Coca-Cola" stood for the growing importance of consumption—both images and icons of, above all, youth culture. In a handy title Godard integrated what many contemporaries had discerned as an evident characteristic of the time: that political transformations and changes within the culture of everyday life were evolving simultaneously and were merging with each other. In a report of the West German news magazine *Der Spiegel*, it was apparent that contemporaries were having a hard time coming to terms with this unfamiliar combination:

> The spectacle is confusing. Participants are a consuming and a demonstrating, a narcissistically self-involved and an activist engaging youth, Chelsea-girls and Red Guards, Rudi Dutschke and Twiggy.[1]

The reception of medially promoted youth idols—the Beatles for instance —and the international proliferation of new patterns of expression—the consumption of music for instance—as well as students' new forms of political protest ("1968") were considered as core elements of a new youth culture. Increasing focus on consumption and a coinciding increase of politicization—a relationship full of contradictions and tensions—were the unmistakable characteristics of the 1960s and the 1970s. Contemporaries of the period observed a particularly striking contradiction in this situation, which would play a large part in increasing social tensions during these two decades: on the one hand, youth were striving towards individual self-actualization like never before (because consumer society was presenting an unprecedented variety of possibilities towards achieving this goal); on the other hand, the rapid expansion of consumer choices (as touted by the industry) was developing into the guiding principle of mainstream life. This in turn was often seen as "manipulative," not least by the tone-setting cliques of the future elites.

Subcultures such as the hippies embodied a protest against mainstream society, which perpetuated the endless cycle of work and consumption. At the same time, members of these subcultures were using elements of consumer culture in the creation and promotion of their own styles. Many of these elements were in themselves neither political nor apolitical, but rather simply ingredients of a lifestyle revolution; as such, however, they became loaded with definite political subtexts. The consumer industry would then co-opt these subcultural impulses, making them available to a much larger audience of young people. In this way, subcultures infiltrated mass culture; but the subcultures regarded this as a commercial appropriation of originally oppositional styles, which destroyed their revolutionary potential. Therefore, new deviant styles had to be developed, to stand outside the established ones. This confrontation between mass culture and counterculture fostered an ongoing process of innovation. This contradictory state, which is still characteristic today, was particularly pronounced during its initial phase of evolution and, in numerous countries, it was at the center of vehement and controversial debates. Therefore, within this tense relationship between consumption and political interest—between overbearance by the cultural industry and self-realization—a transnational scope of problems becomes discernable, which is suitable as a backdrop for a comprehensive assessment of the various societies.

This volume intends to highlight, within an international comparative framework, some of the impacts of Western and Northern European youth cultures and their developing "partial culture" (Friedrich Tenbruck) in its "golden age" (Eric Hobsbawm) beginning in the late 1950s.[2] The 1960s and 1970s are generally held as decades of generational upheaval. On the whole, this process of upheaval has been understood as an internationally pertinent phenomenon and, in particular, it has been closely associated with the emergence of a postindustrial modernity.[3] As this assumption has not yet been studied in detail, this volume aims to look more closely at the extent to which these new kinds of youth cultures impacted the various national cultures at large, how far this process reflected instances of a "change in values," and to what extent this process was international in character. The goal of this volume is to create a multifaceted picture of the European youth cultures during a secular period of transition differentiated by gender, regional manifestation, social origin, and educational status.

The idea for such a systematic study developed in the wake of a conference on the societal transformation of the Federal Republic of Germany and the German Democratic Republic during the 1960s, which took place in Copenhagen in 1998.[4] This conference was part of an international effort occurring during that year to historicize the phenomenon "1968." It became apparent that members of younger age groups had to a significant degree impacted the beginning of the "postindustrial" transformation. This was discernable not only in the essentially simultaneous emergence of student movements the world over and in the development of specific youth cultures, but also in the fact that youthfulness evolved into an ideal—particularly in terms of beauty, patterns of consumption, and political styles—for societies at large. As such, for the study of the European youth cultures between 1960 and 1980, we adopted the hypothesis that extensive societal transformation and the development of new kinds of youth cultures could be a theme of strategic and central importance for the study of recent cultural history. We thus deliberated on this topic in our conference in Copenhagen in May of 2002, organized by the German Studies Department of the University of Copenhagen and the Forschungsstelle für Zeitgeschichte in Hamburg. Most of the contributions to this volume were presented at the conference. Other chapters were added to broaden the volume's thematic scope at those points where we thought it specifically necessary. This volume combines contributions from colleagues from Great Britain, Denmark, Italy, the Netherlands, the United States, and Germany, who all dealt with the trends of European youth cultures during the 1960s and 1970s from various perspectives. Their chapters include the debates inherent to many larger research endeavors—above all dissertations and "second books"—as well as analyses specifically written for this publication.

The lines of inquiry will unfold in five general directions. Part I examines the interrelationship between politics and consumption by using three interpretive strategies, which are central to understanding the time period under investigation. From varying points of departure, they converge upon the theme of this volume: Arthur Marwick begins by using the guiding principle of "Cultural Revolution" to explore the long years of the 1960s; Detlef Siegfried continues by discussing how the eruption of "1968" inserted itself into the dynamic upheavals of the "Golden Years"; and then Rob Kroes uses a broader chronological framework to deconstruct the concept of "Americanization," which seemingly found its most obvious expression in the Coca-Cola logo.

Part II uses various examples to show how new styles established themselves in the contested space between social discourse and consumer practice, altering societies in their self-perceptions. Peter Wicke describes this process by investigating pop music as a central component in the construction of youth leisure; Konrad Dussel examines the driving forces and counterforces that established the dominance of English-language pop music in German media; Axel Schildt shows how the spatial and experiential territories of youth expanded over time; and Uta Poiger describes how anti-consumerism became conflated with anti-imperialism in the analyses of the West German student movement, giving rise to a new, (self-)conscious mode of consumption.

Part III covers youth-influenced political protest movements, which were particularly strong in the 1960s and 1970s. Wilfried Mausbach looks at the West German movement against the Vietnam War, and how elements of consumer society combined with elements of a counterculture to create new cultural styles, which in turn developed their own politically explosive force. In his two-country comparison, Henrik Kaare Nielsen discovers national differences in techno-critical movements against nuclear power. Steven L.B. Jensen describes how Danish youth and student movements developed in the contested space between political rebellion and lifestyle revolution, while Thomas Etzemüller analyzes the specifics of the Swedish student movement.

Part IV highlights the transformation of gender definitions (of one's self and of others) in the 1960s and 1970s, which occurred partly under the banner of "the sexual revolution." Dagmar Herzog examines the introduction of the birth-control pill in the context of a consumer society: how it was portrayed, hotly debated, and also to some degree understood as part of a larger process of revolution. Barry Doyle describes changes in the conception of masculinity in Northern Soul, a subculture oriented towards music and dance; meanwhile, Julian Bourg shows how, in debates around pedophilia in the early 1970s, traditional sexual norms were thrown into flux by the foreshadowings of liberalism and emancipation.

Finally, Part V uses the examples of several counter- and subcultures to show how various significant trends in the development of youth cultures could be gathered and focused like light rays in a magnifying glass. Thomas Ekman Jørgensen describes the paradoxical relationship between consumerism and politics in Copenhagen's counterculture. Franz-Werner Kersting examines how the radical left attempted to undertake further reform projects which were at the same time bound up with the concept of revolutionizing society. In conclusion, Klaus Weinhauer takes the example of drug consumption, in which even a forbidden product found an enormously expanded market in consumer society, but which at the same time was restricted in its propagation—thus giving it political overtones.

Understanding Youth Culture

"Youth" and "youth culture" are terms that have been in use since the late nineteenth century, and assumptions about their meaning can vary significantly at times depending on the countries and the respective historical period. At the center of our interests are individuals roughly 14 to 25 years of age with divergent education, religion, social origin, social status, and gender. Within this diverse grouping, a mass culture was evolving in the late 1950s which was primarily defined by the young age of its proponents and by their particular tastes in music, fashion, hairstyles, political practices, etc.; this "youth culture," however, was itself very heterogeneous. Although various subcultures within this "youth culture" attempted to distance themselves from the norms of society (in part by establishing a "counterculture"), they remained connected to the larger society by various bonds: familial connections, cognitive principles, the media, and institutions such as schools and universities. It was precisely these bonds which enabled youth to contribute significantly to society's transformation. Therefore, the idea of "youth culture" is only useful when informed by this understanding of its internal diversity as well as its external interactions with society at large. However, the label "youth culture" remains appropriate for the project at hand as a convenient shorthand for this complex topic, because it succinctly signifies the core subject: young people's cultural and political preferences, which were to play a significant role in hastening social developments during the time period under scrutiny.

Whereas already during the first half of the twentieth century youthfulness and youth represented a foil for projections of political initiatives demanding renewal, these processes were reinforced even more so after the end of the Second World War. In numerous European societies, it was hoped that the younger generation would produce the desired awakening that would overcome the ceaseless alternation of war and crises which hitherto had characterized the history of Europe. During the 1960s and 1970s, this hope was apparently materializing itself when economic prosperity and political détente were becoming realities—trends that within this context were both connected to the younger members of society. The opposite point of view existed as well, manifest in concerns that the young generation could not fulfill such high expectations and would disperse in inopportune directions. Such concerns were becoming especially apparent when at the end of the 1960s the radicalization of a number of subcultures was progressively questioning the limits of the acceptable.

Because of the divergence of European societies, this volume cannot claim an all-encompassing systematic comparison. Instead, exemplary studies intend to determine problems within the field of study so that future research efforts encounter more familiar grounds. Notwithstanding, to examine the various European societies as specifically as possible, the collection of countries studied has been limited to core states of Western and Northern Europe: Sweden, Denmark, West Germany, Great Britain, and France. Thereby, the focus has been on that part of Europe, which, in general, has been understood as the major entry point for transatlantic cultural transfer usually associated with the term "Americanization."[5] At the same time, this volume does not dogmatically stick to this regional limitation. Numerous contributions also tie in other Western European countries—at times also the United States. The Northern and Central European countries stand at the center of this volume because that is where the processes of societal transformation in question found their strongest manifestation. In these countries, a high material standard of living, extended periods of education, secularization, and postindustrial lifestyles came about first and gained acceptance. Modern youth cultures proliferated extensively in these areas early on and often were given pertinent impetus for their further development. "Post-adolescent" spaces of freedom, in which such styles could develop and be practiced for an extended period of time, had an impact on young people's social realities in Scandinavia and in the aforementioned Western European countries stronger than, for instance, in Portugal, Italy, or Ireland, where poorer material and social conditions, lower educational status, as well as more restrictive religious and family bonds impeded the development of such spaces of freedom. However, by the end of the 1970s, these countries had closed the gap in most of these realms.[6] Processes of material improvement and "change in values" did not bypass Eastern European countries either, where youth cultures and cultural revolutions were mostly visible perhaps in Czechoslovakia and Hungary. Nevertheless, in these countries, severe political restrictions as well as economic and cultural-political measures caused significant impediments, which led, compared to the evolution of Northern and Western European societies, to different developments and manifestations.[7]

Still, although there were common features in the chosen time period which distinguished Europe and in particular the Western and Northern European countries from, for instance, the United States or Japan, a uniform manifestation of trends should not be expected.[8] Various societal patterns and specific national traditions had consequences on the concrete manifestation of the youth cultures in these countries so that a distinctive picture emerged in each country, regardless of their common features.

Similarly, the keystone years 1960 through 1980 have only been drawn coarsely, intended as soft demarcations so that enough leeway could be given to do justice to each country's individual caesuras. Significant supraregional transformations already began to occur during the latter third of the 1950s, notably the expansion of the educational sector and of mass communication, an improved supply of consumer goods as well as the emergence of popular youth magazines and new mass cultures for young people.[9] By the close of the 1970s and at the beginning of the 1980s, radical changes again occurred in the economic, political and youth-cultural realms: in many countries young voters in particular gained a new kind of political representation through the emergence of "green" parties. Pollution of the environment, intensified confrontation of the superpowers, another economic crisis including rising rates of unemployment as well as a societal loss of utopias denoted the conditions of an "ice age," which found its fitting atmospheric expression in occurrences such as punk music, squatting, and sinking election turnouts.[10] In regards to the time frame at hand, it was the start of the economic crisis in 1973/74 which finally marked the end of the long 1960s. However, the effects of the 1960s continued to be felt, only gradually transforming themselves. Therefore, the general time frame of the volume at hand was deliberately extended beyond the caesura of 1973/74 into the historiographic no-man's-land of the 1970s, in an attempt to capture these subsequent transformations.

Politics

Contemporaries had already realized that the post-Second World War societal evolution of Western industrialized nations were following increasingly similar patterns. While national specifics certainly remained, the process of European integration, the gradual establishment of democratic systems in all European states, and the development of consumer societies had led to significant convergences within the economic, the political, and the cultural realms and had pushed differences vis-à-vis the United States into the background. This process of convergence proceeded across some decades and it evolved in anything but a harmonious pattern so that there were times when its future course was unpredictable. In the political sphere, the process of modernization on the one hand ensued under the dominance of the Social Democrats—for instance, in Sweden and in Denmark—on the other hand, under conservative dominance—for instance, in France. Then again, it was accompanied by—temporary—changes of governments. In West Germany, the transition from the Adenauer administration's traditionalism via the conservative modernization under Chancellor Erhard to the modernization efforts of Brandt and Schmidt's social-democratic-liberal cabinets indicated that the societal impetus for modernization was putting pressure of accommodation on all major political parties which led to new political concepts. Within the progression of societal modernization, the integration within the European Union, the complete sealing off of the Eastern Bloc, and the breadth of mass media brought about the phenomenon that Western and Northern European spaces of engagement and mental horizons were predominantly oriented towards the West, encompassing other Western European countries as well as the United States.[11] Not until the mid-1960s would this scope also extend beyond the described boundary, when countries from the "Third World" and from beyond the "Iron Curtain" were drawn into an international frame of reference, pertinent for efforts of self-definition. At the same time, the de-escalation of the Cold War facilitated an internal liberalization of Western societies. During this situation of radical changes towards a "postindustrial" society, the aforementioned "change in values" came about, which, during the 1970s and 1980s, altered a number of behavioral standards as well as the collective self-images of Europeans.[12] The expansion of the scopes of opportunity stood in a dynamic relationship to the expansion of the scopes of expectation: because social agents utilized these new opportunities, new aspirations for the future as well as new expectations for reform materialized, which impacted the specific climate of these dynamic times. This phase came to an end when economic, ecological, and political "limits to growth" had apparently been reached.[13] Certainly, the economic crisis of the mid-1970s curbed the general euphoria for reforms, however, because the crisis denoted the material limits of the possible more clearly than before, it fostered the emergence of "postmaterialistic" attitudes, which focused less on the accumulation of consumer goods and focused instead on the improvement of the quality of life.

It was within this context that young people became considerably more interested in politics. However, this interest was expressed in diverse forms and to varying degrees, depending (not only, but above all) on the differences between the political cultures of various European nations. Therefore, election turnout and contentment with democracy (which reflected political interest, at least in part) were significantly higher in Denmark and West Germany than in France and the United Kingdom, during the time period under investigation.[14] Numerous empirical findings indicate that political interest rose with society's prosperity, the ratio of employees in the service sector, and with educational standing. At any rate, citizens' political interest grew dramatically between the late 1950s and the early 1970s. For instance, less than 30 percent of the population professed to be interested in politics in West Germany up until the year 1960. By the year 1973, this share had risen to nearly 50 percent where it would remain until the decade's end.[15] Young people showed considerably more political interest than the respective populations at large. Between the years 1963 and 1974, the share of those people who could envision themselves joining a political party rose most significantly among men up to the age of 24 years.[16] Within the younger age group, it was not just the men who set themselves apart in terms of their political interest but also those of above-average education. As part of a 1968-inquiry undertaken in West Germany, a comparison of the population at large, university-attending youths, and young people who were not enrolled determined that while 8 percent of the non-academic youths considered themselves to be "very strongly interested" in politics, 25 percent were among their enrolled age-peers, and 5 percent among the population at large. Still, as many as 17 percent of the non-academic young people considered themselves to be "strongly interested" (students 33 percent, population at large 9 percent).[17] In the year 1980, when this comparison was repeated, 25 percent of the citizenry expressed a "strong interest" in politics, 30 percent of young people, and 55 percent of students.[18] An international comparative study undertaken in 1976 asserted that 2.7 percent of the 12- to 23-year-olds interviewed in Germany, Great Britain, and France professed to be "very strongly" interested in politics, and another 8 percent were "strongly" interested. Political interest increased with age and differed between countries: according to this study, political interest was most developed among the French youths ("strong" and "very strong" accounted for a combined 13 percent) and German youths (12 percent); significantly less interested were youths of the British Isles (7 percent). The same scenario was true of the readiness for political engagement, which was the most manifest in France and barely developed in Great Britain.[19] Additionally, discrepancies along lines of social origin and gender were dramatic: in general, the political interest of older, better educated, and male youths was more pronounced than the interest of youths with little education or that of girls. A diachronic section over the years indicates that, on the whole, young people's political interest rose until the early 1970s, decreased slightly until the close of this decade, and picked up again during the early 1980s.

Demands for more direct democracy and individuals' readiness to become active were transforming the appreciation of politics during these years. From 1958 and far into the 1960s, the political activities of young people were particulary evident in for example the British "Campaign for Nuclear Disarmament" and in movements with similar objectives which ran parallel to or came about later in other European countries.[20] From the mid-1960s, the Vietnam War in particular drew a lot of the young people's protest efforts,[21] and they were also protesting against a number of specifically national issues such as the passage of the Emergency Laws in West Germany or racism in the United States, spearheaded by the Civil Rights Movement. During the course of the 1960s, various protest factions solidified and grew more radical resulting in a comprehensive critique of society such that between the years 1967 and 1969 reinforced by the proliferation of countercultural sentiments—the impression of an explosive "youth rebellion" came about.[22] By and large, the political upheaval was maintained by student protest at the universities or at institutions for secondary education, later also, albeit in different degrees, by a number of trainees and young employees. Another significant amalgamation of issues did not emerge until the environmental movement, which from the early 1970s onwards unfolded in the new form of grassroots-democratic citizen's initiatives.[23] In a number of countries, for instance in West Germany, such initiatives were associated with political elements of a wide-ranging alternative culture; in other countries such as Sweden, however, they were largely removed from such alternative cultures.[24] Roughly from the year 1969-at times in combination with such political movements, often, however, separate from them—movements of cultural upheaval had become more distinct from each other resulting in a sheer boundless colorful youth scenery, which attracted large crowds with hardly a common denominator nor really clear-cut political maxims.[25] British and French youths, to a much larger degree than young Germans, exercised fundamental criticism of their respective forms of government. In the year 1976, while 41 percent of 17- to 18-year-olds in Great Britain and 32 percent of their French age-peers had "a lot to complain," about only 11 percent of German 17- to 18-year-olds felt the same way. Also the degree of those who considered "everything [to be] in order," was significantly higher in Germany than in France and in Great Britain.[26] A significant share of the youth culture split from their respective adult societies were congregations around distinct styles of music which often developed idiosyncratic style repertoires in terms of clothing, hair fashion, social conduct, etc.[27]

Although the "long 1960s" had provided hitherto unknown opportunities for self-realization, processes of diversification, de-traditionalization, and individualization, these opportunities were realized within a flexible framework, impacted by origin of class and social stratum, by gender, by affiliation with certain social milieus, by experiences of war and migration, etc. Certainly, this framework was flexible within certain limits, but was not, however, arbitrarily variable. Indeed, the extreme class differences of the first half of the century had diminished in large areas; differences had become slighter due to the overall increase in quality of life. Still, lifestyles were still largely determined by social origin.[28] In the late 1960s and early 1970s, traditionalist attitudes were very common—not in the least, because societies were evolving increasingly and faster from their fundamental norms, thereby impeding societal transformation, sometimes dramatically. At the same time, however, they fell under increasing pressure. The rise of the extreme right-wing Nationaldemokratische Partei Deutschlands (established in 1964) in West Germany since the year 1966 and the British National Front (established in 1966) since the year 1972 signaled that not insignificant sections of the populations who stood against political and cultural westernization, increased immigration, and the rapid transformation of moral norms became radicalized—in particular during the latter half of the 1960s and the first half of the 1970s. During the course of the 1970s, revolutionary-nationalistic movements also attracted young people. From the point of view of the predominantly leftist young intellectuals, these developments indicated a threat for the democratic foundations of European societies, in particular because they appeared to coincide with the continuation of fascist dictatorships in Spain and Portugal as well as the Greek Obrist putsch under Colonel Georgios Papadopoulos of 1967. However, it was not just the Far Right that garnered success in mobilizing individuals for their causes under these conditions. A counter-reaction was developing during the 1960s within the moderate conservative camp as well that was forced to accommodate due to these rapid transformations, which it did more or less quickly. In a number of countries this strategy was quite successful and led to conservative majorities and changes of government, as for instance in Denmark in 1968, in the United States in 1969, and in Great Britain in 1970.[29] This political and cultural counter-reaction against a significantly increased pressure for modernization also became discernable in the enduring force by which de Gaulle's authoritarian regime maintained its position in France.

The Rise of Consumer Culture

Whereas the material, political, and cultural opportunities of the Western and Northern European societies were relatively restricted during the 1950s and were being questioned after their enormous expansion as of the mid-1970s, the decade in-between provided societies with apparently boundless possibilities so that contemporaries already spoke of the "golden years."[30] These years stood in stark contrast to the previous era because since the late-1950s the evidence of the postwar situation—which had severely imprinted the Central European countries—diminished and the fundamental patterns of political culture and lifestyles began to change radically,[31] as drives of prosperity and liberalization began to progressively overlay the deep-seated underlying patterns of European societies, in particular those affected by National-Socialistic policies of expansion and extermination as well as by war, exile, and banishment. In terms of economics, contemporaries benefited from a boom as of the latter third of the 1950s, manifested in qualitatively expanded safeguards—provision of food and shelter, secure old-age pensions, and full employment. Because the economic circumstances had by and large been stabilized, contemporaries had additional means at their disposal, which could be utilized for interests that were not essential for the assurance of one's existence. In most European countries, not only did the weekly hours of work decrease and weekends expand due to the free Saturday, but the numbers of vacation days also increased: in Germany and in Denmark by six days between the years 1958 and 1973, in France by as much as ten days on average.[32] The increasing budget for leisure activities was accompanied by an explosion of opportunities for the use of leisure time: television, increased mobility, and tourism served as the material basis.[33] Moreover, working conditions were transforming and the service sector was significantly gaining ground vis-à-vis the industrial sector and, above all, in relation towards the agricultural sector.

During the 1950s and 1960s, mass consumption took hold in the Western and Northern European countries after a roughly twenty-year lag in relation to the United States.[34] Once the essential means for livelihood had been safeguarded and citizens' financial means could be allocated for non-essential goods and services, the relative expenses for food decreased while the relative expenses for transportation, communication, and leisure rose, as did the expenses for rent and housing.[35] In West Germany between the years 1960 and 1970, the number of privately owned automobiles tripled from 4.5 million to 14 million; by the year 1980, there were 23 million privately-owned cars. In Great Britain, in France, and in Sweden, there were roughly twice as many cars in 1970 as in the year 1960 and by 1980, this number had increased further, even though by a lesser ratio than in West Germany.[36]

The socially underprivileged classes also benefited from this economic boom. Above all it was their increased purchasing power that contributed to the dramatically increased distribution rates of high-quality consumer goods and which led to a convergence of standards of living. In West German working-class households, the ownership of automobiles rose from 22 percent in 1962 to 66 percent in 1973, the ownership of television sets rose from 41 to 92 percent, of record players from 18 to 46 percent, and of telephones from 22 to 34 percent.[37]

The impact of such material improvement on European social cultures becomes apparent across the underlying conditions of consumption and the construction of lifestyles.[38] The materialization of 1960s' and 1970s' consumer society included improved methods of mass production and a broad range of goods, increasing international competition that resulted in falling prices, improved federal welfare measures that took the burden of individual households, a normative image of the citizen as an independently acting individual, and finally the competitive interaction with State Socialism, in which the weapon of "mass consumption" also played an increasingly important role.[39] Consumption no longer focused on the safeguarding of basic survival such as shelter, clothing, or food, but on, strictly speaking, dispensable things and possessions which could be arbitrarily combined: the nicer apartment, the more palatable food, the different clothes. It was the combination of excess and arbitrary selection that determined the distinct lifestyles— and that also revealed the "slight differences." The generational differences became very obvious in the different patterns of consumption, where young people certainly functioned as trendsetters. For among older people, frugality and thrift as well as an "ideology of saving up," which had been authoritative for a long time, still served as normative patterns of behavior. Consumer society was inevitably defined by a "culture of waste," which quickly—and in its stereotypical form—began to determine young people's standards of behavior.[40] Contemporary interpretations such as the one by the British publicist Peter Laurie highlight this phenomenon:

> The distinctive fact about teenagers' behaviour is economic: they spend a lot of money on clothes, records, concerts, make-up, magazines: all things that give immediate pleasure and little lasting use.[41]

Whereas older people were evaluating new consumer goods based on interpretative schemes which had evolved in times of war and times of crises, younger people were attaching their own interpretations which were "unspoiled" by any historical baggage. Beyond the purely material process of purchasing specific consumer goods, of interest is the extent to which these patterns helped shape the evolution and perception of following youth generations with respect to themselves and their perception of others. Materialism provided youths of the time with the potential for dissociation from constraints and for expansion of social and imaginary ties and scope of experiences. Consumer goods appeared to contribute to ideals such as social balance and justice; individualism and participation were becoming a reality.[42] Thus, the reception of mass media and increased motorization, for instance, facilitated a considerable increased mobility, an improved incorporation into communicative networks, and a cultural approximation of rural and urban age peers. Increased sizes of apartments afforded young people with separate spaces in which they could arrange themselves—unbothered by parents or siblings—according to their taste, could listen to their choice of music and pursue their hobbies. The increased use of cosmetics by girls and young women was a process of emancipation—it underscored their physical attractiveness and made them grow up earlier.[43] The emergence of new and diverse styles of fashion, often initiated by young rising stars of the fashion industry such as Mary Quant or Yves Saint-Laurent, contributed to soften considerable social discrepancies and promote an individualistic sense of life.[44] In addition, for some distinct subcultures, the consumption of drugs, which had been practiced mainly by young people since the latter half of the 1960s, became an essential element of their respective lifestyles, not the least because it triggered unconciliatory responses from older generations and from the state authorities.[45] While there existed dominant trends within this spectrum, there were no norms. The diversity of consumer goods at people's disposal afforded them with boundless varieties of combinations, which individuals utilized to distinguish themselves from others and to define their own identity. The creation of distinct styles evolved progressively more and more independently from parental oversight, from public institutions, or from youth organizations; instead they evolved among age peers—the importance of peer groups increased dramatically. In West Germany, for instance, the share of young people who considered themselves to be part of an informal group of peers—a clique—rose from 16.2 percent in the year 1962 to 56.9 percent in the year 1983.[46]

The emergence and spread of pop music played a central role for the formation of independent youth cultures.[47] Adding to the explosion of new styles from bands to electronically amplified music, as well as their distribution by radio, record, and television, was the development of new kinds of technology, from the portable battery-powered radio to the introduction of the music cassette in 1965, which further promoted mobility and significantly facilitated the independent production and reproduction of pop music. Finally, the introduction and proliferation of home stereo systems as a means for the superior enjoyment of music established new quality standards for the reception of music.[48] By noting to such devices as well as varieties of music, their respective clubs and concerts and their respective trends in clothes and haircuts, one could delineate boundaries of styles and social distinctions. To a considerable degree within this realm, young people's generational awareness developed and they separated themselves from the older generations. Numerous pieces of evidence indicate that the industry did by no means deal with their focus group in an arbitrarily "manipulative" manner. Rather, in a ceaselessly renewing spiral, the industry adopted cultural elements that had developed within youth subcultures, distributed them in modified shapes and in return influenced the taste of the masses.[49] At the same time, young recipients adopted such elements independently and combined them in a process of *bricolage* to suit very individual styles. By 1976, listening to music was the primary leisure activity of German, British, and French 17- to 23-year olds. Roughly 70 percent cited this as their primary hobby—listening to music ranked even higher than television and social outings.[50] However, pop culture, which had been establishing itself during the 1960s, did not evolve into a true mass culture until during the course of the 1970s, in particular during the 1970s' latter half when numerous styles coexisted and the disco wave was celebrating its breakthrough as a new mass trend.[51] Whereas pop music's important impulses had particularly originated in Great Britain in the early 1960s and since 1967 to a larger degree in the United States, as of the early 1970s, national styles progressively increased in European countries. These national styles were, on the whole, modifications of existing styles, however, with thoroughly independent profiles, which in part linked up with previously existing national traditions.[52]

A central characteristic of consumer societies is the existence of mass media, and of those increasingly sophisticated institutions which are responsible for loading consumer goods with signified meanings, and also for promoting the widespread dissemination of these meanings. Young intellectuals during the 1960s and 1970s specifically targeted the consumer goods industry, the advertising industry, advertisements in the mass media, and, thus, consumer society as a whole. Although they hardly drew on the Christian conservative *Kulturkritik*,[53] they did link up with the *Konsumkritik* of the Frankfurt school, which—based on a Marxist-inspired analysis of totalitarian tendencies—had been developed in American exile during the 1940s and had influenced the American social sciences significantly in the 1950s, via the highly acclaimed critical works of authors such as David Riesman, Vance Packard, and John Kenneth Galbraith. This criticism of the alienating effect of the "externally-led" individual by the presence by advertisements, media, and consumption gained footing on the European continent.[54] The "New Left" in all countries adopted this critique and made it more popular. During the 1960s, above all Theodor W. Adorno and Herbert Marcuse provided the theoretical inventory for the *Konsumkritik* of the Left—the latter, moreover, allied himself with students and evolved into a theoretical figurehead of the student movement in many countries. Their perception was that consumption did not contribute to the individual's emancipation, but on the contrary led to the individual's absorption into a conformist mass society and to the citizenry's depoliticization. General contemporary perception, however, contrasts significantly with this impression: consumer society did not limit the individual's agency, but on the contrary expanded it. Moreover, consumer expansion progressed hand in hand with increasing political interest.

Such ambiguities also became discernable in the practice of youth cultures that were critical of consumption. Among them, there were a number of such subcultures that adopted elements of the consumer society into their repertoire of conduct. This was even the case when youths such as American hippies or their European manifestations elevated defiant rejection of consumption to a core element of their agenda. Not only were specific kinds of pop music and the consumption of drugs parts of their stylistic repertoire but these youths also attended cinemas and pop concerts, purchased records and home stereo systems, buttons, posters, and jeans, traveled, used specific brands of automobiles, etc. Thereby, it became evident that there was no easy return to asceticism, but rather a differentiation of consumption. In these cases, consumption was provided with an "alternative" claim and thus remained compatible with the fundamental *Konsumkritik*. Inclinations towards American indigenous peoples, towards Far-East Asian religions, and in general the interest in the "Third World" as well as the romanticizing of the simple life were heaped together within this counter-movement against society's apparent addiction to consumption.[55]

Already during the 1970s, a tendency was making inroads that advocated critical consumption, not in the least, because the boundaries of the ecologically sustainable had become progressively apparent within this counter-movement. In the United States, a movement of "consumerism" had formed around the lawyer Ralph Nader that exposed self-interested advertisements of the industry, drew the attention to the unsafety of automobiles, organized boycotts of specific goods and services, and initiated actions for the protection of the environment.[56] This movement's impact was also felt in Europe and, consequently, the issues of consumer rights and consumer protection gained public interest, magazines dealing with these issues were published, and—in some European countries even more so than in the United States—an environmental movement, which was no youth movement per se, but dominated by young people, came about. The trend of politically motivated selective consumption was reinforced by the economic crisis in the years 1973/74, which also had a substantial impact on young people's lives.

Education

The significance of the influence of youth within the European societies of the 1960s and 1970s can in part be understood in the postwar "baby boom." The 1960s and 1970s were thus certainly socially affected by large youth generations. By the mid-1960s, Europe as a whole experienced a demographic decline, however, which had rather different longterm consequences on national developments. In Denmark and in France, the birthrates had already been declining since the beginning of the 1950s; in Great Britain and in West Germany, a significant drop was being recorded during the mid-1960s; and in Sweden, such a phenomenon was noted at the beginning of the 1950s and then again at the beginning of the 1970s. Roughly until the year 1980, the total number of births had considerably decreased, then subsequently slightly increased in some areas or remained stable at a low level.[57] Within the respective national public forums a gradually growing discourse was taking place, drawing increasing attention to the consequences of a gradually aging society (also due to the decline of the death rate). From the close of the 1950s until the years 1979/80, the share of those younger than 15 years old and the 15- to 29-year-olds averaged roughly 22 percent for the former, and together roughly 44 percent. In the years 1970/71, French (49 percent) and Danish populations (47 percent) were especially young; while West German (43 percent) and Swedish populations (44 percent) were relatively old.[58] Yet in this process, the respective demographic developments differed extremely from one another. For instance, in West Germany and in Great Britain, the share of those younger than 15 years old had increased during the course of the 1960s (even though, by the close of the 1970s it had diminished again), whereas in Denmark, Sweden, and France an uninterrupted decline was being recorded. Comparable fluctuations and dis-synchronicities could be observed for young adults aged between 15 and 29 years old: whereas their share in West Germany had declined until the years 1970/71 and was rising until the close of the 1970s, the development in Sweden and Denmark was the exact opposite. There, the 15- to 29-year-olds' demographic share rose until the years 1970/71 and then declined again until the years 1979/80. For Great Britain, a continuous increase was recorded. On the whole, the "long 1960s" were characterized in particular by the fact that European societies perceived themselves as young societies. Thus, the "growing 'visibility' of youth"[59] was not necessarily tied to demographic trends, but also to the fact that young people functioned as trendsetters of the general change in values (*Wertewandel*).

Still, the baby boom had consequences for European societies insofar as the generations coming of age "over-saturated" the existing educational institutions, not to mention the Cold War's political pressure, which demanded a rise in educational standards, and finally, prospering economies that were providing the necessary material basis for the expansion of the educational sector. Whereas the all-encompassing provisioning of elementary schools in Western and Northern European countries had already been secured during the first half of the twentieth century, access to secondary schools and, in turn, to the universities was opened wide during the 1960s and 1970s. In this realm, the starting positions in Great Britain were by far the best. Already during the first half of the 1950s, 34.3 percent of the 10- to 19-year-olds attended a secondary school, ten years later there were 43.4 percent, and by the first half of the 1970s, 51.1 percent.[60] In France, their share increased from 29.3 percent during the first half of the 1960s to 45.9 percent during the first half of the 1970s. In Denmark during the same time span, their share increased from 18.5 to 31.4 percent, in West Germany from 18.3 to 30 percent. Yet, such numbers hold only limited comparative value because the national educational systems differed from one another, notably even in terms of what was understood as secondary education. For example, the Scandinavian countries introduced a new schooling standard in the 1960s in which children spent nine years together in comprehensive school, with the subsequent option of attending three years in a school preparatory to university entrance; meanwhile, German children spent four years together in elementary school, with the subsequent option of nine years in *Gymnasium.* Nevertheless, the massive expansion of secondary education, which is clearly discernable in these figures, not only led to an improved level of education but also to the expansion of universities. In West Germany, the number of university students quadrupled from roughly 212,000 in 1960 to 818,000 in 1980; in France, this increase was even more pronounced from 211,000 to 864,000; in Great Britain from 130,000 to 340,000; and in Denmark from 10,800 to 49,100. The largest rates of increase were generally recorded during the 1960s. By the mid-1970s, the share of university students among 20- to 24-year-olds represented 10 percent in Great Britain, nearly 19 percent in the Netherlands, more than 19 percent in Sweden, 22 percent in Denmark, and almost 23 percent in France.[61] If one defined tertiary education more loosely and also included those who were studying at institutions that were training prospective teachers, the share was even higher: in 1978, the Federal Republic of Germany counted approximately 25 percent, Denmark and the Netherlands 28 percent, and Sweden nearly 36 percent. Altogether in Europe, the share of students in this age group rose at large from 7 percent during the year 1960, to 14 percent during the year 1970, and to 24 percent during the year 1978. Because of the increasing prevalence of advanced education, the younger age-groups were becoming more and more dominated by students attending school and university. Their share among the 5- to 24-year-olds was between two-thirds and four-fifths in the various countries of the European Community at the beginning of the 1980s.[62] Women in particular benefited from this expansion of the educational sector. 1980, the share of female university students generally represented 50 percent in the selected countries, with only the Federal Republic of Germany (41 percent), the Netherlands (40 percent), and Great Britain (37 percent) deviating from this ratio. The goal of also providing new opportunities for the classes that typically enjoy little formal education was only reached in part. Certainly, their opportunities for advancement increased positively; however, children from socially less-privileged classes remained under-represented among the students as well as among the leading elites of the European societies. In France for instance, only 15 percent of working-class daughters obtained a high-school diploma, whereas 72 percent of "upper-class" daughters acquired such a diploma, which was obligatory for admission to university.[63]

Sexual Liberation

One of the most striking characteristics of this age of radical change was that the variety of possible lifestyles for young people expanded dramatically. On the whole, the binding force of traditional social milieus—which had been determined by regional and familial bonds as well as by membership in social classes and affiliation with religious confessions—was slacking off. Next to traditional paradigms, in particular during the 1970s, new social milieus, which distinguished themselves through alternative styles of living, evolved.[64] Whereas children and youths during the first half of the twentieth century had grown up within larger families, often within a three-generation household, family sizes decreased thereafter. The share of households with five or more persons reduced between the years 1960 and 1980 from 14 to 8 percent in the Federal Republic of Germany, in Great Britain from 16 to 11 percent, in France from 20 to 12 percent, and in Sweden from 13 to 6 percent.[65] The share of smaller families and one-person households increased. Moreover, until the beginning of the 1980s, young people in most of European countries progressively moved out of their parental homes earlier; only afterwards did this trend turn around again. In contrast to the 1960s, cohabitation of unmarried partners was establishing itself as a generally accepted style of living during the course of the 1970s, in particular for young people. The Nordic countries were avant–garde in terms of actually practicing this style of living: in 1975, in Sweden and in Denmark as many as 29 and 30 percent respectively of 20- to 24-year-old women lived in nonmarital partnership. Other West European societies followed by a significant time lag and exhibited this phenomenon to a lesser degree. Whereas during the year 1972, for instance, only 1 percent of young women in West Germany lived with their partners without being married, by the year 1982, this share increased to 14 percent; in France, the share rose from 4 to 12 percent between the years 1975 and 1982; and in Great Britain, between the years 1975 and 1980 an increase from 4 percent to 6 percent was recorded.[66] Apartment-sharing communities, propagated by specific groups, predominantly young "counterculture," in West Germany, the Scandinavian countries, and the Netherlands as an alternative to conventional family structures played a central role for a certain period, remaining a more or less pragmatic form of living during the course of the 1970s particularly suitable for specific periods of individuals' lives such as the university years.[67] The diversification of lifestyles is a good indication that in many societal spheres accepted and relatively firmly established patterns of behavior were losing their inevitable obligation. The norms themselves were not dissolving in principle however, they were complemented with alternative options of behavior so that individuals had more choices than before and could combine different elements resulting in relatively unique styles.

One social movement that particularly contributed to transforming social realities was the "new women's movement," which developed within as well as outside of the student movement and specifically mobilized young women.[68] In contrast to the theoretical castles in the air of numerous luminaries of the student movement, the conflict between the sexes was, as Ulrike Meinhof put it,

> not imagined by reading: those who have families know [this conflict of the sexes] by heart, with the difference that, for the first time, it has been made clear that this private matter is no private matter at all.[69]

As a matter of fact, the new self-understanding of women, which initially intended to tackle all political problems with the "child question" in mind and which by these means demanded the transformation of societal standards, changed Western society more lastingly than the ideology-prone group fights of male revolutionaries. Political protests against traditional stipulations by proponents of the Rødstrømperne in Denmark, the Grupp 8 in Sweden, or the Women's Liberation in Great Britain went beyond achievements of a detached avant-garde; they were part and parcel of larger social and mental processes of transformation, which the relationship of the sexes had been undergoing since the late 1950s. The share of working women rose, not in the least because of the economy's need for labor, from 26.4 percent in the Federal Republic of Germany during the year 1950 to 36.5 percent in 1961 and to 40.9 percent in 1970—particularly in the service sector.[70] In the Scandinavian countries, this share rose much faster—due especially to federal initiatives. There, the imperfect equalization of the sexes was considered to be a deplorable state of affairs and the caring welfare states established schemes of legislative mechanisms and institutions, which facilitated the ability to enter gainful employment for women, such as adequate child care facilities and all-day schools, individualized taxation and generous regulations for receiving leaves. They were also advanced with respect to legislating sexual liberation—for instance, Sweden introduced sex education in 1955 and Denmark legalized pornography in 1967—without, however, necessarily leading to the capsizing of the citizenry's sexual norms in their day-to-day lives. Whereas in West Germany, women represented 37.8 percent of the gainfully employed persons in 1960, their share declined during the next decade to 36.6 percent in 1970 and then rose again to 38.1 percent in 1980. In Denmark, this share increased uninterrupted from a much smaller initial position of 30.9 percent during the year 1960 to 39.4 percent in 1970 and 44.5 percent in 1980.[71] These developments unfurled hand-in-hand with a transformation of consciousness. Whereas still as many as three-fourths of all West German men and women were of the opinion that women belonged into the home in the middle of the 1960s, one decade later, this had changed: in the 1970s, only 42 percent of men and 35 percent of women held on to the traditional gender roles.[72]

The protest against traditional gender roles became ignited, not least by the question of abortion. Already during the 1960s, the introduction of the "pill" had revolutionized a mechanism that until then had significantly defined the relationship of the sexes: sexuality could now be separated from reproduction more safely and women's fertility could be better controlled, thereby altering the self-image and the perception of, in particular, young, unmarried women.[73] The legalization of abortion, which had been prohibited in most of Western European countries, would additionally contribute to the process of progressively separating sexuality and reproduction and, thus, of further transferring these realms to individual control. A campaign of French women in 1971, which targeted the prohibition of abortion, also triggered a wave of protests in other European countries. During the course of the 1970s, a widespread network of initiatives against prohibition developed, usually organized by women's houses and women's centers and not necessarily inspired by feminism. In the wake of the "bloodless revolution" that traditional gender roles were experiencing, homosexual relations were also gradually more accepted.[74] The debate concerning sexual relations between adults and children, which was occurring throughout a number of European countries, possibly indicates most obviously how far the aversion against patronizing concepts of education and the conviction of each subject's autonomy reached.[75]

Mass Media

Mass media influencing norms of consumption and political-cultural norms, assumed a magnitude that can hardly be overestimated. The breakthrough of the television is one distinctive characteristic of the "long 1960s," which facilitated the general goals of democratization as well as the improved participation of the citizenry. In terms of the provision with television sets, Great Britain led the pack, already in the 1950s; by 1960, more than 10 million television sets had been reported—so that the rate of increase in the subsequent decade was smaller than in most of the other European countries—and in 1970, practically 16 million television sets were found in British homes.[76] The rest of Europe followed with a considerable time lag. In West Germany, the provision of households with television sets rose from 17.6 percent to 80.3 percent between the years 1960 and 1974.[77] Even more substantial than the rates of increase in West Germany—where the absolute number of households with television sets had a little more than tripled during the course of the 1960s—were those of Sweden, where the number increased more then fourfold; and in France, more than five times as many television sets were in homes in 1970 than ten years before—even though by 1967, the share of French households with television sets had amounted to only 53.5 percent (West Germany 58.7 percent).[78] Until the year 1980, the number of reported television sets further increased in all countries, although by considerably smaller rates.

Young people were not the main recipients of television programs; they watched less television than children or adults. On the one hand, this situation came about because activities outside of their homes were rather important to people of this age, but also on the other hand, because attractive programs for young people were few and far between. Young people watched news broadcasts and music shows that in particular and increasingly drew them to the small screens. Again, Great Britain was setting the example early on with shows such as *Six Five Special* (1957), *Oh Boy!* (1958), or *Ready, Steady, Go!* (1963). In France, *Salut Les Copains* (1959) followed with a small time lag. In West Germany, the *Beat Club* appeared on the small screen in 1965; a show that would evolve with the concept of an "authentic English Beat-show"—as the *New Musical Express* surmised at the beginning of the year 1968— into "the best of the bunch" and that would actually outperform the British competition.[79] In 1968, every show reached 75 million viewers. A number of television shows thereafter tried to combine pop and politics, but most of them did not survive past 1971.[80]

To a much larger extent than on television, pop music was present on the radio, in particular, on the programs of the American and British armed forces radio stations—AFN or BFBS—and, also very importantly, on pirate stations.[81] The latter's steep rise began during the year 1960 with the Dutch Radio Veronica, which broadcast also in German as of the year 1963, and with Radio Nord, the station that was located offshore of the Swedish coastline. In the following years, there were additional stations offshore of the Danish coastline.[82] During the year 1964, Radio Caroline and Radio London started their programs, which were exclusively based on pop music and financed through commercials. Radio Caroline broadcast daily between 6 AM and 6 PM and its broadcasts could be received in Southern England, in the south of Scandinavia, and on the European continent as far as the northwest of Germany. In May 1964, Radio Atlanta appeared as the second British pirate station. Both stations reached approximately 7 million listeners daily. One month later, in June 1964, "Screaming Lord" David Sutch, who had created quite a sensation because of his spectacular appearances at the Hamburg "Star Club," established a third British pirate station in the mouth of the River Thames. As of the summer of that year, the European Council intended to put a stop to this—not in the least also commercial—success resulting out of a boom of establishing pirate stations. For these private stations were serious competition for the publicly owned stations, above all with regard to the young audience, which held promises for the future and were setting future fashions. On 22 January 1965, seven member states of the European Council signed a European agreement on the prevention of radio broadcasts outside of national territories. During the month of August in 1966, the British Government—against the resistance of the conservative opposition—introduced a draft bill against pirate stations, of which ten existed in Europe broadcasting predominantly pop music, some of them twenty-four hours daily. In December 1966, the BBC announced that it would soon counter this tremendous competition with an own pop station, BBC Radio 1, which aired as of the fall of 1967. Within this period of time, the passage of a law in the British House of Commons dealt the decisive blow against the pirate stations, becoming effective on 15 August 1967, by declaring the provision of the ships and the broadcast of commercials illegal.

Meanwhile, pirate stations had shown the broadcast of pop music to be commercially successful precisely because there was such a large interest on the listener's side. Nonetheless, Radio Luxembourg remained among young people by far the most popular station.[83] A 1971 study of young radio listeners in North Rhine-Westphalia, West Germany's most populous state, concluded that 90 percent of all questioned had listened to Radio Luxembourg at least once in a while, a much larger share than all other stations could claim.[84] Responding to the question of which station they would chose if they could receive only one, two-thirds responded in favor of Radio Luxembourg.

Besides radio stations and the few youth shows on television, youth magazines evolved into important mediators of consumer culture and political standards within the young generation during the course of the 1960s. In West Germany, the magazine *Bravo*, which had been serving, above all, the younger audience since 1956 and which focused almost exclusively on pop music, stars, and the problems of teenagers, dominated the market, whereas the older and more intellectual youth were targeted by *Twen* between the years 1959 and 1971. As of the year 1964, the magazine *Konkret*, which was affiliated most closely with the student movement and the *Außerparlamentarische Opposition* (extra parliamentary opposition), had been evolving into a political lifestyle magazine. In France, this market developed a bit later in 1962 with the hugely successful magazine *Salut les Copains*. The following year saw the appearance of *Nous les Garçons et les Filles*, closely associated with the Communist Party, which combined pop culture and politics. Similar magazines also appeared in Italy (*Nuova Generazione*) and in the Federal Republic of Germany (*Elan*). The Catholic Church in France and in West Germany attempted to keep up with youth culture's contemporary developments by relaunching their respective youth magazines. Pure music magazines such as *Melody Maker*, and later *Pop* or *Popfoto*, served the increasing market of pop music consumers. Around about 1968, music magazines began to appear that also assumed a political stance such as the West German magazine *Sounds*. An entirely separate market developed through the emergence of numerous underground magazines, which popped up all over the place during the latter half of the 1960s. Among them were magazines such as the *International Times*, *Oz* (both from Great Britain), *Hotcha* (Switzerland), *Päng* (West Germany), or *Superlove* (Denmark), some of which had large circulations.[85] However, the variety of youth-oriented print-media outlets, which were flooding the magazine market during the 1960s and 1970s, should not obscure the fact that a considerable share of the target group rarely picked up such periodicals. In the year 1976, 63 percent of the British, 45 percent of the French, and 27 percent of the West German 12- to 23-year-olds declared they had never read youth magazines. On a regular basis, youth magazines were read only by 17 percent of German youths, 5 percent of British youths, and 4 percent of French youths.[86]

Travel

Following the end of the Second World War, exchange relations between European countries increased considerably, in part a result of the Cold War and in part by the process of European integration. In the economic sphere, these trends were fostered by the proliferation of mass consumption and of mass culture, which initially originated from the United States. During the course of the 1950s, opinion polls in West Germany ascertained that three-fourths of the West German population had never been to a foreign country. And 70 percent of the German men who had been abroad, had been there during times of war—a great number of them as soldiers of the *Wehrmacht*. Only 26 percent had been outside their native country for work–related reasons or because of tourism.[87] This scenario was to undergo fundamental changes during the 1960s and 1970s—propelled by the young generation—with, however, significant national differences. By the year 1976, 76 percent of West German, 67 percent of French, and 56 percent of British youths had traveled to foreign countries. Thirty-two percent of young West Germans had been to France and 15 percent had been to Great Britain. In Great Britain, this ratio was rather similar—32 percent had been to France and 12 percent to West Germany—whereas in France, it was more evenly distributed—24 percent had been to West Germany and 20 percent to Great Britain.[88]

Since the end of the 1950s, student exchanges increased as well. Whereas in 1960, 117,000 foreign students were enrolled in European universities, in 1973, they rose to 279,000.[89] For instance, roughly 7,000 West German students were enrolled in universities in other European countries during the 1960s, while some 11,000 students from those countries were attending West German universities.[90] In particular, the 1963 established and well-endowed Deutsch-französisches Jugendwerk—one core element of the institutionally promoted European integration—increased the rapid growth of international youth encounters. In 1975, the Nordic Council introduced an initiative to improve inter-Scandinavian student exchanges. In the following year, roughly half of all foreign students enrolled in Danish universities were from the other Scandinavian countries. During this time, the political focus on Western Europe was also impacted on the level of day-to-day experiences.[91] London and Paris became the most popular destinations among West German youths. Above all, the expansion of English education in schools, but also the attendance of British-language schools tremendously fostered communicative abilities. The share of those West Germans who could communicate fairly well in English rose from 13 percent to 20 percent between the years 1958 and 1966 and to 30 percent by 1975, with considerably higher shares among young people amounting to 37 percent in 1966 and 55 percent in 1975. However, until the year 1990, this share rose only by a little bit to 60 percent.[92] In 1976, 53 percent of the 17- to 18-year-old Germans declared themselves able to read an English newspaper, a feat that also 33 percent of their French age peers felt capable of. However, only 19 percent of Germans felt they had comparable knowledge of French, compared to 27 percent of the British. Finally, German-language news reports hardly reached French youth (10 percent) or British youth (8 percent).[93]

Whether travel to foreign countries and improved knowledge of foreign languages contributed to the decline of intercultural prejudices is still contested. At any rate, a causal connection of these phenomena cannot be assumed. However, it can be said that the mutual perceptions of the various national populations improved during the course of the 1960s and 1970s. For instance, at the end of the 1960s, West German prejudices were without exception more positive than at the end of the 1950s, manifest particular in their attitudes towards the French and the Russians, although less pronounced vis-à-vis the Americans.[94] This already indicates that the apparent "openness" towards American cultural imports, particularly by young people, does not (by extension) imply an unconditional "Americanization" of West German culture. Between the polar extremes of cultural "Americanization" and political "anti-Americanism" there developed a great many hybrid styles in everyday culture, mixing various elements of various Western and specifically national traditions.

Concluding Remarks

Our succinct *tour d'horizon* of Western and Northern European youth cultures of the 1960s and 1970s indicates that the tense relationship between a rising focus on consumption and a rising politicalization provides a fruitful analytical approach for the investigation of this age's specific signature. The simultaneity of these two developments was one of its central characteristics, heuristically combining the political, social, and cultural realms. Moreover, this combination may provide clues for the understanding of the various lifestyles' diverse and distinguishing characteristics.

So far, it has been largely sociological research which has put forward (and also partly challenged) the claim that generational procession was a major factor in the "value shift" from materialistic to more postmaterialistic values. This particular research has generally focused on time frames which begin in the early 1970s. Similar time frames are treated by those sociological studies which have examined the process of transformation from the more stable and fixed sociocultural milieus of the classical modern period to more unstable and fluctuating social milieus marked by subcultural influences. A historiographic assessment of these sociological theses—as this volume attempts by focusing on the relationship of politics and consumption—practically confirms the assumptions of a considerable societal transformation, which has been advanced and strongly imprinted by the young generation. Nevertheless, there is still plenty of research to be done. In particular, there is a lack of studies that assess and specify these sociological theses, which are mainly based on quantitative research, by expanding their quantitative data's time frame through the inclusion of the "long 1960s" as well as by the inclusion of qualitative data. For such studies, there are a variety of available sources, among them, for instance, numerous contemporary studies of the empirical social sciences, which need to be analyzed anew, based on the current knowledge of the longterm developments. Studies which deal within a national or international comparative framework with the processes of transformation within socially, politically, or culturally marked milieus, should be very worthwhile. Not in the least to discern such longterm processes of transformation, it makes a lot of sense to even go beyond the periodical limits of the "long 1960s."

Based on previous and current research, a number of future paths for research become apparent. So far, only a few studies have dealt empirically with the question in which relationship cultural changes "from above"—initiated by the media and the cultural industry—and those "from below"—initiated by young people as instigators of this development —related to one another. Part of this question is also how public discourses on and about youth related to young people's perception of themselves. Moreover, it still needs to be studied how and why the evolution of specific styles and subcultures occurred, based on which determining factors, under which temporal conditions, and by which means these processes of material improvement were culturally realized. Whereas the "Americanization" of European youth cultures drew a significant amount of attention during the previous years, it has been hardly studied to what extent specifically Western European and national cultural trends blended with this impetus for "Americanization" or to what extent they could establish themselves as independent cultural spheres or—as the case may be—even as realms of opposition. European youth cultures also provide a rather worthwhile research corpus for the question of how the relationship of the public and the private spheres changed without apparently destabilizing the democratic patterns of the European societies—actually, it resulted in very much the opposite. And finally, regardless of the impetus to historicize nearly everything that has to do with "1968," it is still not satisfactorily explained how cultural liberalization and political radicalization related to one another.

Notes

1. *Der Spiegel* 20 (1967), 41, 156.
2. For recent studies that focus on transforming youth cultures within the given time frame, see Arthur Marwick, *The Sixties, Cultural Revolution in Britain, France, Italy, and the United States, c.1958–c.1974* (Oxford, 1998); Bill Osgerby, *Youth in Britain since 1945* (Oxford, 1998); Niels Martinov, *Ungdomsprøret i Danmark. Et portræt af årene, der rystede musikken, billedkunsten, teatret, litteraturen, filmen og familien* (Copenhagen, 2000); Detlef Siegfried, "Vom Teenager zur Pop-Revolution. Politisierungstendenzen in der westdeutschen Jugendkultur 1959 bis 1968," in *Dynamische Zeiten. Die 60er Jahre in den beiden deutschen Gesellschaften*, ed. Axel Schildt, Detlef Siegfried, and Karl Christian Lammers (Hamburg, 2000), 582–623; Thomas Etzemüller, *Ein 'Riß' in der Geschichte? Gesellschaftswandel und 68er-Bewegungen in Schweden und Westdeutschland* (Konstanz, 2004).
3. Alain Touraine, *La Société post-industrielle* (Paris, 1969); Daniel Bell, *The Coming of Post-Industrial Society: A Venture in Social Forecasting* (New York, 1973); Claus Leggewie, "A Laboratory of Postindustrial Society. Reassessing the 1960s in Germany," in *1968. The World Transformed*, ed. Carole Fink, Philipp Gassert, and Detlef Junker (Washington D.C., Cambridge, 1998), 277–94.
4. The results of this conference are documented in Schildt, Siegfried, and Lammers, *Dynamische Zeiten*.
5. R. Kroes, W. Rydell, and F. J. Bosscher, eds., *Cultural Transmissions and Receptions. American Mass Culture in Europe* (Amsterdam, 1993); Kaspar Maase, *Bravo Amerika. Erkundigungen zur Jugendkultur der Bundesrepublik in den fünfziger Jahren* (Hamburg, 1992); Rolf Lundén and Erik Åsard, eds., *Networks of Americanization. Aspects of the American Influence in Sweden* (Uppsala, 1992); Alf Lüdtke, Inge Marßolek, and Adelheid von Saldern, eds., *Amerikanisierung. Traum und Alptraum im Deutschland des 20. Jahrhunderts* (Stuttgart, 1996); Tom O'Dell, *Culture Unbound. Americanization and Everyday Life in Sweden* (Lund, 1997); Anselm Doering-Manteuffel, *Wie westlich sind die Deutschen? Amerikanisierung und Westernisierung im 20. Jahrhundert* (Göttingen, 1999). See also Rob Kroes's contribution in this volume, ch. 3.
6. Compare Victor Scardigli, *L'Europe des modes de vie* (Paris, 1987).
7. For the differences and commonalities, see these works which present East and West Germany on a comparative basis, which is especially fruitful in this context: Michael Rauhut, *Beat in der Grauzone. DDR-Rock 1964 bis 1972—Politik und Alltag* (Berlin, 1993); Uta G. Poiger, *Jazz, Rock, and Rebels. Cold War Politics and American Culture in a Divided Germany* (Berkeley, Los Angeles, and London, 2000).
8. Hartmut Kaelble, *Auf dem Weg zu einer europäischen Gesellschaft. Eine Sozialgeschichte Westeuropas 1880–1980* (Munich, 1987); Kaelble, "Europäische Vielfalt und der Weg zu einer europäischen Gesellschaft," in *Die westeuropäischen Gesellschaften im Vergleich*, ed. Stefan Hradil and Stefan Immerfall (Opladen, 1997), 27–70.
9. Axel Schildt and Arnold Sywottek, *Modernisierung im Wiederaufbau. Die westdeutsche Gesellschaft der 50er Jahre* (Bonn, 1993); Marwick, *The Sixties*; Schildt, Siegfried, and Lammers, eds., *Dynamische Zeiten*. For West Germany, compare also Ulrich Herbert, ed., *Wandlungsprozesse in Westdeutschland. Belastung, Integration, Liberalisierung 1945–1980* (Göttingen, 2002).
10. On the 1970s in Great Britain, see George McKay, *Senseless Acts of Beauty: Cultures of Resistance Since the Sixties* (London, 1996); for West Germany, see the contributions in *Archiv für Sozialgeschichte* 44 (2004). "*Eiszeit*" was the title of a song released in 1980 by the West German band Ideal.

11. Anselm Doering-Manteuffel, *Wie westlich sind die Deutschen?* Also, see Axel Schildt, "Sind die Westdeutschen amerikanisiert worden? Zur zeitgeschichtlichen Erforschung kulturellen Transfers und seiner gesellschaftlichen Folgen nach dem Zweiten Weltkrieg," *Aus Politik und Zeitgeschichte* 50 (2000): 3–10.

12. Ronald Inglehart, *Kultureller Umbruch. Wertewandel in der westlichen Welt* (Frankfurt am Main and New York, 1989); Helmut Klages, ed., *Werte und Wandel. Ergebnisse und Methoden einer Forschungstradition* (Frankfurt am Main and New York, 1992); Ronald Inglehart, *Modernisierung und Postmodernisierung. Kultureller, wirtschaftlicher und politischer Wandel in 43 Gesellschaften* (Frankfurt am Main and New York, 1998).

13. Donella H. Meadows and Dennis L. Meadows, eds., *The Limits to Growth: A Report for The Club of Rome's Project on the Predicament of Mankind* (New York, 1972).

14. On this issue, compare studies dealing with European societies' different "political cultures." For Great Britain, the Federal Republic of Germany, and Italy see Gabriel A. Almond and Sidney Verba, *The Civic Culture. Political Attitudes and Democracy in Five Nations* (Boston, 1965); Gabriel A. Almond and Sidney Verba, *The Civic Culture Revisited. An Analytic Study* (Boston, 1980); for a focus on EU-nations see Peter Reichel, ed., *Politische Kultur in Westeuropa. Bürger und Staaten in der Europäischen Gemeinschaft* (Frankfurt am Main and New York, 1984); Oscar W. Gabriel, "Politische Einstellungen und politische Kultur," in *Die EG-Staaten im Vergleich. Strukturen, Prozesse, Politikinhalte,* ed. Oscar W. Gabriel (Opladen, 1992), 95–131.

15. Elisabeth Noelle and Erich Peter Neumann, eds., *Jahrbuch der öffentlichen Meinung 1968–1973* (Allensbach and Bonn, 1974), 213; Thomas Gensike, "Sozialer Wandel durch Modernisierung, Individualisierung und Wertewandel," *Aus Politik und Zeitgeschichte* 42 (11 October 1996): 12.

16. From 28 percent to 42 percent, while the average percentage for the population at large rose only from 11 percent to 12 percent (Roland Ermrich, *Basisdaten zur sozioökonomischen Entwicklung der Bundesrepublik Deutschland* [Bonn-Bad Godesberg, 1974], 594).

17. Rudolf Wildenmann and Max Kaase, *"Die unruhige Generation." Eine Untersuchung zu Politik und Demokratie in der Bundesrepublik* (Mannheim, 1968), 34f.

18. Walter Jaide and Hans-Joachim Veen, *Bilanz der Jugendforschung. Ergebnisse empirischer Analysen in der Bundesrepublik Deutschland von 1975 bis 1987* (Paderborn, 1989), 197.

19. Jugendwerk der Deutschen Shell, ed., *Jugend in Europa. Ihre Eingliederung in die Welt der Erwachsenen. Eine vergleichende Analyse zwischen der Bundesrepublik Deutschland, Frankreich und Großbritannien,* vol. 2 (Hamburg, 1977), 77. Also, compare the overview in Henk Dekker, "Political Socialization in Europe," in *Politics and the European Younger Generation. Political Socialization in Eastern, Central, and Western Europe,* ed. Henk Dekker and Rüdiger Meynberg (Oldenburg, 1991), 318–50.

20. Nick Thomas, *Protest Movements in 1960s West Germany: A Social History of Dissent and Democracy* (Oxford and New York, 2003).

21. For the movement against the Vietnam War, see Wilfried Mausbach's contribution in this volume, ch. 8.

22. See Detlef Siegfried's contribution in this volume on the issue of youth rebellion, ch. 2.

23. See Henrik Kaare Nielsen's contribution in this volume, ch. 9.

24. Etzemüller, "Gesellschaftlicher Umbruch," 207f. For an examination of the Swedish student movement see Thomas Etzemüller's chapter in this book, ch. 11.

25. Thomas Ekman Jørgensen's and Steven L.B. Jensen's contributions in this volume, ch. 15 and 10, present impressive examples of local countercultures from different perspectives.

26. Jugendwerk der Deutschen Shell, *Jugend in Europa,* vol. 2, 80.

27. Barry Doyle's chapter in this volume, ch. 14, presents an instructive example of such a subculture.

28. Pierre Bourdieu, *Die feinen Unterschiede. Kritik der gesellschaftlichen Urteilskraft* (Frankfurt am Main, 1987; originally published in French in 1979).

29. For the United States, see Mary Brennan, *Turning Right in the Sixties. The Conservative Capture of the GOP* (Chapel Hill and London, 1995); for Great Britain see Dominik Geppert, *Thatchers konservative Revolution. Der Richtungswandel der britischen Tories 1975–1979* (Munich, 2002).

30. Noelle and Neumann, *Jahrbuch der öffentlichen Meinung,* 209. On the role of youth in this cultural revolution of the 1960's see Arthur Marwick's chapter, ch. 1, in this book.

31. Klaus Naumann, ed., *Nachkrieg in Deutschland* (Hamburg, 2001). Compare also Robert G. Moeller, *War Stories. The Search for a Usable Past in the Federal Republic of Germany* (Berkeley, 2001).

32. Roland Ermrich, *Basisdaten,* 322.

33. Axel Schildt, *Moderne Zeiten. Freizeit, Massenmedien und "Zeitgeist" in der Bundesrepublik der 50er Jahre* (Hamburg, 1995); Hartmut Kaelble, "Europäische Besonderheiten des Massenkonsums 1950–1990," in *Europäische Konsumgeschichte. Zur Gesellschafts- und Kulturgeschichte des Konsums (18. bis 20. Jahrhundert),* ed. Hannes Siegrist, Hartmut Kaelble, and Jürgen Kocka (Frankfurt am Main and New York, 1997), 169–203.

34. For a seminal contemporary analysis, compare George Katona, *The Mass Consumption Society* (New York, 1964); Jean Baudrillard, *La société de consommation. Ses mythes. Ses structures* (Paris, 1970).

35. Hartmut Kaelble, ed., *Der Boom 1948–1973. Gesellschaftliche und wirtschaftliche Folgen in der Bundesrepublik Deutschland und Europa* (Opladen, 1992); Sabine Haustein, "Westeuropäische Annäherungen durch Konsum seit 1945," in *Gesellschaften im Vergleich. Forschungen aus Sozial- und Geisteswissenschaften,* ed. Hartmut Kaelble and Jürgen Schriewer (2nd rev. ed., Frankfurt am Main, 1999), 353–90. For the significance of the improved provision of goods of the material culture, see Wolfgang Ruppert, ed., *Fahrrad, Auto, Fernsehschrank. Zur Kulturgeschichte der Alltagsdinge* (Frankfurt am Main, 1993).

36. B.R. Mitchell, *International Historical Statistics Europe 1750–1993* (4th ed., London, 1998), 735ff.

37. Roland Ermrich, *Basisdaten,* 559. For pertinent statistics on the development of the time period's social culture in Europe, see Alexander Szalai, ed., *The Use of Time. Daily Activities of Urban and Suburban Populations in Twelve Countries* (The Hague, 1972); Statistisches Amt der Europäischen Gemeinschaften, ed., *Sozialindikatoren für die Europäische Gemeinschaft 1960–1975* (Luxembourg, 1980); Michel Gyory and Gabriele Glas, *Statistiken der Filmindustrie in Europa* (Bruxelles, 1992).

38. Already the Dutch sociologist Ernest Zahn studied the connection of rising material prosperity and the transformation of lifestyles in Europe. See Ernest Zahn, *Soziologie der Prosperität. Wirtschaft und Gesellschaft im Zeichen des Wohlstandes* (2nd ed. Munich, 1964; originally published in 1960). Also, compare Axel Schildt, "Europa als visionäre Idee und gesellschaftliche Realität. Der westdeutsche Europadiskurs in den 50er Jahren," in *Das europäische Projekt zu Beginn des 21. Jahrhunderts,* ed. Wilfried Loth (Opladen, 2001), 99–117.

39. Mary Douglas and Baron Isherwood, *The World of Goods. Towards an Anthropology of Consumption* (New York, 1979); Michael Wildt, *Am Beginn der "Konsumge-*

sellschaft. "Mangelerfahrung, Lebenshaltung, Wohlstandshoffnung in Westdeutschland in den fünfziger Jahren (Hamburg, 1994); Siegrist, Kaelble, and Kocka, *Europäische Konsumgeschichte*; Arnold Sywottek, "From Starvation to Excess? Trends in the Consumer Society from the 1940s to the 1970s," in *The Miracle Years: A Cultural History of West Germany, 1949–1968*, ed. Hanna Schissler (Princeton, N.J, 2001), 341–58. For the history of pertinent terminology, consult Ulrich Wyrwa, "Consumption, Konsum, Konsumgesellschaft. Ein Beitrag zur Begriffsgeschichte," in *Europäische Konsumgeschichte*, ed. Siegrist, Kaelble, and Kocka, 747–62.

40. Jürgen Reulecke of the University of Siegen (Germany) drew attention to this phenomenon at the conference in Copenhagen.

41. Peter Laurie, *The Teenage Revolution* (London, 1965), 9, cited in Osgerby, *Youth in Britain*, 37.

42. For the significance of material culture in the 1960s, see Wolfgang Ruppert, ed., *Um 1968. Die Repräsentation der Dinge* (Marburg, 1998).

43. For aspects of gender in the history of consumer cultures, compare Victoria de Grazia, with Ellen Furlough, ed., *The Sex of Things. Gender and Consumption in Historical Perspective* (Berkeley, 1996); Erica Carter, *How German Is She? Postwar West-German Reconstruction and the Consuming Woman* (Ann Arbor, 1997).

44. Compare Marwick, *The Sixties*, 404ff; for a sketch on France compare Dominique Veillon, "Corps, beauté, mode et modes de vie: du 'plaire au plaisir' à travers les magazines féminins (1958–1975)," in *Les Années 68. Le temps de la contestation*, ed. Geneviève Dreyfus-Armand et al. (Brussels, 2000), 161–77. Also, see Paul Yonnet, *Jeux, modes et masses. La société française et le moderne 1945–1985* (Paris, 1985), 295ff.

45. This topic is discussed by Klaus Weinhauer in this volume, ch. 17.

46. Klaus R. Allerbeck and Wendy J. Hoag, *Jugend ohne Zukunft? Einstellungen, Umwelt, Lebensperspektiven* (Munich, 1985), 38ff.

47. See Peter Wicke's contribution in this volume, ch. 4.

48. On home stereo systems, consult Stefan Gauss, "Das Erlebnis des Hörens. Die Stereoanlage als kulturelle Erfahrung," in *Um 1968*, ed. Ruppert, 65–94.

49. Detlef Siegfried, "Modkultur, kulturindustri og venstrefløjen i Vesttyskland 1958–1973," *Den Jyske Historiker* 101 (2003): 68–94. More on the development of the music industry can be found in R. Serge Denisoff, *Solid Gold. The Popular Record Industry* (New Brunswick, 1975); for Great Britain see Michael Cable, *The Pop Industry Inside Out* (London, 1977).

50. Jugendwerk der Deutschen Shell, *Jugend in Europa*, vol. 2, 47.

51. Imports of records could serve as indicators: in West Germany, they amounted to $27 million in 1970, $90 million in 1975, and $346.9 million in 1980 (in France for the same years: $25.3 million, $66.6 million, and $206.5 million; in Great Britain $28.3 million, $98 million, and $313.2 million). Compare Marianne Beisheim et al., *Im Zeitalter der Globalisierung? Thesen und Daten zur gesellschaftlichen und politischen Denationalisierung* (Baden-Baden, 1999), 98.

52. For such national counter-reactions, compare Victoria de Grazia, "Amerikanisierung und wechselnde Leitbilder der Konsum-Moderne (*consumer-modernity*) in Europa," in *Europäische Konsumgeschichte*, ed. Siegrist, Kaelble, and Kocka, 109–38.

53. Which lamented the dissolution of traditional systems of maintaining orderliness, which in many instances had still been setting the tone during the previous decade, and which had also raised its voice loudly and clearly during the 1960s. See Michael Ermath, "'Amerikanisierung' und deutsche Kulturkritik 1945–1965. Metastasen der Moderne und hermeneutische Hybris," in *Amerikanisierung und Sowjetisierung in*

Deutschland 1945–1970, ed. Konrad H. Jarausch and Hannes Siegrist (Frankfurt am Main and New York, 1997), 315–34.

54. David Riesman, *The Lonely Crowd. A Study of the Changing American Character* (New Haven, 1950); Vance Packard, *Hidden Persuaders* (New York, 1957); John Kenneth Galbraith, *The Affluent Society* (New York, 1958). On the increasing proliferation of societal-critical ideas, compare the essay by Michel Trebitsch, "Voyages autour de la révolution. Les circulations de la pensée critique de 1956 à 1968," in *Les Annèes 68*, ed. Dreyfus-Armand, 69–88.

55. See Uta G. Poiger's and Franz-Werner Kersting's contributions ch. 7 and 16 in this volume for more information on these topics.

56. David A. Aaker and George S. Day, eds., *Consumerism. Search for the Consumer Interest* (New York, 1982; originally published in 1971).

57. Ansley J. Coale and Susan Cotts Watkins, eds., *The Decline of Fertility in Europe: The Revised Proceedings of a Conference on the Princeton European Fertility Project* (Princeton, 1986); Wolfram Fischer, ed., *Europäische Wirtschafts- und Sozialgeschichte vom Ersten Weltkrieg bis zur Gegenwart* (Stuttgart, 1987), 23; Beisheim et al., *Im Zeitalter der Globalisierung?*, 492ff.; Charlotte Höhn, "Bevölkerungsentwicklung und demographische Herausforderung," in *Die westeuropäischen Gesellschaften*, ed. Hradil and Immerfall, 71–96.

58. Statistisches Bundesamt, ed., *Statistisches Jahrbuch für die Bundesrepublik Deutschland 1959* (Stuttgart and Mainz, 1959), 21*; ibid., *Statistisches Jahrbuch für die Bundesrepublik Deutschland 1973*, 29*; ibid., *Statistisches Jahrbuch für die Bundesrepublik Deutschland 1981*, 635f.

59. Osgerby, *Youth in Britain*, 17ff.

60. Fischer, *Europäische Wirtschafts- und Sozialgeschichte*, 75ff.; Gerold Ambrosius and William H. Hubbard, *Sozial- und Wirtschaftsgeschichte Europas im 20. Jahrhundert* (Munich, 1986), 102ff.

61. Mitchell, *International Historical Statistics*, 894ff.; Fischer, *Europäische Wirtschafts- und Sozialgeschichte*, 79ff.

62. Stefan Hradil, "Sozialstruktur und gesellschaftlicher Wandel," in *Die EG-Staaten im Vergleich*, ed. Gabriel, 50–94, here 73.

63. Gérard Mauger, "France," in *International Handbook of Adolescence,* ed. Klaus Hurrelmann (Westport, Conn., 1994), 146–59, here 149.

64. Michael Vester et al., *Soziale Milieus im gesellschaftlichen Strukturwandel. Zwischen Integration und Ausgrenzung* (completely revised, expanded, and updated edition, Frankfurt am Main, 2001).

65. For these figures as well as the following, see François Höpflinger, "Haushalts- und Familienstrukturen im intereuropäischen Vergleich," in *Die westeuropäischen Gesellschaften*, ed. Hradil and Immerfall, 97–138.

66. Höpflinger, "Haushalts- und Familienstrukturen," 105; Beisheim et al., *Im Zeitalter der Globalisierung?*, 482ff. Also, see Sibylle Meyer and Eva Schulze, "Nichteheliche Lebensgemeinschaften—Alternativen zur Ehe? Eine internationale Datenübersicht," *Kölner Zeitschrift für Soziologie und Sozialpsychologie* 35 (1983): 725–34.

67. In the year 1979, 18 percent of Westgerman students lived in apartment-sharing communities. Compare Michael Mitterauer, *Sozialgeschichte der Jugend* (Frankfurt am Main, 1986), 114. Also see Gudrun Cyprian, *Sozialisation in Wohngemeinschaften* (Stuttgart, 1978); Ernst Haider, *Wohngemeinschaften in Österreich. Daten und Tendenzen einer gegenkulturellen "Institution"* (Frankfurt am Main, 1984).

68. For Denmark, compare Drude Dahlerup, *Rødstrømperne. Den danske rødstrømpebevægelses udvikling, nytænkning og gennemslag 1970–85*, 2 vol. (Copenhagen, 1998); for West Germany and France with an emphasis on the 1970s, see Kristina Schulz,

Der lange Atem der Provokation. Die Frauenbewegung in der Bundesrepublik und in Frankreich (Frankfurt am Main and New York, 2002); for Sweden, see Elisabeth Elgán, ed., *Kvinnorörelsen och '68 — aspekter och vittnesbörd* (Huddinge: Samtidshistoriska institutet, Södertörns högskolan, 2001). For a more international comparative scope, consult Drude Dahlerup, ed., *The New Women's Movement. Feminism and Political Power in Europe and the USA* (London, 1986).

69. Ulrike Meinhof, *Die Würde des Menschen ist antastbar. Aufsätze und Polemiken* (West Berlin, 1980), 150.

70. Ute Frevert, "Umbruch der Geschlechterverhältnisse? Die 60er Jahre als geschlechterpolitischer Experimentierraum," in *Dynamische Zeiten*, ed. Schildt, Siegfried, and Lammers, 642–60, here 643f. For a more detailed analysis, see Christine von Oertzen, *Teilzeitarbeit und die Lust am Zuverdienen. Geschlechterpolitik und gesellschaftlicher Wandel in Westdeutschland 1948–1969* (Göttingen, 1999).

71. Gabriel, *Die EG-Staaten im Vergleich*, 499.

72. Ute Frevert, "Frauen auf dem Weg zur Gleichberechtigung—Hindernisse, Umleitungen, Einbahnstraßen," in *Zäsuren nach 1945. Essays zur Periodisierung der deutschen Nachkriegsgeschichte*, ed. Martin Broszat (Munich, 1990), 113–31, here 122f.

73. For this topic, see Dagmar Herzog's contribution in this volume, ch. 12.

74. Christina Florin and Bengt Nilsson, "'Something in the nature of a bloodless revolution …' How new gender relations became gender equality policy in Sweden in the nineteen sixties and seventies," in *State Policy and Gender System in the Two German States and Sweden 1945–1989*, ed. Rolf Torstendahl (Uppsala, 1999), 11–77.

75. Julian Bourg explores this topic in ch. 13 of this volume.

76. Mitchell, *International Historical Statistics*, 775ff.

77. Ermrich, *Basisdaten*, 576.

78. Marwick, *The Sixties*, 369.

79. *New Musical Express*, 3 February 1968.

80. Detlef Siegfried, "Draht zum Westen. Populäre Jugendkultur in den Medien 1963 bis 1971," in *Buch, Buchhandel und Rundfunk: 1968 und die Folgen*, ed. Monika Estermann and Edgar Lersch (Wiesbaden, 2003), 83–109.

81. For this topic, compare Konrad Dussel's contribution in this volume, ch. 5.

82. For a detailed chronicle of pirate stations, see *Fc-Archiv* 31, 3 August 1967. Also, compare Paul Harris, *When Pirates Ruled the Waves* (London, 1968).

83. Richard Nichols, *Radio Luxemburg: The Station of the Stars* (London, 1983).

84. Infratest, *Der jugendliche Radiohörer. Nordrhein-Westfalen 1971* (Munich, 1971), 40f.

85. Christoph Schubert, "Alternative Literaturszene in der Bundesrepublik Deutschland," in *Literaturbetrieb in der Bundesrepublik Deutschland. Ein kritisches Handbuch*, ed. Heinz Ludwig Arnold (Munich, 1981), 126–41; Elisabeth Nelson, *The British Counter-Culture 1966–73: A Study of the Underground Press* (New York, 1989); Richard Neville, *Hippie Hippie Shake: The Dreams, the Trips, the Trials, the Love-Ins, the Screw Ups … The Sixties* (London, 1995); Marwick, *The Sixties*, 102ff.; Steven Llewellyn Bjerregaard Jensen and Thomas Ekman Jørgensen, "Studenteroprøret i Danmark 1968. Forudsætninger og konsekvenser" (unpublished manuscript, Copenhagen: 1999), 125ff.

86. Jugendwerk der Deutschen Shell, *Jugend in Europa*, vol. 2, 44.

87. Kaelble, "Europäische Vielfalt und der Weg zu einer europäischen Gesellschaft," 55f.

88. Jugendwerk der Deutschen Shell, *Jugend in Europa*, vol. 2, 86. See also Axel Schildt's contribution in this volume, ch. 6.

89. Martin Kirsch, "Entwicklung der Erfahrungsräume von Europäern im Bereich des höheren Bildungswesens seit 1918," in *Gesellschaften im Vergleich*, ed. Kaelble and Schriewer, 391–429, here 413.

90. Kaelble, "Europäische Vielfalt und der Weg zu einer europäischen Gesellschaft," 50.

91. Compare Jürgen Reulecke, ed., *Rückkehr in die Ferne. Die deutsche Jugend in der Nachkriegszeit und das Ausland* (Weinheim and Munich, 1997).

92. *Emnid-Informationen*, no. 32 (1966); Jugendwerk der Deutschen Shell, *Jugend in Europa*, vol. 3 (Hamburg, 1977), 96f. The penultimate figure refers to 16- to 21-year-olds; the last figure refers to 16- to 19-year-olds. For the figure in 1990, see Heiner Timmermann and Eva Wessela, eds., *Jugendforschung in Deutschland. Eine Zwischenbilanz* (Opladen, 1999), 154. In France, the population's knowledge of English increased between the years 1969 and 1987 from 10 percent to 20.1 percent. Knowledge of French among the West German population in 1969 amounted to 10 percent and in 1987 to 6.9 percent, and among the British it amounted to 15 percent in 1969 and to 20 percent in 1987; in Beisheim et al., *Im Zeitalter der Globalisierung?*, 103.

93. Jugendwerk der Deutschen Shell, *Jugend in Europa*, vol. 2, 84.

94. *Emnid-Informationen*, no. 2 (1969).

Part I

Politics and Culture in the "Golden Age"

Chapter 1

Youth Culture and the Cultural Revolution of the Long Sixties

Arthur Marwick

By the 1950s West European countries were beginning to enjoy some of the fruits of the affluence that had previously characterised only the United States, as recognized by the French historian Jean Fourastié with respect to the thirty glorious years between 1946 and 1975 or again by Eric Hobsbawm who describes "the golden age" between 1945 and 1973.[1] It took time for affluence to translate into the cultural transformations described in this book, and then only because affluence *converged* with other crucial demographic, technological, ideological and institutional factors. The most important of the demographic factors was the working through of the 1940s "baby boom," which resulted in unprecedentedly high proportions of young people in all countries by the early sixties. Thanks to continuing economic growth these young people had equally unprecedented security and self-confidence. As other factors, which I shall discuss in detail in the course of the chapter, took effect, a universal youth culture began to take shape.

   In the 1950s, prior to this convergence, Western societies, afflicted by the miasma of Cold War and threat of nuclear annihilation, were profoundly convention-bound and conformist. The triumph of the Allies over the forces of Nazi brutality and obscurantism by the end of the Second World War, a triumph in which workers, peasants, women, resistance movements and partisans, colonial peoples and ordinary citizens participated, had held out the promise of a greatly changed postwar world; some reforms were implemented, which, particularly in the sphere of education, would eventually have significant results, but in the severe

conditions of reconstruction, austerity and international tension, many
of the hopes for change were frustrated. West European societies were
preoccupied with their own problems; while American personnel and
American customs might have been familiar (particularly in West Germany), as, of course, were American films and American popular music,
American society itself might as well have been a million miles away,
both its rampant consumerism and its family and school rituals, affecting adolescents in particular.[2] However, all Western societies did, in one
way or another, share certain highly conservative characteristics, such as:
rigid social codes and class distinctions; the subordination of women to
men and children to parents; racism—standing out all the more starkly
in America as a result of the few brave and isolated challenges to segregation taking place in the fifties, just perceptible on mainland Britain
(where the non-white population was still tiny) in what was known as
"the colour bar" imposed in employment, housing and leisure facilities,
blatant in Northern Ireland where the indigenous Irish Catholics were
treated as second-class citizens, and very apparent in the behaviour of the
French towards the North Africans in their midst; repression, guilt and
furtiveness in sexual attitudes and behavior, constantly overshadowed by
the fear of pregnancy; unquestioning respect for authority in the family,
education, government, the law, and religion, and for the nation-state,
the national flag, the national anthem, all of this approaching hysterical
dimensions in the United States during the McCarthyite era; a pronounced paternalism in the running of such "top-down" facilities for
young people as youth clubs and youth hostels (one has only to reflect on
the connotations of the German word, *Herbergsvater*), young people
themselves being generally conformist and apolitical; a strict formalism
in language, etiquette, and dress codes, strongly marked among young
people and the prescribed and separate roles of young males and young
females; dull and cliché-ridden popular culture, most notably in American popular music with its boring big bands and banal ballads, epito-
mised in the song, "Love and Marriage, Go together like a Horse and
Carriage" (continental European countries were more successful than
Britain in preserving indigenous traditions in popular music); a very hap-
hazard distribution of the amenities of modern society, with only a few
families in Western Europe with refrigerators or television sets, many
without electricity, inside bathrooms, or even running water.[3]

By the mid 1970s transformations had taken place in all of these
areas. Most tangibly, modern domestic conveniences and consumer
goods were being enjoyed in the remoter rural areas of Western Europe,
as well as in the big cities. The 1960s had been a decade of rising living
standards and enhanced lifestyles, involving a much-remarked-upon

growth in "consumerism"—a word widely and loosely used, less often defined; I use it to signify a condition in which relatively high levels of income throughout society make possible a high level of consumption of goods of all types, which go beyond basic necessities and include "modern conveniences," "consumer goods" and "domestic luxuries," and where, indeed, preoccupation with such consumption becomes a characteristic feature of society." But the decade had also been one of political protest and violent confrontation, in which the main proponents were young people, particularly students; the events of 1968 had seemed to carry the threat of the overthrowal of established society and could be read as testimony to the politicization of a whole student generation. One of the most significant phenomena was the way in which students and other young people who were generally uninterested in politics and certainly resistant to radical and Marxist ideas became swept up in protest movements as they perceived the authorities, and particularly the police, as acting with illegitimate force (often trying to provoke the police into "demonstrating the illegitimacy of the capitalist system" as a deliberate tactic of certain student radicals).[4] It must always be borne in mind that many students who demonstrated were concerned mainly with grievances against the university authorities, against the police, etc., rather than with overt political causes.

Before going any further, my notion of the cultural revolution of the long 1960s, the "long 1960s" running from roughly 1958 to roughly 1974, deserves elucidation and examination, as does the concept of a single, transnational youth culture: how far it was independent of the rest of society; how influential in determining the basic character of the "Cultural Revolution"; how far, if at all, subject to a basic tension between, say, consumerism and politicization. The final section of the chapter, prior to a brief conclusion, will look in more detail at relationships between young people and their elders, broadly arguing that, while there were instances of bitter confrontation, it is wrong to think in terms of a "conflict of generations."

Too little attention is still given to the legislative enactments that were in fact among the culminating achievements of the cultural revolution. First in importance are the measures giving young people the vote at the age of eighteen, coming in 1974 in France and Italy, 1972 in West Germany and the United States, and 1968 in the United Kingdom; these scarcely betoken bitter hostility between the older generation and the younger, or a total disjunction between "youth culture" and the rest of society. It was during these same years in the early 1970s that crucial decisions were made with respect to the rights of women. In October and November 1972 the celebrated abortion trials took place at

Bobigny on the outskirts of Paris, resulting in the de facto acquittal of the women concerned, in the cessation of all such prosecutions, and in the Abortion Law Reform of early 1975.[5] The American Supreme Court ruling that made it clear that it was possible for abortions to be carried out legally was announced on 22 January 1973. In Italy, on 12 May 1974 a different referendum was passed when, to the surprise even of Socialist leader Pietro Nenni,[6] 59.1 percent of Italian voters defied the Catholic Church to endorse the Divorce Law enacted in November 1969. Permissive attitudes and behavior throughout society, though not necessarily permissive legislation by governments, continued and expanded throughout the later 1970s, the 1980s and 1990s, and on into the twenty-first century. It seems to me apposite to perceive the cultural revolution itself as coming to an end around 1974, as it does to perceive it as having its beginnings in the late 1950s, when the phenomenon of the "affluent teenager" began to be noted, when the world view of "the beats" began to spread, when young people began to form music groups of their own to play skiffle and rock, when Mary Quant first began designing clothes specifically for the student-age group, when Herbert Marcuse and others integrated Marxist revolt with Freudian rejection of sexual repression, when postwar educational reforms were beginning to produce greater numbers of young people open to intellectual and cultural influences,when liberals recovered their faith in tolerance, democratic rights, and due process, and when a reaction began to develop against the stifling and authoritarian conventions and taboos of the earlier 1950s.[7] Technological developments relating to travel and communications, the creation and diffusion of popular music, and the production of consumer goods were approaching critical mass. After the privations of the war and postwar periods, and as the postwar welfare reforms took effect, the process whereby young people were becoming sexually mature at an ever earlier age was again accelerating. As recovery gave way to affluence and some aspects of the Cold War faded, there was a revival of wartime aspirations; in some circles, among young and old, the spirit of protest was ignited over the threatened deployment of nuclear weapons and over neo colonialism in Latin America, Africa and South East Asia. Great historical transformations are not confined neatly to years or decades. It is a minor weakness in the excellent *Dynamische Zeiten: Die 60er Jahre in den beiden deutschen Gesellschaften*[8] that it sticks so rigidly to the decade of the 1960s, ignoring, in particular, the important developments of the early 1970s. And it should be noted that while, for reasons given, it is appropriate to perceive the transformations as actually beginning in the late 1950s, the year 1980 does not form a distinctive terminal point, the revolutionary changes that culminated in the early 1970s simply continuing steadily throughout the later 1970s and on towards the twenty-first century.

So what precisely were these "revolutionary developments"? First, it is essential to be clear on the fact that the cultural revolution was in no sense a revolution on the Marxist model, and indeed that there was never any possibility of such a revolution taking place. This consideration influences my conclusions about the long term significance of "politicization." One can admire those young people who were determined to involve themselves in the major issues of the day and who demonstrated on behalf of what they believed to be right, but one has to recognize that they were completely mistaken in their faith that their actions would bring about the overthrow of "bourgeois" society—the great events of 1967/69 really had remarkably little in the way of long term consequences, and it is well worth noting that the senior Bonn diplomat, Ulrich Sahm, commented that while the student demonstrations did worry him, he considered the student movement "marginal" and of no danger to the existing political order.[9] What actually did take place in the "long sixties" was something far more important, a revolution that transformed the lives of ordinary people, one that can most clearly be explicated by identifying seven distinct, but constantly interacting phenomena. The unprecedented influence exercised by young people, partly through a tiny minority of them becoming icons of the age, mainly through the spending power of the overwhelming majority in a new market entirely devised with them in mind, and through their being, in part at least, arbiters of taste in that market, was important, but we do have to understand that other phenomena developed largely independently of young people and that indeed these phenomena themselves operated as contextual influences on youth culture.

First in importance was the great profusion of new movements, new ideas, new social concerns and new forms of social participation, the passion for experimentation, for pushing matters to extremes, and for, of course, challenging established ways of doing things, exemplified by experimental drama, art, poetry and music groups, New Left, civil rights, anti war and environmental-protection movements, the philosophical pronouncements of the structuralists and post structuralists, the situationists and of Marshall McLuhan and Timothy Leary, in which excess was succeeded by still further excess. Closely associated with all of this were outbursts of entrepreneurialism, individualism, hedonism, doing you own thing, as seen in the founding of clubs, boutiques, pornographic magazines, etc., the development of uninhibited fashions (short skirts, long hair, for example) which defied convention and gloried in the natural attributes of the (youthful) human body. Second, and

related to all of these, was an upheaval in personal and family relationships and in public and private morals, subverting the authority of men
over women and parents over children, and entailing a general sexual liberation, involving "permissive" attitudes and behavior, and a refreshing
frankness, openness, and indeed honesty in sexual matters.

And so, thirdly, we come back to the rise of the unprecedented influence of young people, most clearly expressed in the formation of a
potent youth culture. Inextricably bound in with the forces of commercialism, this youth culture had a steadily increasing impact on the rest of
society, dictating taste in fashion, music, and popular culture generally.
The central component was pop/rock music, which became a kind of
universal language, its performers being young in comparison with the
crooners and band leaders of the 1950s, and the audiences mainly
(though far from exclusively) being very young. "Youth," in any case,
was not monolithic: in respect to some developments one is talking of
teenagers, with respect to others it may be a question of everyone under
the age of thirty or so. Such was the growing prestige of youth and
appeal of the youthful lifestyle that it became possible to remain "youthful" at more advanced ages than would ever have been thought proper in
previous generations. While the origins of youth culture lay in America,
the distinctive character it took on owed much to developments in the
United Kingdom. Late in 1960 Mary Quant and her aristocratic partner, Alexander Plunkett-Green took their new youthful fashions to
America. Responses ranged from astonishment that the staid English
could produce anything like this, to a glimmering recognition that this
new English fashion was poised for universal conquest. *Life* (5 December 1960), in a feature entitled "British Couple's Kooky Styles,"
remarked on the shortness of the skirts (in fact they went up to just
below the knee. Quant did not introduce miniskirts to the world until
1964). *Women's Wear Daily* was more percipient: "These Britishers have
a massive onslaught of talent, charm and mint-new ideas." Anticipating
the way in which Mary Quant fashions would soon be a vital part of
American youth culture, the American teenage magazine *Seventeen* prepared a special Mary Quant spring promotion.[10] For nearly forty years
now *everybody* has known everything there is to know about the Liverpool group, The Beatles (consisting of three working-class lads, and
lower-middle-class John Lennon). However, a special insight into the
appeal of the group, and of their kind of music—in this case to a young
adult—is contained in a letter, written (on 3 January 1964) by a Cambridge academic recently returned from a spell at the University of California at Berkeley, to his senior colleague there:

for health and sanity these last months, I've been going to twist and shake clubs which have sprung up all over London. We have a new group who may be visiting America soon, and here are worshipped as I think no other entertainer ever has been … Called the Beatles 4 kids from Liverpool, rough, cheeky, swingy, very much war-time kids, and full of gutsy energy. I must say I fell for their stuff when I got back. I never thought to twist and shake—but I have and I do … it is a relief to lose oneself in the unconscious hypnotic euphoria of the music. [11]

The British influence on youth culture in other countries can be clearly seen in such magazines as *Salut les copains* in France, and *Ciao amici* and *Big* in Italy.[12]

As youth culture expanded from being relatively inward-looking and basically confined to *teenagers* into being increasingly integrated with, and, at the same time, reactive against, the rest of society, with university students more and more the dominating constituent, the cultural revolution presented varied, seemingly contrasting, aspects: from violent would-be revolution to passive hippiedom, pervaded by psychedelic drugs and oriental religion; from organized paramilitary formations on city streets to newly founded paperback bookshops, galleries, experimental theaters, nightclubs and underground magazines. French historians focus on what they call "the years of *contestation*," a word that sounds odd in English, but which draws attention to the dramatic events on the streets of Paris and elsewhere.[13] Equally, one may legitimately, as already mentioned, stress the marked politicization of sections of the student populations. But whether there really was a deep tension, or paradox, at the heart of youth culture seems to me rather doubtful. It is true that most young people, like their elders, enjoyed the benefits of affluence and of consumer society, while it was fashionable among young revolutionaries and radicals to denounce "consumerism" as the evil capitalist trap that lured the workers away from their historical destiny of overthrowing "the bourgeoisie."[14] The burning down of the department store, L'Innovation, in Brussels on 22 May 1967, resulting in the deaths of nearly three hundred people, was only the most lethal of several direct attacks on "consumerism" in various countries; but only very small minorities of extremists were involved, and as political action faded in 1969 (when, for example, the German Extra Parliamentary Opposition disintegrated) and 1970 (when the German SDS was wound up), the hard core of irreconcilables coalesced into the dangerous, but numerically tiny terrorist groups of the 1970s. To understand the essential unity of youth culture, despite the different levels of intensity with which different young people held, and acted out their principles, we have to grasp the two slogans, infinitely flexible, but immensely potent, which, as a mass of contemporary documentation and subsequent reminiscence testifies, lay at the heart of what most young people believed, or wanted to believe: "Changing the World" and "Having a Good Time." Rather than a tension between hedonists and activists, or between consumerism and politicization, youth culture presented a shifting accommodatation between these two imperatives. Most young people were able to persuade themselves that for most of the time they could do both, but some actually believed that they were changing the world simply by having a good time; and can one say they were totally wrong when one considers the austere, gloomy, authoritarian world of the 1940s and 1950s? For some, "changing the world" simply meant changing personal lifestyles and relationships. Even the irreconcilables believed in enjoying themselves—with sex, drugs and the consumer products, records, record-players, amplifiers, etc.—indispensible to youth culture itself), believed in sharing in the irreverent humor that was such a characteristic of the youth movements, and seen strikingly in the pranks of situationists, provos, yippies, Kabouters and Onda Verde (it was for their lack of appropriate Politburo seriousness that the student left were excoriated by the official Communist Parties).[15]

In introducing the exhibition, "I Want to Take You Higher: The Psychedelic Era 1965–1969," to commemorate the thirtieth anniversary of the San Francisco summer of love at the Rock and Roll Hall of Fame and Museum in Cleveland, James Henke, one of the central figures in American youth culture struck a familiar note:

> … this period, unlike the Nineties, was a time of hope, a time of optimism. It was a period when people valued personal freedom and social equality. It was a time when anything seemed possible. People thought they could change the world—and they did.[16]

Jim Haynes, the American who launched Europe's first new-style paperback bookshop in Edinburgh in 1960, then played leading roles in setting up Edinburgh's experimental theater, The Traverse, and subsequently London's Arts Lab, expressed some of the same ideas, though overlaid by later disillusionment. He referred to:

> the innocence and naivety of the decade when everybody thought that they were changing the world, that we could change the world. Then maybe a few people began to realise that maybe through the music, through long hair and colourful costumes, through our attitudes, hopes and fears, we weren't going to change the world. We could only maybe change ourselves a bit.[17]

Innocence, naivety and optimism are frequently mentioned, and these certainly existed by the bucket-load; but optimism is not necessarily a bad quality, and young people, particularly students, could plausibly argue that they were, as an entire generation, facing up to issues that previous generations had largely avoided: the involvement in higher education of young men from all social classes and of unprecedented numbers of women, for instance; the rise of the civil rights movements and the challenges to traditional racial attitudes; neo colonialism, nuclear weapons, new domestic technologies. Unquestionably, the faith in, and the desire for change was palpable. Here is the recollection of a woman who was a teenager in Liverpool during the 1960s:

> ... did all that upheaval in the living standards, in attitudes and fashion have a lasting effect on the lives of the adults who were teenagers in Liverpool in the sixties? I believe it did. It gave us tolerance for new ideas, and brought us a step nearer to equality of rights, removing many prejudices of sexual, racial and moral origin. It gave us the freedom to accept or reject things on their own merits and according to our own individual preferences. I believe that the sixties were a mini-renaissance in which the right of individual expression was encouraged, applauded, and nurtured by a generation whose naïve belief was that all we needed was love.[18]

Apart from having a good time, another basic foundation of youth culture was, despite the primacy of "doing your own thing" and "individual expression," the sense of "being there" and of "belonging." And, of course, of "being outside established adult society" (however unavoidable links to that society were in reality). Barry Miles, founder of Indica paperback bookshop in London, and friend and biographer of Alan Ginsberg, William Burroughs, and Paul McCartney, has defined the ethos of San Francisco's Haight-Ashbury hippy district in these words:

> ... it was like a coalescence of the free sexual revolution, the marijuana revolution, the drug revolution, political revolution, liberation movements of all kinds. We were getting together to have a be-in. The purpose was just to be there. That was the whole point. This was after the sit-ins, and the idea was more Buddhist influenced: to be there, to simply be there, not having to do anything particular except to enjoy the phenomenon of being together outside of the realm of the state. [19]

One of London's more famous psychedelic clubs was UFO, about which cofounder John "Hoppy" Hopkins wrote:

> UFO was done from the heart with a purpose, which was to have a good time. We decided to run UFO all night, and it was a piece of all-night cul-

ture suddenly flashing into being that really made it popular. People would stay till it was light outside. You could stay out of your head all night.[20]

And to put with that, here is the recollection of the guitarist in Tomorrow, one of the UFO rock groups:

> Going into the UFO club when you were on the bill made you feel great…It was a mass happening, day after day, week after week. You were part of something; you felt like you belonged somewhere.[21]

The 1960s youth culture is, of course, indelibly associated with sex and drugs, which can very nearly be explained by the key notion of "Having a Good Time," mixed in with the prevailing notions of experimentation and challenging authority. The spread of drug-taking was greatly accelerated by the absurd belief in the mind-expanding qualities of psychedelic drugs.

One development that was contributing greatly to the knowledge and understanding of the world possessed by young people was the increased availability and, therefore, popularity, of travel. It was highly noticeable that the great political demonstrations faded out with the onset of summer, as the traveling season began. Changing the world did not necessarily mean taking part in political demonstrations: many young people joined with their elders in such humanitarian bodies as Amnesty International, in the various civil rights' movements, the environmental movement, the campaigns for the homeless, even the consumer movement ("consumers," as I shall shortly show, far from being wicked representatives of the bourgeoisie, were simply ordinary people living life as best they could, who themselves needed protection from capitalist exploitation). In Amsterdam the provos, rather than political activists, were "radical pacifists" with a highly developed sense of fun, and plans for "white bicycles" (free of charge, to combat environmental pollution) and "white chimneys" (smokeless). They were succeeded in 1970 by the kabouters, who distinguished themselves by their peaceful work in combating air pollution, in forcing the city to make empty houses available for occupation by the homeless, and helping the elderly cope with bureaucracy.[22] Overwhelmingly the evidence is that in all countries the Beatles were regarded as *the* group that represented the interests and concerns of the young, but the appeal was entirely visceral, directly through the music, not through any political programs or activities associated with the "fab four" (a well-loved song, of course, was "All You Need is Love").[23] The point in respect to rock music in general was made crudely but graphically by American female pop star, Janis Joplin: "My music isn't supposed to make you riot. It's supposed to make you fuck."[24] The variegated mix that made up youth culture was most fully displayed at the major rock festivals, most impressively perhaps at the Essen International Song Days of September 1968, almost, you could say, a festival of consumerism enlivened (not contradicted) by protest songs.[25]

After that long disquisition on the rise of youth and youth culture, I come to my fourth phenomenon, again closely tied in with the others: the enormous growth in the international exchange of cultural products and practices. America continued to be the mass producer of what film critics refer to as "classical" films,[26] but these were now being rivaled, in prestige if not popularity by "modern" films from Europe, many of these coproductions from several European countries. Curiously some of the most internationally famous experimental theater came from America, but also from European countries, notably Norway, West Germany, France and Italy. Basically the American monopoly of cultural exports was broken, and, of course, Britain acquired a special position in regard to pop music, fashion, film and television. Among developments that had their origins in the 1950s or earlier, but which now permeated to all parts of Western Europe, were motor scooters (significant agents in the liberation of young women) and espresso machines (essential adjuncts to the coffee-bars central to early youth culture) from Italy, discos from France, and juke boxes from America. Again it must be stressed that the fifth, and absolutely fundamental phenomenon of the cultural revolution was the spread to all sections of society of decent living conditions (which is linked to, but not the same thing as, consumerism). In an important survey of a rural commune in Brittany, the French sociologist, Edgar Morin, after noting that the commune had been without running water in 1950, remarked on a "wave of change" in the 1960s which "brought wash-hand basins, showers, sometimes bathtubs, inside WCs, refrigerators, and washing machines." He added that:

> Diet became richer and more varied. Gruel was abandoned, the pancake had returned as a delicacy, potatoes remained as a basic element, but people were starting to eat steaks, vegetables, desserts … Italian raviolis and tinned paellas began to appear at the grocer's. [27]

Turning to the country of origin of one of these interesting components of international cultural exchange (ravioli!), we can refer to the three-part survey of a village seventy kilometers south of Rome conducted by the American sociologist Feliks Gross, with the assistance of Professor G.N. del Monte of the sociology department at Rome University. The first survey took place in 1957/58, the second in 1969 and the third in 1971. The first survey made clear both the lack of amenities in the village itself and the constrast between the existence of at least basic facilities within the village and their total absence in the habitations dotted about the surrounding countryside. In his interview with Gross, the mayor of the village put matters succinctly. The village, he said

> ... is about 60 to 80 km from Rome, but it seems that it is about 80,000 km. We are living in very primitive conditions and I don't know if we really belong to a civilized country, or whether we should be considered a part of the African region ... We have not enough direct communication with Rome and with other great cities such as Naples.[28]

In his 1969 survey, Gross reported a stunning transformation. The people now had roads, electricity and water; the elderly had old-age pensions; men, by dint of getting up early, were using the new travel facilities to take up employment in Rome. National statistics show a sharply increasing proportion of personal expenditure going on transport.[29] Professor del Monte provided this colourful piece of information:

> ... a friend, who is also a peasant, showed me his toilet; leading the way, he said with pride: "We have a toilet, the Roman type." It was all plastered with tiles. I asked him: "You remember not so long ago—we used to go in the middle of the field—not to a toilet. How do you feel today when you go to the toilet?" Said he: "I feel like a human being, like the others, not like an animal as I felt before."[30]

When does the acquisition of the basic amenities of civilized living become consumerism? Some authorities declare that consumerism began as far back as the seventeenth or eighteenth century.[31] However the hard statistics both of sales of the new consumer goods based on advanced technology, and of the definitive swing away from expenditure being taken up with basic foodstuffs, demonstrate conclusively that a new intense phase of consumerism began in the 1960s.[32] The famous novel of that decade which both celebrates and criticizes the advent of consumerism was *Les Choses: une histoire des années soixante* (1965) by a former sociology student who had worked for a time as a market researcher, Georges Perec. A similar function is often attributed to the simultaneous and related arts movements, Pop Art and Nouveau Réalisme.[33] For the hard everyday realities of consumerism we can hardly do better than consult the series of interviews with ordinary French families published in *L'Express* of 21–28 September 1968. As we see it in the five extracts I am about to quote, consumerism scarcely connotes luxurious self-indulgence and shows only faint elements of servitude to "the capitalist system" in the extent to which goods are bought on credit, and in the constant rather discontented striving after yet more purchases (a central theme of *Les Choses*). Since, at the end of the 1960s, the over-whelming evidence is that most French people thought they were better off and happier than they had been ten years previously,[34] we do not nec-essarily have to believe all the grumbles of the married couples.

> Robert B., is an agricultural worker, aged 42, with a wife, Simone, aged 38 and six children. He is paid 950 francs a month for twelve months, with double pay in one month and certain bonuses. To supplement the family income his wife does a little outside housework. In total, includ-ing family allowances, the household has an income of about 1,900 francs per month. Electricity, being paid for by the farmer who owns the house, is free and there is no rent.

> In the kitchen there is a veritable arsenal of modern machines: an electric waffle iron, an electric mixer, coffee mill, and mincer, 250-liter refrigera-tor, a butane gas cooker and a washing machine. All bought on credit. In the rest of the house, emptiness with the exception of a transistor radio. Their pride is their car, a 4L, also on credit. "It's prosperity, and us, we want to catch a little of it. By working hard, we have now got there."

> Pierre M., aged 45, is an employee in a food-processing factory in a Paris suburb. He has three sons, and earns 499.40 francs a fortnight. Monique, his wife, does two hours a day of house-cleaning to augment their income. There total, per month, is 1,365.49 francs.

> They find it tough. They live in a three-room unfurnished flat, without a bathroom, in a very old building, paying 100 francs a month (the three boys all have to sleep in one room). They have a refrigerator, electric cooker, and television. "We have bought everything on credit. We have a basic principle: when the instalments on one gadget are paid off, we immediately buy another one." She makes some clothes herself; clothes are passed from boy to boy (they are aged 15, 13 and 9). She says: "On Sundays, from time to time, the boys go to the pictures. Us, we go for a walk, play cards with neighbours. Or else my husband stays at home doing odd jobs about the house." Holidays are with a cousin in a little village in the Sarthe. "It's not the seaside, but the three boys enjoy themselves." M. reckons he's better off than he was ten years ago, though conscious of rising prices.

> Pierre G., son of an agricultural laborer, has risen to the position of salaried executive in a commercial firm, and earns 2,800 francs a month, with 1,000 francs for the thirteenth month, which, with family allowances for his two children aged 7 and 2, rises to about 3,150 francs a month.

> He has a four-room, fourth-floor flat, without a lift, in the outer suburbs of Paris. He has a week's holiday at Easter, which he spends at home, and four weeks in the summer, when he books a holiday away from home. They have a refrigerator, a cooker (with four burners, the latest model), a washing machine, a rotisserie, a camera, a television, a three-band tran-

sistor radio, a record-player, 30-odd records, 100-odd books. Madame G. gave up work as a secretary on the birth of her second child, but would like to take up part-time work "in order not to just go on dreaming about the luxury world presented in the women's magazines." They are "profoundly dissatisfied."

Patrice D. is an industrial designer; his wife, 28, is a secretary in a record company. They live at Bois-Colombes, near Paris, and have one 4-year-old child. D. gets thirteen monthly payments of 1,900 francs the calendar year, and a summer holiday bonus of 1,100 francs. She gets 1,155 francs a month over thirteen months, and a holiday bonus of 900 francs, This gives them a total of 3,818 francs per month.

They run a Simca 500. "It is beyond our means, but it is our only luxury." Their television has been bought on credit. They have a battery of modern conveniences, plus a record player, and ordinary camera and a film-camera, a hair-drier, and a radio in the car. But she dreams of a bigger apartment, holidays away from relatives, better clothes, fine books. She believes that, because of rising prices, their standard of living is going down.

S., aged 32, is an employee in a big Paris shop, earning 1,050 francs per month. He and his wife, Genevieve, have three children.

She is 28 and, apart from looking after her own children, she takes other people's children into her own flat after dinner twice a week. With family allowances, they make 1,530 francs a month. Half of this goes on food; they have a small refrigerator, a second-hand television, and no car. Madame S. dreams of having a washing machine.[35]

Sixth is a phenomenon to which I attach great importance, but which is completely neglected in traditional Marxist-leaning accounts of the 1960s: the expansion and strengthening of a liberal, progressive presence, privileging tolerance and due process, within institutions of authority. This I label "measured judgment," believing that it should completely replace the misconceived notion of "repressive tolerance" invented by Herbert Marcuse.[36] Unwittingly, Tom Hayden, leader of the American socialist student party, SDS, while wittingly intending to attack the federal government, revealed "measured judgment" at work in the American judiciary (and a contrast with the 1950s):

> It was remarkable that in these several years of political trials on conspiracy charges, the federal government failed to win against *any* of the sixty-five conspiracy defendants. Such defendants as the Harrisburg Seven, the Camden Seventeen, and the Gainesville Eight always managed to win, either before juries or appeals courts, a dramatic difference from the McCarthy era, only fifteen years before. [37]

Much of what was most innovatory in British popular culture was in fact fostered by two key establishment figures, John Trevelyan at the British Board of Film Censors and Sir Hugh Carleton Greene at the BBC.[38] In France, the abolition of rules intended to prevent male/female cohabitation at the main University of Paris student residences at Antony was carried through by Jacques Balland, the director of the residences, appointed by the Gaullist Government in January 1966.[39] In West Germany the judiciary ruled that SDS files seized by the police in January 1967 must be returned; on Easter Sunday, 1968, *Justizminister* Heineman made his famous call for "*zukunftsgerichtete Toleranz.*"[40]

Against "measured judgment" we must immediately place, seventhly, and lastly, the existence of circumstances leading readily to dogmatism, rigid intolerance and extreme violence. Bigoted, reactionary attitudes in some institutions of authority, including most police forces and some university administrations, were nothing new, but the sight of change taking place all around them incited certain upholders of the status quo into resistance on a vicious scale. At the same time many of the radical protesters themselves believed in the violent overthrow of existing society, while some, as previously mentioned, deliberately provoked police violence on the assumption that this forced into the open the repressive nature of "capitalist" society. The view of the 1960s as an era of violent confrontations that did determine some of the characteristics of the decade is not, therefore, erroneous; only, as I have stressed, violent confrontation was, in the end, much less important than the positive transformations that took place throughout society.

It was a common statement among young people that it was not possible to trust anyone over the age of thirty. Germany's Nazi past, France's collaborationist past, Britain's continuing imperial adventures, nuclear weapons, Vietnam, the authoritarianism rampant in the 1950s, all inspired a great deal of hostility among the younger generation towards the older. Hysterical attacks by old reactionaries against all aspects of youth culture are to be found throughout the long 1960s. But what the detailed evidence brings out is the great extent to which young people had the support of their own parents, and of other adults, including lawyers and academics. Popular culture would not itself have had the impact it did had it not been for the presence of certain adult mediators who catered to the youthful market and sponsored young performers. France's first great open air pop concert was organized at La Nation in Paris, to coincide with the start of the Tour de France on the night of 22/23 June 1963, by Daniel Filipacchi, founder, first, of the radio programme aimed exclusively at young people, *Salut les copains*, and, then, the teenage magazine of the same name. Expected to attract 20–30,000 participants, it actually attracted five times that number; also 2,000 police, and a vast amount of viciously hostile comment, including an astonishing reference to Adolf Hitler. "There are laws," said *Paris Presse,* "police and courts. It's time to make use of them before the savages of the place de la Nation turn the nation's future upside down." "What difference," asked *Figaro,* "is there between the twist ... and Hitler's speeches in the Reichstag, apart from the leaning towards music?"[41] For the actual state of relationships between students and adults there is rich evidence in the collections of letters preserved at the University of Berkeley at California, scene of the Free Speech Movement from 1964 onwards, and Cornell University, subject to particularly violent disturbances in the Spring 1969. The events at Cornell, and particularly the occupation of the students' union by black students in April, together with the restrained handling of the situation by President Perkins and the almost uniquely liberal administration, provoked many bitter denunciations by Cornell alumni and their withdrawal of financial support from the university. In response, one Cornell student wrote to the Cornell *Alumni News* one of most carefully reasoned denunciations of the older generation to be found anywhere, one which points out that students are now coping with the sorts of social changes their elders had been completely oblivious of:

> I note with interest in the letters column of your July issue that there seems to be a direct relationship between the amount of time an alumni has been away from Cornell, and the degree of outrage expressed by him over the April crisis ... These men and women who attended college in the "Golden Days" of Cornell when they buried their little heads in the sands of academia, sneaked booze into the football games, and joined fraternities and sororities that were openly discriminating and proud of it ...

> While I disagree to a great extent with the issues the blacks were raising, and, to a degree, with the way in which the confrontation was handled by the administration, I have nothing but contempt for the men and women who tried to second-guess the actions of Perkins and the rest of the administration ...

> ... none of these writers had to face the social issues we are now facing. For instance, how many blacks attended Cornell when Mr. Dryden ... was there? Times, and society change with the passage of years. Cornell and the rest of the world are not the simple straight-forward things they were decades ago. But, at least we are trying to cope with our world ... today's Cornellians are ten times as concerned with the outside world, and trying to influence it, than was his generation. We may not be right all the time, and we may be misguided much of it, but we're in there giving the old college a try ...

> ... When people detract from the things today's college students are say-
> ing and doing, I can only turn and point the finger at our parents' gener-
> ation. After all they were the ones who made us what they wanted us to
> be. If we are all wrong, then so were they ... Our parents made us, and
> the world, what we are today. I wish they, and the generation preceding
> them would go light on the criticism they level at us when we try to deal
> with the world they willed us and occasionally stumble in the process.[42]

This student clearly belongs to the moderate majority at Cornell, a supporter of the liberal values that he believes "the old college" should stand
for, but far from a total supporter of black liberation. What the wealth
of correspondance between students, their parents, and other adults
brings out is the great amount of support there was for student protesters. When several hundred Free Speech Movement students were
arrested at Berkeley on 2 December 1964, parents, lawyers and academics immediately formed the Parents' Committee for Defense of Berkeley Students, which declared its support for those arrested:

> because we recognize their high moral purpose in peacefully asking to
> maintain and defend constitutionally-guaranteed rights and princi-
> ples ... We believe the students acted in the best tradition of American
> democracy ... .[43]

It is often argued that the persistent insistence by young people on sexual freedom unknown to their parents was a major cause of conflict
between the generations, and there can be no doubt that some older people were shocked by what they saw as the immorality of their juniors,
and that some of the more politically active young people deliberately
flaunted sexual promiscuity in order to provoke their elders into even
more reactionary positions. Yet there is much evidence of conciliation on
sexual matters also—again the actions of Jacques Balland in France are
relevant. The street violence of 1968 was perhaps a more serious test of
tolerance on the part of the older generation towards the younger,
although in many cases (this happened in all countries) the vicious
actions of the police swung sympathy round to the side of the student
demonstrators.[44] One striking discovery made by Professor Michael Seidman in the Paris police archives, which supports my long-held position
that there was cooperation as well as "contestation," even between students and police, is that student marshals did inform the police about
demonstrators who were armed and dangerous.[45] In some cases the
drama and the "trauma" of the events of May/June 1968 brought parents
and children closer together. A particularly valuable document in this
connection is the special, skeletal edition that the French women's mag-

azine, *Elle*, managed to bring out on 17 June, while Paris was still almost totally paralyzed. The editor, Helen Gordon-Lazereff, spoke directly to her readers, recognizing how "traumatic" their experiences had been, the difficulty they had often had in understanding the children who participated in protests, but noting also how some had become involved through their children and came to understand the rightness of their actions.[46] In a later lycée demonstration, pupils, parents, teachers and workers stood shoulder-to-shoulder against a police cordon.[47] Some adults gave their support to young people throughout the long 1960s; others never withdrew their hostility. Some took offence at greater extremism, greater violence, greater obscenity. Some, as *Elle* suggested, came through to a new understanding. A particularly interesting case is that of the widowed Italian school teacher, Anna Avallone, whose son, Sergio, from 1968, was a student activist at Turin University. In her diary she records some general sympathy towards the ideas of her son and his friends, but she is personally estranged from him, offended by the polemic students are aiming at teachers like herself, hurt by his casual attitude towards her, and shocked that he is sleeping with his girlfriend, Giulia. Eventually, influenced in particular by Giulias's feminism, she is won over, beginning to see her own colleagues and neighbors as hypocrites, seeking understanding of the attempted collaboration of students and workers through reading *The Communist Manifesto*, and happily celebrating her son's wedding, at which Giulia wears a miniskirt.[48]

Anna Avallone might seek enlightenment in *The Communist Manifesto*, but to grasp what happened, and what did not happen, during the cultural revolution it is vital to keep firmly in mind that there was never any possibility of a revolution on the Marxist model. Because it is no longer viable to use the word "revolution" in that sense, we are now free to talk of all kinds of other "revolutions"—"a youth revolution," "a rock revolution," "a standard of living revolution," "a consumer revolution," "a sexual revolution," "a communications revolution," "a paperback revolution." Perhaps the best way of summarising the cultural revolution of the long 1960s is by saying that it consisted of a simultaneous series of overlapping revolutions of that type. There was no overthrowal of one type of society by another: what happened was that new ideas, new developments, new practises, some emanating from youth culture, some from other sources, and all assisted by the processes of measured judgement, *permeated* society.

Notes

1. Jean Fourastié, *Les Trentes Glorieuses ou la révolution invisible de 1946 a 1975* (Paris, 1979); Eric Hobsbawm, *The Age of Extremes: The Short Twentieth Century, 1914–1991* (London, 1994).

2. See in particular, James S. Coleman, *The Adolescent Society: The Social Life of Teenagers and its Impact on Education* (Glencoe, New York, 1961).

3. Arthur Marwick, *The Sixties: Cultural Revolution in Britain, France, Italy and the United States, c.1958–c.1974* (Oxford, 1998), 31–38.

4. I make these points in ibid, 536–63.

5. Ibid. 706–11.

6. Reported in *Epoca*, 25 May 1974.

7. Marwick, *Sixties*, 3–38.

8. Axel Schildt, Detlef Siegfried, and Karl Christian Lammers, eds. *Dynamische Zeiten: Die 60er Jahre in den beiden deutschen Gesellschaften* (Hamburg, 2000).

9. Quoted by Gottfried Niedhart, "Ostpolitik: the Role of the Federal Republic of Germany in the Process of Détente," in *1968: The World Transformed*, ed. Carole Fink, Philip Gassert, and Detlef Junker (Cambridge, 1998), 178.

10. Mary Quant, *Quant on Quant* (London, 1966), 105.

11. H.N. Smith Papers, Box 6 F8, Bancroft Library, University of California at Berkeley.

12. I quote extensively from these and other youth magazines in *The Sixties*, 105–10, 461–74.

13. Genevieve Dreyfus-Armand et al., eds. *Les Annees 68: Le temps de la contestation*, (Brussels: Editions Complexe). Politics and conflict are also stressed in the most recent book on America in the sixties, Maurice Isserman and Michael Kazin, *America Divided: The Civil War of the 1960s* (New York, 2000).

14. In particular, see documents printed in Rene Viénet, *Enragés et situationistes dans le mouvement des occupations* (Paris, 1968).

15. Marwick, *Sixties*, 104–5, 110, 354–55, 606–7.

16. James Henke, "Introduction" to *I Want to Take You Higher: The Psychedelic Era 1969–1969*, ed. James Henke with Parke Puterbaugh (San Francisco, 1997), 11.

17. Jim Haynes, *Thanks for Coming! An Autobiography* (London,1984), 174.

18. Moureen Nolan and Roma Singleton, "Mini-Renaissance," in *Very Heaven: Looking Back at the Sixties*, ed. Sara Maitland (London, 1988), 25.

19. Barry Miles, in Henke, 33. Much of what is in Henke is repeated and elaborated in Barry Miles, *In the Sixties* (London, 2002).

20. John "Hoppy" Hopkins, in Henke, 86.

21. Steve Howe (guitarist), in ibid., 88.

22. Frederick George Friedmann, *Youth and Society* (London, 1971), 25–26.

23. Marwick, *Sixties*, 461–64.

24. Quoted in Godfrey Hodgson, *America in Our Time* (New York, 1976), 341.

25. There is a good account in Wolfgang Kraushaar, *1968: Das Jahr das alles verändert hat* (Munich, 1998), 277–79.

26. See Pierre Sorlin, *The Film in History: Restaging the Past* (Oxford, 1988).

27. Edgar Morin, *Commune en France: la métamorphose de Plodémet* (Paris, 1967), 71–72.

28. Feliks Gross, *Il Paese: Values and Social Change in an Italian Village* (New York, 1973), 45.

29. Gisele Podbielski, *Twenty-Five Years of Special Action for the Development of Southern Italy* (Milan, 1978).

30. Gross, *Il Paese*, 126.

31. The latest example is Peter N. Stearns, *Consumerism in World History: the Global Transformation of Desire* (London, 2001).

32. Marwick, *Sixties,* 257–59, 269–70.

33. Ibid., 185–92, 316, 319–20, 324.

34. *L'Express,* 24 February–2 March 1969.

35. All of these quotations are from *L'Express,* 21–28 September 1968.

36. Herbert Marcuse, "Repressive Tolerance," in *A Critique of Pure Tolerance,* eds. Robert Paul Wolff, Barrington Moore, Jr. and Herbert Marcuse (Boston, 1969), 81–123.

37. Tom Hayden, *Reunion: A Memoir* (New York, 1988), 452.

38. Marwick, *Sixties,* 118, 123–24, 131, 136, 143, 527.

39. Michael Seidman, "The Pre-May 1968 Sexual Revolution," *Contemporary French Civilization* XXV, 1 (Winter/Spring, 2001), 28.

40. Klaus Hildebrand, *Von Erhard zur Großen Koalition 1963–1969* (Wiesbaden, 1994), 381.

41. *Paris Presse,* 23 June 1963; *Figaro,* 23 June 1963.

42. Marsham Papers, Box 2, Division of Rare Books and Manuscripts, Cornell University Library, Ithaca, New York. Among several collections at Cornell, The Challenge to Governance Project Papers and the Perkins Papers are specially useful.

43. Malcolm Burnstein Papers, Box 1 F1.15, Bancroft Library, University of California at Berkeley. The Free Speech Movement Participant Papers at Berkeley are also very rich on adult-student relationships.

44. Marwick, *Sixties,* 604–8.

45. Information generously supplied by Professor Michael Seidman, University of North Carolina at Wilmington.

46. *Elle,* special issue, 17 June 1968, in "Brochures mai 68," 14 AS. 238, Archives Nationales, Paris.

47. Marwick, *Sixties,* 745.

48. Anna Avallone, "Il mio sessantotto: ricordi di una 'madre' e 'insegnante,'" Archivio Diaristico, Pieve Santo Stefano, Tuscany.

Chapter 2

Understanding 1968: Youth Rebellion, Generational Change and Postindustrial Society

Detlef Siegfried

When examining the events of 1968 contemporaries as well as later interpreters have continuously focused on the generational aspect of the revolt, often interpreting it in terms of a "youth rebellion" or a "student revolt,"[1] that is, a sudden uprising of young people subverting essential structures of society. On an international level one of the most influential interpretations of this type was Charles Reichs' *The Greening of America*, published in 1970, which immediately topped the nonfiction bestseller list in the United States and constituted a kind of agenda that announced the world's postmaterialistic renewal by means of a youth revolt.[2] The protagonists saw themselves as persons involved in a generational departure. The younger age groups and those with a higher level of education had a tendency to interpret the events of 1968 as involving a substantial part of the young generation—although only a small part was active in the disputes.[3]

Therefore, a point of view that had already come into existence at the beginning of the 1960s completely prevailed by the end of the decade. Hardly any other intellectual trend reflected the *Zeitgeist* more clearly than what was summarized by the term "New Left." For the New Left the entire old classes' economism was passé; instead, politics and culture became the center of attention—spheres in which and through which society could be changed. Their theorists demanded more political participation, freer intellectual and aesthetic development, and a strengthening of the individual. Even among the proponents of radical change in society, the New Left was in a leading position. The American sociologist C. Wright Mills had given up the notion that the working class could achieve a change in society and viewed the young generation, especially young intellectuals, as a decisive factor for change.[4] The American Students for a Democratic Society (SDS) in particular quickly took up this position and incorporated it into their program, the "Port Huron Statement," which was written in 1962. An avant-garde art movement of the late 1950s and 1960s known as Situationism also attached the same importance to the youth. From the point of view of the Dutch *provos,* young urban outsiders would change the world while the proletarians would degenerate watching television. "Third World" revolutionary movements, such as Castrism or the Maoist Cultural Revolution, defined themselves as young movements and were also perceived as such. After his death in 1967, Che Guevara became an icon of youth rebellion, more than any other leaders of such movements. By 1968 the organizations of the New Left had reached a large degree of unity with regard to their general direction. This also materialized in their political praxis and differentiated them substantially from groups of the Old Left. The anti-authoritarian wing of the *Sozialistischer Deutscher Studentenbund (SDS)* increasingly viewed the young generation as a potentially revolutionary subject. In August 1967 leaders Reimut Reiche and Peter Gäng opined that every oppositional metropolitan movement should be primarily based on "the young" and deemed that it would be most promising to politicize and discipline "the youth's apolitical position of protest."[5] The "fringe group strategy" (*Randgruppenstrategie*), which was favored by some, focused in praxis on working with young outsiders. People who later on became members of the Red Army Faction, such as Ulrike Meinhof, Andreas Baader, and Gudrun Ensslin were active in this field. At the beginning of 1968, the German SDS defined itself as part of a "revolutionary youth movement," and the International Vietnam Congress that was held in Berlin in February 1968 thought of itself as a congregation of the world's revolutionary youth.[6] The biggest Danish underground paper *Superlove* declared a "new class struggle between the old and new generation," and aimed for the transformation of the "unarticulated youth culture into an articulated youth rebellion."[7] Within the American SDS at the end of 1968, an anti-authoritarian Revolutionary Youth Movement formed that aimed to expand the social basis from students to pupils and working class youths.[8] Abbie Hoffmann and Jerry Rubin had already formed their Youth International Party ("yippies") who wanted to combine the hippie counterculture with the New Left and placed their hopes entirely on the young generation's revolutionary role. The blurb of Jerry Rubin's manifesto "Do it!" of 1970 does not lack clarity: "Jerry Rubin has written The Communist Manifesto of our era.

'Do it' is a declaration of war between the generations—calling on kids to leave their homes, burn down their schools and create a new society upon the ashes of the old."

Statements like these pointedly expressed a process of generational disbanding that was already in motion—without, however, actually having the rigidly confrontational posturing here being postulated. Nevertheless, much potential for confrontation remained—even when one ignores the fist-waving and war rhetoric. Such expressions were explosive because they were articulated by the generation that had a future leading role. It was clear to the public and the ruling political classes of all countries, not only the Western ones, that the young generation played a larger role than previously, that it shaped the dynamic present a lot more strongly than older generations, and that they would soon be running society's destiny. In France, even the conservative Gaullists had already in 1959 placed their hopes on young people: "France is now the most dynamic country in the old continent in Europe because it possesses the largest number of young people…," and in 1964 *Paris Match* reported with regard to youths between 16 and 24: "They will be our rulers tomorrow."[9] The horror with which conservatives and liberals from all European countries observed the radicalization of precisely the intellectual youth in the late 1960s stemmed from their awareness that this here was the future elite. Because of the manner in which the students presented themselves to the public, massive criticism was directed towards them, claiming that this future elite did not live up to their exemplary role.[10]

The fact that the youth and student movement was an international, even worldwide, phenomenon was one of its most prominent characteristics. Student protests were registered in fifty-six countries, especially in Western Europe, the United States, and Japan but also in countries of the so-called Third World, and in Eastern Europe.[11] The global simultaneity of a political cultural impetus for renewal with similar goals, methods, and incarnations, represents an extraordinary phenomenon. Certainly it is questionable whether the description of the network of events of "1968" as a global "revolution" is accurate. At any rate these events did not immediately lead to any profound changes of economic or political systems, in many cases not even to changes of government in the preferred direction. Political cultures and lifestyles, however, did change significantly so that the term "cultural revolution" is probably the most suitable. This "cultural revolution" was not, however, an eruptive and temporarily confined event, as suggested by the terms "revolution," "revolt," and "1968" in general, but more a kind of multilayered phenomenon of a longer duration that showed different points of acceleration and radicalization. This "cultural revolution" was about the radical

secular changes of "affluent societies" (John Kenneth Galbraith), which
stretched themselves over the period of the long 1960s, and received a
certain dynamic through situational factors and national problems.[12]
Without a doubt, conditional factors consisting of global-political
upheavals played an important role since the end of Second World War,
not to mention the social and cultural historical changes that took place
since the middle of the century: the reconstruction of relatively stable
national economies, the explosive expansion of consumption, the media
and the educational system, and the change of work and social structures. At the same time, a well-developed sense of crisis persisted due to
the experiences of the previous decades, and an insecurity about how
long the succession of "Golden Years" would continue. In addition, profound processes of national self-realization took place. These represented
adjustments to new conditions and shifts in power relations as well as situations of radical change in domestic politics, which were the results of
worldwide decolonialization, the fascist past of Germany, Italy, and
Japan, the Vietnam War, and racism in the United States. The international character of the "68 movement" thus resulted both from the com-
parability of situations of radical change, the political demands, the
forms of action, and from the similarity of social supporters and their
cultural styles. Which is not to say that significant national differences
did not exist—for example, with regard to the percentage of young
workers or more "apolitical" countercultural elements, to the degree of
militancy in the debates, political systems' potential for integration, etc.
Whereas the United States, West Germany, France, and Italy witnessed
conflicts that bordered on civil war, the protests in Great Britain and in
the Scandinavian countries were far less militant. In the corporatist states
of Northern Europe the impulses of the student movement were incorporated into society relatively unproblematically, while within single
states, strong regional and local differences existed. Larger issues, such as
the expansion of horizons beyond national borders, the juvenalization of
society and politics, as well as the yearning for stronger political participation remained characteristic.

While Ingrid Gilcher-Holtey recently asserted that the protests at the
end of the 1960s constituted "more than a 'student rebellion' or a 'generational revolt,'" the question remains as to the exact meaning of the
generational movement and the extent to which the term "revolt" is justified.[13] While the events of 1968 are concentrated in a relatively limited
segment of time—in reality from 1967 until 1969—they are embedded
in a period of accelerated change spanning from ca. 1958 to ca. 1973.[14]
My goal in the following is to situate the generational aspect of the network of events of "1968" within the background of this broader period
of time—as a radicalization of a process of cultural change, wherein

young people, from the beginning, occupied a trendsetting function—based on the thesis that in the "code 1968,"[15] transformational tendencies of the Modern Age intensified because the young generation constituted the prime proponent of change within society with regard to penetrating consumer society and implementing new cultural standards —for example, concerning consumption of media, sexuality, race relations, education as well as political renewal. In this respect the "social movement" in the narrower sense that also becomes apparent here is only a part of a much more far-reaching mechanism of transformation.[16] For this reason, the view must be directed beyond certain innovative models of order and single protagonists, and instead towards mass trends. In this context it will be assumed that the different political cultures of the various national societies of this time changed very quickly and profoundly in astonishing synchronicity, and that an important motivating force of this transformation consisted of a changing of the generations condensed in the symbol of 1968.[17]

Juvenilization in Western Societies

The increase in influence of the young generation in Western societies throughout the 1960s can be linked to several factors. The 1950s had already shown that, with the improvement of economic circumstances, youths now also possessed substantial spending power.[18] Primarily in the United States but thereafter also in West European countries, a diverse consumer goods industry exploded which saturated the market for youths with jeans, cosmetics, records etc. The consumer goods industry adopted stylistic elements that came into existence in various youth scenes, enriched them, experimented with new products and in doing so, functioned as synchronizer in the development of a new and diverse international youth culture. In turn, social trendsetters took up these impulses and recombined them into new styles, often in creative ways.[19] As youth cultures became attractive to the older generations, consumerism began to influence the nations' cultural self-image. The global confrontational situation caused by the Cold War formed an important background for contemporary interpretations of the youth's patterns of consumption. In any case it shaped the older generations' point of view, while the youth itself viewed the situation with more equanimity. While there may have been disagreement with respect to whether youth consumerism constituted a weakening of the West or whether it was one of its essential strengths, unity reigned with regard to the fact that the strengthening of young people's intellectual abilities would be a decisive criteria for the victory in the Cold War.[20] Since nobody knew how long economic prosperity would last, it was especially important to consoli-date this belief system among the youth, and educate them to be stead-fast democrats who would remain that way in times of economic instability. While material wealth enabled the expansion of the educa-tional system, it received its political direction through its catching up with the supposed lead of the East in the field of education. This is why the hopes for the future were associated more strongly with a well-edu-cated and politically stable young generation than in other times.

In addition, the percentage of young people in the population had increased since the end of the Second World War, in some countries up until to the mid-1960s: the percentage of youths under 15 in West Ger-many at the end of the 1950s was 21 percent, in 1970/71, 23 percent. In Denmark it decreased slightly during this period from 26 to 23 per-cent, in France from 26 to 25 percent. In many countries the share of 15- to 29-year-olds increased in the meantime, in Great Britain by 2 percent, and in Denmark, Sweden, and France by 4 percent each. In 1970/71 43 percent of Germany's, 47 percent of Denmark's, 44 percent of Sweden's, 49 percent of France's and 45 percent of Great Britain's pop-ulation were under 30 years old.[21] In the course of this decade the age group of youths in some European countries became younger in itself. It was a very relevant piece of information for the advertising clients of the West German teenager magazine *Bravo* that between 1963 and 1968 the segment of 21- to 24-year-olds shrank by a third, whereas by 1968 the 14- to 17-year-olds increased.[22] Western societies were young societies, not only due to the high birthrate but also to international processes of migration caused by increasing wealth and mainly mobilized younger age groups. In this way many protagonists of the student movement were young immigrants: in West Germany for example, Rudi Dutschke came from the German Democratic Republic, in Great Britain Tariq Ali was born in Pakistan, and in the United States Mario Savio was of Ital-ian origin.

In comparison to the 1920s, however, the percentage of young peo-ple in the 1960s was smaller. Its increasing importance could not be explained only by demographic factors. To a larger extent than ever, rel-atively young people took on economic or political responsibilities. In Great Britain, but also in Germany, they reached influential positions firstly in the explosively developing mass media and in various branches of the culture industry.[23] In addition, the period of youth was extended due to the large expansion of the educational system. Nearly twice as many people completed a college degree in West Germany and Great Britain in 1968/69 than in 1960, in Sweden more than double as many, in France the amount of students at universities nearly tripled during this period, and in Denmark it more than tripled.[24]

The number of those living in an independent phase between youth and adulthood thus increased significantly. In the Western and Northern European countries the percentage of pupils and students in the total population amounted to nearly 20 percent in 1970.[25] The marriage age of young people between 1960 and 1970 was also lower than in any other postwar decade.[26] In addition, at the end of the decade social realities that had prevailed several years before were legally codified. Young people could now influence basic political decisions and act as sovereign legal subjects earlier than ever before. Great Britain was the first West European country to lower the voting age to 18 in 1968. The Federal Republic of Germany followed in 1970, France and Italy in 1974. In 1972 the European Council of Ministers went a step further and recommended to its member states to lower the age of majority to 18 as well, a trend in all industrialized states reflected by the fact that the limit for adulthood demanded by European Union already existed in nearly all "East Block" states, the GDR included.[27]

Social Mixing and Individualization

A higher degree of social permeability was an essential characteristic of the post-1950s youth generation. In his book *Absolute Beginners,* published in 1959, the British journalist Colin MacInnes showed his enthusiasm for the specific absence of class distinctions in youth subcultures, in which protagonists of various social classes mixed.[28] A similar finding was reached in Germany although MacInnes' tone of euphoria when describing his observations was less shared. In 1962 the West German youth sociologist Friedrich Tenbruck discusses a "decontourization of the social roles," a "radical social release [*Freistellung*]," dangerous since he believed that the costs of individualization would be high and "a virtual gain of liberty" would actually result "in the destruction of the core of personality."[29] Social origin was however by no means irrelevant for young people. Differing traditional and cultural preferences due to social backgrounds still had a strong impact. In fact, under the conditions of mass consumption it continued to be the basis for the development of segmented subcultures partially along the lines of social boundaries, as for example the mods and rockers in Great Britain, hippies in America or *Gammler* in West Germany. The main tendency, however, accurately described by both MacInnes and Tenbruck, was that all in all the new youth cultures disassociated themselves from the adult world and social borders progressively loosened within subcultures. This led to a new mixing of socially determined cultural and political styles, in which the rise of subcultures and the expansion of the "counterculture" which began in 1967 produced deviating styles that transcended corresponding social confines and reached great masses of people.[30] Some working-class youths incorporated stylistic elements of bohemian origin into their dresscodes and social conduct, while upper-class youths simultaneously discovered stylistic elements of a rather proletarian popular culture.

Despite the progressive cultural change throughout the 1960s, most observers and protagonists were taken by surprise by the political radicalization that culminated in the years around 1968.[31] Hardly anybody had expected the youth to become politicized in such a far-reaching way, especially in the left-wing direction. Even in 1965 observers considered the American youth to be uncommitted, in 1966 West German youth was thought to be conformist, and the same view prevailed in Denmark in 1967. And as upwellings began in many places, even in March 1968 directly before the May riots, French commentators stated that things were happening everywhere but in France, where people were sleeping and missing everything.[32] Not least because of their unexpected character the events of 1968 gained the interpretation of a "rebellion." The impression of a surprise emerged because sociologists from San Francisco to West Berlin interpreted the increasing consumption by youth as conformist behavior, political conformity included. Western opinion leaders increasingly accepted young people's informal and experimental lifestyle as a central ideal, but they wanted to correct their assumed political abstinence by a more or less moderate politicization from above.[33] Most sociologists did not notice or misinterpreted the developments because there were no models of interpretation available for these completely new patterns of social conduct. Indeed the satisfaction of basic physical and material needs not only opens up space for cultural experiments but also for the formation of political consciousness, and the so-called "postmodern" principle of montage is not only found in the culture of consumption but also in the political field and did not only point to indifference but also to self-confidence. The surprising character of the events of 1968 also had to do with the fact that the new mass cultures had developed into organizational patterns that, up to then, were only known to deviant minorities, in other words not big organizations and associations or even the state, but small circles and informal groups were giving impulses for the ongoing modernization, and represented the cores of the emerging subcultures with the culture industry as their powerful ally.

Young intellectuals played a very important role in these processes of transformation, both as leaders of change within mass culture and as interpreters. Non-academically educated youths did not play such an important role, although young workers, to a varying degree, took part in the activities around 1968. In France and Italy, for example, they

formed the activist core of the strike movement, whereas in the Federal
Republic of Germany and in the Scandinavian countries, they obviously
became active later and in smaller numbers.[34] The extent to which they
were part of different national opposition movements differed from
country to country—to a certain degree social heterogeniety was even
characteristic for these movements—but usually the position of leadership was held by peers with a higher degree of school education and
often from respectable middle-class families. Having better material prerequisites, they were much more interested in politics and ready for
political activity; they also had more foreign experience, spoke more foreign languages and also spoke these more fluently. They also had a larger
interest in various elements of popular culture—especially in certain
genres of pop music, which inspired esoteric debates and enabled yet further claims to distinction.[35] Differentiations are also discernible within
the classes with a higher level of education. Not until its escalation and
broadening did the political protest movement significantly spread to
the younger cohorts of the educated classes. This was only the case since
roughly 1967 and to an increasing extent 1968/69, as observed for Germany and Italy for example.[36] Even though the political climate at
schools only changed drastically at the end of the 1960s, also the opposition movements of the early 1960s lived off a proportionally high participation of not only university students but also students from
secondary schools. For example, already in 1962 students constituted 35
percent of the Danish "anti-nuclear movement."[37] Another indication is
that many protest careers began in the early 1960s, even though the
movement had its breakthrough at the end of the decade.

The political interest of highly educated youths differentiated them
from their peers with a lower level of education. In the 1950s young
workers supported rock'n'roll which, as a cultural style, was viewed as
something with a rebellious character by the public as well as by the protagonists. At the beginning of the 1960s, however, highschool and university students increasingly discovered such niches and used them for
cultural experiments, attaching a notion of rebelliousness and increasing
political energy to certain elements of the popular culture that was in
and of itself nonpolitical.[38] Whereas popular culture was first and foremost a big social and cultural melting pot, it underwent increasing differentiation beginning in the mid-1960s, due in part to a succession of
new styles exported principally from the United States to Europe and in
part to an increasing political radicalization primarily among secondary
school and university students. Working-class youths were involved in
politics to a far lesser degree.[39] A German survey shows that in 1964, the
percentage of people who had a negative attitude towards the state stayed
at a relatively low level, under 3 percent of secondary school students

and 5 percent of elementary school pupils. Until 1968, the share of self proclaimed enemies of the state within the latter group grew slowly, up to 7 percent. In the case of the group of young intellectuals, however, it shot up dramatically to 16 percent.[40] Basically, the protest movements remained "movements of university students and small minorities of youths outside universities." American and German sociologists assumed an "underclass conservatism" which was in strong contrast to the intellectuals' main "progressive" tendency.[41] It is true that at the high point of the student movement, the attitude of West German working-class youths towards the deeds of their peers was more positive than that of their older colleagues. But it cannot be said that a rebellious attitude transcended all class boundaries within the whole generation.[42]

"Don't Trust Anyone Over 30"?
Relationships Between Generations

The existence of such social differences does not belie the fact that large segments of the adult generations tolerated or even supported the students' political demands—within reason they also supported their radicalization as elements of a wide-ranging cultural change that led to the youth generally developing a more liberal and permissive style and making participatory demands. All in all, the relationships between the generations were a lot more balanced than the confrontational rhetoric and actual confrontational situations at the peak of the student movement would suggest. Surveys in France, the United States, and the Federal Republic of Germany have shown that most parents got used to their children's increasing freedom relatively quickly. Various clues indicate that relatively harmonious conditions outweighed bitter conflict in family relationships.[43] Counter-examples that were often eagerly picked out by the media and became well known must not be generalized. Only a few parents attempted to subdue their increasingly independent children, usually unsuccessfully.[44] Studies over a long period have shown that in West Germany tolerant models of education had never increased as drastically as between the early 1960s and the mid-1970s.[45]

On the other hand the impression of a conflict between the generations was not completely wrong: relatively harmonious relationships existed in the family unit as well as a generation conflict relating to society as a whole. In fact this simultaneity was an essential characteristic of this period of radical change. Conflicts and processes of detachment in various segments of society increased in the 1960s, they were manifest in many ways, not only in different cultural styles. Political parties underwent a generational change. In many countries new parties were

founded, shaped by youth and almost exclusively positioned left of the
Social Democrats. For example, in the Netherlands *Demokraten 66*
(named after the year of their foundation, in Denmark) *Venstresocialisterne* (at the end of 1967), and also the myriad of leftwing radical groups
and small parties mushrooming at the end of the 1960s were nearly
entirely assemblies of very young age groups. In order to decode the contradictory relationship between generations, Norbert Elias has suggested
differentiating between individual generation relations—those of the
private sphere—and social generation relations—apparent in the public
sphere.[46] In this way the vexing picture painted by contemporary youth
studies becomes clearer: while parts of the older generations had
difficulties adapting to the new times and while it was sometimes easier
and sometimes harder to succeed them, at the same time, however, it was
possible that trust and tolerance dominated the climate of the family
unit.

A close examination also shows that everyday life adhered far more
strongly to traditions than public discussion on the youth phenomenon
would suggest. The mass of young people did relate to the modernization that their avant-garde displayed, with a certain delay and in more
tolerable mixtures. As cool as Eric Clapton, as sexy as Brigitte Bardot, as
libertarian as Rainer Langhans—many wanted to be a bit of everything,
but not too extreme, more for home usage so it could be arranged with
other conditions in school, at work and in the parental home. Representative polls at the end of the 1960s show that youths as well as adults
idealized certain concepts of youth as the norm. These, however, never
needed to be identical with the more traditional everyday life of youths.
Most of the elements of a consumer society that the mass of youths
incorporated into their everyday life were easily compatible with the
adults' concept of modernity. For instance, with regard to fashion, vacation, purchasing of household goods etc., in many cases youths' opinions
were a decisive factor for the choice of purchases. Public opinion
believed that, with regard to cosmetics, sports goods and technical
devices, neither the father nor his wife were the biggest experts but the
adolescent children. In this context parents placed their children in leading positions on purpose and explicitly. To a certain degree they felt
often insecure, but did not question the authority of youth tastes. A
study on the conduct of youths and adults with regard to consumption
in 1970 summarized the situation in a formula: "A more youth-orien-
tated paradigm is making its demands without adults being able to
adjust with full sails."[47] This resulted in a substantial need for interfa-
milial communication, which was apparently often satisfied. This study
showed that both parties viewed the atmosphere in the family as good,
and that parents rejected too harsh a criticism of the youths. In this

respect, it is not that surprising that adults adopted a far more friendly manner and attitude towards their offspring between the late 1950s and the mid-1970s: in 1950 only 24 percent of the questioned West Germans, in 1960 already 44 percent and in 1975 no less than 62 percent replied that they had a favorable impression of the young generation.[48] In this period the social basis of the new mass cultures had changed thoroughly—from the marginal underclass culture of the "*Halbstarken*" ("rowdies"), which was perceived as inferior and dangerous or the elitist outsiders of a middle-class bohemia, to a celebrated class-transcending lifestyle of an "experimental society."[49]

Most activists of the student movement defended themselves against an interpretation of their political protest as an expression of age-induced energy surplus. The representatives of the liberal "establishment," who were setting the tone, reacted calmly and in an understanding way to the slogan "Don't trust anyone above 30" which had quickly spread from the United States to Western Europe. They believed that the rebellious spirit would evaporate with age. This was also meant as a counter-argument to conservative cultural pessimism. The protagonists of the student movement, however, viewed this stance mainly as a paternalist gesture, an expression of the opinion leaders' "repressive tolerance." Jerry Rubin, the founder of the yippies, responded with an almost postmodern slogan to the fact that many student activists were about to cross the critical 30-year border: "You're only as old as you wanna be. Age is in your head."[50]

The assignment of age was not really arbitrary but constructed and determined by a historical caesura. For Rubin, the middle of the century constituted a generation border—that turning point around 1950 in which for the Western world the continuum of war and crisis of the first half of the century ended and was gradually replaced by political liberalization, economic prosperity and a culture of consumption: "Those who grew up before the 1950s live today in a mental world of Nazism, concentration camps, economic depression and Communist dreams stalinized. A pre-1950s who can still dream is very rare. Kids who grew up in the post-1950s live in a world of supermarkets, color TV commercials, guerrilla war, international media, psychedelics, rock'n'roll and moon walks. For us *nothing is impossible*. We can do *anything*. This generation gap is the widest in history. The *pre*-1950's generation has *nothing* to teach the *post*-1950's […]."

Decline of Authority and Incline towards Provocation

Rubin's statement is not only a good example for the almost unlimited optimism that was widespread among the activists of 1968, it also exposes the central argument that questioned the leading function of the older generations as well: their patterns of conduct were no longer adequate. Socialized in the "Age of Catastrophe," they could hardly deliver guidelines for how to find one's way and to behave in the "Golden Age."[51] This point of view is hardly deniable. How does a society mentally adjust to drastically changed material conditions, and which role do generational aspects play in this context? Contemporaries of the 1960s and 1970s already pointed to discrepancies in the development of different spheres of society. In the France of 1968, for example, Regis Debray describes an unusually large difference between the rapid development of material conditions and the habits and values of the population that were only slowly changing. From his point of view, the necessary harmonization of this gulf resulted in the dynamics of 1968, which were full of conflict.[52] In fall 1966, Theodor W. Adorno, faced with the electoral successes of a right-wing radical party in West Germany, stated in a very similar way that one had to reflect on "the collision of modern mass media with a consciousness that by far has not reached that of nineteenth century bourgeois cultural liberalism."[53] Even though these interpretations may seem exaggerated, relevant studies on the long term "change in values" in postindustrial societies do confirm that in this context, processes of cultural assimilation were slightly delayed reactions to changed material living conditions. Those processes described by Daniel Bell, Alain Touraine, Ronald Inglehart and Helmut Klages were sparked by the worldwide boost of material improvement since the end of the Second World War.[54] These adjustments could be conducted by younger people much more quickly than by older people who had grown up under completely different conditions. In this respect, Rubin's, Debray's and Adorno's contemporary observations on a discrepancy between the mentality especially of the older generations and the changed social and material realities are confirmed by sociological research.

As discussed, the adaption of the old to the new did not occur explosively in 1968 but progressed from the end of the 1950s and reached a "starting phase"[55] at the beginning of the 1960s, without leading to the radical change desired by some young intellectuals. It was about a "'spreading out' or 'differentiating' of previously underdeveloped patterns of meaning, life or option" which occurred due to the current "change of economic, technological, social and political conditions."[56] Even though one cannot assume that youths' social praxis was profoundly changed in one go, many elements of disintegration were rather strong on the threshold to 1968, for instance with regard to race- or gender relations, acceptance of an autonomous youth culture, sexual conduct etc. The traditional cultural conservatives who tried everything to prevent the radical cultural change in the 1950s no longer had a say in the discourse on the modern age. Conversative modernizers and liberal intellectuals had taken the leading opinion, with "measured judgment" (Arthur Marwick) dominating.[57]

In politics, a change of generations had also been taking place since the early 1960s, as politicians such as John F. Kennedy, Willy Brandt or Olof Palme set off to remove the generation of Eisenhower and Adenauer from power. The speed and extent of these processes of replacement were different in various European countries, however, and overall it is obvious that not only economy, technology and media but also politics and traditional cultural norms were already undergoing a radical change when the student protests escalated. These protests themselves were part of an accelerated development towards "values of self-realization" that began around the mid-1960s.[58]

Here the younger generation took the lead even though this change of values had a grip on all generations. Inglehart quite accurately observed that "due to the wealth that was without example in history and the continuing peace since 1945, younger age groups in Western countries appreciated their higher degree of economic and physical security less highly than older people who had experienced bigger economic insecurity. Vice versa, the priority of members of the younger generation for nonmaterial needs such as a communal feeling and quality of life was higher."[59] "Postmaterialistic" values represented by younger people received a substantially great role in society due to the increasing replacement of the older generation by the younger generation in all fields of society but also by the effects of broadcasting.

There are many factors which speak in favor of interpreting "1968" as an exaggerated expression of this fundamental process of generation succession. This climax cannot only be explained by situational factors alone—such as the Vietnam War or a fascist past—for the structural factors such as norms and values had been undergoing a process of radical change for several years. In his analysis, Norbert Elias pointed out that revolts do not occur when "oppression is strongest but just when it becomes weaker."[60] And the German sociologist Karl Mannheim already concluded in 1928 that a specific element of youthful consciousness of the present did not solely consist in "being closer to current problems," but also "to experience the process of loosening up as a prime antithesis" and to push the development further from this point while "the older generation remains in their earlier position of a new orientation."[61] This explains why student activists' criticism was so strongly directed against liberals who were striving for a modernization and were in the process of realizing it. Not only conservative and liberal politicians were subjects of massive criticism from the student movement but also nineteenth and twentieth century oppositional movements who had established themselves in the field of power politics. In the late 1950s and early 1960s, as social democratic parties learnt to value the economic potential of capitalism and communist parties dealt more or less critically with Stalinism, many young intellectuals split from these parties. The West German SDS was disassociated from the Social Democratic Party and Trotskyist and Maoist groups left the youth organization of the French Communist Party. In Denmark, the *Socialistik Folkeparti* splintered off from the Danish Communist Party and became the first party of the New Left, and Henri Lefebvre, E.P. Thompson, Ulrike Meinhof left the Communist Parties of their countries in these years as well.

Expanding the existing limits through provocation was a distinct strategy for popular youth culture, not least for the media. The concert promoter Fritz Rau, for example, who held a key role in importing American popular culture to the European continent, explained the success of his work with "an instinctive evaluation of the just about possible."[62] The situationist-inspired strategy of provocation went further by intentionally pushing the limits too far. The plan was to break through the shell of a supposedly hermetically sealed off society and in this way kick off consciousness-forming processes by nonconformist actions. Such provocations were not confined to political actions but included politics, everyday life, and art.[63] "Revolution is Poetry. There is poetry in all those acts which break the system of organization"—so read the catalog of the famous exhibition of the Stockholm *Moderna Museet* on revolutionary art in 1969, explaining the mechanism in which artistic creativity, social praxis and political change become melted into one.[64]

The results of these strategies of provocation were ambivalent. On the one hand they polarized the population and partially caused massive counter-reactions, which were desired by the protagonists in order to make the existing potential for conflict perceptible by all. On the other hand, they did not always lead to the desired results. In France, for instance, the majority voted for de Gaulle's government in the June elections immediately after the events of May 1968. In the following year Richard Nixon, a Republican politician, became president of the United States. A similar counter-reaction can be observed in the case of the student demonstrations in the Federal Republic of Germany between 1967 and 1969. Until March 1968, a third of the West German population considered the breath of fresh air with which the students revitalized political culture to be positive. Another third believed that it carried the danger of revolution within and the other third was indecisive.[65] The number of critics grew not so much after the Easter riots following the attempted assassination of Rudi Dutschke but rather after the further escalation of violence during the second half of 1968. The percentage of people in favor of a ban of the SDS increased from 19 percent in May 1968 to 57 percent by the beginning of 1969.[66] The share of those who considered the police's reaction too weak also increased strongly from 8 percent in 1966 to 44 percent at the beginning of 1969. In this context it is striking that the youngest age group and persons with a university-track high school diploma supported the demonstrations by far the most, with approximately 60 percent.[67] Substantial generational and social discrepancies and conflicts did therefore exist, although did not impede the process of cultural change: the relations between the generations relaxed and became less formal on a society-wide basis.

A Youth Rebellion?

Can one therefore speak of a "youth rebellion"? First of all, such a label already reflects a certain contemporary mindset, making it problematic as a scholarly category. Furthermore, it is not in fact entirely applicable: firstly because intergenerational relations were more equable than thereby suggested, and secondly because of the varying degrees to which youth of different social classes took part in this "rebellion."[68] As working-class youths were not active to a comparable degree as university students and because those students received the strongest support from more educated adults, some social scientists argued against speaking of a youth revolt in favor of a revolt of the intellectuals—a label which, however, did not survive. Nevertheless, in the character of the young intellectual as an ideal type, two traits that especially shaped the change to a postindustrial society combined: youthful age and intellectual interventionism. Already in 1963, the author George Paloczi-Horvath in an international overview discovered what he called a "new race": the "superintellectuals" were an especially cool and critical section of the youth, which never existed before and now figures as a committed proponent of the generational conflict.[69]

Such descriptions do indeed contain appropriate observations, but they also indicate how hard it was to recognize the accelerating forces in the midst of a situation of radical change, one in which obviously known social ties of the individual began to loosen. In this context, it is not surprising that the category "generation" entered the field as it pushed social differences into the background and was in conformity with the self-interpretation of Western societies as socially balanced "middle-class societies" that had supposedly overcome class division. The interpretation as a "rebellion" was in tune with the *Zeitgeist* in which breaks from the seemingly cemented norms of the preceding 1950s were basically considered legitimate. Furthermore, it was part of a construction which gave meaning to a multitude of more or less synchronous events.[70] The term "youth rebellion," however, was not entirely a construct. On the one hand, the emotionalism contained within this term is more likely a distortion of the overall character of what it wishes to depict. On the other hand, it reflected—if in an exaggerated way—actual shifts. Not only did the student movement most clearly formulate a new line of political thinking, its cultural demands and participatory ideas promised a multitude of new chances for upward social mobility, for nonstudents as well. In this context it was a generational movement for upward social mobility that took place within the traditional leading classes as well as between the classes. The reception and rapid expansion of international youth cultures account for the correct impression that the development was taking place on a global level and its major upholders were youths. This significantly invigorated the protagonists' self-confidence. When in 1968 various currents of transformation coincided and "everything seemed to be in motion," the Danish provo and son of the social democratic minister of finance, Ole Grünbaum, uttered the firm conviction that the end of the known order was imminent and that the young generation was accelerating this almost physical process: "Today an 18-year-old knows more about the Vietnam War than a 50-year-old. Nowadays, the majority of youths speak two or more languages, whereas at the same time hardly more than ten members of the *Folketing* (the Danish parliament) regularly read larger international papers and magazines. The youth is much better educated than previous generations and more competent than ever in using their knowledge and ability to acquire power. A decisive reason, however, is that the youth is the only relatively large group in our society that can deal with *wealth* and modern life naturally. Wealth is taken literally. For the youth wealth is not a status symbol, but something they take for granted."[71] The young protagonists did not act according to a plan with a clearly defined aim but they were the first to use the playing fields of consumer society and to explore its borders. Especially the intellectuals among them gave the diffuse structural change of postwar societies a subjective expression and a direction.[72] Between 1967 and 1969, young intellectuals spoke out loud for the first time, articulating their take on the ongoing upheavals: publicly, en masse and simultaneously around the world. This phenomenon is too significant to be simply subsumed into the continuum of the 1960s and its cultural revolution. This is why, even today, the whole long decade of radical change is frequently abbreviated by the figure "1968"—a label which means so much, but explains so little.

Youth were not just agents of abstract structural changes. On the contrary: the dawning era presented each individual with far more opportunities for self-actualization than had ever existed before, and it was young people who exploited these to the fullest. Their activities were symptomatic of an emerging individuality and informality in social relationships, which in the process irritated more than a few of their contemporaries. Hardly anyone could say where it would all lead, but they were united on one final goal: a better life for each and everyone. Everything else was open for debate.

Notes

1. Ronald Fraser, ed., *1968. A Student Generation in Revolt* (New York, 1988); Uwe Bergmann, Rudi Dutschke, Wolfgang Lefèvre, and Bernd Rabehl, *Rebellion der Studenten* (Reinbek, 1968); Erling Bjurström, *Generationsupproret. Ungdomskulturer, ungdomsrörelser och tonårsmarknad från 50-tal till 80-tal* (Stockholm, 1980); Niels Martinov, *Ungdomsoprøret i Danmark. Et portræt af årene, der rystede musikken, billedkunsten, teatret, litteraturen, filmen og familien* (Copenhagen, 2000). On 22 April 1968 the French magazine *L'Express* published an article entitled "Europe: Young Rebels" and also in Italy "youth revolt" began to appear (Arthur Marwick, "Die 68er Revolution," in *Große Revolutionen der Geschichte. Von der Frühzeit bis zur Gegenwart*, ed. Peter Wende [Munich, 2000], 312–32, here 317; Jan Kurz, "Die italienische Studentenbewegung 1966-1968," in *1968—Vom Ereignis zum Gegenstand der Geschichtswissenschaft*, ed. Ingrid Gilcher-Holtey [Göttingen, 1998], 64–81, here 64.).
2. Charles Reich, *The Greening of America* (New York, 1970). The title of the German edition was *The World is Becoming Young. The Nonviolent Uprising of the New Generation* (*Die Welt wird jung. Der gewaltlose Aufstand der neuen Generation* [Vienna, 1970]). The title of the Swedish translation is also symptomatic: *Towards a New World. How the Youth Revolt Creates a Society that Places Quality of Living before Economic Progress* (*Mot en ny värld: hur ungdomsrevolten skapar ett samhälle där livskvalitet går före ekonomisk framgång* [Stockholm, 1971]).
3. This was shown by contemporary surveys in West Germany: *Emnid-Information*, no. 3 (1969), 2ff.
4. For an intensive profile of the New Left: George Katsiaficas, *The Imagination of the New Left. A Global Analysis of 1968* (Boston, 1987). Also compare Maurice Isserman, *If I Had a Hammer. The Death of the Old Left and the Birth of the New Left* (New York, 1987); Lin Chun, *The British New Left* (Edinburgh, 1993). On the intellectual spokesmen see Ron Eyerman, and Andrew Jamison, *Seeds of the Sixties* (Berkeley, 1994).
5. Reimut Reiche and Peter Gäng, "Vom antikapitalistischen Protest zur sozialistischen Politik," in *Neue Kritik*, no. 41 (April 1967), 22, 24.
6. Compare the call for an "international conference on Vietnam" and the final declaration in: *Provokationen. Die Studenten- und Jugendrevolte in ihren Flugblättern 1965–1971*, ed. Jürgen Miermeister and Jochen Staadt (Darmstadt and Neuwied 1980), 113–15; Lutz Schulenburg, *Das Leben ändern, die Welt verändern! 1968. Dokumente und Berichte* (Hamburg, 1998), 125–27.

7. *Superlove* 5 (March 1968), 4.

8. See Ingo Juchler, *Die Studentenbewegungen in den Vereinigten Staaten und der Bundesrepublik Deutschland der sechziger Jahre. Eine Untersuchung hinsichtlich ihrer Beeinflussung durch Befreiungsbewegungen und -theorien aus der Dritten Welt* (Berlin, 1996), 306ff.

9. Arthur Marwick, *The Sixties: Cultural Revolution in Britain, France, Italy, and the United States, c.1958–c.1974* (Oxford, 1999), 97 and 99.

10. As in the reactions of the West German public to student demonstrations: *Emnid-Information*, no. 3/4 (1968).

11. Katsiaficas, *Imagination*, 44f. Also consult Michael Kidron's and Ronald Segal's overview, printed in *1968. The World transformed*, ed. Carole Fink, Philipp Gassert, and Detlef Junker (Washington D.C., Cambridge, 1998), 14f.

12. See Wolfgang Kraushaar, "Die erste globale Revolution," in *1968 als Mythos, Chiffre und Zäsur*, Kraushaar (Hamburg, 2000), 19–52. Also compare Immanuel Wallenstein, "1968, Revolution in the World-System: Theses and Queries," *Theory and Society* 18 (1989): 431–49; Beate Fietze, "'A spirit of unrest.' Die Achtundsechziger-Generation als globales Schwellenphänomen," in *Der Geist der Unruhe. 1968 im Vergleich Wissenschaft-Literatur-Medien*, ed. Rainer Rosenberg, Inge Münz-Koenen, and Petra Boden (Berlin, 2000), 3–25. On the character of a "cultural revolution" see Christoph Kleßmann, "1968—Studentenrevolte oder Kulturrevolution?," in *Revolution in Deutschland? 1789–1989*, ed. Manfred Hettling (Göttingen, 1991), 90–105; Pascal Ory, "Une 'Révolution culturelle'?," in *Les Années 68. Le temps de la contestation*, ed. Geneviève Dreyfus-Armand et al. (Brussels: Éditions Complexe, 2000), 219–24, as well as Arthur Marwick's essay in this edition.

13. Ingrid Gilcher-Holtey, *Die 68er Bewegung. Deutschland—Westeuropa—USA* (Munich, 2001), 10.

14. For the historicization of the long 1960s, in which 1968 is more or less strongly embedded, see in addition to Marwick: Lars Mjøset, "Det lange 1960-tallet i Norden," in *Nordiskt 60-tal. Uppbrott och konfrontation* (Helsinki, 1990), 14–18; David Farber, ed., *The Sixties. From Memory to History* (Chapel Hill and London, 1994); Fink, Gassert, and Junker, *1968*; Gilcher-Holtey, *1968*; Dreyfus-Armand et al., *Les Années 68*; Axel Schildt, Detlef Siegfried, and Karl Christian Lammers, eds., *Dynamische Zeiten. Die 60er Jahre in den beiden deutschen Gesellschaften* (Hamburg, 2000); Jürgen Heideking, Jörg Helbig, and Anke Ortlepp, eds., *The Sixties Revisited: Culture, Society, Politics* (Heidelberg, 2001).

15. Detlev Claussen, "Chiffre 1968," in *Revolution und Mythos*, ed. Dietrich Harth and Jan Assmann (Frankfurt am Main, 1992), 219–28.

16. Friedrich Neidhardt, and Dieter Rucht, "The Analysis of Social Movements: The State of the Art and Some Perspectives of Further Research," in *Research on Social Movements. The State of the Art in Western Europe and the USA*, ed. Dieter Rucht (Frankfurt am Main, 1991), 421–64; Ron Eyerman, and Andrew Jamison, *Social Movements. A Cognitive Approach* (Cambridge, 1991).

17. Ronald Inglehart, *The Silent Revolution. Changing Values and Political Styles Among Western Publics* (Princeton, 1977).

18. Compare the classic study for the United States, Eugene Gilbert, *Advertising and Marketing to Young People* (Pleasantville/New York, 1957); for Great Britain, Mark Abrams, *The Teenage Consumer* (London, 1959).

19. Thomas Frank, *The Conquest of Cool. Business Culture, Counter Culture, and the Rise of Hip Consumerism* (Chicago, 1997). In this context also compare my essay, Detlef Siegfried, "Modkultur, kulturindustri og venstrefløjen i Vesttyskland 1958–1973," *Den Jyske Historiker*, 101 (June 2003): 68–94.

20. In all European countries the debate on the non-materialistic side-effects of a consumer society was closely linked to the question whether they constitute an "Americanization" of national and European patterns of conduct. See Heide Fehrenbach and Uta G. Poiger, eds., *Transactions, Transgressions, Transformations. American Culture in Western Europe and Japan* (New York and Oxford, 2000).

21. Statistisches Bundesamt, ed., *Statistisches Jahrbuch für die Bundesrepublik Deutschland 1959* (Stuttgart and Mainz, 1959), 21*; 1973, 29*. For details on the course of the development see the introduction to this volume.

22. *Bravo-Einkaufs-Panel,* Annual 1968/69 (Munich, 1968), 248.

23. For pop-business in Great Britain compare Simon Frith, and Howard Horne, *Art Into Pop* (London and New York, 1987). For France this is impressively described with the example of the "jeune cadre" in Kristin Ross, *Fast Cars, Clean Bodies. Decolonization and the Reordering of French Culture* (Cambridge/Mass., 1995).

24. B.R. Mitchell, *International Historical Statistics Europe 1750–1993,* (4th ed., London, 1998), 894ff.

25. In Denmark 18.8 percent, West Germany 18.4 percent, France 19.7 percent, Great Britain 19 percent. Oscar W. Gabriel, ed., *Die EG-Staaten im Vergleich, Strukturen, Prozesse, Politikinhalte* (Opladen, 1992), 492.

26. Marianne Beisheim et al., *Im Zeitalter der Globalisierung? Thesen und Daten zur gesellschaftlichen und politischen Denationalisierung* (Baden-Baden, 1999), 488.

27. Heinz Schäfer, *Die Herabsetzung der Volljährigkeit: Anspruch und Konsequenzen. Eine Dokumentation* (Munich, 1977).

28. Colin MacInnes, "Absolute Beginners," in *The Colin MacInnes Omnibus. His three London Novels* (London, [1959] 1985).

29. Friedrich H. Tenbruck, *Jugend und Gesellschaft. Soziologische Perspektiven* (Freiburg, 1962), 38f.

30. Theodore Roszak, *The Making of a Counter Culture: Reflections on the Technocratic Society and Its Youthful Opposition* (Garden City, New York, 1969); Walter Hollstein, *Der Untergrund. Zur Soziologie jugendlicher Protestbewegungen* (Neuwied and Berlin, 1969); Helmut Kreuzer, *Die Boheme. Analyse und Dokumentation der intellektuellen Subkultur vom 19. Jahrhundert bis zur Gegenwart* (Stuttgart, 1971); Elisabeth Nelson, *The British Counter Culture 1966–73: A Study of the Underground Press* (New York, 1989); Jonathon Greene, *All Dressed Up. The Sixties and the Counter-Culture* (London, 1998).

31. "Without doubt this problem between the generations is a big surprise in the time after the war, probably the biggest surprise of all unforeseen events." *Welt am Sonntag,* 18 May 1969.

32. Klaus R. Allerbeck, *Soziologie radikaler Studentenbewegungen: Eine vergleichende Untersuchung in der Bundesrepublik Deutschland und in den Vereinigten Staaten* (Munich, 1973); Viggo Graf Blücher, *Die Generation der Unbefangenen. Zur Soziologie der jungen Menschen heute* (Düsseldorf and Cologne, 1966); Ole Bert Henriksen, and Erik Hogh, *Storbyungdom* (Copenhagen, 1970); Ingrid Gilcher-Holtey, *"Die Phantasie an die Macht." Mai 68 in Frankreich* (Frankfurt am Main, 1995).

33. This tendency was very strong in Germany. See Detlef Siegfried, "Vom Teenager zur Pop-Revolution. Politisierungstendenzen in der westdeutschen Jugendkultur 1959 bis 1968," in *Dynamische Zeiten*, ed. Schildt, Siegfried, and Lammers, 582–623.

34. Such discrepancies are exemplified by Marcia Tolomelli, *"Repressiv getrennt" oder "organisch verbündet." Studenten und Arbeiter 1968 in der Bundesrepublik Deutschland und in Italien* (Opladen, 2001).

35. Various examples in international comparison can be found in Jugendwerk der Deutschen Shell, *Jugend in Europa. Ihre Eingliederung in die Welt der Erwachsenen. Eine vergleichende Analyse zwischen der Bundesrepublik Deutschland, Frankreich und Großbritannien*, ed., 3 vols. (Hamburg, 1977). Also Heinz Bonfadelli, *Die Sozialisationsperspektive in der Massenkommunikationsforschung. Neue Ansätze, Methoden und Resultate zur Stellung der Massenmedien im Leben der Kinder und Jugendlichen* (Berlin, 1981), 373f.; Infratest, *Der jugendliche Radiohörer. Nordrhein-Westfalen 1971* (Munich, 1971), 84.

36. Luisa Passerini, "1968 in Italien: Eine Geschichte der 'langen Dauer,'" in *1968—ein europäisches Jahr?*, ed. Etienne François, Matthias Middel, Emmanuel Terray, and Dorothee Wierling (Leipzig, 1997), 79–88, here 83.

37. Steven Llewellyn Bjerregaard Jensen and Thomas Ekman Jørgensen, *Studenteroprøret i Danmark 1968. Forudsætninger og konsekvenser* (unprinted manuscript, Copenhagen 1999), 87f.

38. See Peter Wicke's essay in this volume.

39. For pop culture see Helmut Salzinger, *Rock Power oder wie musikalisch ist die Revolution? Ein Essay über Pop-Musik und Gegenkultur* (Frankfurt am Main, 1972); Simon Frith, *Sound Effects. Youth, Leisure, and the Politics of Rock'n'Roll* (New York, 1981); Sheila Whiteley, *The Space between the Notes. Rock and the Counterculture* (London and New York, 1992); Ron Eyerman, and Andrew Jamison, *Music and Social Movements* (Cambridge, 1995).

40. *Emnid-Information*, no. 9/10 (1969), 13.

41. The first quote is from Günter C. Behrmann, "Politische Einstellungen und Verhaltensweisen Jugendlicher," in *Jugend zwischen Auflehnung und Anpassung. Einstellungen, Verhaltensweisen, Lebenschancen*, ed. Hans-Georg Wehling (Stuttgart et al., 1973), 63–88, here 77. The second quote is from: Walter Jaide, "Über die Unruhe in der jungen Generation," *Aus Politik und Zeitgeschichte* B22/69 (31 May 1969): 3–13, here 8ff. Compare Seymour M. Lipset, *Political Man: The Social Basis of Politics* (New York, [1960] 1963).

42 Emnid-Insitut für Meinungsforschung, *Junge Intelligenzschicht 1968/69. Politische Meinungen, Einstellungen und Verhaltensbereitschaften* (Bielefeld, 1969), 88.

43. Compare Allerbeck's comparative study of West Germany and the United States, Allerbeck, *Soziologie*. For Sweden, see: Bengt-Erik Andersson, *Generation efter generation. Om tonårskultur, ungdomsrevolt och generationsmotsättnigar* (Malmö, 1982). In 1976, 61 percent of West German 22- to 23-year-olds described their relationship to their fathers as "good" or "excellent," in France 62 percent, in great Britain 68 percent; with respect to their relationship to their mothers the percentage was over 70 percent in all three countries (*Jugend in Europa*, vol. 2, 8f).

44. Marwick, *Sixties*, 382.

45. Thomas Gensicke, "Sozialer Wandel durch Modernisierung, Individualisierung und Wertewandel," *Aus Politik und Zeitgeschichte* B 42/96 (11 October 1996): 3–17.

46. Norbert Elias, "Der bundesdeutsche Terrorismus—Ausdruck eines sozialen Generationskonflikts," in Elias, *Studien über die Deutschen. Machtkämpfe und Habitusentwicklung im 19. und 20. Jahrhundert*, ed. Michael Schröter (Frankfurt am Main, 1994), 300–89.

47. Institut für angewandte Psychologie und Soziologie, ed., *BRAVO. Meinungsmacher Junger Markt* (Frankfurt am Main, 1971), 17.

48. Elisabeth Noelle-Neumann, ed., *The Germans. Public Opinion Polls, 1967–1980* (London, 1981), 53.

49. Gerhard Schulze, *Die Erlebnisgesellschaft. Kultursoziologie der Gegenwart* (Frankfurt am Main, 1992).

50. This and the following quote in Jerry Rubin, *Do it! Scenarios of the Revolution* (New York, 1970), 90f.

51. Eric Hobsbawm completely confirms Rubin's contemporary impression from a historiographical view, Eric Hobsbawm, *Age of Extremes. The Short Twentieth Century 1914–1991* (London, 1994).

52. Debray is quoted in Giovanni Arighi, Terence Hopkins, and Immanuel Wallerstein, "1989—Die Fortsetzung von 1968," in *1968*, ed. François, Middell, Terray, and Wierling, 147–64, here 149.

53. Theodor W. Adorno, "Erziehung nach Auschwitz," in Adorno, *Erziehung zur Mündigkeit. Vorträge und Gespräche mit Hellmut Becker 1959–1969*, ed. Gerhard Kadelbach (Frankfurt am Main, 1971), 92–109, here 98.

54. Alain Touraine, *La Société post-industrielle* (Paris, 1969); Daniel Bell, *The Coming of Post-Industrial Society: A Venture in Social Forecasting* (New York, 1973); Inglehart, *Silent Revolution;* Helmut Klages, *Traditionsbruch als Herausforderung. Perspektiven der Wertewandelgesellschaft* (Frankfurt am Main, 1993); Ronald Inglehart, *Modernisierung und Postmodernisierung. Kultureller, wirtschaftlicher und politischer Wandel in 43 Gesellschaften* (Frankfurt am Main, and New York, 1998).

55. Compare Klages, *Traditionsbruch*, 72, pointing out the years 1963 to 1965. The precise periodization of the change of values is left up to historical research, which has only just begun.

56. See, ibid., 15, for the first; Ronald Inglehart, *Kultureller Umbruch. Wertewandel in der westlichen Welt* (Frankfurt am Main and New York, 1989), 22, for the second.

57. Marwick's central argument has been confirmed for West Germany by Uta G. Poiger, *Jazz, Rock, and Rebels. Cold War Politics and American Culture in a Divided Germany* (Berkeley, Los Angeles, and London, 2000).

58. For this periodization see Klages, *Traditionsbruch*, 45.

59. Inglehart, *Umbruch*, 77.

60. Elias, *Terrorismus*, 307.

61. Karl Mannheim, "Das Problem der Generationen," in Mannheim, *Wissenssoziologie. Auswahl aus dem Werk* (Neuwied and Berlin, 1970), 509–65, here 539f.

62. Kathrin Brigl, and Siegfried Schmidt-Joos, *Fritz Rau. Buchhalter der Träume* (Severin, 1985), 151. On the general role of the media: Todd Gitlin, *The Whole World Is Watching. Mass Media in the Making and Unmaking of the New Left* (Berkeley et al., 1980). However, with regard to protest cultures there were substantial national differences. This is shown comparing the United States and Italy: Alessandro Portelli, "The Transatlantic Jeremiad: American Mass Culture and Counterculture and Opposition Culture in Italy," in *Cultural Transmissions and Receptions. American Mass Culture in Europe*, ed. R. Kroes, R.W. Rydell, and D.J.F. Bosscher (Amsterdam, 1993), 125–38.

63. Roberto Ohrt, *Phantom Avantgarde. Eine Geschichte der Situationistischen Internationale und der modernen Kunst* (Hamburg, 1990).

64. Quoted by Daniel Bell, *The Cultural Contradictions of Capitalism* (New York, 1976), 131.

65. *Emnid-Information*, no. 3/4 (1968).

66. Emnid, *Junge Intelligenzschicht*, 79 and 84f.

67. Institut für Demoskopie, Allensbach, *Untersuchungen über die Studentenunruhen in Deutschland* (September 1969), Bundesarchiv Koblenz, Zsg.132/1624, table 13.

68. In the 1970s the last aspect was especially pointed in Stuart Hall and Tony Jefferson, eds., *Resistance Through Rituals: Youth Subculture in Postwar Britain* (London, 1976).

69. George Paloczi-Horvath, *Jugend—Schicksal der Welt. Eine Dokumentation aus vier Erdteilen* (Zurich, 1965), 214ff. In the Spanish translation of this book which was

published in 1969, "fate" (Schicksal) had become "hope" of the world (*La juventud, esperanza del mundo* [Barcelona, 1969]) and in 1971 this author finally published: *Youth Up In Arms: A Political and Social World Survey, 1955–1970* (London, 1971).

70. In this context compare the thoughts of Thomas Etzemüller, *Ein 'Riß' in der Geschichte? Gesellschaftswandel und 68er-Bewegungen in Schweden und Westdeutschland* (Konstanz, 2005).

71. Ole Grünbaum, *Emigrér. Lærestykker om det tiltagende kaos* (Copenhagen, 1968), 117. The first quote is from Kjell Östberg, *1968 när allting var i rörelse. Sextiotalsradikaliseringen och de sociala rörelserna* (Stockholm, 2002).

72. Claus Leggewie, "A Laboratory of Postindustrial Society. Reassessing the 1960s in Germany," in *1968*, ed. Fink, Gassert, and Junker, 283.

Chapter 3

American Mass Culture and European Youth Culture

Rob Kroes

In Europe's lasting encounter with American mass culture, many have been the voices expressing a concern about its negative impact. Cultural guardians in Europe saw European standards of taste and cultural appreciation eroded by an American way that aimed at a mass market, elevating the lowest common denominator of mass preferences to the main vector of cultural production. This history of cultural anti-Americanism in Europe has a long pedigree. In its earlier manifestations, from the late 19th century through the 1950s, the critique of American mass culture was highly explicit and had to be. Many ominous trends of an evolving mass culture in Europe had to be shown to have originated in America, reaching Europe under clear American agency. An intellectual repertoire of Americanism and Americanization evolved in a continuing attempt at cultural resistance against the lures of a culture of consumption. Never mind that such cultural forms might have come to Europe autonomously, even in the absence of an American model. America served to give a name and a face to forces of cultural change that would otherwise have been anonymous and seemingly beyond control.

Today this European repertoire is alive and kicking. Yet, ironically, as a repertoire that has become common currency to the point of being an intellectual stereotype rather than an informed opinion, America nowadays is often a subtext, unspoken in European forms of cultural resistance. A recent example may serve to illustrate this. A political poster for the Socialist Party in Salzburg, in the run-up to municipal elections, showed us the determined face and the clenched fist of the party's candidate. He asked the voting public whether the younger generation would not be losers, and called on the electorate to "fight, fight, and fight." What for? "In order to avoid that young people get fed up with the future." (*Damit unsere Jugend die Zukunft nicht satt wird.*) In a visual pun, at the poster's dead center, the getting fed up is illustrated by the blurred image of a hamburger flying by at high speed. Fast food indeed. The call for action is now clear. Austrians should try and fend off a future cast in an American vein. American culture is condensed into the single image of the hamburger. It is enough to trigger the larger repertoire of cultural anti-Americanism.

We may choose to see this poster as only a recent version of cultural guardianship that has always looked at the younger generation as a stalking horse, if not a Trojan horse, for American culture. In fact, historically, it has always been younger generations who, in rebellion against parental authority and cultural imposition, opted for the liberating potential of American mass culture. Yet interesting changes may have occurred in this pattern. Today young people as well, in their concern about forces of globalization, may target America as the central agency behind these global trends. They may smash the windows of a nearby McDonald's (and there is always a McDonald's nearby), or may choose more creative and subtle forms of protest. Yet again America tends to be a mere subtext in their resistance against global cultural icons.

One more example may serve to illustrate this. I have a music video, a few years old, of a Basque group. The video, in its own right, is an act of cultural emancipation. The lyrics are in the Basque language and the station broadcasting the video has all-Basque programming. This may suggest localism, if not cultural provincialism. Nothing would be farther from the truth. What we have here is a perfect example of "glocalisation," to use Roland Robertson's neologism.[1] The music used is "world music," hailing from the Caribbean and popularized through the British music industry. The format of the music video itself is part of global musical entertainment. Yet the message is local. What the video shows is a confusing blend of the traditional and the modern. The opening shot is of a man using a scythe to cut grass. The camera moves up and shows a modern, international style, office block. A mobile phone rings, and the grasscutter answers the call. More images show modern life. We see an old man talking into a microphone strapped to his head, as if he is talking to himself. We see a group of young men working out in tandem, yet in complete isolation, like a transported glimpse of an American gym. Then the protagonists of the video appear, with a rickety van, getting ready to sell the local variety of Basque fast food, a sausage on a roll. The very smell breaks the isolation of people caught in the alienating life of modernity. They all flock to the sausage stand to get a taste of true Basqueness. They come to life, spurred by an alleged authenticity of traditional Basque life. The lyrics repeat the refrain: "Down with McDonald's, Long live Big Benat"(the name of the Basque delicacy).

The claim made in this video is on behalf of the authenticity of regional cultures struggling to survive in a world threatened by the homogenizing forces of globalization. Yet the medium of communication testifies to the impact of precisely those forces as much as it protests against them. There is much irony in all this, but most important is the fact that what is shown as modernity truly revives a long repertoire of European cultural anti-Americanism. America is modernity and the long history of European resistance to America is truly a story of resisting the onslaught of modernity on Europe's checkered map of regional and/or national cultures.

In the following I propose to do two things. First I shall examine the history of Europe's encounter with and reception of forms of American mass culture, if not of American modernity. The encounter changed the ways in which Europeans have come to conceive of themselves and of their own history. Then I will proceed to analyse the central question of cultural imperialism, radiating from America, and the freedom of reception crucially entailed in the encounter.

American Mass Culture and the European Sense of History and Identity

I have three vignettes to set the stage for our discussion. All three are taken from European films. Each represents a formative moment, if not an epiphany, in the lives of the films' protagonists. In each, it is America that provides the ingredients for these moments of revelation. Dramatically, these moments serve as epic concentrations, condensing into a single moment what normally is a continuing process of identity formation. The first example is from Jacques Tati's 1949 film, *Jour de fête*, the second from Alan Parker's *The Commitments*, released in 1991, and the third from Bernard Tavernier's *Around Midnight*, which came out in 1986.

In *Jour de fête* Tati satirizes the modern obsession with speed, presenting it as a peculiarly American obsession, but one that is highly contagious. In later work, like *Mon oncle*, he would satirize other American infatuations, like the love of gadgets, labor-saving devices, automation and remote control, showing them to have already invaded France, providing French appetites for a life of ostentation and invidious distinction with the snob value of American contraptions. Interestingly, in his *Jour de fête*, he shows us the moment of contagion. The protagonist of the film, a French provincial postman, is at one point shown peeking through a crevice in the canvass of a big tent. Inside a film is shown dealing with speedy American postal techniques involving virtuoso time-saving feats. The feats themselves are satirically transformed into nonsensical dare-devil acts of motorized mail delivery men jumping through hoops of fire, and of airplanes dropping mailbags that are picked up by postmen on motorbikes driving at full speed. Never mind. Many of the propaganda films shown in Europe under Marshall-aid auspices and meant to instill a sense of American efficiency in the minds of Europeans, may well have been perceived and remembered as equally fantastic. In fact, what we see we see vicariously, as if through the eyes of our astounded postman. The images shown to us may well be the product of his eager imagination rather than conveying anything in the actual documentary film. Later hilarious sequences then show the way in which Tati's postman has creatively adopted the American model, adapting his bicycle delivery act, while experiencing a new mail (male?) identity.

The other two film vignettes are variations on this theme of Europeans looking in from the outside, undergoing a culture shock, while experiencing it as a moment of conversion. In Bertrand Tavernier's film it is the encounter of a young Frenchman with American jazz in the late 1940s. Unable to afford the price of admission to a Paris jazz club where one of his cultural heroes is playing, we see him hunched outside a window, literally eavesdropping on a world of meaningful sounds, coded messages from an enticing, but far-away culture. As it happens, he manages to get in touch with the revered musician, recasting his own life into a mission of support and protection of the drug-ravaged career of his tragic hero. In Alan Parker's *The Commitments* another musical encounter makes for a moment of epiphany. A group of poor Irish boys is casting about for a musical form that would allow them to express their working-class sense of themselves. Much of the American pop music that blared from radios in Ireland they critically rejected as irrelevant to their quest. But at one point, early in the story, they are watching James Brown on television do his trade-mark soul act. When the show is over the leader of this small group instantly translates the experience into terms relevant to the lives they lead in Ireland. "We have to become like him. He is like us. The Irish are the Blacks of Europe, the Dubliners are the Blacks of Ireland, and we Northenders are the Blacks of Dublin. Say it once and say it loud: we are Black and we are proud." In disbelief his friends silently repeat the last words, their lips moving to form the words of the punch line. "We are Black and we are proud." Slowly the message sinks in. Yet another appropriation of American culture has taken place, affecting the sense of identity of these youngsters. They are cast in the role of celebrants in a ritual of cultural conversion.

These moments of voluntary affiliation with American lifestyles and cultural models are a recurring feature of postwar European cultural production, in film, on television, and in literature. A more comprehensive study of other examples would give us a sense of the many settings in which these critical encounters with American culture took place. They are like moments of remembrance as everyone growing up in postwar Europe will have them. They are the condensed memorable versions of the more continuing exposure to American culture that Europeans have all experienced. When taken together they are like an album of vignettes vividly illustrating the ongoing process not only of the forms of reception of American culture, but also of its selective appropriation, which is to say of the ways in which American culture was redefined and made to serve the cultural needs of Europeans. Settings of reception, defined in such terms as class, age, gender, or ethnicity, then become the crucial focus for analysis.

Whatever the precise setting, it was always a matter of people finding themselves relatively at the margin of established mainstream cultural modes and molds, people who were not, or not yet, fully integrated into these dominant conventional forms. American culture, as they read it, provided them with alternatives of non-conventionality, informality, and a sense of freedom of choice, all in marked contrast to cultural conventions they were expected to make their own.

If this would be one reason to create our album of vignettes, there is a second one. In cultural studies the exploration of the process of reception, or of cultural consumption, is a nut devilishly hard to crack. Whatever area of mass cultural production one takes, whether it is world fairs, film, television soap operas, or literary forms like the romance, we are always dealing with mass audiences consuming these products. It is one thing to explore the programmatic strategies of the organizers and producers of such forms of mass culture; it is a totally different thing actually to gauge what the audience chooses to get out of them. Interesting response studies have been done in these areas, such as of housewives watching soaps, or of readers reading romances. But the larger the issue becomes, as in the case of the European postwar reception of American mass culture, the more formidable are the problems of how to study the process of reception. That is where a study of vignettes as I have suggested them above might play a role.

After all, as narrative moments in stories told by Europeans, they are like second-order evidence of the reception of American culture. They tell stories of reception. They are recycled, or reconstructed, moments meant to convey remembrances of critical encounters with American culture. In that sense they are explicit indications of a process of reception. As such they are more open to research than questions of first-order reception. It is harder to see someone eating a hamburger in Paris as making a cultural statement, expressing an identity challenging established conventions, than it would be to interpret a narrative passage, in a film or a book, presenting hamburger consumption in precisely the light of a cultural peripety, wilfully subverting European conventions of eating out. Or, for that matter, it would be harder to find proof of a direct, first-order American influence in Alan Parker's style of film-making than it would be to trace his awareness of such influences taking place. After all, he turns them into the stuff of narration himself. This much may be clear, then: if moments of the reception of American culture, presented in the dramatic light of moments of epiphany, have become a recurrent feature of European story-telling, they testify to a degree of self-conscious awareness of the American cultural impact which it would be unwise to neglect.

Condensed into single moments, points in time serving as *lieux de mémoire*, to use Pierre Nora's felicitous phrase, all vignettes of the reception of American culture in Europe highlight what has truly been an ongoing process. Whatever conversion moments Europeans may vividly remember, they have all been more continuously exposed to an environment of free-floating cultural signifiers made in America. Confronted with an ongoing stream of vistas of the good life, as carried by media such as film, advertisements, television, music videos, they have walked through a duplicate world of images as a continuing accompaniment to their lives. They never walked alone. Highly private as the consumption of American culture may have been, eavesdropping on AFN broadcasts late at night and against parental wishes, watching a Hollywood movie, or shutting out one's environment through the use of a Walkman, the cultural products that made for such private moments were at the same time consumed by many others, constituting a mass audience. These private moments, then, may well be seen as forms of collective behavior typical of contemporary mass societies. The very fact that the private consumption of mass culture is necessarily shared with many others gives mass culture its paradoxical quality of setting the public stage, giving an era its particular cultural flavor. Reminiscing, individual people become aware that they share similar cultural memories with others. They are able to reconstruct the feel of years past, evoking moments of cultural consumption that it turns out they shared with others. Everyone knows the exhilarating moments discovering that others enjoyed the same film or rock song one thought to have enjoyed privately. There is the sudden sense of a joint return to a past that briefly comes to life again.

In that sense modern mass culture, much of it in an American mold, has given our sense of history a particular coating. If Dutch historian Johan Huizinga bemoaned the fact that history as he conceived of it was losing form, and escaped his capacity to recognize patterns of coherence and meaning, he must have been unaware of contemporary mass culture giving our sense of history this new coat. As a shared repertoire of recollections, allowing people to call forth an image of their own collective past, the mass cultural mold of an era is certainly a new form that history has assumed. It serves people as a switch that allows them to connect private memories with public memories. More importantly, as in neural networks, such recollections often connect to historical events of a more traditional nature. If, for instance, in the years following The Second World War, most strongly so in the 1950s, there was a marked reconstitution of the domestic sphere, in the context of the rapid sub-urbanization of the United States, these were large-scale, and anonymous forces of social change that it would be hard for historians to render in vivid forms of historical narrative. Huizinga, for one, would have felt at a loss, using the traditional tools of his craft, to come up with narrative forms tellingly catching these processes. Yet, as he himself surmised in some of his musings concerning mass culture, the story of America's return to domesticity found its narrative forms precisely at that level. As it is, the process of social change was accompanied, if not actively promoted, by a host of Hollywood movies and television productions centering on the family home, presented as the "natural" setting for the way that Americans structured their private lives. Collectively they set the cultural tone and gave the cultural feel to an era. To the extent that Americans now remember the era, it is by means of these mass-cultural representations. To the extent that Europeans remember the era, it is doubly vicarious: not only did these films and television programs allow them to look in on American family life, they also provided European audiences with views of the good life, of single family homes, cars in the driveway, "American kitchens," and of husbands happily returning to the family fold. "Honey, I'm home!"

We all, it is my contention, remember such historical configurations through the images that the mass media brought right to our homes, and which are now the stuff of our historical memory. But there are additional ways in which mass culture mediates and shapes contemporary history. It is not only a matter of fictional representations, as in film or television sitcoms, that imaginatively reflect and capture the social and cultural trends of an era. Much of what actually happens in terms of the day-to-day events that make up the daily news, and that are conventionally seen as the real stuff of history, now reach us almost instantly through the modern mass media, in the form of newspaper photographs, or television news flashes. Some of these images gain an iconic status, recapitulating an event in ways that leave an indelible imprint on our minds, as if on an etcher's plate. Often such images start leading their own lives, serving as summary recapitulations of recent history.

And given America's centrality in the history of the post-Second World War world, given also its central position in communication networks spanning the globe, America not only is centrally involved in many events making up recent history, it is also a central provider of images representing these events. There is, to give just one example, the case of Nick Ut's photograph of napalmed Vietnamese children running in terror towards the eye of his camera. Many, in the United States and Europe, vividly remember the photograph. And interestingly the photograph was able to spawn its own afterlife as a factor of newsworthy history. Having become an emblem of the atrocities of the Vietnam War, it remained at the same time the picture of an individual girl in pain, creating an interest in her individual fate. In the fall of 1996, on Veteran's Day, the public's reading of the photograph suddenly moved from the emblematic to the personal. The girl in the photograph re-appeared on the stage of history as a woman of flesh and blood, individualized, no longer solely an icon. On Veteran's Day she came to a ritual of remembrance at the Vietnam War monument in Washington D.C., offering forgiveness.[2] A new meaning was added to an icon of mass culture that had long allowed us to give shape and form to our understanding of the Vietnam War.

There are yet other ways in which the coat of mass cultural memory is used to recreate the past. They resemble the ways in which the reception of American mass culture is recycled into individual vignettes, into those single moments of conversion that I talked about before. They are like a second-order, conscious use of the mass-cultural coat of history for the reconstruction of historical events. Again, the Vietnam War may offer apposite illustrations of what I have in mind. Surely, Vietnam War movies in their own right are mass-cultural products adding to the sediment that mass culture leaves on our sense of history. Trying to evoke images of the Vietnam War, we often do so with the help of Hollywood's attempts at rendering the war. Nor does Hollywood shrink from adding iconic heroes to our store of recollections, for instance in the form of Rambo as a latter-day raging Roland. Yet the very way in which many of these films go about taking us back to the historical event is through the use of collectively remembered mass-cultural products of the era. The music of the Rolling Stones and the Doors in Francis Ford Coppola's *Apocalypse Now* trigger historical connections in the minds of contemporary audiences. Similarly, the heart-rending finale of Michael Cimino's *The Deerhunter* has the remaining protagonists join in the singing, with voices wavering, of Irving Berlin's "God Bless America." For the re-assertion of their mutual bonds, grieving over those they have lost, they use a popular song richly evocative of their larger bonds with America. Yet, tellingly, European audiences were strongly moved as well because they vicariously shared the musical repertoire and its associative force. Barry Levinson, in his *Good Morning, Vietnam,* made this connecting strategy the central ploy of his narrative. The high point of his film, of a wellnigh transcendent force, is his combined use of various tools from the realm of mass culture. In a sequence following Robin Williams' announcement of just another song in his radio program for the American forces in Vietnam, we hear the voice of Louis Armstrong singing "What a Wonderful World." Accompanying the lyrics there is a jumble of images of the Vietnam War as any prime-time television news from Vietnam would show these. Yet the structural logic of the sequence does not only resemble television news flashes. It is at the same time structurally similar to the standard music video, more often than not equally a jumble of images made coherent only by the accompanying sound track. Ironically, the clip from the film became a hit as a music video, following the release of the film, and disseminated worldwide through MTV, an American pop music channel. Merging the evocative force of Armstrong's voice with the logic of television footage into something that clearly appeals to our familiarity with music videos, Levinson manages to use all these mass-cultural triggers to produce a moment of transcendence, a bitter comment on the horror of the war. It makes us sit back and reflect, in spite of what pre-Second World War critics of American mass culture had argued in their mood of cultural pessimism.

Were these critics alive today, what would they have to say to these new forms that now play a role in shaping our sense of the past? Many undoubtedly would have seen it as the ultimate victory of a cultural inversion they had been the first to see as typically American, an inversion that replaces reality with its fake representations. From Georges Duhamel and Simone de Beauvoir to more recent observers of American culture like Jean Baudrillard and Umberto Eco, the language may have changed from the straightforward invective to more esoteric formulae like *simulacrum* or *hyper-reality,* but the diagnosis remains essentially the same. They all come up with their own variations on the old Marxian theme of false consciousness. A man like Huizinga too might have been reluctant to see present-day forms of historical awareness as worthy replacements of the historiographic forms whose decline and ultimate demise he observed or foresaw. Yet he may have come closest to a historiographic perspective that has been gaining adherence in recent decades. His almost sociological sense of the role and function of rituals, ceremonies, and public spectacles in late medieval Europe, his keen sense also of the role that modern mass media played in providing frameworks for identification and self-definition to mass audiences, took him to the threshold of an epistemological seachange in the historiography of collective consciousness. Huizinga would have had no quarrel with a current relativism that sees collective identities, of nations, of ethnic groups, of regional cultures, as just so many constructions. Precisely the invented rituals of celebrating and memorializing such identities he would have recognized as dramatic forms of history that he himself had studied. Yet he may have disagreed as to the implied voluntarism of this perspective and its attribution of historic agency. In Huizinga's case in fact the agency rested with historians. It was they who shaped history into larger narrative forms. Much current historiography, however, places the agency in history itself and explores it in terms of group strategies, struggles for cultural hegemony, and the invention of rituals meant to rally people around strategic readings of their collective identity.

This takes us back to a problem I raised earlier. Exploring the strategic agency behind the formation of group identities and frameworks for identification is one thing. But there is always the further question as to why, at the level of individual reception and appropriation of the rival constructions, people opt for particular readings of their collective identity. How do we explore the meanings and significance, at the point of reception, of such rival appeals? What messages and representations of reality do people store and digest to render meaningful life histories?

If indeed mass cultural products, produced and disseminated under American auspices, do function as the markers of time and the molders of the collective historical recollections not only of Americans but of Europeans as well, we need to make one further point. The sense of history as I have explored it here is necessarily of a transient nature. It applies only to history as a shared experience, remembered collectively. As generations succeed each other on the stage of history, there is unavoidably a point in the past beyond which this repertoire of shared memories cannot stretch, a point following them like a ship's back wash. A century hence none of the markers of time and triggers of historical recollection, as I have explored them here, will be operative any more. Does that mean that our history for future historians will be just like any other and older stage of history?

Today, at any rate, the challenge to study the mass-cultural coat of our age is eagerly taken on by contemporary historians. When they are involved in the production of television documentaries about recent historic episodes they consciously draw on the repertoires of mass culture produced at the time. There are many more instances of increased awareness among historians of the mass cultural forms of history. In search of audiences that want to see their personal histories displayed, books, special exhibits, and, yes, entire museums are now devoted to the everyday lives of common people, showing the advent of mass cultural products into their homes, work, leisure time pursuits, and so on. If mass culture has provided people with the rituals and ceremonies for the public display of their collective identities, its time has now come to be displayed in its own right.

Cultural Imperialism and the Freedom of Reception

Students of Americanization are in general agreement as regards the semantic transformations that attend the dissemination of American cultural messages across the world. Depending on their precise angle and perspective, some rather tend to emphasize in their explorations the cultural strategies and auspices behind the transmission of American culture. Whether they study Buffalo Bill's *Wild West Show* when it traveled in Europe, Hollywood movies, or World Fairs, to name just a few carriers for the transmission of American culture, their focus is rather on the motifs and organizing views that the producers were trying to convey rather than on the analysis of what the spectators and visitors did with the messages they were exposed to. All such cultural productions taken as representations of organizing world views do tend to lead researchers to focus on senders rather than receivers of messages. Yet, given such a focus, it hardly ever leads these researchers to look at the process of reception as more than merely one of passive imbibing. Whatever the words one uses to describe what happens at the point of reception, words such as hybridization or creolization, current views agree on a freedom of reception, a freedom to re-semanticize and re-contextualize meaningful messages reaching audiences across national and cultural borders. Much creativity and inventiveness go into the process of reception, much joy and exhilaration spring from it. Yet making this the whole story would be as fallacious as a focus centered solely on the schemes and designs of the senders of messages. Whatever their precise angle, researchers agree on the need to preserve balance in their approach to problems of Americanization.

Furthermore, some researchers, like Robert W. Rydell in a contribution to the 1998 Lisbon conference of the European Association for American Studies,[3] tend to conceive of Americanization as a process tied to an early American economic expansionism, or, more recently, to an emerging global economy structured by the organizing logic of corporate capitalism, still very much proceeding under American auspices. The main area in which Rydell sees Americanization at work is in the "commodification of culture which colonizes the leisure time of people worldwide." World Fairs and other transmitters of America's commercial culture conjure up a "veritable 'dream world' of mass consumption, a simulation through spectacle of the good life afforded by the technological advances associated with modernization."[4] He goes on to contrast this simulacrum of the good life with the ravages wrought by corporate capitalism in many parts of the globe. He explicitly wants to keep the concept of Americanization in our critical lexicon as a useful reminder of what American economic expansionism has meant in terms of advancing the interests of American corporate culture overseas.

I am not so sure whether this is the right tack. Rydell seems unduly to read the autonomous rise of global corporate capitalism as due to American agency. It is a common fallacy in much of the critique of Americanization to blame America for trends and developments that would have occurred anyway, even in the absence of America. From Marx, via Hobson and Lenin, all the way to the work of the Frankfurt School, there is a long line of critical analysis of capitalism and imperialism, highlighting its inner expansionist logic. Surely, in our century, much of this expansion has proceeded under American auspices, receiving an American imprint, in much the same way that a century ago, the imprint was British. The imprint has often confused critics into arguing that the havoc wreaked by an overarching process of modernization, ranging from the impact of capitalism to processes of democratization of the political arena or the rise of a culture of consumption, were truly the dismal effects of America upon their various countries. From this perspective the critique of Americanization is too broad, exaggerating America's role in areas where in fact it was caught up in historic transformations much like other countries were.

From a different perspective, though, this view of Americanization is too narrow. It ignores those vast areas where America, as a construct, an image, a fantasma, did play a role in the intellectual and cultural life of people outside its national borders. There is a repertoire of fantasies about America that even predates its discovery. Ever since, the repertoire has been fed in numerous ways, through many media of transmission. Especially in our century America has become ever more present in the minds of non-Americans, as a point of reference, a yardstick, a counterpoint. In intellectual reflections on the course and destiny of their countries and cultures, America became part of a process of triangulation, serving as a model for rejection or emulation, providing views of a future seen in either a negative or a positive light. America has become a *tertium comparationis* in culture wars elsewhere, centering on control of the discourse concerning national identity and national culture. When America was typically rejected by one party in such contests, the other party saw it as a liberating alternative.

Undeniably, though, in the course of this allegedly "American Century," America has assumed a centrality that one might rightly call imperial. Like Rome in the days of the Roman Empire, it has become the center of webs of control and communication that span the world. If for such reasons we might call America's reach imperial, it is so in a number of ways, in the economic sphere, in the political sphere, and in the cultural sphere. If it is still possible to use the word in a relatively neutral way, describing a factual configuration rather than the outcome of concerted effort and motive, we might speak of an American imperialism, of its economic imperialism, political imperialism, and cultural imperialism. Trying to accommodate themselves to their diminished role and place in the world, European countries have at times opted to resist particular forms of America's imperial presence.

Yet, suggestive as the terms are of neat partition and distinction, the three forms of imperialism do in fact overlap to a large extent. Thus, America in its role as the new political hegemon in the Western world, could restructure markets and patterns of trade, through the Marshall Plan, which guaranteed access of American products to the European markets. Political imperialism could thus promote economic imperialism. Opening European markets for American commerce also meant preserving access for American cultural exports, such as Hollywood movies. Economic imperialism thus translated into cultural imperialism. Reversely, as carriers of an American version of the "good life," American products, from cars to movies, from clothing styles to kitchen appliances, all actively doubled as agents of American cultural diplomacy. Thus, trade translated back into political imperialism. And so on, in endless feedback loops.

In my own work of recent years I have chosen to focus on the cultural dimension in all these various forms of an American imperial presence. American culture, seen as a configuration of ways and means that Americans use for expressing their collective sense of themselves—their Americanness—is mediated through every form of American presence abroad. From the high rhetoric of its political ideals to the golden glow of McDonald's arches, from Bruce Springsteen to the Marlboro Man, American culture washes across the globe. It does so mostly in disentangled bits and pieces, for others to recognize and pick up, and re-arrange into a setting expressive of their own individual identities, or identities they share with peer groups. Thus, teenagers may have adorned their own bedrooms with the iconic faces of Hollywood or rock music stars in order to provide themselves with a most private place for reverie and games of identification, they have also been engaged in a construction of private worlds that they share with countless others. In the process they re-contextualize and re-semanticize American culture to make it function within expressive settings entirely of their own making.

In the following I propose to explore a few ways in which we might reflect on the intricate ways in which, in the post-Second World War period, American mass culture, reaching a Europe that more than ever before had come within America's imperial sway, may have affected European cultures. My focus will be on advertising, seen as a peculiar blend of economic and cultural imperialism.

American Advertising in Europe

A nation that stops representing itself in images stops being a nation. It is doomed to lead a life of derivation, vicariously enjoying worlds of imagery and imagination imported from abroad. Or so President Mitterrand was reported to have been musing. In a mood of cultural protectionism, against the backdrop of a seemingly unstoppable conquest of Europe's cultural space by American images, Mitterrand's France called for—but failed to get—a clause exempting cultural goods from the free-trade logic of GATT. The episode is reminiscent of earlier defensive ploys by France in the face of a threat of Americanization. There is the story, as told by more than one author,[5] of the fight that France chose to pick to keep Coca-Cola out of the country. Coca-Cola became the symbol of everything that a certain intellectual discourse in Europe had always rejected in America, as the country that had succeeded in mass-marketing bad taste. If there was much to be envied in America as a model of modernity, it offered an example that France should be following selectively and on its own terms—under strict "parental guidance," so to speak. Yet the example as set by America was tempting, precisely because it undercut parental authority and cultural guardianship, promising the instant gratification of desire rather than its sublimation, consumption rather than consummation. Coca-Cola was the item that the French chose to symbolize this pernicious pleasure principle in the global transmission of American mass culture. The soft drink, in this French campaign, was turned into an icon of an alleged American strategy of cultural imperialism. It also gave the strategy a name: Coca-Colonization.

More recently, in the early 1990s, another soft-drink commercial, for Seven Up, illustrated the seductive semiotics that underlies so many of the messages that reach us from across the Atlantic Ocean. It did this without drawing on the repertoire of American icons. There was no Marlboro Man roaming the open space of an American West, no Castle Rock, no Statue of Liberty. Instead it introduced a streetwise little brat, a cartoon character by the name of Fido Dido. Only few among the European audience watching the commercial would have been aware of its American auspices. As it happened, however, the cartoon character was American, and so was the commercial itself. Yet, to all intents and purposes, it could have been produced by advertising agencies anywhere. The only clearly American referent in the commercial was the product it tried to promote, a soft drink that saw its market share slipping and felt in need of a new image.

In the first instalment of what turned out to be a little series of narrations centering on Fido Dido, we see him meeting the hand of his maker. Briefly it may seem like a lighter, cartoon version of the scene in the Sistine Chapel where a drowsy Adam, touching fingers with God, is brought to life. But Fido Dido's meeting is of a different kind. His confrontation is with parental authority, with the commanding hand of social propriety. The hand of the maker, "in living color," holds a pencil and gets ready to retouch Fido Dido. First his unkempt hair gets neatly combed and partitioned. Fido Dido indignantly shakes his hair back into its previous state. The pencil continues the attack and dresses Fido Dido in jacket and tie. It moves on to the object in Fido Dido's right hand, also in full color, as real as the hand and pencil: the can of Seven Up. The pencil tries to erase it, yet the can is beyond such manipulation. Fido Dido meanwhile has moved towards full rebellion. Jacket and tie have already been thrown off; a well-aimed kick hits the pencil. Its tip breaks and hangs limply—a fitting symbol of parental impotence. Victoriously Fido Dido walks off the screen. In final retaliation his yo-yo now hits the pencil. The broken point falls off. His victory prize is a taste of the elixir of freedom: cool, sparkling Seven Up. The semiotics all merge into one message: a simple soft drink has been turned into a symbol of freedom. Much as the product, as well as the commercial and the cartoon character itself, may be American, the message is understood internationally.

We may see in this one example the end stage of a process of internationalization and generalization—decontextualization, if one wishes—of a sales pitch that was developed in America and, in its earlier stages, relied on much more explicit American iconography. We mentioned the Marlboro Man as a contemporary case of strong American symbolism— the West as open space, a realm of freedom—used to connect the sense of freedom, of being one's own man, to a simple item of merchandise like a cigarette. Yet the Marlboro Man is only a recent version of the commodification of American symbols of freedom that as a process has gone on for over a century. America as empty space, the epic America of the frontier, America as a mythical West had long before the consumption revolution been turned into a symbol of freedom. The West as a beckoning yonder had kept alive the dream, in far-away corners of Europe, of a life lived in freedom and independence. As the promise of a new world and a new era, it could vie with contemporary utopian views offered by Marxism or similar emancipation movements. Posters, produced for shipping lines, emigration societies, and land development agencies, contributed their imagery to the continuing construction of America as the very site of freedom and space. For many people such imagery must have represented the promise of freedom and escape offered by America.

If such is the central appeal of "America" as an image, we need not be surprised at the craving for material that could visualize the image. Chromo lithographs, photographs, stereographs and their suggestion of three-dimensionality, all tried to still this hunger. They allowed people to move beyond the limited horizons of their daily lives and to enter into an imaginary space, a fantasy world. They offered reality and illusion at the same time.

Apparently, well before the decade of the "roaring twenties," commerce had appropriated the allegorical repertoire of the American dream. The images that now flooded across the country through techniques of mechanical reproduction could be endlessly re-arranged to render new symbolic messages. The West as a realm for the imagination could connect with the world of trite consumption goods such as tobacco or cigarettes. Advertising developed into an art of symbolic alchemy that has continued to retain its potency. The symbolic connection that advertisers sought to establish hinged on the concept of "freedom." This linking of evocative images of American freedom and space tended to work best with leisure time articles, such as cigarettes, beer, an automobile or a motorbike, a pair of blue jeans. Consumption, leisure time, and "freedom" thus became inextricably interwoven. And even today "America" can be counted on to trigger an association with freedom. The iconography of America has become international. Italian jeans manufacturers now advertise their wares in Germany on posters depicting Monument Valley. The German cigarette brand West mounted an international advertising campaign whose central metaphors revolve around the American West. The Dutch non-alcohol beer Stender used the imaginary West of American road-movies for its television commercials, including brief encounters at gas stations in an empty West, an exchange of glances between the sexes, the half-inviting, half-ironic sizing up, the beginning of erotic tension. The release of tension occurs, surprisingly, when he or she, in gleaming black leather, irrespective of gender, in the true macho style of the West, flips the top of a bottle of Stender and takes off again on a shiny motorbike, into the empty distance.

America's national symbols and myths have been translated into an international iconographic language, a visual lingua franca. They have been turned into free-floating signifiers, internationally understood, free for everyone to use. Yet it is only a replay, on an international scale, of what had previously occurred in the United States. Given the characteristic American bent for dis-assembling whatever presents itself as an organically coherent whole, only to re-assemble the constituent elements differently, this American leadership role need not surprise us. In their production of commercial messages this same cultural bent has been at work, removing symbols from their historical context and re-arranging them into novel configurations. The appropriate metaphor may be that of Lego construction, which uses the individual pieces as just so many "empty signifiers," combining them into ever-changing meaningful structures. Commerce and advertising are but one area where we can see these rituals of cultural transformation at work. For indeed, consumption goods as well can freely change their meaning, appearing in ever-changing configurations, furnishing a realm of virtual reality, turning into simulacra at the hands of the wizards of advertising. They become true phantasmas set free by the human imagination.

No bastion of conventional order is immune to this erosive freedom. In the area of advertising as well as in other areas of cultural production we can discern a moving American frontier, affecting an ever-increasing number of social conventions with its "deconstructing" logic. Recent shifts in this frontier have affected the established constructions of gender, re-arranging at will reigning views of what constitutes the typically male and female, the masculine and feminine. "Genderbending" is the word that American English has invented for describing this process. Pop culture heroes like Michael Jackson, Grace Jones, or Madonna, project invented personae that are strangely androgynous. Hollywood is busy bending gender in films like *Alien II*, where the enemy computer is called *Mother* and the heroine copes as if she were a man. Commercials like those for Stender also play on the repertoire of accepted gender definitions. The best recent example is a television commercial for Levi's 501. A young, chocolate-skinned woman, invitingly dressed, her midriff bare, is shown taking a New York cab. While the driver is ogling her in his rear-view mirror, his lips moving a toothpick back and forth, suggestively, as if engaged in a mating ritual, she coolly adds a few final touches to her make-up. But then the tables are turned. What gives the driver a start and brings his cab to a full stop, is the sound of an electric razor and the sight of his passenger shaving. The last shot is of the passenger walking away, the victor in another battle of the sexes, the Levi's as snug and inviting as ever. As the text reminds us, in case we didn't know already: "Cut for Men Since 1850." Thus, in all these cases, an entire new area has opened up for fantasies of freedom to roam.

There may be a cultural "deep structure" underlying such developments that is characteristically American, yet our point is that the appeal of such cultural *bricolage* is international. Even in the absence of clearly American markers, as in the case of our Fido Dido commercial, the underlying logic of recombination, tying "freedom" to a soft drink, is American. The appeal, though, is worldwide. In that sense we have all become Americanized. We have grown accustomed to a specific American mode of cultural production, or rather to the ways in which American culture reproduces itself, through endless variation and recombination. Not only have we cracked American cultural codes and can we read them flawlessly, we have also appropriated these codes. They have become part of our collective imaginary repertoire.

One illustration will make an additional point. In the spring of 1994, on walls all over Italy, there were posters displaying a scene taken from the history of the conquest of the West. We see a covered wagon in what is clearly a Western landscape, dry and desolate. A few men gather together in front of the wagon. The scene is one of relative relaxation. Clearly, the day's work has been done. The poster's color is sepia, suggesting a reprint of an old photograph. The legend informs us that *Vendiamo un' autentica leggenda*—We sell an authentic legend. Clearly a variation on Coca-Cola's claim of being "the real thing," the viewer is left wondering what the authentic legend might be. Is it the Levi's blue jeans? The answer must be yes. Is it the American West? Again: the answer is yes. A commodity, a piece of merchandise as down-to-earth as a pair of workingman's trousers, has become a myth, while the West as a myth has become commodified. And Levi's, as the poster honestly tells us, sells it. Yet there is more to this poster. There is an ironic *sous-entendu*, an implied wink to the audience. After all, the audience has long since got the message. They *know* that Levi's is a myth and they *know* what the myth represents. It represents more than the West, it represents their own collective memory of growing up in a Europe filled with American ingredients. Generation upon generation of Europeans, growing up after the war, can all tell their own story of a mythical America as they constructed it, drawing on American advertisements, songs, films, and so on. Ironically, these collective memories—these imagined Americas where people actually spent part of their past growing up—are now being commodified: to all those who on the basis of Jack Kerouac and a pop song remember Route 66 without ever having crossed the Atlantic, a Dutch travel agency now offers nostalgic trips down that artery. The road may no longer exist, it re-occurs as a replica of itself, a simulacrum in the great Disney tradition.

The point is clear: generation upon generation of Europeans have grown up, constructing meaningful worlds that they shared with their peers and which crucially drew on American ingredients. Mythical "Americas" have become part and parcel of the collective memory of

Europeans. This takes us back to Mitterrand's musings. It seems as if he has fallen victim to a misreading of the way the collective memory of Europeans was built in the postwar period. Why indeed must a collective memory be a matter of, as Mitterrand has it, a country depicting itself in images? Why not admit that the collective memory of national populations is crucially a matter of the appropriation and digestion of foreign influences? One could ignore these only at the peril of centrally imposing definitions of what constitutes the nation. And in fact many of the arguments in favor of the cultural exemption clause, protecting national cultural identities, seem to betray this narrow paternalist view of the nation and its identity.

Commercial messages have been only one of the transmission belts of American culture abroad. Modern media of mass reproduction and mass distribution, like film, photography, the press, radio, television, sound recordings, have filled the semiotic space of people everywhere with messages made in America. Americans themselves, through their physical presence abroad, in the form of expatriate colonies, of armies, of business men, have equally contributed to the worldwide dissemination of their culture. Yet commercial messages, in the way they transmit American culture, are a particular case. They are not simply neutral carriers, conveying American culture for others to consume and enjoy, but give a particular twist to whatever ingredients of the American imagination they use. A recent illustration of this process can be seen in a commercial message broadcast by CNN, the worldwide cable news network, and paid for by the "Advertising Council" in London. In what is in fact an advertisement for advertising, the point is made that without advertising we all would be worse off, getting less information through the media, whether the press or the electronic media. Advertising is presented as a necessary prop for the continued existence of a well-informed public in a functioning democracy. The little civics lesson, offered by this commercial, ends with the slogan: "Advertising—The Right to Choose."

What we see happening is the commodification of political discourse. The language of political ideals, of rights and freedoms, is being high-jacked in order to dress purposeful commercial action in stolen clothes. Whether dressed as a freedom or a right, a commodifying logic appears in pure form, unconnected to any particular product. Yet it is a logic we met before in particular cases, which tied the promise of freedom to cigarettes or soft drinks. It is a logic that commodifies, and pedestrianizes, political ideals by putting them in the service of commercial salesmanship. In that sense, we seem to have struck upon just another instance of the vulgarizing impact of American culture, corroborating a point made by so many European critics of American mass culture.

Yet this is not the whole story. The very slogans chosen by sales departments, affirming our "Freedom of Choice," or our "Right to Choose," are semantically unstable and may well convey a message different from the one the salesmen had in mind. A word like choice, when left unspecified, sits uneasily astride the divide between the political and the economic spheres. "Freedom of Choice" in particular may well read as the "Choice of Freedom," a simple inversion that may well put political ideas into the heads of an audience that is addressed in its role as consumers. Paradoxically, then, advertising stratagems cooked up by commercial sponsors may well have the effect of a civics lesson, if not of a subversive and anti-authoritarian call. Precisely there, it seems, lie the secrets of the appeal that so many American commercial messages have had, domestically as well as abroad. Exploring frontiers of freedom, of children rebelling against parental authority, of sexual freedom, of freedom in matters of taste and in styles of behavior, American consumer goods have been instruments of political and cultural education, if not of emancipation. Generation upon generation of youngsters, growing up in a variety of settings in Europe, West *and* East of the Iron Curtain, have vicariously enjoyed the pleasures of cultural alternatives conjured up in commercial vignettes. Simple items like a pair of blue jeans, Coca-Cola, a cigarette brand, thus acquired an added value that helped these younger generations to give expression to an identity all their own. They have been using American cultural language and have made American cultural codes their own. To that extent they have become Americanized. To the extent, though, that they have "done their own thing," while drawing on American cultural repertoires, Americanization is no longer the proper word for describing what has gone on. If anything, those at the receiving end of American mass culture have adapted it to make it serve their own ends. They have woven it into a cultural language, whose grammar, syntax and semantics—metaphorically speaking —would still recognizably be French, Italian, or Czech. All that the recipients have done is make new statements in such a language.

There are more instances of such recontextualization. Surrounded as we are by jingles, posters, neon signs, and billboards, all trying to convey their commercial exhortations, we all at one point or another ironically recycle their repertoires; we quote slogans while bending their meaning; we mimic voices and faces familiar from radio and television. We weave them into our conversations, precisely because they are shared repertoires. Used in this way, two things happen. International repertoires become national, in the sense that they are given a particular twist in conversations, acquiring their new meanings only in particular national and linguistic settings. Secondly, commercial messages stop being commercial. A de-commodification takes place in the sense that the point of the conversation is no longer a piece of merchandise or a specific economic transaction. In this ironic recycling of our commercial culture we become its masters rather than its slaves.

The European Reception of American Mass Culture

Many things have happened along the way since American mass culture started traveling abroad. American icons may have become the staple of a visual *lingua franca* that is understood anywhere in the world, yet their use can no longer be dictated solely from America.

For one thing, as we saw before, it is clear that European commercials made for European products may draw on semiotic repertoires initially developed in and transmitted from America. Yet, in a creolizing freedom not unlike America's modularizing cast of mind, Europeans in their turn now freely re-arrange and recombine the bits and pieces of American culture. They care little about authenticity. T-shirts produced in Europe are as likely to say "New York Lions" as they are "New York Giants."[6] What is more, American brand names, as free-floating signifiers, may even be de-commodified and turned into carriers of a message that is no longer commercial at all. Admittedly, the T-shirts, leather jackets and baseball caps, sporting the hallowed names of Harley Davidson, Nike or Coca-Cola, still have to be bought. Yet what one pays is the price of admission into a world of symbols shared by an international youth culture. Boys or girls with the word Coca-Cola on their T-shirts are not the unpaid peddlers of American merchandise. Quite the contrary. They have transcended such trite connotations and restored American icons to their pure semiotic state of messages of pleasure and freedom. Within this global youth culture, the icons that youngsters carry are like the symbol of the fish that early Christians drew in the sand as a code of recognition. They are the members of a new International, geared to a postmodern world of consumerism rather than an early modern one centered on values of production.

There are many ironies here. What is often held against the emerging international mass, or pop culture, is precisely its international, if not cosmopolitan character. Clearly, this is a case of double standards. At the level of high culture, most clearly in its modernist phase, there has always been the dream of transcending the local, the provincial, the national, or in social terms, to transgress the narrow bounds of the bourgeois world, and to enter a realm that was nothing if not international: the transcendence lay in being truly "European," or "cosmopolitan." But clearly what is good at the level of high culture is seen as a threat when a similar process of internationalization occurs at the level of mass culture. Then, all of a sudden, the defense is not in terms of high versus low, as one might have expected, but in terms of national cultures and national identities imperiled by an emerging international mass culture. There is a further irony in this construction of the conflict, contrasting an emerging global culture seen as homogenizing to national cultures seen as havens of cultural diversity. In the real world, of course, things are different. There may be a hierarchy of taste cultures, yet it is not a matter of higher taste cultures being the more national in orientation. It seems to be the case that this hierarchy of taste cultures is itself transnational, that indeed there are international audiences who at the high end all appreciate Beethoven and Bartok, or at the low end all fancy Madonna or Prince. Yet in a replay of much older elitist tirades against low culture, advocates of high art see only endless diversity where their own taste is concerned, and sheer vulgar homogeneity at the level of mass culture. They have no sense of the variety of tastes and styles, of endless change and renewal in mass culture, simply because it all occurs far beyond their ken.

There is a further point to be made about the forms of reception of American mass culture abroad. What was new and seen as typically American in the late 1940s and 1950s became the acquired repertoire of an international youth culture in the 1960s. At the receiving end people henceforth used the ingredients of American mass culture to express new collective identities and to re-arrange the ingredients as they saw fit. From the point of view of American mass culture traveling abroad, in many cases the exploration of cultural frontiers is taken to more radical lengths than anything one might see in America. Whereas sexual joy and freedom are merely hinted at in American commercials, where Coca-Cola at best holds the promise of more intimate intercourse in its vignettes of rapturous boys and girls, on the beach, in boats, floating down rivers, European posters and television commercials often are more explicit. There is a brooding, erotic Italian wallposter of a macho guy, bare-chested, standing astride a scantily clad, sexually aroused young woman crouched between his legs. She wears a crown reminiscent of the Statue of Liberty, there is an American flag. The commercial is for the one piece of clothing on the man's body, his pair of blue jeans. Similarly, in the Netherlands, in a poster and television campaign sponsored by the government, inviting (in small print) people to become organ donors and to wear a donor codicil, we see a young couple making love, both naked, she sitting on his lap, curving backwards in rapture. The text, in large print, reads: "Give your heart a new lease on life." Pasted across the country, on railway platforms, on bus stops, the poster must have made visiting Americans bashfully turn their heads away. To them the campaign would not appear as the outcome of a process of Americanization taken a few daring steps further. Nor for that matter would another poster campaign, again sponsored by the Dutch government, on behalf of safe sex. Graphically, for everyone to see, couples are shown, taking showers or engaged in similar forms of foreplay. Shocking stuff indeed, but nor is this all. Yet another frontier is being explored, if not crossed: in addition to hetero couples, gay couples are shown.

Admittedly, these poster campaigns no longer convey commercial messages, although in fact the Dutch government, in order to get its messages across, has adopted advertising techniques and in fact uses advertising billboards, rented, one assumes, at the going market rate. In a sense we have come full circle. Where the CNN advertisement drew on republican language to claim the freedom of the advertiser, we now see advertising space being reclaimed for statements *pro bono publico*. If democracy is a marketplace, it has become inseparable from the economic market. It is in fact one indivisible and noisy place with cries and calls vying for the public's attention, echoing back and forth. The perfect illustration of this was being pasted all across the Netherlands, in January 1995. A huge poster, produced by a Dutch advertising agency solely for the Dutch market, advertised the Levi's 508, yet playfully drew on American political language for its commercial message. What the poster showed was the lower part of a half-nude male torso, covered from the waist down by a pair of jeans. Intertextuality abounded. The poster was reminiscent of famous album covers such as the Rolling Stones' *Sticky Fingers,* designed by Andy Warhol, or the Bruce Springsteen album *Born in the USA.* But there is more. Playing on the classic version of the Four Freedoms the poster rephrased them as follows: freedom of expression, freedom of thought, freedom of choice, and—Levi's 508—freedom of movement. The third freedom, as we have seen, already makes the transition from the political to the commercial; the fourth, political though it may sound, is meant to convey the greater room of movement provided by the baggier cut of the 508. The picture illustrates the point by showing the unmistakable bulge of a male member in full erection, casually touched by the hand of its owner. Clearly, the semiotics of American commercial strategies has been taken to lengths, so to speak, that are inconceivable in America. America may have been less embarrassed in exploring the continuities between the political and the commercial, Europe later on may have been more daring in its pursuit of happiness, graphically advertising it all across its public space.[7]

For indeed, as European examples from the political and the economic marketplace serve to illustrate, the logic of a choice of freedom knows no bounds, once set free from controlling American standards of taste and decency. As is a *lingua franca*'s wont, it moves in a realm of free creolization, where the controlling authority of a mother culture no longer holds. Americanization then should be the story of an American cultural language traveling and of other people acquiring that language. What they actually say in it, is a different story altogether.

Notes

1. Roland Robertson, "Globalisation or Glocalisation?," *The Journal of International Communication* I, 1 (1994).
2. See the report by Jan Scruggs, "A child of war forgives...," *New York Times,* 11 November 1996.
3. R.W. Rydell, "The Americanization of the World and the Spectacle of the American Exhibits at the 1900 Paris Universal Exposition," in *Ceremonies and Spectacles: Performing American Culture*, ed. Teresa Alves, Teresa Cid, and Heinz Ickstadt (Amsterdam, 2000), 93–101.
4. Ibid., 99.
5. See Richard F. Kuisel, *Seducing the French: The Dilemma of Americanization* (Berkeley, 1993) and Mark Pendergrast, *For God, Country and Coca-Cola: The Unauthorized History of the Great American Soft Drink and the Company That Makes It* (London, 1993).
6. As pointed out in a piece on United States pop culture in Europe, by Elizabeth Neuffer, in the *Boston Sunday Globe,* 9 October 1994, 22.
7. In this connection it is of interest to point out that the campaign for Levi's 508 was produced by a Dutch advertising agency solely for the Dutch market. The video for the 501s that I referred to earlier was made by a British agency for the European market.

Part II

Leisure Time and New Consumerism

Chapter 4

Music, Dissidence, Revolution, and Commerce: Youth Culture between Mainstream and Subculture

Peter Wicke

Youth culture and pop music have long become synonymous, but this has not always been the case. In the year 1942, when the American sociologist Talcott Parsons coined the term "youth culture,"[1] music figured only marginally in its understanding. Instead, youth phenomena largely referred to points of view, attitudes, and common sets of values, which boiled down to a premature state of adulthood within the age-specific context of adolescents. The dynamic of their cultural behavior was characterized by their desires to appear as early on as possible as what adolescents understood as "adult," in particular, to partake in their seniors' pastimes and diversions. Not until the emergence of rock'n'roll did music gain its symbolic function, which has ever since become characteristic of the culture of adolescents and youths. Music was thereafter the medium that enabled youth culture to gain the autonomy that it maintains today, and it was music and its cultural manifestations as a globally circulating mass medium that, at the same time, concealed the cultural connections that linked—behind commercial phenomena such as hits and stars—socially structured lifestyles of youths to concrete realms, places, and settings. Youth culture is a lived practice that exists only in the plurality of social and geographical settings in which it takes place. It is paradigmatic for youth cultures and their vitality that this plurality adjusts ceaselessly to the transnational machinery of commercially organized cultures without losing their relative autonomy. This feature became apparent for the first time in the early 1960s, when along with the Beatles also a place and various settings, Liverpool and its cavern clubs, made history.[2]

This caesura however through which also Europe returned to the realm of commercialized culture, cut deeper. As a matter of fact, nothing within pop culture was after this caesura as it had been before. *Before* referred to a music business run by professionals, who—despite Elvis' frenetic hip shaking and the countless teenage-stars in his wake—had set their minds on restrained entertainment. Somewhat wild was considered acceptable, because it fostered business. In general, however, a ubiquitous consensual arbitrariness defined the structures of the media and markets, which had remained largely unaffected by the youths' enthusiasm for rock'n'roll in previous years. The emergence of rock'n'roll during the 1950s had been spectacular, yet its impact had been only short-lived, occurring only in the years 1956/57 and, contrary to popular myths, with only marginal consequences. The music business considered the newly discovered teenager market merely as an extension of existing market structures. The development of material for this new segment and the expansion of the existing music repertoire followed established routines. The same professional songwriters, who had written songs before, created material for this new segment. Only the singers themselves were consistently younger. In the year 1962, artists such as Mike Sarne and Wendy Richard, Frank Ifield, Helen Shapiro, and the Tornados dominated the British charts. In Germany, Gerd Böttcher's "*Für Gaby tu ich alles*" (For Gaby I'd do Everything), Béla Sanders' "*Gartenzwerg-Marsch*" (Yard Dwarf March), and the Germany-residing American Bill Ramsey's "*Ohne Krimi geht die Mimi nie ins Bett*" (Mimi Never Goes to Bed without a Crime Novel) were the music highlights of that year. In the United States, among all the number one hits of 1962, Elvis Presley could only be found once, with the song "Good Luck Charm" that did not dovetail with his earlier work. Otherwise, the celebrities among the American teenage-stars were Ricky Nelson, Fabian, Bobby Rydell, Bobby Darin, Connie Francis, Paul Anka, and Frankie Avalon. Elsewhere, the scenario did not present itself in a much different fashion. If anything, youth culture was a concern for social workers and pedagogues. Rock'n'roll, now usually called twist, had turned into a form of gymnastic party entertainment with the aim of shedding off extra pounds gained by members of the affluent society in the wake of the economic boom of the 1950s.

The first signs that something groundbreaking was occurring were of commercial nature. During the month of September 1963, the Beatles, a band of barely 20-year-old music autodidacts from England's northwestern province, achieved something that had never been done before nor has ever been achieved ever since: their long-playing record *Please, Please Me*, and EP (extended player, a vinyl record with twice the single record length) "Twist and Shout" as well as their single "She Loves You," all topped the bestseller list in their respective categories in Great Britain. Certainly, at first sight this appears to be just one out of many superlatives, which are, after all, part of music industry's history, which ceaselessly rewrites its book of records, many of which are not worth mentioning. Nevertheless, by October 1963, this seemingly insignificant incident, besides drawing the attention of the music industry's accountants, had quickly triggered a nation-wide debate within the British media, that subsequently spread to the European continent. While for some, this new scenario epitomized the "apotheosis of inanity,"[3] for others, such as the conservative member of the House of Commons Norman Miscampbell, it was

> an outlet for many people who find it difficult to integrate themselves into society when they move into adolescence. The Beatles, and groups like them, are giving such people an outlet, and are taking up the slack, which ought to have been provided by a deeper education.[4]

Writing in the London *Sunday Times* during the month of December 1963, Richard Buckle on the contrary went so far as to argue that the Beatles, taking their commercial success into account, were "the greatest composers since Beethoven."[5] Already during November 1963, the Beatles were honored to be invited to the *Royal Variety Show*—Great Britain's most important show-business event annually staged since 1912—and to perform for the Royal Family. This caused a tense controversy because the *Royal Variety Show* was understood as a platform exclusively for the very best British show business had to offer. And to a large number of show-business representatives, the young ruffians with their idiosyncratic haircuts were not part of this elite group. That they ultimately did perform in London's Prince of Wales Theatre on the same stage as, among others, Marlene Dietrich and Maurice Chevalier, however, was not solely the result of their spectacular record sales. Certainly, show business's credibility would have been on the line if the market— one of show business' primary tools to measure and legitimize aesthetic value—had been ignored by excluding the most successful newcomer band of the year only on the basis that numerous show business professionals considered the Beatles's appearance and their music infantile. More important were the implications of the Beatles' sales records, and the buyers of Beatles records were exclusively young people. These young people literally "bought" this huge success and utilized it in the development of a new self-esteem. Youth had become the central topic within the commercial fabrication of the social sphere.[6]

A similar scenario emerged in the United States. For instance, the American show-business periodical *Billboard* listed only weeks later in their 31 March 1964 issue the Beatles's song "Can't Buy Me Love" at the top of the American pop charts; in second place was the Beatles' "Twist and Shout" followed by another Beatles record "She Loves You"; in fourth and fifth place were two further Beatles recordings, "I Want to Hold Your Hand" and "Please, Please Me" respectively. This feat even eclipsed the self-proclaimed "King of rock'n'roll" Elvis Presley. The sale of Beatles records amounted to roughly 60 percent of all record sales in the United States during this time. In the year 1964, young buyers of records made up almost a 40 percent share of all record sales worldwide, by the end of the decade, this share increased to roughly 80 percent.[7] It seemed something groundbreaking was occurring in the Beatles' challenging "Yeah, yeah, yeah" and their juvenile and yelling fans. In 1983, Iain Chambers made this diagnosis:

> Around 1964/5, there occurred a decisive shift in the economy of public imagery surrounding pop music. Pop stopped being a spectacular but peripheral event, largely understood to be associated with teenage working-class taste, and became the central symbol of fashionable, metropolitan, British culture.[8]

Youth—which since the coining of the term "teenager" by American sociologists during the 1950s had begun to appear as a product of the cultural realm as well as a socio-demographic category[9]—left its social-work niche and became a societal event. The 1950s "teenager rebellion" was too quickly absorbed—by the Hollywood movie industry or the music industry that had both capitalized on this topic—to be more than a marginal historical phenomenon.[10] British Beat Music turned youth culture into a public matter, more than just a commercial trend. On Easter and Pentecost 1964, the traditional British bank holidays, when so-called "rocks" and "mods" met for their first ritual battles in the south-English beach resorts Brighton, Clacton, and Margate, such events became testimony to a process of change, initiated by the media, in public awareness of the increasing autonomy and culture of youths.[11] Their idiosyncratic leisure rituals out of enthusiasm for music, their disorderly conduct and deliberate provocative acts, their formation into small informal groups along certain styles of clothing, as well as their devotion to certain material objects—the motorcycle for the rocks or the Lambretta TV 175 motor scooter for the mods—were now the basis for a new youth discourse that proliferated quickly. The media did not only offer an outlet for youth self-presentation but also a forum for evaluation and interpretation. Within its representation in the media, youth began to become aware of itself as a societal force, albeit at first only marginal and predominantly apolitical. The resulting publicity, however, helped to bring down customs that had demoted adolescents to the status of pedagogical objects. Roughly at the same time throughout all European industrialized nations, youth and youth culture were emerging as an issue of public concern.[12]

Various European societies had reached a stage at which they started to project their own transformation onto their young generation and their offspring's culture. On 19 June 1964, during a session of the House of Commons dealing with the consequences of the increasing automation of production, it did not take long, while debating the issues youth and education within the context of rapidly changing social realities, for the Beatles to be cited as an example epitomizing transformations resulting from these new realities. Issues such as young people's culture and their habits of consumption, which previously had been of only marginal interest, were now a focal point of sociopolitical considerations. During this House of Commons session, William Deedes, the speaker of the government, declared:

> They [the Beatles] herald a cultural movement among the young, which may become part of the history of our time. ... For those with eyes to see it, something important and heartening is happening here. The young are rejecting some of the sloppy standards of their elders, by which far too much of our output has been governed in recent years. ... [T]hey have discerned dimly that in a world of automation, declining craftsmanship and increased leisure, something of this kind is essential to restore the human instinct to excel at something and the human faculty of discrimination.[13]

While Deedes' contention did not remain unopposed and, in retrospect, may appear as far too lofty, it did initiate what the sociologist Claus Leggewie later somewhat mockingly called the "*immerwährende Jugendkonferenz*" (eternal youth conference).[14] The triad youth, youth culture, and pop music had evolved into the symbolic figure for societal processes of change. The journalist George Melly, the author of one of the first more thorough analyses of "Beatlemania" under the telling title *Revolt Into Style* (1970) argued:

> [Pop] presents, with an honesty based on indifference to any standards or earlier terms of reference, an exact image of our rapidly changing society, particularly in relation to its youth.[15]

Dieter Baacke,[16] author of the influential and widely-read *Beat—die sprachlose Opposition* (Beat—the Voiceless Opposition), thought along similar lines and proposed a handy formula, which in variations until today has been accompanying considerations concerning youth culture and pop music. Moreover, regardless of the emergence of essentially wordless techno music during the 1990s, his formula succeeded in maintaining an unexpected up-to-dateness.

However, the *topos* "youth = opposition" is as old as the term youth itself[17] and it is just as correct as it is false. As a consequence of the accelerated pace of societal transformation, which as of the 1950s increased dramatically following the Second World War's major ramifications, expectations and hopes of the various generations deviated more rapidly. Furthermore, the generations' social realities, because of this increased rate of change, also began to grow more disparate resulting in diverging sets of values and forms to associate as well as to socialize with others. This had in turn the consequence that adolescents sought out their own paths into as well as within this increasingly complex societal reality. The cultural realm was the only sphere where these endeavors faced relatively little risks. Consequently, within this context, the quest for "*Anderssein*" (the state of being different)—as is well known, "to make a difference" became one of rock cultures' main principle—reverberated loud and clear. Some attentive sociologists such as Friedrich Tenbruck had already diagnosed by 1962 that an autonomous "*Teilkultur Jugendlicher*" (a separate culture of young people) was evolving which he had interpreted as a "*Sozialisierung in eigener Regie*" (self-directed socialization).[18] "Beatlemania"—again to contemporaries a seemingly inexplicable as well as anxiety-stimulating phenomenon—had its share in adolescents' new experience of gaining more social power, an effect of accumulated spending power[19] and their potential as future customers in a society that was progressively more determined by commercialization, mass consumption, and mass-media outlets. Thus, it did not come as a surprise that this development was first tied to and analyzed within the context of young people's habits of consumption.[20]

However, the changes of young people's leisure habits had nothing to do with opposition or rebellion. Actual changes remained limited to the sphere of the production of culture symbols,[21] that is, as Ian Birchall already depicted it at that time, "an attitude of rebellion within a framework of acceptance."[22] To show society its own transformation, images of juvenile acts of rebellion produced by the media were certainly indispensable. This transformation would have been less discernible if it had been dealt with in the more adequate context of changing structures of the industrial production of goods (due to rapid technological innovation) resulting in fundamental social changes of all Western industrialized nations, as well as in the context of the alteration of social identities and forms of representation based on new cultural means. The discourse on youth, which evolved during the 1960s and which was predominantly tied to visible changes of young people's habits of leisure and consumption as well as fashion, trends, and music, was the context within which youth, not the least through music, manifested itself as a cultural construct that found expression in a highly differentiated youth culture. Without this discourse on youth, which developed at the beginning of the 1960s and was projected onto adolescents—often crudely or ludicrously overstated—basically every single societal transformation that was discernible, music may have remained a harmless stimulant to shake a leg. Instead, in the wake of headline news depicting the occurrence "Beatlemania," music evolved into an extraordinary medium of cultural communication, one of the fundaments of societal production of individuality and subjectivity: "[T]he level of attention and meaning invested in music by youth is still unmatched by almost any other organized activity in society, including religion."[23] Henceforth, "youth" [read young people] began to define itself peculiarly through music.

Music and Society

For numerous reasons, music was particularly suited to solidify within the society at large the initially diffuse and vaguely defined generational consciousness. Portable radios, which were introduced during the 1950s, offered young people an autonomous access to this medium, through which they began to explore and encounter cultural spaces independently from their parents. In West Germany, by the beginning of the 1960s, already one youth out of six between the age of 12 and 16 had such a portable radio at his disposal.[24] Every third youth had access to a record player.[25] However, socioeconomic differences were significant: 45 percent of all record players were in households with monthly incomes of above DM 1.000, only 3 percent were in households with a monthly income of less than DM 250.[26] Since the vinyl record was the medium in which the evolving youth culture revealed itself most plainly, children of the upper-middle class were the ones who set the tone. This is also true for television. Television played a major, although often underestimated role in the formation of the triad youth, youth culture, and pop music. The Beatles were not only a product of Liverpool's cavern clubs but also of London's media industry with television at its center: *Ready, Steady, Go!*—a television-show for pop music, introduced in 1963 by England's commercial television-station ITV, following in format Dick Clark's *American Bandstand*[27] with live performances in front of a young, dancing audience—helped both the Beatles as well as numerous other bands of the Liverpool-Mersey-Beat tradition to break through. On 1 January 1964, the BBC began broadcasting the pop-music show *Top of the Pops*, also copying the *American Bandstand* format and similar programs, which targeted 12- to 16-year-olds and which lived off the live presentation of popular hits, could be found across Europe. In West Germany, the *Beat Club*'s inaugural show—broadcasted by German television during the afternoon hours of 25 September 1965—institutionalized the amalgamation of youth and pop music.

Within this context, music carried for adolescents, among others, two main advantages with it. First, music provided them with a platform from which they could proactively engage themselves in as well as shape the society at large; two things they did with rising self-esteem. And second, music was the most democratic besides other established forms of media within a mass culture highly penetrated by different media outlets. Until today, pop music has been the least censored branch within the cultural realm. Time and again, musicians as well as their audience, found spaces and means to express themselves, their real feelings, and how they perceive themselves. There has been no other cultural branch permitting similar access to the industry of cultural mass production without pertinent knowledge and experiences. During the first half of the 1960s, amateurs produced the British beat bands (even the Beatles' productions, regardless of their close partnership with the experienced business insider George Martin). These amateurs were able to persevere in spite of existing professional standards and contrary to their representatives' predictions; a process that has recurred time and again in countless variations down to today's techno music. Musical creativity is not tied to requirements that need investors, even though the music business succeeded repeatedly in securing such developments for itself. Not even a pertinent musical education is a requirement as countless successful young musicians have proven, who did not study formally, but knew how to play music in a self-directed and at the same time curious way. The flair of "making-music-yourself" was an instrumental aspect for the function of music in the context of youth culture and has remained so until today.

Ultimately, music ideally suited to absorb the developing system of young people's values and their interests because music's symbolic function was neither reliant on the unambiguous meaning of words nor on ideologies, but rather based on emotional impulses. This aspect was already noticeable during the 1950s within the groups of British Teddy Boys or the German *Halbstarken* (a group of leather-clad young rowdies), with the difference that in those days values were projected onto music that was by and large beyond the young people's influence. Even rock-

'n'roll music was part of a repertoire that was originally produced for adults; only later would professional radio disc jockeys present songs such as those of Bill Haley, Little Richard, or Fats Domino in special broadcasts to teenagers. That this repertoire would later be appropriated by one of "theirs," as in the case of Elvis Presley, was the grand exception with all its known consequences. Since the early 1960s, however, all kinds of music, which were relevant for the evolution of youth culture, originated in the sociocultural network of same-age youths. In this network, based on immediate contact with the audience as well as a constant process of responding to previously produced material, various sound patterns were charged with cultural values and significance, which then were professionally arranged in the studios. Within British beat music, diversity arose at first often diffuse or barely articulated, challenging society's leveling tendencies, that were the result of mass consumption's first wave during the 1950s. In this process, traditions and standards of musical entertainment were broken. Instead of creating familiar sound patterns—as was the case with German Schlager (popular songs, usually with German lyrics) productions, which followed standard procedures that aimed at easy commercial success—artists searched for extreme sounds (noise, piercing sounds, rhythmic-metric intensity), that both polarized society but also simultaneously promised listeners a high-intensity experience and ultimately became the tonal insignias of this process. Group singing, which during the 1960s was heard strikingly frequently and which probably appeared initially for pragmatic reasons (within a group it is easier to carry the right tune), figured prominently in this development taking the place of the, hitherto, for pop music, usual solo singing by one vocalist.[28] Out of this choral sound, the sense of group was more emphatic in terms of an experience of mutuality than any genuinely articulated concrete experience, and in this way social gaps between the various fractions of the young audience could be bridged. While social differences did not disappear, as for instance, in the highly publicized difference between the Beatles and the Rolling Stones, which the media usually portrayed as diametrical opposites, these differences did not stand in the way of the, albeit, illusionary, yet passionate search for the essence of a communal generational experience. Already at that time, it was noticed that the Beatles succeeded in bridging social differences of young people's daily realities through their music.

> [M]ore than most pop-singers, they [the Beatles] have bridged the class-gap within youth between student and worker, massing them against the largely unresponsive adult world.[29]

The new sound patterns of music now carried with them both patterns of integration but also symbolic patterns of segregation for young people. The line between "us" and "them" was henceforth drawn on the basis of music. At first, this line was drawn along lines of age, later, separating different social realities, and ultimately today, dividing people on the basis of virtual realities of highly differentiated social networks around scenes and subcultures, which are as fragile as they are variable in terms of their composition, orientation, patterns of communication, and cultural codes. This underlying logic has been discussed by Lawrence Grossberg as a

> mode of productivity that can be described in the following terms: affective (rather than ideological); differentiating (us versus them); a celebration of fun (where 'fun' takes on different meanings depending on what it is opposing); politicized, primarily within the realm of everyday life; and operating as a mode (or practice) of survival in the face of the very conditions that called it into existence.[30]

One of this youth-cultural productivity's idiosyncrasies was its evolution within a sphere of interests that was determined by the opposition of the local and the global, i.e., a bipolar realm excluding the national plane, which during the 1960s and 1970s was still the predominant plane of social, cultural, and political integration. Within Europe, this process was dealt with under the catchphrase "Americanization."[31] Even British beat music's roots were primarily American. On the local level, in youth as well as cavern clubs, this music was played, performed, and ultimately altered in such a way that a seemingly original kind of music developed, which through channels of commercial transmission was reintroduced to the global marketplace of popular music. The Beatles' first album consisted for almost one half of cover versions of contemporary U.S.-hits (Arthur Alexander, Cookies, Shirelles, Isley Brothers), but the other half was so similar to American examples (even though the songs were listed as original Beatles composition) that they were highly reminiscent of contemporary American songs. Love Me Do, for instance, the song that initiated the Beatles's amazing career, was clearly based on Carl Perkins' 1956-country-ballad Sure to Fall. With other British beat music bands of the 1960s such as the Rolling Stones, the share of United States material of their song repertoires was significantly above 80 percent. This process repeated itself in basically the whole of Europe—even behind the so-called "Iron Curtain"[32]—with the difference that now British songs and the impetus to pick up and play the guitar served as the examples for local music scenes. However, the perception of one-sided and one-dimensional causes for globalization was based merely on isolated observations of different record markets, thus reducing complex cultural behaviors to a hotchpotch of isolated products in the shape of goods.[33] While this commercial side was certainly important for the evolving youth culture of the 1960s, youth culture is made up of a complex web of activities, in which the purchase of records indeed figured prominently, however, not predominantly. After all, the social contact with music cannot be reduced to the mere act of purchasing records. Particularly for adolescents, who by and large had no own income at their disposal, the purchase of records was only a subordinate feature within a large variety of activities related to the enjoyment of music, which principally took place within their direct social environments of peer groups.[34] And it was socially that essential transformations occurred, even though these transformations initially were noticed in sales records and in young people's habits of consumption.

Musical practices, which had originated as acoustic backgrounds and which had assumed the function of coordinating motional patterns important for dance and background entertainment (which, particularly, radio broadcasts had made possible), evolved then into a comprehensive form of cultural communication that was taken very seriously. The shift of sound patterns' aesthetic focal point from the dance floor to the concert auditorium and on to the studio—from technically reproduced to technically produced sounds[35]—were part of this evolution, which was soon to be called revolutionary. When in 1967, the Beatles released their album *Sgt. Pepper's Lonely Hearts Club Band*, the "Fab Four" were seen as the avant-garde of a cultural revolution, which while it objected to any form of conventional politics, opened up spaces for entirely new experiences. The disturbances brought about by the Beatles and other likeminded bands of rock music into which British beat music had evolved by that time, were due to the mere shift of certain cultural features. While the Vietnam War led to the radicalization of parts of the young generation in the United States as well as in Europe, the "*musikalische Revolution*"[36] (musical revolution) followed a different path, much to the regret of the political activists' of the youth and student movements. Yet in retrospect, John Savage remarked pertinently:

> Youth culture was turning into a youth utopia: by the end of 1966, the fusion of drugs, sexual, social, and political forces led baby boomers to confuse purchasing power with political power.[37]

Certainly, this revolution caused a radical renovation of the world of sounds' aesthetic inventory, in which new technical possibilities for the spheres of sound's synthetic expansion were consistently utilized. In an expanded and intensified sensuality of sounds, new experiences could be encountered, not only but especially in relations to one's own body as well as societal processes of its disciplining. These new experiences enabled individuals to counter social realities within a somewhat self-determined fashion. It was at this point that these developments intersected with the various drug cultures as well as with those processes, which during the 1960s' climate of constant change, were subsumed under the catchphrase "sexual revolution."

Politics versus Consumerism: The Rise of the Music Industry

The relationship between commercially organized youth culture on the one side and the political youth and student movement on the other side remained, in spite of numerous situations of contact full of disagreements and extremely problematic. The few direct and immediate contacts that occurred between the politicized youth and the representatives of the cultural youth movement—for instance, the 1968/69 debate between John Lennon and John Hoyland, one of the leaders of the British student movement, which appeared in the Marxist periodical the *Black Dwarf*—bespeak as much the misunderstanding as they do the insurmountable ideological differences. John Lennon defended himself with a harsh rhetoric against the previously published attack on the Beatles-song "Revolution," whose lyrics were quite clearly on the topic of revolution: "Don't you know that you can count me out." Lennon responded to criticisms of taking an apolitical stance removing himself from responsibility for the young people, with these words:

> I don't worry about what you, the left, the middle, the right or any fucking club boys think. I'm not that bourgeois. ... I'm not only up against the establishment but you too. I'll tell you what's wrong with the world: people—so do you want to destroy them? Until you/we change our heads, there's no chance. Tell me of one successful revolution. Who fucked up communism, Christianity, capitalism, Buddhism, etc. Sick heads, and nothing else.[38]

Certainly, it is indicative that Lennon rephrased these lyrics for the re-recording of the double album *The Beatles*—which due to its all-white cover design by Richard Hamilton is also known as the *White Album*—adding to the controversial passage an "in": "Don't you know that you can count me out/in," an attempt to satisfy listeners from the two ideological camps. The suspicion that commercial rationales played a role cannot be contested; in fact, it is one of the fundamental misconceptions about the 1960s that youth culture and its music possessed an anticommercial impetus. The commercial form of organization was of central importance and a prerequisite for its social functions. After all, it connected adolescents' production of cultural meaning with the symbolic center of a societal formation shaped by capitalism. Paul McCartney's response "We're the world's number one capitalists,"[39] during a 1968-interview to the question of whether the Beatles considered themselves as revolutionaries, was meant quite seriously. After all, the exciting aspect of pop culture is that the entire commercial buzz is aimed at young people, who usually experience society under the impression that they are a liability.

From the very beginning youth culture was located precisely in between mainstream and subculture, just as much characterized by subcultural as well as countercultural patterns of segregation as it was characterized by mechanisms of integration of the markets for music, media, and fashion. This in-between authentic rock on the one side and commercial pop on the other side that in the mid-1960s, represented unique bilateral boundaries by the end of the decade diversified into groupings such as "underground," "progressive music," or "progressive rock," and by the 1970s into even more diverse subcultures, from punks to poppers.

> Thus Rock emerges in a stratification that is accomplished through the making of distinctions, within the mainstream, between the "serious" and the "trivial," the "oppositional" and the "complicit," the "truthful" and the "fraudulent," the "anti-mass" and the "mass," the "authentic" and the "alienated." The second term of each of these oppositions describes qualities Rock ascribes to "Pop."[40]

In that sense, it is not contradictory that musicians such as Jimi Hendrix, who, through eccentric electric guitar play, had become a figurehead of the "Underground" music scene by the end of the 1960s, or Janis Joplin for that matter catered more or less as stipulated their creative outputs to the record industry for the sale within the capitalist music business. An underground that nobody knew about would have had to renounce its most important dimension of impact: publicity. Commerce is essential for a culture whose bearers hold, albeit merely symbolically, the status of an independent and autonomous social group. Nonetheless adolescents then as now were caught in a contradictory web of dependencies and relations, which were impressed by considerable social differences. The more successful the product youth culture was, the larger the awareness grew how diverse adolescents' culture truly was.

By the end of the 1960s, it became apparent that society at large, which music had once represented, was in fact the product of this music, the result of its successful commercial utilization and professional marketing. Simultaneously, youth culture began to separate into various fractions, each with its "own" kind of music serving as an emblem, not only between young and old, but now as means of segregation and social demarcation within youth culture itself. The young African-Americans in the United States were the first to draw attention to themselves through their own version of rock music, which in the latter half of the 1960s had evolved into a musical youth-idiom. When some of these young African-Americans, for instance, Jimi Hendrix or Sly & the Family Stone, tried to escape white middle-class kids' attempts to romanticize them as exotic city-guerillas, their sound became more radical. They had the rich legacy of Black music at their disposal and created their musical version of youth, which expressed their experience growing up in America's inner-city ghettoes. In James Brown's "Say It Loud I'm Black and I'm Proud," this process found its paradigmatic manifestation. With the close of the 1960s and the beginning of the 1970s, further streams within music emerged. As a reaction to the sound experiments of psychedelic rock as well as a countermeasure to the bombastic music of art rock (both these kinds of music had their primary base within the student scene), a new form of rock music, primarily European in origin, evolved in the shape of so-called hard rock. Hard rock bands such as Led Zeppelin, Black Sabbath, and Deep Purple or the Canadian Bachmann-Turner-Overdrive appealed explicitly to youths of those social backgrounds, in which the Rock music's strength and energy encountered social realities, which together were released in fantasies of violence. In a review of the British band Black Sabbath, Lester Bangs, in reference to a William Burroughs' text, coined at the beginning of the 1970s the term heavy metal, which is still being used today.[41] Sociological categories, however, can no longer be used for these intra-youth-cultural differentiations because they are experientially based on emotions, and, even though socially structured, the realm is nonetheless relatively autonomous.[42] Henceforth, agglomerations of young people of different dimension as well as of diverse social backgrounds stood behind rapidly differentiating musical styles:

> Youth as community ... becomes replaced by youth as a category constructed by the market.[43]

Next to fan cultures—which arose around musicians or genres (heavy metal, glam rock, etc.) with a partly remarkable degree of self-organization (fan clubs, fanzines, etc.) and which developed scenes[44] with more or less independent infrastructures in forms of clubs, local media outlets, or informal social networks—there is evidence of other subcultures of young people during the 1970s such as the punks, the rudies, the skinheads (who had the hard mods as their precursors), or the new romantics, who defined themselves primarily as communities of common styles or common ideas. Within these communities, which appropriated autonomous cultural spaces for themselves, music was but one element besides others in their own symbolic universe.[45] In the midst of these diverging images of young people and their culture, the image of "youth" also changed:

> Youth itself is transformed from a matter of age into an ambiguous matter of attitude, defined by its rejection of boredom and its celebration of movement, change, energy, i.e., fun. And this celebration is lived out and inscribed upon the body—in dance, sex, drugs, fashion, style and even the music itself.[46]

By the close of the decade, "youth" had seemingly transformed into a conglomerate of minorities, in which the ostensibly lost national allusion returned under the label "new wave." In 1978, a process started in Germany that for a short period of time caused a significant increase of national productions in the music market. Between 1978 and 1982, the repertoire category "*Pop Deutsch*" (pop german)—as the crude language of the music business calls it—garnered more than 40 percent of all record sales, with a 47.9 percent high in 1982.[47] Similar trends occurred in all European countries.[48] However, these transformations mirrored, above all, new economic strategies elicited by changing demographic and social structures of the record market. Particularly influential was the consolidation of an independent sector of regional micro-labels, which maintained distribution and licensing affiliations on a joint venture-basis with the global media-conglomerates.[49] The commercial as well as the medial representation of youth culture in its social and regional diversity, which had been characteristic since the 1960s and which was now ever more present and obvious, stood behind this development. The criteria language, which in this context has been raised frequently, influenced this process only marginally and instead was based on the concept of a national culture, which had never played a role in the context of youth culture. Usually, song lyrics merely provided listeners with audible means with which to attach their own ideas or most of all, functioned as a framework for vocal sound production. Furthermore, because of advanced means of production, vocal sound patterns obtained such an unambiguous clarity and strength of imagination that their verbal message became redundant. Faced with rapidly changing technological, economic, and societal conditions, it was important for cultural practices to constantly ensure the link between informal patterns of organization with their commercial patterns of organization. In 1981, the creation of the American Music Television (MTV) impacted this process, begun in the 1950s and which has continued since. Within this new setting, a new phase of cultural evolution—the continued connection of youth-cultural practices with the cultural industry, of social realities with the world of the media, and of subculture and mainstream—was inaugurated.

Notes

1. Talcott Parsons, "Age and Sex Roles in the United States," reprinted in Talcott Parsons, *Essays in Sociological Theory* (Chicago, 1964), 89–102.
2. Comp. Sara Cohen, *Rock Culture in Liverpool: Popular Music in the Making* (Oxford, 1991).
3. Paul Johnson, "The Menace of Beatlism," *New Statesman* 28, 2 (1964): 326.
4. Cited in Elizabeth Thomson and David Gutman, *The Lennon Companion: Twenty-five Years of Comment* (London, 1987), 49.
5. Richard Buckle in *The Sunday Times*, December 1963; cited in Iain Chambers, *Urban Rhythms: Pop Music and Popular Culture* (Hampshire, 1985), 63.
6. However, numerous points became blurred in the distorting mirror of media representation at that time. Certainly from 1960 to 1969, the returns of the record industry doubled not only in the United States but also in Great Britain, from $600 million to $1.3 billion and from £15 million to £32 million respectively (analogous developments have been recorded for other Western industrialized nations). Yet, in the context of the national economies, for instance for Great Britain by the end of the 1960s, these numbers made up less than a 0.2 percent share of the entire production of consumer goods. Compare Dave Harker, "Still Crazy After All These Years," in *Cultural Revolution? The Challenge of the Arts in the 1960s*, ed. Bart Moore-Gilbert and John Seed (London and New York, 1992), 238.
7. Simon Frith, *The Sociology of Rock* (London, 1978), 12.
8. Iain Chambers, *Urban Rhythms*, 57.
9. The term appeared for the first time in the American media during the Second World War, at that point still in the hyphenated form "teen-ager." In the middle of the 1950s, sociologists such as Shmuel Noah Eisenstadt used the term also in academic texts. Shmuel Noah Eisenstadt, *From Generation to Generation: Age Groups and Social Structure* (Glencoe, Ill.,1956).
10. See Grace Palladino, *Teenagers: An American History* (New York, 1997).
11. Compare Stanley Cohen, *Folk Devils & Moral Panics: The Creation of the Mods and Rocks* (London, 1972).
12. Compare Dieter Baacke, *Jugend und Jugendkulturen. Darstellung und Deutung* (Weinheim and Munich, 1987).
13. Cited in Thomson and Gutman, 39.
14. Claus Leggewie, *Die 89er. Porträt einer Generation* (Hamburg, 1995), 7 passim.
15. George Melly, *Revolt Into Style* (Harmondsworth, 1970), 5.
16. Dieter Baacke, *Beat—die sprachlose Opposition* (Munich, 1968).
17. See John Gills, *Youth and History: Tradition and Change in European Age Relations, 1770–Present* (New York, 1974).
18. Friedrich H. Tenbruck, *Jugend und Gesellschaft. Soziologische Perspektiven* (Freiburg, 1962), 92.

19. For Germany in the year 1959, the economic research institute DIVO determined a spending power of DM 180 million within the hands of 10- to 15-year-olds. According to the Hamburger Institut für Wirtschaftsforschung (Hamburg Institute for Economic Research), there would be another DM 300 million of spending power for the year 1959, if one were to consider also the 15- to 19-year-olds. See Axel Schildt, *Moderne Zeiten. Freizeit, Massenmedien und 'Zeitgeist' in der Bundesrepublik der 50er Jahre* (Hamburg, 1995), 160.

20. Mark Abrams, *The Teenage Consumer* (London, 1959).

21. The ceaselessly raised increase in the crime rate for adolescents, at that time in this context, proved, in retrospect, to be a mere problem of statistics. Disorderly conduct within the setting of music concerts as well as curfew violations made up a share of up to 80 percent of such statistics. See Mike Brake, *Comparative Youth Culture* (London and New York, 1985), 43.

22. Ian Birchall, "The Decline and Fall of British Rhythm and Blues," in *The Age of Rock: Sounds of the American Cultural Revolution,* ed. Jonathan Eisen (New York, 1969), 98.

23. Andrew Ross, "Introduction," in *Microphone Fiends: Youth Music & Youth Culture,* ed. Andrew Ross and Tricia Rose (London and New York, 1994), 3.

24. Compare Arne Andersen, *Der Traum vom guten Leben. Alltags- und Konsumgeschichte vom Wirtschaftswunder bis heute* (Frankfurt am Main and New York, 1997), 32.

25. Compare DIVO-Institut Frankfurt ed., *Der Westdeutsche Markt in Zahlen: Ein Handbuch für Forschung, Werbung und Verkauf* (Frankfurt am Main, 1962), 32.

26. Ibid.

27. WFIL-TV (Philadelphia) broadcasted *American Bandstand* for the first time in 1952 and in 1957, ABC-TV began broadcasting it nationally on a weekly basis. The original pattern of the show—pop as well as rock stars performing their current records in front of a choreographed live audience with brief talk-show sequences in between—has been replicated countless times ever since.

28. Exceptions such as the doo-wop-bands or the early motown-sound remained, on the whole, limited to the United States and served British beat bands, above all for the Beatles, as inspirations or as a repertoire for cover-versions.

29. Terry Eagleton, "New Bearings: The Beatles," in *Blackfriars* 45 (April 1964), 15.

30. Lawrence Grossberg, "Same As It Ever Was? Rock Culture. Same As It Ever Was! Rock Theory," in *Stars Don't Stand Still in the Sky, Music and Myth,* ed. Iren Kelly and Evelyn McDonnell (London, 1999), 112.

31. For the Federal Republic of Germany, see the informative study by Kaspar Maase, *Bravo Amerika* (Hamburg, 1992); for France Richard F. Kuisel, *Seducing the French: The Dilemma of Americanization* (Berkeley, 1993); for Great Britain the article by Dick Hebdige, "Towards a Cartography of Taste," in *Popular Culture: Past and Present,* ed. Bernard Waites, Tony Bennett, and Graham Martin (London, 1982), 194–218.

32. Compare Peter Wicke, "Rock Around Socialism. Jugend und ihre Musik in einer gescheiterten Gesellschaft," in *Handbuch Jugend und Musik,* ed. Dieter Baacke (Opladen, 1998), 293 passim.

33. See Deanna C. Robinson, Elizabeth B. Buck, and Marlene Cuthbert, *Music at the Margins. Popular Music and Global Cultural Diversity* (Newbury Park, 1991).

34. Compare John Connell and Chris Gibson, *Sound Tracks. Popular Music, Identity and Place* (London and New York, 2003).

35. Compare Peter Wicke, "Von der Aura der technisch produzierten Klanggestalt. Zur Ästhetik des Pop," in *Wegzeichen. Studien zur Musikwissenschaft,* ed. Peter Wicke and Jürgen Mainka (Berlin, 1985), 276 passim.

36. Compare Helmut Salzinger, *Rock Power oder Wie musikalisch ist die Revolution?* (Frankfurt am Main, 1972).

37. John Savage, "The Enemy Within. Sex, Rock and Identity," in *Facing the Music*, ed. Simon Frith (New York, 1988), 160.

38. John Lennon, "A Very Open Letter to John Hoyland from John Lennon," in *Black Dwarf*, 10 January 1969, no page number.

39. Cited in Barry Miles, *Beatles in Their Own Words* (London, 1978), 62.

40. Keir Keightley, "Reconsidering Rock," in *The Cambridge Companion to Pop and Rock*, ed. Simon Frith, Will Straw, and John Street (Cambridge, 2001), 128.

41. Compare Lester Bangs, *Psychotic Reactions and Carburetors Dung. Rock 'n' Roll as Literature and Literature as Rock 'n' Roll*, ed. Greil Marcus (New York, 1987).

42. Deena Weistein proved this in her study empirically: *Heavy Metal. A Cultural Sociology* (New York, 1991).

43. Alan Tomlinson, *Consumption, Identity & Style. Marketing, Meanings, and the Packaging of Pleasure* (London and New York, 1990), 31.

44. Compare Will Straw, "Systems of Articulation, Logics of Change: Communities and Scenes in Popular Music," *Cultural Studies* 5, 3 (1991): 368-87.

45. Compare Dick Hebdige, *Subculture: The Meaning of Style* (London, 1979).

46. Lawrence Grossberg, "Is Anybody Listening? Does Anybody Care? On 'the State' of Rock," in Ross and Rose, *Microphone Fiends*, 51.

47. Figures taken from Rolf Moser and Andreas Scheuermann, eds., *Handbuch der Musikwirtschaft* (Starnberg and Munich, 1992), 87.

48. See. Michèle Hung and Esteban Garcia Morencos, *World Record Sales 1969-1990. A Statistical History of the World Recording Industry* (London, 1990).

49. Warner merged into the newly created 1969 corporation of Warner Communications (today's Time-Warner AOL); Columbia merged into the Columbia Broadcasting System (CBS, which on the basis of company purchases was rapidly expanding and rising to the realm of global players) and served as the spine for the CBS Recording Group (today's Sony Music Entertainment); RCA Victor was part of a diversified company that united under one roof everything that had something to do with electronics, from home utilities to electronic weaponry (in 1986, Bertelsmann purchased RCA Victor and made it one core of the Bertelsmann Music Group, BMG); in 1979, EMI was integrated into Thorn Electronics (in 1996, after a rare occurrence of de-merging, EMI was once again independent); Philips and Siemens united their record efforts, Polydor and Deutsche Grammophon respectively, in the holding PolyGram, which until 1980 had risen to be the third largest producer of records because of its aggressive purchasing activities (today PolyGram is part of Universal Vivendi).

Chapter 5

The Triumph of English-Language Pop Music: West German Radio Programming

Konrad Dussel

In his *Age of the Extremes*, Eric Hobsbawm identifies the "emergence of a specific and extraordinarily powerful youth culture" as one of the central characteristics of a worldwide "cultural revolution" in the second half of the twentieth century. For him, the point of departure were the United States, whose "youth lifestyle was transmitted either directly or (as if by osmosis) through the intermediary of the United Kingdom." Hobsbawm mentions various channels of transmission, such as youth tourism, the global network of universities, and the influence of fashion. However, first and foremost were "music records and, later, cassettes … whose most important promotional medium was, then as now, old-fashioned radio."[1]

This essay examines the role of "old-fashioned radio" as the "most important promotional medium"—not for music records in general, but for beat and rock music in particular, which stood at the core of the era's youth culture. Central questions include: What was offered to youth in the 1960s and 1970s? And how and why did this change? The focus will be on the German context, especially on the example of Baden-Baden's Südwestfunk (SWF), which has since been incorporated into *Südwestrundfunk* (Southwest Broadcasting). However, "real" youth broadcasts, such as those produced as more or less educational fare by the editors of Baden-Baden's "school and youth radio," will not be dealt with: the central theme here will be music programming.

Limiting the focus does not mean losing sight of the wider context. The developments in England cannot be ignored, and the interconnections that exist between countries are a particularly important aspect which should not be underestimated. However, the broader effect of global socioeconomic change can here only be summarized in one sentence: if the American and Western European economies had not expanded so dramatically after the Second World War, then there would not have been the increase in prosperity and leisure time—which were necessary preconditions for the mass media developments which concern this essay.

In addition, one must resist the temptation to focus only on the major state-organized public broadcasters of the United Kingdom and West Germany. Although official sponsorship actually allowed them a certain autonomy, they were not free from the impact of evolving technologies. It was precisely in this area that massive changes occurred after 1945, the most important being television's technological coming of age as it took its place beside radio broadcasting. At the same time, the music record received a technological makeover, with the replacement of old-fashioned shellac by modern vinyl, as well as the introduction of new long-playing and single formats; these in turn provided the recording industry with totally new avenues for marketing and profit-making, which could not help but have an effect on radio programming.

My goal is to describe the effects of the most important, immediate changes in the "external" environment of radio broadcasting, and then to examine the "internal" consequences. Audience response is the connecting link which forms the actual band of transmission.

Since the magnitude of these radical changes can be easily obscured by various background factors, constants, influences, and lines of development, "snapshots" of two years will be introduced as the best likely way of providing an initial impression of the kinds of changes that took place in radio programming.[2]

SWF Programming in 1959 and 1979

Just a quick glance at old broadcast guides reveals how different the media landscape once was, even as recently as 1959. For example, the leading German radio and television guide *Hör zu* (Listen Up) dedicated two full pages to radio programming every day. This totaled fourteen pages per week; in comparison, television programming warranted just four pages per week.[3]

Nearly all German radio stations produced two "programs": a main "first program" for AM as well as FM transmission, and a supplemental "second program" for only FM transmission. However, the content of the two programs was not strictly differentiated. Both tried to offer something for everyone, just at different times of day. At SWF in 1959/60, this meant that music constituted 59 percent of the first program, and 58 percent of the second; the first program had 28.7 percent dance and popular entertainment music, while the second had 25.2 percent.[4] Ideally, the first program would play classical music while the second played popular music, and vice versa.

In reality, however, the listeners' choices were not really choices, as FM reception was not very common (even though most radios included this capacity). When the ARD (the association of public broadcasters in West Germany) commissioned a study of radio listening habits in 1960/61, the SWF second program was found only on rare occasions to have attracted more than a one percent audience share; at times the figures were so low as to be barely measurable. In contrast, the first program registered low audience ratings only during certain times of day; during peak hours (early morning, midday, and evening), figures of up to 10 percent were recorded.[5]

In those days, a considerable proportion of music entertainment was produced by the broadcaster's own orchestras. In the case of SWF, these were primarily Willi Stech's *Kleines Unterhaltungs-Orchester* and Emmerich Smola's *Großes Unterhaltungs-Orchester* (smaller and greater orchestras for popular entertainment, respectively). It is not really possible to stylistically summarize their broad repertoires;[6] however, one cannot help but make a few critical comments. Even among Stech's ensemble recordings, only a quarter were vocal numbers; in Smola's case, the proportion could be presumed to be even less. Foreign tunes were hardly to be heard at all, unless discreetly repackaged by German composers such as Werner Drexler. In 1959, Stech recorded not only Drexler's slow waltz "*Bin verliebt*" ("I'm in Love"), but also seven other pieces such as the "dancelike intermezzo" of "Pizzeria," or the "South American sketch" of "Cosi, Cosi."[7]

It was nearly impossible to find a radio program which targeted a youth audience, at least going solely by the titles. In the autumn of 1959, there was just one: "*Teenager-Party! Rhythmus für junge Leute*" ("Teenager Party! Rhythms for Young People"), hosted by Horst Uhse. The show was broadcasted on the SWF second channel every Wednesday from 9 to 10 p.m.

Twenty years later, in 1979, the situation had changed in almost every respect. Only the organizational structure had remained the same: as before, West German radio was transmitted solely by state-organized public broadcasters. Their offerings had, however, changed remarkably. By this time, television had grown to three channels, taking center stage in the public spotlight; this new focus was mirrored by the programming guides, in which announcements for radio shows were becoming progressively shorter.

However, radio's offerings had also significantly increased, a major reason being the acceptance of FM radio as a matter of course. Like almost every other German station, SWF was now broadcasting three different programs around the clock, and each program was defined by distinctly different formats and content. According to the broadcaster's own guidelines, "The first channel is a family program, geared towards the greatest possible audience. … The focus is on entertainment and information. … The entertainment emphasizes the program's family character. The music ranges from contemporary to traditional, from hits to comic opera, but not beyond." The second channel's target audience were "listeners who demand and expect, on the one hand, education, edification, entertainment and instruction (reflecting a cultural imperative), and, on the other hand, deeper information and critical orientation as a guide towards self-actualization. … Music entertainment which reaches out from the classical-romantic repertoire should predominate." The third program was mainly defined according to "the expectations and behavior of listeners who use radio mainly for background music." This music was "catchy, modern entertainment, predominantly in the original language, with mainly vocal titles, both German and international."[8]

In 1979, the radio programs of SWF1 and SWF3 differed primarily in the ratio of talk to music, and also to a small extent in the music's tone or color. Between the hours of noon and 2 p.m., which had become the time slot with the greatest audience, SWF1 had seventy minutes of talk with only fifty minutes of music, while SWF3 had twenty minutes of talk and one hundred minutes of music. SWF1 played more instrumental music and had a wider international range, while SWF3 was clearly dominated by English-language pop music; this was especially true for programs defined by the audience and not by the editorial staff.[9]

The Pop Music Revolution in Germany

Between 1959 and 1979, a radical change had occurred which completely restructured the landscape of music entertainment, reaching almost all corners of the world. The center of this change can be precisely dated to the period 1964/65. This change is particularly easy to pinpoint in the German-speaking countries, since the language of the lyrics provides a simple criterion for measuring the basic shift. However, rather than offering just a vague general impression,[10] a meaningful—perhaps even the most meaningful—example will be presented.

A look at the "*Bravo-Jahres-Musicbox*" (the annual music charts compilation published in *Bravo*, West Germany's biggest youth magazine) provides a precise indication of this profound sea change.[11] In his summary of the 1960s, Thommi Herrwerth describes the early days: "Back then, Germans listened almost exclusively to hits sung in German," because "foreign hits generally received German adapted lyrics."[12] This was still the case in 1963, when the *Bravo* charts featured nineteen German titles and just one American song: Elvis Presley at No. 11 with "Devil in Disguise." Undisputed No. 1 was the German pop-singer Freddy, who also placed another song at No. 6 on the charts. The British singer Cliff Richards was also in the Top 20, but he obediently sang his hit in German translation ("*Rote Lippen soll man küssen*"). Only on the B-side of his single could his song appear in the original English version ("Let's Make a Memory").[13]

By 1964, the tide had dramatically turned. Cliff Richards reached No. 1 with two German titles, but then followed five English-language songs by the Beatles: "A Hard Day's Night," "I Want to Hold Your Hand," "She Loves You," "I Should Have Known Better," and "Twist and Shout." Furthermore, three other foreigners and even a German sang in English (Drafi Deutscher with "Shake Hands," the "first original German beat hit in the history of pop music").[14] With nine out of twenty entries, English-language songs now accounted for nearly half of the hits.

That was just the beginning. In succeeding years, German-language songs fell even more by the wayside. In 1965, the Beatles were once again on the *Bravo* charts with five hits, and the Rolling Stones charted with two (including the legendary "[I Can't Get No] Satisfaction"). On top of that were yet another five English titles, plus one Italian and one French, so that room remained for only six German titles (including "Du bist nicht allein" by Gerd Höllerich, who, however, was already building his career under an English pseudonym: Roy Black).[15] In the following year, 1966, the ratio was sixteen to four in favor of English-language titles. In 1967 it was almost exactly the same, except that Roy Black had managed to move into the top two places with two of the four German titles which charted that year. But the other two German-language songs were sung by Englishmen, prompting this rather plaintive comment in *Bravo*: "And Roy Black is the only German performer in this year's *Musicbox*. Yes, unfortunately: Germany was hung out to dry in 1967 too. Foreign stars continue to set the beat."[16]

By 1968—in tune with the general mood of social unrest—German pop had reached its low point. Only Roy Black still had a hit in German, although at a respectable No.2 with "*Bleib bei mir*." Everything else was in English. The Beatles still had three songs in the Top 20, and there were four by the Bee Gees. However, the top was reserved for soft pop: "Delilah" by Tom Jones, and "Congratulations" by Cliff Richards (who was no longer in need of German translation).[17]

Hard times had begun for German-language singers. There is evidence to indicate that the launch on 18 January 1969 of the program *Hitparade* (on the second national West German television channel, ZDF) was in part an attempt to ensure "that German and Austrian performers do not disappear from the picture completely."[18]

In the beginning, this trend toward English received little or no support from the German mass media. Even *Bravo* magazine was amongst its detractors. However, its readers thought differently, and the consequences were inevitable: "*Bravo* had no other choice: if it did not want to risk losing readership, it had to turn a new leaf. As a result, this youth magazine, which previously promoted good manners, decency and irreproachable behavior, suddenly underwent an emergency makeover to become the central forum for fans of beat music."[19]

Unlike *Bravo*, state-sponsored public radio stations were not directly dependent on audience ratings. They could attempt to cultivate their own programming ideas and ignore beat music whenever they wanted. They pursued this strategy at first, although they were undoubtedly well aware of the wishes of their audience. *Hessischer Rundfunk* (HR), for example, had "*Die Frankfurter Schlagerbörse—notiert nach Angebot und Nachfrage*" ("The Frankfurt Hit Exchange—Rated by Supply and Demand"). There, the requests for German pop music were continually decreasing. When the program director read the program report for December 9, 1965, the prognosis was clear: the Rolling Stones and Chris Andrews were firmly on top of the charts, followed by the Lords and the Yardbirds. A German title occupied fifth place, receiving only about half as many votes as the Yardbirds and an eighth as many as the Rolling Stones.[20] However, it was not until the autumn of 1967 that HR produced not only "*Teenager Melodie*" without shame, but also its own one-hour weekly pop music series for young people called "Teens-Twens-Top Time," subsuming English-language tags into the very titles of the programs.

(West) German public broadcasters did not really stand a chance at successfully quarantining beat music and English-language pop to specialty niches. The international trends had already become too strong, and in the highly competitive mass media market, their own position was too weak.

Radio in the Shadow of Television

Television dealt a final death blow to traditional radio programming when the battle for audience ratings was unconditionally decided in its favor. Whoever owned a television watched television, whenever there was something to watch—and in the 1950s and 1960s, that was primarily in the evenings. Radio was completely written off. This was true in the United States as well as in the United Kingdom and West Germany. Radio broadcasting was in a deep crisis in the 1950s, as people turned the radio off and the television on.[21]

However, this generalized statement should be qualified in at least one respect: television may have proved itself to be the new family medium, but the family no longer assembled around the receiver with quite the same single-minded focus that they still exercised during the war years. Television did not fascinate youth nearly as much as it did adults. This helped define a new target audience for radio.[22]

From the beginning, considerable differences existed in patterns of television consumption. However, it was many more years (even decades) before broad empirical data were gathered in which certain necessary distinctions were included. For example, in the extensive mass media survey first commissioned by the ARD in 1964, more weight was placed on variables such as "educational level" and "political leanings" than on "age." Even in 1974, the youth audience was subsumed into the larger category of "under 30s." Nevertheless, the differences between older and younger groups were already noticeable. (Incidentally, the figures table 5.1 also indicate that the radio programming reforms of the 1970s were already beginning to bear fruit).

Table 5.1 Media consumption in minutes, in West Germany on an average weekday[23]

	Television		Radio	
	1974	1980	1974	1980
Under 30 years old	102	86	125	145
50 years and older	145	158	90	110

At first, the strategy of radio management amounted to simply building on radio's advantages over television, by offering "what television cannot: topical immediacy, news reports and music." In practice, that meant doing away with the "something for everyone" concept of variety programming. Instead, two very distinct programming streams were to be established. At the end of 1960s, it could be summarized that "usually, the first program (which was broadcast on both AM and FM) should contain light music and information, while the second program should primarily consist of cultural broadcasts and special programs for the more refined and demanding minority."[24]

Another emerging factor to consider was that the era of the "one-radio household" was coming to an end. Between 1968 and 1978, the proportion of West German households which possessed a radio (if at all) had changed only minimally; what *had* changed was the number of radios in each household. In 1968, 72 percent had one radio, and only 24 percent had two radios; in 1978, this had changed to 36 and 61 percent respectively. The reasons for this change were clear: "The driving force behind the increase in multiple-radio households was … the younger family members, the children and youths, who demanded their own listening opportunities."[25]

Radio programming underwent fundamental changes in the 1960s and 1970s—not only in Germany, but also in large parts of Europe. Two processes of restructuring overlapped each other: on the one hand, the broader trend toward programming based on popular entertainment (observable since the 1930s) reached a temporary high point,[26] with traditional variety programming becoming progressively more distinctive and organized around the two main poles of "high culture" and "popular entertainment"; on the other hand, the tone of popular entertainment in general underwent a profound shift, becoming more geared toward young people.

The reorientation of radio programming (at least in part) towards youth seemed a logical response, but, in practice, was fraught with complications. The most obvious was that youth preferences in music had gradually grown apart from traditional standards of taste since the end of the Second World War. Rock and beat music were phenomena that provoked almost virulent resistance from many older people.

New Sounds on Vinyl

The assumption that the success of new forms of music entertainment on state-organized public radio was primarily the result of strategically targeted manipulations on the part of multinational media corporations cannot be supported empirically. On the contrary, it can be shown that there were serious reservations at the center of the capitalist entertainment industry (that is, within the large American record companies). In the end, they were only won over by the sales figures of smaller independent labels which recognized and supported new trends from the start.[27]

In this regard, the changing context of record playing (and of television) also played a role. Simon Frith described the fading era thus: "From the 1920s until the beginning of the 1950s, the products of the music industry were aimed at a family audience, and records were heard through the family-owned radio and the family-owned gramophone; in most households, there was only one of each."[28] However, increasing prosperity led to better-equipped households: television sets appeared beside radios, and more record players were purchased on top of that. There was also a shift of emphasis in usage patterns: as television became the family medium, radios and record players were "freed up" for youth.

In 1966, an Infratest survey found that, on average, every second household in West Germany had a record player. However, the distribution was very uneven. Among households containing youth (aged 14 to 19), 88 percent had a record player, whereas among households consisting of elderly couples (over the age of 60), only 35 percent had one.[29] Youth were gradually becoming the main consumers of vinyl records, in the United States and elsewhere. In West Germany in 1969, customers under the age of 25 accounted for 88 percent of record purchases.[30]

Internationally, music consumers priorities were, at least in one respect, crystal clear: so-called "serious" music was continually losing ground to "popular" music. Worldwide figures would show that the market share of classical music slipped from 10 percent to 6 percent between 1960 and 1980; even in the relatively favorable German market, classical music shrank from a 20 percent to a 13 percent market share, just in the period 1964 to 1968. By 1980, it had to content itself with just under an 8 percent market share.[31]

There is little research into how vinyl records altered the broad landscape of popular music.[32] Nonetheless, one can say that radio was not the instigator of the latest trends, which were then later taken up by record companies; instead, it was the other way around. Furthermore, this did not happen without conflict. Radio station managers continued resisting new forms of popular music: even in the United States, harsh battles were fought over the broadcast-worthiness of (in particular) rock'n'roll.[33] However, radio stations could not function completely independently of the record labels or (especially) of audience tastes.

Even in Germany, where radio stations and record companies were not commercially interdependent,[34] record labels were not completely at the mercy of radio programmers. Much was sold without ever receiving airplay; music could be popularized through restaurant jukeboxes, for example, or through magazine articles and even just word of mouth. The importance of the jukebox in particular should not be underestimated. In West Germany in 1972, there were approximately 80,000 of these machines. They were filled with singles which were restocked at regular intervals: some simply became outdated, while others became worn out through excessive demand. Around 10 million singles were put into jukeboxes every year, accounting for at least a quarter of all singles sold in West Germany.[35]

"Pirate Stations" Set New Standards

Beat and rock music increasingly proved themselves to be number one sellers. The demand for LPs and singles was enormous, and profits were considerable. In the attempt to earn even more, American companies tried to break down the defensive wall of European state broadcasting. Their weapons were the so-called "pirate stations," which began broadcasting off the British coast in 1964. Acknowledging the role of US corporations here is not to question the enthusiasm and idealism of the local young organizers, whose efforts quickly became the focus of heated debate. However, the economic background cannot be ignored in an otherwise detailed examination of their campaign; in the case of Ronan O'Rahilly, it can be mentioned briefly that he "had had little difficulty in finding the necessary £250,000 for the project," as if it was no big deal for a relative "nobody" in his late twenties to raise an (at the time) considerable sum of money in order to buy a ship and fit it out with radio broadcast equipment.[36]

Although there had already been pirate stations for several years (off the Danish, Swedish, and Dutch coasts), the launch of Radio Caroline on 29 March 1964 nonetheless represented a caesura. Other pirates emerged soon after: Radio Atlanta, Radio Sutch, Radio Invicta, Radio London.[37] These small stations had in common not only their boat-based strategy (anchored outside British jurisdictional waters), but also a completely new style of radio programming: the hosts simply played one song after another, using the longer breaks only for advertising. This was an adaptation of the Top 40 format that was developed in the United States in the 1950s, which was far removed from the stodgy style of the BBC. Current pop and rock music filled the waves—in both senses of the word![38]

The pirate radio stations achieved great commercial success. According to listener surveys, the best-known stations (Radio Caroline and Radio London) reached over a million listeners in the spring of 1966. At the same time, the advertising earnings of Radio London alone were estimated at approximately £600,000 per year.[39]

The structure of the British record market also underwent considerable changes. After ruling the domestic market until 1964 with a combined share of roughly 75 percent, the British corporations EMI and

Decca lost about half their market share in the succeeding years, while the big American labels CBS, Warner and RCA more than tripled their market share, going from 8 to 28 percent market share.[40]

The pirate stations posed the biggest threat not, however, to the BBC, but to Radio Luxembourg, which suddenly seemed like yesterday's news. Europe's oldest commercial radio station had already lost a large slice of the English market through the introduction of commercial television in the United Kingdom in 1954, forcing it to convert its family programs into youth programs;[41] now it was also under threat from competition in its original home territory. In response, Radio Luxembourg quickly adopted the style of the pirates. Then, just in time, relief came courtesy of the British Government: a new law was adopted in the summer of 1966 forcing all pirate radio stations to close by August 1967.

To a certain extent, the BBC itself took over the pirate inheritance.[42] In the autumn of 1967, a new structure was introduced at the BBC: in addition to the original three radio programs, there was a new "fourth" channel, which was given the flagship name "Radio 1"; its now legendary programming included "Top of the Pops."

Radio programming was in flux, and the pace of change accelerated under pressure from the competition. In the heart of Europe, it was "Ö3" (founded also in 1967 by *Österreichischer Rundfunk*, the Austrian public broadcaster)[43] which rattled the managers of neighboring stations—especially those at Bayerischer Rundfunk, the public broadcaster in Bavaria. In Western Europe, it was Radio Luxembourg which challenged the competition.

Even East Germany's state radio found itself increasingly under pressure from the special programming style of Radio Luxembourg. This style was consciously adopted at first by the East German covert propaganda stations *Deutscher Freiheitssender 904* and *Deutscher Soldatensender 935* (German Freedom Station and German Soldier Station, respectively),[44] in order to secure a broader reach among Western listeners. That the East German state could not adopt this style in its own territory without problematic consequences became clear by 1964, when it decided to devote more time toward programming aimed at its own youth. After a successful 99-hour special program marking the *Deutschland-Treffen* (All-Germany Convention) of the FDJ, the youth organization of the SED (governing party of East Germany), "DT 64" was established as a permanent afternoon show of *Berliner Rundfunk*, the East Berlin broadcaster.[45]

All in all, reactions toward "DT 64" were rather ambivalent. Surveys of listening patterns were also conducted in East Germany (starting in the second half of the 1960s), providing a great deal of empirical data.[46] A major summary was also published in 1971.[47] On the positive side, "DT

64" reached by far the largest audience: among youth aged 15–18 and
19–24, market shares of 50 and 45 percent were achieved, respectively. In
contrast, Western stations only attained 30 and 27 percent shares of these
two groups. However, among those who did not tune into Berliner
Rundfunk, the station of choice was Radio Luxembourg, and the reason
was clear: a 1973 survey showed that 74 percent of youth respondents
agreed with the statement "Western stations are chosen because they play
the latest hits and beat music"; other more identifiably political statements met with only a maximum 50 percent agreement. In addition,
specifically Western beat music was in demand; among East German
youths, domestically produced beat music received about as much enthusiasm as the social-realist inspired *Singebewegung* (Singing Movement).

In the analysis of their own local programming (which at the time
reflected completely opposite priorities), the East German researchers
passed clear judgment: "This real and present desire to listen to beat
music is only insufficiently satisfied by our own radio programming.
Therefore, a section of our youth is forced to seek other sources." In
addition, the researchers rejected the notion that this "real and present
desire" was only the result of targeted (external) manipulation. Instead,
they maintained the position that "beat music, in the form currently
produced abroad, meets the desires of our youth: desires which exist relatively independent of corresponding artistic products, and which result
from youth lifestyles and their concrete environmental conditions, from
which arise the desires as well as the very means by which they may be
satisfied. Therefore, one cannot exclude the possibility that beat music
represents an appropriate means for satisfying specific youth desires
which have arisen from existing developmental conditions."

The question of beat music on East German radio remained a difficult topic, because the responsible ideologues never managed to formulate a consistent and strictly enforceable policy.[48]

Radio Luxembourg's programming style also presented a major challenge to its more immediate neighbors, the West German public broadcasters *Saarländischer Rundfunk*, *Südwestfunk*, and *Westdeutscher
Rundfunk* (Saarland, southwestern and western broadcasters, respectively). When *Westdeutscher Rundfunk* (WDR) commissioned a study of
listening patterns on an average weekday in North Rhine-Westphalia in
1970, they were able to successfully report that their two channels still
accounted for more than half of actual listening hours, whereas Radio
Luxembourg had to make do with a third. But the outlook was totally
different when differentiated by age group: among 14–29-year-olds,
Radio Luxembourg had as many listeners as both WDR programs combined.[49] These warning signals could not be ignored. What would the
situation be in a couple of years? Programming reform was inevitable. In

the early 1970s, West German broadcasters began to follow the BBC's example of 1967.

From "Pop-Shop" to SWF3

West German developments are especially well illustrated by the programming changes at Baden-Baden's Südwestfunk, which was at the time still independent. The station had been in a state of upheaval since 1965. The results of extensive audience surveys had caused the management a great deal of disquiet, and the appointment of politically conservative journalist Helmut Hammerschmidt as station director marked the beginning of profound programming reforms.[50] These were also underscored by a generational turnover, particularly in the area of popular entertainment. For example, 1970 saw the retirement of both Oskar Haaf (head of popular entertainment radio) and Willi Stech (director of the SWF *Kleines Unterhaltungs-Orchester*), both of whom were members of the generation born in 1905. Stech's ensemble was immediately dissolved: the "drab, introspective in-house productions in traditional-sounding formats" were simply no longer competitive.[51]

At the time, SWF's third program was still being used as a kind of dumping ground for anything that did not fit in the other two programs; on this third channel, younger people were now preparing something new. The man in charge was Walther Krause, who had been with SWF since 1965: he was of the generation born in 1937. His close associates Frank Lauffenberg and Karl Heinz Kögel were born in 1945 and 1946, respectively.

By 1969, preparations were in full swing for a new programming stream on the third channel. In November of that year, Krause (who would later become managing director) made a trip to London, where he studied the leading example set by the BBC. In his report, Krause criticized Radio 1 for "not catering to the particular wishes of England's youth; instead, it adapts itself much more to the conventional tastes of a wider audience. … In this respect, BBC 1 cannot serve as an example for us." However, he then added: "Nonetheless, the opportunities that BBC offers to its disc jockeys are exemplary. There are three DJ studios at BBC 1's broadcasting complex, each of which contain the following equipment: three turntables for the use of the host, three so-called Jingle Cases [these are players for prerecorded announcements on easy-to-manage cassettes], three telephones, an echo machine, and other purely technical devices. Only under these conditions can a really engaging youth program be produced."[52]

SWF's new program was launched on 1 January 1970. "*Pop-Shop und Teenage Magazin*" was the title of the daily three-hour program, which followed a standardized script from the start. The first hour was called "*Stars und Hits,*" and was devoted to introducing new German records, including not only German-language songs (whether from a German or a foreign singer), but also anything that was in some way produced in Germany. The third hour belonged to "Top!—Pop!—Beat!," which featured new foreign productions. In contrast, the second hour changed its focus everyday, from "golden oldies" to listener requests, as well as in-house productions (such as those from the station's dance orchestra). After just three months, the program was expanded to a fourth hour (mostly for instrumental music), while the third hour was renamed "Hit-In." In addition, the standardized scheme was interrupted every Thursday for "Pop-Shop-International," running from 12:03 until 3:45 p.m.[53]

However, the original quota reserved by SWF3 for *Schlager* (German-language pop hits) was quickly limited and defined in a very specific way. In *Bunte* magazine, Karl-Heinz Kögel was quoted thus: "We don't play Freddy Breck, Roy Black, Heino, or other similar singers," and the disc jockeys were instructed to follow a new slogan: "Down with Roy Black, up with Hannes Wader!"[54] More importantly, German titles were being given less and less airtime, regardless of whether they were from left-wing protest singers or *Heile-Welt-Sänger* (singers who presented the world through rose-colored glasses).

Audience reaction to the new programming stream was not statistically overwhelming, but that was primarily an effect of the unfavorable early afternoon time slot.[55] In 1974, the program's average hourly market share was measured at 0.4 percent, which was the second worst result in a survey of eleven public broadcast programs, and only a sixth of the market share achieved by Radio Luxembourg. However, the results were substantially better in the target markets of youth aged 14–19 and 20–29; SWF's scores of 1.2 and 0.9 percent (respectively) was only bettered by *Bayerischer Rundfunk* and its modern new service "*Bayern 3,*" and the difference with the scores of Radio Luxembourg (3.9 and 3.7 percent, respectively) was reduced by roughly one-quarter.[56]

More importantly, the programming provoked much discussion within SWF itself. This can be traced only to a certain extent back to the transmission context. Almost nothing is left of the actual "Pop-Shop" broadcasts of the early 1970s: neither recordings, scripts nor playlists. This is hardly surprising, considering the "live" nature of the show. On the contrary, what *is* surprising is that some material *did* survive, and in a somewhat unexpected context. To be precise, the director of *Südwestfunk* commissioned the Allensbach Institute (for public opinion research) to analyze "Pop-Shop" broadcasts. To this end, six shows in January and May of 1972 were recorded and transcribed, to be finally assessed for content. In this undertaking, however, music played absolutely no part at all: singers and titles were only marginally mentioned.

The overall context of this undertaking requires a short explanation, as it shows (not least of all) how difficult it is to separate entertainment from politics—particularly during the pivotal juncture between the 1960s and the 1970s. The latter decade was marked by the debate around political balance in broadcast programming. SWF's director took a controversial position in his *Richtlinien-Entwurf für die politische Programmarbeit* (proposed guidelines for political programming work), which caused a furor as the so-called *Hammerschmidt-Papier*. This paper was originally published on 23 November 1970 simply as a starting point for discussions at the ARD directors' conference; nonetheless it caused a storm. In the end, Hammerschmidt's position failed to convince the majority of the ARD, which finally passed the *Grundsätze für die Zusammenarbeit im ARD-Gemeinschaftsprogramm "Deutsches Fernsehen"* (basis for cooperation in the ARD communal program "German Television") on 9 July 1971. This vague and terse document was light years from the articulate (but nonetheless relatively rigid) reasoning of Hammerschmidt.[57]

Hammerschmidt's intellectual point of departure was the observation "that in the same way that informational departments use entertainment formats for their own ends, entertainment departments also use informational segments in their broadcasts," as well as the related postulate, that "to an increasing degree, political effects can be aspired to and exercised by other departments, and that these effects can be longer-lasting than those produced by informational items in classical formats."[58]

Of interest to the discussion at hand is the question of how Hammerschmidt's proposition was applied to the youth program "Pop-Shop." The Allensbach Institute was not required to deliver an "impact analysis," but rather an "analysis of the program, the way it was transmitted, and the way it left the broadcaster."[59] The goal of the text analysis (which expressly ignored the musical two-thirds of the program) was to research how far "the program conveyed *biased* criticism, *biased* choices of topics, and *biased* recommendations."[60] The approach was in-depth, since "explicit criticism, or criticism by choosing negative words and negative images is rare. Strategies for criticism are far more subtle, or to put it in a more fashionable term: 'subliminal.'"[61] Sentence after sentence was scrutinized for possible critical contents, and the results were graded on a seven-point spectrum, from "far left" to "far right." However, even the Allensbach Institute was not itself immune from expressing "subliminal" criticism. The first pages, prior to any introduction of the study's underlying methodology, state early on that "a great deal of the texts engage in criticism, which is certainly unsurprising in a program geared towards youth."[62] Considering the mood of the times, then, the verdict pronounced under "results" is also unsurprising: "The spectrum of critical argumentation (reaching from 'far left' to 'far right') shows that when critical arguments are presented on 'Pop-Shop,' they primarily stem from the perspective of the left." The only more surprising statement is the one inserted at the end: "The number of explicit left-wing statements has decreased, from 29 percent in January to 15 percent in May." Equally noteworthy is the fact that at first 71 percent and then 85 percent of all statements were graded as neutral: so what happened to the "great deal of texts" which engaged in criticism?[63]

One could certainly examine the Allensbach analysis in greater detail, challenging (for example) the gradation system and the articulation of the results. In the present context, it is sufficient to say that "Pop-Shop" was classified (according to political criteria) as being "left-wing." Despite its political orientation, the new style at SWF definitely found great favor among neighboring broadcasters. However, they did not exclusively rely on a youth audience. *Bayern 3*—*"die Servicewelle aus München"* ("the Service Wave from Munich")—had been targeting the increasing number of motorists with easy listening music since 1 April 1971, as did hr3 (the third program of *Hessischer Rundfunk*, the public broadcaster in Hesse) after 23 April 1972.[64]

These experiences were incorporated in turn by the reformers of SWF's third program. When SWF3 started the new season in January 1975, it too was not specifically a youth channel; instead, it was conceived as a general public service for varying audiences—basically for anyone who wanted popular music as a background to other activities.[65] On the one hand, "Pop-Shop" was quantitatively reduced, broadcasting only two hours on weekdays; on the other hand, its time slot was more favorable, shifting from midday to early evening, 7 to 9 p.m. The show even claimed the weekend evenings, with "Pop-Shop-Party" on Saturdays (7 p.m. to midnight), and a four-hour edition of "Pop-Shop" on Sundays (7 to 11 p.m.) The remaining hours were largely filled with radio magazines: for example, "*Funk-Boutique*" (Monday to Saturday, 10 a.m. to noon) and "*Radio-Kiosk*" (Monday to Saturday, 2 to 4 p.m.)

As previously mentioned, SWF3 was not a station exclusively for young people; instead, it was a youthful station which set itself apart from the two other SWF stations mainly by its choice of music. And its audience success was remarkable, with average ratings tripling between 1974 and 1980. The ratings gulf between SWF3 and Radio Luxembourg also shrank dramatically. However, the age-group breakdown was also changing, with a gradual loss of the youth audience. In 1974, the age groups of 14–19 and 20–29 had each registered equally at 28 percent of the SWF3 audience; by 1980, this ratio had clearly polarized, with figures of 21 and 33 percent, respectively. Incidentally, Radio Luxembourg had itself lost a great deal of its sparkle by 1974, when only 17 percent of its audience were youth aged 14–19; in 1980, this figure was down to 16 percent. For the age group 20–29, Radio Luxembourg's corresponding figures were 21 and 20 percent, respectively.[66]

Youth was increasingly turning to new sources: in particular, television. This did not go unnoticed by the Luxembourg broadcaster. When private commercial television was introduced in West Germany in 1985, RTL (Radio Television Luxembourg) jumped in right away. Its early participation was later justified by its subsequent success, especially with children and youth. Among households with cable television in the first half of the 1990s, RTL was only at third place (along with private broadcaster Sat.1), being easily beaten by the two biggest public stations in Germany. However, this score can be directly attributed to the relatively large proportion of older viewers, particularly those over age 50. The younger the viewers, the more they favored RTL (and to a lesser degree, Sat.1); among viewers under age 30, RTL occupied the top position.[67]

It was only in the mid-1990s that radio managed to regain some ground in the German youth market. The northern and western public broadcasters produced two new market leaders: NDR's "N-Joy Radio" (launched on 4 April 1995), and "*WDR Eins Live*" (launched on 1 April 1995), which were both tailored specifically for listeners aged 14–19.[68] As before, such programs were characterized by specially targeted playlists; however, the rock and beat music of the 1960s and 1970s were now a thing of the past.

Conclusion

Eric Hobsbawm was not the first to recognize the particular importance of music (especially beat music) in the emergent youth culture of the 1960s and 1970s. Early on, beat music was already being interpreted as "a novel, certainly unfamiliar, and therefore often unnoticed expression of a particular type of opposition," an opposition which "in contrast to the protests of politically engaged and activated youths" expressed itself precisely where youth "expressed their conformity by confirming the consumer impulse, seemingly without reservation." Their method was therefore not "criticism of society, … but rather, dissociation from it."[69]

This style of politicization was completely congruent with an increasingly consumerist orientation. However, it does not mean one can speak of youth being "taken in by the culture industry." On the contrary, researchers into the development of youth culture in Austria concluded that "the empirical evidence does not suggest youth were manipulated victims and puppets of the culture industry; instead, youth were gradually learning to functionalize media, to integrate it instrumentally into everyday life, and to use it for their own cultural emancipation."[70]

This idea can be supported by an analysis of the supply structures of the radio market. In the context of Western Europe, this reveals realities and developments which cannot be reconciled with the suggestion of an almighty, homogenous "culture industry." At the very least, one must (on the one hand) differentiate between the state-organized and the purely commercial branches of media production, and (on the other hand) also concede that audience tastes exercised a considerable measure of influence.

One fact cannot be overlooked: modern forms of pop music (from classic rock'n'roll through beat music to contemporary rock), were established as phenomena of the masses, largely against the will of the communications arbiters. The recording and radio industries were themselves in a structural crisis, due to the growth of television.

Classic rock'n'roll was not initially launched by the culture industry, and neither were the new genres of beat music and modern rock. It was not just state-organized public radio, but also commercial record labels that had difficulties with this new music, trying to prevent its popularization. In the long run, however, profit making always won out, causing the scene to shift fundamentally in the course of the 1960s. As it became clear how much money could be made in the new genres of popular music, a major reorientation occurred, from the effects of which (due to various intermediate connecting links) not even the state-organized broadcasters could escape. However, it was only after 1970 that West German stations began accepting new styles of popular music to an appreciable extent. Furthermore, it was another ten years before the decision was widely reached to establish programs with a consistent focus. For example, hr3 (which began broadcasting as early as 1972) did not change its "quite oppositional blocks of music into an overall unified sound" until the late date of May 1981.[71]

A type of music that had largely defined itself as a protest against traditional thinking and business practices gradually became the very thing it protested. Was this, however, inevitable? Gert Haedecke, one of the fathers of SWF3, gave a particularly succinct summary of this complex situation: "Music which promoted protest and rebellion became good business, and business further disseminated this music and with it the spirit of rebellion, which found further expression in music, which in turn became business, and so on."[72]

The degree to which politicization flourished in its narrower sense, and to which the symbolic date of 1968 signified more than just a relatively superficial phenomenon, is still a matter for debate. The thesis that "the 1960s were (to a certain extent) an exceptional time, and that youth (as well as rock music) normalized themselves in the 1970s,"[73] and that the emancipatory promise of the 1960s was lost in the 1970s and 1980s, has one central weakness: the lack of the necessary comparative empirical studies. This lack suggests further possible avenues for exploration which could be particularly fruitful for future research.

Notes

1. Eric Hobsbawm, *Das Zeitalter der Extreme. Weltgeschichte des 20. Jahrhunderts* (Munich, 1998), 406, 411.
2. The following chapter is based on my contribution to the conference, whose participants provided numerous stimuli which found their way into the revised version. My special gratitude goes to Arthur Marwick.
3. Additionally compare: Lu Seegers, *Hör Zu! Eduard Rhein und die Rundfunkprogrammzeitschriften (1931–1965)* (Potsdam, 2001).
4. Südwestfunk, *Geschäftsbericht 1959/60*, unpaginated leaflet *"Gliederung des Hörrundfunkprogramms."*
5. Infratest, *Der Rundfunkhörer, seine Lebensgewohnheiten, sein Hör- und Sehverhalten. Teilauswertung SWF*, 17–20. In August 1960, 74 percent of the radios in SWF's transmission area were fitted with an FM receiver, in West Germany an average of 81 percent (ibid., 1).
6. Wolfgang Behr himself refrained from making such an attempt. See Wolfgang Behr, *Das Kleine Orchester des Südwestfunks unter der Leitung von Willi Stech. Untersuchungen zur Aufgabe und Bedeutung eines Rundfunkunterhaltungsorchesters. Mit Beiträgen zu den Anfängen der unterhaltenden Musik am Südwestfunk* (Baden-Baden, 1994).
7. Ibid., 347.
8. General description of the SWF programs in Konrad Dussel and Edgar Lersch, eds., *Quellen zur Programmgeschichte des deutschen Hörfunks und Fernsehens* (Göttingen and Zürich, 1999), 302, 304.
9. Due to SWF's own lack of statistics on this subject, one must analyze the detailed transmission reports which are stored in SWF's historical archive (HA-SWR) in Baden-Baden. I would like to thank the archivist Jana Berendt for providing this and other material. A random sample survey of titles from *"Extra Drei"* and its successor "Musicbox," in both of which a specific segment of the audience chose the songs, reveals that in both cases the percentage of German-language songs remained persistently under 10 percent. In fact, "Musicbox" really only had English-language songs, with songs in other languages being rare exceptions; on *"Extra Drei,"* however, these came closer to the 20 percent mark.
10. For example: Hanna Brunhöber, *Unterhaltungsmusik*. Compare Wolfgang Benz, ed., *Die Geschichte der Bundesrepublik Deutschland. Volume 4: Kultur,* (Frankfurt am Main, 1989), 168–99.
11. The following is supported by the reproductions and detailed comments in Thommi Herrwerth, *Itsy Bitsy Teenie Weenie – Die deutschen Hits der Sixties* (Marburg, 1995). An examination of *Musikmarkt Hitparaden* of the 1960s provides very similar results.

12. Herrwerth, *Deutsche Hits*, 15. Incidentally, the same observation holds true for the Austrian scene: Kurt Luger, "Jugendkultur und Kulturindustrien im Österreich der 50er Jahre," in *Modernisierung im Wiederaufbau. Die westdeutsche Gesellschaft der 50er Jahre*, ed. Axel Schildt and Arnold Sywottek (Bonn, 1993), 493–512; Wolfgang Wittmann, *Österreichisches Hitlexikon* (Graz,1984).

13. Herrwerth, *Deutsche Hits*, 55.

14. Ibid., 72f.

15. Ibid., 86ff.

16. Ibid., 108.

17. Ibid., 116f.

18. Ibid., 111.

19. Ibid., 87. Also compare Thommi Herrwerth, *Partys, Pop und Petting—Die Sixties im Spiegel der Bravo* (Marburg, 1997).

20. *Hessischer Rundfunk* (HR) historical archive 5123. Notes about HR were provided courtesy of Stefan Kursawe, who recently published his dissertation *Vom Leitmedium zum Begleitmedium. Die Radioprogramme des Hessischen Rundfunks 1960–1980* (Cologne, 2004).

21. Marie-Luise Kiefer, "Hörfunk- und Fernsehnutzung," in *Mediengeschichte der Bundesrepublik Deutschland*, ed. Jürgen Wilke (Bonn, 1999), 426–46, here: 431–34.

22. Jürgen Zinnecker, *Jugendkultur 1940–1985* (Opladen, 1987), 189.

23. Klaus Berg and Marie Luise Kiefer, eds., *Massenkommunikation II. Eine Langzeitstudie zur Mediennutzung und Medienbewertung 1964–1980* (Frankfurt am Main, 1982), 33.

24. Henning Wicht, "Der Hörfunk im Zeitalter des Fernsehens. Die Programme der ARD-Anstalten," in *ARD-Jahrbuch 1969*, 63–70, quoted in Dussel and Lersch, *Quellen zur Programmgeschichte*, 287, 289. Compare Konrad Dussel, "Vom Radiozum Fernsehzeitalter. Mediumumbrüche in sozialgeschichtlicher Perspektive," in *Dynamische Zeiten. Die 60er Jahre in den beiden deutschen Gesellschaften*, ed. Axel Schildt, Detlef Siegfried, and Karl Christian Lammers (Hamburg, 2000), 686ff.

25. Walter Klingler, "Hörfunk und Hörfunknutzung seit 1945," in *Medienrezeption seit 1945. Forschungsbilanz und Forschungsperspektiven*, ed. Walter Klingler, Gunnar Roters, and Maria Gerhards, (2nd ed., Baden-Baden, 1999), 121.

26. Konrad Dussel, *Hörfunk in Deutschland. Politik, Programm, Publikum (1923–1960)* (Potsdam, 2002).

27. In detail: Steve Chapple and Reebee Garofalo, *Wem gehört die Rock-Musik? Geschichte und Politik der Musikindustrie* (Reinbek, 1980), especially 44, 57f., and 66; Simon Frith, *Jugendkultur und Rockmusik. Soziologie der englischen Musikszene* (Reinbek, 1981), 122f.

28. Frith, *Jugendkultur und Rockmusik*, 40.

29. Infratest archive, Munich.

30. Werner Mezger, *Schlager. Versuch einer Gesamtdarstellung unter besonderer Berücksichtigung des Musikmarktes der Bundesrepublik Deutschland* (Tübingen, 1975), 168.

31. Brunhöber, *Unterhaltungsmusik*, 169; Hans Hirsch, *Schallplatten zwischen Kunst und Kommerz. Fakten, Tendenzen und Überlegungen zur Produktion und Verbreitung von Tonträgern* (Wilhelmshaven, 1987), 210f.

32. Werner Zeppenfeld, *Tonträger in der Bundesrepublik Deutschland: Anatomie eines medialen Massenmarktes* (Bochum, 1978); Walter Haas, *Das Jahrhundert der Schallplatte. Eine Geschichte der Phonographie* (Bielefeld, 1977).

33. Philip K. Eberly, *Music in the Air: America's Changing Tastes in Popular Music, 1920–80* (New York, 1982), 212ff.

34. This is not to deny that, especially in the field of popular music, the beginnings of a "problematic symbiosis overlapping private interests with those of public broadcasters" could be observed (Mezger, *Schlager*, 49); with a stronger emphasis on the structural background: Zeppenfeld, *Tonträger*, 150ff.

35. Günter Kleinen, "Die Musikbox," in *Schlager in Deutschland. Beiträge zur Analyse der Popularmusik und des Musikmarktes*, ed. Siegmund Helms (Wiesbaden, 1972), 308f.; Mezger, *Schlager*, 65f.

36. Paul Harris, *Broadcasting from the High Seas: the History of Offshore Radio in Europe 1958–1976* (Edinburgh, 1977), 17.

37. In addition to Harris, *Broadcasting from the High Seas*, also compare, Stephen Barnard, *On the Radio. Music Radio in Britain* (Milton Keynes, Philadelphia, 1989), 41ff.

38. Jeremy Turnstall, *The Media in Britain* (London, 1983), 45ff.; on the Top 40 format: Eberly, *Music in the Air*, 199ff.

39. Harris, *Broadcasting from the High Seas*, 80, 86.

40. Turnstall, *Media in Britain*, 50.

41. Richard Nichols, *Radio Luxembourg. The Station of the Stars. An Affectionate History of 50 Years of Broadcasting* (London, 1983), 102; Barnard, *On the Radio*, 33ff.

42. Barnard, *On the Radio*, 50ff.

43. Viktor Ergert, Hellmut Andics, and Robert Kriechbaumer, *50 Jahre Rundfunk in Österreich. Vol. 4: 1967–1974* (Salzburg, 1985).

44. Jürgen Wilke and Stephan Sartoris, "Radiopropaganda durch Geheimsender der DDR im Kalten Krieg," in *Pressepolitik und Propaganda. Historische Studien vom Vormärz bis zum Kalten Krieg*, ed. Jürgen Wilke (Cologne, 1997), 292–331; Jürgen Wilke, "Radio im Geheimauftrag. Der Deutsche Freiheitssender 904 und der Deutsche Soldatensender 935 als Instrumente des Kalten Krieges," in *Zwischen Pop und Propaganda. Radio in der DDR*, ed. Klaus Arnold and Christoph Classen (Berlin, 2004), 249–266.

45. Andreas Ulrich and Jörg Wagner, eds., *DT 64. Das Buch zum Jugendradio 1964–1993* (Leipzig, 1993), especially 16ff.; Heiner Stahl, "Agit-Pop. Das Jugendstudio DT 64 in den swingenden sechziger Jahren," in Arnold and Classen, *Zwischen Pop und Propaganda*, 229–247.

46. Liselotte Mühlberg, "Hörerforschung des DDR-Rundfunks," in *Mit uns zieht die neue Zeit... 40 Jahre DDR-Medien*, ed. Heide Riedel (Berlin, 1994), 173–81; Konrad Dussel, "Der DDR-Rundfunk und seine Hörer. Ansätze zur Rezeptionsforschung in Ostdeutschland (1945–1965)," *Rundfunk und Geschichte* 24 (1998): 122–36.

47. "Zur Rezeption von Jugendprogrammen des Rundfunks," Deutsches Rundfunk-Archiv Potsdam, Schriftgut Rundfunk, Staatliches Komitee für Rundfunk, Abt. Soziologische Forschung, Signatur 1.2.7.1. I would like to thank Christian Könne for relevant studies drawn from his dissertation project on the development of East German radio in the 1960s.

48. Michael Rauhut, "'Wir müssen etwas Besseres bieten.' Rockmusik und Politik in der DDR," *Deutschland Archiv* 30 (1997): 572, 587. Also compare Michael Rauhut, *Beat in der Grauzone. DDR-Rock 1964 bis 1972—Politik und Alltag* (Berlin, 1993).

49. "*Hörfunknutzung und Spartenpräferenzen in Nordrhein-Westfalen. Durchschnittswerktag 1970*," 24 and 26 (a copy of this study, conducted by Infratest for WDR, is stored at the Infratest archive in Munich).

50. The research situation is completely asymmetrical: whereas the political contexts have been analyzed extensively (Ralf Fritze, *Der Südwestfunk in der Ära Adenauer. Die Entwicklung der Rundfunkanstalt von 1949 bis 1965 unter politischem Aspekt* [Baden-Baden, 1992]; Konrad Dussel, *Die Interessen der Allgemeinheit vertreten. Die Tätigkeit der Rundfunk- und Verwaltungsräte von Südwestfunk und Süddeutschem Rundfunk 1949–1969* [Baden-Baden, 1995]; Stefan Rechlin, *Rundfunk und Machtwechsel. Der*

Südwestfunk in den Jahren 1965-1977. Eine Institutionsgeschichte in rundfunkpoli-tischen Fallbeispielen [Baden-Baden, 1999]), the historical programming dimension of this radical change has only been superficially analyzed (Roland Hügel, "Hörfunkprogramm unter Fernsehkonkurrenz. Auswirkungen des Fernsehens auf Umfang, Struktur, Sendeformen und Programmplanung des Hörfunks in den Jahren 1958–1973 am Beispiel des Südwestfunks und des Süddeutschen Rundfunks" [unpublished MA thesis, Mainz, 1985]).

51. Behr, *Kleines Orchester des Südwestfunks,* quote 209.

52. HA-SWR/SWF P 13238.

53. Undated compilation *"Das ist Pop-Shop!"* with SWF radio directory's receipt stamp dated 12.8.70, ibid.

54. Wilfried Richartz, "Bei den Hitparaden darf noch lange nicht jeder!," *Bunte,* 30 August 1973 edition, 22.

55. Gert Haedecke, "SWF 3—Lebensweg eines Radioprogramms," in *Hörfunk-Jahrbuch 98/99,* ed. Stephan Ory and Helmut G. Bauer (Berlin, 1999), 65–80, 66.

56. *Media-Micro-Zensus der Arbeitsgemeinschaft Media-Analyse,* 155. For this undertaking compare Michael Meyen, *Mediennutzung, Medienfunktionen, Nutzungsmuster* (Constance, 2001), 75ff., and Hansjörg Bessler, *Hörer- und Zuschauerforschung* (Munich, 1980), 187 ff.

57. Hammerschmidt's "Richtlinien-Entwurf" in: Helmut Hammerschmidt, *Zur kommunikatiospolitischen Diskussion. Reden und Aufsätze 1965–1976,* ed. Henner Faehndrich and Wolfgang Hempel (Berlin, 1978), 76–84; the "Grundsätze," in *ARD-Jahrbuch* 71, 256f.; for discussion compare Rechlin, *Rundfunk und Machtwechsel,* 245ff.

58. Hammerschmidt, "Richtlinien-Entwurf," 76.

59. Allensbach Institute (for public opinion research), *Pop-Shop im Südwestfunk. Programm-Inhaltsanalyse einer Sendereihe im 3. Programm des Hörfunks,* 1 (copy at historical archive of SWR/SWF).

60. Ibid., 9 (my emphasis, KD).

61. Ibid., 4f.

62. Ibid., 3.

63. Ibid., 11.

64. Compare Walter von Cube's strongly promotional text which refers to both programs: Walter von Cube, "'Bayern 3.' Ein Hörfunkprogramm für Autofahrer," in *ARD-Jahrbuch* 1972, 63–65. Reprinted in Dussel and Lersch, *Quellen zur Programmgeschichte,* 293–96.

65. Compare former SWF director Helmut Hammerschmidt's "Notizen zur Hörfunkstruktur," as well as the "Generalbeschreibung der SWF-Programme" which is undated, but probably from 1975, printed in Dussel and Lersch, *Quellen zur Programmgeschichte,* 296ff.

66. Data taken from the "Media-Analyse" (media analyses) of 1974 and 1980, prepared by the Arbeitsgemeinschaft Media Analyse (study group for media analysis).

67. *DLM Jahrbuch 89/90. Privater Rundfunk in Deutschland* (Munich, 1990), 311–13.

68. Michael Keller and Walter Klingler, "Jugendwellen gewinnen junge Hörerschaften. Ergebnisse der Media Analyse 1996," in *Radioperspektiven. Strukturen und Programme,* ed. Christof Barth and Christian Schröter (Baden-Baden, 1997), 65–82.

69. Dieter Baake, *Beat—die sprachlose Opposition,* (2nd ed., Munich, 1970), 9, 15.

70. Kurt Luger, *Die konsumierte Rebellion—Geschichte der Jugendkultur 1945–1990* (Vienna and St. Johann, 1991), 308; similarly: Zinnecker, *Jugendkultur,* 322ff.

71. hr3 brochure *"Zehn Jahre hr3—Die Servicewelle aus Frankfurt,"* 7.

72. Haedecke, *SWF 3,* quote, 68.

73. Frith, *Jugendkultur und Rockmusik,* 224.

Chapter 6

Across the Border: West German Youth Travel to Western Europe

Axel Schildt

Although youth tourism plays a central role in defining perceptions of the self and of the foreign, it has neither been thoroughly researched as an integral part of youth culture, nor as part of the burgeoning of mass tourism since the 1960s. Youth tourism was a new phenomenon, as can be inferred from the seminal works in pedagogy and sociology published between 1963 and 1970;[1] in Germany, the term "youth tourism" appeared in scholarly literature for the first time during the mid-1950s.[2] The following sketch, using West Germany as a case study, intends to highlight a single important topic within the scholarly field of youth cultures in Europe.

This is not to say that prior to this young Germans did not travel. Considering the two World Wars, one can speak of a rather mobile twentieth century; however, this mobility rarely encompassed civil tourism. At the turn of the century, and particularly during the inter-war years, cross-border traveling by youth groups were part of endeavors such as *Grenzlandarbeit,* whose political intentions enabled German youths to meet German minorities primarily in eastern and southeastern Europe.[3] As late as 1967, a volume entitled *Deutsche Jugendbewegung in Europa* (The German Youth Movement in Europe) was published which drew attention to this sphere of nationalist interest in neighboring European states.[4] As early as the 1920s, there were already tendencies towards "thinking beyond the border" (*Denken über die Grenze*) and the idea of *Begegnung* (encounter) with the youth of former enemy states emerged during this time.

After the Second World War, observers reported a great longing among West German youths to overcome the isolation brought about by the war. There was perhaps no other Western European country in which school children and students were as enthusiastic about Europe as in Germany. Countless newspaper articles recorded symbolic acts protesting against existing borders. During November 1950, some three thousand German, French, Belgian, Italian, Dutch, Danish, and Norwegian youths assembled outside the European Parliament in Strasbourg and demanded the unification of all European states; one banner carried by German students read "*Stürmt die Bastille Nationalstaat*" ("Storm the Bastille National State").[5] German youth also met their foreign counterparts while visiting neighboring countries under a "Work Camp" program (for example, when they went to France to maintain the graves of German soldiers). Although such activities are worth noting in this discussion,[6] they were certainly not representative of West German youth experiences in general. Political commitment remained within the traditions of the up-and-coming members of the educated classes and academics; the opportunity for organized youth travel proliferated only slowly during the 1950s. Between 1949 and 1959, roughly thirty non-profit *Ferienwerke* (vacation organizations), which efficiently organized and offered cross-border journeys, developed. In 1950 and 1953 respectively, the two largest providers of cross-border journeys, the Office for Foreign Affairs (*Auslandsstelle*) of the German National Student Association (*Deutscher Bundesstudentenring*) and the German Association for International Youth Exchange (*Deutsche Gesellschaft für internationalen Jugendaustausch*), were founded.[7] In addition, schools, youth groups, and social and athletic clubs offered a variety of activities. Nonetheless, general travel restraints were the rule for the large majority of German youths, which was also the case for society in general—only roughly 20 percent of German citizens were passport-holders in the mid-1950s, obligatory for travel to European states, with the exception of the so-called *kleiner Grenzverkehr* (cross-border travel for residents within close proximity to the national border).

In the 1960s, rapid change took place.[8] According to polls, only one-third of West German citizens went on vacation in 1960. Another third of this group, i.e., only roughly 10 percent of all Germans, traveled to destinations across the national border. At the end of the 1970s the percentage of citizens going on vacations had doubled to the figure of roughly 60 percent; within this figure, the share of cross-border journeys had also increased to 60 percent. Thus, at the end of the 1970s, more than one-third of Germany's citizens had been on vacation outside their country. However, cross-border journeys were not equally distributed within society. Residents of large cities traveled twice as often as residents of rural towns, a strong indicator of tourism as an urban phenomenon, and employees and civil servants traveled twice as often as blue-collar workers.[9] This statistical snapshot suffices to give an impression of the dynamic developments within the field of mass tourism, which were a component and an expression of the general trend towards prosperity, and characteristic of an "affluent society."

Within this general development of mass tourism, youths functioned as trendsetters due to their above-average travel frequency, their advanced knowledge of foreign languages, as well as their larger willingness for interaction and communication. In this sense, the 1960s were the golden age of youth tourism. Based on various studies, at the end of the 1950s, the percentage of travelers in their teens or twenties was significantly above the national average. At the beginning of the 1980s, however, their share was only slightly higher than the national average. By this time, vacations (especially in foreign countries) had become a given for West German society in general. In 1978, two-thirds of all 14- to 19-year-olds and even as many as three-quarters of all of 20- to 29-year-olds took vacations in foreign countries (at the beginning of the 1990s, the share had increased to four-fifths); thus, roughly half of the 14- to 29-year-olds had crossed a national border within one year. By this time, there was hardly a youth that had not been to a foreign country. On average, at the beginning of the 1990s, 17- to 19-year-olds had already visited seven to eight countries.[10]

It has been pointed out that by the beginning of the 1980s a historical era came to an end. Large organizations did not dominate the field any longer, instead, numerous smaller alternative vacation organizations were founded and a number of "drifter"-tourists began to look for "marginal paradises" outside Europe. Today, to a larger extent than ever before, European youths travel outside their home continent.[11] Looking back to the early 1960s, when youth tourism to European countries began to develop into a mass phenomenon, the arguments about the ramifications of youth tourism were rather heated. On all sides, people began to realize that leisure figured more prominently with youths than *Völkerverständigung* (international understanding) and that youth tourism was but one manifestation of severely criticized contemporary consumerism. Heinz Hahn, a psychologist and one of the experts participating in the debate over youth tourism, stated in an article in the mid-1960s: "Thirty years ago, young people became acquainted with the art of vacationing in youth hostels and youth summer camps. Nowadays, travel initiation starts in Daddy's car, as he takes the family to Italy for Pentecost holidays; it continues at some beach resort, where you can observe 'how one must act on vacation'; and it reaches its conclusion in a film like *Blond muß man sein auf Capri* ('One Must Go Blond on

Capri'), or in the latest summer special of a glossy magazine."[12] Various sociological and psychological studies of the period may be summarized as follows: youths expected 90 percent leisure activities and only 10 percent educational activities. It was even more likely for young people than adults to adopt certain patterns of tourist behavior as suggested by the mass media; youths wanted to go on vacation with peers to find unrestricted interaction as well as to escape their elders' control, at least a little; and they did not want to be bothered by structured programs during their vacation. A Franz Kafka quote best captures youth desire: "Away from here—that is my goal"; also an "escape from the daily routine" was desired.[13] However, these attitudes were only marginally different from those of adults, among whom the need for familiar surroundings (even on vacation) may well have been greater.[14]

Nonetheless, pedagogical professionals, clerics, and youth experts in general remained concerned, for, while many youth journeys were, in terms of the participants' motivation as well as the providers' pedagogical-political conception, recreational journeys embellished by educational ideals, youth travel underwent quick commercialization. The creation of so-called "collective trips to foreign countries" (*Sammelfahrten ins Ausland*) by train, bus, plane or boat was considered particularly dubious. At the beginning of the 1960s, these trips enabled hundreds of thousands of youths to travel to Istanbul, Naples, Barcelona, London or Stockholm at reduced rates without having to join an organized travel group. During the mid-1960s young vacation vagrants in various regions of Greece and southern France had allegedly turned into a serious nuisance. Their behavior was not considered to be ideal for young people exploring and experiencing their "fatherland Europe."[15] However, little is known about the actual behavior of these youths traveling through Europe individually. There is not a single contemporary study on vagrants, hitchhikers or similar groups. In 1962, individually planned trips by young people accounted for roughly three-quarters of all their travels to foreign countries; however, many of them went on vacations with their parents.[16] And even those young people who went on vacation with their peers to foreign countries by bike, by train, by hitchhiking (hitchhiking left an identifying mark on youth tourism during the 1960s and the early 1970s), by motorcycle,[17] or even by car largely exhibited behavior that probably deviated only slightly from the norm, if at all.[18] Youth hostel culture, for example, with its emphasis on social discipline, was already well-established in most Western European countries as early as the 1960s.[19]

In particular, vacations planned and offered by youth tourism companies caused concerns, when sociologists and psychologists, making use of participatory observation methods and questionnaires, published studies about German youths' behavior as exhibited at holiday camps in foreign countries. Above all, works by Helmut Kentler and his close associates, particularly their account of a vacation in Catania (Sicily), shocked the West German public, actually leading to a debate in the *Bundestag*, (the West German parliament). In these studies, the young individual, using categories of the contemporary and very influential American sociologist David Riesman,[20] was described as a "*total aussen-geleiteter Typ*" ("externally directed type"),[21] usually of middle-class origin: female secretarial and other petty clerks, prospective school teachers, sons and daughters of store or restaurant owners, as well as young singles), who had enough money to afford extras. Their daily routines did not amount to more than the monotonous succession of swimming, suntanning, and eating, as well as late-night parties, which exhibited loose sexual morals. Helmut Kentler interpreted these forms of conduct as the "subculture of a repressive society,"[22] and other participants in the ongoing debates forecasted the decline of the *Abendland* (the Occident), especially in terms of sexual morals.

It is a well-known fact that at the beginning of the 1960s, double rooms for unmarried couples were out of the question. Experts agreed that for youths, the interest in foreign countries, their people and their culture did not figure prominently in deciding on vacation destinations. Indifferent towards the actual geographical destination, they usually associated southern latitudes and plenty of sun with a successful vacation. Foreign countries signified the *other* in terms of *patterns of behavior* and, above all, it promised possible sexual relations, which were generally impossible at home.[23] Yet, sexual relations typically came about within the all-German peer group, where foreigners were considered obtrusive. A study about an Italian resort quotes a female member of an organized travel group who found her prejudices about male Italians as more or less cunning womanizers confirmed: "To the Northern European, the Italian male's tendency of turning from their usual lethargy to a courting rooster at first sight of any female human being, is indeed the rarely pleasant and most striking quality of Italy's sons. [And making matters worse:] On a daily basis, a male Italian is more often well-groomed than freshly-washed."[24] Tour guides tried to explain that Italians did shower frequently, and were constantly washing their laundry and disinfecting their homes, even in the poorer neighborhoods; but obviously their words had little effect. It must be mentioned that the *Italiener* (Italian male) had a particularly low standing in West Germany at the time, due to the recent immigration of new *Gastarbeitern* (guest workers), which resurrected old stereotypes from the Second World War. However, similar presumptions were also reported for a group of the *Deutsche Landjugend* (German Rural Youth) traveling through France, who were simply rude; upon arrival at their accommodation, these youths first checked the beds for cleanliness, often in the presence of the owners.[25] Thus, participants of numerous youth vacations went home finding their prejudices confirmed by personal experiences, a fact which has been affirmed by a number of contemporary studies (and hardly a sphere of social behavior has been so thoroughly studied during the 1960s as this one).[26]

In the debate over Catania and other studies, the *Jugendferienwerke* (Youth Vacation Organizations) were targeted, at times vehemently.[27] The training workshops for youth travel counselors were expanded (within the *Bundesjugendplan* [Federal Youth Program] of 1965, financial resources being provided for this measure for the first time)[28] just as the counselors' supervisory responsibilities were expanded, and inspections of the young travelers' sleeping quarters were now obligatory at night. The previously dominant position that foreign travel in itself could have positive intercultural effects (often referred to as a "contact hypothesis"), sometimes became radically reversed: critics claimed that foreign travel actually reinforced negative stereotypes, rather than dissolving them. Therefore, the state should instead increase its support for intercultural education through journeys to foreign countries based on educational objectives—increasing knowledge about countries and their people, dismantling of prejudices as well as developing tolerance among neighbors, promotion of a spirit of supranational community as a contribution for peace, etc.[29] The foundation of the *Deutsch-Französisches Jugendwerk* (German-French Youth Organization) in 1963, initiated at governmental levels, symbolized this new way of thinking. Studies that were part of the development and the preparation of the German-French exchange indicated that by 1963, 64 percent of the German youths had already been to a foreign country, while among the French youths only four out of ten had left their country.[30] Moreover, these studies also indicated tremendous differences in terms of self-perception and the perception of foreigners. It is worth mentioning that French youths thought more positively of their West German peers than vice versa.[31] Attempts to create a European youth organization failed during this period.[32]

Nevertheless, acceptance grew for foreign travelers that did not exclusively and directly serve an interest in foreign countries and *Völkerverständigung*.[33] The stark contradiction between commercial and non-commercial youth tourism had decreased since the beginning of the 1970s, and at this point in time offers became more diverse on the basis of the awareness that the adventure-tourists of *Völkerverständigung* and the less adventure tourists desiring southern sun could not be addressed in the same way. Simultaneously, youth protection legislation was loosened throughout most of Europe: opening hours of youth hostels were extended, regulations on alcohol and tobacco consumption were relaxed, and moreover, boys and girls could now spend the night in the same room without facing moral censure. Intriguingly, the few polls of the 1970s conveyed the impression that journeys to foreign countries now positively influenced young travelers' opinions of their countries of destination. However, some differences were still characteristic: young West Germans held France in lower esteem than young French did West Germany, and young Germans associated England primarily with crises and strikes. This is an indication that increasing knowledge of other West European countries may have coincided with the emergence of new stereotypes. In spite of this, a general pattern that the growth of youth tourism led to a refinement of a previously crude understanding of other European countries and peoples can be highlighted. In 1976, 54 percent of all West German youths between the age of eighteen and twenty-four had had contact with foreign youths. Studies completed in 1978 point to the fact that young people knew only insignificantly less about foreign countries than the older population did, even though the older people had had more time to travel. And while traditional vacation destinations such as Austria and Italy remained the favorites of young and old Germans, a number of noteworthy differences emerged. Particularly Great Britain and Scandinavia were visited considerably more often by younger than by older tourists, due to the growing foreign-language competence of the younger age group. In 1985, 96 percent of all students of grades 5 through 13 had English as a school subject and another 26 percent were learning French as a foreign language. Obviously, youths visited these countries, mainly to brush up their foreign language-skills. However, they also returned with new and vivid impressions,[34] not the least of foreign youth cultures when they witnessed different relationships to adults, rights, duties, and prohibitions.[35] Youth tourism, combined with other elements of popular cultural exchange, such as music, fashion, and other aspects of consumption, thus greatly increases our understanding of West German youth culture.[36]

The Impact of Travel on West German Youth Culture

As late as during the 1960s, youths who had been abroad gained tremendously in terms of their exposure to and experience of foreign cultures. Any West German youth, who during the summer of 1966 had been to the southern coast of England and had spent time in one of the beach resorts between Margate and Ramsgate to take part in language courses, became immersed in a fascinating world of cinemas, gambling halls, ice cream parlors, and live concerts by bands like The Who, The Kinks, or The Small Faces. Moreover, they had gained a reliable preview of whatever would become a trend in their own country within the next half year after their return home.[37] On the other hand, one must also take into consideration the idea (recognized particularly by researchers at the British School of Cultural Studies) that new trends in music, fashion, movies, etc., are idiosyncratically adapted and modified by (and eventually incorporated into) distinct national, regional and socially differentiated lifestyles. Moreover, mass-media radio and television played a progressively more decisive role within this process. By the mid-1960s, moralizers of the *öffentlich-rechtlichen* (publicly-funded) radio stations, controlled by political parties, the churches as well as other societal groups, could no longer disregard English Beat music and had to provide it—and soon music from the American West Coast as well—with significant air time. Commercial youth magazines reported extensively from London's Portobello Road as well as other legendary places where new fashion trends originated. Even within department stores catering to the taste of the general public, departments for young fashion were introduced. On television, the show "Beatclub" aired once a month and showed what was "in." While youth travel to England, France, and other European countries increased progressively, the advantage gained on such trips vis-à-vis those youths that did not travel decreased as foreign products became increasingly available at home. While in the beginning—as late as during the mid-1960s—there were obvious and significant time lags in terms of access to such products between metropolitan cities of northern Germany and provincial towns in Germany's south, these began to disappear very quickly. Another important development, especially in the latter third of the 1960s, was the emergence of political protest movements, especially those inspired by foreign models; this triggered even more travel between European countries, particularly by high school and college students. For them, London was no longer the desired destination but rather Paris, Rome, and Amsterdam. As of the 1970s— with the demise of the Fascist dictatorships in Portugal, Spain, and Greece—the sunny beaches of southern European countries also became extremely popular with politically active or at least politically interested youths. On the coast of Portugal's southern province Algarve or on the Greek island Crete, German youths met youths from other European countries—as well as from the United States—that shared with them similar political and aesthetic priorities. Even if such encounters affected just a small portion of the travel market (which was not only expanding among youth, but in all age brackets), their importance in mediating the transmission of new youth culture and practices cannot be ignored. Yet, the study of these processes is still incomplete. It would not only facilitate a more differentiated comprehension of West German youth culture but it would also open up various European and international perspectives for comparison.

Notes

1. Heinz Hahn, ed., *Jugendtourismus. Beiträge zur Diskussion über Jugenderholung und Jugendreisen* (Schriftenreihe der Arbeitsgemeinschaft für Jugendpflege und Jugendfürsorge 11) (Munich, 1965); Hermann Giesecke, Annelie Keil, and Udo Perle, *Pädagogik des Jugendreisens* (Munich, 1967).

2. Anton Grassl, "Jugendtourismus: Zeitgeschichtliche Beobachtungen (1955)," in *Jugendtourismus*, ed. Heinz Hahn, 33–40.

3. Compare Werner Müller, "Von der 'Völkerverständigung' zum 'interkulturellen Lernen'. Eine Aufarbeitung inhaltlicher Bestimmungsfaktoren des internationalen Jugendaustauschs in der Bundesrepublik Deutschland" (Ph.D. diss., University of Hamburg, 1985), 32–35.

4. Peter Nasarski, ed., *Deutsche Jugendbewegung in Europa. Versuch einer Bilanz* (Cologne, 1967).

5. Refer also to the documentation of newspaper articles and photographs in the anthology, *Das haben wir zusammen gemacht. Erinnerungen, Projektberichte, Vorschläge zum 70. Geburtstag von Heinz Hahn* (Starnberg, 2000).

6. Compare Horst W. Opaschowski, *Jugendauslandsreise. Geschichtliche, soziale und pädagogische Aspekte* (Neuwied/Berlin, 1970), 115; Jürgen Reulecke, ed., *Rückkehr in die Ferne. Die deutsche Jugend in der Nachkriegszeit und das Ausland.* (Materialien zur historischen Jugendforschung) (Weinheim and Munich, 1997).

7. Werner Müller, "Inhaltliches Engagement und professioneller Rahmen: Zur 'dualen Legitmation' des Jugendreisens," in *Jugendreisen: Vom Staat zum Markt. Analysen und Perspektiven*, ed. Thomas Korbus, Wolfgang Nahrstedt, Bernhard Porwol, and Marina Teichert (Bielefeld, 1997), 88–101.

8. Scholars position the point of departure of West German mass tourism in this era. For contemporary studies see, above all, Hans-Joachim Knebel, *Soziologische Strukturwandlungen im modernen Tourismus* (Stuttgart, 1960); Heinz R. Scherrieb, "Der westeuropäische Massentourismus. Untersuchungen zum Begriff und zur Geschichte des Massentourismus, insbesondere der Verhaltensweisen bundesdeutscher Urlaubsreisender" (Ph.D. diss., University of Würzburg, 1975); historiographical analysis by Axel Schildt, *Moderne Zeiten. Freizeit, Massenmedien und 'Zeitgeist' in der Bundesrepublik der 50er Jahre* (Hamburg, 1995), 180–202; Haus der Geschichte der Bundesrepublik Deutschland, ed., *Endlich Urlaub! Die Deutschen reisen. Begleitbuch zur Ausstellung im Haus der Geschichte* (Cologne, 1996); Wolfgang König places the beginning of mass tourism in the middle of the 1970s, when roughly half of Germany's population traveled at least once a year: Wolfgang König, "Massentourismus. Seine Entstehung und Entwicklung in der Nachkriegszeit," *Technikgeschichte* 64 (1998): 305–22; see the debate concerning the beginning of mass tourism and the bibliographical references in Matthias Frese, "Naherholung und Ferntourismus. Tourismus und Tourismusförderung in Westfalen 1900–1970," in *Verkehr und Region im 19. und 20. Jahrhundert. Westfälische Beispiele*, ed. Wilfried Reininghaus and Karl Teppe (Paderborn, 1999), 339–85, in particular 340 passim; see also Rudy Koshar, *German Travel Cultures* (Oxford and New York, 2000).

9. Hans-Werner Prahl, and Albrecht Steinecke, *Der Millionen-Urlaub. Von der Bildungsreise zur totalen Freizeit* (Darmstadt and Neuwied, 1979).

10. Compare, among others, Franz Pöggeler, "Entwicklungstendenzen des Jugendtourismus," in *Moderner Tourismus—Tendenzen und Aussichten* (Materialien zur Fremdenverkehrsgeographie 17), ed. Dietrich Storbeck (Trier, 1988), 527–47; Studienkreis für Tourismus, ed., *Reiseanalysen 1971–1991* (Starnberg, 1992).

11. Compare E. Cohen, "Marginal paradises. Bungalow tourism on the islands of Southern Thailand," in *Annals of Tourism Research* 9 (1982), 189–228; Tracey Skelton and Gill Valentine, eds., *Cool Places: Geographies of Youth Cultures* (London, 1998).

12. Heinz Hahn, "Ferienwerke und Reisedienste für junge Leute," in *Jugendtourismus*, 41–53, quote on 41.

13. Helmut Kentler, "Urlaub als Auszug aus dem Alltag," *Deutsche Jugend. Zeitschrift für Jugendfragen und Jugendarbeit* 11 (1963): 118–24; also, see Dieter Danckwortt, "Jugend geht auf Reisen. Eine Untersuchung von Ferienreisen der 14- bis 18jährigen Schuljugend einer Großstadt in Norddeutschland im Jahre 1956," in *Jahrbuch für Jugendreisen und Internationalen Jugendaustausch* 4 (1962), 75–99; Wolfgang Böhm, "Zur Motivation junger Auslandsreisender. Ein Bericht über eine empirische Studie," in ibid.: 112–22; Hans C. Dechêne, "Über jugendlichen Reisedrang. Eine motivationspsychologische Studie," in *Zeitschrift für experimentelle und angewandte Psychologie* 8 (1961): 461–507; Ottmar L. Braun, "Sozial- und motivationspsychologische Aspekte des modernen Jugendtourismus," *Gruppendynamik* 27 (1996): 39–50.

14. Compare Birgit Mandel, "'Amore ist heißer als Liebe.' Das Italien-Urlaubsimage der Westdeutschen in den 50er und 60er Jahren," in *Goldstrand und Teutonengrill. Kultur- und Sozialgeschichte des Tourismus in Deutschland 1945–1989,* ed. Hasso Spode (Berlin, 1996).

15. Hahn, "Ferienwerke," 41.

16. Compare Brigitte Gayler, "Das Reiseverhalten junger Deutscher in den siebziger Jahren," in *Jahrbuch für Jugendreisen und Internationalen Jugendaustausch* 21 (1979), 61–77; Gayler, "Entwicklungsperspektiven im Jugendtourismus," in *Innovationen und künftige Entwicklung des Fremdenverkehrs,* limited print for the Studienkreis für Tourismus (Starnberg, 1981), 156.

17. The first empirical study encompasses only the beginning of the 1980s: Renate Nötzel, *Junge Motorradtouristen. Beobachtungen bei acht selbstorganisierten Fahrten von Motorradclubs* (Starnberg, 1983).

18. S. Cohen and L. Taylor, *Escape Attempts* (Harmondsworth, 1976).

19. Compare "Jugendstätten in westeuropäischen Ländern" in *Jahrbuch für Jugendreisen und Internationalen Jugendaustausch* 5 (1964), 89–115.

20. David Riesman, *Die Einsame Masse* (Reinbek, 1958), published in English as *The Lonely Crowd. A Study of the Changing American Character* (New Haven 1950).

21. Kentler, *Urlaub als Auszug,* 64.

22. Kentler, "Urlaub als Subkultur," in *Jugendtourismus,* 73–86, quote on 75.

23. Burkhard Schade, "Erleben und Verhalten junger Auslandsreisender," in *Jugendtourismus,* 87–101.

24. Helmut Kentler, *Urlaub auf Sizilien. Beobachtungen in einem Jugendferienlager am Mittelmeer* (Munich: Studienkreis für Tourismus, 1963), 46; also, compare Kentler, Thomas Leithäuser, Helmut Lessing, *Jugend im Urlaub* (Weinheim, Berlin, and Basel, 1969), 64–66.

25. A. Degen, "Bericht über eine Reise des Bundes der Hessischen Landjugend nach Südfrankreich," *Jahrbuch für Jugendreisen und Internationalen Jugendaustausch* 8 (1966).

26. Also, see Udo Perle, *Urlaub in Port Issol. Beobachtungen eines Gruppenpädagogen in einem Jugendferienlager an der französischen Riviera* (Starnberg: Studienkreis für

Tourismus, 1961), 21–22; Konrad Schön, "Urlaub auf Mallorca. Beobachtungen eines Pädagogen in einem Jugendferiendorf am Mittelmeer," in *Jahrbuch für Jugendreisen und Internationalen Jugendaustausch* 5 (1963), 87–99; Udo Perle, "Urlaub in Cervia," in ibid., 101–15; Anitra Karsten, *Vorstellungen von jungen Deutschen über andere Völker. Ein Bericht über die bisherige Forschung* (Schriftenreihe der Stiftung für internationale Länderkenntnis der Jugend 1) (Frankfurt am Main, 1966); Horst W. Opaschowski, "Urlaub in Imperia. Beobachtungen eines Jugendreiseleiters in einem Hotel an der italienischen Riviera," in *Jahrbuch für Jugendreisen und Internationalen Jugendaustausch* 10 (1968), 31–63; Armin Ganser, *Junge Leute im Urlaub auf Ibiza. Beobachtungen in Ferienclub-Anlagen* (Starnberg: Studienkreis für Tourismus, 1979); for general information see Jürgen Reulecke, "Kommunikation durch Tourismus? Zur Geschichte des organisierten Reisens im 19. und 20. Jahrhundert," in *Die Bedeutung der Kommunikation für Wirtschaft und Gesellschaft,* ed. Hans Pohl (Stuttgart, 1989), 358–78; Ulrike Hess, "Die Debatte um die Völkerverständigung durch Tourismus: Entwicklung einer Idee und empirische Befunde," in *Der durchschaute Tourist. Arbeiten zur Tourismusforschung* (Tourismuswissenschaftliche Manuskripte 3) (Munich and Vienna, 1998), 106–5.

27. Compare, for instance, Willi Weber, "Jugendtourismus heute," in *Jahrbuch für Jugendreisen und Internationalen Jugendaustausch* 6 (1965), 35–56.

28. See the interesting eyewitness account of Catholic youth programs as documented by the historian Jürgen Reulecke, "'Mit Hirn, Charme und Methode.' Zur Ausbildung von Jugendreiseleitern in den 1960er und 1970er Jahren," *Bildung und Erziehung* 53 (2000): 171–82.

29. Karsten, *Vorstellungen von jungen Deutschen über andere Völker*, compare Werner Müller, "Interkulturelles Lernen beim Jugendaustausch," in *Tourismuspsychologie und Tourismussoziologie. Ein Handbuch zur Tourismuswissenschaft,* ed. Heinz Hahn and H. Jürgen Kagelmann (Munich, 1993), 270–74.

30. Viggo Graf Blücher, *Die Generation der Unbefangenen. Zur Soziologie der jungen Menschen heute* (Düsseldorf and Cologne, 1966), 240–41.

31. Compare Klaus Dieter Hartmann, *Wirkungen von Auslandsreisen junger Leute auf Länderkenntnis und Völkerverständigung. Ein Überblick über Ergebnisse der sozialpsychologischen Forschung* (Starnberg, 1981), 108–20; Anita Orlovius-Wessely, *Viel gereist und nichts gelernt? Wirkungen von Auslandsreisen bei Jugendlichen* (Bensberger Studien 9) (1997).

32. For this debate, compare Harry Liehr, "Für ein europäisches Jugendwerk," *Deutsche Jugend* 12 (1964): 367–70, as well as numerous other articles in this periodical during the following years.

33. See *Jugend. Bildung und Freizeit. Dritte Untersuchung zur Situation der Deutschen Jugend im Bundesgebiet, durchgeführt vom EMNID-Institut für Sozialforschung im Auftrag des Jugendwerkes der Deutschen Shell* [Youth. Education and Leisure Time. Third Inquiry into the Situation of the German Youth within West Germany: Carried out by the EMNID-Institute for Social Research, commissioned by the Youth Association of the Shell Corporation in Germany] (1966), 266–76; Hartmann provides a synopsis for the debates' development during the 1960s and 1970s: Hartmann, *Wirkungen,* 10–20.

34. In general, compare Christoph Köck, ed., *Reisebilder. Produktion und Reproduktion touristischer Wahrnehmung* (Münchner Beiträge zur Volkskunde 29) (Münster, New York, Munich and Berlin, 2001).

35. For instance, see Wolfgang Nahrstedt and Ralf Amrhein, "Jugendklubs in England," *Deutsche Jugend* 13 (1965): 129–36; Blücher for the Youth Association of the Shell Corporation in Germany, ed., *Jugend in Europa: Ihre Eingliederung in die Welt der*

Erwachsenen—eine vergleichende Analyse zwischen der Bundesrepublik Deutschland, Frankreich und Großbritannien. 7. Untersuchung zur Situation der Jugend, durchgeführt vom EMNID-Institut für Meinungs- und Marktforschung [Youth in Europe: Their Inclusion into the World of Adults; A Comparative Analysis between the Federal Republic of Germany, France, and Great Britain; 7th Inquiry into the Youth's Situation Carried Out by the EMNID-Institute for Public Opinion and Market Research] (Hamburg, 1977).

36. For the connection of tourism and consumption in Austria see Kurt Luger, *Die konsumierte Rebellion. Geschichte der Jugendkultur 1945–1990* (Neue Aspekte in Kultur- und Kommunikationswissenschaft 1) (Vienna, 1991); for general information see Hartmut Berghoff, "From Privilege to Commodity? Modern Tourism and the Rise of the Consumer Society," in *The Making of Modern Tourism. The Cultural History of the British Experience, 1600–2000,* ed. Berghoff, Barbara Korte, Ralf Schneider, and Cristopher Harvie (New York, 2002), 159–79.

37. Here, I report from my own perspective as a then 15-year-old eyewitness. The only risk existed in the aggressiveness of English pubpatrons during the viewing of the 1966 Football World Cup Final between England and Germany, which the host country England won because of an irregular goal.

Chapter 7

Imperialism and Consumption: Two Tropes in West German Radicalism

Uta G. Poiger

In November 1968, a few days after her conviction in the fire bombing of two Frankfurt department stores, Gudrun Ensslin made the following statement in a television interview:

> The people in our country and in America and in every West European country, they have to eat like animals, in order not to think about what we have to do for example with Vietnam [...] Wonderful, I too like the cars, I too like all the things one can buy in department stores. But when one is compelled to buy them, in order to remain unconscious, then the price is too high. Then one doesn't have to look to Vietnam to see the misery; then it is enough to really look at our society and to see the lack of consciousness, which I would simply call inhuman.[1]

Ensslin's actions raise questions about the ways in which West German leftist radicals of the late 1960s and 1970s drew a link between the power of consumption in the West and attitudes towards the Third World. What made West German department stores into arson targets to protest the Vietnam War? What analysis did radicals develop of consumer society and imperialism? And how did they make a connection between the two? Attending to these issues will not only add to our understanding of West German radicalism and its vision of consumption and politics; it might also point to ways in which histories of consumer culture in modern Germany (and Europe) need to be revised with international frameworks in mind.

Consumption was not a new, but an increasingly important issue after 1945, in both Cold War Germanies. The import of foreign commodities, but also the export of German-produced commodities and German capital were crucial for maintaining German prosperity. Politicians like Ludwig Erhard counted access to consumer goods and proper consumption among the rights and duties of the citizens of the West German democracy.[2] This happened at a time when anticolonial movements rose up against European colonizers, "modernization" and "development" discourses replaced biologically based racism and formal empires, and each Germany was itself drawn into the informal empire of a superpower, the United States or the Soviet Union.

By the 1960s, certain references to colonialism were no longer acceptable in West German consumer culture, while others persisted. Thus the terms *Kolonialwaren* and *Kolonialwarenläden*, colonial goods and colonial goods stores, used since the late nineteenth century, disappeared. But in 1970 the German company Beiersdorf advertised its global face cream NIVEA in West Germany in a way that hearkened back to the idea of Western civilizing missions that had been part of various imperial projects. The ad showed a hut in Guatemala, and was titled in big letters "NIVEA: The German Message."[3]

During these same years, from the mid-1960s onward, the West German consumer culture, always viewed with unease by many cultural critics, came under increased attack from the radical left. At a time when Third World imports such as coffee or exotic fruit had become staples of the West German diet, West German radicals attacked the West as imperialist and relying on the exploitation of the Third World. Many of these radicals had come of age in the relative prosperity of the late 1950s and early 1960s; by the 1960s many of them were participants in a youthful and multifaceted West German counter culture. Their analysis of the politics of contemporary imperialism focused heavily on the interventions made by Western countries, especially the United States, in decolonizing nations. Several areas of the world in particular gained the attention of West German radicals: Vietnam, Latin America, Cuba, Congo, and Iran. Members of radical groups read Third World liberation theorists, and saw them and the armed struggles of liberation movements as inspiration for resistance in the capitalist world.

The radical student group SDS (Socialist German Student Federation) for example claimed a position of solidarity with Third World liberation movements. Members of SDS followed Herbert Marcuse's arguments that intellectuals, youth, and to some degree ethnic minorities could show real opposition in Western industrial nations and, through the power of their "reason" and "sentiment," could work in solidarity with liberationists in the Third World. West German radicals agreed with Marcuse that the working class in industrial nations had achieved relative wealth and conformed to the system. In Germany Marcuse had made these arguments at a convention organized in May 1966 by the SDS on "Vietnam—Analysis of an Example."[4] By 1967, many young West German radicals also followed the logic of Black Power, and saw African-Americans as victims of internal colonization within the United States, who would play a particularly important role in exposing and fighting Western imperialism. And by 1968/69, Israel too became a target of radical anti-imperialist criticism for its treatment of Palistinians.[5]

Many of these analysis of imperialism included a critique of consumer culture in the West. In the 1960s radicals made the connection between their criticisms of Western, and often also Soviet, exploitation of the Third World and consumption in Germany, Europe, and the United States by focusing on the alleged manipulative aspects of consumer culture in the West, including the Federal Republic. In the concluding remarks to their 1967 book *Modelle kolonialer Revolution*, SDS leaders Peter Gäng and Reimut Reiche found, for example, that at the current "late stage of capitalism," manipulation through the advertising and culture industries put increased pressure on the individual in the West. This form of oppression remained relatively abstract, as the disintegration of the father-centered nuclear family and the strategies of the culture industry created a sense of dissatisfaction, but made it difficult for the individual to recognize his oppression as a political issue. However this could change in the current "world political situation." Highly industrialized socialist states posed no credible alternative, while there was the possibility of solidarity between movements of intellectuals and youth in the capitalist metropole and Third World liberation movements. With this analysis, Reiche and Gäng were clearly indebted to arguments made by Marcuse in his work and by American economists Paul A. Baran and Paul M. Sweezy in *Monopoly Capital,* a book widely received in West Germany. In another study, on sexuality from 1968, Reiche changed this analysis somewhat and identified both the sphere of production and the sphere of consumption in the metropoles as spheres of exploitation. In rather vague terms he saw these phenomena as part of "world imperialism."[6]

The link between imperialism and consumer culture also became a topic in relation to spectacular fires in department stores, first in Brussels in May 1967 and a year later in Frankfurt with the fire bombings in which Ensslin participated. After the fire in a Brussels Department Store, in which 300 people died, the Berlin anti-authoritarian Kommune 1 published and distributed a flyer, in which they made the connection between consumer culture in the West and imperialist practice, in this case the Vietnam War. Kommune 1 was one of the most visible groups of the West German counter culture; members commented on current politics and also argued for radical change through transformed styles of living and dress.

In the pamphlet, which like so many of its utterances was characterized more by a provocative tone than a clear logic, Kommune I asked: "Why are you burning, consumer?" The pamphlet cynically described the fire as a "new gag in the multifaceted history of American advertizing strategies." According to Kommune 1, "the burning department store with burning people revealed for the first time in a European metropolis that crackling Vietnam feeling (being there and burning along), that we still have to do without in Berlin." Some might wonder whether it was a good idea to "burn 'King Customer,' the consumer who is so clearly privileged and courted in our society." The fire allowed "saturated" citizens to experience what was going on in Hanoi, rather than just feel abstract sorrow for the American "poor pigs" who were dying in the Vietnamese jungle, or for the poor Vietnamese people. While claiming some sympathy for the pain of the mourners in Brussels, the pamphlet ended by sarcastically recommending similar actions in Berlin department stores and also the blowing up of barracks.[7] Apparently such action allowed closer identification with the struggle in Vietnam.

Following the publication of the pamphlet, seven members of Kommune 1 were put on trial for trying to incite criminal behavior, but were ultimately acquitted. During the trial, it became publicly known that three members of the Kommune I had been convicted earlier in 1967 for stealing in a supermarket. Members of the Kommune 1 also participated in demonstrations against longer opening hours for stores on Berlin's main shopping street Kurfürstendamm in August 1967.[8] Anticonsumerism was clearly a component of Kommune 1's efforts to find new forms of living and of political expression.

The connection between anti-imperialist ideologies and attacks on consumer culture was also made explicit in the first actions of what would soon become the terrorist group *Rote Armee Fraktion*, RAF. In April 1968, Ensslin, along with Andreas Baader, Thorwald Proll, and Horst Söhnlein planted bombs at two Frankfurt department stores. The explosions caused damage to goods and buildings, but no one was physically harmed. Both the bombings and the trial that followed in October 1968—in the aftermath of the May events in Paris, the assassination attempt on radical SDS leader Rudi Dutschke, and escalating confrontations between West German police and protesters—garnered national attention. The SDS initially denounced the bombings as "counter-revolutionary."[9] In a pamphlet published in *Der Spiegel* in

April, Kommune 1 also distanced itself from the bombing, at least partially: they argued that, while political arson was a daily necessity for Blacks in the United States, at present better targets existed in West Germany. However, Kommune 1 expressed "sympathy for the psychological situation that led some to employ such means" in West Germany.[10]

Ensslin in particular justified the bombing as an attempt to criticize both West German consumer culture and the Vietnam War. During the trial she claimed: "We did it in order to protest the indifference with which the people watch the genocide in Vietnam."[11] In November 1968, a few days after her conviction, she supplemented this argument on German television with her critique of consumer society. In Ensslin's view, the pressures of consumption prevented people in the metropoles, and in West Germany in particular, to notice their own lack of consciousness, to notice the involvement of their states in Vietnam, and become aware of the general misery in the Third World. Apparently the department store burning, for Ensslin an effort to deploy guerilla tactics in the metropole, was designed to wake West Germans out of their apolitical consumer stupor. Ensslin's views on guerilla tactics in the metropole were influenced by her readings on the *Black Power* movement in the United States. Thus Ensslin herself had translated Andrew Kopkind's article on the inevitability of African-American guerilla groups for a 1967 West German publication on *Black Power*. For Ensslin and other West German radicals, *Black Power* signified the need and possibility for militant struggle in industrialized nations.[12]

Others on the left highlighted the history of National Socialism as a motivating factor for the arson attack. Andreas Baader's defense attorney, Horst Mahler, for example, argued that the inaction of the parents' generation under National Socialism was now forcing the protest movement to take action in order to draw attention to the crimes committed in Vietnam.[13] Radical writer and editor Bernward Vesper, Ensslin's estranged husband, went even further and criticized the judge and the prosecutor in the trial as members of a generation who in 1938, presumably in reaction to the attacks on Jews in the Night of Broken Glass, had failed to "light department stores in protest against fascism."[14] Vesper and Ensslin appeared unaware of the position department stores held in the 1920s and 1930s in antisemitic Nazi propaganda; the Nazis had at times demanded the destruction of department stores, which they alleged were tools of the exploitation of German workers and shopkeepers by Jewish capitalists.[15]

In 1968, at least *Der Spiegel* in its commentary ignored the attempts at connecting the dangers of consumption and the Vietnam War, while others on the radical left made arguments similar to those of Ensslin.[16] After the trial, the West Berlin chapter of the SDS announced in a declaration of solidarity with the arsonists, that the "genocide in Vietnam" was a "result of the capitalist way of production in its highest, imperialist form" and "the brutal expression of a society, which attempts to suppress the true needs of the masses for autonomy through a system of *Scheinfreiheiten* (illusory freedoms)." The Berlin SDS criticized that the Vietnam War was part of attempts to secure the Third World by military means for the export of capital, the exploitation of cheap labor, and high profit margins. All this in turn was designed "to exploit the masses in capitalist countries all the more securely." The Berlin SDS described the "fireworks" in the Frankfurt department stores as a "helpless symbol" for the "crimes" "with which this imperialism covers us daily."[17] In this manifesto, the Berlin SDS made reference to the economic dimensions of First and Third World relations, and drew a close link between exploitation in both places, but with little attention to differences between the two.

The radical left columnist Ulrike Meinhof, who had not yet gone underground in 1968, also discussed the issue of consumption and the department store bombing and was fairly critical. In a commentary published in the Spring of 1968 in the leftist journal *Konkret*, she explained that such an "attack on the capitalist world of consumption" did not undermine this world of consumption, because the destruction of goods was in fact compatible with the logic of planned wear and tear in capitalism. What made the burning of a department store progressive according to Meinhof was the fact that it violated the law that protected private property, a law that was frequently used by the owners of private property to exploit those who were producing others' wealth through their labor and consumption. Meinhof doubted that this progressive vision could be transmitted to the people in the West German context. Referring to rioting and looting in the United States, Meinhof explained that "the ghetto negro, who is looting burning stores, experiences that the system does not break down ... and he can learn that a system is foul that does not provide him with what he needs to live." West Germans, clearly wealthier than poor Black Americans, could only pilfer goods from the department stores that they already owned. Citing André Gorz, Meinhof argued that, through looting, the number of goods in households would be increased which "only served as substitute satisfaction *Ersatzbefriedigung*, [and] perfected the 'private microcosm.'" The individual's reign over this private microcosm was designed "to pacify and distract from the conditions under which he has to work as a producer in society." She added that "[c]ollective desires, which remain unfulfilled in rich capitalist countries, ... would not enter people's consciousness through the burning of department stores." Like others on the left, Meinhof was sympathetic toward the anticonsumerist and anti-imperialist impulses behind the department store bombings, but doubted their effectiveness.[18]

In this article and in a second one for *Konkret* a few months later, Meinhof gave her critique of consumer society a gendered twist. The products she found worth looting were dishwashers. According to Meinhof they were still much too rare and much too expensive, but would be useful for the millions of working women; unfortunately they were also too heavy for looting.[19] In the second article in early 1969, Meinhof criticized the interests of West German capital in Iran that supported an oppressive regime there and, through pressure on West German government institutions, the oppression of protesters in West Germany. Meinhof concluded that the left had recognized the connection between "consumption terror and police terror here and the interest of German capital in the exploitation of the Persian people," but the "link between the desire for profit on the part of German capital and the oppression of women and children" remained little understood. Meinhof argued that the oppression of women needed to become part of the overall critique of the capitalist and imperialist system.[20]

In the early 1970s, after members of the RAF—joined by Meinhof and Mahler—had switched the targets of their attacks from department stores to United States military installations in West Germany, they continued to deploy references to imperialism in their analysis of the potential for revolution in industrialized capitalist countries and their identification with Third World liberation movements. But clearly none of them any longer viewed direct attacks on department stores or other symbols of capitalist consumer culture as effective. Rather, they saw their attacks on United States installations as part of the avant-garde struggle against imperialism. Taking a term from Lenin's analysis of imperialism, Horst Mahler, for example, explained in 1972 that the West German working class was among the "worker aristocracy of imperialism," profited from the exploitation of the world, and was therefore unlikely to become a revolutionary subject.[21] This analysis distinguished Mahler from the ones made by Ensslin or Meinhof earlier, where they had focused on the exploitation of workers through consumption.

Like Mahler, Meinhof in the 1970s also strongly identified with the armed liberation struggles in the Third World and believed that RAF activities were designed to hit imperialists in the metropole. But Meinhof's analysis of the situation of workers in West Germany remained different from Mahler's. According to Meinhof, workers suffered from physical exploitation in factories and also from the exploitation of their "feelings and thoughts, desires and utopias." The despotism of the capitalists became visible in the factories as well as in all other areas of life including mass consumption and the mass media. Meinhof hoped that through an act of will, workers and people on the left would overcome their apathy and join in the armed anti-imperialist struggle.[22]

From the late 1960s and into the 1970s, "consumption" and "imperialism" (like "fascism") were tropes in the critiques that leftist radicals leveled against the society of the Federal Republic and the politics of the West more generally, often without a detailed engagement with either phenomenon. For example, Members of Kommune 2, in a 1969 publication about themselves, also listed "disgust with the capitalist consumer world" and the "brutality of the imperialist system" among the factors motivating them to search for new forms of living in their efforts to undermine and change the existing social and political system.[23]

It is striking that most critiques of consumer culture that made a link between capitalism and imperialism in the late 1960s and early 1970s paid little, if any attention to the conditions of agricultural or industrial production in Third World countries. Of the voices listed above, only the Berlin SDS and Horst Mahler followed Marcuse in attacking the exploitation of workers in the Third World. To be sure, Germany was importing little from African countries in this period, but agricultural imports from South America could certainly be found on the shelves of German stores, and East Asian industrial imports were also increasing. Many West German radicals focused on the manipulation of citizens in the metropole through their engagement with consumer culture without analyzing where and how the consumed goods were produced.

But a different radical tradition also persisted, and indeed gained significance, one that criticized West German involvement in "development aid," and in this context drew attention to labor conditions in the Third World.[24] These critiques would have important repercussions in the course of the 1970s. Along with the radical criticism of Western political and social systems, demands for consumer knowledge of the conditions of production for various imports emerged. What would be considered as part of the conditions of production could range from the situations on farms or in factories, to environmental dangers, to political regimes under which producers lived. Such demands intersected with demands that consumer advocates like Ralph Nader made in the United States and West European countries. Efforts to gain the attention of companies and raise the consciousness of consumers about unsafe products, false advertising, and conditions of production made "politically motivated selective consumption" into a tool in a range of political causes.[25]

For many young people who found themselves influenced by both the radical critiques of the manipulative aspects of consumer culture and the demands for consumer responsibility for conditions of production, striving for "authenticity" appeared like a logical response in the 1960s and 1970s. Searching for authenticity took a number of routes in West

Germany and often had international dimensions, including for example the adoption of some forms of United States music and fashions, such as blues or jeans, and the consumption of music or fashions from the Third World. The search for authenticity and the demands for consumer knowledge of conditions of production in the Third World went hand-in-hand with the founding of so-called Third World stores, which imported "artisan" clothing, jewelry, and home furnishings from different parts of the globe. These stores attracted and attract customers with exotic, usually hand-made products and by associating their imports with social programs for the producers abroad. However, such desires for authenticity also can have problematic dimensions, since they frequently seek to fix an unchanging "other" untarnished by industrialization, capitalism, Westernization, or modernity more generally.[26]

Radical critiques of consumption and imperialism and the searches for authenticity through foreign imports also had an impact on larger companies and their strategies of appealing to consumers. Coffee companies for example began to show happy, independent Colombian coffee growers in their advertisements. And by the late 1980s large corporations emerged for whom attention to the conditions of production in the Third World became an organizing principle and marketing strategy. For example, the British-based chain Body Shop, present in Germany and many other countries, has used references to the conditions of production for the ingredients of its beauty products in its marketing strategies and stresses that the all-natural ingredients are produced under ecologically sound conditions. The company also responds to global feminist concerns by emphasizing that female producers in the Third World receive crucial resources through Body Shop's responsible purchases of raw materials. All this has not happened without a few scandals, and one can certainly wonder about new forms of exoticization in Body Shop's marketing strategies. Nonetheless Body Shop is part of important changes in the politics of consumption over the last thirty or so years.[27]

What I would like to argue for with this brief analysis of various ways in which links between consumer culture and international relations have been made, is a modification in studies of German consumer cultures. While histories of consumption have fruitfully connected modes of self-articulation for different groups (for example workers, or youth) and national politics,[28] we urgently need to add another dimension—how understandings of consumption relate to the understanding and obscuring of international relations and inequalities. While the reception of American imports has received considerable attention, most histories of European consumption in the twentieth century have thus far failed to take other international dimensions seriously.[29] Even analyses of American imports and Americanization need to be reformulated. My brief inquiry shows that we need to consider issues of race and West German engagements with African-American oppositional movements and their position in the United States consumer culture and political system, when we try to understand Americanization and visions of consumer culture in West Germany.

More generally, we need to explore how ideologies of consumerism have been transformed in interaction with changing foreign relations and changing relations within the nation—between women and men, between different classes and generations, and among different ethnic groups. Thus we need to examine how various groups of Germans—among them policy makers, business leaders, producers of mass culture, intellectuals, and consumers—constructed, analyzed, and contested the links that the flow of images, goods, and people forged between Germany and the world. In other words, we need to ask how Germans have reformulated the politics of consumption in transnational contexts.

In the 1960s and 1970s leftist radicals in West Germany deployed two strands of thinking about the relationship between consumption in the metropole and manifestations of imperialism abroad. In one, imperialism was a trope for immoral Western political and military action in the Third World. According to radicals, most citizens of Western countries did not resist this imperialism because their consciousness was dulled by consumer culture. In this logic department stores could become targets of arson for some on the radical left. From the 1960s onward we also see the emergence of a different stance that seeks to address international divisions of labor and wealth and urges the Western consumer to take responsibility for the conditions of production in the Third World. The latter is one of the lasting ways, in which the "children of Marx and Coca-Cola"—and some of the enterprises that cater to them—have tried to give consumption explicit political meaning.

Notes

1. Gudrun Ensslin on 4 November 1968, cited in Ingo Juchler, *Die Studentenbewegungen in den Vereinigten Staaten und der Bundesrepublik der sechziger Jahre: Eine Untersuchung hinsichtlich ihrer Beeinflussung durch Befreiungsbewegungen und -theorien aus der Dritten Welt* (Berlin, 1996), 361. On the department store arson, see also Wolfgang Ruppert, "Zur Konsumwelt der 60er Jahre," in *Dynamische Zeiten: Die 60er Jahre in den beiden deutschen Gesellschaften*, ed. Axel Schildt, Detlef Siegfried, and Karl Christian Lammers (Hamburg, 2000), 752–67, 766–67. For research assistance on this chapter, I would like to thank Katrina Hagen.
2. See Erica Carter, *How German is She? Postwar West German Reconstruction and the Consuming Woman* (Ann Arbor, 1997); Volker R. Berghahn, ed., *The Quest for Economic Empire: European Strategies of German Big Business in the Twentieth Century* (Providence, 1995).

3. Cited in Harm G. Schröter, "Marketing als angewandte Sozialtechnik und Veränderungen im Konsumverhalten: Nivea als internationale Dachmarke, 1960–1994," in *Europäische Konsumgeschichte. Zur Gesellschafts- und Kulturgeschichte des Konsums, 18. bis 20. Jahrhundert*, ed. Hannes Siegrist, Hartmut Kaelble, and Jürgen Kocka (Frankfurt am Main, 1997), 615–47, 641.

4. See Herbert Marcuse, "Die Analyse eines Exempels," in *Neue Kritik*, no. 36/37 (June 1966): 29–40. See also Herbert Marcuse, *One Dimensional Man: Studies in the Ideology of Advanced Industrial Society* (Boston, 1964); German edition: Marcuse, *Der eindimensionale Mensch: Studien zur Ideologie der fortgeschrittenen Industriegesellschaft* (Neuwied, 1967).

5. See Juchler, *Die Studentenbewegungen*.

6. Peter Gäng and Reimut Reiche, *Modelle der kolonialen Revolution* (Frankfurt am Main,1967); Paul A. Baran and Paul M. Sweezy, *Monopoly Capital: An Essay on the American Economic and Social Order* (New York, 1966); Reimut Reiche, *Sexualität und Klassenkampf: Zur Abwehr repressiver Entsublimierung* (Frankfurt am Main, 1968). Marcuse himself referenced Baran/Sweezy. On the reception in West Germany, see also Frederico Hermanin, Karin Monte, and Claus Rolshausen, *Monopolkapital: Thesen zu dem Buch von Paul A. Baran und Paul M. Sweezy* (Frankfurt am Main, 1969).

7. Kommune 1, "NEU! UNKONVENTIONELL!," 1967 May 24, Stanford University Libraries, Special Collections M 613 (hereafter cited as M 613), Box 35, Folder 1.

8. Rainer Langhans und Fritz Teufel, *Klau mich* (Frankfurt am Main, 1968).

9. Cited in Bernward Vesper's afterword to Andreas Baader, Gudrun Ensslin, Thorwald Proll, and Horst Söhnlein, *Vor einer solchen Justiz verteidigen wir uns nicht* (Frankfurt am Main, 1968), 19.

10. "Stellungnahme der Berliner Kommune I für den *Spiegel*," *Der Spiegel*, 8 April 1968.

11. Gudrun Ensslin, quoted in Juchler, *Studentenbewegungen*, 361.

12. *Black Power: Die Ursachen des Guerillakampfes in den Vereinigten Staaten. Zwei Analysen* (Berlin, 1967). See Juchler, *Studentenbewegungen*, especially 249–55.

13. See Juchler, *Studentenbewegungen*, 361, 362.

14. Vesper's afterword, 19.

15. See for example, "Program of the National German Workers' Party," 1920, in *Documents on the Holocaust: Selected Sources on the Destruction of the Jews of Germany and Austria, Poland, and the Soviet Union*, ed. Yitzhak Arad, Yisrael Gutman, and Abraham Margaliot (Jerusalem, 1981), 15–18.

16. "Prozesse: Kaufhausbrand," *Der Spiegel*, 4 November 1968, 67.

17. Erklärung des Landesverbandes Berlin des SDS zum sogenannten Brandstiftungsprozess, in Baader, Ensslin, Proll, and Söhnlein, *Vor einer solchen Justiz verteidigen wir uns nicht*, 26–27. See also Juchler, *Studentenbewegungen*, 362.

18. Ulrike Meinhof, "Warenhausbrandstiftung," *Konkret*, no. 14 (1968), reprinted in *Ulrike Meinhof: Dokumente einer Rebellion* (Copenhagen, 1972), M 613, Box 38.

19. Meinhof, "Warenhausbrandstiftung."

20. Ulrike Meinhof, "Alle reden vom Wetter," *Konkret*, no. 4 (1969), reprinted in *Ulrike Meinhof: Dokumente*.

21. Horst Mahler, "Erklärung zum Prozessbeginn," cited in Iring Fetscher and Günter Rohrmoser, *Analysen zum Terrorismus 1: Ideologien und Strategien* (Opladen, 1981), 48ff.

22. Ulrike Meinhof, "Die Aktion des Schwarzen September in München," cited in Fetscher and Rohrmoser, 56–57. See also Fetscher and Rohrmoser, 53-61.

23. Kommune 2, *Versuch der Revolutionierung des bürgerlichen Individuums* (Berlin, 1969), 13.

24. See for example, Republikanischer Club, "Entwicklungshilfe als Geschäft: Vietnam-Informationen 1," no date (1967) in LOG Sondernummer: Dokumentation Berliner Flugblätter II, M 613, Box 35, Folder 5.

25. See the the introduction to the volume by Axel Schildt and Detlef Siegfried.

26. On the quest for authenticity in the 1960s and 1970s, see Detlef Siegfried, "White Negroes: Westdeutsche Faszinationen des Echten," in *Bye Bye Lübben City. Bluesfreaks, Tramps und Hippies in der DDR*, ed. Michael Rauhut and Thomas Kochan (Berlin, 2004), 333–344.

27. See the Body Shop company website at http://www.thebodyshop.com/web/tbsgl/about.jsp.

28. See for example, Victoria de Grazia, ed., *The Sex of Things: Gender and Consumption in Historical Perspective* (Berkeley, 1996); Uta G. Poiger, *Jazz, Rock, and Rebels: American Culture in a Divided Germany* (Berkeley, 2000); Alon Confino and Rudy Koshar, "Regimes of Consumer Culture: New Narratives in Twentieth-Century German History," *German History* 19 (2001):135–61; Konrad H. Jarausch and Michael Geyer, *Shattered Past: Reconstructing German Histories* (Princeton, 2002), 269–314.

29. On this point see also Craig Clunas, "Modernity Global and Local: Consumption and the Rise of the West," *American Historical Review* 104 (1999): 1497–511; Volker Wünderich, "Zum globalen Kontext von Konsumgesellschaft und Konsumgeschichte: Kritische und weiterführende Überlegungen," in *Europäische Konsumgeschichte*, ed. Siegrist, Kaelble, and Kocka, 793–810.

Part III

Political Protest

Chapter 8

"Burn, ware-house, burn!" Modernity, Counterculture, and the Vietnam War in West Germany

Wilfried Mausbach

When, in the spring of 1967, West Berlin's notorious "drop out" group Kommune 1 (K1) adapted the rallying cry of African-American ghetto rioters from Watts to Detroit, their slightly crooked English hardly confused readers of their leaflet: the targets of their wrath were not warehouses but department stores, the shrines to consumerism. There is a certain irony in this. After all, one of the motives for poor blacks in America's urban ghettos in setting cars and white-owned businesses ablaze was "to assert their unrequited plea for all the decencies and dignities possessed by other Americans."[1] They rioted partly, then, to partake in the very consumerism that the K1 scolded for seducing the masses. The communards of West Berlin felt that the desires created through marketing and advertising diverted people from their real interests and numbed them with regard to moral outrages like the Vietnam War.

This strand of antimaterialism and cultural criticism took its cue, of course, from the writings of the Frankfurt School of social philosophers, who, as emigrants to the United States, had developed their ideas against the backdrop of America's rapidly expanding consumer society. In a way, however, the Frankfurt School's cultural criticism represented only the estranged sibling of a much older tradition of German cultural pessimism that dated back to at least the early nineteenth century and that had always employed America as a cipher for the disquieting aspects of modernity. Both varieties bemoaned the alienation of mass man brought about by industrial society. Their prescriptions, to be sure, turned out to be diametrically opposed; but the diagnosis nevertheless reveals important similarities. Among them was a preoccupation with technology and bureaucratization as well as a deep mistrust of consumer society and popular culture. This chapter will trace some of these currents in West German protests against the Vietnam War, including the activities of the K1.

More than any other faction of the West German student movement, the K1 also exemplifies the countercultural suffusion of the movement. As we shall see, this is not least apparent in the group's anti-war leaflets, which recycled particular aspects of consumer society in order to ironically comment on the apathy of West Germans in the face of Vietnamese suffering. In borrowing, recontextualizing, and redirecting principal forms of consumer culture, the K1 thus reflected an important characteristic of the counterculture. Hippies and other youths, though still vaguely informed by cultural criticism, actively used certain features of consumer society to mark out spaces for themselves and develop their own identities. In fact, counterculture and consumer society fed on each other, and this symbiosis may well have done more than anything else— and certainly more than intellectual prophecies of doom—to spread the cultural revolution of the 1960s.

Of Ants and Americans

Modernity, according to Max Weber, was characterized by the spread of markets, democracy, technology, and bureaucracy. Mid-twentieth-century sociologists regarded especially technology and bureaucracy as closely intertwined. To be sure, human anxiety about the former considerably predates concern about the latter, going back at least as far as Gutenberg's printing press. People's worries grew rapidly, however, with the advent of industrial machinery at the close of the eighteenth century. In nineteenth-century Germany, the debate about the promises and pitfalls of industrialization unfolded with constant reference to the most advanced technological society of the age: the United States.

As Volker Depkat has shown, many Germans began to identify America as the land of technological progress only after it had lost its appeal as the standard-bearer of Enlightenment principles, i.e., of humanistic progress.[2] More and more visitors professed to be shocked by a crass materialism that stood in stark contrast to the idealistic notions formerly held about the United States. Wrote Nikolaus Lenau in 1832: "Brother, the petty-mindedness of these Americans stinks to high heaven. Dead when it comes to spiritual life, dead as a doornail."[3] Stereotypes like these provided a convenient "other" against which the German bourgeoisie could develop a clearly circumscribed image of itself. If Americans reduced the idea of progress to mere material improvement, which they strove to achieve through technical devices, the German *Bildungsbürgertum* was concerned with a higher, humanistic progress, which it strove to achieve through aesthetic and intellectual education.

Here we can sense, of course, the fateful dichotomy between civilization and culture which became a hallmark of German intellectual thought from the late nineteenth to the mid-twentieth centuries. In this view, civilization was seen as outer-directed, mechanical and shallow, whereas culture embodied inner values, organic growth and spiritual depth. This antithesis lay at the heart of a German cultural pessimism that ranted against modernity, democracy, and the West—all prominently epitomized by the United States.[4] Around 1900 Friedrich Gundolf voiced concern that "the last remains of all substance will vanish in fifty more years of incessant progress …, when the urban-progressive infection of traffic, dailies, schools, factories, and barracks will have penetrated the most remote corner of the world, when the satanic topsy-turvy America-world, the ant-world, will have arrived for good."[5] To Gundolf and many like-minded critics, the fragmentation of society and the mechanization of life resulted in isolation and atomization. Not only did industrialization force humans to bustle around mindlessly in monotonous work processes, but huge machines, massive tenements, and tremendous skyscrapers also made them shrink to ant-like proportions.

Cultural pessimism did not necessarily entail opposition against all aspects of modernity. Jeffrey Herf has demonstrated that many German intellectual and cultural conservatives actually embraced modern technology during the 1920s and 1930s.[6] Even more pointedly, he has argued, "technological pessimism in the tradition of radical, that is, illiberal and antidemocratic German conservatism is less a product of the famous revolt against modernity of the period 1870 to 1945 than of the unconditional, unambiguous defeat of Nazi Germany in 1945."[7] This proposition, however, tends to minimize the considerable ambiguity that characterized German attitudes toward technology in the interwar period and it ignores strong continuities from the 1920s to the 1950s, instead identifying the New Left of the 1960s as the resuscitator of technological pessimism. To be sure, businessmen, engineers and even some conservative intellectuals welcomed technological rationalization or at least acknowledged it as inevitable.[8] As Herf makes clear, however, they sought to insulate this rationalization from other concomitants of modernity lest social leveling, democratization or mass consumption threaten existing hierarchies. Thus, German proponents of technocracy took pains to portray their ideas as originating in genuinely German traditions.[9] Similarly, National Socialist modernizers presented technology as a means for cultural uplift, thereby relocating it from the seamy sphere of civilization to the noble realm of culture.[10] Reactionary modernists, then, aimed to integrate technology into traditional German political, social and cultural patterns rather than adjust those patterns to a modernizing world. This in itself is a sure sign of the shadow cultural pessimism still cast on debates about technology. After all, liberal and reactionary modernists faced an equally numerous and probably even more vocal coalition of antimodernist writers, journalists and intellectuals.[11] Gottfried Benn complained that "all German literature since 1918 has been trading on the slogans 'tempo,' or 'jazz,' or 'cinema,' or 'overseas,' or 'technical activity,' while all problems of the mind and the emotions have been pointedly dismissed."[12] The cover of Adolf Halfeld's influential book *Amerika und der Amerikanismus* bore the inscription: "The culture of Europe, in particular of Germany, developed by tradition, is threatened by America with its concentration on materialism and the mechanization of life. Rationalization on the American example is trump, regardless of whether it kills the human in mankind."[13] In 1931, Karl Jaspers identified technology and the machine as the most threatening phenomena of the time, profoundly rupturing human existence.[14] Two years later, Theodor Haecker explained that human dignity and technical functionality were incompatible. Because man's rhythm of life was subjected to the beat of the machine, he was forced to step out of "the order of being" and subordinate himself to the order of the machine.[15] Finally, in 1934, Werner Sombart set the tone already for the postwar period when he warned that technology acquired a life of its own, independent of and not controllable by mankind.[16]

This notion was picked up by many cultural critics after 1945.[17] Friedrich Georg Jünger, less famous than his brother Ernst, published a book that included a chapter titled "Technology Serves Not Mankind but Itself."[18] In a study that was very influential in Germany, the French sociologist Jacques Ellul radicalized the concept of technology by systematically exploring how technology developed autonomously and how it eventually shaped the course of society rather than the other way round.[19] The modern industrial state regarded human beings no longer as full persons but only as functions in the realms of production, consumption, and administration. In a seminal work published in 1955, the prominent German sociologist Hans Freyer termed these realms "secondary systems" (*sekundäre Systeme*), implicitly setting them apart from a primary social order that was supposedly more appropriate to human nature.[20] The domination of "secondary systems," therefore, resulted in loneliness and alienation.

But the conclusions Freyer drew from this diagnosis differed significantly from his prewar position, when he had already identified technology as a threat to cultural unity and accused modernity of destroying identity and meaning. Whereas during the interwar period he had called for a conservative revolution and hoped that an authoritarian state could stabilize the traditional order, he now resigned himself to the domination of life by "secondary systems" and merely recommended a commitment to tradition in order to alleviate the inevitable alienation.[21] This deradicalization of German conservatism is also apparent in the work of Freyer's most prominent students, Arnold Gehlen and Helmut Schelsky. In his first major postwar work, Gehlen had analyzed how technology rode roughshod over primary human instincts and how technological rationality had imposed itself even in non-technical contexts.[22] As a remedy, he called for the re-establishment of a system of social rank. His later work, however, is characterized by a resignation similar to that of Freyer. Gehlen no longer advocates alternative designs to overcome the domination of technology but rather accepts that progress will henceforth only be possible on a stationary basis.[23] At most, people could retire into an individual asceticism. Like Gehlen and Freyer, Helmut Schelsky, probably the most influential German sociologist of the 1950s and early 1960s, observed that societal development had ceased to be determined by ideologies or political norms and was now completely driven by technological requirements or *Sachgesetzlichkeiten* with inherent goals which did not need any further legitimation.[24] Domination no longer had any subject, and criticism remained without practical consequences—a mere ritual to sooth the soul.[25] In the characterization of the times, intellectuals and politicians alike referred to traditional images without advocating the old solutions. Even Ludwig Erhard, the revered father of West Germany's economic miracle, warned of the threatening termite-state, while personifying the extent to which Germans had made themselves comfortable in the modern world.[26]

It is true, then, that the German discourse on technology had markedly shifted by the early 1960s. While conservatives still lamented the imperatives of the technological age, calls to transcend it originated mainly from the political left. However, there is a strange and not as yet thoroughly analyzed interchange of concepts and ideas between technological pessimists on both sides of the ideological aisle. Perhaps most remarkable is the proliferation of the Hegelian-Marxist concept of alienation among conservative intellectuals. At the same time, it has been occasionally observed that the diagnosis of cultural crisis provided by the Frankfurt School of critical theorists is almost indistinguishable from its conservative counterparts.[27] Already in the 1950s, Edward Shils summarized this diagnosis, calling it "at bottom, romanticism dressed up in the language of sociology, psychoanalysis and existentialism. ... [T]he ordinary citizen ... is standardized, ridden with anxiety, perpetually in a state of 'exacerbated' unrest, his life 'emptied of meaning,' and 'trivial-ized,' 'alienated from his past, from his community, and possibly from himself,' … depersonalized and degraded to the point where he is a cog in an impersonal industrial machine."[28] To be sure, the critical theorists of the Frankfurt School—contrary to their reactionary opposites—had no intention to turn back the clock or even to contain the consequences of modernity. Instead, they tried to reach beyond it—to a society where human beings would be freed from what Max Weber had termed the "iron cage" of modernity. If, during the 1920s and early 1930s, Hans Freyer believed that only a conservative revolution could save cultural unity, Max Horkheimer, appointed director of the Frankfurt Institute of Social Research in 1930, hoped that a proletarian revolution would overcome the problems of modernity.[29] Yet Horkheimer and his colleagues shared with conservatives an indebtedness to Hegel's philosophy and a deep pessimism of the legacy of the Enlightenment. Following Max Weber, they believed that reason had lost its liberatory potential. The logic of technological mastery over nature and humanity alike had led to the exclusive domination of mere instrumental rationality in society. Wrote Herbert Marcuse in 1941: "As the laws and mechanisms of technological rationality spread over the whole society, they develop a set of truth values of their own which hold good for the functioning of the apparatus—and for that alone. … Rationality here calls for unconditional compliance …" Technology was thus also "an instrument for control and domination."[30] In fact, members of the Institute of Social Research regarded National Socialism in no way as a relapse into premodern behavior but rather as the apotheosis of technical rationality. "The Third Reich is indeed a form of 'technocracy,'" stated Marcuse, while Horkheimer assured him that he himself viewed National Socialism as the "triumph of reason purified by scepticism."[31] This is a preview, of course, to Horkheimer and Theodor W. Adorno's classic *Dialectic of Enlightenment*, in which instrumental reason figures as a key to understanding Auschwitz.[32] It is also another parallel to conservative interpretations after 1945, which similarly looked to universal trends rather than to the peculiarities of German history in order to explain the rise of National Socialism.[33] For both Adorno and Martin Heidegger National Socialism represented an effort to arrive at a totality of technical production (*Totalisierung des technischen Herstellens*).[34]

Martin Heidegger's considerable early influence on Herbert Marcuse has sometimes been cited as a source for the latter's technological pessimism.[35] It was indeed Marcuse who returned with a vengeance to his earlier work on technological rationality during the 1960s. In his *One-Dimensional Man*, unquestionably one of the most influential books of the decade, he warned that a "false consciousness has become embodied in the prevailing technical apparatus which in turn reproduces it …

Today, domination perpetuates and extends itself not only through technology but *as* technology, and the latter provides the great legitimation of the expanding political power, which absorbs all spheres of culture."[36] Marcuse's propositions had a tremendous impact on the New Left. He has been called a spiritual father to German student leader Rudi Dutschke and identified as "the most widely discussed thinker within the American left" of the 1960s; it has even been suggested that he himself became "something of a commodity" to the movement.[37] There can be no doubt that Herbert Marcuse was crucial in shaping the movement's perception of technology. As Andrew Feenberg has observed, "Technology was the enemy in the way the state had been in an earlier era; to revolt was to reclaim humanity against the machine."[38]

The American war machine in Vietnam occupied a prominent place in this worldview. This is true in several distinct though interrelated respects. First, the tools of war implemented by the United States in Vietnam epitomized the dark side of technological progress. Not surprisingly, indignation at the American type of warfare imbues the literature of anti-war activists. When protest in Germany was still in its infancy, the Berlin chapter of the German Socialist Students League (*Sozialistischer Deutscher Studentenbund,* SDS) disseminated a leaflet that focused in particular on the techniques and gadgets of destruction from carpet bombings to defoliation to remote control bombs and extremely light automatic rifles.[39] The lyricist Arnfried Astel explained in a poem called "New Weapon" how new munitions supposedly used by American soldiers in Vietnam spun like a top in the victim's body, triggering a hydrodynamic shock that would paralyze the entire nervous system.[40] The International Vietnam Tribunal in Stockholm heard testimony on American cluster bombs, stressing their indiscriminate and devastating effects.[41] Indochina hearings held by an umbrella organization of German anti-war groups dealt extensively with technological aspects of the war. Newspaper clippings later compiled about the testimony reported a switch to electronics in what was termed "the American death machinery."[42]

Vietnam was generally portrayed as a field of experimentation for new American weaponry in much the same way the Spanish Civil War had been for Nazi Germany in the 1930s. The widely read journalist Bernard Fall maintained in 1965 that "the situation in Vietnam isn't Munich; it is Spain. ... above all, there is a test of military technology and techniques and military ideas."[43] The parallel proliferated quickly also among German protesters; but it did not stop there.[44] Writing under the pseudonym Georg W. Alsheimer, the physician Erich Wulff, who taught and practiced at the University of Hué in Vietnam, accused the Americans of making a hypocritical distinction between technologically primitive murder committed by Vietnamese guerrillas and the neat and orderly industrial extermination they carried out themselves. In the latter case, he added scornfully, a man could of course keep his personal decency.[45] This thinly veiled reference to an infamous remark by SS chief Heinrich Himmler signified an increasing tendency among German anti-war protesters to compare Vietnam to Auschwitz, the epitome of technological mass murder.[46]

The stark contrast between primitive jungle warriors and "the American technico-military Behemoth"[47] also furthered a romantic identification with Vietnamese guerrillas. These tenacious peasants perfectly fitted the image of ant-like human beings struggling ferociously against the results of technological rationality. Their adhesion to nature only underscored this impression that was captured by Günter Kunert in a poem:[48]

> One so small, the other
> so huge: Mr. Goliath, professional colossus,
> swinging the cudgel of tactical air wings
> against David, his green armor the jungle

Anti-war activists were fascinated by the sight of America's "shiny war machine bogged down in the underbrush in Vietnam."[49] Neither was the contrast lost on Herbert Marcuse. In a letter to Max Horkheimer he stressed that "the rulers of the West, with the whole brutally efficient technological perfection of Western civilization," were systematically starving out, incinerating and destroying the pitiful life of their Vietnamese opponents—a life which, "through dreadful toil and with enormous sacrifices," had just become a little more human.[50]

But Marcuse and many of his admirers within the New Left linked an additional and important aspect to this struggle between primitive freedom fighters and high-tech American forces: the former would help to break the spell of technological rationality captivating the advanced industrial world. This could be accomplished if, as Marcuse told students at the Free University of Berlin in July 1967, the Vietnamese guerrillas demonstrated "that the human will and the human body with the poorest weapons can keep in check the most efficient system of destruction of all times." Vietnam was then "in no way just one more event of foreign policy but rather connected with the essence of the system, [and] perhaps also a turning point in the development of the system, perhaps the beginning of the end."[51] In a broader cultural sense, Marcuse hoped that the traditions of non-Western societies might work to sever the fatal link between technology and domination in Western countries.[52]

The Banality of Evil

Technological determinists, who believed that technology shaped the development of society, also found that it reinforced tendencies toward bureaucratic centralization. The study of bureaucracy started from Max Weber's proposition that it represented the form of administration congenial to societies that legitimate power through rational-legal authority. Bureaucracies try to minimize, if not to eliminate, the influence of personal interests, individual predilections and moral considerations upon the efficient completion of assigned tasks. The heartless and faceless bureaucrat was a major topic of intellectuals and sociologists throughout the 1950s. On the left, the Frankfurt School exaggerated Weber's diagnosis in theories of an administered society (*verwaltete Welt*). Among the public at large, the figure of the bureaucrat owed his prominence mostly to the gloomy fictional accounts of George Orwell and Franz Kafka. A German translation of Orwell's *1984* was published in 1950, at about the same time that a complete edition of Kafka's work reached the bookstores.[53] This helped to prepare the ground for the minor sensation caused by the renowned sociologist Alfred Weber in 1953, when he warned of the so-called "fourth man," a robot-like bureaucratic terror machine.[54] Weber's book can be seen as the German counterpart to William H. Whyte's immensely popular description of *The Organization Man* three years later.[55] Both evoked the nightmare of a technocratic class capable of any task and able to follow any command without moral misgivings.

In the early 1960s this scenario received a dramatic boost with the trial of Adolf Eichmann, head of the Gestapo section in charge of the extermination of European Jews, and the publication of Hannah Arendt's controversial book about the trial. Eichmann came across not as the demonic monster many people expected but as the quintessential *Schreibtischtäter*—a mindless paper-pusher, an utterly ordinary if all-too-efficient bureaucrat. Hannah Arendt captured this glaring absence of any particular wickedness, pathology, or ideological conviction in her succinct and catchy phrase "the banality of evil."[56] The fierce controversy that erupted in the wake of Arendt's book ensured that the notion of administrative mass murder was rapidly popularized.[57] Christopher Browning later stated concisely what more and more people came to accept during the 1960s: "The Nazi mass murder of the European Jewry was not only the technological achievement of an industrial society, but also the organizational achievement of a bureaucratic society."[58] This, of course, had wider implications, as Daniel Bell pointed out in his review of Arendt's book: "The frightening prospect it disclosed was that, given the structural tendencies of modern societies to centralize power and to manipulate vast numbers of men through the agencies of state coercion, the totalitarian potential was an ever-recurrent one."[59] And indeed, the New Left wasted no time in applying this lesson to the Vietnam War.

In the United States, Carl Oglesby, president of the Students for a Democratic Society (SDS), conjured up Adolf Eichmann's image when he exclaimed at an anti-war rally in November 1965: "Think of the men who now engineer that war—those who study the maps, give the commands, push the buttons, and tally the dead: Bundy, McNamara, Rusk, Lodge, Goldberg, the President himself. They are not moral monsters. They are all honorable men."[60] The critic and historian Lewis Mumford lamented: "In every country there are now countless Eichmanns in administrative offices, in business corporations, in universities, in laboratories, in the armed forces: orderly obedient people, ready to carry out any officially sanctioned fantasy, however dehumanized and debased."[61] Sociologically, a major problem of large administrative units is the separation of tasks, "which distances the contributor from the job performed by the bureaucracy of which he is a part. ... It is one thing to give a command to load bombs on the plane, but quite different to take care of regular steel supply in a bomb factory."[62] As Herbert Marcuse pointed out, however, even the pilot who releases the bombs was fatefully removed from the plight of his victims under the conditions of modern technological warfare. "The new forms of aggression destroy without somebody getting his hands dirty, his body besmeared or his conscience burdened."[63] The New Left on both sides of the Atlantic therefore concluded that it was surrounded by Eichmanns who were conducting or abetting a modern genocidal war in Southeast Asia.[64]

The battle lines were drawn, then, not just between Americans and Vietnamese, but between technocrats everywhere in the industrialized world and those who tried to overcome the stale and bureaucratic one-dimensional society. As Richard Shaull wrote in a book that was also quickly published in a German translation: "The new revolutionary has made his appearance at the moment of most extraordinary advance in technology. Thus we have two prototypes of the new man who is emerging in our time: the revolutionary and the technocrat. They look at the modern world from very different perspectives and represent two sharply contrasting styles of life; and both are products of our Western history."[65] The German writer Martin Walser thus welcomed the incoming Nixon administration as "the new technocrats," though he also indicated that it was exactly their and their predecessors' behavior in Vietnam, which had broken the hitherto all-encompassing numbing of conscience.[66] To this numbing of conscience and its cause we will now turn.

The Cunning of Consumerism

Technological change involved yet another epochal transformation: the advent of mass production and, along with it, mass consumption. Conservatives saw therein one more threat to social order. Mass consumption tended to level social hierarchies and to shift the power to define societal values from closely circumscribed circles to the average consumer. As Ernest van den Haag observed in 1960: "Initiative, and power to bestow prestige and income, have shifted from the elite to the mass. ... the elite is no longer protected from the demands of the mass consumers."[67]

While critical theorists shared their conservative counterpart's disdain of consumer society, they did so for diametrically opposed reasons. Whereas conservatives attributed to consumerism an almost revolutionary potential, many on the political left countered that it in fact absorbed any progressive energies. To the members of the Institute of Social Research, this link provided an answer to the haunting question of why the working class had failed so miserably in the face of fascism. The experience of a fully developed consumer society in the United States convinced the Frankfurt emigrants that revolution was impossible under the conditions of mass production and mass consumption, or what they called advanced industrial society.[68] Consumerism, they felt, neutralized the alienation experienced in the workplace. In supplying an illusion of freedom (i.e., freedom of choice) and pleasure, it provided a palliative for repression and deadened the capacity to conceive of a better world or even to note the nightmares of the contemporary world.

It was in an effort to break this consumerist lock on human conscience, that the K1 designed a series of leaflets in the spring of 1967. The occasion was a tragedy in Brussels, where a department store had burnt down, killing hundreds of customers and arousing great sympathy in Germany. Responding to the discrepancy in the German public's reaction to the events in Belgium and Vietnam, the K1 disseminated its own ironical comments on the catastrophe. In doing so, the authors of the leaflets deliberately recycled the very strategies they held responsible for the public's apathy toward the Vietnam War. Thus the headline of one leaflet imitated ticker-like headers of mass tabloids and the language of aggressive advertising campaigns: "New! Unconventional! New! Breathtaking!" The text then went on to praise the creativity of American advertising: "Coca-Cola and Hiroshima, the German economic miracle and the Vietnamese war ... represent the fascinating and exciting feats and world-famous trademarks of American energy and American inventive genius." The leaflet portrayed the fire in Brussels as "a new gimmick in the versatile history of American publicity gags," and an innovative one at that: "For the first time, a burning department store with people ablaze has conveyed to a European metropolis this crackling Vietnam feeling."[69] Casting off the mantle of advertising manager, the group in its next pamphlet reiterated this cynically inverted longing for a connection between events in Southeast Asia and Europe: "Our Belgian friends have finally gotten the knack of letting the public really partake in the funny hustle and bustle in Vietnam; they set a department store on fire, three hundred prosperous citizens lose their exciting lives, and Brussels becomes Hanoi. ... burn, ware-house, burn!"[70]

When Berlin prosecutors indicted the presumed authors of these lines, Rainer Langhans and Fritz Teufel, on charges of instigating arson, the defense asked several professors sympathetic to the movement to act as expert witnesses with regard to the meaning of the leaflets. In his brief, Peter Szondi of the Free University's German Department stressed that the ironic nature of the leaflets ruled out the possibility of taking the incriminating passages at face value. The authors were, in fact, putting words into the mouths of supporters of the American policy in Vietnam. By borrowing these words from the realm of advertising, they implied that those convictions stemmed not from rational deliberation but rather from the sort of dubious emotions that, in modern advertising, increasingly displaced the actual qualities of a product. The said supporters were, then, actually enjoying the war, and the leaflet simply promised an intensification of this pleasure by way of a more direct involvement. Such promises, wrote Szondi, were typical of advertisements for television sets; applied to the Vietnam War they meant that the "consumer" would be put in a position in which he or she was able to experience *in reality* the fate of bombed Vietnamese citizens.[71]

Conspicuously absent from the sympathetic expert witnesses was Theodor W. Adorno—the critical theorist whose thinking had clearly informed the authors of the leaflets. In fact, Adorno had been asked to prepare a brief, but declined. When he visited the Free University for a guest lecture shortly thereafter, students were openly scornful of his refusal. An SDS leaflet remarked that someone who had written so eloquently on the commodity structure of society and on the culture industry would have been predestined to explain the K1's motivation.[72] To the students, Adorno's refusal demonstrated once again how stubbornly the Frankfurt philosophers shied away from following up their critical theories with personal action—a failure that was rapidly alienating the antiauthoritarians from their spiritual fathers.[73] Unbeknownst to the students, Adorno had in fact commented on the K1 pamphlets. However, he had not done so for the benefit of the proceedings in Berlin, nor would the students have much liked what he had to say. In a letter to Max Horkheimer, he had accused the movement of an unreflected, pure and simple actionism (*puren begriffslosen Praktizismus*) and had found that the Kommune's leaflets had "truly crossed the line of what we may tolerate, even in the sense in which Wotan was forbearing with Siegfried's smashing his spear."[74] This reference to the *Nibelungenlied,* the most Germanic of myths, perfectly encapsulates the distance between Adorno and the anti-authoritarians of the 1960s.

What irritated Adorno at least as much as the bizarre notion to create Vietnamese conditions in Europe, were the forms the K1 used to express its ideas. As Alexander Kluge, who later became a renowned film producer, pointed out in his brief for the Berlin proceedings, these forms derived from pop-literature.[75] The K1 was thus simply reflecting the infatuation of youth with pop culture, i.e., with the artifacts and urban lifestyles of contemporary consumer society. Starting in the early to mid-1950s and encouraged by flagging parental control and increasing amounts of money at their own disposal, teenagers and young adolescents had managed to carve out an autonomous subculture of their own, delimited from the larger society by conspicuous tastes in music, hairstyles, and fashion.[76] While advertisers discovered therein "a caste, a culture, a market,"[77] the wider public viewed this new phenomenon with apprehension, and Germans in particular feared the manipulation of youth through consumerism. As Uta Poiger has shown, however, experts and authorities in the Federal Republic attempted to recast the discourse on youthful deviance during the latter 1950s in order to make consumption central to West German identity.[78] At the same time, young artists and writers throughout the Western world began to incorporate expressions of consumer society into their work in ways that ranged from celebratory to cynical.[79] It is this ambiguous interaction of youth culture and contemporary consumer society that provided the background for the manifestations of the K1.

There is no question that the K1 was one of the major catalysts for a youthful counterculture in Germany, even though this might have been due more to the fantasies that many young people projected into the group than to its own activities.[80] Certainly the communards aggressively cultivated their image as the vanguard of playful provocation and sexual liberation. The mass media played an indispensable part in this endeavor. Most important in this regard were the tabloids of the conservative Springer publishing house, which—in an effort to both reflect and further incite public outrage—hurled abuse after abuse at the communards. Soon, the K1's increasing notoriety attracted other dailies and weeklies as well as domestic and international television crews. In the end, there were regular teenage pilgrimages to the building at *Stuttgarter Platz.* When Uschi Obermeier, Rainer Langhans' girlfriend and a model, moved in with the group, the couple perfectly embodied the Kommune's symbiosis of counterculture and mass culture.

Movement participants who favored earnest theoretical discussions over happenings and hedonism observed the prominent splinter group with open suspicion. Klaus Rainer Röhl, in an insert to his leftist magazine *Konkret*, filed the following report: "Such is life in the Kommune. In the midst of overloud beat music, fug, and chatter left and right, I try to find out what they want and what they mean. That's hard, because the talk is confused … Having understood neither Mao, nor Marx, nor Marcuse, they are talking drivel with shining eyes. Their language is childish-teenage-like." Nevertheless, Röhl warned, the popularity of the communards threatened to drown out more serious voices: "None of Rudi Dutschke's brilliant analyses, no dynamic action of the SDS that could not be brushed aside with a reference to the Kommune 1."[81] Not surprisingly, Dutschke's own attitude toward the communards remained ambivalent, and the SDS had in fact already expelled the group prior to the leaflets episode.[82]

Meanwhile, however, the number of communes seeking to disrupt the system through personal lifestyles rather than political agitation had mushroomed. Less prominent than the K1, they were certainly more important for the diffusion of movement ideas and alternative lifestyles into society at large, i.e., for the cultural revolution.[83] But at the same time, many leaders of the New Left feared that those commune-dwellers, often immersed in the broader counterculture, would dilute the revolutionary determination of the movement. Bahman Nirumand, the prominent Persian dissident within the German New Left, offered the following calibration of the movement: first, the great mass of people who no longer wanted to be part of a trained civilization; then, the smaller group of jazz enthusiasts who, although quite opinionated, dismissed the stupidity of politicians and rather discussed the split-tone multiphonics of John Coltrane; finally, an elite of happening-aficionados, oppositional artists and anti-philosophers, who "know their Marx and their Adorno, Winnie, Zen, and Superman." To Nirumand, all these subcultures were themselves conformist. "Truth is the latest fashion. Commitment gets paid in coin of the realm … The shamelessness of sing-out puppets returns multiplied in the guitar as the fetish of a hypocritical rebellion."[84] When the movement splintered into myriads of groups with Marxist-Leninist, Maoist, Trotskyist or some other outlook, anxiety became even more pronounced. Many activists–turned–doctrinaires bemoaned the rampant growth of a leftist subculture that allegedly offered perfunctory pleasures to those who had to wage an anti-authoritarian struggle full of privation. In view of the seeming intensification of class struggle, some therefore worried that "only a few comrades are subjectively capable to muster the necessary realistic revolutionary asceticism and discipline."[85]

It was exactly the absence of asceticism and earnestness, the homage to hedonism and playfulness among the communards and their like that put off Adorno. Himself a prototypical product of the *Bildungsbürgertum* tradition forged in the nineteenth century, Adorno insisted that only strenuous effort could produce anything of value. Even his difficult prose has been interpreted as "a direct challenge to the reader to respond with commensurate seriousness."[86] Not surprisingly, Adorno also adhered to a classical concept of leisure which valued aesthetic education in the fine arts instead of the modern variant of idle consumerism. Indeed, elaborating on Marx's suggestion of a dialectical relationship between consumption and production, he argued that the mass cultural diversions "occupying men's senses from the time they leave the factory in the evening to the time they clock in again the next morning" did bear the same "impress of the labor process they themselves have to sustain throughout the day," thus infecting leisure time with the same economically structured and profit-oriented activity that dominated work hours.[87] Consumption, then, was nothing but a concealed continuation of production by other means. In joining technologically driven and bureaucratically controlled economic and cultural mass production (including consumption), the culture industry overwhelmed any idea of protest and created a society that was integrated to a much larger degree than heretofore imaginable.

For many within the New Left, the Vietnam War opened up the possibility that this total integration of advanced industrial societies might be relieved from the outside. A victory of the National Liberation Front in Vietnam would encourage other Third World countries to resist integration into the capitalist system, thus undermining the reproductive capacities of that system. This would in turn make it impossible for capitalism to maintain the consumerist strategies that had arrested class antagonism within advanced industrial countries.[88] Herbert Marcuse supported this analysis and even contributed to it through a talk he gave at an SDS congress in Frankfurt in May 1966, the first anti-Vietnam event in Germany with countrywide participation.[89] His former colleague Theodor W. Adorno, on the other hand, would not pin his hopes on the underdeveloped world.

Adorno saw one last refuge for social negativity: art. Interestingly, Martin Heidegger arrived at the same conclusion, viewing art as the last possible salvation from the technological stance.[90] And indeed, there is in Adorno's understanding of art a good deal of the high esteem for inwardness which was a hallmark of conservative German cultural pessimism. Mass culture, Adorno believed, was depreciating the inwardness that had still characterized earlier cultural manifestations.[91] In a similar vein, Adorno's young assistant, Jürgen Habermas, distinguished between

culture and consumption, noting that culture was something that could
lead humans to "meet the real in its high reality," whereas consumption
merely reflected the possibility to instantly satisfy demands. Habermas
proclaimed: "The satisfaction of demand is a process on the skin of the
consumer, whose heart stands in need of nothing."[92] Since popular culture is an item of both mass production and mass consumption, it could
of course not contain any contradictory potential, any seeds of emancipation. The latter, according to Adorno, could only be found in avant-
garde works, "whose formal difficulty sharply contrasts with the
frictionless entertainments of the culture industry."[93] Consequently his
enthusiasm for Arthur Schönberg's atonal music and his simultaneous
diatribes against jazz and other forms of popular music as commodified
products of the culture industry.[94]

One of the most problematic results of the culture industry is that it
virtually replicates in the realms of culture and leisure the alienation
caused in the workplace by the division of labor. It separates culture
producers from culture consumers, thus cutting off the latter's experience of a work of art from the social processes in which it is produced.
In addition, it discourages human beings from engaging in cultural
activities themselves. As Ernest van den Haag observed, "Culture
becomes largely spectator sport, and life and experience become exoge-
nous and largely vicarious. (Nothing will dissuade me from seeing a difference between a young girl walking around with her pocket radio
listening to popular songs and one who sings herself)."[95] Most important, cultural experience not only becomes passive and atomized, but
also standardized. In music, memorable melodies and repetitive rhythms
are turned out for a preconditioned audience. This completes the abolition of autonomy. Whereas the world of art had hitherto existed apart
from the sphere of labor as a refuge for truth and negativity, modernity
had led to its integration into the realm of domination. As Herbert Marcuse put it, "It is good that almost everyone can now have the fine arts
at his fingertips, by just turning a knob on his set, or by just stepping
into his drugstore. In this diffusion, however, they become cogs in a cul-
ture-machine which remakes their content. Artistic alienation succumbs,
together with other modes of negation, to the process of technological
rationality."[96]

Marcuse, to be sure, eschewed the traditional notion that pleasure
itself was somehow morally suspect. His idea that the bureaucratically
controlled pleasures of the consumer society could be overcome by a
"Great Refusal" that would reopen a space for unalienated pleasures,
held an enormous attraction for the student and countercultural movements of the 1960s. Marcuse himself, in turn, saw in the beatnik and
hippie movements "quite an interesting phenomenon, namely the sim-

ple refusal to take part in the blessings of the 'affluent society.' … The need for better television sets, better automobiles, or comfort of any sort has been cast off. What we see is rather the negation of this need."[97] Less attached to asceticism than Adorno or Horkheimer, Marcuse believed furthermore that the hedonism of the counterculture was directed at unalienated pleasures. Consequently, he was much more sympathetic to the movement than his former collaborators. Yet in his cautious optimism for such delicate signs of refusal, Marcuse missed the extent to which the counterculture in fact appropriated items and forms of mass culture and consumer society—be it in leaflets against the Vietnam War or in a New York underground newspaper that featured an "Adventures of One-Dimensional Man" comic strip.[98] As much as this process was apt to amplify Adorno's wariness of the movement, it seems to have escaped Marcuse's attention. That it might play an important, if not crucial role for the cultural revolution of the 1960s did not occur to either conservative or critical intellectuals.

Of Ants and Agency

What the Frankfurt School and its followers did not realize was that human beings are not just passive victims of manipulation but also active subjects who appropriate and make use of cultural forms for their own purposes. Many supporters of the student revolt were alarmed when colorful happenings, experimental lifestyles, and rock music festivals, which heralded the mutual penetration of counterculture and mass culture, pushed anti-war and other demonstrations to the sidelines. "Here we confront the champions of two debilitating and medically hazardous drugs," wrote one observer, "TV and LSD." Both the drug that Timothy Leary had taken from the shady flats of Haight-Ashbury to the glossy pages of *Playboy* magazine and the technology airing shows of which Adorno had said that they reproduced "the very same smugness, intellectual passivity, and gullibility that seem to fit in with totalitarian creeds" were thus combined to demonstrate the perils of mass culture. And the author continued: "I would rather miss a flower in the jungle of mass culture (possibly the Beatles are such a flower) than lose myself in that jungle."[99] Radical teachers discovered with consternation that "far from sharing our contempt, and fear, of mass culture, many students are now embracing it … There is a belief abroad that changes in hair style, in dress, in sexual habits constitute a rejection of the social order and prepare you for revolution. The new style is supposed to be more 'authentic'; the fact that it is also fashionable does not seem to occur to its defenders."[100] In Germany, Martin Walser warned of the danger "that, through pop and pinball, society helps the needs of the young to a laxative effect without political consequences."[101]

If anyone at all could venture to get into the all-devouring culture industry, it was the intellectual himself. The author Hans Magnus Enzensberger, noting that the mind industry could digest and reproduce anything from slogans and works of art to fashion and esoteric cults, nevertheless implored his colleagues to engage the enemy. Enzensberger criticized the prevalent fixation on the pressures of materialistic society (*Konsumterror*). Consumerism did not create false needs, he argued, but rather distorted real needs. In order to do so, it had to rely on the very cultural and intellectual elites that were most eager to produce alternatives to existing conditions. This confronted the intellectual with a special responsibility. "To opt out of the mind industry, to refuse any dealings with it may well turn out to be a reactionary course … It might be a better idea to enter the dangerous game, to take and calculate our risks … [The intellectual] must try, at any cost, to use it for his own purposes, which are incompatible with the purposes of the mind machine. What it upholds he must subvert."[102]

Sociologists and other intellectuals did not believe, on the other hand, that ordinary youths were capable of cannibalizing the culture industry for their own purposes. Especially teenagers were regarded as mere puppets, virtually functioning as a lobby for the economic interests of producers. In this view, the culture industry eagerly supplied the products that would both get youngsters to part with their money and serve as ideological pacifiers.[103] It was only from the mid-1970s on, that scholars began to pay attention to the ways in which subcultures *as consumers* become themselves active manipulators, appropriating consumer products and transforming them into tools of their own identity construction—up to the point that consumers themselves have lately been identified as a threat to capitalism.[104] One need not subscribe to such a seemingly paradoxical notion to accept the less provocative insight that different (sub)cultures, far from being just alienated by the culture industry, in fact alienate cultural products themselves in order to use them for their own objectives. British Teddy Boys turned Edwardian suits into signs of non-conformity; German youths used Hollywood-style American coolness to set themselves off against the clipped-militaristic body language of their elders, while at the same time they used rock'n'roll and jazz to challenge the cultural hegemony of the *Bildungs-bürgertum* and draw demarcation lines not only separating generations but also one particular social stratum from another.[105] The portable radios so despised by cultural critics were eagerly received by youngsters whose musical taste was now liberated from parental vetoes at home, while television brought a breathtaking transformation of leisure activities, which—as far as it kept parents glued to the screen—created additional autonomy for adolescents.[106]

Mass cultural technologies and the consumerist strategies accompanying them were, then, actively employed by youths both to distance themselves from different "others" and to construct in-group identity. Occasionally, we can find traces of this fact quite early in the literature, left in particular by members of the younger generation, who reflected on the communal spirit of their age cohort. Greil Marcus, for example, explained how he and his friends used rock music to develop a shared body of myths and metaphors, games and contests, which conveyed meaning and a sense of belonging. This became possible, however, only because rock'n'roll was "a medium that [was] everpresent, thanks to the radio, and repetitive, thanks to Top Forty and oldies and record players." He also pointed out that, "the metaphor isn't even principally the 'meaning' of the words to a song; more often it is that the music, or a phrase, or two words heard, jumping out as the rest are lost, seem to fit one's emotional perception of a situation, event, or idea."[107]

This observation should protect us from assuming that matters of lifestyle and political protest were clearly distinguishable—or, for that matter, that only anti-war songs provided a sounding-board for anti-war sentiments. In the United States, Phil Ochs' folk songs against the Vietnam War, which could not and would not deny their roots in the labor movement, were not all that popular within a movement that soon turned to the snotty escapism of the Animals' "We Gotta Get Out of This Place."[108] Nevertheless, most listeners instinctively related the latter, too, to Vietnam, although its lyrics actually referred to a poor district.[109] Given the fact that words to a song were often not taken literally but rather adapted to a preconceived context, the conclusion that the Vietnam War received only minimal attention from musicians and the recording business does not tell us a lot about the relationship between the protest movement and popular music.[110] This is doubly true for West Germany. Here the countercultural infatuation with Anglo-American beat and rock music also relegated the mostly intellectual enthusiasts of American folk, French chansons, and German singer-songwriters to the sidelines.[111] But the fact that listeners had to contend with a foreign language multiplied the possibilities to take words out of context, even though some tried to memorize the lyrics very assiduously. As one participant remembered, "It was pop and rock music, where individual experiences, personal destiny, and existential desire came together. Beatles songs were the tunes of the revolt's early light—songs of existential radicalism, in the magic of the lyrics, the glory of utopian realms of freedom: individual loneliness ('I [sic!] look at all the lonely people'), moving out ('She's leaving home'), fancying the liberating action ('Rocky had [sic!] come equipped with a gun'), the explosion of discovering your inner universe ... ('In [sic!] a glass onion')."[112] Rock'n'roll might not have spurred on the protest, but it definitely reflected the movement's feeling of being alive. When the movement grew into a market, the recording industry started to promote appropriate rhythms and rhymes. Political criticism had never before been articulated so frequently in commercial products.[113]

Much more important for the communal spirit of the revolt than inspiration from rock music's lyrics, however, were the physical gestures and bodily emotions that accompanied the music. As John Sinclair, a political activist and manager of a rock band in Detroit, proclaimed: "MUSIC IS REVOLUTION ... —it blows people all the way back to their senses and makes them feel good, like they're *alive* again in the middle of this monstrous funeral parlor of western civilization."[114] Though not everyone might subscribe to the idea that the physical impact of rock music saves people from the clutches of the one-dimensional society, it is altogether plausible that listeners experienced feelings of emotional salvation—however passing. Most important, as Susan McClary has argued, music can give rise to bodily experiences which, if translated into a widely shared vocabulary of expressions, can challenge political and social conventions.[115] This is yet another way in which the counterculture of the 1960s has certainly actively manipulated commercial products.

Even reservations with regard to technology, which had been especially pronounced among German conservative as well as critical philosophers, received a marked transformation within the counterculture. John Sinclair, for example, noted that "The members of a rock and roll family or tribe ... work on the frontiers of modern technology to produce a new form which is strictly contemporary in all its implications." This appreciation of modern technology reveals that the counterculture actively engaged not only mass culture but also its principal prerequisite. Kingsley Widmer saw therein a prime characteristic of the counterculture, asserting that "its newness comes from its curious relations to technology and its mass spread by way of the electronic media." He identified a peculiar "electric increment" residing in every countercultural form or practice that became popularized. "These electric-increments characterize a post-technological popular and protesting culture which turns the media to its own imperatives, and thus carries out considerable humanization. Much of what stands out here seems to be the playful use of technology. The technical gets turned into the fantastic, humorous, grotesque."[116]

The counterculture, then, did not—as some will have it—reject the project of modernity. Unlike their more theoretically concerned co-conspirators within the movement, the majority of rebellious youths did not want to assault technology, mass culture, and consumerism but outflank and outwit it. On the one hand, this was a long way from the conservative demeanor of fatalism and withdrawal into tradition. On the other hand, however, it also abandoned the idea that the wholesale integration of society could be overcome only by a political revolution. As Widmer put it, "In the usual cultural theory, change in power allows change in institutions which then allows a change in sensibility, from political to social to cultural revolution. However, our present cultural conflicts imply that the last be first, that a change in sensibility will change the order of the world."[117]

Notes

1. Harvard Sitkoff, *The Struggle for Black Equality 1954–1992*, rev. ed. (New York, 1993), 192.
2. Volker Depkat, "The Birth of Technology from the Spirit of the Lack of Culture. The United States as 'Land of Technological Progress' in Germany, 1800–1850," in *Technologie und Kultur: Europas Blick auf Amerika vom 18. bis zum 20. Jahrhundert*, ed. Michael Wala and Ursula Lehmkuhl (Cologne, 2000), 23–53.
3. Nikolaus Lenau to Anton Schurz, 16 October 1832, in Nikolaus Lenau, *Werke und Briefe. Historisch-kritische Gesamtausgabe*, vol. 5: Briefe 1822–1837, ed. Hartmut Steinecke (Vienna, 1989), 228–31, 230.
4. The classic study on German cultural pessimism is Fritz Stern, *The Politics of Cultural Despair: A Study in the Rise of the Germanic Ideology* (Berkeley, Calif., 1961).
5. Quoted in Rolf Peter Sieferle, *Fortschrittsfeinde? Opposition gegen Technik und Industrie von der Romantik bis zur Gegenwart* (Munich, 1984), 278f., fn. 70.
6. Jeffrey Herf, *Reactionary Modernism: Technology, Culture, and Politics in Weimar and the Third Reich* (New York, 1984).
7. Jeffrey Herf, "Belated Pessimism: Technology and Twentieth-Century German Conservative Intellectuals," in *Technology, Pessimism, and Postmodernism*, ed. Yaron Ezrahi, Everett Mendelsohn, and Howard Segal (Dordrecht, 1994), 115–36.
8. See Mary Nolan, *Visions of Modernity: American Business and the Modernization of Germany* (New York and Oxford, 1994).
9. Stefan Willeke, *Die Technokratiebewegung in Nordamerika und Deutschland zwischen den Weltkriegen. Eine vergleichende Analyse* (Frankfurt am Main, 1995).
10. Philipp Gassert, "Nationalsozialismus, Amerikanismus, Technologie: Zur Kritik der amerikanischen Moderne im Dritten Reich," in *Technologie und Kultur*, ed. Wala and Lehmkuhl, 147–72.
11. Frank Trommler, "The Rise and Fall of Americanism in Germany," in *America and the Germans: An Assessment of a Three-Hundred Year History*, ed. Frank Trommler and Joseph McVeigh, 2 vols. (Philadelphia, 1985), 2: 332–42.
12. Quoted in Detlev J.K. Peukert, *The Weimar Republic: The Crisis of Classical Modernity*, trans. Richard Deveson (New York, 1992), 185.
13. Quoted in Earl R. Beck, *Germany Rediscovers America* (Tallahassee, Fl., 1968), 161.
14. See Dagmar Barnouw, *Weimar Intellectuals and the Threat of Modernity* (Bloomington and Indianapolis, 1988), 13.

15. See Erich E. Geißler, *Welche Farbe hat die Zukunft? Über politische Kultur im technischen Zeitalter* (Bonn, 1986), 36.

16. See Sieferle, *Fortschrittsfeinde,* 214f.

17. For a lucid discussion of the German discourse on technology in the 1950s see Axel Schildt, *Moderne Zeiten: Freizeit, Massenmedien und 'Zeitgeist' in der Bundesrepublik der 50er Jahre* (Hamburg, 1995), 324–50; see also idem, *Zwischen Abendland und Amerika: Studien zur westdeutschen Ideenlandschaft der 50er Jahre* (Munich, 1999), 91ff.

18. Friedrich Georg Jünger, *The Failure of Technology: Perfection without Purpose,* trans. F. D. Wieck (Hinsdale, Ill., 1949).

19. Jacques Ellul, *The Technological Society,* trans. John Wilkinson (New York, 1964). On Ellul see Wolfgang Schluchter, *Aspekte bürokratischer Herrschaft. Studien zur Interpretation der fortschreitenden Industriegesellschaft* (Frankfurt am Main, 1985), 187–91.

20. Hans Freyer, *Theorie des gegenwärtigen Zeitalters* (Stuttgart, 1955).

21. Jerry Z. Muller, *The Other God That Failed: Hans Freyer and the Deradicalization of German Conservatism* (Princeton, N.J., 1987), 339–54. See also Paul Nolte, *Die Ordnung der deutschen Gesellschaft: Selbstentwurf und Selbstbeschreibung im 20. Jahrhundert* (Munich, 2000), 287–90.

22. Arnold Gehlen, *Man in the Age of Technology,* trans. Patricia Lipscomb (New York, 1980). The German original, first published in 1949 and in a revised edition in 1957, bore a title that more clearly reflected the traditional German emphasis on inwardness and spiritual values: *Die Seele im technischen Zeitalter* (literally, The Soul in the Age of Technology).

23. Arnold Gehlen, "Über kulturelle Kristallisation," in idem, *Studien zur Anthropologie und Soziologie* (2nd ed. Neuwied and Berlin, 1971), 283–300; Schluchter, *Aspekte,* 206–21; Nolte, *Ordnung,* 285ff.

24. Helmut Schelsky, "Der Mensch in der wissenschaftlichen Zivilisation," in idem, *Auf der Suche nach Wirklichkeit. Gesammelte Aufsätze* (Düsseldorf and Cologne, 1965), 439–80.

25. See Schluchter, *Aspekte,* 193–206; Nolte, *Ordnung,* 281ff.

26. Nolte, *Ordnung,* 285, 296. For a general outline of German conservative thinking after 1945 see Axel Schildt, *Konservatismus in Deutschland. Von den Anfängen im 18. Jahrhundert bis zur Gegenwart* (Munich, 1998), 213–42.

27. See e.g. Barnouw, *Weimar Intellectuals,* 37; Herf, "Belated Pessimism," 134, fn. 45; Helmut Dubiel, *Was ist Neokonservatismus?* (Frankfurt am Main, 1985), 15f.; Leon Bramson, *The Political Context of Sociology* (Princeton, N.J., 1961), 34, 43.

28. Edward Shils, "Daydreams and Nightmares: Reflections on the Criticism of Mass Culture," *Sewanee Review* 65 (1957): 587–608, 596f.

29. Michael Grimminger, *Revolution und Resignation. Sozialphilosophie und die geschichtliche Krise im 20. Jahrhundert bei Max Horkheimer und Hans Freyer* (Berlin, 1997), 26 and *passim.*

30. Herbert Marcuse, "Some Social Implications of Modern Technology" (1941), in idem, *Technology, War and Fascism* (Collected Papers of Herbert Marcuse, ed. Douglas Kellner, vol. 1) (London and New York, 1998), 41–65, 49, 41.

31. Ibid., 41; Horkheimer to Marcuse, 26 November 1941, quoted in Rolf Wiggershaus, *The Frankfurt School: Its History, Theories and Political Significance,* trans. Michael Robertson (Cambridge, 1994), 297. See also Max Horkheimer, "The End of Reason," *Studies in Philosophy and Social Science* 9 (1941): 366–88.

32. Max Horkheimer and Theodor Adorno, *Dialectic of Enlightenment,* trans. John Cumming (New York, 1987).

33. See Sebastian Conrad, *Auf der Suche nach der verlorenen Nation: Geschichtsschreibung in Westdeutschland und Japan 1945–1960* (Göttingen, 1999), 169–74; Kurt Lenk, "Zum westdeutschen Konservatismus," in *Modernisierung im Wiederaufbau: Die westdeutsche Gesellschaft der 50er Jahre,* ed. Axel Schildt and Arnold Sywottek, (Bonn, 1993), 636–43.

34. Hartmut Schröter, "Technik und Kunst—Adorno: Heidegger. Zur Einführung," in *Technik und Kunst. Heidegger : Adorno,* ed. idem (Münster, 1988), 7–15, 9.

35. See Martin Jay, *The Dialectical Imagination: A History of the Frankfurt School and the Institute of Social Research 1923–1950* (Berkeley, Calif., 1996), 272. Others have discerned a "disturbing affinity" of Marcuse's "technological determinism" with Freyer, Gehlen and Schelsky's thinking. See Claus Offe, "Technik und Eindimensionalität: Eine Version der Technokratiethese?," in *Antworten auf Herbert Marcuse,* ed. Jürgen Habermas (Frankfurt am Main, 1968), 73–88, 81; see also Wolfgang Trautmann, *Gegenwart und Zukunft der Industriegesellschaft. Ein Vergleich der soziologischen Theorien Hans Freyers und Herbert Marcuses* (Bochum, 1976), esp. 50–53.

36. Herbert Marcuse, *One-Dimensional Man: Studies in the Ideology of Advanced Industrial Society* (Boston, 1964), 145, 158 (emphasis in original).

37. Gretchen Dutschke-Klotz, "Die vier Väter: Lukacs, Gollwitzer, Marcuse, Bloch," in Rudi Dutschke, *Die Revolte. Wurzeln und Spuren eines Aufbruchs,* ed. Gretchen Dutschke-Klotz, Jürgen Miermeister, and Jürgen Treulieb (Reinbek, 1983), 10–17, 12; Paul Breines, "Marcuse and the New Left in America," in Habermas, *Antworten,* 133–51, 137; Martin Jay, "The Metapolitics of Utopianism," in idem, *Permanent Exiles: Essays on the Intellectual Migration from Germany to America* (New York, 1985), 3–13, 3.

38. Andrew Feenberg, "The Critique of Technology: From Dystopia to Interaction," in *Marcuse: From the New Left to the Next Left,* ed. John Bokina and Timothy J. Lukes (Lawrence, Ks., 1994), 208–26, 221.

39. "Informationen über Vietnam und Länder der Dritten Welt, no. 2, June 1966," reprinted in *Freie Universität Berlin 1948–1973: Hochschule im Umbruch (Dokumentation),* vol. 4: *Die Krise 1964–1967,* ed. Siegward Lönnendonker and Tilman Fichter, with Claus Rietzschel (Berlin, 1975), 325ff.

40. Arnfried Astel, "Neue Waffe," in *Gegen den Krieg in Vietnam: Eine Anthologie* Riewert Qu. Tode, ed., (Berlin, 1968), 19.

41. Bertrand Russell and Jean-Paul Sartre, *Das Vietnam-Tribunal oder Amerika vor Gericht* (Reinbek, 1968), 93–99.

42. "Indochina-Hearings 1971 der Initiative Internationale Vietnam Solidarität, Berichte und Kommentare," folder 04601, Dokumentationsstelle für unkonventionelle Literatur, Bibliothek für Zeitgeschichte, Stuttgart (hereafter: BfZ-Doku). Interestingly, it has recently been argued with regard to an important segment of American anti-war protest that it was the impersonal and deadly imposition of technological overkill which inspired the creation of the Vietnam Veterans Against the War. See Dolores McCabe, "Vietnam Veterans Against the War, Inc.: Technology, Idealism and Rebellion" (Ph.D. diss., City University of New York, 1997).

43. Bernard B. Fall, "This Isn't Munich, It's Spain," in *"Takin' It to the Streets": A Sixties Reader,* ed. Alexander Bloom and Wini Breines (New York and Oxford, 1995), 206–11, 207. On the predilection of policymakers to justify the American intervention in Vietnam with reference to the futility of British and French efforts to appease Hitler at the 1938 Munich Conference, see Yuen Foong Khong, *Analogies at War: Korea, Munich, Dien Bien Phu, and the Vietnam Decisions of 1965* (Princeton, N.J., 1992), 174–205.

44. See e.g. Wilhelm Bauer, "Positionen in Vietnam," *Neue Kritik* 6 (1965), no. 29: 6ff.; Georg W. Alsheimer, "Amerikaner in Vietnam," *Das Argument* 8 (1966), no. 36: 2–43; see also the declaration of a group of well-known writers and intellectuals supporting the international congress on Vietnam held in Berlin in 1968, quoted in Ingo Juchler, *Die Studentenbewegungen in den Vereinigten Staaten und der Bundesrepublik Deutschland der sechziger Jahre: Eine Untersuchung hinsichtlich ihrer Beeinflussung durch Befreiungsbewegungen und –theorien aus der Dritten Welt* (Berlin, 1996), 258; and, of course, Hans Magnus Enzensberger's letter to the president of Wesleyan University: "On Leaving America," *New York Review of Books*, 29 February 1968, 31f.

45. Alsheimer, "Amerikaner in Vietnam," 30.

46. For a discussion of Himmler's speech to SS leaders in Posen on 4 October 1943 see Richard Breitman, *The Architect of Genocide: Himmler and the Final Solution* (New York, 1991), 242f. For more on the Auschwitz-Vietnam analogy see my "Auschwitz and Vietnam: West German Protest Against America's War During the 1960s," in *America, the Vietnam War, and World: Comparative and International Perspectives*, ed. Andreas W. Daum, Lloyd C. Gardner, and Wilfried Mausbach (New York, 2003), 279–98.

47. Breines, "Marcuse and the New Left," 134.

48. Günter Kunert, "Fernöstliche Legende," *Gegen den Krieg in Vietnam*, ed. Riewert Qu. Tode, 83.

49. Breines, "Marcuse and the New Left," 134.

50. Marcuse to Horkheimer, 17 June 1967, in *Frankfurter Schule und Studentenbewegung: Von der Flaschenpost zum Molotowcocktail 1946–1995*, ed. Wolfgang Kraushaar, 3 vols. (Hamburg, 1998), 2: 262.

51. Herbert Marcuse, "The Problem of Violence and the Radical Opposition," in idem, *Five Lectures: Psychoanalysis, Politics, and Utopia*, trans. Jeremy J. Shapiro and Shierry M. Weber (Boston, 1970), 83–108, 87.

52. Everett Mendelsohn, "The Politics of Pessimism: Science and Technology Circa 1968," in *Technology, Pessimism, and Postmodernism*, Ezrahi, Mendelsohn and Segal, 151–73, esp. 162f.

53. See Hermann Glaser, *Kleine Kulturgeschichte der Bundesrepublik Deutschland 1945–1989* (2nd ed., Bonn, 1991), 184f.; Schildt, *Moderne Zeiten*, 328.

54. Alfred Weber, *Der dritte oder der vierte Mensch. Vom Sinn des geschichtlichen Daseins* (Munich, 1953).

55. William H. Whyte, *The Organization Man* (New York, 1956).

56. Hannah Arendt, *Eichmann in Jerusalem: A Report on the Banality of Evil* (New York, 1963).

57. For a detailed account of the controversy see Elizabeth Young-Bruehl, *Hannah Arendt: For Love of the World* (New Haven and London, 1982), 328–78; see also Peter Novick, *The Holocaust in American Life* (Boston and New York, 1999), 127–45. To be sure, Raul Hilberg's seminal study on *The Destruction of the European Jews* (Chicago, 1961) had interpreted the Final Solution as an administrative and bureaucratic process already in 1961. But Hilberg's work had been largely ignored in Germany, and it was only Arendt's trial report that let this notion come to the fore, thereby admittedly also drowning out Hilberg's contribution. See Nicolas Berg, "Lesarten des Judenmords," in *Wandlungsprozesse in Westdeutschland: Belastung, Integration, Liberalisierung 1945–1980*, ed. Ulrich Herbert (Göttingen, 2002), 91–139, esp. 92f., 110ff.

58. Christopher R. Browning, "The German Bureaucracy and the Holocaust," in *Genocide: Critical Issues of the Holocaust*, ed. Alex Grobman and Daniel Landes (Los

Angeles, 1983), 148, quoted in Zygmunt Bauman, *Modernity and the Holocaust* (Ithaca, N.Y., 1992), 13.

59. Daniel Bell, "The Alphabet of Justice: Reflections on 'Eichmann in Jerusalem,'" *Partisan Review* 30 (Fall 1963): 417–29, 427.

60. Carl Oglesby, "Trapped in a System," in Bloom and Breines, *Takin' It to the Streets*, 220–25, 220f.

61. Lewis Mumford, *The Myth of the Machine*, vol. 2: *The Pentagon Power* (New York, 1970), 279.

62. Bauman, *Modernity and the Holocaust*, 100.

63. Herbert Marcuse, "Aggressivität in der gegenwärtigen Industriegesellschaft," in idem, Anatol Rapoport, Klaus Horn, Alexander Mitscherlich, Dieter Senghaas, and Mihailo Marković, *Aggression und Anpassung in der Industriegesellschaft* (Frankfurt am Main, 1968), 7–29, 25.

64. See Klaus Naumann, "Sympathy for the Devil? Die Kontroverse um Hannah Arendts Prozeßbericht 'Eichmann in Jerusalem,'" *Mittelweg 36* 2/1 (1994): 65–79, 69.

65. Carl Oglesby and Richard Shaull, *Containment and Change* (New York, 1967), 199. The German edition was published as *Amerikanische Ideologie: Zwei Studien über Politik und Gesellschaft in den USA* (Frankfurt am Main, 1969), with the quote on page 226.

66. Martin Walser, "Zur neuen Taktik der US-Regierung. Rede auf einer Vietnam-Veranstaltung der KDA München, July 1969," *Tintenfisch* 3 (1970): 65–70.

67. Ernest van den Haag, "A Dissent from the Consensual Society [1960]," in *Mass Culture Revisited*, ed. Bernard Rosenberg and David Manning White (New York, 1971), 85–92, 91.

68. Detlev Claussen, "Die amerikanische Erfahrung der Kritischen Theoretiker," in *Keine Kritische Theorie ohne Amerika*, ed. Detlev Claussen, Oskar Negt, and Michael Werz (Frankfurt am Main, 1999), 27–45.

69. "Warum brennst Du, Konsument?" (leaflet no. 7), 24 May 1967, reprinted in *Freie Universität Berlin 1948–1973*, 4: 442. The anthology does not convey, however, the visual character of the headline. A copy of the original leaflet is in Kommune 1, "Quellen zur Kommune-Forschung," D0895, Bfz-Doku.

70. "Wann brennen die Berliner Kaufhäuser?" (leaflet no. 8), 24 May 1967, reprinted in *Freie Universität Berlin 1948–1973*, 4: 442

71. Peter Szondi, "Aufforderung zur Brandstiftung? Ein Gutachten im Prozess Langhans/Teufel," *Der Monat* 19, no. 227 (1967): 24–29.

72. Sozialistischer Deutscher Studentenbund, "Flugblatt zu Adornos 'Iphigenie'-Vortrag an der Freien Universität Berlin, 7 July 1967," in Kraushaar, *Frankfurter Schule und Studentenbewegung*, 2: 265f.

73. See Wolfgang Kraushaar, "Kritische Theorie und Studentenbewegung," in idem, *Frankfurter Schule und Studentenbewegung*, 1: 17–32; Wiggershaus, *Frankfurt School*, 609–36; Ingrid Gilcher-Holtey, "Kritische Theorie und Neue Linke," in *1968 – Vom Ereignis zum Gegenstand der Geschichtswissenschaft*, ed. Gilcher-Holtey (Göttingen, 1998), 168–87.

74. Adorno to Horkheimer, 31 May 1967, in Kraushaar, *Frankfurter Schule und Studentenbewegung*, 2: 233.

75. "Auszüge aus den gutachterlichen Äußerungen zum Prozess gegen Langhans/Teufel wegen Aufforderung zur Brandstiftung," folder 00135, BfZ-Doku.

76. Schildt, *Moderne Zeiten*, 152–79; Arthur Fischer, Werner Fuchs, and Jürgen Zinnecker, *Jugend der fünfziger Jahre* (Opladen, 1985). Average real incomes rose 69 percent in West Germany from 1950 to 1960 and another 57 percent during the

following decade. See Gerd Hardach, "Krise und Reform der Sozialen Markt-wirtschaft. Grundzüge der wirtschaftlichen Entwicklung in der Bundesrepublik der 50er und 60er Jahre," in *Dynamische Zeiten: Die 60er Jahre in den beiden deutschen Gesellschaften,* ed. Axel Schildt, Detlef Siegfried, and Karl Christian Lammers (Hamburg, 2000), 197–217. For similar trends in the United States, see James T. Patterson, *Grand Expectations: The United States, 1945–1974* (New York and Oxford, 1995), 311ff., 369–74.

77. See Arthur Marwick, *The Sixties: Cultural Revolution in Britain, France, Italy, and the United States, c.1958–c.1974* (Oxford and New York, 1998), 45ff.

78. Uta G. Poiger, *Jazz, Rock, and Rebels: Cold War Politics and American Culture in a Divided Germany* (Berkeley, Calif., 2000), 106–23.

79. See Marwick, *The Sixties,* 181–93.

80. See the perceptive, though at times all too polemical discussion in Gerd Koenen, *Das rote Jahrzehnt: Unsere kleine deutsche Kulturrevolution 1967–1977* (Cologne, 2001), 150–71.

81. Klaus Rainer Röhl, "Sie küßten und sie trennten sich," *Konkret,* no. 8 (1967), unpaginated.

82. Ulrich Chaussy, *Die drei Leben des Rudi Dutschke. Eine Biographie* (Berlin, 1993), 150f.; "Dutschke-Interview with Der Spiegel, 10 July 1967," reprinted in Dutschke, *Die Revolte,* 20–38; Wolfgang Lefèvre, "Referat zur Begründung des Antrags auf Ausschluß der Kommune 1 aus dem Berliner SDS, 12 May 1967," in *Freie Universität Berlin 1948–1973,* 4: 436ff.

83. For a first effort to weave together the many threads that make up this phenomenon see Marwick, *The Sixties,* which unfortunately, however, excludes West Germany.

84. Bahman Nirumand, "Die harmlose Intelligenz: Über Gammler, Ostermarschierer, Adorniten und andere Oppositionelle," *Konkret,* no. 7 (1967): 23ff.

85. Klaus Behnken, Reiner Geulen, Udo Knapp, and Reinhart Wolff, "Revolutionäre Disziplin: Zur Organisation der radikalen sozialistischen Opposition," *Konkret,* no. 8 (1969): 16–19, 18.

86. Jay, *Dialectical Imagination,* 176.

87. Horkheimer and Adorno, *Dialectic of Enlightenment,* 131. Marx's reflections on production and consumption are in Karl Marx, *Grundrisse: Foundations of the Critique of Political Economy* [1857], trans. Martin Nicolaus (New York, 1973), 83–94.

88. See e.g. Rüdiger Griepenburg and Kurt Steinhaus, "Zu einigen sozioökonomischen und militärischen Aspekten des Vietnamkonflikts," *Das Argument* 8 (1966), no. 36: 44–61.

89. Herbert Marcuse, "Die Analyse eines Exempels," *Neue Kritik* 7 (1966), no. 36/37: 30–38.

90. Schröter, "Technik und Kunst," 14.

91. Douglas Kellner, "Kulturindustrie und Massenkommunikation. Die Kritische Theorie und ihre Folgen," in *Sozialforschung als Kritik: Zum sozialwissenschaftlichen Potential der kritischen Theorie,* ed. Wolfgang Bonß and Axel Honneth (Frankfurt am Main, 1982), 482–515, 497.

92. Jürgen Habermas, "Notizen zum Missverhältnis von Kultur und Konsum," *Merkur* 10/3 (1956): 212–28, 213ff.

93. Craig Calhoun and Joseph Karaganis, "Critical Theory," in *Handbook of Social Theory,* ed. George Ritzer and Barry Smart (London, 2001), 179–200, 190.

94. See e.g., Max Paddison, *Adorno, Modernism and Mass Culture: Essays on Critical Theory and Music* (London, 1996), 81–105; Heinz Steinert, *Die Entdeckung der Kulturindustrie: oder: Warum Professor Adorno Jazz nicht ausstehen konnte* (Vienna, 1992); Harry Cooper, "On *Über Jazz:* Replaying Adorno with the Grain," *October* 75 (1996): 99–133.

95. van den Haag, "A Dissent from the Consensual Society," 91.

96. Marcuse, *One-Dimensional Man*, 65.

97. Herbert Marcuse, "The End of Utopia," in idem, *Five Lectures*, 62–82, 75.

98. See Breines, "Marcuse and the New Left," 141.

99. Bernard Rosenberg, "Mass Culture Revisited," in *Mass Culture Revisited*, ed. Rosenberg and White, 3–12, quotes: 4 and 11; T. W. Adorno, "Television and the Patterns of Mass Culture," in *Mass Culture: The Popular Arts in America*, ed. Bernard Rosenberg and David Manning White (Glencoe, Ill., 1957), 474–88, 479. On the counterculture and drugs see David Farber, *The Age of Great Dreams: America in the 1960s* (New York, 1994), 172–82.

100. Alan Trachtenberg, "Culture and Rebellion: Dilemmas of Radical Teachers," in *Mass Culture Revisited*, ed. Rosenberg and White, 120–30, quotes: 125 and 128.

101. Martin Walser, "Kapitalismus gegen Demokratie," *Tintenfisch* 4 (1971): 30–35, 35.

102. Hans Magnus Enzensberger, "The Industrialization of the Mind," *Partisan Review* 36/1 (1969): 100–111, 110f.; see also idem, *Palaver: Politische Überlegungen (1967–1973)* (Frankfurt am Main, 1974), 91–129, esp. 108ff.

103. See the excellent summary of these debates in Detlef Siegfried, "Vom Teenager zur Pop-Revolution. Politisierungstendenzen in der westdeutschen Jugendkultur 1959 bis 1968," in *Dynamische Zeiten*, ed. Schildt, Siegfried, and Lammers, 582–623, esp. 584–90. Siegfried imaginatively argues that, as a result of this diagnosis of exploitation, authorities themselves attempted to politicize the young in the early 1960s in order to make them less receptive to consumerism. When this "politicization from above" was supplemented, however, with a "politicization from below," it took a turn that they had not anticipated.

104. See in particular Dick Hebdige, *Subculture: The Meaning of Style* (London, 1979); Michel de Certeau, *The Practice of Everyday Life* (Berkeley, Calif., 1984); Daniel Miller, *Material Culture and Mass Consumption* (Oxford, 1987), and the recent article by George Ritzer, "Obscene from Any Angle: Fast Food, Credit Cards, Casinos and Consumers," *Third Text* 14 (2000), no. 51: 17–28.

105. Tony Jefferson, "Cultural Responses of the Teds: The Defence of Space and Status," in *Resistance through Rituals: Youth Subcultures in Postwar Britain*, ed. Stuart Hall and Tony Jefferson (London, 1976), 81–86; Kaspar Maase, *BRAVO Amerika: Erkundungen zur Jugendkultur der Bundesrepublik in den fünfziger Jahren* (Hamburg, 1992); idem, "Amerikanisierung von unten. Demonstrative Vulgarität und kulturelle Hegemonie in der Bundesrepublik der 50er Jahre," in *Amerikanisierung: Traum und Alptraum im Deutschland des 20. Jahrhunderts*, ed. Alf Lüdtke, Inge Marßolek, and Adelheid von Saldern (Stuttgart, 1996), 291–313.

106. Schildt, *Moderne Zeiten*, 169ff., 220, 278ff.; Werner Polster, "Wandlungen der Lebensweise im Spiegel der Konsumentwicklung – Vom Dienstleistungskonsum zum demokratischen Warenkonsum," in *Gesellschaftliche Transformationsprozesse und materielle Lebensweise. Beiträge zur Wirtschafts- und Gesellschaftsgeschichte der Bundesrepublik Deutschland (1949–1989)*, ed. Klaus Voy, Werner Polster, and Claus Thomasberger (Marburg, 1991), 193–261, esp. 222–33.

107. Greil Marcus, "Who Put the Bomp in the Bomp De-Bomp De-Bomp," in *Mass Culture Revisited*, ed. Rosenberg and White, 444–58, 454f.

108. See Terry H. Anderson, "American Popular Music and the War in Vietnam," *Peace and Change* 11 (1986): 51–65; Ray Pratt, "'There Must Be Some Way Outta Here!' The Vietnam War in American Popular Music," in *The Vietnam War: Its History, Literature and Music*, ed. Kenton J. Clymer (El Paso, 1998), 169–89.

109. See Kevin Hillstrom and Laurie Collier, *The Vietnam Experience: A Concise Encyclopedia of American Literature, Songs, and Films* (Westport, Conn., 1998), 291–95.

110. Cf. Kenneth J. Bindas and Craig Houston, "'Takin' Care of Business: Rock Music, Vietnam and the Protest Myth," *The Historian* 52 (1989): 1–23.

111. See Siegfried, "Vom Teenager zur Pop-Revolution," 610f.

112. Peter Mosler, *Was wir wollten, was wir wurden. Zeugnisse der Studentenrevolte* (exp. ed. Reinbek, 1988), 99f.

113. George Lipsitz, "Who'll Stop the Rain? Youth Culture, Rock'n'Roll, and Social Crises," in *The Sixties: From Memory to History*, ed. David Farber (Chapel Hill, N.C., and London, 1994), 206–34; Pratt, "'There Must Be Some Way Outta Here,'" 172.

114. John Sinclair, "Rock and Roll Is a Weapon of Cultural Revolution [1968]," in *Takin' It to the Streets*, Bloom and Breines, 301 (emphasis in original).

115. Susan McClary, "Same As It Ever Was: Youth Culture and Music," in *Microphone Fiends: Youth Music and Youth Culture*, ed. Andrew Ross and Tricia Rose (New York and London, 1994), 29–40.

116. Kingsley Widmer, "The Electric Aesthetic and the Short-Circuit Ethic: The Populist Generator in Our Mass Culture Machine," in *Mass Culture Revisited*, ed. Rosenberg and White, 102–19, 104f.

117. Ibid., 118.

Chapter 9

Youth and the Antinuclear Power Movement in Denmark and West Germany

Henrik Kaare Nielsen

Youth, Modernity, and Politics

A general characteristic of the modernization process in highly developed Western countries is that social praxis is differentiated in several respects. Thus, historically a number of relatively autonomous fields of praxis have arisen that have operated according to their own rationalities (politics, economy, art, etc.); also the life-world[1] of the population and the everyday cultural patterns of orientation belonging to it are in ongoing processes of change and segregation, creating new social and cultural relations between individuals and social groups and redistributing resources and life possibilities.

In a life-world perspective, across these segregations of subpopulations and subcultures, modern individuals are in general confronted with experiences of ruptures. These experiences are fundamentally ambivalent: on the one hand, the disruption of accustomed life contexts generates pain and longing after the reestablishment of familiar frameworks for life development, but on the other hand the same process also contains a great liberating potential through its tearing down of narrow-minded norms and social ties. This fundamental ambivalence in modern cultural development involves a dialectical movement between regression and progression in the subcultures, between backwards directed pain and the forward-directed expansion of life potentials, between an orientational crisis and the gains of liberation.

The actual youth cultures (as opposed to the traditional adult-organized cultural offerings for youth) that have been developing in modern Western societies since the 1950s thus express collective adaptations of a new youth situation. The differentiation of youth as a social category was motivated by the general extension of the length of education, itself determined by the changes in the qualification demands of the labor market. This development was further supported by the general increase in the purchasing power and made industry, advertising business, and media capable of staging and cultivating the youth as a new consumer group with its own needs and preferences.

For the youths themselves this process was tantamount to being marginalized from the adult world and from the social relations of working life. On the one hand, this made the formation of social identity a fundamentally problematic process, in which youth lacked useful traditions, norms, and ideals to orient themselves when faced with challenge—and thus they were largely left to themselves and one another in developing rough ideas of adequate forms of social identity—on the other hand, as an isolated ghetto, this new youth situation also contained a space of possibilities of historically unprecedented dimensions. With collective, subjective ways of adapting to this ambivalent youth situation, the youth cultures have demonstrated a corresponding ambivalence: in part, in the form of a symbolic staging that clearly distinguishes individual subcultures from one another and from the surrounding world generally, they have served as essential frameworks for an autonomous search for social identity, for testing new drafts and props for an adequate youth self-image; in part they have, as sheltered spaces of possibilities, served as forums for pleasurable self-realization, for sensually exploring the many life possibilities that highly developed modernity implies and that present themselves to the youth's life situation in a concentrated form.

The collective identity work of youth cultures does not necessarily assume a political character. The discourse of self-realization that is their central feature can in principle be oriented toward the modes of societalization of both the market and political civil society and thus unfold in the role of the consumer or the citizen, respectively. The concrete interaction between the specific universe of youth culture and the contemporary historical conditions is decisive for whether the dynamics of youth culture has an effect on market transactions or democratic participation.

When this cultural dynamic is actually politicized it is—due to its diffuse, identity-seeking character—initially a fragile process that in times of adversity will either tend to assume fanatical forms or turn into disillusionment. Furthermore, by virtue of the character of the underlying needs of youth culture, it will look for forms of participation that combine a clearly profiled social position of identity with a pleasurable intensity in the struggle for—or against—the "issue." In any case, however, the development depends on the interplay of the concrete politicization process with its specific context.

This context is especially determined by the specific society's constellations of interests, the predominant power balances in the current area of politics, and the historical experiences of conflict that have shaped the political culture in the space of social praxis where the politicization process unfolds—in the current context this is mainly the framework of the nation-state. From this point of view, I shall examine similarities and differences between the antinuclear power movements in Denmark and West Germany in the 1970s, drawing upon a major comparative analysis of political culture and new social movements in the two countries.[2]

By way of introduction, it should be noted that the antinuclear power movement cannot be designated as an actual youth movement in Denmark or West Germany, as were, for instance, the youth and student uprisings in the 1960s. The protest against nuclear power was not expressed in generational terms, but united citizens across age differences. It was nonetheless youth that made a decisive mark on the self-conception and cultural forms of the movement—in part because by far the majority of the participants were young and the characteristic features of the politicization processes of youth culture influenced the movements' formation of identity, and in part because the youth uprising of the 1960s had created new forms of political commitment and participation that the antinuclear power movement also used as inspiration.

In addition, the anti-hierarchical and anticonsumerist ideals of the uprising in the 1960s had achieved a hegemonic position among the vast majority of activists in the movement during this period, and the protest against nuclear power was thus culturally accompanied by a lifestyle that stressed egalitarian values and a casual and "natural" staging of the self (no make-up, parka coats, flat shoes, backpacks), and that correspondingly rejected the "artificial" differentiations of the fashion industry, which were considered hopelessly consumerist and oppressive to women. In other words, the struggle against nuclear power became inscribed in a broader conflict concerning cultural values, and in an avant-garde way the youth uprising's distinct rupture with the norms of established society had created new ideals and forms of interaction, forms that oriented the broader popular movements in the 1970s.

The West German Antinuclear Power Movement

In West Germany the protest against nuclear power grew from a broader ecological movement that in turn was rooted in a variety of decentralized "civic initiatives" that started to emerge at the end of the 1960s.[3]

The extraparliamentary organization of civic initiatives, which indicated the beginnings of a change in the political patterns of behavior of wide sections of the population, was in part inspired by the direct actions of the political uprisings of the 1960s, but beyond this shared organizational feature the two currents in this phase had nothing in common. While the uprisings of the 1960s demanded major, revolutionary upheaval "here and now," viewing the extraparliamentary actions as part of the construction of a counter-force that would overthrow the established system, the ideas of the civic initiatives remained entirely inside the framework of the parliamentary system and established society: in principle the system was satisfactory, only the citizens' direct influence on their own life circumstances should be bettered, quality of life should be ignored, and the inappropriate consequences of capitalism should be removed by means of rational planning and reforms. The civic initiatives mainly recruited their members from the middle-class—especially from the highly educated groups—but included peasants and workers, where the concrete problem concerned their life situation.

The ecological movement that grew out of these decentral civic initiatives around the middle of the 1970s had its dynamic center in the opposition to nuclear power—but beyond this it concerned itself with many other ecological topics. The main organization *Bundesverband Bürgerinitiativen Umweltschutz* (BBU) was established in 1972 and eventually gathered approximately 1,000 civic initiatives supported by around 100,000 members. BBU stood alone as the most important grassroots organization in West Germany in the 1970s and as such served among other things as the central coordinator for the major actions against nuclear power. BBU sought to unite the ideals of decentral, direct democracy and the autonomy of the individual civic initiatives with the effort to guarantee a certain amount of efficiency in the umbrella organization—which encompassed pragmatic and more fundamentalist positions; social-democratic, conservative, "green" and socialistic points of view constantly took to the field against one another on the level of principles, but in practice, in the concrete campaigns and actions, BBU was the framework for wide-ranging and mutually stimulating cooperation between theses various currents.

As mentioned above, it was the question of nuclear power that became the uniting theme for the ecological movement. Nuclear power became a topic for political debate in West Germany in 1973/74, but in truth it had been part of state policy-making ever since 1955, when as part of the Paris agreements the Federal Republic was allowed to do research in nuclear energy. In order to maintain the position of the electro and machine industry on the world market—and as far as the state was concerned also in order to be included in the development of the field of nuclear weapons—the state and industry made considerable investments in research and development in the area of nuclear power technology in subsequent years.[4]

The state had supported this expansion by developing the home market for the reactor industry, which thus initially played an essential role as a display window to the world market. But when the "oil crisis" in 1973/74 raised practical doubts about the opportuneness of the Western countries' strong dependency on oil as an energy source, the Federal Republic saw the point of converting much of the Western power supply to nuclear power: a conversion of this kind would at once strengthen the West German nuclear industry and decrease dependency on the apparently uncertain oil supply. A large-scale program for developing the nuclear power capacity of West Germany was thus adopted; beyond the nine nuclear power plants already in operation, an additional ten reactors were thus under construction in 1976, and an extra eighteen were projected. The goal was that more than 40 percent of West German power consumption was to be supplied by nuclear power by 1985.

The interest in further developing nuclear power in West Germany related to a joint platform for weighty, prospering branches of industry, for strategic state planning with regard to the position of national capital on the world market and with regard to ensuring the supplies on the home market, as well as for the labor movement's efforts to guarantee jobs in the energy sector and in industry in general. It was a strong front, and in consideration of the mass of capital already placed in nuclear power technology, it had de facto a lot to lose.

At first, opposition to nuclear power turned up as a theme for individual civic initiatives, that is, in the local areas where the nuclear plants were to be situated. The broad commitment among the movement of civic initiatives and the other currents that eventually joined it thus also arose in continuation of these local conflicts. The conflict that above all triggered the generalization of the opposition to nuclear power was the struggle in Wyhl in Baden-Württemberg. At this village in the wine country of Kaiserstuhl the authorities intended to start building a nuclear power plant in 1973. The local winegrowers and other concerned citizens opposed the plan and formed civic initiatives—which the state parliament ignored. The conflict came to a head and in February 1975 the local civic initiatives, which were gradually supported by the entire surrounding area and by activists from the surrounding cities—proceeded to occupy the construction site. The authorities had the site cleared by a strong and hard-hitting police force, but a few days later 30,000 demonstrators broke through the barricade and the occupation continued for several months. Under the impression of this large-scale opposition, the administrative court in Freiburg later put a stop to the building of the plant in Wyhl.

The prolonged and sometimes highly radical struggle in Wyhl attracted a great deal of public attention throughout West Germany, and in the broad movement of civic initiatives and the other oppositional currents, the example of Wyhl created considerable motivation to fight against the Federal Government's nuclear power program. This widespread readiness to protest was developed for the first time in the confrontations related to the projected power plant in Brokdorf in Schleswig-Holstein in 1976/77, and thus it is not until this point that one can speak of an actual *movement* against nuclear power in West Germany, even though the opposition had long since matured decentrally in the civic initiatives and the various political and subcultural offshoots of the uprising in the 1960s.[5]

The confrontations in Brokdorf became quite violent. Taught by their experiences in Wyhl, the authorities concentrated on keeping the construction site from being occupied. To this end the site was transformed into a regular fortification with broad moats and high, solid barbed wire fences. Likewise, for many of the demonstrators the struggle in Wyhl held a paradigmatic status: occupying the site was regarded as the only way to victory, and each time the actions thus accelerated to civil war scenarios, where a ten-thousand-persons-strong crowd of demonstrators was driven away by an almost equally as numerous, paramilitarily organized police force equipped with clubs, tear gas, chemical clubs, water canons and helicopters.

The same scene unfolded in 1977 at the construction sites in Grohnde, Kalkar and Gorleben, and the radicality increased on both sides. The police increasingly made use of "pre-emptive" attacks on the demonstrators: for instance, by barricading access roads they could keep demonstrators from even reaching the demonstration, or the same effect could be achieved by organizing comprehensive search and seizure actions against the recently arrived demonstrators with the excuse that they were suspected of being in possession of "passive weaponry" (a concept invented for the occasion, comprising everything from lemons to car tools to crash helmets). Finally, the police increasingly made use of provacateurs in order to escalate the actions and thus the division between the demonstrators.[6]

The antinuclear power movement recruited broadly: from the younger, educated middle-class, which constitutes the "classic" basis of new social movements, from the groups directly affected by the concrete conflict (often farmers in the local area who saw their livelihood or social status threatened), and finally—and gradually as the conflicts got worse—from the small leftwing groups and other offshoots of the uprisings in the 1960s. The movement thus contained a spectrum ranging from conservative environmental advocates to Christians and social democrats to Maoists and anarchists. In the struggle against nuclear power these socially, culturally, and politically diverse groups joined in a broad consensus, which beyond the immediate theme also gradually included a general opposition to industrial society's principle of blind economic growth and the ensuing environmental destruction, as well as a profound distrust of the state and the technocratized political institutions. As we shall return to below, the movement oriented itself as positive counter images to ideas about ecological balance, quality of life, and decentral, direct democratic structures—and here the "alternative movement's" themes and practical attempts to create new ways of living came to play a central role as an inspiration for the broader ecological movement's formation of identity.[7]

Notwithstanding all its actual inner contradictions, the ecological movement remained a joint, extraparliamentary force at first with nuclear power as a central theme, but it also dealt with a variety of ecological problems and carried out large and small actions related to other issues. The interests that the movement was up against in the field of nuclear power were nevertheless so massive that it ultimately suffered defeat. Since the ecological movement and the established political system had diametrically opposed interests in this field and were practically at war with each other, it was primarily the courts that regulated the conflicts, and as the movement grew stronger it became capable by these means of winning certain concessions such as the building stop in Wyhl, but never victories; the plans were merely put on hold, and as later developments have demonstrated, they were largely resumed after several years. In connection with this partial displacement of the battle from the sphere of politics to that of the law, the movement was confronted with a large number of legal and bureaucratic attempts to marginalize it, where complicated procedural rules, regulations concerning the right to make complaints, and so on systematically came in the way of achieving the goal of the movement: stopping nuclear power.[8]

The power balances surrounding the nuclear power issue in West Germany thus remained adverse to the ecological movement. Yet it was not a spirit of defeat or disillusionment that led to the movement being particularized and partially divided at the end of the 1970s, but rather the increasingly violent character of the big actions. This development had two causes: first, the brutal conduct that the state (supported by the media, the business sector, and the labor movement) manifested toward all extraparliamentary activity. The political climate in West Germany was utterly and completely determined by the Red Army Faction's terror actions and the state's attempts to obviate them. Even though the ecological movement was in no way part of these processes, at its demonstrations it was forced to pay for them in the shape of a police effort entirely out of proportion to the task. For the authorities it was a question of erasing the difference between terrorism and extraparliamentary political activity in a broad sense in this period, and beyond the use of violence at the demonstrations the opponents to nuclear power also became increasingly criminalized: demonstrations were forbidden, random individuals were made responsible for the demonstration as a whole, the penalties were made more severe, and so on.

Secondly, a minority of the demonstrators contributed to fuelling the fires of violence. To a certain extent it was youth from the anarchistic subculture who let themselves be provoked by the police brutality, but above all it was the cynical, calculated use of violence by a number of minor communist groups (the so-called "K-groups"). For years these groups had been waiting in vain for the working class to rise and take revolutionary action. With the ecological movement something finally happened; surely, it was not the working class that marched against the nuclear power plants, but still: it was the masses. The K-groups saw the opportunity of accomplishing the historical mission that their theory of revolution assigned to them, namely, leading the people's final showdown with state and capital. Parallel to the terrorists' strategic considerations, the "K-groups" use of violence at the demonstrations served "pedagogical" aims in this context: by radicalizing the struggle they would force the state to openly "follow suit" and thus cause the clear fronts of the class struggle to appear behind the fog formations of the ecological struggle. In the course of this process the masses would then gain insight into the reality of the class struggle and the necessity of revolution. The K-groups' commitment to the ecological movement was in other words purely tactical and expressed an attempt to instrumentalize the popular movement in respect to a version of the politico-cultural paradigm of the radicalized uprisings of the 1960s. Later many people from the K-groups—concurrently with the disintegration of the groups—participated constructively in the ecological movement, for one thing in forming the environmental party *Die Grünen*; but at the height of the struggle against nuclear power, they screwed up the spiral of violence in a fatal interaction with the police and authorities, thus causing the movement irreparable damage.

The violent confrontations scared sympathizers away and drew a negative picture of the movement in the media; in addition to this, the vast majority of the activists were opposed to the use of violence, and even for more radical elements, already during the Brokdorf demonstrations it had become clear that struggling against the well-equipped police forces was pointless. In 1977 the ecological movement was thus in a situation where it had to seek new ways if it wished to avoid division, defection, and disillusion.

Without it coming to a dramatic disintegration of the movement, the different tendencies now began to separate from one another and go their own ways. A small, autonomous and strongly anti-institutional direction crystallized that contained the most radical elements of the movement. A more far-reaching tendency endeavored to keep together the broad, popular spectrum of the ecological movement, and to support and coordinate these basic activities. This tendency viewed itself as purely extraparliamentary, and BBU served as its general organizational framework. Finally, part of the movement drew the conclusion that the perspective in the former extraparliamentary work was blocked and that the only way forward for the ecological struggle now was to lead it into the parliaments. Eventually the environmental party *Die Grünen* grew out of these efforts.[9]

Nuclear Power in Denmark?

While the new environmental movement in West Germany grew from below as a synthesis of a heterogeneous variety of individual grassroots initiatives, and was not really in touch with the currents of the 1960s until much later on, the core of the Danish environmental movement arose as a regular offshoot of the anti-authoritarian youth uprising. The Danish movement was started "from above" in the shape of the environmental group NOAH, which a group of critical students and young natural science graduates at the University of Copenhagen established in March 1969. As a critical group of experts, NOAH rebuked the Danish authorities' and decision-makers' scanty knowledge and awareness of the environmental field, and due to the obvious necessity of this critique, in the beginning of the 1970s NOAH was able to develop into an actual movement with local groups throughout the country.[10] From this point onward NOAH thus no longer served as an exclusive group of experts, but as an open grassroots movement. Being active in a local group was the only membership requirement. The group's leadership was collective and its organizational form distinctly decentral and oriented towards direct democracy.

From an ecological point of view they worked with such topics as environmental pollution in general, the work environment, harmful substances in foodstuffs, recycling, technology and planning, the global distribution of resources, etc. And they attempted to influence planning by criticizing the local and the state authorities' dispositions and basis for decisions and by making formal complaints. Beyond an extensive informational campaign in respect to the population, the NOAH groups carried out a number of happening-like actions that were effective in the media and whose aim was not only to communicate information, but—like the actions of the provo movement in the 1960s—to provoke the spectators to think and become active themselves.

The reception of NOAH was mixed. Large parts of the population welcomed the environmental advocates, and parts of the established press also supported the protests against the rampant pollution. It was especially an important public breakthrough for the movement when the major daily *Politiken* invited NOAH to be in charge of a correspondence column on pollution in 1969. Authorities and politicians were perplexed—especially due to a lack of knowledge regarding ecological issues—and in the beginning sought to the best of their ability to marginalize or ignore NOAH. At the same time, they started to direct state politics towards being able to meet the environmental demands that were now clearly becoming urgent on a widespread front in society: in the period from 1969 to 1974 a comprehensive bill was drafted in respect to the environmental field and a number of government agencies were established to handle it. The intensified international debate on environmental problems, which among other things was triggered by the Club of Rome's "Limits to Growth" from 1972, further contributed to this initial integration of the ecological complex of problems into established politics.[11]

NOAH carried out lobbyism in concrete cases in respect to both local and central authorities, but as a matter of principle they refused to be part of any formalized collaboration with the newly created, rapidly expanding environmental authorities; they thus declined the offer to hold a position in a central state environmental agency. The background for this position is to be found in NOAH's anchorage in the student movement and its neo-Marxist conception of science, for although NOAH's development from the beginning of the 1970s had widened both the basis for recruitment and the political spectrum of the movement, the anticapitalistic and Marxist current clearly remained predominant. Its resistance to formalized cooperation with the authorities was thus rooted in a fundamental critique of the system that considered the institutions of the system as objective guardians of capital interests and thus as unfit in the perspective of an environmental struggle. NOAH saw this basic position confirmed in the limited scope of the environmental bills with regard to possibilities for effectively preventing pollution, as well as in the bureaucratic marginalization they met on the part of the authorities as these were gradually established and started to regulate more and more areas: the right to make complaints in environmental cases was limited, an immensety complicated complaints procedure was established, and so on.[12]

In connection with this course of events, it is possible to observe if not a radicalization, then an expansion and clarification of NOAH's self-conception. While in 1969 its preamble read: "through informative and analytical activities to contribute to the struggle against pollution," in 1973 it read: "to fight pollution and its causes," and in 1976 the perspective had been extended to "improve the living environment by actively fighting against environmental destruction and its causes—and indicating alternatives."[13]

The general raising of the public consciousness in environmental questions, for which NOAH had paved the way, also benefited the Danish opposition to nuclear power—to the extent that in the last half of the 1970s the opposition to nuclear power tended to place NOAH's broad ecological perspective in the shadows.

The emergence of the nuclear power issue on the political agenda in 1973/74 took the established parties and the public by surprise. At this point only *Ventre socialisterm*, (VS) a small leftwing party, had developed knowledge about the problems of this energy source and based on this had taken a clear stance against nuclear power; the other parties all represented a more or less warm approval of nuclear power, but in the debate their level of information with regard to this technology turned out to be very low—evident in the fact that *Socialistisk Folkeparti*, (SF) a broad leftwing party, and the *Radikale Venstre*, a center party, quickly did a 180-degree about-face and created an image for themselves as opponents of nuclear power.

Even though the theme was basically unknown in the public debate, the idea of nuclear power in Denmark had a history that stretched all the way back to the establishment of the Nuclear Energy Commission in 1955. Especially the producer organization ELSAM kept the idea warm in the power plant circles in the following years, and from the middle of the 1960s, industry and Risø, the nuclear research plant, also started to create an image for themselves as advocates of nuclear power. However, since the oil prices were falling during this period, attempts to put the ideas into action at first were not made, but in 1973/1974, when the oil crisis all at once raised the price of crude oil by 112 percent the adherents of nuclear power suddenly held excellent cards, and they played them with a hard offensive effort towards an unprepared general public. The incentive to quickly decide to convert the power supply so that it was largely based on nuclear power was all the stronger since, at the outbreak of the oil crisis, 90 percent of the Danish supply of electricity was based on oil. In addition—just as in West Germany—the interest in liberating the national energy supply from its dependence on the OPEC countries and the plans for converting to nuclear power had at the start broad political support.[14]

Although the Danish and the West German opposition to nuclear power developed concurrently and demonstrated strong parallels with regard to themes of struggle and organizational forms, it is possible to note crucial differences in the overall conditions of the respective movements: while the West German movement challenged an already established reality in West German society with an accompanying network of organized social interests with many ramifications, the object of the Danish movement still only existed on the drawing board, and consequently it all belonged to the future rather than it being immediately palpable needs and interests that led the forces planning nuclear power in Denmark. Also enormous differences in the weight with which nuclear power entered into the national economy as a whole existed: as we have seen above, the West German reactor industry was a particularly important branch in the 1970s, with a strong competitive position on the world market, and as such it was the object of large-scale public and private investments. By contrast, in Denmark the investments in nuclear power were limited to research expenses and the expenses held by the power plants for planning and analyses made regarding waste disposal and reserving areas for construction sites. These very different overall conditions for the struggle against nuclear power have not in themselves determined its outcome, but they have, for instance, had the effect that in Denmark, to a much greater extent than in West Germany, the struggle could be conducted as a genuine *debate*—without strong pressure from major organizations, urgent economic regards or vital state interests and without the strong marginalizing mechanisms with which pressure like this is often connected.

The Organization for Information on Nuclear Power (OOA) did not define itself as an opposing organization upon being founded in 1974, but merely demanded that the decision to introduce nuclear power be postponed for three years in order for there to be an objective public debate on the subject. OOA was an initiative "from above"; indeed, just like NOAH, OOA was an unusually unspontaneous, well-prepared organization that a group of twelve to fifteen people had worked systematically toward for about one year. Through self-organized study, this group—which included individuals associated with, among others, an ecumenical church organization, NOAH, and an environmental organization for youth—had gained some of the knowledge of nuclear power that the scanty Danish debate had lacked, and moreover it had made extensive organizational and politico-tactical considerations regarding OOA's way of functioning internally and in respect to the public.[15]

Due to the generally raised environmental consciousness in wide population groups and the strength with which nuclear power advocates recited their demands for a quick decision for nuclear power, after its establishment as a small "avant-garde organization" the OOA developed quickly into a broad, national grassroots movement: already by March

1974 fifteen local groups had formed, and in 1980 the number had reached 130. The local groups were autonomous and the entire organization operated according to the principles of direct democracy; there was no representational system and no voting, but rather a "democracy of presence," whereby those present at a given meeting made the decisions, not by majority decision, but by consensus—measures that should counteract the formation of factions. But in contrast to NOAH, the OOA was equipped with an efficient national secretariat that was empowered to take initiatives and make statements on behalf of the entire organization—without consulting the local groups first. The reason for this structure was that their adversary—the state, industry, and the power plants—was centrally organized and the OOA thus had to be effective on this level. This peculiar mixture for a grassroots movement of radical direct democracy and centralism/avant-gardism turned out in practice to work effectively, and as it was never the object of any serious criticism, it must also be assumed to have been satisfactory for the activists.

The OOA's resonance in the general public put pressure on parts of the established political world, and especially due to the Social Democrats the demand for a three-year moratorium was quickly met, as well as the effort to revert the decision-making competency from the Ministry of Education to the parliament. In this way, the nuclear power issue ceased to be an administrative and became a political issue.

While the opposition to nuclear power in West Germany was formed on the basis of a multiplicity of small grassroots organizations, each of which also worked on other areas of the environmental struggle, and which displayed considerable differences among themselves, in Denmark there was thus one organization, which limited its field of activity to the theme of nuclear power and energy planning. The cornerstone of the OOA's strategy was information campaigns in respect to the population and authorities, and they constantly tried to be a little ahead of nuclear power advocates with regard to objective argumentation and well-founded knowledge. They thus also refrained from participating in ideologically or party-politically biased polemics, and there is hardly any doubt that precisely this objective course oriented toward a single issue was decisive for the OOA's broad penetration in the public. Another main theme in the work of the movement was presenting concrete alternatives to nuclear power considered in terms of their ecological and social consequences. In cooperation with a number of researchers they thus presented an alternative power plan for Denmark in 1976, advocating— as a contrast to the government's power plan from the same year—that nuclear power be dropped, pointing out extensive possibilities for energy efficiency and giving high priority to the use of sustainable energy sources. As regards the planning and realization (e.g., in the form of windmills, natural gas plants, etc.) of these concrete alternatives in the field of energy, the Danish movement was far ahead of the West German one in the 1970s. Along the lines of the West German movement, the OOA was additionally concerned with the close connection between the civil and military use of nuclear energy, as well as with the wider political and social perspectives of nuclear power, seeing the danger of authoritarian state development take shape in the light of the more severe demands on control and safety that accompanied this technology.

During its first two years the OOA's information campaigns focused on collecting signatures, distributing campaign newspapers, informational meetings, and so on. Starting in 1976 they organized major demonstrations and marches against nuclear power, cooperating among others with the Swedish antinuclear movement in the struggle against the Barsebäck plant and with the West German movement in opposition to the Brokdorf plan. Their biggest campaign was distributing the informational newspaper *Denmark Without Nuclear Power* to all households in Denmark in 1979/80.

In the second half of the 1970s, the arguments of the advocates of nuclear power slowly crumbled: the asserted security of supplies turned out to be at the very least doubtful, inasmuch as the world's uranium resources were limited and mostly under the control of the United States and the Soviet Union. The actual experiences with nuclear power plants seriously weakened their arguments about cheaper power and more jobs, and there still wasn't anyone with a plausible solution to the waste problems. Finally, the danger of breakdowns with incalculable consequences became entirely palpable with the accident on Three Mile Island in the United States in March 1979.

Under the impression of these conditions and the OOA's continued information campaigns, the opposition grew among the general public in Denmark, the majority of which was opposing nuclear power as early as 1976. This development created a schism in the basis of most of the supporting parties, and especially in the Social Democrats this resulted in strong tensions between the nuclear power-oriented party leadership and the growing minority of opponents. The party pushed this internal conflict ahead of itself for years by initiating a large number of reviews to create a clear and satisfactory basis for making decisions regarding all aspects of nuclear power. When these reports were finally available in 1984, the Social Democrats no longer formed the government and the opposition of its members could thus come to the front in the politics of the party— even though the reports they themselves had ordered took a positive attitude to the introduction of nuclear power in Denmark. With this slide in the Social Democrats' position an alternative majority in parliament arose in the area of energy policy, adopting in the spring of 1985 an energy policy without nuclear power and revoking the reservations of areas of land linked to this. The conservative government remained an advocate of nuclear power, but kept—probably due to the many indications that nuclear power was not such a good piece of business after all—low profile in respect to the shelving. The OOA had won—so far.

Experiences of Conflict and Politico-Cultural Patterns

Entirely like the reactions to the uprising in the 1960s, the leading parts of the established political world in both Denmark and West Germany sought to meet the challenge from the environmental movement by sowing seeds of doubt on their legitimacy and democratic disposition. In West Germany the opponents of nuclear power were stamped as radical leftists and anarchists; they were from time to time accused of receiving money from East Berlin and running errands for the Eastern bloc, and the media had a penchant for portraying the movement in the light of the violent confrontations into which the major demonstrations escalated.

Even though the historical and current Danish contexts were quite different, the same kind of marginalization flourished in the Danish debate by the casting of doubt on the movement politically. It was insinuated that the OOA and NOAH stood behind terrorist activities and were the instrument of the extreme left. This idea of a fundamental contradiction between the environmental movement and democracy played implicitly or explicitly a key role in the concrete local conflicts, serving to expel the movement's protests and demands from the field of positions with a claim to political consideration.

Beyond these tendencies, in Denmark the established political world generally presented the protest of the environmental movement as emotional and hence amateurish and unqualified. In addition, the environmental movement encountered a less calculated and articulate—but for all that no less active—kind of opposition from the side of the established system: that of bureaucracy. Thus, issues such as the right to make complaints, procedures, and so on were woven into a complicated net of regulations, knowledge of which laymen could acquire only with great difficulty and which in many cases excluded the environmental movement from influence on a purely technical level.

In West Germany, however, the established political system dealt with the conflicts with the environmental movement primarily by means of a variety of repressive measures. As mentioned above, these conflicts took place in a political climate highly influenced by the clash between state and terrorism, and by still active remains from the absolutist state on several different levels. The West German State's general approach to extraparliamentary activity was characterized in this period by "authoritarian legalism,"[16] which in continuation of the German tradition regarded unauthorized political movements as a potential security risk for the state and thus as phenomena that should be neutralized. Civil disobedience was thus in advance precluded from being able to invoke any kind of legitimacy.[17]

The environmental movement became familiar with this basic state attitude: in part in the form of bans against demonstrations, a hard, criminalizing court practice towards civil disobedience, and infiltration and surveillance on the part of the political police, *Verfassungsschutz*, in part in the form of the use of both pre-emptive and direct, confrontational force. This distinctly repressive dimension in the established political world's way of dealing with conflict was—as was the case during the uprising of the 1960s,—of crucial importance in the politico-cultural processes, causing profound ruptures in the worldview of the activists.

Superficially, the West German authorities' repressive way of dealing with the environmental movement was fundamentally dissimilar to the course of events in Denmark, for while sporadic attempts were also made here to place obstacles in the way of the environmental movement,[18] neither NOAH's or OOA's actions escalated at any point in time into violent clashes with the police, and the authorities' general course of action towards civil disobedience was tolerant and mild.

As opposed to West Germany, it was not a fundamental, authoritarian legalism that determined the authorities' way of dealing with the "difficult" movements, but rather pragmatic considerations of the concrete situation and the interests and considerations defining this. Again, the fact that the Danish movements had allies in the parliaments and in the established public, and that parts of the nascent environmental administration also took a sympathetic view of the movements' work played a not insignificant role in procuring and maintaining this pragmatic course.

While the uprising in the 1960s originated with the relatively narrow needs and interests of the life situation of youth in the process of education, the environmental movement of the 1970s organized the effects of transformations in the life-world of wide sections of the population. With its revolutionizing of traditional life-world structures, the advancing societalization of the conditions of reproduction problematized the life situation of increasingly larger sections of the population, thus producing a growing but latent potential for social conflict.[19] But whereas the more specific problems in the 1960s uprising became the driving force in an offensive-expansive politicization process—whose rallying cry to start with was a universalistic confidence in progress and a desire to realize the modern, democratic project, only criticizing the aspects of the modernization process that got in the way of this—the wider opposition in the life-world that the environmental movement organized and politicized was rather of a defensive kind in the beginning.

The opposition was directed toward the experienced *dangers* that the capitalistic modernization process inflicted on the life-world and the interests connected to this, and it had a diffuse, emotional critique of modernity as its basic theme. Unlike the uprising from 1960s it was not based on a radical experience of ruptured identity, which gave the universe fixed contours, but on an underlying, vague sense of distaste over the enormous social and cultural changes. This distaste, which on the individual level could be experienced as feelings of loneliness, anxiety, and alienation, remained in the politicization process an essential socio-psychological sounding board for the environmental movement's treatment and formulation of its themes.[20] But in the concrete struggles for specific, regionally and thematically limited life-world interests, and upon encountering the reactions of the established political systems outlined above, the contours of this diffuse emotional opposition towards the consequences of modernization for the life-world became even more distinct, and it was in these processes that the environmental movement's experience of conflict was organized and its politico-cultural profile took shape. The concrete course taken by the conflict slowly undermined the political worldview that was predominant among well-functioning citizens.

On the basis of a concrete conflict of interests that involved life-world interests experienced as burdensome, wide sections of the population went through learning processes in which the antagonism between a traditional, authorized worldview and real experience became so critical that the former had to start disintegrating. People commonly experienced that the politicians they themselves had elected openly disregarded their interests, that the experts they had formerly believed were objective and unprejudiced suddenly proved to be willing instruments for political interests, and that the mass media they had regarded as being neutral communicators of objective information revealed themselves to be misrepresenting, tendentious agents for established interests.[21]

Dealing with these experiences involved extensively revising the former worldview. If one risks being called an extremist or communist merely for defending one's elementary interests, it is also possible that the authorities acted unjustly in all sorts of other situations, and that the media lied. These experiences, which gradually crystallized through prolonged and frequent connections with authorities and the media, shook the movements and the worldview of the individual activists.

Along with the other bureaucratic, verbal and—especially in West Germany—violent experiences of conflict, these reality shocks created a crisis of identity in the environmental movement, which did not have the monomaniacal character of the radicalized uprising in the 1960s, but which however became a primary driving force in developing and determining the form of the politico-cultural patterns according to which the movement thought and acted.

The main tendency in Denmark and West Germany was that the environmental movement dealt with its experience of conflict in a dichotomous figure with implications that were highly critical of the system. As mentioned above, the offshoots of the youth and student uprising played a not insignificant role in the environmental movement's work and the formation of its consciousness, and these currents have thus also made a distinct impression on the aspects of the movement's self-conception that are critical of the system, but they would not have been able to achieve this status if their critique of the system had not been capable of gathering and organizing general experiences in the broad movement.

In contrast to the formation of consensus in the uprising of the 1960s, the critical consensus that crystallized in the course of the environmental movement's struggles was founded on broad life-world interests, but like the former movement it created an image of itself as an absolute "otherness" in respect to the system. The fundamental values in this consensus were thus generally defined in sharp contrast to the functional principles of the established political and economic system, but the various concrete formulations of this conflict of interests actually insert it in different scenarios—and it is these scenarios that are decisive for the politico-cultural perspectives in the formation of consensus.

The movement's orientation toward decentral, direct democracy therefore contained relatively different views of parliamentarian democracy. In the opinion of many currents in the West German environmental movement, in the course of the conflict parliamentarian democracy had become identical to the politics and the dynamics of blind economic growth that they were fighting against. The negative experiences of conflict were thus in the view of the movement largely centered around the parliamentarian system, making this into a problematic entity with which to deal.

The course of events surrounding the West German environmental movement was thus in a politico-cultural sense an expression of the fact that a broad yet diffuse democratic potential in the population by way of an authoritarian-legalistic state practice of marginalization was driven into a position that was no longer founded on or reflected politico-consensual ideologies. Instead, they sought legitimization in ideas about a completely different, "true democracy" whose logical conclusion implied a totalitarian attitude to political disagreement and to the institutional democratic process as such. In principle, this "alternative" democratic self-conception could thus end up appearing counter-productive in respect to the development of a democratic political culture in West Germany.[22]

Throughout the course of events the established political world strongly supported this counter-productive developmental direction, in part through the continuity of its marginalizing efforts in respect to the environmental movement's demands and actions, in part because it confirmed the movement's self-conception as a "counter-force" precisely by only—fleetingly—taking it seriously when it resorted to militant actions like occupying construction sites and the like. In a structural sense, this is the same fatal dialectic between the systemic blocking of conflicts and the displacement of the worldview of a life-world movement that could be observed in connection with the development of West German terrorism.[23]

In the predominant Danish environmental organizations, however, the aim of their expressed self-conception was fundamentally for the extraparliamentary work to create public opinion that would thrust the movement's demands onto the political agenda and force parliamentarian politics to give priority to environmental interests. Consequently, on the programmatic level, here it was more a question of a dialectical concept for the relationship between parliamentarian and extraparliamentarian politics, between representative democracy and direct democracy. But actually the Danish movements' understanding of democracy was a complex and ultimately confused entity. NOAH's and OOA's own organizational structure was for instance developed in sharp contradistinction to the principle of representation—they explicitly distinguished between "real" and "formal" democracy, referring to direct democracy and the representative system, respectively—and the perspectives that this distinction contained for the development of society and democracy were not considered in further detail. Likewise, a variety of comments and evaluations in NOAH's and OOA's ongoing debate attest to their fundamental doubts about the ability of the representative system to solve the problems that the movement considered urgent.

Next to its fundamentally dialectical approach to the authorities regarding the practical work, the Danish environmental movement thus also contained—although in a less prominent position than the West German—politico-cultural ideologies that abstractly negated parliamentarian democracy, viewing direct democratic life-world institutions as the forums where politics rightly belonged, and therefore back to which the movement should deliver it. But whereas in the West German context these tendencies were up front and structured the political universe, in the Danish context they belonged to an underlying, emotional level as a cultural sounding board for critique and visions at the base of the movement, not on the manifest, political level.

These tendencies in the antinuclear power movements' formation of their identity stem from, as we have seen, the interaction between the life-world needs politicized in the cultural process of modernization and the various constellations of interests, power balances and politico-cultural traditions characterizing the specific national space of praxis. The question is then whether the tendencies mentioned, which demonstrate elements of ideological affinity with totalitarian currents, actually contained elements of danger to democracy in West Germany and Denmark.

There is nothing to indicate that this was the case. Even though ambiguities exist as concerns their exact understanding of democracy, all the currents explicitly defined themselves within a democratic horizon, where the focus was on the anti-authoritarian attitude and the demand for empowerment of citizens. If anything, in its social effects the movement helped democratization and the development of a modern political culture—not to mention its concrete merits as an environmental advocate.

As the thematic framework for extensive changes in wide needs and interests of the life-world, the antinuclear power movement raised the level of consciousness in large sections of the populations in Denmark and in West Germany, strengthening a democratic, political self-consciousness on a basic level. In Denmark the movement furthermore exercised a powerful influence on the established political system, both in respect to the political agenda and the authorities' openness and willingness to listen to protests and demands from the life-world. In West Germany, however, the established political system in the 1970s maintained its marginalizing efforts in respect to extraparliamentarian protests and likewise only to a very limited extent allowed the environmental movement's themes to gain a foothold in institutional politics. Not until the parliamentarian efforts of *Die Grünen,* the environmental party, in the 1980s and 1990s have these extreme oppositions been mitigated.

Translated by Stacey Cozart

Notes

1. The term "life-world" is here used according to Jürgen Habermas' definitions, *Theorie des kommunikativen Handelns,* vol. 1–2 (Frankfurt am Main, 1981); English version: *The Theory of Communicative Action,* vol. 1–2 (Cambridge 1995/97) in which he conceptualizes the life-world as the historically specific horizon of meaning in which communicative interaction takes place.
2. Henrik Kaare Nielsen, *Demokrati i bevægelse* (Aarhus, 1991).
3. Peter Mayer-Tasch, *Die Bürgerinitiativbewegung* (Reinbek, 1981).
4. Herbert Kitschelt, "Kernenergie und politischer Konflikt," in *Leviathan,* no. 4 (Berlin, 1979).
5. Karl-Werner Brand et al., *Aufbruch in eine andere Gesellschaft* (Frankfurt am Main, 1983)

6. Enno Brand, *Staatsgewalt* (Göttingen, 1988).
7. Joseph Huber, *Wer soll das alles ändern* (Berlin, 1980).
8. Herbert Kitschelt, "Justizapparate als Konfliktlösungsinstanz?," *Demokratie und Recht*, no. 1 (Köln, 1979).
9. Richard Stöss, ed., *Parteienhandbuch* (Opladen, 1984).
10. Peter Gundelach, *Sociale bevægelser og samfundsændringer* (Århus, 1988), 236.
11. Jeppe Læssøe, The Making of the New Environmentalism in Denmark, manuscript (Copenhagen, 1989).
12. NOAH, *For miljøets skyld* (Copenhagen, 1989).
13. Ibid.
14. Niels Christian Sidenius, "Hvorfor er der ikke atomkraftværker i Danmark?," *Politica* 18, no. 4 (Aarhus, 1986).
15. Siegfried Christiansen, *Den danske oplysningskampagne om atomkraft 1974–1977*, unpublished script (Copenhagen, 1977).
16. Jürgen Habermas, *Die neue Unübersichtlichkeit* (Frankfurt am Main, 1985), 97.
17. Sebastian Cobler et al., *Das Demonstrationsrecht* (Reinbek, 1983).
18. OOA, "aldrig gi'r vi op." (Copenhagen, 1978); OOA: *Atomkraft?*, no. 1–45 (Copenhagen, 1974/84).
19. Habermas, *Theorie des kommunikativen Handelns*; Joachim Hirsch, *Der Sicherheitsstaat* (Frankfurt am Main, 1980); Joachim Raschke, *Soziale Bewegungen* (Frankfurt am Main, 1985); Roland Roth and Dieter Rucht, *Neue soziale Bewegungen in der Bundesrepublik Deutschland* (Frankfurt am Main, 1987).
20. Bjarne K. Herskin, *Aktivisten—på vej til en ikke-ideologi*, working paper, from Institut for Organisation og Arbejdssociologi (Copenhagen, no indication of year).
21. Nina Gladitz, ed., *Lieber heute aktiv als morgen radioaktiv* (Berlin, 1976).
22. Alternative Liste, Dokumentation über die Gewaltdiskussion in der Alternativen Liste Berlin (Berlin, 1983).
23. Nielsen, *Demokrati i bevægelse*.

Chapter 10

"Youth Enacts Society and Somebody Makes a Coup": The Danish Student Movement between Political and Lifestyle Radicalism

Steven L.B. Jensen

In August 1968 a group of 130 people from the Copenhagen student activist movement gathered for a week long retreat to discuss and plan the future directions of the movement. The movement had during the Spring—after successful actions by a large group of psychology students followed up by the broader activist movement—initiated widespread reform of how Danish universities were to be governed. Now the student movement needed to define a way forward in matters of university policy in a political environment that within a few short months had changed a stagnant reform agenda, in which the input from the elected student representatives was sidelined, to one dominated by students demonstrating, questioning their professors about the quality and relevance of the education they were receiving and challenging the undemocratic nature of the governing bodies. On these governing bodies not just the students but also the non-professorial academic staff had no representation or formal influence. The events in the Spring of 1968 culminated with the psychology students occupying the university, followed by a large scale demonstration in front of the University of Copenhagen situated in the center of the city.

Events had moved so quickly that the activist movement had not really defined itself beyond describing itself as open and anti-hierarchical in nature. It had been an effective channel for mobilizing parts of the student community but it had already in its short lifespan shown its weaknesses. The organizational memory can be short in a movement of this nature and on several occasions during its Spring meetings discussions that had been settled at an earlier point were reopened. This was at least partly due to the constant flux of participants and a lack of clear records of what had been decided earlier.

As the 130 students gathered on Mors—a small island far from Copenhagen—these were some of the issues to be addressed. Above all it was to provide the activist movement with its purpose and aims. The students did not lack ambition or media attention as three national newspapers chose to report from the retreat.

As it turned out the retreat was ridden with internal conflicts. The dividing line was between those arguing for focused political activism and those who argued for lifestyle radicalism as the movement's *raison d'être*. These conflicts were already in the making during the planning process but became full-blown during the week itself. This tension between political and lifestyle radicals is well-known from other countries. It is most famously captured in a remark by the German activist Dieter Kunzelmann in *Der Spiegel* in 1967 where he stated "The Vietnam War does not interest me—only my problems with orgasms do."

The retreat was not a defining moment in the history of the 1960s Danish student movement. Actually it failed completely to meet its intended aim and it might well be argued that it was an irrelevant event in the Danish student revolt. However, as the Anthropologist Clifford Geertz famous dictum goes, "small facts speak to large issues" and the reasons for the failure are significant in order to understand the development, political nature, and paradoxes inherent in the Danish Student Movement.

The aim of this chapter is therefore to place the activist movement's retreat in the larger context of the Danish student revolt as it developed before and to a minor extent after the retreat itself. Furthermore, at the end of this chapter key themes and concepts that were part of the dividing lines at the retreat will be placed in the wider context of "1968" political and lifestyle youth rebellion.[1] This will be done by exploring more closely the concepts of alienation, revolution and emancipation and their relationship in the self-perception of the "counterculturals." However, before embarking on this it is necessary to present some background to the development of the student revolt and the activist movement prior to the August 1968 gathering on Mors.

The Start of the Student Revolt in Denmark

The student revolt in Denmark started on 21 March 1968 when a group of psychology students gathered for a demonstration in Studiegården—a courtyard enclosed by university buildings. Loud music was played live by the popular "hippie" band Burnin' Red Ivanhoe to ensure that classes would be interrupted and the demonstration would get the attention necessary from both students and professors. The concert was followed by speeches from a number of students putting forward demands for "Democracy in the workplace" (a trade union slogan of the time) and "Academic freedom—also for the students." On a gable facing the courtyard some students had the night before painted in large letters, "Bryd Professorvældet. Medbestemmelse nu" (meaning: Destroy the monopoly of power held by the professors. Power sharing now). The demonstration caught the attention of quite a few students and also some professors who went to see and stayed to listen to the spectacle. It was also covered extensively by leading Danish newspapers—thereby initiating an important strategic link for the students between the organization of political manifestations and success in attracting media attention thereby disseminating their messages throughout the population. The need for university reform had been discussed on several occasions in the years preceding 1968 but without leading to any real changes. The media liked the news value and novelty of the methods being used in student politics, though not all the newspapers were in agreement with the demands put forward by the students.

The demonstration was followed up the same evening with an "action meeting" for psychology students in order to plan the way forward. The demonstration had been planned in some secrecy and the organizers had not wanted to define the agenda beyond the initial manifestation. It was up to the psychology students in an open forum to define the agenda for future manifestations. They decided to focus on actions that would quickly mobilize members of the student community instead of focusing on long term objectives. The momentum had to be kept going.

The students decided to go on strike the next day (a Friday) and make the following week (25–29 March) "a debating week" where teachers were to be forced to discuss the form, contents, and purpose of the specific courses they were teaching as well as the overall contents of the degree in Psychology. If the teachers did not accept this proposal the students were to leave classes. This proposal was a way of engaging all students in the discussions raised by the activists. The idea did receive widespread support with only very few students and teachers not accepting the ultimatum.

During the debating week the psychology students also decided to go beyond their own department and called students from all university faculties to a meeting on 27 March to inform them about the actions taken within the previous week. Their hope was that similar processes would be initiated at the other departments. The psychology students had realized that they would only succeed in their demands for a reform of the governing structures of the universities if other students raised the same demands. With one day's notice they managed to gather 200 students for this interdepartmental meeting. The aim of the meeting was to organize and mobilize students and establish a broader based activist policy that would both attack the power monopoly of the professors and in the longer term lobby for improved teaching facilities and better qualified teachers. Furthermore, it was decisive for the psychology students that it should be done outside the Student Council—the official political body with elected student representatives—as this council was regarded as being a failure. This meeting on 27 March was in effect the birth of the Copenhagen student activist movement.

The next day, 28 March, there was a meeting of the Student Council. At the meeting the council had to fight for its legitimacy and authority. They had as elected representatives pursued a strategy of negotiation with the university authorities and had been represented on the University Administration Committee established by the Danish Government to provide suggestions on how to reform and modernize the universities and how to make them more efficient. Their views had been ignored by the majority of professors on this committee.[2]

Two strategies stood in opposition to one another. The negotiation strategy supported by the Student Council versus the activist strategy, and it was the activist strategy that was gaining credibility. The activists saw themselves as being spontaneous and in closer contact with the student community and therefore a more legitimate political player than the Student Council and its careerists. The latter were regarded as technocrats and politically ambitious students that were using the council as a springboard for a career after finishing university. Furthermore they had been incapable of getting a political breakthrough for the student's demands for reform. It was therefore absolutely necessary to make use of other political means.[3]

Posed with this challenge it was decisive for the council to regain the initiative by being the coordinating body for the activists. The chairman of the council, Christian S. Nissen, used a strategy of being accommodating and expressing agreement with the views held by the activists. Thereafter he integrated the criticism into Student Council style of politics with interesting formulations like, "Spontaneity is a necessary thing but it must necessarily take place within the framework of the plan laid out beforehand."[4]

The psychology students did not intend to allow the initiative to pass to the council. They found it authoritarian and not in accord with the people they represented. The political manifestations would be watered down if the council was to coordinate them and the momentum for change would be lost.

After lengthy discussion a resolution was agreed upon in which the Student Council moved closer to the activist strategy. The resolution was an attempt by the council to catch up with an important political initiative from the student community that had left them sidelined, it having been partly directed against the council itself due to its perceived failures. The activist students—at this stage mainly the psychology students—had succeeded in influencing the Student Council but it was not a success that was regarded as relevant. The ambition was to mobilize students at department level and engage as many as possible in discussing the future of the revolt. It was large-scale, open and supposedly non-hierarchical meetings that were to be the organizational form and not representative democracy. At least for now the Student Council remained sidelined.

The psychology students now entered a period of negotiation on power-sharing with the professors at the Department of Psychology. They had the support of the chancellor to their efforts to find an interim arrangement before a more comprehensive solution could be found for the whole of the university. Knowing well that such an arrangement would have widespread influence on the broader solution to be found for the university, the students dismissed the outcome of the negotiations on 19 April. The draft proposal outlining a departmental board with representation of both professors and students was not far-reaching enough. In response the students decided to occupy the university (or rather their department). This action should not be seen solely as dissatisfaction with the draft proposal but also in the light of internal politics in the movement. The initial organizers of the demonstration on 21 March were worried that the period of negotiation had led to a loss of momentum. Another political manifestation would create a new political situation and at the same time strengthen the efforts to mobilize students.

The occupation turned out to be successful. The students regained the initiative and a new proposal was drafted that largely accommodated the psychology students on the outstanding issues, e.g., influence on the content of the courses taught. The occupation was the climax of events in Spring 1968 and when the psychology students left the barricades at noon on 25 April their role as the leading force in the revolt came to an end. It was thereafter up to the broader activist movement to take over.

The Making of the Activist Movement—March-May 1968

The activist movement was to be an interfaculty coordinating forum for students. Though the minutes from the meeting on 27 March do not give a clear picture of the birth of a movement, it is evident that students who did not normally discuss student politics had been brought together for the first time. Not before April did a clearer outline of the activist movement emerge.

On 23 April about 5,000 students demonstrated in the Cathedral square in front of the main university building in the heart of Copenhagen. The demonstration had been organized in fourteen days and only a month had passed since the start of the revolt. In that month the political deadlock had been broken and a comprehensive public debate on the future of the universities and on the revolt itself had taken place in the printed and broadcasting media. The activist movement was on a high. The movement lived off these manifestations as they provided a clear target for its work and secured the internal coherence of the movement. The fact that the demonstration took place at the same time as the occupation of the university and the successful completion of the psychology students' revolt was clear confirmation of the success of the activist strategy. It also made necessary the definition of new demands and objectives if the movement were to continue to have a reason to exist.

A group tried to develop a policy paper on the objectives of the movement.[5] The aim of the political manifestations was to achieve full openness and real influence on student politics to secure the active participation of the larger student community. A restructuring of the student organizations was necessary to ensure close contacts with this community. It is striking that the long term political aims over and above the educational system are not mentioned. The closest they came to this was when they—in rather vague terms—defined the main purpose of education as acquiring, "a critical attitude towards the sciences and other aspects of society." The reasons given for the demand for change was that tuition was outdated with one-sided scientific traditions being the basis of too many subjects and outdated teaching methods and too much irrelevant literature being part of the course work. This work was according to the students based solely on knowledge accumulation and not the objective of developing an independent and critical understanding of the subject one was studying.

Among the long term aims and purposes the following were also mentioned: "The process of democratization is a necessary condition for the renewal of the structure and purpose of the university which societal developments have long since demanded ... The university should not be an isolated enclave in society but an integrated and creative part ...

Education of students should not be an adjustment to the once accepted administration of society but should provide the students with the skills to critically take part in the dynamic development of present and future society."[6]

More debates took place during May but without moving the agenda forward. On several occasions the debates started all over due to new people attending the meetings and to their being no clear minutes of discussions from earlier meetings. The loosely organized but highly active movement with no membership and no official leadership provided freshness into student politics but the loose structure was also an Achilles heal. The "collective memory" was vague and lead on several occasions to discussions of a principle nature having to start all over again. It also indicates a problem in finding a focus. The activist strategy had hitherto been a success and would be an obvious strategy also in the future. But what would the objectives be? And what political issues should the activists engage themselves in? The activist movement had an awareness of the problems caused by the organizational structure. The fact that there was a long summer holiday between the end of the Spring semester and the beginning of the Autumn semester which brought in a large influx of new students that needed to be mobilized also posed problems. These challenges were what the August retreat on Mors was supposed to solve.

Planning the Retreat

During the planning process a presentation outlining the purpose of the retreat was prepared. In this document one of the ambitions mentioned was to discuss the conflict between the generations and the different roles they played at the universities. Were the conflicts between the activists and the Student Council members decided "by the different roles that the system had assigned to them"? Was there an innate tendency in all systems toward conflict "between the highest authority, the delegates and their constituents"?[7] This aspect of the retreat indicated an ambition to discuss how interactions took place between different groups at the university, it also including interactions within the student community itself. The thinking on the nature of the "system" is worth taking note of. It is presented as a conscious agent in the perception of the students, i.e., "roles that the system had assigned to them."

In addition to this the activists were to discuss the objectives of the universities, their internal organization in light of the new future structure that was to be developed, their dependence on other societal institutions, and the position of science and academic research in society. As regards the activist movement itself the debates would focus on: "when should actions be used? Which actions should be used? Should actions be an independent means or should they support negotiations, democratic methods: how will we ensure being represented on all standing committees and political bodies?"[8] Apart from the planning of actions controversial issues were not really discussed and there were no references to political movements outside the university institutions.

As the planning went ahead commitments were made by leading activists and Student Council members in support of the retreat. Even the chairman of the council was planning to participate. However, suddenly things changed.

On to the scene came two school teachers, Bo Dan Andersen and Søren Hansen, known as provo teachers. They had achieved significant media coverage because of a number of actions they had carried out in school circles. They were supposed to contribute to the retreat with "pedagogy and creativity." Instead they took control of its direction and decided to make it an experimental micro-society. The objectives changed dramatically: "during the construction of this experimental society we will study the conditions that will give the greatest possible development and satisfaction for the individual ... Through the creation of a society built on trust, openness, personal expression and organizational efficiency the participants will gain experiences to be used in the situation back home."[9]

Self-realization through teamwork, inter-group relations, experimenting with new methods for learning and personal development to secure an expansion of individual, group and societal expression all became part of the agenda. This new direction alienated a number of students and in the weeks running up to the retreat several of them withdrew from participating. They wanted a clearer political focus and felt the retreat would be a waste of time.

Life on Mors: The August Retreat and the Activist Movement

The first days were organized with group meetings before the participants embarked on building their experimental society. The organizational efficiency promised by the provo teachers proved to be wishful thinking. At the end of the third day a meeting was held to decide how the experiment was to continue. Now the conflicts surfaced with the dividing line to be found between freak and anarchy on one side and on the other participants wanting political organization and discipline in order to clarify the objectives of the continued student revolt. The latter group had organized a written response demanding an alternative to this anarchy. They felt focus had been completely lost and wanted to restore a sense of direction. They wanted to politicize the retreat.

In their coverage one of the national newspapers used the following words to describe this conflict, "Youth enacts society and somebody makes a coup." This playful or teasing tone was some distance from the rather self-assertive and solemn tone used by the students involved in the discussions. The debates from the meetings spilled over and escalated in the daily publications that came out as part of the retreat. These publications remain the best sources of the content and nature of the conflict and will be quoted at length below.

What also ignited the debate—apart from how the retreat progressed—was the concept "Ego-power" introduced by the two school teachers. The concept was indicative of their self-analytical and personal development agenda. Ego-power was about making personal needs the focus of everything in order to analyse one's personal motives before taking action. They wrote,

> *Something on personal motives.* We have identified the need to put you in a learning situation. We want to teach you what we ourselves have learnt. We have learned this through analyzing our own actions and believe for the time being you must follow the same method … At the retreat a useful excuse has been to postulate that one was revolutionary for the sake of others. We believe it must be like this: we are revolutionary for our own sake. A good revolutionary must recognize this. He must recognize the problems immediately before him and not project them into all kinds of utopias. Mao=escapism. Hippie=escapism and until now all talk about the university crisis has been escapism … How do we as revolutionaries channel our personal needs in a manner that is acceptable to ourselves and others?[10]

This attitude aggravated the anti-anarchists, especially one of the participants called Finn Ejnar Madsen.[11] He understood this as a call for individuals to become egoists in order to emancipate themselves from the norms of authoritarian society. According to Finn Ejnar Madsen it was a denial of the "planned revolutionary effort"—an effort that for him equalled reason. He replied:

In this attempt at emancipation from the norms of authoritarian bourgeois society he

> [Bo Dan Andersen] unfortunately also denies human reason. He worships spontaneity apparently in a reaction against authoritarian bourgeois reason … Spontaneity should not be anyone's basic life philosophy. If it becomes so it leads to a frustration of a number of human needs as it is impossible for spontaneity to organize itself strongly enough so as to pro-

vide an effective alternative to combating the existing system of repression. Paradoxically, it takes a lot of self discipline to fight for the liberation of humankind.[12]

Finn Ejnar Madsen had on several occasions during the retreat presented his views on the relation between revolution and reason. The response came instantly from one of the other students, Steffen Larsen, who found Madsen's views to be an outcome of "revolutionary consciousness which had ordered him to deliver another proof of how things operate and that repeated attempts to point out flaws in his analysis of the revolutionary process had obviously failed. It is recommendable if student rebels ... would make their personal motives clear—that is one of the most fruitful things this retreat can teach us. This may initially restrain our revolt but at least we will be sure to be lead along *the right track*."[13]

Finn Ejnar Madsen responded the next day and took issue with the notion of analyzing one's personal motives before taking action: "The revolutionary acts like all other efficient human beings with a rational singleness of purpose. He makes his final objectives clear before he through an analysis reaches the understanding that he achieves his objectives through a revolution ... The revolutionary's motives are therefore rather uninteresting while what really characterizes him is his ability to find the paths to [reach] his objectives: the qualitative change = the revolution."[14]

It is striking how a revolutionary in this understanding is reduced to an identity label one has decided to wear or not and how with the correct analysis revolution almost becomes a quick fix. The self-assertive tone was profoundly utopian and remarkably emancipated from any critical self-reflection. Instead of solving the problems the retreat ended in frustrations and divisions internally in the activist movement. It failed to produce any results that could bring the student movement forward. The retreat did have a life after it ended. *Politisk Revy* and *Superlove*, the leading magazines of respectively the New Left and the hippie movement, both published several articles on it. In an article in *Superlove* Steffen Larsen followed up his contribution to the discussions at the retreat. He believed that the:

> Student activist meeting had clearly demonstrated that a new style of thinking was necessary. It may seem strange that almost every day (except for half a day) was spent on discussing personal problems. In reality this was the most positive thing. Because it was, perhaps reluctantly, realized that there were personal motives for starting rebellions. Because it was gradually admitted that these personal motives did not stand in a reasonable relationship with the cause. And finally because it was toward the end to a wide extent accepted that these motives and needs must be

explained before one could address societal problems ... Should one develop an imaginary universe filled with ghastly creatures like the authority problem, capitalists, guerrilla heroes and the world wide greedy, omnivorous and asexual imperialism. Or should one save the revolt until the day when one is mature and has the "need" for it? Should one start with a personal revolution? It is that simple.[15]

Politisk Revy had several articles relating to the retreat including an interview with two of the participants who had been teamed up with two others who had not been there but had participated in a "summer camp on Cuba." One of the former explained that the retreat had been an example of the perfect anarchistic society. One of the Cuba travelers responded promptly that anarchism was nothing but petit bourgeois individualism. After it had been denied that there had been shooting practice as part of the summer camp on Cuba, as some Western media had reported, the following exchange took place:

> Cuba visitor 1: "... what is needed at the present time in Denmark is a guerrilla of the mind—to raise awareness"
> Cuba visitor 2: "a revolution would in the final stage become bloody—it will be the machine guns that will decide who will be in power"
> Retreat participant 1: "there will be no need for machine guns in Denmark"
> Cuba visitor 2: "Of course there will be"
> Retreat participant 1: "Who says so?"
> Cuba Visitor 2: "I don't know"
> Retreat participant 2: "Then keep your mouth shut."

It was not an interview that made for consensus. This was deliberate on the part of the two student activists. They applied their anarchist approach with the clear intention of destroying the structure of the interview as well as do all they could to try and undermine the seriousness of their opponents' views.[16]

The Unbearable Lightness of Revolution

How come revolution was a topic that was spoken about with such an air of both seriousness and casualness at the same time? The coming revolution was described in dramatic terms but it was also a concept that was used casually in the political rhetoric of the time by both the political and the lifestyle radicals, but as shown above normally with very different meanings. It was often mentioned in the same context and as a factor that would lead to liberation or emancipation or with the sense of alienation being the motivating factor for the revolutionary ambition. The question is where does this utopian thinking originate from? Here the rhetoric in the debates at the gathering on Mors may be the, "small facts that speak to larger issues" referred to in the introduction.

There seems to be a linkage between the three concepts of alienation, revolution and emancipation that may explain the nature of the utopian thinking that was so widespread in the youth revolt of the 1960s. The three concepts offer a narrative structure that seems to reflect an important part of the self-perception among both the political and lifestyle radicals. They describe the process the revolt should go through.

Alienation is referred to in many sources from the 1960s to the extent that it may be regarded as a notion or even social experience with which many identified. Alienation can be said to express a gap or a discrepancy between place/situation and identity: "Dilemmas of alienation highlight the twin poles of location and identity; to be alienated: to be displaced from oneself."[17] This displacement could be numbing but as it became an experience shared by many the social movements of the era became a mediating force that helped turn individual problems into public issues.

The process could have stopped here. However, as many of the movements radicalized, alienation became part of a political process that linked it to the concept of revolution. The passion for revolution came from different sources both within the private spheres of the countercultural scene as well as from global political conditions with conditions in the Third World and their wars of independence inspiring and radicalizing many young leftists. These types of revolutions of the mind, in lifestyles, in political thinking, and in political conflicts were all closely related to the idea of emancipation or liberation.

Emancipation was the point where the synthesis between place/situation and identity would be recreated ending the sense of alienation. Emancipation became the great objective of the countercultural movements of the 1960s. It was also an integral part of their utopian illusions.

The continued conceptualization of alienation, revolution, and emancipation lent both intellectual vigor and rigor to the movements. From this came a large part of the passionate imagination and innovation of the 1960s movements, but also the dogmatism and self-deceit that can be seen both in the debates at the retreat and in the wider political upheavals reflected in the symbolic term "1968."

As the retreat gradually disintegrated the political and life-style radicals stood strongly opposed with no possibility of agreement. It was not external factors but internally conflicting world-views that had led to the unraveling of the activist movement. It had no organizational structures to withstand the hijacking of its agenda. The open and anti-hierarchical structure of the movement had offered an easy entry point enabling the manipulation of the agenda and university politics was sidelined as the conflict between the two groups radicalized into the absurd. This situation had been foreseen by a number of the students, who before the retreat had cancelled their participation. It is significant that a number of these became prominent student politicians from the autumn of 1968 because they had understood that the continued revolt needed organizational structures. They got elected to key positions in the Student Council and took their activist agenda with them to radicalize student politics from within. The activist movement and the Student Council had de facto merged by the end of 1968.

With a radicalized agenda the Student Council then worked to influence the legislation deciding how the universities were to be governed. During the period of negotiations that lasted until the Spring of 1970 the students used actions on a number of occasions but without the success they had experienced in the early part of 1968. The law that was passed in Parliament offered the students influence in many areas of university rule. However, it was not sufficient for the students who became increasingly radicalized. In March 1970 they occupied the university again protesting that the law took away the Student Council's monopoly on representing students by opening up for elections between different student groupings. This time they had made a political miscalculation and instead of applying political pressure they alienated their last political allies. The paradox is that the law that became known as the world's most liberal law on university rule was passed with the students strongly opposed to it. The Student Council even went so far as to boycott the first elections for the new representative governing bodies.

Final Remarks

How does the Danish Student Revolt compare in the broader context of international student revolts in the years around 1968? In simple terms this question may be addressed by focusing on three levels on which the international student revolts operated.

Firstly, there is an international level where revolts became a source of mutual inspiration between countries. Often references were made in one place to revolts elsewhere in order to legitimize action and underline the broad basis for student and youth dissent. In Copenhagen in March 1968 references were made to West Berlin, Berkeley, Manchester, Turin, and Warsaw. This was at the same time that students from the University of Nanterre—a Parisian suburb—were meeting in frustration over the study and life conditions at their university and student housing. This eventually led to the dramatic events in May 1968 that changed the discourse on the student revolts. These events gave feedback also to the discussions in Denmark where France had played no role until then.

Secondly, the student revolts also operated within a national political context that often set the ground rules for how radicalized the revolts became. The dramatic events in Germany had a lot to do with a generational revolt against a fascist past. The revolt in Germany and also in France was reciprocated violently by state authorities and escalated the revolts into challenges to the political order. It never reached these levels in the Nordic countries. If a national political context played a role in Denmark it was almost supportive to the students. The political parties were in favor of university reform and though the parties did not encourage the revolt they did have a lot of sympathy for the student's actions—at least in the early months of the revolt. As the students became radicalized their political support and goodwill dwindled.

Thirdly, it is important to emphasize that the revolts often took place in very specific institutional settings and situations, i.e., at the Psychology Department in Denmark, Student Unions in Sweden, gender-divided dormitories at universities in Britain and France. These specific settings played a crucial role in conditioning the students to take up direct action. Therefore the specific institutional settings deserve detailed attention in order to fully understand the genesis of the battles over authority and legitimacy that is a large part of the 1968 revolts.

I believe that these three levels shaped the emergence of and events during the majority of the 1968 student revolts. Sometimes all three were in play, other times the first and the third was in play while the challenge to the national political culture was limited. The latter was the case in Denmark. Still, the events received national attention through the interest of the print and broadcast media and the universities were reformed. In this sense they did contribute, alongside the lifestyle radicalism and the leftwing political activism in the wider society, to alter important aspects of the national political culture in Denmark.

Notes

1. The use of the categories political versus lifestyle radicals are to be understood as descriptive categories that emphasize the most dominant feature of the views held by members of the two groups. It does not imply that lifestyle radicalism is not also political in nature or that the political radicals did not experiment with alternative ways of living.
2. There was only one exception—the chancellor of the University of Copenhagen, Mogens Fog. He was an avid reformer and strongly disappointed with the Committee Report released in January 1968—the work having been initiated as far back as in 1964—and therefore Fog expressed his dissenting views on the report which largely maintained the status quo.

3. "Studenterrådet har spillet fallit," *Information*, 23–24 March 1968.

4. Rigsarkivet, "Studenteroprøret," U6, BII, "Notat vedrørende 'aktionspolitik,'" Jnr. 1149/949 CSN. 24 March 1968, 3.

5. Rigsarkivet, "Studenteroprøret," A.I.1., "Oplæg til en diskussion om studenteraktionernes mål og midler."

6. Ibid.

7. Rigsarkivet, "Studenteroprøret," U.1, A.I.1, "AKTIVISTSEMINAR." Document undated, probably from mid May.

8. Ibid.

9. Rigsarkivet, "Studenteroprøret," U.4, A.V, "Til deltagerne på seminaret på Morsø Ungdomsskole fra den 5.–12. august 1968." Written by the two teachers Bo Dan Andersen and Søren Hansen and dated 16 July 1968.

10. Rigsarkivet, "Studenteroprøret," U.4, A.V, "Noget om egne motiver." Undated publication from the retreat. English title: "Something on personal motives."

11. A few months later in November 1968 at the Annual Celebration of the University of Copenhagen Finn Ejnar Madsen rose to national fame when in front of the Danish royal family and a surprised audience he occupied the speaker's platform pushing aside the principal of the university (no violence was used as the principal stood back and allowed Finn Ejnar Madsen to make a declaration). He held a short speech announcing that this bourgeois ceremony should be ended. This manifestation is still the best-known of all the student manifestations in the period 1968–70.

12. Rigsarkivet, "Studenteroprøret," U.4, A.V, MOD SELDYRKELSE. *Avis* nr. 2.

13. Rigsarkivet, "Studenteroprøret," U.4, A.V, MOD SELDYRKELSE (- for jeg-power). *Avis* nr. 2. Italics added.

14. Rigsarkivet, "Studenteroprøret," U.4, A.V, "Revolution og sygdom," *Avis* nr. 4.

15. Steffen Larsen, "Hvad skal vi lave," *Superlove*, September 1968, 11.

16. The two activists who had been at the retreat were Henning Prins and Leif Varmark. They were both part of the group that established the "New Society" in the early Spring of 1968 and at least Henning Prins played a significant role in the 1970 Thy Camp with 25,000 participants. For more on the "New Society," Thy Camp, *Superlove* and *Politisk Revy*, see Thomas Ekman Jørgensens contribution to this book.

17. Kristin Ross, *Fast Cars, Clean Bodies. Decolonization and the Reordering of French Culture* (Cambridge, 1994), 150.

Chapter 11

A Struggle for Radical Change?
Swedish Students in the 1960s

Thomas Etzemüller

One can read a lot about the student protests of the 1960s in West Germany, Italy, France, the United States, or even Great Britain and the "Third World." But astonishingly, some important—and well known!—countries are always missing: Denmark, Finland, Norway, and Sweden.[1] One never reads anything about them—is it because there is nothing to report? Were the Scandinavian countries islands of peace within a sea of unrest? Had the Scandinavian Governments long since reformed society to true egalitarian democracies so nothing was left to protest against in 1968? To turn it the other way round: what is there to report, what happened in the north during the 1960s?[2]

In this article I am concentrating on Sweden, a country that since the 1930s served as an "imaginary landscape" (Tom O'Dell) for many Europeans and Americans to project their desires and fears upon. First, in the 1930s, its social politics symbolized an ideal "Middle Way" between socialism and capitalism. Then, in the 1950s, it suddenly became the country of moral decline, inhabited by sexually depraved teenagers and irresponsible politicians who invented sex education in schools. Later on, in the 1970s and 1980s, it counted as one of the most successful welfare states. But hardly anyone has more than this blurred impression of Sweden. Almost nothing is known about its society and history, even amongst most professional historians. And yet a closer look at Sweden will reveal interesting similarities and also some differences to Continental history.[3]

First of all there are some chronological coincidences to observe. Like the rest of the Western world Sweden became an industrial nation—a little bit later than other countries, in the late nineteenth century—but with all the same problems: worker unrest, bad living conditions, fear of racial degeneration. Then Social Democracy came to power in 1920 and has ruled the nation since 1932 with barely any interruption. After the Second World War Sweden too became a modern consumer society, as a result of the postwar economic boom. Cities grew and underwent modernization; the first motorway was opened (which connected Lund and Malmö); in Stockholm a subway was built; households got washing machines, electric cookers and fridges; the agricultural sector—which decreased further—and industry were mechanized and rationalized; people had more money and the *köp-slit-släng-samhälle*, the "buy-wear out-throw away-society" took form.[4] Reactions to that were quite similar to reactions in other newly born consumer societies. On the one hand, Swedes enjoyed their prosperity. They could buy more and more consumer products, and the average pensioner for the first time could live on his pension. Social policy no longer had to relieve poverty, it could secure living standards. On the other hand, this radical change caused fears. After the war many Swedes imagined, in a similar vein to "McCarthyism" in the United States, a systematic subversion and destruction of society, not by a communist but by a homosexual conspiracy. This reflected the same postwar feeling of crisis, insecurity, and uncertainty about the future in Sweden as in the United States.[5] Some years later rock'n'roll came to the north and a teenage culture began to emerge—baby boom, "rebellious youth," (called *raggare* in Sweden), youth riots from 1948 on, and no explanation for this phenomenon. In this respect, and despite other differences, the 1950s looked much the same in the United States, West Germany, and Sweden.[6] Protests against—Swedish!—nuclear weapons, if not as forceful as in Denmark, Great Britain, or West Germany, the (comparatively late) emergence of a (comparatively weak) "New Left," and the rise of teenage culture also corresponded with Western developments.[7] Observed on that level, one can see some fundamental similarities in economic and social developments, and a similar perception and reaction to them. This is important, because it helps to explain why events in Sweden bore a resemblance to the Continent and the United States—though the Swedish way into modernity without doubt is a very special one.

Then came the 1960s. As in other countries the number of university students rose during the 1950s and exploded in the next decade, from 20,000 students in 1953 to 45,000 in 1962, 115,600 in 1968 and more than 124,000 in 1970. In 1955 one of the many state investigations that are typical of Sweden had recommended a heavy extension of the system of higher education; so the government decided to increase the number of teachers automatically in proportion to the increasing number of students of the humanities. This measure proved unsuccessful, however and soon there was a lack of teachers and facilities. In the early 1960s newspapers discussed how many humanists society needed, and a planning group published a worrying prognosis about future student figures. Initially, university reforms should have enabled everyone to have access to higher education, as a means to erase class barriers. Now that goal faded and it was decided that university courses should be investigated and tightened, studies should be accelerated, and students should "flow through" much more faster. In early 1968 a heated debate about power and influence in society, about democracy as well as educational and cultural ideals took place. For new university branches all over the country Humboldt's principle of the unity of teaching and research was abolished; university teachers warned of uncalculable results as students became stressed; student representatives accused reformers of putting education at the disposal of monopoly capitalism. The government backtracked, tried to increase student influence in the reforms, and softened its plans. Nevertheless reform was necessary and a new investigation again recommended a new structure for higher education, its orientation to the labor market and the participation of representatives of "general interest" in the universities' management. The New Left spoke of an industrialization of education, the government investigated its investigation—but after a few more years of discussion reforms came into force.[8]

In Stockholm courses had to be given in churches or hostels for the homeless; the university's Rector consoled himself with the fact that at least they had not had to take place in the open air. Interestingly enough these difficult learning conditions did not politicize students. All involved conceded that the situation was intolerable and had to be solved. In that respect, students and university heads cooperated well. Criticism of reforms was sparked off by sociopolitical reasons. And although history in Sweden followed similar paths, it differed from what one saw in Berlin, Frankfurt, Paris, or Chicago. One important reason for that is the sociopolitical constitution of Sweden. It can be called *Den korporativa staten*, the corporate state, which means that besides government and parliament all relevant social groups in Swedish society are involved in legislative work and implementation of laws. This makes the political system highly consensus-oriented, flexible, and receptive to change. As soon as something is regarded as an anomaly, a commission is appointed by government, consisting of representatives of all concerned groups. The commission investigates the problem and proposes reforms. Then the government—again in close cooperation with all relevant groups—designs and enacts reform laws that are implemented by the administration. But unlike most Western countries these groups are not only lobbygroups. In fact, they are integrated into the whole system of governance and even administration, that is, the execution of state duties is partially delegated to social groups. This is too brief a description to really appreciate how exceptional this kind of ruling system is. It is deeply rooted in the collective mentality of Swedes, and it provides nearly all governmental acts with a large measure of legitimacy. Its price is a weak separation of powers (the justice belongs to the administration), a far-reaching subordination of Swedes to authority, and an absolute priority of consensus over dispute that is responsible for the near pathological avoidance of conflict, as Susan Sonntag once wrote.[9]

Students are part of that corporate constitution. What seems peculiar to us is political duty to them: as a matter of course, student associations at their annual meetings discussed general political matters. The Liberals, for instance, asked the government in 1962 to prescribe doorlocks on cars because car theft would be the first step to youth delinquency. Social Democratic students wanted private driving schools to be nationalized because the *state* would then be responsible for education. Twenty-one requests on domestic, seven on foreign issues, fourteen on organizational questions and six on student politics as an agenda for a student congress was in no way unusual. The government asked students just as other groups to submit their view on bills or final reports of state investigations, not only on those concerning education. It therefore appeared as a harsh break with tradition when the student parliament in Lund in fall 1968 refused to deliver a statement on university reforms—after a long discussion and as a protest against those reforms. Student activists thought, students could best defend their interests by forming some kind of trade union. Political activism certainly was necessary, but within the system and as long as it aimed at educational questions. Left-wing students criticized this as self-isolation from society, and in the newly invented student parliaments began marathon sessions about protests against the Franco regime or the war in Vietnam, about a support for Greek students or a collection in favor of the Liberation Front of South Vietnam (FNL). In substance leftists and "unionists" often agreed; quarrels were about whether that had anything to do with student politics or to what extend student politics had to be general sociopolitics. "Unionists" often lost majority in parliaments, but could block decisions in the executive committees. Thus a dramaturgy of its own originated, with long, complicated debates, shady moves, ignored decisions, postponed meetings, elections, and shifting majorities. Unintentionally, "unionists" in their fight against politicos helped to politicize student politics.[10]

Some incidents received quite a lot of public attention. In Stockholm, for example, in May 1968 students occupied their own *kårhus* (students' center). The board of the student corps considered this illegal, but refrained from calling the police in order to avoid an escalation. Olof Palme, at that time minister for education, was called upon for a debate. Self-confident as ever, he left no doubt about his desire to push through university reforms. He left to applause. Nevertheless the occupants had some feeling of "May '68." Rooms were crowded, the atmosphere heated and for a moment everything seemed possible to them. Their house was guarded by police to hold off some thousand counter-demonstrators who asked the police to throw out the students. From within policemen were directed to beat away the troublemakers. After three days the occupation was brought to an end, students left for a demonstration through the city, shouting "It is Right to Rebel" and "Smash Capitalism," and singing the "Internationale," whilst their opponents sang the old patriotic song "Du gamla, du fria fjällrika Nord" to mark their disgust. In comparison with the Continent, happenings were quite peaceful—but for Swedish society students had committed an act of violence. They were disobedient against society and had broken the consensus that all problems should be solved by sensible cooperation. Therefore *kårhusokkupationen* went down in the history of the student left and counted for public opinion as a decisive step to radicalization respectively.

Similar events happened in Lund, a university with a radical tradition. In 1968/69 events were condensed to the label "Red Lund." In June 1968 students disturbed celebrations of the 300-year anniversary of Lund's university. They linked their protests after the French and German model to the war in Vietnam, the university reform, and the universities' function within capitalism. Again no violence occurred, but professors, it is said, while passing the double lines of shouting students and guarding policemen, were reminded of the Bastille and the French Revolution. In September initially peaceful action against the conscription board escalated through the use of mounted police; papers exaggerated this to a real battle, while students again could recognize capitalism's "true face"—as in November the same year, when they disrupted the visit of South African diplomats in the Lund Cathedral by shouting "Black Power" and singing "We Shall Overcome" and "Black and White Together." In the evening they forced their entrance into a reception. The Rector, sympathizing with them, turned down an offer of help by the police and later informed the ministry of foreign affairs that the university did not feel compelled to apologize to anyone: students were not subject to disciplinary control, and, besides, representatives from South Africa had to expect protests of that kind. Justice was of another opinion and took them to court. This trial drew huge public attention and also went down in history, especially for its many transcription failures. The most grotesque possibly was the conversion of the "black American

author James Baldwin" into the "black African author James Bond."
Students transformed the court to a forum for their affairs and were convinced that justice stood under political influence, while newspapers
started a discussion about whether the state or students threatened freedom of opinion.[11]

In Göteborg, Stockholm, Lund, Uppsala, even at the young university
of Umeå in the far north, leftist students tried to politicize their fellow
students. Their concentration on university reform, department organization, content of courses or reading material proved a skillful mobilizing strategy, because it both integrated "student as such"-defenders and
could be linked into a wider sociopolitical framework. All universities
experienced the same chaotic struggles in student parliaments between
politicos and unionists that tried to prevent a wrongly led politicization.
That produced an effect precisely to the contrary. More and more students got involved in leftist politics, and the war in Vietnam radicalized
them. But in contrast to, for example, West Germany, student protests
and protests against the war constituted two separate strings, both dominated, though, by students. Because of "unionists'" resistance at universities world politics could only fought for on a reduced scale. But from
the "Third World" study groups at the universities a Vietnam movement
emerged in the mid-1960s. This movement called itself *FNL-rörelse,*
named after the *Front National de Libération du Viêt-nam du Sud.* From
February 1965 the leftist student organization *Clarté* held regular
demonstrations in front of the United States embassy in Stockholm, but
no one really cared. At that time the Swedish Postal Service thought that
Vietnam was in Northern Africa while the ministry of justice spelled its
name "Vietnamn" (*namn* means *name* in Swedish) and the leftist
monthly *Zenit* predicted a quick end to the war. Soon, this situation
changed. Swedish media were in any case skeptical toward United States
racial politics and gradually became less positive toward its warfare—
stimulated not least by the increasingly hardening attitude of the Swedish
Government toward the United States. And when the *Clarté* moved its
protests to the *Hötorget,* the inner city, a "critical event" (Pierre Bourdieu)
occurred that left nothing to be desired. Police tried to break up one of
these quite small demonstrations; some demonstrators resisted because
they had gotten permission for their rally. Police called in reinforcements
that with much noise drew public and press attention. The next day
front pages ran the story with bold headlines, depicting Sköld Peter
Matthis, being held in a stranglehold by the police. That picture became
an icon of the movement, Matthis an activist like Dutschke in Germany
(if not as radical), and the movement's initials FNL were instantly known
all over Sweden. The resulting trial against Matthis (for resistance to the
police) lasted for four years, and proved to be another mobilizing factor.[12]

A crack appeared between pacifists of the older antinuclear-weapons movement and students of the *Clarté*. The former supported a general peace in Vietnam, the latter a peace on the conditions of the FNL. The former established the "Swedish Vietnam Committee," the latter set up the "Working Group for the Support of the FNL." Local groups emerged in Uppsala, Göteborg, Linköping, Lund and Örebro, all college locations, then rapidly nearly all over Sweden. In 1966 there existed eight, a year later twenty, in 1969 ninety and in 1973 150 groups, with approximately 10,000 members in 1972. Even in small villages high school students engaged in FNL groups, and all of them joined together in "The United FNL-Groups" (DFFG). They centralized their work, and their organization became more and more bureaucratic. One cannot underestimate the mobilizing force of that movement. Thousands of teenagers invested their spare time in setting up, printing, and distributing leaflets, internal bulletins, training letters and other publications, collecting money, recording music, selling the movement's products, demonstrating, discussing with citizens or visiting schools and even old people's homes. As no other social movement of the 1960s, DFFG succeeded in mobilizing an army of collectors, demonstrators, sellers, and house-callers. Their hard work introduced the movement to society and created identity within itself. Working conditions were chaotic, disputes erupted, groups ceased to function, and twice Marxist-Leninist splinter-groups, the socalled "rebels" or "liquidators," tried to conquer the movement and had to be beaten off under heavy losses of material and members. Those groups emerged in opposition to the "Marxist-Leninist Communist Association" (KFML), founded in 1967 and working heavily for revolution in Sweden. KFML gained much influence in DFFG, regarding it as a means to reach the masses and to set up a proletarian dictatorship. Consequently it started to train young FNL members to become consciousness Marxist-Leninist-cadres. On the other hand, though, it supported efforts within the DFFG to create some kind of "Popular Front," for despite its radicalization and its revolutionary cause it tried to integrate even nonrevolutionary groups to forge as broad as possible an alliance against the War in Vietnam. To the "rebels" of 1968 this betrayed the fight against imperialism, while the "liquidators" of 1970 intended to strengthen socialist ideology and proletarian influence within the DFFG. This was not only a question of the "right" ideological consciousness and revolutionary way, it also touched on political strategy.[13]

In 1965 the DFFG became irreconcilable to the "establishment." The government's stance toward the United States intervention in Vietnam was characterized as mere eyewash and staged radicalization; in fact, it was said that the government tried to murder the movement with police

truncheons and speeches by Olof Palme. That last remark was aimed at
some modest words in Gävle, where Palme had mentioned the war in
Vietnam. The media interpreted them as a sharp if indirect attack on the
Washington government, covered by Prime Minister Tage Erlander himself. After that the Swedish and the American positions became
entrenched. In 1967 Sweden broke off diplomatic relations with South
Vietnam; in 1969 it acknowledged North Vietnam; and up to 1972 its
criticism intensified ever more. The United States had already had
enough when in 1968 Palme led a demonstration side by side with the
ambassador of North Vietnam. Instead of apologizing, he indifferently
declared this incident to be a pure coincidence. The United States
ambassador left the country; Sweden did not back down. Its attitude was
very much motivated by what can be called the "Palme Doctrine": the
superpowers intended to divide the world into interest spheres, which
meant hegemony over small nations like Vietnam and Sweden. To support Vietnam therefore meant to defend Sweden's own national interests
and needs for security.[14] Nevertheless, the government's policy was not
unambiguous. Its stance changed with concessions, and that irritated the
DFFG. The "establishment," i.e. Social Democracy, on the other hand,
was also annoyed because in their eyes the Vietnam movement attracted
the youth too much. The party had to act since it always had channeled
radical trends, as Tage Erlander once said. So it founded the "Swedish
Committee for Vietnam" (SKfV) to compete for students. It consisted
mainly of prominent figures like Alva and Gunnar Myrdal and quickly
started to lobby intensively among diplomats and decision makers in
Sweden. As the DFFG and the government SKfV demanded a bomb
halt and the retreat of United States forces from Vietnam; its first public
manifestation was the aforementioned demonstration with Palme and
the North Vietnam ambassador. That torchlight procession the committee not only understood as a protest against the United States but
also as a reaction of "democratic opinion" to egg-throwing leftists—who
participated in that very same demonstration, but decided not to speak
at the final rally because they were angry about what they felt were
obstructions by Palme and Gunnar Myrdal. Later on they criticized the
committee's lottery for awarding prizes instead of relying on the solidarity of donors (they themselves collected 8,2 million crowns up to 1973).
Myrdal called them "elements" and "confused brains," thereby marking
the depth of the gulf between the old order and the winds of change, as
author Peter Weiss remarked.

Indeed two generations and two ways of political working met. On
the one side was the established culture of organization: the founding of
a movement by grown-ups and elder statesmen, reasonable argumentation, lobbying with the help of small talk and opulent dinners,

respectable and proper processions, and the usual political day to day work, ritualised and bureaucratic. On the other side were the teenagers who drew attention to their matters by percussion, music, colorful clothes, cheeky slogans, sit-ins, and egg-throwing. In public, such breaking not only of ancient campaign traditions but *rules* were condemned as totally unrespectable manners if not mere violence. Of course, youngsters had to learn to behave like that; to demonstrate was for many of them in the beginning an embarrassing experience, especially as they regarded demonstrations to a great extent as an ineffective device for political work. After a while they got used to it because they rejected the way the adults acted. After some early clashes between demonstrators and the police, who were not used to wildcat marches, elder Swedes too became accustomed to the new phenomena, particularly when the DFFG gradually tamed its rallies as not to disturb traffic and to avoid "violence" like egg-throwing that public opinion condemned as loutish. In 1969 the SKfV had tried to establish some kind of cooperation with the DFFG to carry out a joint demonstration. Though negotiations failed both sides thought a collaboration necessary to influence public opinion. The DFFG cooled off conflicts in order to create the popular front, and in 1972 it declared its former attempts to destroy the SKfV as a mistake. Politics of the SAP (Social Democratic Party of Sweden) seemed to have changed for the better and the government no longer looked imperialistic. On 1 May 1972 Stockholm saw the biggest anti-war demonstration so far with some 50,000 participants under the auspices of Social Democracy, Stockholm's FNL-group, the Communist Party, KFML, and SKfV. For FNL members this was a chance to get in touch with Social Democrats—and to reach the masses that should be transformed into a powerful anti-imperialistic front. However, that never really worked out. A sign-in only produced 360,000 signatures in support for the slogan "United States out of Vietnam." At the same time the five parliamentary parties, without any difficulty, collected 2.7 million signatures. The KFML and DFFG even engaged in this action as a means to spread their opinion. Despite all that, collaboration with the "establishment" always remained precarious. Both sides regarded each other with skepticism.[15]

After having read this brief description of Swedish student protests and the FNL movement, and comparing it with the countless stories of confrontation and brutality from the United States, France, or Western Germany, one could consider Sweden to be some kind of paradise, where opponents cultivated a rhetoric and carried out symbolic acts of confrontation but *in reality* collaborated in a reasonable manner. This is not untrue. Let us take a closer look at the escalation of violence in Sweden. Again we can detect similarities to the Western countries that at the same time turn out to be different. A series of violent incidents started in the mid-1960s: first, the already mentioned arrest of Sköld Peter Mattis, who became a symbol for the fight between the old system's repression and the young generation's revolution; the occupation of the *kårhus* in Stockholm; in Lund the "battle" in front of the conscription board; the *domkyrkoaktionen* against the South African diplomats; and the disturbance of the 300-year anniversary of the university, which many Swedes felt to be the sad peak of illegitimate violence—outdone only by "The Case of Båstad" in May 1968 and a demonstration in Stockholm on 20 December 1967. On that lovely winter day rallies in forty places all over the country, on the occasion of the seventh anniversary of the FNL in Vietnam, were organized. In Stockholm the local FNL group announced its intention to march to the United States embassy, without permission. Police and media prepared appropriately, and when after the official rally individual groups went off to the embassy, police awaited them. Photographers were able to take pictures of the skirmish, throughout which a leading figure of the movement, Jan Myrdal, was put through the hoop in public. A picture shows him with broken glasses, taken away by the police—another icon. *Dagens Nyheter*, which otherwise had been well disposed toward the protesters, harshly condemned their breaking of democratic rules. This was to be the beginning of militancy. Demonstrators, on the other hand, had long complained of militancy, on the police side. In January 1968 they questioned witnesses who drew a picture very much the same as their German comrades' testimony after the death of Benno Ohnesorg and the attempted assassination of Rudi Dutschke:[16] beating and underhand policemen who did not care for press cards and used the "well-known 'Sköld-Peter-Matthis-grip'"; mounted attacks from out the darkness; ill-treatment by the police, even of elderly citizens; demonstrators who roamed the scene and ended under swinging clubs; innocent teenage girls who vanished amongst hordes of beating policemen; clubs, whips, shock attacks and, of course, peaceful demonstrators who always followed the orders of the police and did not know what was happening to them. 20 December for both sides, counted a high-point of confrontation that they would again and again come to evoke (though many witnesses did *not* see the decisive moments when whips and clubs were said to have hit demonstrators).[17]

In Båstad, a small town in southwestern Sweden, an international tennismatch took place. One of the teams came from Rhodesia (as it was then known), and soon from all over the country young people gathered, while police occupied the arena. Some photographs and a film reveal what newspapers later called "the worst after 1909"—meaning the heavy labour conflicts of that time—or the "most compelling case of political violence in Swedish postwar period." As a result of a scrap one poorly secured gate became loose. Demonstrators remained indecisively on one side, three policemen on the other. Some more came, and after a while they tentatively started to fight at the gate. Some policemen used their clubs, others observed this with scepticism and warned demonstrators of overeager colleagues. After the gate was closed, demonstrators sat down, the fire service used a hose as water-cannon (police in Sweden had none) and outrage about such excessive measures arose. But all the time policemen and demonstrators talked to each other, and some constables complained about having been compelled to take part in that operation. In the end the match was canceled, much to the anger of local inhabitants who depended on the revenues. Exhausted, drenched, and satisfied, some protesters chatted with the police, some withdrew, a Danish girl with the feeling of 5 May 1945—the day of Denmarks liberation from the German occupation. For them "Båstad" became another mythical and mobilizing event, in parliament and the press a long debate about political violence began.[18] And when in 1970 a new United States ambassador, Jerome Holland, came to Sweden, he, while leaving the plane, met demonstrators who were said to have shouted "Nigger go home." The demonstrators denied that, but the Swedish government had to pronounce its first in a long series of excuses. Wherever Holland then went, he was greeted by demonstrations, eggs, and tomatoes, for the FNL movement tried to destroy normal relationships between Sweden and the United States. Allegedly, seventy-five policemen had to protect him when he went fishing. In 1972, unnerved he returned to his home country. Despite its critical attitude to United States politics, the Swedish Government and the press condemned attacks like these with utmost sharpness.

Even when the "system" did not really care to be repressive, the danger at least was evoked. On two occasions police in Lund would not have dared to intervene. *Clarté* in Stockholm prepared for a situation similar to Berlin where the police confiscated the directory of the SDS but was forced to return it. This had to be expected even in Sweden. And in Uppsala the FNL group missed "organized fascists" and attacks on the group; only one meeting was sabotaged. Newspapers did not fail to report activity. From 1967 articles about demonstrations, egg-throwing, flag-burning, attacks on American institutions, and riots piled up; more and more they appeared like reports from the front line. Did this correspond to reality? In a film[19] one can see some scrapping between Swedish demonstrators and policemen. Then there are clubbing policemen and water-cannons in Germany. Then, in France, policemen armed with shields and steel helmets, carrying guns on their backs, standing within a devastated city-landscape of burned cars and broken-up streets; and at last the National Guard driving back demonstrators with fixed bayonet.

Nothing makes clearer where Sweden is to be located on the international scale of violence. Newspaper pictures and internal reports of FNL groups concerning "police brutality," confirm this. Except for Lund and Stockholm, confrontation in most cases was limited to quarrels about permissions for demonstrations and collections. Bystanders of demonstrations sometimes swore at students and pupils, but mostly they were reported to be friendly or uninterested. The "reactionary petit bourgeois" that students in Berlin so often were confronted with, was lacking in the north. On the contrary: The government took "The Case of Båstad" as reason to send the prime minister and five ministers to a discussion with fifty-nine youth groups. And in 1973 for the first time the FNL flag was run up in a municipality.[20]

However, even if the "establishment" reacted thus and violence in comparison to other countries was negligible, the scare of "violence" was in no way exaggerated. This type of political confrontation between the state and a section of its population was something completely new in postwar Sweden. It reminded people of times they thought were gone: of the heavy labour conflicts of 1909 and "Ådalen '31," when the military shot five workers—that had been the last time in Swedish history, that political violence had occurred. Therefore many Swedes considered student actions against university and state institutions as extremist violence not suitable to Swedish traditions of reasonable and peaceful conflict resolution. Notwithstanding the aims of any political action, one had to follow the rules of political decision making that were in force in the Swedish democracy: reason, matter-of-fact argumentation, parliamentary work, and the face-to-face contact of authorities and those affected. One had to draw a decisive distinction between one's political opinion and violence as a means to carry through that opinion. That principle the Swedish Labour Movement had defended even in the most unfavorable and humiliating circumstances, a newspaper wrote. These tried and tested ways of rational reconciliation of interests were being carelessly jeopardized by politicized students and pupils. They, on the other hand, experienced the comparatively modest police interventions and judgments of courts as naked repression of the capitalist system, similar to the rest of the Western world. They took it for granted that the Swedish government and justice both conspired with Nixon, and that courts quite naturally broke the rule of law; processes were clearly arranged by American pressure, and it was only due to public opinion that too obvious violations did not pass and that higher courts had to moderate sentences. The Swedish way of conflict resolution they regarded as just a poor cover for underlying repressive mechanisms of the worldwide "capitalistic system," which also ruled Sweden. Therefore it did not seem ridiculous when the movement for example called the "prisoner of political consciousness" Yvonne Hoogendoorn a martyr for her twenty days in prison. In the United States civil rights activists were murdered, but to Swedish students this was only a difference in quantity not in quality. The system seemed to be the same.

Each side perceived a radicalization of the other that up to now was unknown to them, so each side felt itself to be the victim of either "extremism" or "repression" respectively; and despite all the differences from Western countries they observed in Sweden the same quality of "irrational" or "repressive" behavior as on the Continent or in the United States. This perception was certainly fueled by a perception of the clashes in France, West Germany, or the United States. The media reported foreign clashes and let it look nearly all the same in Sweden—entirely to the students' delight, who now felt on an equal level with their Western comrades. But in reality no one really went outside the Swedish framework of appropriate behavior. Politicians and university heads tried to de-escalate confrontations, often successfully, because "radicals" went along with them. The latter restrained their way of acting when they discovered that public opinion did not appreciate it. So, despite all the heated rhetoric and actions both sides in principle were willing to collaborate—because *this* was the Swedish principle of *all* politics. Perhaps it was symptomatic that Henry Thoreaux's classic "On Civil Disobedience" was published in Sweden first in 1977. In the afterword to this edition Thoreau was linked to Ghandi, the *Ruhrkampf*, the Danish and Norwegian resistance in the Second World War, the antinuclear-movement in West Germany, the protests against the war in Vietnam, the civil rights movement in the United States, and finally to Sweden: to refuse to do military service was to act in Thoreaux's mind.[21] Seen from a Swedish point of view, their violence grew in line with other countries; seen from their point of view, the same pattern indeed was visible in Sweden—but much of it existed only in imagination.

Now, what about the revolution in Sweden? Why was there none, and what was there instead? First we have to recognize that protests at the universities and against the war in Vietnam were dominated by students; they never constituted a "Popular Front" or really agitated workers. But through the media perception of the international student movements, a tight network of personal contacts, and the translation of texts of the international left, they adapted themselves to what they considered a global revolutionary movement that was near to overthrowing the capitalist and imperialist system. The media reassured them that society thought something similar (if not quite the same), and "police brutality" as well as a justice system submissive to the "capitalist system" confirmed to them that this "system" had to be fought against in Sweden as well. *Structurally* the Swedish "1968" resembled events worldwide. Some peculiarities, though, obstructed students in Sweden. At the universities the "unionists" prevented—in spite of their unintended politicizing effect—a fundamental politicization of the colleges. It was "unionist" themes that mobilized the average student, not the general political ones. More important was the FNL movement that linked Vietnam to capitalism and Sweden but was obstructed by the fact that there was no real enemy. There were only opponents like the SAP that tried to outstrip the students by reforms, the communist party that did not differ much from Social Democrats, or the Swedes of whom many were offended by the modes of protest but who did not regard the demonstrators with hate (as for example inhabitants did in Berlin). Last, but not least, even the students were Swedes who preferred "rational" methods of resolving conflicts. Hidden behind a language of warfare in "establishment" papers and movement bulletins, both sides *did* the same: they behaved reasonably and collaborated. The language only reflected their uneasiness about new and unknown ways to advocate political opinions.

Instead of a revolution there was something different, namely a critique of modern society. As mentioned before Sweden after the Second World War underwent rapid change, from an industrial to a consumer society. That caused new lifestyles and a "silent revolution" of values.[22] Reflected for example in art, theatre, and literature,[23] those changes also caused feelings of unease about the condition of the Social Democratic welfare state. Despite the extensive social reforms of the 1950s, more and more shortages came to light and the "Welfare Queues"—the waiting for flats, a stay in the hospital, apprenticeships, university courses, etc.— grew longer and longer; even the dismantling of class society stagnated. Rationalization of work, the new satellite towns in concrete and without adequate communications to the cities, drug abuse, or the question of gender-equality produced worries about the future, criticism of Social Democracy, or anger that culminated in a series of wildcat strikes in 1969 (mistakenly taken as a harbinger of revolution by the young leftists[24]). To this Social Democrats responded with even more reforms, but in 1966 they suffered disastrous losses in local elections. Two years later they gained an absolute majority in general elections, lost it again in 1970, and had to quit power in 1976—for the first time in forty-four years. The party had identified itself so much with the country's development that this seemed unbelievable. Worries stirred within the party that perhaps it could not offer a solution for all the complicated problems that had emerged in the last twenty years.[25]

Indeed, the "student uprising" had been a signifier that problems now were negotiated in another language and at least partly in other ways than before. The Swedish tradition of *folkrörelser* was too strong to let emerge powerful *Bürgerinitiativen* as in West Germany. There the

Bürgerinitiativen established themselves beside administrations and politics and influenced them from the outside. In Sweden there still was no real "outside" of politics: most politicos still worked within the system. No strong counterculture came into being, no Christiania, no Kreuzberg, where alternative ways of living and political action could be developed, as a model for the rest of society. A few communes in the countryside tried to lay the basis for a "new society," while teenagers organized in groups such as "Campaign Conversation," "Alternative Society," or "Campaign to Stop Christmas," there criticizing the rising consumption, the commercializing of Christmas, or trying to improve living conditions. Most important was the "All Activity Movement" that intended to establish "All Activity Houses," where people of all ages and classes should meet, as a base in the enemy's camp, to foster "saboteurs" and the "New Man." The houses should be financed by the state but be freed from administrative supervision. Local administrations were entirely willing to support this new movement but wanted to keep control. Youngsters occupied the newly established All Activity Houses to snatch them from authorities; they were closed down, vacated and reopened. Authorities did not like anti-organizational movements; the movement on the other hand became more and more bureaucratic and died.[26] Anyhow, these events show that the ideas of the New Left gained a foothold outside the universities. And even if many FNL members did not appreciate the Beatles, the Rolling Stones, and the teenage culture in general, which they considered a product of international capitalism—whereas traditional dance was understood as a genuine Swedish way of expression—, they remained not uninfluenced. After all revolutionary hopes had faded, some musicians set up the "Tent Project." It was a rock musical that preached the old revolutionary messages by telling the history of the Labour Movement from the viewpoint of the Second and Third International. This project combined influences from modern art, politics, aesthetics, and new lifestyles with a popular mixture of political entertainment. It toured through the country and could not have been performed without the help of countless groups of the small alternative scene. In that respect, the political and the lifestyle revolution fused at least a bit.[27]

Compared to other countries, Sweden had a similar history of "1968": first, a deep change in economic and social relations that required new modes of interpreting society; then Marxist theory, the emergence of the consumer society and decolonization in the Third World that were amalgamated by leftist students to an overall theory of modern society. This theory helped to detect and to name negative consequences of the affluent society, as for example bad housing or working conditions. Its connection to the language of generation conflict opened the front line between "young" and "old," "progressive" and "reactionary," "freedom" and "repression." That is, a *perception* of their own position in society—trying to live their own way, "oppressed" by the elders—was intermingled by students with a theory corresponding to that perception—the oppression of the people by "capitalism."[28] By that they transcended their own totally new situation: for the first time youth had the opportunity to create a lifestyle of their own that completely differed from that of their elders, and met their resistance. In effect, this was a confusion of *Lebenswelt* and "system" which produced two results: a wrong recipe and positive consequences. For the problems revealed, students proposed an explanation—the "capitalist system"—and a solution—revolution—that did not convince many and was not to be realized. People did not really have problems with the "system" but with their living environment. At the same time the *modes* of protest in order to change society outlived their student inventors and were adapted by others, because these new ways to negotiate problems with authorities enabled them to change things for the better in their form. Also in this respect, "1968" in Sweden resembled events on the continent, despite all differences.

Notes

1. Cf. Carole Fink, Philipp Gassert, and Detlef Junker, eds., *1968: The World Transformed* (Cambridge, 1998); Ingrid Gilcher-Holtey, *Die 68er Bewegung. Deutschland, Westeuropa, USA* (Munich, 2001); Ingrid Gilcher-Holtey, ed., *1968—vom Ereignis zum Gegenstand der Geschichtswissenschaft* (Göttingen, 1998); George N. Katsiaficas, *The Imagination of the New Left. A Global Analysis of 1968* (Boston, 1987).

2. I examine this in more detail and in comparison to Western Germany in my book: *1968—Ein Riss in der Geschichte? Gesellschaftlicher Umbruch und 68er-Bewegungen in Deutschland und Schweden* (Constance, 2005) .

3. For the other Scandinavian countries see Steven L.B. Jensen and Thomas E. Jørgensen, "Studenteroprøret i Danmark," *Historisk Tidsskrift* [Copenhagen] 101 (2001): 435–70; Terje Tvedt, ed., *(ml). En bok om maoismen i Norge* (Oslo, 1989); Johannes Nordentoft and Søren Hein Rasmussen, *Kampagnen mod Atomvåben og Vietnambevægelsen 1960–72* (Odense, 1991); Tapani Suominen, *"Verre en Quislings hird". Metaforiska kamper i den offentliga debatten kring 1960- och 1970-talens student- och ungdomsradikalism i Norge, Finland och Västtyskland* (Helsinki, 1996); Guri Hjeltnes, ed., *Universitetet og studentene. Opprör og identitet. Foredrag fra en nordisk konferanse om studenthistorie* (Oslo, 1998).

4. Stig Hadenius, Björn Molin, and Hans Wieslander, *Sverige efter 1900. En modern politisk historia*, 12th ed. (Stockholm, 1991); Yvonne Hirdman, *Vi bygger landet. Den svenska arbetarrörelsens historia från Per Götrek till Olof Palme*, (2nd ed., Stockholm, 1990); Sven E. Olsson, *Social Policy and the Welfare State in Sweden*, 2nd ed. (Lund, 1993); Lennart Schön, *En modern svensk ekonomisk historia. Tillväxt och omvandling under två sekel* (Stockholm, 2000).

5. Göran Söderström, "Kejne- och Haijbyaffärerna," in *Homo i folkhemmet. Homo- och bisexuella i Sverige 1950–2000*, ed. M. Andreasson (Göteborg, 2000), 92–117.

6. Erling Bjurström, *Generationsupproret. Ungdomskulturer, ungdomsrörelser och tonårsmarknad från 50-tal till 80-tal* (Stockholm, 1980); Erling Bjurström, "Raggare. En tolkning av en stils uppkomst och utveckling," in *Spelrum. Om lek, stil och flyt i ungdomskulturen*, ed. Peter Dahlén and Margareta Rönnberg (Uppsala, 1990), 207–28; Jonas Frykman, *Dansbaneländet. Ungdomen, populärkulturen och opinionen* (Stockholm, 1988); Tom O'Dell, *Culture Unbound. Americanization and Everyday Life in Sweden* (Lund, 1997); Lars B. Ohlsson, *Bilder av den "hotfulla ungdomen." Om ungdomsproblem och om fastställandet och upprätthållandet av samhällets moraliska gränser* (Lund, 1997); Hans-Erik Olson, *Statens och ungdomens fritid. Kontroll eller autonomi?* (Lund, 1992); Bill Osgerby, *Youth in Britain since 1945* (Oxford, 1998); Grace Palladino, *Teenagers. An American History* (New York, 1996); Uta G. Poiger, *Jazz, Rock and Rebels. Cold War Politics and American Culture in a Divided Germany* (Berkeley, 2000); Berit Wigerfelt, *Ungdom i nya kläder. Dansebanefröjder och längtan efter det moderna i 1940-talets Sverige* (Stockholm, Stehag, 1996).

7. Per Ahlmark, *Den svenska atomvapendebatten* (Stockholm, 1965); Alvar Alsterdal, *Den nya vänstern* (Stockholm, 1963); Edward J. Bacciocco jun., *The New Left in America. Reform to Revolution, 1956 to 1970* (Stanford, 1974); April Carter, *Peace Movements. International Protest and World Politics since 1945* (London, New York, 1992); Lin Chun, *The British New Left* (Edinburgh, 1993); Göran Therborn, ed., *En ny vänster. En debattbok* (Stockholm, 1966); Per Anders Fogelström, *Kampen för fred. Berättelsen om en okänd folkrörelse*, 2nd ed. (Stockholm, 1983); Klaus Jørgensen, *Atomvåbnenes rolle i dansk politik. Med særligt henblik på Kampagnen mod Atomvåben 1960–1968* (Odense, 1973); Anna-Greta Nilsson Hoadley, *Atomvapnet som partiproblem. Sveriges socialdemokratiska kvinnoförbund och frågan om svenskt atomvapen 1955–1960* (Stockholm, 1989); Johs Nordentoft and Søren H. Rasmussen, *Kampagnen mod Atomvåben; Nordiskt 60-tal. Uppbrott och konfrontation* (Helsinki, 1990); Lawrence S. Wittner, *Resisting the Bomb. A History of the World Nuclear Disarmament Movement, 1954–1970* (Stanford, CA, 1998).

8. Ronny Ambjörnsson, Gunnar Andersson, and Aant Elzinga, *Forskning och politik i Sverige, Sovjet och USA* (Stockholm 1969); Sven-Olof Josefsson, *Året var 1968. Universitetskris och studentrevolt i Stockholm och Lund* (Göteborg, 1996), 64–86; Kjell Östberg, *1968 när allting var i rörelse. Sextiotalsradikaliseringen och de sociala rörelserna* (Stockholm, 2002); Olof Ruin, *Studentmakt och statsmakt. Tre studier i svensk politik* (Stockholm, 1979), 137–86; Bengt Hansson and Erik Janson, eds., *UKAS—en utmaning* (Stockholm, 1968); Marina Stenius Aschan, ed., *UKAS och samhället. En sammanställning av dokumentationen kring och kritiken av UKAS-förslagets första del* (Stockholm, 1968).

9. Göran Ahrne, Christine Roman, and Mats Franzén, *Det sociala landskapet. En sociologisk beskrivning av Sverige från 50-tal till 90-tal*, 2nd ed. (Stockholm, 2000); Åke Daun, *Swedish Mentality* (University Park, PA, 1996); Ulf Hannerz, *Den svenska kulturen* (Stockholm, 1983); Leif Lewin, *Samhället och de organiserade intressena* (Stockholm, 1992); Leif Lewin, *Votera eller förhandla? Om den svenska parlamentarismen* (Stockholm, 1996); Michele Micheletti, *Det civila samhället och staten. Medborgarsammanslutningarnas roll i svensk politik* (Stockholm, 1994); Bo Rothstein, *Den korporativa staten. Intresseorganisationer och statsförvaltning i svensk politik* (Stockholm, 1992). Susan Sonntag is quoted by Daun, *Swedish Mentality*, 81–3.

10. Kim Salomon and Göran Blomqvist, eds., *Det röda Lund. Berättelser om 1968 och studentrevolten* (Lund, 1998); Josefsson, *Året var 1968*, 89–117, 190–213, 226–33, 274; Lena Lennerhed, *Välfärdens rebeller. Sveriges Liberala Studentförbund och kul-*

turradikalismen under 1960-talet (Stockholm, 1989); Bo Lindberg and Ingemar Nilsson, *Göteborgs universitetets historia*, 2 vols. (Göteborg, 1996), vol. 2, 61–73; Sven Nygren, *Ur Uppsala studentkårs historia*. *Från revolution till revolt* (Uppsala, 1983); Sven Nygren, "I spåren efter 1968. Ur Uppsalastudenternas tillvaro 1968–1979," in *Världen i Uppsalaperspektiv*. *Uppsala studentkår 1930–1990*, ed. Torgny Nevéus (Uppsala, 1998), 119–78.; Ruin, *Studentmakt och statsmakt*, 87–136; Kersti Ullenhag, "Kontrasternas decennium. Uppsalastudenten åren 1960–1967," in *Världen i Uppsalaperspektiv*, ed. Nevéus, 97–118.

11. Salomon and Blomqvist, eds., *Det röda Lund;* Josefsson, *Året var 1968*, 135-80; Per-Erik Lindorm, *Ett folk på marsch 1960–1977* (Stockholm, 1978), 115; *Världsproblem och kyrkofred. Domkyrkoaktionen i Lund november 1968. Dokument och kommentarer till en rättegång. Materialet sammanställt av en redaktionsgrupp under ledning av Anders Westerberg* (Lund, 1970).

12. Kim Salomon, *Rebeller i takt med tiden. FNL-rörelsen och 60-talets politiska ritualer* (Stockholm, 1996), 94–107; Eva Block, *Amerikabilden i svensk dagspress 1948–1968* (Lund, 1976); Eva Queckfeldt, *"Vietnam." Tre svenska tidningars syn på vietnamfrågan 1963–1968* (Lund 1981); *FNL i Sverige. Reportage om en folkrörelse under tio år* (Stockholm, 1975), 6, 11; *Zenit* 9 (1965), no. 1, 18f.

13. Torbjörn Sävfe, *Rebellerna i Sverige. Dokumentation, kritik, vision* (Göteborg, 1971); Salomon, *Rebeller i takt med tiden*, 107–38, 147–67.

14. Björn Elmbrant and Erik Eriksson, *Det bidde en tumme. Historien om den svenska Vietnamhjälpen* (Stockholm, 1970); Yngve Möller, *Sverige och Vietnamkriget. Ett unikt kapitel i svensk utrikespolitik* (Stockholm, 1992); Carl-Gustaf Scott, "Swedish Sanctuary of American Deserters During the Vietnam War. A Facet of Social Democratic Domestic Politics," *Scandinavian Journal of History* 26 (2001): 123–42.

15. Salomon, *Rebeller i takt med tiden*, 168–83, 210–22, 231; Gunnar Myrdal et al., *Röster för Vietnam. Den fullständiga ordalydelsen till de tal, som hölls vid det möte som anordnades av Svenska kommittén för Vietnam den 21 februari 1968 på Sergels torg i Stockholm, samt mötets uttalande till president Lyndon B. Johnson* (Stockholm, 1968); Olof Palme, *USA-kriget i Vietnam* (Stockholm, n.d., [1968]); Svante Lundberg, Sven-Axel Månsson, and Hans Welander, *Demonstranter. En sociologisk studie* (Stockholm, 1970).

16. Cf. Knut Nevermann, *Der 2. Juni 1967. Studenten zwischen Notstand und Demokratie. Dokumente anläßlich des Schah-Besuchs*, ed. Verband Deutscher Studentenschaften (VDS) (Cologne, 1967), 12–27; Klaus Benneter et al., *Februar 1968. Tage, die Berlin erschütterten* (Frankfurt am Main, 1968); Heinz Grossmann and Oskar Negt, eds., *Die Auferstehung der Gewalt. Springerblockade und politische Reaktion in der Bundesrepublik* (Frankfurt am Main, 1968), 81–96.

17. Cf. *Förhör om polisbrutaliteten 20 december 1967* (I have to thank Kjell Östberg at Södertörns högskola, Stockholm, for a copy of this unprinted manuscript); Möller, *Sverige och Vietnamkriget*, 93–95.

18. Bo Lindblom, ed., *Fallet Båstad. En studie i svensk opinionsbildning* (Stockholm, 1968); *Året var 1968* (film, Sweden, 1986).

19. *Året var 1968.*

20. Möller, *Sverige och Vietnamkriget*, 95–99, 237–46; Elmbrant and Eriksson, *Det bidde en tumme*, 18–79; Salomon, *Rebeller i takt med tiden*, 216–26, 261–66; reports of the FNL-groups in 1967/68 (National Archives, Stockholm, 730031, E2A:1).

21. Henry David Thoreaux, *Om civilt motstånd* (Knivsta, 1977).

22. Ronald Inglehart, *The Silent Revolution. Changing Values and Political Styles Among Western Publics* (Princeton, NJ, 1977).

23. Leif Nylén, *Den öppna konsten. Happenings, instrumental teater, konkret poesi och andra gränsöverskridningar i det svenska 60-talet* (Stockholm, 1998); Per Ringby, *Avantgardeteater och modernitet. Pistolteatern och det svenska teaterlivet från 1950-tal till 60-tal* (Gideå, 1995).

24. Salomon, *Rebeller i takt med tiden*, 185–200; Christer Thörnqvist, *Arbetarna lämnar fabriken. Strejkrörelser i Sverige under efterkrigstiden, deras bakgrund, förlopp och följder* (Göteborg, 1994); Anders Thunberg et al., eds., *Strejken. Röster, dokument, synpunkter från en stor konflikt* (Stockholm, 1970).

25. Hadenius, Molin, and Wieslander, *Sverige efter 1900*, 226–307; Hirdman, *Vi bygger landet*, 301–46; Lennerhed, *Välfärdens rebeller*, 12–16; Schön, *En modern svensk ekonomisk historia*, 366–467.

26. Jonas Anshelm, *Mellan frälsning och domedag. Om kärnkraftens politiska idéhistoria i Sverige 1945–1999* (Stockholm, Stehag, 2000); Bjurström, *Generationsupproret*, 102–5; Carl Holmberg, *Längtan till landet. Civilisationskritik och framtidsvisioner i 1970-talets regionalpolitiska debatt* (Göteborg, 1998); Andrew Jamison et al., *The Making of the New Environmental Consciousness. A Comparative Study of the Environmental Movements in Sweden, Denmark and the Netherlands* (Edinburgh, 1990), 13–65; Britta Jansson, *Alternativa livsformer i sjuttiotalets Sverige* (Uppsala, 1983); Josefsson, *Året var 1968*, 124–35, 216–19; Bertil Nelhaus, ed., *Allaktivitet—ja, men hur? Erfarenheter från försök att förverkliga en vision*, (Stockholm, 1971); Elisabeth Elgán, *Kvinnorörelsen och '68—aspekter och vittnesbörd* (Huddinge, 2001).

27. Johan Fornäs, *Tältprojektet. Musikteater som manifestation* (Stockholm, Göteborg, 1985).

28. In fact, the often-claimed conflict of generations mostly existed in a mutual perception of the generations: Bengt-Erik Andersson, *Generation efter generation. Om tonårskultur, ungdomsrevolt och generationsmotsättnigar* (Malmö, 1982), 115–85.

Part IV

Gender Transformations

Between Coitus and Commodification: Young West German Women and the Impact of the Pill

Dagmar Herzog

The mass availability of birth control pills in the late 1960s coincided with at least three other dramatic developments in the history of sexuality: a thorough saturation of the visual landscape with nude and semi-nude images of women's bodies and the unabashed marketing of a multitude of objects via these images; a liberalization of sexual mores and of the terms of debate surrounding sexuality so profound that it acquired the name "sexual revolution"; and the emergence and rise to cultural prominence of both a New Left movement and an incipient feminist movement, both of which, albeit in different ways, sought deliberately to politicize questions of sexuality. All three of these phenomena were evident throughout Western Europe and the United States, and in many ways West German developments mirrored those in other nations. In the wider context of the Cold War, across the Western world, the initial fifteen or so postwar years had seen a strong emphasis on family values, political quiescence, and conformity to conservative gender norms. And in all these nations in the 1960s and 1970s, countercultural and youth rebellions coincided with and spurred further broader liberalizing trends. Similarly, in all these nations feminist women's organizations, often emerging out of anti-war and student activist groups, not only fought for reproductive control and abortion rights and greater social, economic, and political equality for women, but also made heterosexual sex itself into a political matter.

Yet there were also specificities to the cultural climate of post-Nazi Germany that shaped how all these transformations, and the relationships between them, were experienced and interpreted by contemporaries. Because of the intense salience of issues of sexuality and reproduction to Nazism itself, and because of the ways sexual politics functioned as a main site for coming to terms with, and attempting to master, the Nazi past—in *both* the conservative 1950s *and* the liberal and radical 1960s–1970s—conflicts over sex in Germany were unusually freighted and vehement. This essay will, first, reconstruct key elements of the pre-Pill culture of sex and birth control in the Federal Republic. Next, it will examine how that culture was liberalized, initially in the realm of advertising and subsequently also in official mores, and then explore the ways the distribution of the Pill both contributed to and benefited from other dynamics of liberalization. Finally, the essay will address the radical politicization of sex by New Left men and by the women's movement.

Before the Pill

Postwar West German culture was peculiarly hostile to open discussion of birth control products or practices. In comparison with the United States in the 1950s, for instance, there were in West Germany far fewer family planning clinics, and sales of such objects as diaphragms or spermicidal jellies were proportionally much lower; there was also far less medical literature discussing the subject available to specialists and of what literature there was, much expressed strong criticism of birth control.[1] There were a number of reasons for this. One was that in several of the Federal Republic's states, the Himmler order of 1941 banning the sale and advertisement of all birth control products besides condoms, remained in effect. (Condoms had been exempted from the order during the Third Reich because of their usefulness in preventing the spread of venereal disease.) Yet another was that many of the doctors practicing in postwar Germany had been trained under Nazism and had received no effective education about birth control issues in their medical school years. In addition, there were also more subtle—but no less tenacious—inherited forms of misogyny, and of unreflected anxieties about the declining German birthrate, that affected physicians' willingness to educate themselves or their patients about effective strategies.

The hesitation to defend fertility control vigorously as a basic human right was not only a direct inheritance of Nazism, however. There was also an indirect, but no less powerful, legacy. The effort of Christian conservatives, especially Catholics—with the backing of the Christian

Democratic government under chancellor Konrad Adenauer—to enforce conservative sexual values in the postwar period needs to be understood not only as an extension of the values promoted during the Third Reich, but rather, and far more, as a deliberate backlash *against* Nazism. For while this has been largely forgotten now, Nazism brought with it many incitements and inducements to heterosexual activity— marital, premarital, and extramarital—not only for the sake of repro- duction, but also for the sake of pleasure (or, as it was usually put, "drive-satisfaction," *Triebbefriedigung*). For the duration of the Third Reich, Catholics in particular fought furiously against Nazi assaults on the sanctity of Christian marriage. And in the immediate aftermath of the war, Catholics were the most vocal in criticizing what they saw as Nazi-encouraged licentiousness and libertinage. There was far more con- cern with protecting youth from supposedly corrupting sexual influ- ences—pornography or birth control products—in the postwar period than there had been under Nazism.

Symptomatically, for instance, while condom vending machines had been fairly familiar aspects of the streetscape, or the backs of bars or bar- bershops, in many German towns throughout the Third Reich and in many places also for seven or eight years thereafter, the years from the mid-1950s into the early 1960s saw heated discussion among jurists and journalists over the desirability of these machines and their potential for morally corrupting youth. Even the neutral display of condoms in vend- ing machines could be interpreted—as some courts did—as an offense to "morals and decency" (*Sitte und Anstand*), a particularly vague but for that reason all the more effective traditional legal category employed by conservative jurists in their efforts to constrict youth—and inevitably also adult—access to fertility control.[2] Again, Catholic activists set the tone. In 1951–52 conservative Catholic youth organizations had demonstratively burned down kiosks which marketed porn, and in 1953 they initiated "actions" against condom vending machines. In both instances these campaigns, far from being legally censured, themselves directly inspired conservative jurisdiction.[3] Yet it is crucial also to note that the major opposition party of Social Democrats did not provide much of an alternative to the Christian Democrats on sex-related issues. Clearly very fearful of being associated with the sex radicalism of Weimar-era socialism, postwar Social Democrats displayed a singular lack of imagination and conviction. They might vote against a repressive measure—for example the censoring of pornography in the name of youth protection—but neither in the press nor in the *Bundestag* debates did they offer any truly energetic defenses of individual sexual freedom and self-determination.

The preoccupation with cleaning up sexual mores in postwar Germany had multiple functions. Stressing the importance of premarital chastity allowed postwar Christian commentators to delineate their difference from Nazism in especially stark terms, since Nazis had been so particularly eager to celebrate premarital sex and challenge the churches for their "prudery" on this matter. This postwar emphasis on sexual propriety was not only politically expedient. For many serious Christians, it was the result of a deeply held—and under the circumstances, not unperceptive—belief that sexual licentiousness and genocide had been, quite concretely, linked. Yet at the same time, and disturbingly, the manifest postwar departure from Nazi values with respect to premarital heterosexual sex was often accompanied by unapologetic continuity with Nazism in regard to the ongoing criminalization of homosexuality as well as continuity in adherence to eugenic ideas, as homophobia and eugenics both were refurbished and given renewed legitimacy under Christian auspices. Moreover, the emphasis on postwar Christian sexual morality also deflected attention from the Christian churches' complicity with Nazism during the Third Reich—and not only with its anti-Bolshevism but also with its anti-semitism. In general, the postwar churches worked to redirect moral debate away from mass murder and toward sexual matters. Both Protestant and Catholic church leaders presented sexual propriety as the cure for the nation's larger moral crisis, and thereby implied, in a striking—and telling—displacement, that sexual immorality, not complicity in genocide, was the source of that crisis.

Precisely this complicated combination of rupture and continuity between Nazism and postwar Christian politics, together with the sense that the hyper-preoccupation with sexual morality only thinly veiled some deeper entanglement in national guilt—as well as ongoing anger and resentment at the fact of that guilt—was unnervingly palpable to more critical young people growing up in this climate. And yet at the same time the connections were difficult to decipher. What many young people were left with was a profound sense that their society was marked by hypocrisy.

Moreover, popular mores were not the same as official mores. This was true both with respect to Christian values more generally and with respect to sexual morality per se. Germany was a more secularized society than either the United States or Great Britain, and Nazism had done its part to further that secularization. Only about one-quarter of West Germans attended church regularly in the late 1940s, and the numbers dropped over the course of the 1950s. Meanwhile, even believers and church-goers had their own opinions about sexual matters that diverged from both the churches' official stances and from those advanced by religious conservatives in the government. For example, in a survey conducted in 1949, also among the regular church-goers, fully 44 percent were of the opinion that premarital sex was acceptable. And the numbers were far higher for those who did not attend church regularly. In this same survey, it was found that 89 percent of the men and 69 percent of the women interviewed admitted to having had premarital sex. Among young men under the age of 30, 97.8 percent thought premarital coitus was either permissible or simply necessary.[4] Although the numbers admitting to and endorsing premarital coitus had dropped by approximately ten percentage points by the time the survey was repeated in 1963—and this was no doubt due precisely to the conservative rhetoric and cultural vigilance of the 1950s—numerous more informal estimates offered in the course of the 1950s and early 1960s suggested that anywhere between 80 and 90 percent of young people were practicing premarital coitus.[5] These numbers are much higher than the comparable figures for the United States or Britain. In short, in spite of all of the official rhetoric adamantly insisting on female virginity before marriage, and pleading also for boys to desist from premarital experimentation, actual practices in Germany diverged sharply from the formal norms. In no area of sex-related discussion was there so wide a gap between prescription and actual behavior—even as the prescriptions had profound consequences for how the sex people did have was experienced.

Two national peculiarities, then, came together: a low level of information about and access to birth control and a high rate of premarital coitus. Yet another national peculiarity was crucial as well. While American youth were internationally notorious for the practice of petting—manual mutual sexual play often leading to orgasm, a practice developed for the purpose of combining sexual intimacy and pleasure with pregnancy prevention (and the maintenance of technical virginity)—the conservative publicists who dominated the sex advice market in West Germany were tireless in their insistence that this form of sexuality, while seemingly offering "pleasure without regret" (*Genuss ohne Reue*), would ruin the capacity for future sexual happiness in marriage. They were certain that girls who engaged in petting would prove to be frigid in their marriages.[6] Also more liberal German commentators found American petting practices bizarre. As one postwar journalist disapprovingly summarized the general attitude, "this 'petting' cannot possibly offer any sort of deeper satisfaction."[7] And, strikingly, although interviews with individuals who were adolescents in West Germany in the 1950s reveal quite a lot of activity that could be defined as petting, it was almost always seen—by the participants themselves—as a brief transitional phase before the onset of coital activity and/or as a paltry, even pathologically perverse, substitute for "real" sex, something unnatural.[8] Here the experts and the masses agreed.

The discomfort with petting was undoubtedly exacerbated by the massive postwar campaign against youth masturbation. Although a range of experts in the Weimar and Nazi and early postwar years had emphasized not only the harmlessness of youth masturbation, but even its value as a preparatory experience for later sexual relationships, the majority of 1950s experts, with astonishing forcefulness and unanimity, insisted that masturbation was dangerous and deleterious to one's psychological health. Although most, if not all, experts rushed to assure readers that masturbation did not have the frightening physiological consequences it had once been rumored to have—deterioration of the bone marrow, a wasting-away of energy and health, impotence or insanity—sex-advice authors nonetheless emphasized that masturbation disturbed an individual's capacity for proper relationality. Having become dependent on self-stimulation and on fantasies, experts warned, young men would have trouble making the transition to having sex with an actual woman. Young women, if they became accustomed to clitoral self-stimulation, would in turn have trouble gaining any satisfaction in coitus. Any problems couples subsequently had with each other could be traced back to these early missteps. As one man who had been subjected to these exhortations in the 1950s remembered in 2001, "Of course we all masturbated. But we were *terrified*."[9]

In sum, the ultimate messages conveyed were contradictory. Coitus was treated as the only natural sexual activity. For example, with the exception of one sex advice magazine—which was shut down in 1951— no publication in West Germany in the 1950s ever mentioned oral or anal sex as possible alternatives to coitus. The contrast to Weimar-era sex advice—when for instance the well-known physician Max Marcuse not only endorsed both oral and anal sex as pleasurable ways of avoiding pregnancy, but also noted that their use was widespread—could not be more striking.[10] Yet at the same time, almost all advice writers treated female orgasm during coitus as an important desideratum, and advice literature stoked women's fantasies of being overwhelmed by male strength and tenderness, while it also held out the dream of lifelong passion in bed. Indeed, some of the most sophisticated arguments put forward by medical doctors against birth control practices and products had to do with the idea that these practices or products would inhibit *female* pleasure. Simultaneously, however, the literature, whether Christian or secular, continually elaborated normative notions about gender that either placed the blame for any problems or sexual unhappiness women might feel on the women themselves, or—if it acknowledged that coitus, especially with a selfish man, might not always be a wonderful experience for a woman—did not suggest alternative or even supplementary practices but rather declared that women simply did not like or seek sex as much as men did.

Aside from condoms, birth control products were almost impossible for unmarried people to procure. But birth control was not easily available for married people either. Access depended not only on the laws of the state in which one lived, but also on whether one lived in a big city or a little town, had (or did not have) a sympathetic and well-informed family physician, had (or did not have) a local pharmacist from whom one could purchase spermicidal powders or jellies without embarrassment, and/or had (or did not have) the wherewithal to order birth control products and information from mail-order catalogues. A general atmosphere of shame and secrecy surrounding sex also made conversations with friends or relatives over potentially awkward personal matters much less likely.

The rhythm method, invented and refined in the 1930s with the discovery of how women's cycles actually worked, was the *only* method in 1950s West Germany that was ever energetically endorsed in the medical literature. And although many doctors fiercely attacked the method as (variously) ineffective or unhealthy for a relationship, it was the only form of birth control officially permitted to believing Catholics. A general familiarity with which days were likely to be "safe" and which were not was also fairly common knowledge among all strata of the population. But so too was the knowledge that the method was not exactly fully reliable, especially if one tried to "stretch" the days when coitus might be all right beyond a supersafe minimum, or if any untoward event—stress, illness—threw the cycle off. Widely held beliefs that coitus during a woman's menstrual period was not normal or acceptable shortened the number of available days even more. And again, the hostility to, or ignorance and utter lack of imagination about, possible alternatives to coitus on the "unsafe" days was manifest throughout both the professional medical and the popular advice literature. Thus, for instance, a prominent physician analyzing the value of the rhythm method in 1953 could only recommend the method as a means of family planning "to that group of advice-seekers who have at their disposal a considerable amount of conscientiousness and self-discipline," for—in his opinion—the period of "abstinence" required by the method could prove to be an "unbearable burden" on marriages.[11]

The single most widely used method of birth control in the pre-Pill era, both before and within marriage, was withdrawal during intercourse (i.e. coitus interruptus). "My husband is careful [*Mein Mann nimmt sich in acht*]," was the standard way women phrased it when prodded by a curious doctor about how they managed to space the births of their children.[12] And as a young man who grew up in 1950s West Germany remembered in 2001, speaking of himself and his girlfriend: "We thought this American petting business was *dumb*. We were in love; we talked about it. We decided to use withdrawal." (And then when the girlfriend did get pregnant, this teenage couple married.)[13]

This story was part of a much larger phenomenon of premarital heterosexual activity among teens which led to "early marriages" (*Frühehen*), also colloquially called "must marriages" (*Mussehen*). Marriages among minors—a phenomenon which had reached "outrageous" levels by the late 1950s—were almost always entered into solely because a child was "on the way." Among the approximate average of 500,000 marriages entered into annually in the early 1960s, 88,000 spouses per year were between the ages of 16 and 20; 20,000 brides annually were 17 years old or less. Unsurprisingly, statistics showed that these marriages were also uniquely vulnerable to divorce.[14] But also among young couples who were no longer minors, unplanned pregnancy often led to a marriage that would otherwise have been delayed or not entered into at all. Numerous memoirs and oral history testimonies describe the social pressures within local communities that made rushed marriages the norm. At the end of the 1950s, it was found that approximately one-third of West German brides were pregnant on their wedding day. By the early 1960s, studies variously found that anywhere from 40 to 70 percent of firstborn children were conceived out of wedlock; more than 50 percent of all marriages and fully 90 percent of early marriages (with spouses between the ages of 18 and 21) were entered into solely because the bride was pregnant.[15]

Early marriages—or, if married, another (sometimes only half-wanted) child—were, however, not the only consequences of a climate in which birth control products and information were not easily accessible to everyone. Professional physicians' discomfort with or hostility to dispensing birth control information and products contributed not only to the popularity of coitus interruptus, but also resulted in an environment in which abortion, despite its illegal status under Paragraph 218, was nevertheless widespread.

In the 1950s and early 1960s, abortion was *the* German method for keeping family size small—in stark contrast, as observers noted, to both France and Britain where there was much stronger official support for family planning.[16] As one doctor put it bluntly in 1953, Germany was in the midst of an "abortion epidemic."[17] Another in 1963 matter-of-factly referred to "the abortion plague."[18] Over the course of the 1950s, estimates of abortion rates fluctuated and also varied by region, but there was general agreement among medical professionals that the rates remained extraordinarily high, or were even climbing. Midwives, quacks, and pregnant women themselves performed most of the abortions (sometimes using knitting needles or injections of soapy water or poisonous herbs or chemicals), but it was also no secret that there were doctors who were willing to break the law for a price.[19] As some patients confided, when prodded gently by a trusted physician about what they had done in those instances when withdrawal had not worked: "Well yes, a few times I did let myself get scraped out [*na ja, ein paarmal habe ich mich ausschaben lassen*]."[20] A frequently used technique was to go to a physician for a routine brief walk-in office visit, have him or her induce a miscarriage mechanically, and then be rushed to either a public hospital or a private clinic with "sudden" bleeding.[21] In 1959 alone, 5,400 individuals were each sentenced to several years in prison for performing abortions.[22] Experts assumed that for every case that came to the attention of authorities, either the police or a hospital (where women sometimes ended up not just because of induced miscarriages but also after botched operations or in instances of life-threatening complications), there were at least 100 abortions that went unrecorded. Indeed, in a case that made national news in 1963, a doctor who had served time in prison a year earlier for the first time a woman in his care had died and was now committed to an insane asylum in the wake of his second fatality, admitted to having performed approximately 2,000 abortions over the previous decade.[23] Other ways of obtaining estimates involved asking women about their prior reproductive history, in confidential intake exams during visits to their gynecologists, and then extrapolating from this sample. Based on a total of between ten and eleven million women of reproductive age in the Federal Republic between 1950 and 1957, estimates found that in any given year between 5 and 10 percent of all German women had an abortion. Experts repeatedly spoke of an average, for the duration of the 1950s, of anywhere between 500,000 to one million abortions in the Federal Republic each year. Some studies found that there was a yearly ratio of one abortion to every birth; an oft-quoted 1953 study undertaken by a Hamburg gynecologist identified in his region an annual ratio of three abortions to every birth.[24]

By the early 1960s, the mainstream press and medical journals repeatedly referred to an annual average of anywhere between 750,000 to more than one million abortions, with some physicians even estimating two million per year, and it had also become routine for mainstream periodicals to note as common sense that there was one illegal abortion for every birth in the Federal Republic.[25] Contemporaries variously speculated that one of every two German women faced the decision of whether or not to abort at some point in her life, or indeed that every year one in four women was affected.[26] One prominent gynecologist interviewed in 1964 noted that abortions were available not only in every major city, but also in the smallest villages, and that the methods used, also by nonprofessionals, had become so sophisticated (*geschickt*) that doctors had no chance of keeping track of the rates in their area.[27]

While doctors had pointed out already in the 1950s that death rates from abortion were much lower than they had been in previous decades because of the widespread use of antibiotics, numerous observers in the 1960s still noted that health complications from illegal abortions were nonetheless widespread. This was so not least because the illegality made proper follow-up care unlikely, and there is no question that the furtive and not always clean conditions under which abortions were performed exacerbated the likelihood of both physical and psychological damage. Insurance records from the 1950s also reveal that, every year, an average of 10,000 West German women died from complications due to their abortions.[28] Only the invention and widespread dissemination of the Pill brought an end to this scandalous state of affairs.

Commodification and Liberalization

The Pill did not cause the sexual revolution, however. Mass availability of the Pill brought West German abortion rates down dramatically from the end of the 1960s on. But the medical-technological invention of the Pill alone did not in itself bring about a liberalization of sexual mores. That liberalization depended upon two other crucial dynamics. One was the ever-intensifying use of sexual stimuli in advertising and journalism, in other words a dynamic largely intrinsic to economic processes. The second dynamic—in extraordinarily complex interaction with the first—was a process of political mobilization against the official culture of sexual conservatism. This political mobilization, beginning at the turn from the 1950s to the 1960s and escalating in ardor and strategic effectivity in the first three to four years of the 1960s, involved both prominent liberal public intellectuals and younger, often left-leaning student activists. But there is no question that liberals and leftists, while on the one hand often critical of the commodification of sex and its role in consumer capitalism, were, on the other, able to use the space opened up by the manifest contradictions between conservative norms and sexualized marketing to press their own claims.

The sexualization of the public sphere preceded the 1960s. Despite strict constraints on naked images in the media for much of the 1950s— nudity was rigorously censored under the auspices of the "Law about the Circulation of Youth-Endangering Literature" (*Gesetz über den Vertrieb jugendgefährdender Schriften*), which took effect in 1953—it was clear to observers of all ideological persuasions that sex was being used to sell products. Moreover, the West German film industry, engaging in avid self-censorship through the umbrella organization for film studios, "Voluntary Self-Control of Film" (*Freiwillige Selbstkontrolle des Films*), also eschewed nudity and overt representations of sex—and yet simultaneously milked the "sex appeal" of starlets for all they were worth. In addition, international "bombshells" like Marilyn Monroe and Brigitte Bardot were as iconic and obsessively idealized in West Germany as they were in the United States or in France. For many conservative critics, this purported "hypersexualization" was yet another sign of what they feared was the decline of Western civilization.

Across the ideological spectrum, however, there were also a range of more trenchant interpretations of the effect of sexualized marketing appeals. The respected conservative sociologist Helmut Schelsky, for instance, astutely observed in 1955 that the sexualization of the visual environment so often hysterically criticized especially by conservative religious activists could actually have a rather anti-sexual impact. In Schelsky's opinion, the constant inundation with external stimuli had the tendency not only to encourage conformity rather than individualized fantasies, but also to inhibit an individual's internal desires and drives from developing at all. Forcing sexual images into everyone's field of vision, he thought, ultimately had a de-eroticizing impact.[29] The left-leaning Frankfurt-based student newspaper *Diskus* in 1962 made a no less important observation. Although religious conservatives argued that youth were being "overenlightened" in dangerous ways by the wealth of sexually suggestive images in the media, *Diskus* was convinced that the success of sexualized advertising rested precisely on the fact that sex was still subject to many taboos and that society was only partially enlightened. It was specifically because enlightenment was incomplete that "one can still capitalize on sex," and that politicians, opinion-makers, and advertising specialists alike could successfully appeal to "the sexual arousability of the human being." *Diskus'* big insight was that sex profoundly attracted the ultraconservative "philistines" too. "We are floating in an ocean of sexual stimuli of all nuances, from the direct reference to the private parts to more subtle appeals to the unconscious. … The restorationist forces themselves address the unconscious when they polemicize against 'smut and trash' and appeal to the cleanliness complexes of the anal phase of our childhoods."[30]

A year later, in 1963, the Frankfurt School philosopher and sociologist Theodor W. Adorno argued that the never-ending stimulation brought by mass media and advertising—which permitted sex to be turned on and off, steered *and* exploited—meant that while sex appeared to have become more tolerated, it had also been tamed. In the process sex itself had become desexualized. But rather than just being nostalgic—as Schelsky had overtly been—for a time when sex held more drama, Adorno saw danger precisely in this desexualized, tamed, tolerated sexualization. The hypervaluation of coitus in the name of "an ideal of naturalness" (*ein Ideal des Natürlichen*) had been accompanied by a relentlessly derogatory attitude toward all "perversion" (*Perversität*) or "sophistication" (*Raffinement*). A single-minded emphasis on "pure genitality" (*pure Genitalität*) made sex a pitifully shriveled and dull thing. This single-mindedness was itself a form of profound repression and it had frightening consequences (e.g. it fueled hostility to sexual minorities like homosexuals and prostitutes). Just as bizarre but revealing was the fact that even though taboos against sexuality outside of marriage were becoming so manifestly outdated, the taboos were still mobilizable at any moment. Sexually conservative, even aggressively punitive, messages still reached a wide audience. All the more reason to be suspicious that the one kind of non-genital sexuality that was not just permitted but actively cultivated by the society was voyeurism.[31]

These diverse aperçus from the pre-sexual revolution moment highlight for just how long the changes that would from 1966 on be grouped under the heading of "sex-wave" had already been underway. But more importantly, they foreground the ambiguities that from the start accompanied the sexual revolution as it took shape from the mid-1960s on. For from the beginning the manic explosions of nudity and sex-talk that had erupted over West Germany by 1966 and gathered force for the remainder of the 1960s were accompanied by indeterminate but nonetheless strong feelings that all this hype was not as sexually exciting or personally and socially transformative as people might have hoped.

What ultimately dissolved the former culture of censorship was above all market forces. By 1966, censorship of nudity or sex-related themes in the media had in many ways simply stopped working, for there was no doubt to anyone that West Germany had become home to a "sex-wave" of "pubescent flanks," bellybuttons, and ubiquitous breasts—usually with all but the nipples uncovered—blanketing billboards and magazine covers, and of ever more frank descriptions of sexual matters in periodicals and mass-market books alike. The society was "obsessed with sex." Not only was West Germany full of *representations* of sex, but magazines also showed photos which proved that some young women were starting to go topless at swimming pools, and published articles which announced that nude dancing, or the "American" fashion for partner-swapping, were becoming popular at West German parties as well. "A flood of demonic forces is overwhelming our people. Countless individuals are being lured into unrestrained pleasure and the living-out of their drives," warned the Protestant campaign "Action Concern about Germany" (*Aktion Sorge um Deutschland*), and the archconservative Catholic campaign "Action Clean Screen" (*Aktion Saubere Leinwand*), under the direction of politician Adolf Süsterhenn, sharply denounced the atmosphere of "sexual terror" and called for tightened censorship of film.[32]

Yet media and advertising just kept pushing the boundaries of what it was possible to show. Indeed, the print media—from popular illustrated magazines to serious newspapers—took advantage precisely of the intensifying conflict between liberal and conservative forces over sexual matters in order themselves to profit from the national preoccupation. Articles self-reflexively thematizing the culture of voyeurism—or "sex as spectator sport," as one magazine sardonically phrased it—were inevitably part of the same circuit they criticized.[33] An ever-greater percentage of text space in popular magazines was devoted to sex-related themes. As recently as 1963, the ideal of marriage, and also young and not just older people's devotion to the value of marital fidelity, had been celebrated in the media as *the* West German cultural common sense. Indeed, fidelity had been at the top of the list of qualities most valued in a marriage partner, also among female and male youth.[34] But starting in 1965 and within a few years spreading relentlessly also into the most mainstream of venues, infidelity and its possible benefits became an especially popular media theme. From the left-wing youth magazine *Konkret* to the right-wing tabloid *Bild*, infidelity in general and threesomes in particular (always two women with one man, a familiar constellation in heterosexual porn), were discussed in elaborate detail. Meanwhile, sexual representations in film that two or three years earlier had been considered absolutely shocking, had come to seem utterly routine. By the late 1960s, the bourgeois sex apostle Oswalt Kolle's pseudoscientific "sex enlightenment" movies for the masses—which featured naked couples talking through their sexual problems, framed by expert voice-overs assuring people that marriages could be mended through open communication—functioned for many people more as amusing soft-core pornography than as genuinely educational materials.[35] Yet for all the new heightened visibility of and volubility around sex, enlightenment continued to remain only partial, and simultaneously generated many new anxieties. The yearning for sex to be easier, and more fun, coincided with a powerful awareness that the selling of sex and the sexing of sales involved manipulation and impossible-to-meet expectations.

Liberalization and Politicization

Although it was introduced to European markets in 1961, the Pill had only been taken by about 2,000 West German women by 1964. Initially, many doctors would only prescribe the Pill to married women. Outraged, student radicals publicized the existence and benefits of the Pill, auctioned pills as a form of guerrilla theater, circulated addresses of doctors willing to prescribe to singles, and demanded that universities provide Pill access. "We're not talking about 'the Pill,' we're taking it," announced the sign in a typical student counseling clinic.[36] In addition, the increasing attention to sex in the news made it impossible to cover over any longer the truth of massive youthful sexual activity. Scholarly surveys and journalistic reports on sexual attitudes and practices confirmed what everyone knew. Sex simply was a major part of youth culture. The age at first coitus was dropping. In response to this new/old news, a remarkable range of professionals concerned with youth, among them leading pedagogues, psychologists, sociologists and even—and significantly—theologians, went on line to defend premarital coitus as a normal developmental phenomenon.[37] From the mid-1960s on, these more liberal authorities would set the terms of debate about sex, and conservatives were the ones on the defensive. The publicity surrounding two major scandals involving doctors who provided (in one case) abortions and (in another) sterilizations contributed significantly to turning Pill access into a moral *cause célèbre*.[38] The market-driven sex wave *and* the cultural ascendance of more liberal experts *and* the critical youth insurgency each did its part to legitimate what people were already doing—and to push even further the liberalization of popular mores and behavior.

Under the combined force of all these developments, barriers to Pill use by singles soon crumbled. By 1968, the number of West German women using the Pill had jumped to 1.4 million, and then jumped again to 3.8 million by 1977. By 1975, while 33 percent of fertile women relied on the Pill in West Germany, 47 percent relied on other birth control methods. But among young women, the rates of Pill use were very high. In 1977, fully 80 percent of girls under the age of 20 were on the Pill. Unsurprisingly, abortion rates declined precipitously. Yet the birthrate declined the most. Already by 1974 West Germany had the lowest birth rate in the world, with the GDR close behind. Everyone spoke of a "Pill-induced decline," a "*Pillenknick*." Within the course of one decade, the birthrate in West Germany had dropped 50 percent. "Are the Germans dying out?," became a national discussion.[39]

And yet, the very space opened by the Pill—since this was a birth control method that women controlled themselves—and the fact that the Pill's availability coincided with freer talk about sex in general, also created the circumstances which made it possible for women both to share with each other and to go public with their dissatisfactions about heterosexual relations. The very thing that made heterosexual sex less anxious and potentially far more pleasurable for women, also created the conditions for new conflicts. This was in part due to the way that the Pill's arrival reinforced, rather than challenged, longer-term belief-patterns that saw penetration as the best or only acceptable sexual activity, and reinforced skepticism not only about alternative but also even supplemental practices. It was also due to the fact that the Pill arrived into a culture that was not exactly egalitarian in gender terms, and in which men brought to sexual encounters their own, often not fully reflected, anger, condescension, neediness, and insecurities. And it was not least due to the fact that, having banished the constant dread of unwanted pregnancy, and also—in the context of the general liberalization—having banished at least some of the anxiety about reputation, women's economic and emotional dependence on men was dramatically diminished. Women had gained the chance to have sex become more enjoyable and meaningful for them, and to start to set more of the terms in sexual encounters.

Already in 1966, the influential liberal news magazine *Der Spiegel*, in a major cover story on the sex-wave, was recording massive male ambivalence about the very female orgasms that were now more possible than ever before. "The new pleasure-demands of women," it reported, were leading to a high incidence of "psychological impotence in men." The faddish "overvaluation of the orgasm," as one expert put it patronizingly, was leading women to complain that their men did not know how to satisfy them, and men were responding with inhibition, anxiety, and heightened self-consciousness. Unable to take any female criticism of heterosexual relations seriously, *Der Spiegel* in this instance insisted on seeing women's difficulty in achieving pleasure as an unfortunate but inevitable outgrowth of the monotony of monogamy (thereby rerouting a complaint about male behavior into a challenge to the value of marital fidelity).[40] Yet as research on sex multiplied, mainstream venues like the parenting magazine *Eltern*, and the illustrated news magazine *Stern*, and *Der Spiegel* as well, ended up—though usually only tentatively and in passing—reporting that coitus per se was not fully exciting for many women.[41]

Also among the most educated and politically active youth—precisely the ones who saw themselves as the avantgarde of both the anticapitalist political revolution *and* the sexual revolution—there was considerable heterosexual conflict. Transforming sexual relations was one of the most important tasks the New Left in West Germany set itself. Indeed, the cultural critic Klaus Theweleit, himself a member of the West German New Left "generation of 1968," once retrospectively remarked that in West Germany, "the interest in the political was manifest among many young people as an interest in the sexual. The bodies of young people in the early sixties were sexually charged in a wholly unusual way."[42] Or as the journalist Sabine Weissler summarily noted, after reading numerous New Left materials, the desire to change sexual relations was often *the* spark that led to political activism. "The flood of articles, lectures, discussion events, and reading circles on the question of sexual enlightenment as a part of political emancipation was incredible."

In school and student newspapers, ahead of Vietnam, emergency laws, university reform, etc. sex was "topic number one."[43] Yet almost from the start, gender conflict was evident. Complaining about the "laborious manipulations" demanded by other birth control methods, for instance, male students writing in the Berlin newspaper *FU Spiegel* in 1968 could not figure out why many female students were hesitant to take the Pill. Did not these young women also want a "de-problematization of sexuality"? The only conclusion the authors could reach was that young German women must still have considerable prejudices about and hostility to sex.[44] In the fall of 1968, when young activist women in Frankfurt published the first broadside of the incipient women's movement, they complained specifically about "socialist screw-pressure" (*sozialistischer Bumszwang*), and the ways in which women who did not cooperate got labeled "lesbian," or "frigid," or as suffering from "penis envy."[45]

Those we call "*68ers*" faced a double challenge. On the one hand, the student movement was definitively strongly motivated by sexual rebellion against the conformist postwar culture, fueled by a fervent desire for personal liberation and self-transformation. As a group of young activists in Frankfurt, speaking also about themselves, complained in 1970, "none of the adults in our fundamentally anti-sexual and pleasure-hostile society was able to develop an untroubled relationship to sexuality."[46] But on the other hand, the mainstream sex-wave booming all around them quickly repulsed them as well. As Theweleit remarked, "with repugnance we took cognizance of the partner-swapping tales of bourgeois couples," as "the sex-wave spread in the so-called populace."[47] And yet many members of the New Left engaged in plenty of partner-swapping experiments of their own, perpetually confused about whether fidelity was a bourgeois trap or—now that the bourgeoisie had given up on it also—actually an acceptable leftist value. The discomfort with the mainstream sexual revolution was acutely evident in some of the major New Left texts on sexuality, from former SDS leader Reimut Reiche's 1968 study, *Sexualität und Klassenkampf* (Sexuality and Class Struggle) to the writings of the anti-authoritarian child-rearing movement at the turn from the 1960s to the 1970s. A classic sample of the typical tone— snatches of "materialist" analysis pasted together with inexpressible utopian longings—is provided in a 1970 book from Berlin: "As long as the nuclear family survives—ultimately, for economic reasons—sexual freedom serves as a sad little palliative for daily surfeit and disgust." And: "Even if people humped around ten times more than before, it would not add up to real sexual liberation. For merely to amass orgasms, even if man and woman arrive at them simultaneously, can not yet be seen as a satisfying form of sexuality."[48] What made activist students' perspective on sex unique, in short, was not their advocacy of greater liberality per se, but rather their insistence on connecting liberated sex with progressive politics. No coincidence then that sex rights activists in the New Left within a few years would turn away from the early, and often quite melodramatic, Wilhelm Reich-inspired calls for complete sexual liberation as an antifascist imperative toward more Herbert Marcuse-influenced analyses of the mainstream sexual revolution as just another aspect of repressive desublimation, while continuing to demand a form of sexual freedom linked to social criticism and social justice struggles.

Yet as grandiose as the New Left theoretical reflections often were, both early feminist writings and also New Left men's retrospective memory-writings record quite a bit of more mundane tensions about sexual behaviors. There was fierce rivalry between men within New Left groups not only over who could make the smartest Marxist statements, but also over who got to sleep with the prettiest women. Women were hardly the passive victims of this process. Within the feminist consciousness-raising groups, women too acknowledged that they had measured their own self-worth and expressed rivalry with each other by competing to "catch" the most impressive New Left leaders. Other women acknowledged that women could also have considerable power in erotic relationships with men, and that often it was the man, as much as if not more than the woman, who was the emotionally dependent one. Yet there was clearly often ambivalence on both sides. One woman put the problem poignantly: "I think the fear of being touched and the incapacity to touch others and to do so tenderly, passionately, is a general social phenomenon. It is hard, simply to approach people and hug them; the walls become higher all the time. But the worst thing is—I think—the way in which one tries to master this incapacity. After all, the need has not disappeared. So one does it aggressively, humiliates one another, separates emotionality and sexuality and 'bangs' on forcefully (like machines)."[49] Yet other women struggled to put into words the baggage that both men and women brought to sexual encounters, often inherited from their own parents.[50] As one woman put it in an early reflection, "Until recently I was involved with a man who had horrible fears about his potency and wanted to sleep with me very often, because he believed that otherwise it wouldn't work when he was older. I was rarely asked about my feelings and needs in this, and was at that time also not really capable of expressing these often enough or of refusing him. I have after all also learned 'that a man just needs that' and 'that a woman should subordinate herself in this way' (quote from my mother)."[51]

Many young women were obviously extremely happy with heterosexual sex, especially now that the Pill had simplified it. "We were not a group of sexually frustrated women," one woman affiliated with the New Left remembered in 2002. Instead, she said, many marriages among New Leftists ultimately broke up more because the couples had simply grown apart, or even because the women had outgrown their male partners.[52] And although, as another formerly New Left woman put it, "New Left men were so hung-up and lousy in bed, just dreadful as lovers," she solved the problem at least for herself. "That's when I turned to the working class. That went much better. [*Da hab ich mich an die Arbeiterklasse gewandt, da ging's viel besser.*]"[53]

Yet reading the texts of the time—polemical flyers and mimeographed statements produced in the context of university seminars, study groups on sexual politics and in the first consciousness-raising groups, as well as newspapers, calendars, and handbooks—reveals an astonishing amount of anger, despite or sometimes even because of the Pill, expressed over the terms of heterosexual sex. As one woman in a Frankfurt consciousness-raising group described the benefits of a women's group in contradistinction to her experiences of New Left coed groups: in the New Left groups, there was a feeling of being unable to be real, there was only the ability to "put on a show, to produce myself (clothes, make-up)." In the women's group, by contrast, there was finally "the feeling no longer to be treated like an object as in the mixed groups (suitable for fucking, nothing else)."[54] Others pointed out that women still were so economically dependent on men—because they did not have as saleable skills, they needed ultimately to find a man who would support them—that really sex was not a free exchange: "The market value of the woman, like that of a breeding pig, is determined by age, weight and the firmness of the flesh … . Since usually she has not learned much … . she must therefore behave such that the man wants to fuck her."[55] In 1972, when the Berlin feminist group Bread and Roses published its thoughts on the Pill, it not only listed "leg cramps, blue hands, more pounds, dried-out skin, hair loss or beard growth" as side effects that some women who took the Pill experienced, but also noted: "Many women would love best to throw every Pill one by one into the garbage, but most young men are so incredibly convinced of the Pill's wonders, that one does not even dare to communicate one's worries, out of fear of being considered bitchy, hysterical, or old-fashioned."[56] And as a group of young feminists put it in a contribution to the *Frauen Zeitung* in 1973, under the subhead, "What does the Pill have to do with the Revolution?," men were so egotistical and irresponsible in sexual matters that even if a male pill were to be developed, most men could not be trusted to take it. Men just presumed that the women they slept with were on the Pill, but "it's so shitty, those guys can't be depended on at all, one would have to monitor perpetually to make sure they swallowed it." Moreover, even (or especially) "comrades"—i.e. New Left men—were so hostile to women's emancipation in general that this group of women held out only the faintest hope that someday a complete "revolutionizing of the relationships between women and men" might even be possible.[57]

Problems between New Left-affiliated men and women were clearly reflective of broader conflicts within the society as a whole. Not until the mid-1970s did strategies for achieving better female orgasms—albeit orgasms produced by female masturbation rather than male solicitude—become a national obsession also in the West German mainstream, as the Bertelsmann and Ullstein publishing companies offered German translations of the works of American female sex specialists Shere Hite and Lonnie Barbach. Reluctantly, and while taking side slaps at Hite's research method, *Der Spiegel* did mention Hite's findings that only 30 percent of women achieved climax through penetration alone, and announced that "never before have so many women" freed themselves from the fatalistic and suffering-inducing Freudian belief in vaginal orgasms.[58] *Stern* took a more profeminist line, enthusiastically endorsing the advice of female masturbation guru Barbach, and informed its readers in no uncertain terms that men needed to read her book as much as women, for after all it was "all too often the clumsiness or brutality of sexist men" that was responsible for the "lack of orgasm" in women.[59] And again, even this kind of diversification of sex advice was immediately corralled into the culture of quasipornographic voyeurism. Typical here was the Munich-based sexologist Günter Hunold's study, *Intimreport der deutschen Frau* (Intimate Report on the German Woman, 1978), which shared with readers housewives' detailed descriptions of masturbating with the help of such aids as *Eierlikör*, or vegetables ("I always purchase a bit more asparagus than I'll need for our evening meals").[60] Whether this book provided more of a masturbation aid for men or for women was an open question.

Moreover, this very moment of graphic information and assertiveness about female orgasm coincided almost exactly with an untrammeled, albeit incoherent, backlash against feminism. Already in 1975, *Der Spiegel* was reporting hopefully on what it described as a "return to femininity," while also communicating male rage over having to slave away to bring home money for wives who, because of the Pill, weren't even making any babies anymore.[61] By 1977, *Die Zeit*, under the alarmist caption "Lysistrata everywhere," fretted that women were turning away from *both* men and motherhood.[62] But when *Der Spiegel* reported in 1977 that women were rejecting the Pill in droves, the magazine could not imagine any other reason for this than that women must secretly *crave* motherhood. Any negative side-effects reported by women were dismissed as psychosomatic. *Der Spiegel* could not comprehend what possible pleasant alternatives there might be to the Pill, and mocked the notion of reintroducing the rhythm method—except using oral sex instead of abstaining entirely on the unsafe days—as surely something that only a few "avant-garde" feminists, and their men, might possibly try.[63] The contrast with the American scene at this moment—when for example the mainstream women's magazine *Redbook* was publishing happy statistics about the diverse kinds of fun heterosexual women were having with oral sex, sex combined with marijuana, etc.—is striking.[64]

Yet another, and crucial, aspect of the distinctive West German backlash against feminism involved an upsurge of reports of male sexual dysfunction under heightened performance pressure. Already in 1969, the conservative tabloid *Bild* was reporting on sexually overtaxed men: until the age of 25, the newspaper stated, Germans sought sex daily; after age 30, however, husbands preferred watching television after work, and claimed to be "too tired."[65] But by 1977, precisely in the midst of mainstream perplexity about female resistance to the Pill and major confusion about how to feel about the reports that female orgasms were easier to achieve through masturbation than through coitus, the subject of men's retreat from sex was almost constantly discussed. *Stern* printed a cartoon in which a woman compared a man's lack of energy in bed to nicotine-free cigarettes.[66] *Der Spiegel* declared that performance pressure was rampant especially among men in their late forties and fifties; "fear is the enemy of erection." Men this age put too much emphasis on their work and let their sex lives slide. Taking up sex again at all required an "'especially sensitive female partner'"; rarely was this the wife.[67] And in a different essay, *Der Spiegel* coupled its report on the American Betty Dodson's female masturbation techniques with another reminder that "militant masturbation … means man-hatred."[68] Yet a third essay again educated readers to the fact that for men, "precisely … performance expectations … blocked sexual capacities the most."[69] Depressingly, men's sense that they were under pressure was not leading them to change their ways. On the contrary, a study done by the Hamburg research institute SEAT in 1978 found that "every third woman would be happy if she could at least regularly achieve an orgasm."[70] Meanwhile, *men's* masturbation was avidly defended.[71]

Notably, furthermore, announcements that the sexual revolution was winding down soon followed the anti-feminist backlash. A sequence of article titles and captions in *Stern* said it all: "Between Desire and Frustration: Sex in Germany 1980: After the rush of freedom comes the hangover?" Then in 1982: "Men are becoming chaste. An end to sex …. The German man … is fed up with the women's movement." One man quoted by *Stern* said it outright: "The women's movement has reduced our horniness to zero."[72] Men and women were now widely reported to be having sex not much more frequently than they had been before the introduction of the Pill just twenty years earlier.

Conclusion

One cannot make sense of how the Pill was experienced and interpreted in West Germany without understanding the complex context in which it became widely available. The Pill took away fear of pregnancy, and freed women to enjoy coitus as never before. The Pill was "an incomparable salvation" (*eine Rettung ohnegleichen*), as one young woman who had been involved in both the New Left and the early feminist movement put it.[73] "I experimented around without any inhibitions," said another.[74] Men and women both eagerly sought out the new possibilities the Pill offered them.

Yet it is also striking how quickly the media registered male anxieties about performance pressure. The longing for sexually free women and the fear of those free women came hand in hand. Arriving as it did in conjunction with the sex-wave, this new freedom to enjoy sex also raised female expectations of sex and made it possible for girls and women to make demands for better sex on their male partners. Many men in turn responded with new insecurities and anger. As one woman sarcastically summarized the dilemma in 1980: "The men are constantly calling for the hot-to-trot woman, who shows her desire openly—but woe if she actually shows up. [*Die Männer rufen ständig nach der scharfen Frau, die ihr Begehren offen zeigt—aber wehe, sie kommt wirklich.*]"[75]

Finally, the commodification of young women's bodies that was the main feature of the sex-wave would also be one of the main reasons for many women's ultimate ambivalence about the sexual revolution more generally and the Pill specifically.[76] Certainly, girls and women could experience the pleasures of self-display and of being objects of desire, but they could also find the objectification unnerving. Meanwhile, boys and men could experience the pleasures of looking and fantasizing, but while the Pill also made real sex far more readily available for them, sex with real women, especially when they started to make demands, could also somehow be awfully irritating. As one fed-up man put it in 1980, "Honestly, I am for the peep-show. The women's movement doesn't do anything for me."[77] Feminist anger about the Pill, as it became articulated ever more publicly through the first half of the 1970s, took the mainstream by surprise. And yet that anger was not separable from a larger rage about and deeper sense of discontent with heterosexual relationships in all their dimensions. It would take the next, younger cohort of men—less oppressed by their own upbringings, less threatened by women's intelligence or strength—to develop a different, more expansive approach to heterosexual sex. The Pill, and the liberalization of mores of which it was a part, created the *conditions* for a revolution in gender relations. But it took a great many more battles, both individual and collective, to begin to make that particular revolution real.

Notes

1. See the summary remarks about the differences between West Germany and other Western nations in Hermann Knaus, "Zur Frage der natürlichen Geburtenregelung und ihrer individuellen Anwendung," *Die Heilkunst* 69 (1956): 272–73; K. Saller, "Zivilisation und Sexualität," *Die Heilkunst* 70 (1957): 48; Günter Grund, "Optimale Kontrazeption," *Medizinische Welt*, no. 32 (10 August 1963): 1601; and "Die Antikonzeption—in Deutschland noch ein Stiefkind," *Berliner Ärzteblatt* 78, no. 2 (1965): 73–77.

2. See Clemens Bewer, "Verkauf von Gummischutzmitteln durch Aussenautomaten," *Zeitschrift für ärztliche Fortbildung* 50/6 (1961): 460–62.

3. See "Schwarzer Terror," *Rheinische Zeitung*, 25 January 1951; "Der erste Scheiterhaufen," *Frankfurter Rundschau*, 8 April 1952; and Hans Harmsen, "Mittel zur Geburtenregelung in der Gesetzgebung des Staates," in *Sexualität und Verbrechen*, ed. Fritz Bauer et al. (Frankfurt am Main, 1963), 185.

4. See Ludwig von Friedeburg, *Die Umfrage in der Intimsphäre* (Beiträge zur Sexualforschung), vol. 4 (Stuttgart, 1953), 24, 27, 46, 50; and Udo Undeutsch, "Comparative Incidence of Premarital Coitus in Scandinavia, Germany, and the United States," in *Sexual Behavior in American Society: An Appraisal of the First Two Kinsey Reports*, ed. Jerome Himelhoch and Sylvia Fleis Fava (New York, 1955), 362.

5. See "Theologische Stimmen zur ärztlichen Beratung über Empfängnisverhütung," *Wege zum Menschen* 9 (1957): 193; "Erst die Liebe, dann die Moral? Alles über die Deutschen (15)," *Stern* 48 (1963), 43–52; and Elisabeth Noelle and Peter Neumann, eds., *Jahrbuch der öffentlichen Meinung 1958–1964* (Allensbach, 1965), 589.

6. In this context see also Helmut Schelsky, who—interestingly—gives authority to his own critique of petting by citing anthropologist Margaret Mead's negative assessment of it. Helmut Schelsky, *Soziologie der Sexualität* (Hamburg, 1955), 121–22. For an example of an ordinary citizen who shared these views that "substitute solutions" like petting would have "the most damaging consequences for a later marriage," see Gerda Ruppricht, letter to the editor, *Twen*, no. 10 (1962), 11.

7. L. M. Lawrence, "Der Kinsey Report," *Merkur* 3/5 (1949): 495–99.

8. On the 1950s, see Peter Kuhnert and Ute Ackermann, "Jenseits von Lust und Liebe? Jugendsexualität in den 50er Jahren," in *"Die Elvis-Tolle, die hatte ich mir unauffällig wachsen lassen": Lebensgeschichte und jugendliche Alltagskultur in den fünfziger Jahren*, ed. Heinz-Hermann Krüger (Opladen, 1985). In the early 1960s, 72 percent of young men and 44 percent of young women between the ages of twenty and thirty admitted to having at some point engaged in petting. But only a small minority approved of the practice. While it was "okay for the start of a relationship," it was like "playing with fire," or something "unnatural." See "Erst die Liebe, dann die Moral?," 50. And even into the mid-1960s, with the sex-wave in full swing, West German working-class youths in particular continued to feel that anything outside of coitus was a perversion. See "Die gefallene Natur," *Der Spiegel* 19, 2 May 1966, 50–69.

9. Conversation with F. B., 2001.

10. Max Marcuse was one of the most important and influential sexuality specialists in Weimar. See especially his *Der Präventivverkehr in der medizinischen Lehre und ärztlichen Praxis* (Stuttgart, 1931).

11. H. Dietel, "Möglichkeiten und Grenzen der natürlichen Geburtenregelung," *Hamburger Ärzteblatt* (November 1953): 234–35.

12. Anne Marie Durand-Wever, "Ärztliche Indikationen zur Empfängnisverhütung," in *Die gesunde Familie*, ed. Hans Harmsen (Beiträge zur Sexualforschung), vol. 13 (Stuttgart, 1958), 126–30. For a robust defense of the withdrawal method—after

more than a decade of very hostile attacks on it by numerous physicians—see Herbert Lax, "Methodik der Antikonzeption," *Deutsches medizinisches Journal* 15, no. 8 (April 1964): 261–67.

13. Conversation with F. T., 2001.

14. See R. Hobbing, "Zur Frage der Haltbarkeit von Minderjährigenehen," *Unsere Jugend* 6, no. 8 (1954): 366–68; "Erst die Liebe, dann die Moral?," 46; and "Jung gefreit—Nie gereut," *Twen* (1960), 29; and "Darüber spricht man nicht," *Twen* (1960), 30. The divorce rate for teen marriages was twice as high as that for marriages between 24- and 26-year-olds.

15. See Angela Delille and Andrea Grohn, *Blick zurück aufs Glück* (Berlin, 1985), 124; "Ist der Betrieb ein Heiratsmarkt? Alles über die Deutschen (2)," *Stern* 16/35 (1963), 25; Harmsen, "Mittel zur Geburtenregelung," 175; Gisela Staupe and Lisa Vieth, "Einführung," in *Die Pille: Von der Lust und von der Liebe*, ed. Staupe and Vieth (Berlin, 1996), 14; and "Heiraten nur weil ein Kind kommt?," *Twen* (1960), 26. One feminist text in 1974 stated as self-evident that one out of every two marriages was a "must marriage." Criticizing the block placed by the Federal Constitutional Court in June 1974 on the implementation of a liberalized abortion law that had been preliminarily passed by the *Bundestag* in 1973, feminists summarized the misery of an unwanted pregnancy. Referring to the eight judges, the women wrote: "None of these men … . know the panic of having a monthly period be even only a few days late, none of them knows the crashing breakdown that happens when we finally know that we are expecting a child that we cannot or do not want to raise. None of them know the sense of alienation from one's own body, when the biological mechanism of a pregnancy is moving along against the will of the woman. None of them seem even to know that in such situations marriages are entered into that develop into a terror for the woman, the man, and the children." See "Kundgebungsbeitrag: Frauen und solidarische Männer" (1974), personal archive Sibylla Flügge, Frankfurt am Main.

16. See Hans Harmsen, "Abtreibung oder Empfängnisverhütung?," *Gesundheitsfürsorge* 3 (1953/54): 123; and the very informative essay by A. V. Knack and W. Pieper, "Der Stand der Empfängnisverhütung in der ärztlichen Praxis," *Ärztliche Mitteilungen* 41/14 (May 1956): 388.

17. Hermann Doerfler, "Was kann die Bayer. Ärzteschaft und was der einzelne Arzt zur Bekämpfung der Abtreibungsseuche beitragen?," *Münchener Medizinische Wochenschrift* 95, no. 17 (24 April 1953): 509–11.

18. Harmsen, "Mittel zur Geburtenregelung," 186.

19. See Michael Luft, "Abtreibung in Deutschland: Hilfe, ich kriege ein Kind! (1)," *Konkret* (May 1964), 7–11. One study done in Kiel in the early 1950s suggested that one out of every twenty abortions was performed by a physician. See Doerfler, "Was kann die Bayer. Ärzteschaft." See also Theodor Bruck, *Geburtenregelung* (Flensburg, 1964), 129–30.

20. Durand-Wever, "Ärztliche Indikationen."

21. Luft, "Abtreibung in Deutschland," 9.

22. Delille and Grohn, *Blick zurück aufs Glück*, 123.

23. The case of Dr. Suhr is discussed in Michael Luft, "Paragraph 218 oder Baby-Pille für Alle: Hilfe, ich kriege ein Kind! (2)," *Konkret* (July-August 1964), 7–9, 16.

24. See Delille and Grohn, *Blick zurück aufs Glück*, 123; and the comments about Dr. Hanns Dietel's study in the interview with Dr. Heinz Kirchhoff in "Anti-Baby-Pillen nur für Ehefrauen," *Der Spiegel* 9, 26 February 1964, 87.

25. See Carl Nedelmann, "Abtreibung: Geburtenregelung und Strafrechtsreform," *Konkret* (July 1965), 6.

26. See Heike Rieder, letter to the editor, *Konkret*, Se1964, 2; and the statistics on West Germany in Kühne, "Australiens Frauen und die Pille: Bremswirkung pseudowissenschaftlich erzeugter Karzinophobie," *Berliner Ärzteblatt* 78, no. 7 (1965): 370–73.

27. Kirchhoff quoted in "Anti-Baby Pillen," 87.

28. See Bruck, *Geburtenregelung*, 127–28; and Delille and Grohn, *Blick zurück aufs Glück*, 123.

29. Schelsky, *Soziologie der Sexualität*, 125-26.

30. Christian Crull and Hans Hagedorn, "Sex und Profit," *Diskus* 12, no. 7 (1962), 1.

31. Theodor W. Adorno, "Sexualtabus und Recht heute," in *Sexualität und Verbrechen*, ed. Fritz Bauer et al., especially 299–308.

32. See "Die gefallene Natur," 50, 53–54.

33. Ibid., 58.

34. See "Umfrage in die Intimsphäre: Alles über die Deutschen (13)," *Stern* 16/46 (1963), 56; "Erst die Liebe, dann die Moral?," 52; see also the comments about yearning for twosomeness and for founding a family in Dieter Binder, "Anmerkungen zum Thema Sex on the Campus," *Diskus* no. 7, (July/August 1960), 1; and Anton van der Vet, "Generation ohne Hitler," *Konkret* (1962).

35. Conversation with C. K., 2001.

36. The poster can be seen in Sabine Weissler, "Sexy Sixties," in *CheSchahShit: Die sechziger Jahre zwischen Cocktail und Molotov* (Berlin, 1984).

37. E.g. see the authorities quoted in "Erst die Liebe, dann die Moral?," 50; and "Zur Jugendliebe gehört die Empfängnisverhütung," *Der Spiegel* 35 (1966), 55.

38. See Luft, "Paragraph 218," 7–9, 16; and Moritz Pfeil, "Eine gewisse Presse, eine gewisse Justiz: Der Lehrfall Dohrn," *Der Spiegel* 17/47, 20 November 1963.

39. See Gerhard Döring, "Das erste Mal," *Eltern*, June 1969, 56; "Anti-Baby Pillen," 81; "Last und Lust," *Der Spiegel* 22/32, 5 August 1968, 85; "Ins rechte Mass," *Der Spiegel* 24/12, 16 March 1970, 190, 195; "Die Kinder wollen keine Kinder mehr," *Der Spiegel* 29/13, 24 March 1975, cover page ("Sterben die Deutschen aus?") and 42, 44; and "Das Unbehagen an der Pille," *Der Spiegel* 31/6, 31 January 1977, cover page ("Überdruss an der Pille") and 40.

40. "Die gefallene Natur," 68. For a confident summary assertion, as late as 1964, that the vast majority of young girls were not experiencing anything at all in their coital encounters, see Lax, "Methodik der Antikonzeption," 266–67.

41. For example, see Gisela Schmeer, "Die Aufklärung und wir Frauen (VII)," *Eltern*, July 1969, 119; "Jeder sechste will mit jeder," *Der Spiegel* 13 (1971), 180; and Ingrid Kolb, "Das Warten der Frauen auf den Orgasmus," *Stern* 22 (1980), 132–45.

42. Klaus Theweleit, *Ghosts: Drei leicht inkorrekte Vorträge* (Frankfurt am Main, 1998), 106–7. Or, as Theweleit had put it several years earlier, a "special sort of sexual tension was the 'driving force' of 1968" in West Germany. Klaus Theweleit, … *ein Aspirin von der Grösse der Sonne* (Freiburg im Breisgau, 1990), 49.

43. Weissler, "Sexy Sixties," 99.

44. H. Abholz, H.W. Dräger, and B. Witt, "Lautloses Platzen," *FU Spiegel*, February 1968.

45. The *Weiberrat* quoted in Dagmar Herzog, "'Pleasure, Sex and Politics Belong Together': Post-Holocaust Memory and the Sexual Revolution in West Germany," in *Intimacy*, ed. Lauren Berlant (Chicago, 2000), 139.

46. "Kinderschule Frankfurt," in *Erziehung zum Ungehorsam*, ed. Gerhard Bott (Frankfurt am Main, 1970), 51, 54.

47. Theweleit, *Ghosts*, 129.

48. *Berliner Kinderläden: Antiautoritäre Erziehung und sozialistischer Kampf* (Cologne, 1970), 108.

49. "Psychische Verelendung und Emanzipatorische Selbsttätigkeit" (collective statement produced by a women's group circa 1974), 6. Personal archive, Sibylla Flügge, Frankfurt am Main.

50. See Sibylla Flügge, "1968 und die Frauen—Ein Blick in die Beziehungskiste," in *Gender und soziale Praxis*, ed. Margit Göttert and Karin Walser (Königstein/Taunus, 2002), especially 266-86.

51. "Psychische Verelendung," 6–7.

52. Conversation with T. S., 2002.

53. Conversation with G. T., 2000.

54. "Psychische Verelendung," 5.

55. Elisabeth Skerutsch, "Was soll der Abtreibungsparagraf?," mimeograph flyer, circa 1974, personal archive Sibylla Flügge, Frankfurt am Main.

56. *Brot und Rosen* statement from 1972, quoted in Volkmar Sigusch, "Sexualwissenschaftliche Aspekte der hormonalen Kontrazeption bei jungen Mädchen," in *Sexualität und Medizin*, ed. Sigusch (Cologne, 1979), 91.

57. "Was denn nun: Pille, Spirale oder Gummi? (Beitrag vom Frauenzentrum Berlin)," *Frauen Zeitung*, no. 1, Oct. 1973, 7, 15.

58. "Hite-Report: Abnabeln von Doktor Freud," *Der Spiegel* 5 (1977), 185. Hite also reported that 87 percent of her respondents did still continue to seek penetration, but largely for "the sake of a bodily contact and the feeling of togetherness." In a rare moment of reflectiveness, *Der Spiegel* suggested that this idea of using the penis as "a method of communication, not only an instrument," could perhaps lead the way out of the "genital labyrinth": "But this would mean, as the U.S. psychiatrist Herb Goldberg formulated it, to move men to feel. Goldberg is pessimistic: 'that's as though one would tell a cripple to run.'"

59. Otto Köhler, "Über die Liebe an und für sich," *Stern* 19, 28 April 1977, 74.

60. Günter Hunold, *Intimreport der deutschen Frau: Die sexuelle Befreiung vom Mann* (Munich, 1978), 190–93.

61. "Frau '75: 'Grosse erotische Mutter,'" *Der Spiegel* (1975). The cover displayed a naked woman with a child and announced "Woman '75: Return to Femininity."

62. Viola Roggenkamp, "Lysistrata geht um: Kein Pillenknick, sondern die Emanzipation der Frau lehrt die Gesellschaft das Fürchten," *Die Zeit* 18, 22 April 1977, 57.

63. "Das Unbehagen an der Pille," 40.

64. See Robert J. Levin and Amy Levin, "Sexual Pleasure: The Surprising Preferences of 100,000 Women," *Redbook* (1975), 55; and Robert J. Levin, "The Redbook Report on Premarital and Extramarital Sex," *Redbook*, October 1975, 190.

65. "Bis 25: Täglich Liebe. Ab 30: Ich bin so müde," *Bild*, 24 January 1969.

66. *Stern* cartoon reprinted in "Jüngstes Gerücht," *Der Spiegel*, 28 February 1977, 190.

67. "Jüngstes Gerücht," 191.

68. "Mild bis wild," *Der Spiegel*, 7 March 1977, 207.

69. "Stunde der Wahrheit," *Der Spiegel*, 18 April 1977, 231.

70. Ingrid Kolb, "Zwischen Lust und Frust," *Stern* 21 (1980), 132.

71. E.g. see *Pflasterstrand*, no. 23 (late January-early February 1978), 3.

72. Conrad Zander, "Die Männer werden keusch: Schluss mit dem Sex," *Stern* 51, 16 December 1982, 48–50; "Die verteufelte Lust," *Stern* 47, 17 November 1983, 78.

73. Conversation with R. G., 2002.

74. Conversation with C. H., 1996.

75. Quoted in Kolb, "Zwischen Lust und Frust," 172.

76. For example, see the analysis in "Zum Wandel der Sexualmoral," a paper written by an anonymous woman in a seminar at the University of Frankfurt, probably in the early 1970s. Personal archive, Sibylla Flügge, Frankfurt am Main. Sexual intercourse,

she pointed out, was not just about satisfying sexual drives; it was very much also about ego-confirmation for men who had so few other sources for that confirmation. Since in late capitalism sexuality was meant to function as a compensation for all existential insecurities induced in men by the experiences of daily life, especially at work, the fetishization of female bodies in the media and the recent rhetoric affirming female sexuality—and the presentation of that affirmation as a victory for women's emancipation—really meant nothing but a coercion for women, a constant compulsion "always and above all to be sexy ... always and above all to be available for sex," and "the pressure voluntarily to identify with her role as sex-object for men." The Pill was constantly presented as *the* ticket to women's emancipation, but it came together with insistent duress, and frequent declarations that women were "neurotic, frustrated, or even repressive, if they do not want to sleep with someone." See also the devastating interviews about women's bad experiences of heterosexual sex in Alice Schwarzer's *Der "kleine" Unterschied* (1975), discussed in Leona Siebenschön, "Noch genauso frigide," *Die Zeit* 30, 18 July 1975, 37.

77. Gernot Gailer, "Eine Traumfrau zieht sich aus, " *Ästhetik und Kommunikation* 40–41 (September 1980): 91.

Chapter 13

Boy Trouble: French Pedophiliac Discourse of the 1970s

Julian Bourg

On 28 January 2001, the British newspaper, the *Observer*, broke a story about a former 1960s radical turned Green Party delegate to the European Parliament.[1] Daniel Cohn-Bendit had first achieved prominence as a vocal figure in the French student/worker strikes of May 1968. Thirty-one years later he was elected to the Parliament in Strasbourg, representing France as a dedicated Europeanist. The *Observer* article publicized remarks Cohn-Bendit had made in a 1975 book he wrote on education, *The Big Madness*, and then in a German countercultural magazine in August 1976. Working in an experimental children's school set up by New Leftists, part of the 1970s *Kinderladen* movement, he said that his interactions with students occasionally became sensual or sexual. Sexually curious overtures were made by the children, and in the open, anti-authoritarian ambience of the time, he sometimes indulged them. As he wrote in 1976, "It has happened to me several times that a few children opened the fly of my pants and started to stroke me. I reacted differently each time according to the circumstances, but their desire confronted me with problems. I asked them: 'Why don't you play with each other, why have you chosen me and not other children?' But when they insisted on it, I then stroked them. For that reason I was accused of perverted behavior." When asked by the *Observer* to assess his earlier admission, Cohn-Bendit replied that, although it was correct for public figures to account for their pasts, his remarks should be viewed in the context of their times. As an educator in 1970s Germany, his published remarks had been intended to provoke: teachers had to grapple with the fact that children were sexual. "Our idea was to let [the children] realize their personalities through expression of their needs," he told the *Observer*, "Pedophilia was not what got me going."

The "Cohn-Bendit Affair" of late February and March 2001 proved the rule that scandals usually emerge as a critical mass.[2] Politically charged attacks and defenses of Cohn-Bendit coincided with several highly publicized trials of priests accused of pedophilia as well as with a government-led national campaign against the sexual abuse of children.[3] Cohn-Bendit said he was passing the "worst six weeks of my life" as he was simultaneously implicated in another scandal when *Stern* magazine (January 2001) printed pictures of Joschka Fischer, the former radical turned German Foreign Minister, beating up a policeman in 1973.[4] Cohn-Bendit and Fischer, friends since their student stays, found themselves raked over the coals of media sensationalism. In France, May 1968 itself was on trial for the general excesses of the era.[5]

From the Marc Dutroux scandal in Belgium in 1996 through the pedophilia crisis in the American Catholic Church in 2002, the theme of sex with children has been such a recurrent fixture of contemporary European and North American public culture as to have made it a genuinely historical phenomenon. Recent debates on this theme, ranging from understandable outrage to hysterical and paranoid polemic, can be historicized in a broader context. Generally, they relate to postwar Western sexual politics, and specifically, they reference an eccentric masculinist rhetoric of "intergenerational" relations native to the sexual liberation movements of the 1970s. The Cohn-Bendit Affair is thus an intriguing coda to earlier debates in which the sexuality of children and sometimes sex with children were taken as frontiers of social liberation.

Though appreciated in elite middle-class culture since the late nineteenth century, the facts of childhood sexuality have achieved growing popular acceptance in Europe and North America since 1945.[6] Accepting such facts, though, has in no way resolved what they mean. Especially since the 1960s, the West has endlessly worried over and been obsessed with what to do about childhood sexuality, how to negotiate and regulate it, and what cultural and political meanings to give it.[7] For instance, the series of events grouped under the heading "sexual revolution"—volitional movements as well as demographic and economic transformations—drew on and contributed to the postwar problematization of childhood sexuality. Inasmuch as "youth" stood for a social cohort for whom sexual expression was (and, to some extent, still is) considered illegitimate, the liberalization of sexual norms expanded the numbers of those who count *grosso modo* as socially legitimate sexual subjects. In this respect, age cohorts were social groupings on par with others who have gained via the "sexual revolution": women, homosexuals, transsexuals, etc. Of course, the category of "youth" is not isomorphic with that of "childhood." Sexual legitimation for youth of certain ages has been answered since the 1970s with the reinscription of norms that define illegitimate expressions and experiences of child sexuality.

In the mainstream public spheres of Europe and North America, consensual sexual relations between young adults in their late teen years finds greater legitimacy than those between youth in their early teens; and sexual relations between adults and preteen children are not considered legitimate at all. In fact, the last case has become a limit situation, a rallying cry for advocates of the remoralization of sexuality. For understandable reasons, "liberal" inheritors of the sexual revolution, who might, for instance, advocate the decriminalization of homosexuality or support the free distribution of contraceptives, avoid taking stands on the issue. Rights language has difficulty with children. Should there be highchairs and booster seats at the table of socially legitimate sexuality? One cannot really be *for* sexual relations between adults and children, can one? Suffer the little children. The highly mediatized pedophilia scandals of recent years have been merely the latest episodes in a fairly static historical period characterized by entrenched oppositions: the liberalization of sexuality, on one side, and the reinscription of sexual taboos, on the other side. In such a cultural field, pedophilia seems a *perfect situation* of Weberian rationalization, or better, the situation of *rationalization perfected*: a square-circle, a *cul-de-sac*, an urgent debate whose conclusion has already been decided in advance.

Setting aside the obvious point that adult-minor sexual relations have found various forms of legitimacy since the Greeks, open debate on pedophilia has been widespread since the 1970s, especially in gay male discursive circles.[8] In his generally balanced but ultimately slippery assessment of late-twentieth-century "intergenerational sex," Jeffrey Weeks has correctly noted that common "stereotypes" about pedophilia "obscure a complex reality."[9] Complexity notwithstanding, Weeks's slipperiness derives from the claim that man-boy relationships are somehow free from domination in general because they are free from the type of domination that characterizes man-girl relationships. He turns one feminist argument—girls have a different sociosexual experience than boys—against another—asymmetrical sex/power relations can be exploitative. The conclusion is that boys ought to have a distinctive "nonlegal" regime of protections against abuse. Advocates of intergenerational sexual relations such as Weeks have often focused their attentions on how law governs the spaces where children, adult society, and sexuality intersect. The argument is that adult-minor sexual relations, or at least some of them, ought to be decriminalized in the same manner that, say, abortion and, in some places, homosexuality have been. From this point of view, sexual liberation needs to trickle down into yet-unliberated arenas. Calls for reform of the legal regimes covering adult-minor relationships have frequently been argued on the basis of their "pedagogical" value, a rhetoric that clearly references the model of "Greek love."[10] The issue of consent finds itself sandwiched between (1) a liberational notion that claims the denial of childhood sexuality to be repressive, and (2) a pedagogical notion that finds adult-minor relations to be educative. The theme of "power" often seems elided, a point feminists have championed for some time.[11] As intimated by Weeks's suggestion, gender differences have played out decisively in the articulation of pedophiliac positions.

One telling chapter in this broad postsexual revolution debate on pedophilia, whose popularity and occasional sophistication may surprise the outside observer, emerged in France during the 1970s. Following the student/worker revolts of May 1968, and the women's and gay liberation movements that developed in their wake, calls for legitimizing intergenerational relations were taken seriously by eminent figures on the French intellectual-political Left. In 1970s France, precisely those aforementioned elements of the rhetoric of intergenerational advocacy were foregrounded—sexual liberation against a repressive social order, pedagogy, and homosexuality (the long-standing French term for homosexual, *pédéraste*, had strong intergenerational overtones). There, too, debate turned to the dilemma of consent and the reform of laws barring sex between adults and minors.

Rhetorical Legitimacy

Exemplifying the rhetorical power of arguments for the decriminalization of pedophilia were two widely noted petitions published in the first half of 1977.[12] In January, *Libération* and *Le Monde* published, "For Another Legislation on the Sexuality of Minors," written in support of three men who, after being held in preventative detention in French jails since 1973, were at last coming to trial for "indecent assault without violence on minors" (*attentat à la pudeur sans violence sur les mineurs*).[13] The three men were accused of having had relations, played sexual games with, and photographed a number of boys and girls under the age of 15. Declaring that "three years in prison is enough for caresses and kisses," the petition attacked the "disproportion" between the accuseds' pre-trial punishment and the offenses with which they were charged. The petition furthermore highlighted a presumed disconnect between the law and the "daily reality" of French society. Although the document likely reflected the ease with which those on the independent

French Left at the time signed petitions on the fly, the names of the signatories spoke volumes: Louis Aragon, Roland Barthes, Simone de Beauvoir, Jean-Louis Bory, François Châtelet, Copi, Michel Cressole, Fanny and Gilles Deleuze, Jean-Pierrre Faye, Philippe Gavi, André Glucksmann, Félix Guattari, Daniel Guérin, Jean-Luc Hennig, Guy Hocquenghem, Bernard Kouchner, Jack Lang, Georges Lapassade, Michel Leiris, Jean-François Lyotard, Gabriel Matzneff, Bernard Muldworf, Anne Querrien, Christiane Rochefort, Jean-Paul Sartre, René Schérer, Philippe Sollers, and Jean-Marie Vincent, among others. By the end of the month, the three men in the so-called "Dejager Affair" had been sentenced to five years in prison. A journalist for the Trotskyist *Rouge* noted that, ironically, a rapid judgment had been reached only after the leftist press had taken up the cause of the accused and suggested that the youth had consented to the games and photographs.[14]

The second petition, an "Open Letter for the Revision of the Penal Code," was printed in *Le Monde* on 22 May 1977.[15] The previous month *Libération* had hosted intense and often outrageous debates on sexual violence against women and the pitfalls of "bourgeois justice." Pedophiliac discourse on "consent" coincided temporally and thematically with French feminist mobilization against rape.[16] Also in April 1977, the *Parti communiste français* (PCF) had finally come out in favor of decriminalizing homosexuality.[17] It was a dynamic convergence. The "Open Letter" that appeared in *Le Monde* called for a revision of those portions of the penal code that dealt with intergenerational relations. The three specific provisions in question were: the criminal charge of corruption of youth (*incitation de mineur à la débauche*), the minimum heterosexual age of consent of 15 years, and the minimum homosexual age of consent of 18 years. Again, the lag between laws on the books and the evolution of social mores served as the rationale for a change in legislation. In addition to many of the names mentioned above, one found new additions: Louis Althusser, Jean-Paul Aron, Jacques Derrida, Françoise Dolto, Michel Foucault, and Alain Robbe-Grillet. The petition was not mere fancy, since a state blue-ribbon panel, the Commission de révision du Code pénal, had been formed to oversee an updating of the entire penal code.[18] Foucault, in fact, had been invited to serve as a consultant to the Commission.

Though these notables of the French intellectual-political Left signed their support for the "Dejager Three" and for a reform of the penal code, a much smaller number of individuals made rethinking and decriminalizing intergenerational relations their *idées fixes*, or obsession. The most significant observation to make about this discursive constellation is the simplest: those doing the talking were exclusively men. They included: Jean Danet, Tony Duvert, Michel Foucault, Daniel Guérin, Guy Hocquenghem, Georges Lapassade, Gabriel Matzneff, and René Schérer.[19] To be sure, the theme of adult-minor relations had been present at the birth of the French women's and gay liberation movements. The famous twelfth issue of the Maoist publication, *Tout!* (April 1971), which symbolically marked the emergence of the *Mouvement de libération des femmes* and the *Front homosexual d'action révolutionnaire*, had made adult-minor relations contiguous with the general sexual liberation of young people. Of course, all articles on that topic had been written by men.[20] "Marginal" or alternative sexualities were widely legitimated in the far-left press in the decade after 1968. Guérin and Schérer were both members of the editorial collective of the mid-1970s cultural revolution rag, *Marge*, where they published on man-boy relations between 1974 and 1976.[21] In October 1976, the magazine *Sexpol* printed a special issue on *Childhoods*. It treated prepubescent sensuality, the dilemma of parents having sex in front of their children, and how post-1968 sexual education was introducing new forms of repression. Sex with children appeared in the form of a letter from a self-identified pedophile.[22] Child sexuality and sex with children appeared as subthemes within broader countercultural and sexual-political mobilizations.

Youthful Desires

The status of the *desires* of children and youth lay at the heart of pedophiliac discourse. The "liberation of desire" had been a core slogan during and after the events of May 1968. Herbert Marcuse and Wilhelm Reich had an unprecedented reception in France during the 1970s. In 1972, Gilles Deleuze and Félix Guattari's *Anti-Oedipus* appeared; provocative and ridiculously dense, the book advanced an anti-psychoanalytic revolution of "desiring machines," the essence of desire being the "machinic" processes of immanent and productive coupling, uncoupling, and recoupling.[23] Also in 1972, Guy Hocquenghem published his *Homosexual Desire*, a work written, as it were, within the "anti-Oedipal" field.[24] Hocquenghem was a contributing editor to the twelfth issue of *Tout!* and a key animator of the *Front homosexuel d'action révolutionnaire*. His book championed the "differentialist" sexual politics that came to be associated with 1970s French theory, and among the subversive sexualities he discussed were male intergenerational relations. When he reclaimed for children "their desire to be seduced," Hocquenghem touched upon a fantasy that would be remarkably popular in the mid-to-late 1970s.[25]

Talk of children's desires thus subtended more generalized agitation around the liberation of desire. In 1974, Tony Duvert argued for the decriminalization of child love on the basis of a straightforward application of sexual liberation to an overlooked social class.[26] Gabriel Matzneff called children willful "igniters" [*allumeurs*] since they liked "to please," and suggested that young people make passionate, ardent lovers since they had yet to succumb to the cynicism and detachment that can characterize adult relations.[27] The handsome and smarmy Matzneff saw his own desires for children as a reversion to the polymorphism of his own childhood desires—"I was never so tormented by the thirst for caresses and kisses as when I was twelve or thirteen years old." This reversion represented a willful refusal to join the world of adults.[28] Even those who were skeptical about a simple unchaining of young desires, like Hocquenghem, Foucault, and Schérer, nevertheless placed children's desires at the center of their analyses. Hocquenghem's suggestion, noted above, that children desire seduction needs to be set against his criticism of Duvert for making "the liberty of the child" into the "sufficient reason of sexual liberation."[29] As we will see, Foucault raised the issue of a child's role in seduction, linking it to the important issue of consent, and Schérer's theory of the "puerile erotic" also smuggled children's desire back into the "system of childhood" he criticized.

Whatever the various commitments to some positive view of the desires of children, there was a more general consensus about the regimes of social relations aligned against it. Hocquenghem had mentioned adult-minor sex as one possible means of disrupting the Oedipal order of reproductive sexuality because it "inspired a particular degree of civilized concern."[30] The notion that desire could subvert repressive civilization was related not only to *Anti-Oedipus*, but also to Schérer, who turned to Charles Fourier as a resource in thinking about an "immediate" quasi-anarchistic contestation of "civilizations."[31] Civilization included all that involved the order of normalization and normality: the family, politics, the state, the police, and institutions like schools. More provocatively, Matzneff viewed "adult society" as an order that held a relationship of "exclusive use" with regard to children.[32] Parents, teachers, police, judges, and so forth made children "untouchable" in a kind of age-segregated "caste" system: old with old, young with young.[33] Such segregation—a buzzword in French pedophiliac discourse—had as its "corner stone" the notion that the sexual expression of young people was "harmful and disastrous" to their development.[34] Matzneff went to the extreme in saying that adults authorized to deal with children perpetrated a kind of violence which approached that of "sadists" and "ogres" who "rape and kill" and which was in the end "worse" than the "soft violence" of a "bill note that slips into a blue jean pocket or a panty."[35] He reserved his harshest words, however, for mothers whose animosity to child-lovers such as himself he explained as the jealousy older women felt when men found their daughters more attractive than themselves. The lesson to be learned was that chances were better to seduce a child in a broken home than in a tightly knit one.[36] Matzneff's troubling rhetoric and sensibility disturb the attempt to associate him with Hocquenghem and Schérer's more sophisticated theorizing, even if such linkages are historically sound.

Socratic Sex Lives

Among the many facets of "civilization" to be undercut by intergenerational sex, education and pedagogy were singled out for attack. They seemed the strongest points of convergence for linking male homosexuality, children, and social institutions in 1970s France. The eighth issue of *Tout!* (February 1971) had published an article by a substitute teacher who had been fired when he decided to "let the children do whatever they wanted," allowing their sexuality to "express itself, even physically" as part of an "experiment in non-pedagogy."[37] The March 1973 special issue of the journal directed by Guattari, *Recherches*, entitled "Three Billion Perverts," addressed homosexuality and pedagogy in four different ways: (1) the relationship of homosexuality to institutions, (2) an analysis of a homoerotic Boy Scout cartoon, (3) a petition, signed by activists at the experimental University of Vincennes, in support of a high school teacher who had been fired for being gay, and (4) a discussion of the tension between pederasty and pedagogy and of the "very dangerous" notion that liberating child-child and youth-youth sexual relations alone would re-write adult-child segregation in a new way (i.e., Matzneff's "caste").[38]

The most thorough analysis of the pedophiliac/pedagogical complex was made by Schérer, or rather, at his intersection with Hocquenghem. Schérer had been the younger man's high school philosophy teacher and first amorous relationship. He had joined Hocquenghem at the *Front homosexuel d'action révolutionnaire*, and they had both taught at the University of Vincennes during the early and mid-1970s. In 1976, they co-authored a controversial issue of *Recherches*, entitled, *Co-ire: album systématique de l'enfance*, based in part on Schérer's Vincennes seminars on childhood.[39] When Hocquenghem's last book was published posthumously in 1994, Schérer wrote an affectionate postface invoking their relationship, and he continues today to discuss his own positions in relation to Hocquenghem's.[40] Thus it was with some measure of personal-erotic familiarity with the topic that they wrote on pedagogy and intergenerational relationships.

In a review of Schérer's *Emile perverti* (1974) and Duvert's *Le Bon Sexe illustré* (1974), Hocquenghem argued that "since Rousseau" pedagogues have been "obsessed" with eradicating the pervasive sexuality of the school environment.[41] A mutually segregating—for adults and children—"system of childhood" has developed. Although "pedagogy and pederasty grow out of the same tree," the two branches have offered different possibilities. Pedagogy, instituted by Socrates and exemplified by Rousseau, subjected the child to a disembodied "surveillance-viewing" (*surveillance-vue*) by the "weak and warped body" of the teacher.[42] The bodies of the student and teacher were separated and segregated, a "renouncing master" facing an "ideal child." Pedagogy consisted in the transfer of a "disincarnated" *logos* between them. Knowledge was thus a "deflection" of the pederastic aspect of the pedagogical relation. Haunted by sex on all sides, that asexed relation has become *the* template for other non-familial relations between adults and children. Hocquenghem concluded his essay by foregrounding the Deleuzo-Guattarian aspects of Schérer's project of dismantling the system of childhood. In order to find "a 'pederasty' at last cleared of the pedagogical perversion" and "to weave a multitude of transversal, non-pedagogical relations on cleared (*déblayés*) grounds and bodies," the "cut" of child and adult had to be mended. This reparation had nothing to do with either one's so-called inner child or a recovery of a lost innocence. On the contrary, one must,

> re-establish the continuity of that which was cut, re-open the floodgates of these intensive and *intuitive* fluxes that have bifurcated in compensation for the belief that the child and the adult were separated. ... To circulate [*faire passer*] intensities and not ideas is the beginning of the struggle against pedagogy ... [of] the intuitive, non-segregating drift ... the vast tide of a re-found unity.

To reduce this position, in Freudian language, to a reversion to infantile, polymorphous perversity—or in Lacanian language, to an imaginary search for an elusive Real—such a reduction would betray Hocquenghem's Deleuzo-Guattarian meaning. It seems, however, a reasonable judgment. Despite important qualifications, Hocquenghem and Schérer came close to Duvert and Matzneff's affirmation of child desires when it came to the subversion of normalizing pedagogy.

Schérer followed *Emile perverti* and *Co-ire* with ruminations in the same vein: *Le Corps interdit* (an essay collection co-authored with Georges Lapassade) (1976), *Une Erotique puérile* (1978), and *L'Emprise des enfants entre nous* (1979).[43] These latter two works completed his portrait of the social status of childhood and the logic of adult-child relations. Aiming straight for the heart of pedagogical thinking, Schérer contended not only that the child was treated as a potentiality, a person in formation, but also that as little-big-people, children and childhood played a functional role in the maintenance of social order. The child had a specific social function as a "pivot" and "social organizer" in the ordering of those *intensities* and *intuitive fluxes* mentioned by Hocquenghem.[44] In the same way that psychoanalytic "familialism" had channeled and ordered Deleuze and Guattari's "desiring machines," the child had a familial and pedagogical function for the maintenance of social order. This functionality had become apparent in contemporary talk about children's rights, especially in the debate on whether or not a child could consent to an amorous relationship. There was thus a curious coincidence between the educational/pedagogical regime of *Bildung* and a juridical regime which spoke of the "rights of children" in terms of consensual contract. To Schérer's mind, the paradox was that, on one hand, children were considered "legal subjects" (*sujet du droit*) inasmuch as they were protected by law as non-consenting agents; on the other hand, children were defined as "incapable" of being full juridical subjects because of their status as social works-in-progress.[45] We will see with Foucault how objections to the language of rights and consent served as the *terminus ad quem* for arguments by some adult-minor relationship advocates. Schérer was bothered by two different kinds of talk about children: first, the rhetoric that children needed "rights" as if they were "in a universal state of servitude"; and second, by an optimistic appraisal of "sexual liberation." The latter, *pace* Duvert and Matzneff, failed to account of the possibility that liberalizing social norms might be involve rewriting of norms at other levels, somewhat along the lines of what Herbert Marcuse had referred to as "repressive de-sublimation." In other words, widespread acceptance of childhood sexuality was a prelude to its recanalization—the more one talked about sex, the less one said.[46] In Schérer's half-Fourierist/half-Deleuzo-Guattarian view, the normalizing connection between juridical and pedagogical registers hinged on the fact that the social order was the order of discourse and representation.

Very much in step with the predilections of 1970s French theory, Schérer contrasted this social order with a "puerile erotic" and a "passional universe" that were "outside of" or "indifferent to" discourse.[47] The pre-discursivity of child experience, that is, its not-fully-formed nature prior to entry into the adult social and political world, held liberational potential. As Fourier had maintained, childhood was a time of *gourmandise*, a period of "transition" that did not completely obey the "civilized" order.[48] Though he was careful to point out that he was not advocating a view of the child as an "essential being," Schérer did not completely escape the ironically Rousseauan position that set a pre-social "good" child up against the corruptions of the "bad" social order. In fact,

Schérer's thorough attempt to extricate himself from the Rousseauan-pedagogical position in *Emile perverti* could be seen as a troubled dialogue—troubled for the very proximity of his position to a "naturalism" against which he was arguing.[49] In any case, Schérer had to admit that "in a certain way, one could suggest [the passion of the child] by such expressions" as an "essential being" or the German, *Grund*.[50] A child's passion showed an "inconsistency" and "versatility" that revealed an "incommensurable liberty"—"disordering ... subversive ... erotic ... [and] irreducible to all discourse."[51] Lest this seem like a happily romantic, utopian outlook, Schérer gingerly phrased the child's "puerility" as the "affirmation of simulacra"—signs without reference, meaning without *logos*—and as a "reversal of Platonism."[52]

Notwithstanding this flourish, the endpoint of his analysis was to rework a role for the "pederast," or in Fourier's language, the "ambiguous ones" (*des ambigues*).[53] Pederasts were ambiguous because they played the role of "pivots" between the child and adult worlds, since they too (like children) broke down fixed relations and assigned roles: such "characters ... constantly established the transitions and accords between otherwise divergent classes according to age or disposition in the social order."[54] The virtue of pederasty, concluded Schérer, was the fact that it will never be a generalized social fact or role. Its very lack of generalizability showed how it opened up a way of talking about the sexuality of children that had nothing to do with the language of "rights" and "consent." Borrowing Jean-François Lyotard's notion of a "politics of incommensurables," which he claimed could be found in Fourier as well, Schérer contrasted "a non-Euclidean political space" to politics with more ordinary geometric proportions. A "topological justice" might satisfy a kind of freedom based on "attraction" in ways that rights talk never could.[55] As he had concluded a discussion of Fourier some years earlier: "The revolution can *also* be attractive. In fact, in order *to be*, it must be attractive."[56]

Joining the attack on pedagogized child sexuality, in his own oily way, Matzneff targeted what he called "*philopédie*."[57] "I am horrified by pederasty with pedagogical pretensions," he wrote, "One can caress a young boy without believing oneself obliged to give him a math or history lesson in the half hour that follows."[58] But his personal and practical accounts of his own experiences—vainglorious writings that suffered from the stylistic excesses of someone who takes himself too seriously—tended toward the self-contradictory. He could slip from a discussion of his "Don Juan-esque nature" to the claim that "love is at the antipodes of the vampire egoism of Don Juan-ism."[59] So instead of an anti-pedagogical version of pederasty, Matzneff displayed a contradictory non-pedagogical pedagogy, which nevertheless had certain lessons in mind. He was the author of what might be called, pedophilia rightly understood. And what needed to be understood in his view was that pederasty was about love not violence. Constitutionally incapable of seeing himself as doing any wrong, he was utterly convinced of the transparency between his motives and acts ("I have never wrested the least kiss, the least caress, by either ruse or force.").[60] In a kind of odd Christian metaphysics of incarnated "flesh" and corporeal love, he separated himself from "ogres" who abuse children by saying that he was "one who wakes people up" (*éveilleur*).[61] Waking up young people meant introducing them not only to sexual pleasure, but also to sexual love.[62] Matzneff's vision of love bizarrely combined traditional elements like fidelity and "the leap" with the hard-knock lessons of love 'em and leave 'em.[63] The great tutorial his young lovers received dealt with autonomy—by leaving them or encouraging them to leave him, he gave them the gift of themselves.[64] Young people who had the great fortune of having been with him left "happier, freer, more *realized*."[65] He called this kind of relationship a "special paternity" and offered it as a clear alternative to the familialism he detested.[66]

In part because he wanted to distinguish himself from pedophilia *incorrectly* understood, Matzneff favored a reform of criminal law that dealt with sexual matters. So-called "ogres" who abused children should be punished because they gave well-intentioned pedophiles like himself a bad name. He had to admit that among the numerous pedophiles he had met, few of them were "Socrates."[67]

> Too many pedophiles are tricksters; they lie to kids, they present themselves as they are not, they use pick-ups methods that are extremely dishonest and cynical, justifying the kind of complaints made by feminists who identify pederastic seduction with rape. Pederasts certainly have nothing in common with sexual sadists, but they frequently behave like abusers, and to abuse means not only to deceive and to fool; to abuse equally means to rape. As much as pedophiles mystify children, they incur similar reproaches and don't have the right to be indignant about it.[68]

Legal reform was needed because repressive laws were partially responsible for reprehensible behavior: "The day when we will be free to love those who we love, we will love them better."[69] Although at one point, Matzneff referred to a "we" (himself, Schérer, Hocquenghem, and Foucault) engaged in a "fight" for the amendment of articles 330, 331, and 356 of the penal code; he did not want to go too far in the revision of criminal law.[70] Legalizing intergenerational relations would first of all not address the important pseudo-religious fact that love was a "perilous adventure" and a "leap into the unknown."[71] Furthermore, as Matzneff admitted, he felt in "transgression like a fish in water."[72] The impasse of outside-the-law was preferred to legal legitimation. More toleration and liberalization, yes, but not so much as to spoil his savory transgressions: "the day when we see, in magazines, in the cinema, in the street, everywhere, men or women kissing twelve-year-old kids on the mouth, it will without doubt amuse me much less to pick-up *les minettes et les minons*."[73] Though Matzneff could eke out a critical insight into the regime of Republican law—"the love of the less-than-sixteen-year-old reigned until the French Revolution" and so-called progress had been a downhill slide ever since— in contrast, Michel Foucault brought slightly more nuanced reflection to bear on the juridical impasses of adult-minor sex.[74]

Foucault on Man-Boy Love

It would be a considerable understatement to say that Foucault's mid-1970s-to-early-1980s sexuality project reflected his contemporary ambience as much as it made historical claims about earlier periods. Foucault obviously expressed and added significantly to the sexual politics of that decade. It is by no means an exaggeration to claim that child sexuality lay at the very origins of his history of sexuality project. In his 1974–75 Collège de France lectures on "The Abnormals," he first discussed sexuality as a separate issue, focusing on the late eighteenth-century emergence of the medico-disciplinary figure of the "onanist." New concerns about masturbation emerged at the same time as "the appearance of the sexual body of the child."[75] Children and sex were thus an integral part of Foucault's projected six-volume enterprise, of which only three volumes were published. So his claim in *La Volunté de savoir* (1976) that the "pedagogization" of children's sexuality exemplified the proliferation of talk about children and sex since the eighteenth century, a proliferation accompanying sexuality's simultaneous repression—this claim itself needs also to be read contextually and symptomatically, illuminated within the contemporaneous ambience of the 1970s.[76] The same holds for when Foucault, in the second volume of the *History of Sexuality*, spent time differentiating the cases of sexual girls and boys; and also in the third volume's final section on "boys," where he described how the normative heterosexual reproductive couple borrowed from and supplanted the male pederastic relation, establishing an "order of things which is still ours today."[77] In addition to the light it sheds on earlier historical periods, the sexuality project has a great deal to say about 1970s France as an expression of almost journalistic immediacy (wrapped, of course, in Foucault's smoggy rhetoric). Foucault himself often referred to his work as a "history of the present." In the context of one of his ambiences—and Foucault was a man of many ambiences—one can see perhaps why he took some of the positions and made some of the omissions he did.

Some of Foucault's few direct comments on the pedophiliac discourse occurred in the spring of 1977 and the spring of 1978, in the particular context of the possible reform of the penal code with respect to sex and children. Two round-table discussions—one with David Cooper, Jean-Pierre Faye, Marie-Odile Faye, and Marine Zecca; the other with Hocquenghem and Jean Danet—were significant for their direct handling of the question of sexuality and the law. They are even more important for the ways they join children's sexuality to the question of rape, and thus to a partial feminist perspective. The first discussion took place on 12 May 1977, and was published in October 1977; it was framed as a debate on psychiatry and penalization. Foucault himself raised the problem of sex and legality, explaining that that morning he had received a number of written questions from the *Commission de révision du Code pénal.* Dismissing censorship as a non-problem (presumably for the reason, stated later in the dialogue in a discussion of the social "reformers" of the eighteenth century, that "private life" has "nothing to do with legislation"[78]), Foucault declared that "there are two areas that for me present a problem. One is rape and the other is children."[79] Clearly intending to provoke the two women discussants—Zecca and Faye—he suggested that rape might very well be punished as violence removed from any consideration of sexuality, as if there were "no difference, in principle, between sticking one's fist in someone's face and one's penis into their vagina." Zecca's objection to this prodding led him to conclude that sexuality had a "preponderant place" on the body set apart and given particular legislative protection.[80]

Against this speculation, Zecca and Faye raised forceful objections about sexual violence against children—particularly against "little girls," says Faye—claiming that such acts mixed sex and violence in ways that could not be cleanly separated out.[81] At this point Foucault shifted gears, admitting that rape could be "defined fairly easily" as "non-consent" and "physical refusal of access"—though the vague *refus physique d'accès* implied that a simple "no" was insufficient.[82] He then launched into his "second question": children. The primary issue for Foucault, and he presented it as more a question than an entrenched position, concerned the possibility of distinguishing between rape and seduction. That a child could be an active agent in the situation of seduction—a situation presumed to be a two-way street—raised the dilemma of consent. Though perhaps intending only to provoke, his reasoning on this point was abysmal. In response to Faye's repeated assertion that between adults and children there was a structural "inequality that is difficult to define," Foucault responded, "I'm tempted to say: from the moment that the child doesn't refuse, there is no reason to punish any act." Digging himself in deeper, he further claimed that even persons in positions of "authority" could not make a child "do what he or she doesn't really want to." In a quintessential expression of exhausted anti-familialism, perhaps indebted to *Anti-Oedipus*, he claimed that one exception was the domineering authority of parents, especially wicked "step-fathers."[83] It troubled him that "the legislation concerning the rape of a child" gave authority to the parents, who "usually" turned that power and used their children against other adults.[84] Foucault completely passed over in silence the potential for risks and distortions outside the family, and so too, outside law. Oddly, at this moment Foucault was relatively open to the prospects of reform and saw himself as asking the tough questions:

> People may ask why I've allowed myself to get involved in this—why I've agreed to ask these questions. ... But in the end, I've become rather irritated by an attitude, which for a long time was mine, too, and which I no longer subscribe to, which consists in saying: our problem is to denounce and to criticize; let them get on with their legislation and their reforms. That doesn't seem to me the right attitude.

It was thus in a very different spirit that Foucault, almost a year later, on 4 April 1978, joined Hocquenghem and Danet on a radio roundtable broadcast on *France-Culture*: "The Law of Sexual Decency" (*La Loi de la pudeur*). Not only did this moment immediately precede a highly publicized rape trial in Aix-en-Provence, it also coincided with a press campaign on child prostitution.[85] The density of contemporaneous convergences help situate the talk of children, sexuality, and the law. For Foucault and his interlocutors, it was a moment of dashed hopes. What had looked like a period of reform and increased legal toleration for homosexuals, and perhaps for the specific question of intergenerational relations, had undergone an abrupt shift, said Foucault, "in the opposite direction": the "overall movement tending toward liberalism" had been "followed by a phenomenon of reaction, of slowing down, perhaps even the beginning of a reverse process."[86] As Hocquenghem put it, the "liberal illusion" of reformed legislation had led to the emergence of "new arguments" about the categorical separation of adults and children.[87] Those new arguments facilitated the emergence of a category of social behavior (and with it a new class of criminal perpetrators, or "perverts"): sex with children was bad, but it was "worse when children are consenting."[88] Danet made the same point, emphasizing the way in which emergent "subtle forms of sexual supervision" could coexist with old repressive legislation.[89]

Discussing the history of that legal regime and the new forms of containment, Foucault suggested that the shift underway was from an earlier phase of sexual legislation operating according to vague laws on "decency" [*pudeur*] to the present definition and protection of certain "vulnerable populations."[90] In other times, "acts" had been punished; now "individuals" were caught up in a juridical/medical regime in which psychiatrists and psychologists played key roles.[91] Since the old "repressive hypothesis" was no longer convincing and the sexuality of children had to be admitted, childhood sexuality was made generically distinct from adult or fully developed sexuality. As distinct, it was off limits.[92] If adults were sexual with children, they could be accused of imposing "their" adult sexuality unwontedly. For their part, children needed to be "protected from [their] own desires," since they too might cross the border.[93] To some extent, this diagnosis was premonitory, since 1980s and 1990s discussions of "child abuse" were to recycle sharp distinctions between *predators* and *innocents*. In an impressive rhetorical torrent, Foucault concluded that more or less everything had become "dangerous."[94] Children were vulnerable and in danger, and they needed to be protected from dangerous adults who threatened them. Sexuality itself became a "roaming danger … a threat in all social relations." And finally, these developments Foucault saw—from his critical, if still vaguely ethical position—as dangerous themselves: "I would say that the danger lay there."

Following this presentation, the panel was asked a number of tough questions. The first wasted no time in cutting to the crux of the debate in 1977 and 1978. Given that feminists were focusing on rape and asking for penalization of that crime, how did Foucault, Hocquenghem, and Danet propose to build "strategic alliances" with them?[95] Hocquenghem referred back to the May 1977 petition, *Lettre ouverte pour la révision du Code pénal*, in which, he said, they had been "extremely careful" not to confuse an "indecent assault without violence" (*attentat à la pudeur sans violence*) and "corruption of minors" (*incitation de mineur à la débauche*) with an "indecent assault with violence" (*attentat à la pudeur avec violence*). But such a distinction was clouded over when he next tried to separate the question of "rape in the strict sense," on which feminists were right to take a stand, and the "reactions at the level of public opinion … man-hunting, lynching, or moral mobilization." It may be that Hocquenghem had the campaign against child pornography, with its homophobic overtones, in the front of his mind. Be that as it may, in effect, he dissolved feminist reclamation of law over rape within broader social anxieties, completely dismissing the fact that, unless feminists appealed to public opinion, there could be no change in public policy and attitudes. Hocquenghem's comment was consistent with a long-standing irritation he had with the anti-male echoes of some feminist discourse; the limits of his own capacity to form strategic alliances in the fight against "phallocentrism" emerged at the moment when he was unable to examine the macho dimensions of his own positions. With greater subtly, Danet sought to divide the questions of rape and pedophilia on the issue of consent. Consent was a courtroom discourse, but the courts applied the criterion of consent differently in rape and pedophilia cases. Warning that he did not mean to say that "consent is always there" for children, he stressed that,

> with regard to rape, judges consider that there is a presumption of consent on the part of the women and that the opposite has to be demonstrated. Whereas where pedophilia is concerned, it's the opposite. It's considered that there is a presumption of non-consent, a presumption of violence.

The "system of proof" operated under different assumptions in each case.[96]

This argumentative maneuver, however, could not handle the next direct question, which asked point-blank what age for consent should be allowed. Foucault skirted the question, admitting that it was in fact "difficult to lay down barriers." He commented instead on two underlying issues, the presumed impossibility of childhood sexuality being directed toward adults and the belief that a child was "incapable of explaining what happened and incapable of giving his consent." Against the latter prejudice, he declared, "a child may be trusted to say whether or not he was subjected to violence." Hocquenghem used somewhat stronger language, saying that consent was a "trap" and that "no one signs a contract before making love."[97] The linkage of consent with contract (a point echoed by Foucault) was meant to short-circuit any project of a reform of the penal code. That the parties involved here were suspicious about appeals to consent, contract, and law should be clear. Their own talk of consent, concluded Hocquenghem, was meant as a kind of short-hand to say that "there was no violence, or organized manipulation in order to gain affective or erotic relations." But barring an appeal to a category of limit such as law it is difficult to see how a lack of violence or manipulation could be assessed. Such was the confidence in the transparency of motives among certain French advocates of intergenerational relations, acknowledged "dangers" notwithstanding.

Sexual Law and Contemporary French Masculinity

The discourse of pedophilia, moving forward after the 1979 formation of the Research Group for a Different Childhood (*Groupe de recherche pour une enfance différente*), hit a major setback in the Coral Affair of 1982–84.[98] Personalities such as Foucault, Guattari, and Jack Lang were accused of having had sex with boys at a group home, Le Coral, outside of Montpellier. Fake photographs and documents were circulated as alleged proof. Schérer, who called the controversy "an important moment in the modern legal system's general mobilization against pedophilia," was himself charged for "corrupting the youth," but the charges were dropped. The tenor of the scandal would be echoed by the Cohn-Bendit episode almost twenty years later. In any case, the early 1980s saw a marked decline in the public legitimacy of arguments for intergenerational relations. Newspapers on the Left, such as *Libération*, which had legitimized eccentric sexual debates in the 1970s, became less willing to do so. In the gay male community, the arrival of AIDS forced a reconsideration of sexual ethics. More broadly, a new rhetoric of "abuse" emerged in Europe and North America, abetted in part by the reassertion of cultural conservatism associated with Ronald Reagan, Margaret Thatcher, and, in a slightly different way, François Mitterrand.

The last point should be softened in light of a specific circumstance: the years on either side of Mitterrand's election in 1981 saw the passage of a series of progressive laws that liberalized and equalized sexuality in France.[99] The right to choose was reaffirmed in 1979, making permanent a probationary five-year law. In December 1980, the penal code's statutes on rape were updated for the first time since 1810.[100] In August 1982, homosexuality was decriminalized.[101] New sexual legislation intersected with the issue of age minority. The age of absolute minority had been already lowered in 1974 from 21 to 18. In 1832, the minimum age of sexual consent had been set at 11; in 1863, it was increased to 13 years of age, and in 1945, it climbed to 15.[102] An 1803 law remained on the books stipulating that girls could marry with parental consent at the age of 15.[103] The 1980 legislation on rape reaffirmed a much older provision of *Code Pénal* setting a special regime of penalties for sexual acts committed with minors "not emancipated by marriage"; since 1945, this meant someone older than 15, and since 1974, it meant someone younger than 18.[104] These provisions applied only to heterosexual relations. Before 1942, homosexual acts had never been explicitly named under French penal law, although provisions against indecency and the corruption of minors had been used effectively for prosecuting, as it were, the crime that dare not speak its name. Philippe Pétain had criminalized all homosexuality through the *Ordonnance* of 6 August 1942, and Charles de Gaulle reaffirmed the minimum age of homosexual consent at 21 through the *Ordonnance* of 2 July 1945 [*acte impudique ou contre nature*]. Homosexuality was recriminalized in 1960.[105]

The 1980 legislation on rape set the penalties for an "indecent assault without violence" with a 15-year-old at three to five years in prison and/or a fine of 6,000 to 60,000 francs, and with a 16- to 18-year-old at six months to three years in prison and/or a fine of 2,000 to 20,000 francs. Until the 1982 decriminalization of homosexuality, an "indecent assault without violence" with a "minor of the same sex" brought a prison term of six months to three years in prison *and* a fine of 60 to 20,000 francs. Before 1980, rape of a child aged 15 or younger required the maximum prison term (twenty years), and "indecent assault with violence" against a child of that age also yielded a ten- to twenty-year sentence, the maximum not required. The 1980 legislation removed a section of the law treating children as a distinctive category and included them instead as part of a special section on "vulnerable" persons, alongside pregnant women and mentally or physically disabled persons. One further law related to children and sex was the 1981 revision of anti-prostitution statutes, that part of the *Code Pénal* dealing since the early nineteenth century with "debauchery and the corruption of minors." Since 1946, prostitution with minors had been included with prostitution involving force, weapons, family members, or public officials.[106] In 1981, the National Assembly reaffirmed another aspect of the 1946 code, specifying "attacks on morals by exciting to debauchery or favoring the corruption of minors less than eighteen *or even occasionally less than sixteen.*"[107] This qualification was likely a direct consequence of the pre-existing category, mentioned above, of adolescents older than 15 and "not emancipated by marriage," a category rewritten in the distinction between the "indecent assault without violence" of a child less than 15, on one hand, and a child between the ages of 16 and 18, on the other hand. Of course, all these distinctions were thoroughly revised when a completely new French Penal Code was accepted in the early 1990s.

Two observations can be made through an examination of this battery of legislation from the late 1970s and early 1980s. First, legal liberalization with an eye toward equalization represented the institutionalizing of sexual mores that had evolved since 1968. Feminists and gay activists had played inestimable roles in changing the cultural and legal status quo of France with respect to abortion, rape, and homosexuality. The lowering of majority age from 21 to 18 socially legitimated the sex lives of young people, but the ambiguity of sex with 16- and 17-year-olds was literally written into the *Code Pénal.* Second, in spite of the fact that intergenerational sex underwent important revisions (the despecification of homosexuality), liberalized equalization in the late 1970s and early 1980s also opened an era in which childhood was perceived to need greater protection and, to use the term favored by some of the figures I've discussed, "segregation." Though differences between gay sex with minors and straight sex with minors were effaced, protection of children from "sexual predators" began to gain momentum as a public obsession. The view that children are asexual beings, *tabula rasa* for the desires of perverts, has combined pre-Freudian and post-Freudian perspectives in fascinating ways; children are held at once to be presexual and at the same time to be particularly vulnerable to sexual abuse. In the 1980s and 1990s, discourses of "abuse" would flourish, and sex with children was recalibrated as the kind of *fléau social*, or social blight, that homosexuality or even extramarital sex had been previously considered.[108] One trend bearing a paradoxical relation to this protectionist sensibility has been the substantial revising or dismantling of the category of "juvenile justice."[109] In the United States, teenagers are infantilized, and they can be executed.

I should be clear about the conclusion I want to draw: I have no interest in defending intergenerational sex. For devotees of "French theory" who persistently cling to the "politics of difference," the issue seems a limit case and thus somewhat of a quandary worth considering. What seems pertinent to me, instead, is how those who contributed to 1970s French pedophiliac discourse made some perceptive diagnoses on the emergent remoralization of sexuality already underway during the years following May 1968. Western societies have become more open and tolerant about sexuality since the 1970s, but they have submitted certain behaviors to ever-more-exacting and precise "regimes" of legal, psychological, medical, and social management. This kind of insight was one of Michel Foucault's great contributions, and, as I have tried to demonstrate, we might understand it better by historicizing one of the ambiences where it developed. In the late twentieth century, one became a citizen at a younger age than in the nineteenth century, but one became a socially legitimate sexual actor at an older age than in the nineteenth century.

A final remark to make about 1970s French pedophiliac discourse concerns its masculinity. That discourse fit into a more extensive pattern on the French intellectual-political Left. With a few exceptions, masculine power and masculinity were seldom the objects of self-critical analysis by French men in the 1970s.[110] More easily found were frequent hysterical and paranoid reactions to feminist criticisms of male power, violence, and desire. As mentioned in passing above, the limits of the liberation of child desires were drawn to some extent by feminists along the issues of power and violence. The utter absence of these themes in 1970s French pedophiliac discourse speaks volumes. The writings of Schérer, Matzneff, and company appeared at the same time and within the same political field as feminist mobilizations around sexual violence. In fact, the overlapping of intergenerational discourse with sexual violence discourse was only one case of a broader set of conflicts between men and women on the post-1968 French left. Many male French leftists in the 1970s were slow to become self-critical about violence, often for "revolutionary" reasons.

Gill Allwood has amply demonstrated how French masculinity studies since the 1970s have been "thinner" in France than in the United Kingdom and the United States.[111] To be sure, the incapacity of male leftists to consider the masculinist features of their own positions is neither new nor distinctive to France.[112] It nevertheless remains the case that the incapacity of French pedophiliac discourse to be self-critical about its own masculinity was part and parcel of the delayed or retarded emergence of critical masculinity in France. There is no shortage of examples of how men and women on the post-1968 French Left have responded to criticisms of masculinity, it seems to me, with "bad faith."[113] One might recall that until recently France had a law specifying castration as a capital crime.[114]

Notes

1. Kate Connolly, "Sixties Hero Revealed as Kindergarten Sex Author," *Observer,* 28 January 2001.
2. Jacqueline Remy, "Le remords de Cohn-Bendit," *L'Express,* 22 February 2001; "Génération provoc: retour sur l'esprit soixante-huitard, avec ses utopies et ses erreurs," Dossier in *Libération,* 23 February 2001; Pierre Marcelle, "De la vértu vicieuse," *Libération,* 5 March 2001; Daniel Cohn-Bendit, "'Ma vie est un inventaire permanent': l'ancien leader de Mai 68 entend assumer l'héritage d'une génération aujourd'hui sur la sellette" (Interview with Jean-Michel Helvig and Paul Quinio), *Libération,* 8 March, 2001; René Schérer, "Non à l'amalgame," *Libération,* 13 March 2001. Jean-Paul Dollé, "Mai 68 a existé, certains le haïssent," *Libération,* 26 April 2001.
3. Daniel Licht, "L'Eglise à confesse chez Ségolène Royal," *Libération,* 17 January 2001. "Un évêque rattrapé par la justice," *Le Figaro,* 23 February 2001.
4. Paul Berman, "The Passion of Joschka Fischer," *The New Republic,* 27 August 2001. Lorrain Millot, "Des 'révélations' bien intéressées: la fille de la terroriste Meinhof a ressorti les informations," *Libération,* 23 February 2001.
5. Paul Quinio, "L'Affaire Cohn-Bendit ou le procès de Mai 68," *Libération,* 23 February 2001.
6. The pivotal text in the United States was Benjamin Spock, *The Common Sense Book of Baby and Child Care* (New York, 1946; 7th rev. ed., 1998).
7. Even if he exaggerates and moralizes, Barry M. Coldrey, "The Sexual Abuse of Children: The Historical Perspective," *Studies* 85 (Winter 1996): 340, usefully suggests that the English-speaking modern world became obsessed with children and sex at two specific moments: from the 1880s to the First World War and since the 1960s.
8. Lewis Gannett has called man-boy relations "the closet. final frontier." See his article by that name in *The Gay & Lesbian Review* 7, 31 January 2000, 1. Cf. Daniel Tsang, ed., *The Age Taboo: Gay Male Sexuality, Power, and Consent* (Boston, 1981); Joseph Geraci, ed., *Dares to Speak: Historical and Contemporary Perspectives on Boy-Love* (Swaffham, Norfolk, 1997).
9. Jeffrey Weeks, *Sexuality and Its Discontents: Meanings, Myths, and Modern Sexualities* (London, 1985), 226–29.
10. Ibid., 226. For one feminist account of sex and pedagogy, see Jane Gallop, *Feminist Accused of Sexual Harassment* (Durham, NC, 1997).

11. For French feminist criticisms, see Christiane Rochefort, *Les Enfants d'abord* (Paris, 1976) and Leïla Sebbar, *Le Pédophilie et la maman (L'amour des enfants)* (Paris, 1980). Tony Duvert denounced Sebbar for her "puritanism and dishonesty." Duvert, *L'Enfant au masculin* (Paris, 1980), 45. See also Tsang, ed., *The Age Taboo*.

12. "Pour une autre législation sur la sexualité des mineurs," *Libération*, 26 January 1977. "A propos d'un procès," *Le Monde*, 26 January 1977. Jean-François Sirinelli, *Intellectuels et passions françaises: manifeste et pétitions au XXè siècle* (Paris, 1990), 437–39. Gabriel Matzneff had plaintively called for a petition in November 1976 when he had been brought up on charges for remarks made on the television show *Apostrophes*. Matzneff, "L'amour est-il un crime?," *Le Monde*, 7–8 November 1976.

13. Before the 1992 reform of the entire Penal Code, French criminal law distinguished among "outrage against public morals" *(l'outrage aux bonnes moeurs)*—usually related to publications and the press—"outrage against public decency" *(l'outrage public à la pudeur)*, "indecent assault," either with or without violence *(les attentats à la pudeur)*, and "attacks on morals," "debauchery," and "corruption of minors" *(les attentats aux moeurs, la débauche, la corruption des mineurs)*.

14. P. Verdon, "Procès Dejager: les familles rassurées," *Rouge*, 31 January 1977. Pierre Georges, "L'Enfant, l'amour, l'adulte," *Le Monde*, 29 January 1977.

15. Sirinelli, *Intellectuels et passions françaises*, 439–41. Sirinelli sees these two petitions as symptomatic of a certain "airiness" among French intellectuals in the late 1970s.

16. See my essay, "'Our Sexual Revolution Is Not Yours': French Feminist 'Moralism' and the Limits of Desire," *Love In, Love Out*, ed. Lessie Frazier and Deborah Cohen (forthcoming).

17. The PCF announcement came as a surprise during a film festival (22–26 April) sponsored by the *Groupe de libération homosexuel (Politique et Quotidien)*. There were also heated debates around the festival's final program on "Pederasty and the Sexuality of Children." Michèle Solat, "Une 'semaine homosexuelle' à Paris," *Le Monde*, 22 April 1977; Suzette Triton, "Le PCF déclare officiellement qu'il ne soutient pas l'homosexualité mais condemne toute répression contre elle," *Rouge*, 25 April 1977; C.S., "Ce soir à la semaine GLH-PQ: 'Pédérastie et sexualité des enfants'," *Rouge*, 26 April 1977; Denise Avenas, "La pédérastie: un débat qui bouscule nos édifices moraux," *Rouge*, 28 April 1977; Claire Devarrieux, "Débats sur l'homosexualité," *Le Monde*, 2 May 1977.

18. Commission de revision du Code pénal, *Avant-projet definitif de code pénal (April 1978)* (Paris, 1978).

19. The best critical discussion of some of these figures is Benoît Laprouge and Jean-Luc Pinard-Legry, *L'Enfant et le pédérastie* (Paris, 1980).

20. Un pédé mineur et devenu joyeux, "Les mineurs ont droit au désir: 15 Berges"; Un homosexuel, sale étranger, dangereux communiste, "Le triangle rose: lettre ouverte aux hétérosexuels communistes"; Un militant du FHAR, "Vie quotidienne chez les pédés," *Tout!* 12, 23 April 1971.

21. Daniel Guérin, "Pour le droit d'aimer un mineur," *Marge* 2, July–August 1974; René Schérer, "Pédophilie: notes de lecture," *Homosexualités–Marginalités*, Special Issue of *Marge* 11, October–November 1976.

22. *Enfances*, Special Issue of *Sexpol* 9, October 1976. The journal's title was an homage to Wilhelm Reich.

23. Gilles Deleuze and Félix Guattari, *Anti-Oedipus: Capitalism and Schizophrenia*, preface by Michel Foucault (New York, 1977).

24. Guy Hocquenghem, *Homosexual Desire*, tr. Daniella Dangoor, intro. Michael Moon, preface (1978) by Jeffrey Weeks (Durham, NC, 1993).

25. Ibid., 141.

26. Tony Duvert, *Le Bon Sexe illustré* (Paris, 1974).

27. Gabriel Matzneff, *Les Passions schismatiques* (Paris, 1977), 147. Hereafter *PS*. Matzneff, *Les moins de seize ans* (Paris, 1974), 38 and 41. Hereafter *MSA*.

28. *PS*, 139.

29. Hocquenghem, "L'enfance d'un sexe," *Normalisation de l'école—Scolarlisation de la société*, Special Issue of *Les Temps modernes* 340, (November 1974); repr. in *Le Dérive homosexuelle* (Paris, 1977), 114.

30. Hocquenghem, *Homosexual Desire*, 141.

31. Schérer, "A propos de Fourier: lutte de classes et lutte de civilisations," preface to Charles Fourier, *L'Ordre subversif: trois textes sur la civilisation* (Paris, 1972), 26–28, 36–40. Published the same month as *Anti-Oedipus*.

32. *MSA*, 38. *PS*, 131–33.

33. *MSA*, 30. *PS*, 140.

34. *PS*, 130.

35. *MSA*, 38 and 42.

36. Ibid., 91–98.

37. [Jules Selma], "Jean-Pierre 9 ans: 'Je voudrais embrasser une fille sur le cul'," *Tout!* 8, 1 February 1971.

38. *Trois milliards de pervers: grande encylopédie des homosexualités*, Special Issue of *Recherches* 12 (March 1973). The cartoon was *Pines de Sylphes*. The petition, "Sale race! Sale pédé!," was signed by Daniel Ben-Saïd, François Chatêlet, Deleuze, Guattari, Hocquenghem, Lapassade, Jean-François Lyotard, Schérer, and Henri Weber, among others. The discussion was a four-part dialogue: Max, Truc, Albert, and Jérôme, "La Pédophilie," 181–93.

39. Hocquenghem and Schérer, *Co-ire: album systématique de l'enfance*, Special Issue of *Recherches* 22 (May 1976); 2nd ed. April 1977.

40. Schérer, "Post-face," in Hocquenghem, *L'Amphitéâtre des morts* (Paris, 1994). Interview with René Schérer (May 1999).

41. Hocquenghem, "L'enfance d'un sexe," 109–21. Schérer, *Emile perverti, ou des rapports entre l'éducation et la sexualité* (Paris, 1974).

42. Schérer used this Foucauldian language a year before *Discipline and Punish* (1975) was published. Schérer himself notes this in "Les droits des enfants," in *Le Corps interdit: essais sur l'éducation négative*, Georges Lapassade and Schérer (Paris, 1976), 87. Rather than see Schérer et al. as repeating or applying Foucault's insights (and they certainly borrowed from him), it is worth seeing Foucault himself as operating within an ambience from which he borrowed and to which he contributed. Though he had little to say about Schérer, Foucault remarked in 1981: "With Hocquenghem one encounters many interesting questions, and I have the impression that on certain points we are in agreement." J. François and J. de Wit, "Interview met Michel Foucault" (22 May 1981), *Krisis: Tijdschrift voor filosofie* (March 1984), in Foucault, *Dits et écrits*, ed. Daniel Defert and Françoise Ewald, 4 vols. (Paris, 1994), IV: 663.

43. Schérer, *Une Erotique puérile* (Paris, 1978); and *L'Emprise des enfants entre nous* (Paris, 1979).

44. Schérer, *Une Erotique puérile*, 10, 15–16.

45. Ibid., 185.

46. Ibid., 9–12. Schérer, *L'Emprise*, 233–37.

47. Ibid., 234–37.

48. Schérer, *Une Erotique puérile*, 182–85.

49. This is true of aspects of Deleuze and Guattari's thought as well. "The unconscious if Rousseauistic, being man-nature. And how much malice and ruse there are in

Rousseau!" Deleuze and Guattari, *Anti-Oedipus*, 112. Matzneff declared that "childhood is in the image of the age, at once cruel and Rousseauistic." *PS*, 57.

50. Schérer, *Une Erotique puérile*, 21.
51. Ibid., 17–21. In *L'Emprise* (235), Schérer gives a more balanced view to the extent that, in trying to let children speak for themselves, he admits that among themselves children can be as phallic and repressive as any group of adults.
52. Schérer, *Une Erotique puérile*, 22.
53. Ibid., 182–83.
54. Ibid., 183.
55. The former term is Jean-François Lyotard's in his *Duchamp's trans/formers*, tr. Ian McLeod (Venice, CA, 1990). Schérer, *Une Erotique puérile*, 25–26.
56. Schérer, "A propos de Fourier," 43. Schérer's championing of Fourier as prophet of the sexual revolution was not without sympathizers. Daniel Guérin, *Charles Fourier: vers la liberté en amour* (Paris, 1975). Guérin's own writings on pedophilia appear in *Son Testament* (Paris, 1979).
57. *PS*, 121. The term "pedophile," he said, stinks of "camphor and bromide." Elsewhere he calls adult lovers of children the "Carbonari of love," in reference to the broadly anti-absolutist but otherwise vague secret political societies of the early nineteenth century. *PS*, 145.
58. *MSA*, 30–31. *PS*, 132.
59. Ibid., 125 and 137.
60. *MSA*, 41.
61. Ibid., 140. On sexualized incarnationism, see *PS*, 151. Matzneff was Eastern Orthodox, and his journals from the 1960s and 1970s show doubt mixed with erotic fixation in megalomaniacally "Christian" proportions.
62. Ibid., 137. *MSA*, 45.
63. *PS*, 123–24.
64. *MSA*, 60.
65. Ibid., 59.
66. Ibid., 67.
67. *PS*, 140.
68. Ibid., 141–42.
69. Ibid., 143.
70. Ibid., 126.
71. Ibid., 124.
72. Ibid., 142. Transgression was a "macrobiotic necessity," and he was at home in "marginality, bohemia, and solitude." Ibid., 125. *MSA*, 73–76.
73. Ibid., 75.
74. *PS*, 145.
75. Foucault, *Résumé des cours, 1970–1982* (Paris, 1989), 76–80.
76. Foucault, *The History of Sexuality, Volume 1: An Introduction* (New York, 1978), 104.
77. Foucault, *The Use of Pleasure: Volume 2 of the History of Sexuality* (New York, 1985); *The Care of the Self: Volume 3 of the History of Sexuality* (New York, 1986), 198.
78. Foucault et al., "Confinement, Psychiatry, Prison," 206. Compare Gisèle Halimi: "A sexual choice has nothing to do with the law. It's nobody's business. With one limit. Violence. And that is why children must be protected." Interview with Halimi (March 2001).
79. Michel Foucault, David Cooper, Jean-Pierre Faye, Marie-Odile Faye, and Marine Zecca, "Confinement, Psychiatry, Prison" [12 May 1977], in Foucault, *Politics, Philosophy, Culture: Interviews and Other Writings, 1977–1984* (New York, 1988), 204–5. Org. pub. "Enfermement, Psychiatrie, Prison," *Change* 32–33 (1977).

80. Foucault et al., "Confinement, Psychiatry, Prison," 201.

81. Ibid., 202 and 204.

82. Ibid., 204. Foucault, *Dits et écrits*, III: 355.

83. Foucault et al., "Confinement, Psychiatry, Prison," 205.

84. Ibid., 209.

85. Association Choisir/La Cause des femmes, *Viol: le procès d'Aix*, preface by Gisèle Halimi (Paris, 1978). "La Prostituttion des enfants," *Rouge*, 1–2 April 1978. Marco, "Après l'émission 'Aujourd'hui madame' sur la prostitution des enfants: un point de vue," *Rouge*, 3 April 1978. "La Prostitution des enfants en France," *Le Quotidien de Paris*, 12 April 1978. "Les Enfants qui se prostituent: I. La misère à vendre," *Le Matin*, 21 April 1978.

86. Foucault, Hocquenghem, and Jean Danet, "Sexual Morality and the Law," in Foucault, *Politics, Philosophy, Culture*, 272. Org. pub. "La loi de la pudeur," *Recherches* 37, April 1979.

87. Ibid., 273.

88. Ibid., 277 and 273.

89. Ibid., 275.

90. Ibid., 276.

91. Ibid., 281.

92. Ibid., 276.

93. Ibid., 277.

94. Ibid., 280–81.

95. Ibid., 283.

96. Ibid., 284.

97. Ibid., 285.

98. Corinne Gauthier-Hamon and Roger Teboul, *Entre père et fils: la prostitution homo-sexuelle des garçons* (Paris, 1988), 112–15. On the Coral Affair, see Frédéric Martel, *The Pink and the Black: Homosexuals in France since 1968*, tr. Jane Marie Todd (Stanford, 1999), 142–46.

99. Janine Mossuz-Lavau, *Les Lois de l'amour* (Paris, 1991). Olivier de Tissot, *La Liberté sexuelle et la loi* (Mesnil-sur-l'Estrée, 1984). Antony Copley, *Sexual Moralities in France, 1780–1980: New Ideas on the Family, Divorce, and Homosexuality* (New York, 1989).

100. Rape was newly defined as any kind of "sexual penetration." If "indecent assault" was accompanied by "torture or barbarous acts," the penalty was automatic life imprisonment. Loi ordinaire 80–1041 (23 December 1980), http://www.legi france.gouv.fr.

101. Loi ordinaire 82–683 (4 August 1982).

102. *Code Pénal*, §331.

103. *Code Civil*, §144 (27 March 1803). A 16-year-old can renounce French citizenship. *Code Civil*, §17–3 (8 February 1995).

104. *Code Pénal*, §331–1.

105. *Ordonnance* 60–1245 (25 November 1960), *Code Pénal* §330.

106. Law of April 13, 1946, *Code Pénal* §334, bis. (then §334–1 in 1960). The 1946 law also made French citizens accountable for infractions committed in other countries, a measure reaffirmed in 1998. *Code Pénal*, §222-22 (17 June 1998).

107. My emphasis. Loi ordinaire 81–82 (2 February 1981), *Code Pénal*, §334–2.

108. Martine Bouillon, *Viol d'anges: pédophilie: un magistrat contre la loi de silence* (Paris, 1997).

109. In September 2002, legislation was passed stating that minors between the ages of 10 and 18 who are capable of "discernment"—a term with rich Jesuitical connota-

tions—can be held responsible for their crimes. *Code Pénal*, §122–8 (9 September 2002).

110. Georges Falconnet and Nadine Lefaucheur, *La Fabrication des mâles* (Paris, 1975); Alain Laurent, *Féminin- Masculin: le nouvel équilibre* (Paris, 1975); Pascal Bruckner and Alain Finkielkraut, *Le nouveau Désordre Amoureux* (Paris, 1977).

111. Gill Allwood, *French Feminisms: Gender and Violence in Contemporary Theory* (London, 1998). The work of Daniel Welzer-Lang did much for masculinity studies in France during the 1990s. See also Robert A. Nye, *Masculinity and Male Codes of Honor in Modern France* (New York, 1993).

112. Michael Miller Topp, *Those Without a Country: The Political Culture of Italian American Syndicalists* (Minneapolis, 2001), 18–24, 135–73.

113. Elisabeth Badinter voices a common French view that "the problem of masculinity is less acute in France than elsewhere." Badinter, *XY: On Masculine Identity*, tr. Lydia Davis (New York, 1995), 5. Cf. the comment of Alain Touraine: "In the United States, men and women hate each other. In France, they love each other." Interview with Touraine (April 1999). Pierre Bourdieu ultimately set "masculine domination" within the problematic of social and symbolic domination in general. Bourdieu, *Masculine Domination*, tr. Richard Nice (Stanford, 2001).

114. The crime was excused if "immediately provoked." Before the abolition of the death penalty in 1981, if the male victim died within "forty days," the penalty was death. If the victim did not die, those convicted of "unprovoked" castration were automatically sentenced to life in prison. *Code Pénal*, §316 and §325. The statute was repealed in 1992.

Chapter 14

_____

"More than a dance hall, more a way of life":[1] Northern Soul, Masculinity and Working-class Culture in 1970s Britain

Barry Doyle

The theme of this book is youth between politicization and consumerism at a pivotal moment in the social and political transformation of Europe. Most of the contributors have taken politics as the key element of this axis and have tended to focus on the often contradictory responses of middle-class youth to the perils and possibilities of a commercial popular culture and a new politics.[2] Notwithstanding Nick Thomas' contributions to this area,[3] in general British scholars have shown much less interest in the activities of middle-class youth than in those of young workers.[4] However, for many of those studying British youth in the postwar era there was little obvious politicization to celebrate or even investigate.[5] As a result, many chose to focus on popular culture, and especially youth culture, as a possible arena for the politics of working-class youth. Some identified a form of action, which came to be known as "resistance through ritual." Around the same time, historians on the left were beginning to move away from traditional labor history to explore other aspects of working-class life, sometimes to try to explain the relative quiescence of the British worker and the frequent defeats suffered by radicalism.[6] This historical approach to the link between politics and popular culture produced a strikingly different conclusion—that popular culture was a rejection of politics, a "culture of consolation."[7] This paper will address these contrary interpretations through an analysis of a mainly working-class youth subculture which straddled the years from the mid-1960s to the early 1980s and which provides an opportunity for exploring politicization, consumerism, and conceptions of masculinity in this period.

Youth Subcultural Studies and Masculinity

Youth subcultural studies in Britain remains dominated by the sociology of the mid-1970s Birmingham Centre for Contemporary Cultural Studies, which attempted to give motivation and political purpose to the apparently random and often nihilistic cultures of postwar British youth. Influenced strongly by both conventional Marxism and the writings of Gramsci, the Birmingham School, and especially Phil Cohen, theorized and gave meaning to styles such as the teds, the mods, and the skinheads of 1950s and 1960s London.[8] In the course of their work, two important elements emerged: the first was Cohen's identification of youth subcultures with the bipolar options of upward mobility and proletarianization; and the second was the concept of the "magical recovery of community." They suggested that, in the course of the 1960s specifically, London's working-class youth, faced by massive transformations in the economic, social, and physical dynamics of the capital, explored first the upwardly mobile option offered by the mod—with their sharp suits, scooters, secure skilled and white-collar jobs and West End lifestyle—and then, as the realities of economic decline hit home, switched to the exaggerated lumpen style of the skins with their mimicking of workmen's clothes and language along with an ultra "hard" image. This latter option was taken up by Tony Jefferson in his readings of the Teddy Boys, to suggest that both skins and teds, in their own ways, were somehow attempting to recover magically the lost world of traditional working-class east and south London collapsing in the face of slum clearance and containerization.[9] Thus, the Birmingham School broadly theorized the "subcultural response" as representing, "a synthesis on the level of style of those 'forms of adaptation, negotiation and resistance elaborated by the parent culture' and others 'more immediate, conjuntural, specific to youth and its situation and activities.'"[10] Dick Hebdige took some of these ideas and blended them with the theories of the new cultural studies, appropriating concepts such as bricolage and homology from semiotics and anthropology to emphasize both the creativity and the political significance of youth culture. He foregrounded the significance of the dialogue between black and white youth—with all its contradictions—culminating in the fusion of indigenous black and white in the punk-reggae alliance in late 1970s London and Birmingham.[11]

Through these writings an image was developed of a heroic working-class youth capable of resisting the attempts of school, work, home, planners, and consumer capitalism to force them to conform. Both their creativity and their "hardness" put these working-class youths in opposition to the middle-class, to women, to the "straights" or "divis," to the mass producers of fashion and music, to "scoobies" or "hippies," and to Asians.[12] In their attempts to recover magically a pure form of working-class male resistance, some academics came close to idealizing—or at least legitimizing—the violence of the football terrace and even of racial assaults, as well as the petty turf wars of the estates.[13] But they also followed in the footsteps of Hoggart and Williams in condemning those willing to buy into mass consumption.[14] Thus the only authentic culture was that created—or at least successfully appropriated—by working-class youth.[15] The Birmingham School and their fellow travelers sought the pure form of their youth cultures—the moment of creativity before the style became incorporated by the commercial market, mass produced and exported to the provinces where, in its bowdlerized form, it was purchased in chain stores by the unknowing youth of Swansea or Middlesbrough.[16] Such academics identified periods of creativity and mediocrity in working-class youth styles, with the mid-1950s, the early 1960s, the late 1960s and the period after 1976 as high points, and the late 1950s, and 1972–76, as the nadirs.[17] Although youth in the latter period were clearly fighting—both figuratively and literally—those trying to oppress them,[18] they were also listless and lacking the will to change their lives, an apathy summed up by Phil Cohen:

> The irony of the story is that the imagery of kung fu appeals most strongly to those kids who are often least equipped, in real terms, to master its techniques. The majority of the Wall, for example, had long since rejected the whole ethos of physical self-discipline and sustained effort, which goes with success in organized sport.[19]

This rejection of organized sport was also mirrored in attitudes to dance—a subject largely absent from studies of male youth in this period. Hebdige noted that, whilst music was important to mods, the ace faces rarely did more than tap their toes to rare soul sounds, though he does suggest white kids copied the black lads' willingness to take part in more energetic forms of dance, including "the shake and the hitch hiker."[20] More typical is Geoff Mungham's portrayal of dance hall culture in the early 1970s, where the girls danced and the boys hung round the edges eyeing each other and moving onto the floor only for the pick-up.[21] Solo male dancing never appears in these studies as a possible expression of masculine identity, despite the fact that it was a notable part of ted and skin culture. Instead masculinity, when it is discussed, is often presented as the macho culture of the school gang and the shop floor, shaped by the wage, the culture of the workplace, and the domestic separation of spheres which were reproduced, especially in the lives of the skins and the teds.[22]

The methodology of the Birmingham School has come in for considerable criticism, not least from feminists who attacked their patronizing approach to young women[23] and from others who have condemned both their seeming glorification of the violent aspects of youth culture and their elitist attitudes to the majority of youths who were content to either consume what the market gave them or take up, without ever understanding, the leading styles.[24] In more recent years their class-based methodology has been rejected in favor of a cultural approach promoted by Steve Redhead, which emphasizes the importance of the cultural products of youth, especially recorded music and drugs.[25] Historians have so far contributed little to the debate, with only Bill Osgerby's fine book on postwar youth really challenging the dominance of sociology and cultural studies in this field. But whilst the feminist critique has been the most effective and loud, the metropolitan bias is what will be addressed in this chapter, through a study of the still shadowy cult of Northern Soul which dominated the culture of a substantial proportion of the youth of the Midlands and north of England, and briefly popped its head above ground in the course of 1975.

Northern Soul has a surprisingly limited historiography of its own. Most academic studies which refer to it base their analysis on Tony Cummings's journalistic history of the scene published in the mid-1970s.[26] Since the mid-1990s however, there has been a revival of interest in Northern Soul which mirrors the revival of the scene on the back of CD compilations and the internet. Internet sites like Night Owl have provided a forum for reminiscence and discussion,[27] whilst the growth of Kev Robert's Goldmine business and *Togetherness* movement has led to the opening up of new venues, the release of many important CDs, and the publication of a substantial compendium of the best records.[28] The revival has also seen a number of books published by enthusiasts, participants, and journalists, containing useful information and much opinion but little in the way of analysis and certainly no theoretical discussion.[29] Only Katie Milestone has attempted a serious discussion of the scene and her work is more concerned with representations of the north bound up in discussions of Northern Soul in the media, than in analyzing the scene in the light of youth cultural studies.[30] Thus, the Northern scene remains an underdeveloped area of study and the discussion that follows will add a little more to our understanding.

What was/is Northern Soul?

Northern Soul was a dance-based youth subculture which drew its followers from the north Midlands, the northwest and to a lesser extent Yorkshire and the northeast of England and central Scotland, and which flourished from the late 1960s to around 1981–82. Drawing on a Mod tradition,[31] adherence to the scene usually involved attendance at up to three clubs each weekend with at least one of them being an all-night event. These clubs—which suffered variously from the interests of the police, drug squad, and licensing authorities, as well as the vagaries of fashion—were found both in big cities like Manchester and Sheffield and spread across the medium-sized towns of the Midlands and northwest, including the Catacombs in Wolverhampton and the Green Lantern in Market Harborough. The music played in these clubs was composed largely of black American soul records from the mid- to late 1960s—the rarer the better.[32] Similar in style and tempo to classic Motown or Stax,[33] the scene was characterized by its fetishistic dedication to rarity and authenticity along with deep aesthetic divisions between collectors and dancers.[34]

Through most of this period, the Northern Soul scene was overwhelmingly the province of the young working-class male, with few of the crowd at a venue young women. Nobody went to hang round the edges or try and get off with the girls, and despite suggestions that the clubs—especially the all-nighters—were "dens of iniquity," anyone spotted kissing in anything but a perfunctory manner would be barracked.[35] For the central characteristic of the scene was the high-speed, athletic dancing to obscure black music of the mid-to-late 1960s. As one recent description has put it:

> The very best Northern Soul is often frantic, energetic and emotional and the dancing style of its followers mirrors this. Athletic dancers would glide swiftly around the floor and then suddenly kick out a leg and go into a backdrop or the splits. Those with brilliant coordination and balance could then leap up and go into the sort of fast spin an ice skater would be proud of. Handstands and somersaults were sometimes seen and the top dancers could combine many of these moves in the course of a record.[36]

There are even stories from the early days of dancers running up the walls as a prelude to a backward flip.[37] In addition to the acrobatics, the dancers would punctuate the records with handclaps—a mis-timed clap proving fatal to a newcomer's credibility. In general, the pace was fast, though dancing styles did vary according to the numbers, with fast records generally known as "stompers" and those of mid-tempo as either "floaters" or "shufflers."

How did the Northern Soul scene come into being? The standard history asserts that, as the London Mod scene—which had been shaped around soul music, dance clubs, and all-nighters—turned to psychedelic, cerebral, and progressive forms of music, the "hard mods" broke away to emerge as skinheads, whilst in the North, Mod transformed into a rare soul scene situated in clubs like Samantha's in Sheffield and the Twisted Wheel in Manchester, where DJ Roger Eagle and others began playing increasingly obscure sounds to packed all-nighters.[38] The term Northern Soul was first used by London journalist Dave Godin in an article on the Wheel in *Blues and Soul* magazine in 1970, which also characterized the rare soul scene as friendly, committed to "soul" as a way of life, knowledgeable, great dancers, yet not distinctive in dress or background.[39] Soon after his visit the Wheel closed under the pressure of Manchester police amid rumors of drug dealing, and the focus switched to the Highland Room at the Blackpool Mecca, which would have two periods of prominence, and the Torch, in Hanley, Stoke-on-Trent.[40] Here DJ Ian Levine began to stamp his name on the scene, emerging as the central, and most abused, character in Northern Soul. Thus the scene was well established by the end of 1973 when two events occurred, which made it the subculture of choice for much of working-class youth north of the Severn-Trent. In September, the most famous and longest running all-nighter began at Wigan Casino, continuing every Saturday night for eight years.[41] Two months later a new magazine—*Black Music*—commenced publication, and though not devoted entirely to the northern scene, it became the focal point of information and debate, and a market-place for an increasing number of commercial ventures including pressings of records, clothes, badges, and a range of other products and services provided on a regional basis by mail order.[42]

Given the development of this regional infrastructure, and the fact that the northern scene was beginning to break records into the mainstream charts—especially R. Dean Taylor's "There's a Ghost in My House"—by the end of 1974 metropolitan interests were beginning to get involved, and for around eighteen months Northern Soul went overground. The vehicle for commercialization was white cover versions of classics—most notably Wigan's Ovation's version of "Skiing in the Snow"—followed by the major labels releasing albums and singles from their back catalogues on labels like Pye's Disco Demand.[43] For some this was selling out, for others it was a way of broadening the appeal and providing product for those who could never afford the prices charged for genuine tracks.

What is notable is that this flirtation with the popular did not kill Northern Soul and by late 1976 it had returned to its underground—in the eyes of the metropolis—existence. In 1977 Wigan Casino was voted top disco in the world and was featured in a Granada television documentary, which, allegedly, had twenty million viewers and was one of the most popular programs of the year.[44] This was the zenith and, just as the rise had been consolidated by a media event, so was the fall. The increasing difficulty in finding new sounds and the ageing of the crowd saw Northern Soul go into steep decline and die in 1981.[45]

Northern Soul and Consumption

The Northern Soul scene led young working-class lads into various forms of consumption, some conventional and commercial, some unconventional, and some illegal, but all requiring substantial outlays in terms of time and money.[46] Initially Northern Soul did not have a distinctive dress style, for unlike teds, mods, skins and punks,[47] the focal point was the music and the dancing and not the style[48] mirroring much earlier and much later dance scenes.[49] As such the clothing tended to be either indistinguishable from mainstream fashion—as in the early days at the Twisted Wheel—or a broadly utilitarian style which emphasized the dancing. By 1973 the fashion was for "long trench coats—often leather—baggy 32-inch flares and brogues or loafers. The coats … stripped off to reveal vests or flared-collared T-shirts. Girls favored leather trench coats too and also wore loose-fitting long, strappy dresses (which would flare out when dancing) or sometimes cheesecloth shirts … and denim skirts or jeans."[50] By early 1976 the style, though still conservative, was more distinctive—and widespread across the North. This "compact and uncluttered look," included bowling shirt with short sleeves and name embroidered across a pocket, flat black brogues—"granddaddy shoes"—with leather soles for dancing, pre-faded cord parallels, "extravagantly baggy with ankle flapping 32-inch bottoms, finger-tip patch pockets and high waist-band inset with ticket pockets, zippers and assorted snap fastenings," sweat bands, singlet and the vinyl Addidas holdall.[51] As the scene faded out in the late 1970s it became less distinctive in terms of dress, with skinny black trousers or jeans, capped sleeve T-shirts and white belts.[52] Throughout, the most distinctive element was the flat leather shoes, which as well as being distinctly counter-fashion—this was the era of the stack-heeled shoe—were also very expensive. Overall, clothing was to be "functional and stylish," with those attending venues like the Casino looking askance at the "posers" at the Blackpool Mecca who, by early 1976, were taking their cue from David Bowie and Bryan Ferry.[53] The clothing was often sourced locally in markets or by mail order through advertisements in *Black Music* and *Blues and Soul*,[54] though by the mid-1970s the main elements were available in shops across the Midlands and North. The point of the clothing was not just to keep you cool, but to enhance your image whilst dancing, and though commercially available, there was considerable competition to have the best or the right shoes, and to have the highest waistband with the most buttons.

A more complex form of consumption revolved around the records. To a great extent the scene was divided between dancers and collectors, for whilst dancers valued skill and hard work and rated the records on how good they were to dance to, collectors were more concerned with the records as artifacts.[55] This did not mean that dancers did not appreciate the authenticity of the sounds, but they took a more instrumental approach to them as objects of consumption. Dancers wanted beat, speed, and a structure which allowed them to go through their repertoire of dance moves. Occasionally this led them into conflict with the DJs, who shared many of the values of the collectors yet also needed to satisfy the punters. Thus, on the one hand they needed to acquire a fairly steady stream of new sounds to ensure they got work—venues often advertised the records DJs played—but they also had to play a satisfactory selection of already popular sounds to fill the floor.[56] One of the main criticisms leveled at DJs was that they played records to please themselves and boost their own egos rather than giving the punters what they wanted. On the other hand, the connoisseur DJs came to criticize some of their competitors for scraping the barrel for stompers like the theme from the television series, *Joe 90*.[57]

Dancers and collectors generally shared a check-list of things a record should be: by a black artist, with a sound close to Motown, and it should not have been a hit. Favored labels included Ric Tic, Mirwood, Parkway, and Okeh, as well as a number of records from the Tamla Motown roster. For collectors, acquiring original recordings became of vital importance. Originals of obscure, in-demand sounds, could change hands for up to £50 in the early 1970s, whilst even pressings of the more popular sounds could command price tags of £4–10 when a chart single cost less than 25 pence.[58] This commodity fetishism resembled that of the antique collector, the stamp collector or even the art connoisseur.[59] Authenticity both in style and in proximity to the original was vital, reaching its apogee in Frank Wilson's "Do I Love You?" a track which conformed at both levels—being a classic Motown sound with an excellent structure for dancing, and by having just one extant original copy which is alleged to have changed hands for £15,000 at the end of the 1990s.[60]

Though this clearly was consumption, it was a very masculine form of consumption which subverted the commercial market at certain levels. Thus it distinguished itself from conventional commercial consumption by giving value to the very products the market had rejected.

Minor hits could occasionally make it on to the scene if they conformed in other ways, but in general it was obscurity and failure which were valued. Secondly, records were not identified by conventional methods of advertising and promotion—often the record companies didn't even know the record existed—rather they had to be hunted down, discovered in obscure locations, checked for authenticity through sometimes extensive research, and validated by the grapevine and sometimes the few respected journalists.[61] Admittedly the DJs were the main gatekeepers but they were not the only ones introducing sounds to the scene, nor were they assured of a hit just because it was obscure and they played it. Third, and interrelated, records were rarely bought and sold through record shops, but at clubs either from collectors, other punters, or DJs such as Kev Roberts and Ian Levine.[62] There were some specialist shops—Dave Godin's Soul City, ironically in London—which was very influential in the early days[63] or Nottingham's Select-a-Disc, which specialized in illegal pressings,[64] but most records changed hands privately until they became well known. And, of course, records produced or released specifically for the Northern Soul market, as occurred from about 1974 onwards, were rejected by the faithful, though often snapped up by younger members of the scene. Overall, the consumption of records set the Northern Soul devotee in opposition to the conventional aspects of record consumption in this era, helping to reinforce bipolar distinctions between men and boys, men and women, and men and the market.[65]

The illegal use of drugs further reinforced the distinctive consumption practices of these young men. Alcohol was nearly always a minor part of the scene. All-nighters were not licensed and in any case drinking interfered with the ability to dance. Instead the athletic and non-stop dancing was fueled by copious quantities of speed. As with most working-class youth cultures up to the late 1970s, amphetamines were the drug of choice. Despite the image of the 1960s as an era of marijuana and psychedelic drug use, this was confined to a relatively small middle-class group.[66] Working-class kids, many in strenuous manual jobs, wanted drugs to keep them going, to extend their leisure time, rather than slow them down or expand their minds. Amphetamine use was pioneered by the mods as part of their all-night scene and continued unabated into Northern Soul and on to punk.[67] "Gear," as it was known, was an essential part of the soul fan's accoutrements, though for most it was a lifestyle drug used only at the weekends as part of the overall experience.[68] Most amphetamines were legally produced prescription drugs not tainted by the decadent middle-class image of substances like pot and LSD, and they were incredibly cheap with few antisocial side effects. Yet to the police and adults it was the most unsavory element of the scene and led to the closure of the majority of the main all-night venues (except the Casino).[69] Undoubtedly it did lead some into criminal activities, such as breaking into chemists to get supplies,[70] and it led others on to heroin and in a few cases death, but for most it was just a phase which they packed away with their baggy trousers and patches.

Northern Soul, Masculinity and the Subculture of Working-class Youth

So what did Northern Soul actually mean? How does it fit in with our understanding of masculinity and youth culture in the 1970s?[71] This was a scene which reflected the adult world but unlike the groups portrayed in the metropolitan literature, Northern Soul adopted many of the more conservative and even commendable aspects of the adult culture. At root it required a lot of hard work and indeed valorized a "work hard, play hard" attitude; as suggested by a soul fan in the mid-1970s "the kind of Soul we wanted was fast dance things. We work hard, bloody hard, and we want to work hard on the dance floor. The faster the better."[72] As such the Northern Soul scene required a considerable investment of time, money, and even intellect to acquire the skills, knowledge, and experience required for credibility and respect. The acquisition of appropriate dancing skills required many hours of practice, both at home and in the smaller clubs and discos that played Northern sounds.[73] Far from rejecting "the whole ethos of physical self-discipline and sustained effort" implied by Cohen, even the least adept dancers wanted to be good and tried to emulate the best, whilst the best showed the dedication of professional athletes—a bread delivery man who won the Wigan dancing competition twice in the 1970s went on to be an international martial arts expert.[74] The scene was very hierarchical, with status coming from dancing ability, the best dancers occupying a place at the front of most clubs, aspirants having to work hard to gain entry to the elite.[75] At Wigan, it usually took two to three years for newcomers to make it into the top right-hand corner, with anyone too precocious either elbowed out or humiliated.[76] Many stories refer to older mentors introducing devotees to the scene, sometimes encouraging and bringing them on, and as with hard work, these hierarchies of skill and age reflected the masculine worlds of work, organized sport, and other forms of working-class male leisure.[77]

In other ways, Northern Soul resembled the parent culture. After the dancing, the main element of the scene was the music with its emphasis on rarity and obscurity. Although it was usually the DJs who found and broke the records, many of the dancers were also serious collectors, and even those who were not could sometimes be drawn into paying big prices for favorite sounds.[78] Knowing the hot records, finding out about obscure labels and even more obscure artists, having original pressings, or respectable copies all added to the credibility of the devotee and provided one of the main forms of social cement within the group. This was a very masculine form of leisure, with its emphasis on the personal acquisition of knowledge and the authenticity of the product,[79] but it was also an anti-consumerist form of consumption, which valued rarity and obsolescence at the expense of modernity and allowed the maintenance of an aura of authenticity in a culture of mass production.[80] As a result, the "style" of Northern Soul was in the ability to dance and to speak knowledgeably about the music, rather than in the clothing which came as something of an afterthought. Yet even the clothing could be seen as an assertion of northern masculine pride, which their cloth-cap-wearing granddads would have recognized. As one lad put it, "Everybody seemed to be following London … All of them Southerners telling us what to do. So I suppose the clothes are a bit of a rebellion, if you like, but it wasn't planned."[81] Northern Soul was a rebellion, though aimed at metropolitan consumerism, rather than the parent culture.

Traditional northern working-class conservatism and respectability were also apparent in the temperate, if not teetotal, atmosphere and the occasional messianic zeal shown by the devotees. The demands of the dancing, and the fact that all-nighters could not get liquor licenses, meant that in general the scene involved only limited quantities of alcohol, though, as seen, quite large amounts of drugs. The absence of alcohol helped to account for the almost complete absence of violence, both those involved and even bouncers and the police attesting to the fact that there was very rarely trouble at Northern Soul clubs.[82] In general, the bouncers at the established venues policed drug activities and ensured that those entering were "members," though there could be conflicts in the streets with other youth groups, especially from 1977 onwards with the advent of punk.[83] Combined with this limited alcohol and minimal violence was the continual assertion of a friendly atmosphere and a strong sense of community. As people traveled from all over the country to the big clubs, there was no element of territoriality involved, and the shared hardship and devotion of the fans drew them together.[84] Yet this communitarianism was tempered by a strong sense of individualism and self-expression, with the dance-floor a highly competitive place for those "out on the floor," mirroring, to some extent, the world of labor of the northern working-class. This friendliness also extended to levels of racial tolerance rather more developed than among the adult world. Journalists like Dave Godin and Frank Elson wrote in a sympathetic manner about the plight of black people in America and linked it closely to the roots of the music.[85] Their emphasis on the importance of tolerance to "soul" may have had an impact on the racial politics of some of the followers on the scene, such as the engine fitter who noted "Black is beautiful ... and it is about time the whole world realized it."[86] Both the friendliness and the absence of racial tension were highlighted by west London DJ Norman Jay, who described his first visit to Wigan Casino thus:

> When I went to my first Northern Soul gig I was intimidated. When I first went to Wigan Casino, five of us went up in my mini, there were three black guys and two of my white friends. Bouncers up there gave us real grief, until they realized we were Londoners. 'We came all the way from London for this.' And the people in the queue backed us up. It completely took me aback. They were the friendliest people I have ever met. All my perceptions were shattered in one night. And it was such as fantastic feeling.[87]

Once again the scene challenged many of the characterizations and stereotypes of male youth and masculinity in the mid-1970s.[88]

In all these ways, the scene was a reflection, or a parody, of the adult culture. That the two had much in common was evidenced in 1975 when complaints about drug use at the Wigan Casino led the *Wigan Observer* to defend the club, stating:

> Observers of the Casino scene from this newspaper describe the all-nighters as noisy, repetitive, sweaty, sexless and sometimes boring affairs. Why, people don't even dance together because of the dangers of physical damage from out-flung legs and arms.
>
> It is asking too much to expect everybody to applaud Northern Soul with all its trimmings. Its devotees seem generally to keep themselves to themselves and when all is over return peacefully whence they came, which is more than can be said for some soccer and rugby fans.[89]

Whilst not exactly a ringing endorsement of the scene, the *Observer*, along with many in the North, saw little to criticize in Northern Soul and much to admire in the temperate hard-working young men.

So what does this tell us about subcultures, masculinity, and consumption in the 1970s? Certainly that the image portrayed by the metropolitan studies—of working-class lads kicking against the world and, by the late 1960s, rejecting social transformation for a lumpen, skinhead option or acquiescing in the plastic world of glam and high street consumption—is inappropriate. The Northern Soul scene, as it had developed by the mid-1970s, was a strong reflection of the parent culture, which did attempt to "magically recover" some of those key aspects of northern working-class culture—pride in skill and hard work, conservatism in taste and consumption, faith in something, and supportive communities—whilst at the same time giving them modern twists— especially the drug use and the record collecting. Through virtuoso dancing, it gave young men an alternative way to use their bodies to assert their masculinity and gain respect[90] in an intensely masculine and highly competitive environment, much more reminiscent of the shop floor or the sports field than the street corner or the standard night club. As such it gives a very different vision of youth culture from that captured in those classic texts of the mid-1970s, but also a very different experience of consumption and politicization to that of middle-class youth. Yet ultimately Northern Soul was not a rebellion, it was a culture of consolation, somewhere to escape the reality of work, home, family, and as such had little to do with resistance through ritual.

Notes

1. Clive Gregson, "Northern Soul" (Gregsongs, 1983). I would like to dedicate this article to the memory of my brother, Simon Martin Doyle, 1957–2002, who inspired both a personal and an academic interest in this subject.
2. For a study which addresses similar issues in an international context see Gerard J. De Groot, ed., *Student Protest: The Sixties and After* (London, 1998).
3. Nick Thomas, "Challenging Myths of the 1960s: the Case of Student Protest in Britain," *Twentieth Century British History* 13 (2002): 277–97.
4. The most up-to-date survey of youth in postwar Britain is Bill Osgerby, *Youth in Britain since 1945* (Oxford, 1998). For middle-class youth in this period see chapter 7.
5. See, in particular, the commentaries introducing the chapters in Phil Cohen, *Rethinking the Youth Question: Education, Labour and Cultural Studies* (Basingstoke, 1997), especially "Subcultural Conflict and Working-class Community," first published in CCCS, *Working Papers* 2 (1972).
6. Peter Bailey, *Leisure and Class in Victorian England* (London, 1978); A.P. Donajgrodzki, ed., *Social Control in Nineteenth Century Britain* (London, 1978).
7. This is particularly the position of G.S. Jones, "Working-class Culture and Working-class Politics in London, 1870–1900: Some Notes on the Remaking of the Working-class," *Journal of Social History* 7 (1974): 460–508.
8. Tony Jefferson, "Cultural Responses to the Teds: the Defence of Space and Status"; Dick Hebdige, "The Meaning of Mod," and John Clarke, "The Skinheads and the Magical Recovery of Community," all in *Resistance Through Rituals: Youth Subculture in Postwar Britain*, ed. Stuart Hall and Tony Jefferson (London, 1976), 81–102; Cohen, "Subcultural Conflict"; Dick Hebdige, "Made in England," in *Skinhead*, ed. Nick Knight (London, 1982).
9. Cohen, "Subcultural Conflict"; Clarke, "Magical Recovery of Community"; Jefferson, "Cultural Responses to the Teds."
10. Dick Hebdige, *Subculture: The Meaning of Style* (London, 1979), 56.
11. Ibid.
12. In addition to previous citations, Graham Murdock and Robin McCron, "Scoobies, Skins and Contemporary Pop," *New Society* 547 (1973): 690–92; Paul Willis, *Learning to Labour: How Working Class Kids get Working Class Jobs* (London, 1977).

13. Hebdige, "Made in England"; Geoffrey Pearson, "'Paki-bashing' in a North-east Lancashire Cotton Town: a Case Study and Its History," in Mungham and Pearson, *Working Class Youth Culture*, 48–81; Paul Corrigan, "Doing Nothing," in *Resistance Through Ritual*, ed. Hall and Jefferson, 103–05; Paul Cohen, "Knuckle Sandwich and Sore Thumbs," in *Rethinking the Youth Question*, Cohen, 86–109.

14. Richard Hoggart, *The Uses of Literacy: Aspects of Working-class Life with Special Reference to Publications and Entertainments* (Harmondsworth, 1958); Raymond Williams, *Keywords* (London, 1976). For British cultural studies generally see, Graeme Turner, *British Cultural Studies: An Introduction* (3rd ed., London, 2002).

15. This critique owes much to Gary Clarke, "Defending Ski-jumpers: a Critique of Theories of Youth Subcultures," first published in 1981 and reprinted in *On Record: Rock, Pop and the Written Word*, ed. Simon Frith and Andrew Goodwin (London, 1990).

16. See for example, Hebdige, *Subculture*, 94–96; John Clarke, "Style," in *Resistance Through Ritual*, ed. Hall and Jefferson, 188–89.

17. For the late 1950s see Dave Harker, *One for the Money: Politics and Popular Song* (London, 1980). For the era before punk, Geoffrey Mungham and Geoffrey Pearson, "Introduction: Troubled Youth, Troubling World," in *Working Class Youth Culture*, ed. Mungham and Pearson, 7; Hebdige, *Subculture*, 59–62; Jon Savage, *England's Dreaming: Sex Pistols and Punk Rock* (London, 1991).

18. For a list of oppressors see Susie Daniel and Pete McGuire, eds., *The Paint House: Words from an East End Gang* (Harmondsworth, 1972), 66. For football hooliganism, a major manifestation of youthful violence in the 1960s and 1970s, Eric Dunning, Patrick Murphy, and John Williams, *The Roots of Football Hooliganism: An Historical and Sociological Study* (London, 1988). For violence more generally, Geoffrey Pearson, *Hooligan: A History of Respectable Fears* (London, 1983).

19. Cohen, "Knuckle Sandwich and Sore Thumbs," 93.

20. Hebdige, *Subculture*, 53–54.

21. Geoffrey Mugham, "Youth in Pursuit of Itself," in *Working Class Youth Culture*, ed. Mungham and Pearson, 82–104.

22. Mike Brake, *Comparative Youth Culture: The Sociology of Youth Culture and Youth Subcultures in America, Britain and Canada* (London, 1985), 178–83.

23. Angela McRobbie and Mica Nava, eds., *Gender and Generation* (Basingstoke, 1984); Angela McRobbie, *Feminism and Youth Culture: From Jackie to Just 17* (Basingstoke, 1991); Brake, *Comparative Youth Culture*, ch. 7; Osgerby, *Youth in Britain*, ch. 5.

24. Clarke, "Ski-jumpers"; Stanley Cohen, "Symbols of Trouble: Introduction to the New Edition," in *Folk Devils and Moral Panics: The Creation of the Mods and Rockers* (1st pub. 1972, rev. ed. Oxford, 1980); Osgerby, *Youth in Britain*, ch. 6. See also Bill Osgerby, "'Well it's Saturday night an' I just got paid': Youth, Consumerism and Hegemony in Post-war Britain," *Contemporary Record* (1992).

25. Steve Redhead, *The End-of-the-Century Party: Youth and Pop Towards 2000* (Manchester, 1990); Steve Redhead, ed., *Rave Off: Politics and Deviance in Contemporary Youth Culture* (Aldershot, 1993); Steve Redhead, *Subculture to Clubcultures: An Introduction to Popular Cultural Studies* (Oxford, 1997); Steve Redhead with Derek Wynne and Justin O'Connor, eds., *The Clubcultures Reader: Readings in Popular Cultural Studies* (Oxford, 1997).

26. Tony Cummings, "The Northern Discos," in *Rock File 3*, ed. Charlie Gillett and Simon Frith (St. Albans, 1975), 23–36. See also Iain Chambers, *Urban Rhythms: Pop Music and Popular Culture* (Basingstoke, 1985), 137–38; Simon Frith, *The Sociology of Rock*, (London, 1978), 56–57; Anthony Marks, "Young, Gifted and Black: Afro-American and Afro-Caribbean Music in Britain, 1963–88," in *Black Music in Britain: Essays on the Afro-Asian Contribution to Popular Music*, ed. P. Oliver (Milton Keynes, 1990), 107; Osgerby, *Youth in Britain*, 77–78.

27. http://www.nightowlclub.com. See also http://www.soul-source.co.uk

28. *Northern Soul Top 500*, compiled by Kev Roberts and David S. Carne (London, 2000). For Goldmine, see http://www.goldsoul.co.uk/page.htm

29. Russ Winstanley and David Nowell, *Soul Survivors: The Wigan Casino Story* (London, 1996); David Nowell, *Too Darn Soulful: The Story of Northern Soul* (London, 1999); Mike Ritson and Stuart Russell, *The In Crowd: The Story of the Northern & Rare Soul Scene Volume One* (London, 1999); Pete McKenna, *Nightshift: Personal Recollections of Growing Up in and around The Casino Soul Club, Empress Hall, Wigan Sept. 1973 to Dec. 1981* (Dunoon, 1996); Keith Rylatt and Phil Scott, *CENtral 1179: The Story of Manchester's Twisted Wheel Club* (London, 2001).

30. Katie Milestone, "Love Factory: the Sites, Practices and Media Relationships of Northern Soul," in *Clubcultures Reader*, ed. Redhead et al., 152–67.

31. For links to the mods see "Northern Soul: That Beating Rhythm … The History, the Clubs, the Sounds, the Fans, the DJs," *Black Music* 1/7 (June 1974): 10; Mike Ritson and Stuart Russell, *The In Crowd*; Dave Haslam, *Adventures on the Wheels of Steel: The Rise of the Superstar DJ* (London, 2001), ch. 6.

32. Discussion of the music can be found in Russ Winstanley and David Nowell, *Soul Survivors*, Part II; Roberts and Carne, *Northern Soul Top 500*; "Northern Soul Top Sounds, 1967–74," *Black Music* 1/7 (June 1974), 14; Cummings, "Northern Discos," 24–25; G. Burns, "A Hard Week's Night," *Sunday Times Colour Supplement* 29, February 1976, 28; Ritson and Russell, *The In Crowd*, passim; A. Clark, "A Homage to Mecca," *Mojo Collections* 6 (Spring, 2002), 70–73 and C. Hunt, "The Wigan Casino Story," *Mojo Collections* 6 (Spring, 2002), 64–69.

33. The best history of Stax is Peter Guralnick, *Sweet Soul Music: Rhythm and Blues and the Southern Dream of Freedom* (Harmondsworth, 1991). There are a number of histories of Motown, but see Nelson George, *Where Did Our Love Go? The Rise and Fall of the Motown Sound* (London, 1986). For a rather sour history of soul music generally see Nelson George, *The Death of Rhythm and Blues* (London, 1989).

34. For the importance of rarity and authenticity in male consumption, see Jill Greenfield, Sean O'Connell, and Chris Reid, "Gender, Consumer Culture and the Middle-class Male, 1918–39," in *Gender, Civic Culture, and Consumerism: Middle-class Identity in Britain, 1800–1940*, ed. Alan Kidd and David Nicholls (Manchester, 1999), 183–97; Christopher Breward, *The Hidden Consumer: Masculinities, Fashion and City Life, 1860–1914* (Manchester, 1999).

35. Winstanley and Nowell, *Soul Survivors*, 26–27.

36. Ibid., 25.

37. For example "Chez," "Tales, Stories and Yarns: A Great Crowd," http://www.nightowlclub.com/intro/intro.htm

38. Cummings, "Northern Discos"; Winstanley and Nowell, *Soul Survivors*, 5–14; Ritson and Russell, *The In Crowd*; Haslam, *Wheels of Steel*, 109–18.

39. Dave Godin Column, "Land of a Thousand Dances," *Blues and Soul* 50, December, 1970.

40. Godin provided an equally fulsome account of Blackpool Mecca in "The Dave Godin Column," *Blues and Soul*, March, 1971.

41. Winstanley and Nowell, *Soul Survivors*.

42. *Black Music* changed its name to *Black Music and Jazz Review* in 1978 and was taken over by *Blues and Soul* in 1984.

43. Winstanley and Nowell, *Soul Survivors*, 36–46; "All Singing, all Dancing, all Night," Program 4 with Dave McAleer, BBC Radio 2, first broadcast 4 November 1998.

44. Winstanley and Nowell, *Soul Survivors*, 55–60. See Milestone, "Love Factory," for an analysis of the representations and images used in the program.

45. For the late 1970s scene, which was dominated by increasing hard drug use and more conflict and competition from other youth cultures, see McKenna, *Nightshift*, 75–96.

46. For the growing literature on males as consumers see, Breward, *Hidden Consumer*; Greenfield, O'Connell, and Reid, "Consumer Culture and the Middle-class Male"; Jill Greenfield, Sean O'Connell, and Chris Reid, "Fashioning Masculinity: *Men Only*, Consumption and the Development of Marketing in the 1930s," *Twentieth Century British History* 10 (1999); Katrina Honeyman, "Following Suit: Men, Masculinity and Gendered Practices in the Clothing Trade in Leeds, England, 1890–1940," *Gender and History* 14 (2002); Frank Mort and Peter Thompson, "Retailing, Commercial Culture and Masculinity in 1950s Britain: The Case of Montague Burton, 'The Tailor of Taste,'" *History Workshop* 38 (1994).

47. Dick Bradley, *Understanding Rock and Roll: Popular Music in Britain, 1955–1964* (Milton Keynes, 1991). For the limited importance of reggae to skinheads, see Pete Fowler, "Skins Rule," in *Rock File*, ed. Charlie Gillett (London, 1972); and Savage, *England's Dreaming* for punk.

48. Simon Frith noted that "The Northern Soul scene … has continuities with both the mods (in its emphasis on dancing, its use of pills, its soul cult) and the skinheads (in its self-conscious anti-progressive and pro-working class stance) but the differences reveal what a sub-culture looks like when it's *really* focused on music!" (Emphasis in original), *Sociology of Rock*, 57.

49. For dance cultures in 1940s America which replicated many of the characteristics of Northern Soul, see Steve Chibnall, "Whistle and Zoot: The Changing Meaning of a Suit of Clothes," in *History Workshop* 20 (1985): 56–81. For histories of the rave or house scene, see Osgerby, *Youth in Britain*, 170–83; Sarah Thornton, *Club Cultures: Music, Media and Subcultural Capital* (Oxford and Cambridge, 1995); Simon Reynolds, "Rave Culture: Living the Dream or Living Death?" and Hillegonda Rietveld, "The House Sound of Chicago," in *Clubcultures Reader*, ed. Redhead et al.

50. Winstanley and Nowell, *Soul Survivors*, 17–18.

51. Burns, "Hard Week's Night."

52. Nowell, *Too Darn Soulful*, 125.

53. Burns, "Hard Week's Night."

54. For example advert for "New! French style 30 inch Baggies," *Black Music* 1/7 (June 1974), 57.

55. See the contrasting views expressed in Dave Godin's interviews with soul fans in 1974 and Burns' respondents, as well as more detailed discussion of divisions between collectors and dancers in Winstanley and Nowell, *Soul Survivors*; Nowell, *Too Darn Soulful*; and, defending the collectors, Haslam, *Wheels of Steel*. For a detailed discussion of the increasing fetishization of recorded music from the mid-1970s, see Thornton, *Club Cultures*, ch. 2.

56. Hunt, "Wigan Casino," 66–67.

57. The biggest debate surrounded the play-list of Ian Levine at the Blackpool Mecca in the mid-1970s. See Nowell, *Too Darn Soulful*, ch. 4 and Bob Dickinson, "Soul Searchers," *Guardian*, 23 July 1999.

58. Cummings, "Northern Discos," 26–27; Winstanley and Nowell, *Soul Survivors*, 27–28.

59. For general discussions of the male consumer as collector, see Leora Auslander, "The Gendering of Consumer Practices in Nineteenth Century France," in *The Sex of Things: Gender and Consumption in Historical Perspective*, ed. Victoria de Grazia with Ellen Furlough (Berkeley, 1996), esp. 86–88; Greenfield, O'Connell, and Reid, "*Men Only*."

60. For the story of "Do I Love You?" see Winstanley and Nowell, *Soul Survivors*, 80–82; Milestone, "Love Factory," 161–63 for discussion of rarity and "aura" drawing on Walter Benjamin.

61. Haslam, *Wheels of Steel*, ch. 6; Ritsin and Russell, *The In Crowd*; Nowell, *Too Darn Soulful*; Winstanley and Nowell, *Soul Survivors*.

62. Cummings, "Northern Discos," 26–28.

63. Ritson and Russell, *The In Crowd*, 100–3.

64. Cummings, "Northern Discos," 27–29.

65. See in particular, the section on "Music and Sexuality," in Frith and Goodwin, *On Record*, 369–424; and Thornton, *Club Cultures*, ch. 2.

66. Jock Young, *The Drugtakers: The Social Meaning of Drug Use* (London, 1971); Paul E. Willis, "The Cultural Meaning of Drug Use," in *Resistance Through Ritual*, ed. Hall and Jefferson, 106–18.

67. Osgerby, *Youth in Britain*, 45–46; L. Wilson, "Carnival of Soul," *Mojo Collections* 6 (Spring, 2002), 75; Savage, *England's Dreaming*, 191–96.

68. Although some of those writing about Northern Soul tried to play down the use of speed, more recent accounts have given it more prominence. See Cummings, "Northern Discos" and Winstanley and Nowell, *Soul Survivors*, 47–54 for the optimistic case; Nowell, *Too Darn Soulful*, 84–92 and ch. 6; and McKenna, *Nightshift*, 76–96 for detailed discussion of extensive drug use.

69. Rylatt and Scott, *CENtral 1179*; Milestone, "Love Factory," 154; Nowell, *Too Darn Soulful*, 84–92 for the Torch.

70. Nowell, *Too Darn Soulful*, 184; McKenna, *Nightshift*, 77; A.R. Wilson, "Urban Songlines: Subculture and Identity on the 1970s Northern Soul Scene and After" (Ph.D. dissertation, London, Courtauld Institute of Art, 2000).

71. Martin Francis, "The Domestication of the Male? Recent Research on Nineteenth and Twentieth-century British Masculinity," *Historical Journal* 45 (2002): 637–52; I. Zweiniger-Bargielowska, "Masculinity, the Body, and Mass Consumer Culture in Britain during the Twentieth Century," unpublished paper presented to the Social Science History Association Conference (Chicago, 2001). I am grateful to Dr. Zweiniger-Bargielowska for access to this work.

72. Cummings, "Northern Discos," 25.

73. See the "Tales" and the "Tributes" pages, http://www.nightowlclub.com/intro/intro.htm especially the section on youth clubs, for stories of the process of skill acquisition.

74. Winstanley and Nowell, *Soul Survivors*, 141–45.

75. For hierarchy and dance-floor conventions see "Tales" and "Tributes" pages at http://www.nightowlclub.com/intro/intro.htm; Nowell, *Soul Survivors*, passim.

76. Winstanley and Nowell, *Soul Survivors*, 196–200 for an evocative description of the process of entry into the elite. See also Chibnall, "Whistle and Zoot," 58–59, for the same hierarchy amongst Los Angeles Lindyhoppers in the early 1940s.

77. For discussion of a number of these aspects see Michael Roper and John Tosh, eds., *Manful Assertions: Masculinities in Britain since 1800* (London, 1991); Francis, "Domestication of the Male." For the interaction of skill, leisure, and hierarchy at work, see Paul Thompson, "Playing at Being Skilled: Factory Culture and Pride in Work Skills among Coventry Car Workers," *Social History* 13 (1988): 45–69. Thanks to Stephen Brooke for this reference.

78. See, for example, the reminiscences in Winstanley and Nowell, *Soul Survivors*, 173–220, which are drawn from a number of sources.

79. Frith, *Sociology of Rock*, 191–202; Harker, *One for the Money*, passim. Martin Polley, *Moving the Goalposts: A History of Sport and Society since 1945* (London, 1998),

104–10; Ross McKibbin, "Work and Hobbies in Britain, 1880–1950," in *The Working Class in Modern British History: Essays in Honour of Henry Pelling*, ed. Jay Winter (Cambridge, 1983), 127–46.

80. Both hippy/alternative cultures and punk rock attempted to recover authenticity in the face of mass production. See Angela McRobbie, "Second-hand Dresses and the Role of the Ragmarket," in *Zoot Suits and Second-hand Dresses: An Anthology of Fashion and Music*, ed. Angela McRobbie (Basingstoke, 1989), 34–39; Savage, *England's Dreaming*.

81. Burns, "Hard Week's Night."

82. S. Maconie, "'You'll do yourself a mischief': The Northern Soul Story," *Q* 125 (1997): 64; Chez, "A Great Crowd," "Tales" page of http://www.nightowlclub.com/intro/intro.htm; McKenna, *Nightshift*.

83. McKenna, *Nightshift*, 56–7; Winstanley and Nowell, *Soul Survivors*.

84. Russ Winstanley of the Casino noted, "if you've travelled down from Aberdeen in the freezing cold after working all week, you don't want hassle ... You wanted to meet your new mates from Ipswich, Wolverhampton, wherever, and dance." Maconie, "Mischief," 64. See also Winstanley and Nowell, *Soul Survivors*, 171–220 and stories on Night Owl site.

85. For example, Godin, "Land of a Thousand Dances," *Blues and Soul*, January 1971. Godin apparently pulled out of a deal to start a record-releasing company because one of the backers was a racist. Ritsin and Russell, *The In Crowd*, 103.

86. Dave Godin, "Brothers and Sisters," *Black Music* 1/7, June 1974, 13.

87. F. Broughton, sleeve notes to the CD compilation "Good Times with Joey and Norman Jay" (Nuphonic, 2000).

88. For a rather unpleasant exploration of youth culture and racism in mid-1970s Lancashire, see Pearson, "'Paki-bashing,'" in *Working Class Youth Culture*, ed. Mungham and Pearson.

89. *Wigan Observer*, October 1975, quoted in Winstanley and Nowell, *Soul Survivors*, 49–50.

90. Contrast this with tales of football hooliganism, such as John Williams' observation of Leicester City hooligans around 1980, in Patrick Murphy, John Williams, and Eric Dunning, *Football on Trial: Spectator Violence and Development in the Football World* (London, 1990).

Part V

Cultures, Countercultures, Subcultures

Chapter 15

Utopia and Disillusion: Shattered Hopes of the Copenhagen Counterculture

Thomas Ekman Jørgensen

In the late 1960s, a small but visible group of young, extravagant, and exotic young people caught the attention of the media. They styled themselves as the carriers of a "counterculture," a new way of living opposing the materialist, bourgeois values of the postwar years. Dressed in colorful garments, these self-appointed prophets of love, hedonism, and spontaneity for a short while seemed to embody the spirit of the times. Despite their short appearance, they left a lasting image in the collective memory of the 1960s.

Unlike the many political groups of the 1960s and 1970s, the "countercultural" scene is difficult to define and delimit. The scene was neither defined by any explicit ideology nor by any institution (as were the student revolt or the scene of the *groupuscules*), nor did it have a clearly definable group of followers. Rather it was a stage, which individuals could enter and leave for long or short intervals—from hours to years—as spectators, leading actors or both.

Despite the many names in use for the scene, it is not easy to find or think of a suitable concept that sufficiently covers the phenomenon. Most of the existing concepts are highly loaded with political content, as for example the term "counterculture," which implicitly accepts the scene's self-understanding as being in subversive opposition to the "system." Others, like "hippies," are both too narrow in the sense that the term refers to a specific, American phenomenon (as opposed to, for example, the Dutch *Provos*), and too broad in the sense that it was commonly used to define any long-haired rock fan at the time. Taking the diffuse character of the scene into consideration, the easiest solution is to use these concepts unsystematically as synonyms of the scene or community and not as precise definitions. Thereby one can recognize that the phenomenon did not have a fixed, generative core or structure, but was incoherent and changing; sometimes it was countercultural, sometimes commercial, sometimes political, and at other times purely aesthetic.

Seen in the larger perspective of the 1960s, the existential element of *Les années 68* played a major, although different, role—despite its elusive character. In some countries, notably Italy, it served as a fierce denial of traditional lifestyles; in others, like the United States, it served as protest against materialism, or simply as a space of hedonist experiment with very little explicit political content. Common to these different national experiences is the fragility and—as a consequence—short history of the scene. All over the Western world, the promises of the lifestyle experiments, from drugs to communes, gave way to disillusion and the revival of the revolutionary, Comintern tradition of disciplined Marxism-Leninism.

This road from hedonism to Leninism is clearly visible in a micro-historical perspective. As an example of a greater, international development, focus will be on the small but very active Copenhagen scene in the late 1960s. This scene was in many ways an avant-garde venue, though it did not see itself as such. It consisted of a hard core that formed a taste-community with strong utopian expectations. This network managed to form institutions, which in turn spread its ideas to a broader, more or less devoted audience, from the rock fan in the province to the regular in the Copenhagen clubs. By the mid- and late 1960s, this scene was setting a large part of the agenda on the Danish Left, only to collapse under the burden of its high expectations by 1970. It thus serves as an example of the fragility that characterized the Western existential, or "freak" left.

New Left and Freak Left

By the mid-1960s, the Danish Left—understood as the political landscape left of social democracy—was dominated by the "cultural radical" tradition combined with influences from especially the American New Left. The orthodox communist party had split in 1958 and the first decidedly New Left party, the Socialistisk Folkeparti (SF, Socialist People's Party), was formed. The party distanced itself from the communist *langue de bois* by a factual, down-to-earth political style, which aimed at a moral, practical socialism instead of inflexible and conspiratory Stalinism. It soon became a rallying point for the leftist intellectuals, who in these years were rediscovering the traditions of cultural radicalism. This particular Scandinavian tradition reaches back to the Enlightenment reaction to national romanticism in the late nineteenth century; it stresses rationality and free thought as opposed to traditions and romantic "sentimentality."[1] Thus, the Danish New Left was first and foremost characterized by being rational and factual. It was typically preoccupied with revealing true facts about capitalist society and exposing sentimental lies of consumer culture. The New Left intellectuals saw themselves as an elite who brought enlightening culture and objective facts to the people, which otherwise would be reduced to a state of stupidity by commercial culture in an unholy alliance with the bourgeoisie and its political representatives.

This New Left establishment was very skeptical about the challenge from the existential and emotional tendencies that began to appear on the Danish leftist scene. The concrete challenge came from the Dutch provo movement. In 1966, Duco van Weerlee's Provo manifesto *Wat de provo's willen* (What the provos want) was translated into Danish. Its stream-of-consciousness expressive style stood in stark contrast to the Danish factual and self-righteous rhetoric. Where the Danish New Left was certain and clear about their goals, Weerlee's manifesto was anti-programmatic by principle:

> *Provo* is against capitalism, communism, fascism, bureaucracy, militarism, snobbism, professionalism, dogmatism and authoritarianism.
> *Provo* has to take the choice between desperate revolt and painful destruction.
> *Provo* revolts where it can.
> *Provo* declares itself as a constant loser but won't miss the chance at least to grossly provoke this society.[2]

The provos used the happening as their main means of expression, often with provocation as the main goal. Like the situationists in France and Italy, they explicitly opposed the "argumentist" logic of politics and wanted to replace it with spontaneous action in order to break down existing norms in society. In this spirit, every daily act had political content, either reproducing bourgeois norms or breaking them. As the Italian situationist Luisa Passerini remembers:

> Together we sought to put into practice a revolutionary aspiration. ... The three of us had rented an apartment in the city where we attended university; one room each, very little furniture: beds, tables, lots of chairs, more versatile than any other furnishings. We pursued disorder in a literal sense: the plates remained unwashed for weeks and gigantic mold formed.[3]

In this line of thought, the traditional political practices of speeches and debate were shunned and even sought to be obstructed by spontaneous happenings.

In 1967, the prominent provo Jasper Grootveld visited Copenhagen. During a session at the leftist student organization *Studentersamfundet* (Student Society), he held a "speech" consisting of unconnected phrases like "Nothing exists, everything happens. Everything happens all the time, that which happens does not exist." Afterwards, he and the audience undressed and painted each other's bodies.[4] Grootveld also initiated his own "Love America" campaign, where he went around naked in Copenhagen and washed American cars. All this while the mainstream left was exposing, documenting, and condemning the American war in Vietnam. On the established left, the reactions ranged from uninterested distance—"The message of provo is neither very visionary, nor well thought out"[5] (which of course was missing the point)—over concerned worries—"The revolt could be killed at birth by intoxicated midwifes"[6]—to sarcastic comments about the vanity of individual experiments when the war was raging in Vietnam. Nevertheless, provo soon got a solid foothold in Denmark, and even the New Left flagship, the biweekly *Politisk Revy*, began to change its cultural radical image and open its pages to provo writers.

However, the biggest source of inspiration came from across the Atlantic. Danes returning from the United States, as well as American draft resisters seeking refuge in Scandinavia, brought new music and, not the least, new drugs to Copenhagen. The Beatles and the Rolling Stones had of course been well known for some years, but with the hippie culture came a wave of experimental rock, primarily from the United States and Great Britain, but also from the local Copenhagen music scene. Bands like Country Joe and the Fish, the Doors, Pink Floyd, and the local Burnin' Red Ivanhoe, had considerable success among a wide audience. Thus, music became the foundation of a growing subculture, which copied the lifestyle of the musicians as well as the aesthetics surrounding the rock scene. As the provo Ole Grünbaum put it in his memoirs: "Music becomes our religion, our communication, our dailies, and TV."[7] Long, loose hair, jewelry (especially for men), and colorful clothing became hallmarks of the scene.

Drugs were another cornerstone of the scene, and the one around which the largest utopian expectations existed. Denmark had not known hard drugs before, but from the middle of the 1960s they appeared in Copenhagen, probably brought to the country by American visitors. Particularly hallucinogens such as mescaline and LSD, but also hash and marihuana, were seen as means to expand your mind as well as to become a wiser and better human being. It was a common belief that these drugs would become an integrated part of society, as soon as the broad public became aware of their effects. There was awareness about the possibility of having a "bad trip," but, as *Politisk Revy* reassured its readers, this would only occur under very unlucky circumstances.[8]

Thus, by 1967 Copenhagen had its well-defined version of the international "freak" scene. Though in many ways like its American model, the provo inspiration gave it a more politicized, European element, which linked aesthetics and practices with an, albeit vague, leftist, anti-capitalist element. This link, however, is not easily reduced to one or more key concepts. Rather, it was a very contradictory and incoherent mixture of practices and opinions. Mostly, the aim was to break down the existing society, from the nuclear family to the nation-state. But this critique could take quite different shapes at the same time. On the one hand, as Arthur Marwick has pointed out, there was a strong preoccupation with nature and things authentic,[9] a romantic longing for traditional country living. The people, the countryside, indigenous peoples, and organic, "natural food" all played a large part in the symbols and values of the scene. On the other hand, just as many examples could be found of complete fascination with everything modern and technical, from electric instruments to science fiction:

> By ... synthetic and technical means (and which other means do we have today?), they tried to give back to life its sacredness and deep joy, to recreate the humane [*menneskeliggjorte*] cosmos.[10]

The music scene of the late 1960s is one of the clearest examples of this, from the Beatles' *Sergeant Pepper* album to Pink Floyd's chaotic improvisations and mix of instruments with everyday noises. The rock musicians used their technological possibilities fully and with great enthusiasm, the main point being innovation rather than authenticity. This modern trait existed side by side with the romantic anti-modernism and praise of nature, which often appeared in the lyrics. This tension between criticism of and enthusiasm for modernity was a common international phenomenon, which existed in Height Ashbury and inner Copenhagen alike. It was mirrored in the destructive element, which aimed at tearing down society completely to rebuild it from scratch, and the constructive element, which used the possibilities of the affluence of the Western societies to experiment with new forms of consumption, be it aesthetic or material. It was a representation of the present as utopia and dystopia alike. Contemporary society was seen as an "iron cage" of outlived traditions and cold rationality, or it could be an exciting time of change before the coming of the new age of love and freedom. Both representations, however, pointed towards a utopian future. They implied the message that utopia was possible, that it was possible to liberate one-self from the constraints of the present and attain total freedom. This utopia was not a well-defined goal like the communist society in classic Marxism, rather it was a state of ever-expanding and contradictory desires: everything had to be destroyed while at the same time everything had to be improved; everyone should be as one and everyone should have complete freedom. It was more a "state of desire," a perpetual dialectic of desire, satisfaction, and new desires to be satisfied.[11] This state of desire involved an insatiable hunger for self-fulfillment and lib-eration ("*frigørelse*" was one of the most common concepts of the scene), which implied and required a new society, a new form of living to pro-vide satisfaction.

Rituals, Venues, Institutions

As these ideas gained following during 1967, the Copenhagen scene began to form its own institutions and rituals, a number of practices that defined the scene and bound its members together in a net of cultural markers. These practices were, however, rarely connected by some com-mon defining principle; some were aesthetic, others political (or both), yet most emerged more or less randomly and arbitrarily. This intrinsic incoherence produced a number of paradoxes and tensions within the scene, when a certain practice collided with ideas and other practices from somewhere else. These paradoxes often became visible in the more institutionalized parts of the scene, where the social experiments were carried out.

The scene itself developed a large degree of exclusiveness as a distinct and demanding "taste-community."[12] Towards the outside, there was a clear distinction between the real members of the scene and the "old" outsiders, exemplified by the slogan "All grown ups are paper tigers!"[13] or against those who—even worse—tried to copy the style without truly belonging to the community. "Plastic" was the internationally used term for commercial use of the hippie aesthetics, with, for instance, the "plas-tic world" being a synonym for the artificial bourgeois life.[14] Internally, the scene saw and described itself as a "tribe" or a nation ("Woodstock nation"), apart from the rest of society. This image was mirrored in the focus on the group. Again, the music scene exemplified this: whereas the big idols of the 1950s and early 1960s had been individual stars with an orchestra, the music now was played by groups. The Beatles were the first to present a unified group image, followed by a host of new bands only identified by their common name, not by their lead musician (with the exception of the Jimi Hendrix Experience). The group as a self-contained community became an important element in the identity of the scene. The group could be a major gathering in a public park, a be-in or love-in, a concert in a club or a private get-together. Typically, such a group would form a circle focused inward toward the record player or the performers, while the chillum was passed around. This is very obvious when looking at photographs from the time, where musicians often were positioned on the floor with the audience around them, or the performers would themselves form a circle with the audience around them in a double circle. The concrete group or the larger imagined community became the scene for social and aesthetic experiments, a place where the members could try to make the utopian promises come true.

The imagined community explicitly presented itself as a global one. As in Benedict Anderson's definition, it was a community where the members, although never actually meeting each other, still felt a sense of communion.[15] The members of the scene saw themselves as belonging to a larger international brotherhood of "the young generation." The international music scene, although highly unilateral in its focus on Britain and the United States, created a sense of solidarity and a bond with like-minded fans in other countries. With the rise in income in the 1960s, it was also possible to live out this international solidarity by traveling. The Western hippies would meet and make contacts in far-off places on the way to India or other exotic destinations and confirm their solidarity and their common ideals. However, such travels were for the very hard core of the scene. Most rock fans would be satisfied with listening to live records from Monterey or London. Hence, the counterculture was for the most part lived out in the very local milieu of the big cities, where the local bands were just as important as the great international stars.

In Copenhagen, the scene soon began to develop specific venues and forums. From around 1968 there existed several magazines, which formed a sort of a public sphere outside the concerts and the personal networks. Most important was *Superlove*, which was published by well-known members of the leftist art milieu as well as people from the rock scene. It mostly brought music reviews and interviews with different bands, but also had a debate section and political feature articles. Though not entirely void of commercial interests, the magazine presented itself idealistically as a publication that "tries to serve the youth by finding the things that it is interested in."[16] With this mixture of idealism and commercialism it soon reached the impressive circulation of 10,000 copies sold nationwide.

The magazine *Hætsjj* was an absolute underground publication. Started by the local provos, it had no editing board or agenda; instead anybody could go to the flat where it was made and print an individual issue. The actual printing was done as cheaply and primitively as possible, so that it could theoretically be made from one day to the other. Mostly, it was the organ of the part of the scene centered around the Academy of Fine Art, artists inspired by situationism and the fluxus movement (notably Per Kirkeby and Bjørn Nørgård), but also by the counterculture in general. Sometimes, however, anarchist students or revolutionary groups would make one issue. Though it thus maintained its ideals of integrity and spontaneity, its complete lack of formal organization limited its circulation to the Copenhagen inner circle.

Superlove was also a so-called "head shop" in the area known as "Copenhagen's Height Ashbury" (around Larsbjørnsstræde), where similar international magazines were sold as well as posters and records. The neighborhood also had an Indian Shop selling oriental paraphernalia—standard to hip furnishing—and, close by, *Otto the Long Hair Barber* could be found. These shops were signs of the commercial entrepreneurship, which thrived on the scene. Despite the anti-commercial outlook, the taste-community required commodities to express the group-specific taste: American Indian leather goods, oriental statues, incense, and, not least, music records and drugs; all of which required an organized net of distribution, capital, and a market mechanism to satisfy the demand. The commercial entrepreneurs were thus indispensable but also in conflict with the anti-capitalist and anti-commercial traits of the scene. Though many happily frequented the shops, they at the same time disliked the thought that someone should earn money off them. The new lifestyle was not just another form of consumption; buying a record was an existential statement above the material capitalist exchange of goods.

Other entrepreneurs worked to set up new music venues. In the inner city, *Galleri 101* and *Klub 27* were the preferred music and drug establishments, but other concert venues were being established in the suburbs Gladsaxe and Brøndby. Both the latter areas were dominated by giant, all-concrete apartment buildings built during the 1960s, when Copenhagen experienced a period of demographic growth. The young inhabitants of these suburbs were attracted to the music and the culture surrounding it, making Brøndby Pop Club and Gladsaxe Teen Club very attractive and active music scenes. The Brøndby club especially received big international names like John Mayall's Blues Breakers and the Yardbirds.[17] The identity and sense of belonging to a greater and exclusive community was obviously attractive in communities consisting of people either moving out from the old working-class neighborhoods in Copenhagen or coming to the city from the countryside. The new environment in the all-concrete blocks offered little possibility of identification or reminiscences of pre-established lifestyles. The "tribe" around the music could provide an alternative identity to the traditional forms of identification connected to their prior urban or rural environment. This also points to the modern character of such taste-communities: unlike traditional communities predetermined by professional and social "standard biographies," these were rather communities that individuals chose consciously to become part of. They did not automatically provide identity; however, they offered it as a possibility. They were thus also more fragile and unstable than traditional communities. Instead of being tied to social class or a physical space, they were dispersed and constantly reshaped and reinvented.[18] In the late 1960s, Denmark was quickly passing from a dominantly rural, agricultural society to the postindustrial age. The tensions of this passage were exposed clearly in the suburban blocks that housed both the old, industrial working class and a newly urbanized rural population. Here, the rock scene and its symbols offered the choice of a new community to replace the broken identities. In addition to this, the Copenhagen music scene was extremely active with almost every major international band visiting in the year of 1968, which further increased its general appeal. This was before the age of mega-concerts. The equipment was often light and (in comparison to today) uncomplicated; the musicians would play on 100W amplifiers with very little extra gear, and the cost of hiring a world-known band was hence affordable even for small venues. The attraction of the new rock scene was thus undeniable and its influence went far beyond the inner circle of full-time hippies.

Outside the public space of the music venues, lifestyle experiments were carried out within the private sphere as well. The main testing ground for the utopian aspirations were the communes. As with most of the utopian ideas, the communes were from the beginning more explicit in their negative ambitions than in the positive goals they tried to achieve: it was necessary to break the "holy myth" about the nuclear family as the foundation of society and as the natural way of living together: "[We] use the group family to blow up our social structure. In connection with this, nothing else matters."[19] The utopian alternative was a complete identification with the group:

> [The] dream is every time and everywhere for some reason more people are together to "forget" your identity, immediately to be able to function as a group, a total openness, a total love.[20]

In practice, however, this group identity would not emerge without mediation in the form of a highly negotiated everyday life, where all private habits were submitted to the control of the commune. Cleaning, eating, and—very importantly—sexual relations within the commune had to be negotiated in order to make everyday life work. In contrast to the persistent rumors of the sexual liberty and even group sex in the communes, it was an area of high social control. Because of the problems of living with ex-lovers or partners, this was a much-discussed issue. In some places, it was even agreed not to have sexual relations within the commune, and, in a survey from 1972, 21 percent of those asked agreed that no couples should form themselves within the same commune.[21] Generally, the more ambitiously the individual commune pursued the ideal of the complete community, the greater the necessity to negotiate areas that previously had been considered private, and the greater the possibility of conflicts arising around these negotiations:

> Little everyday situations could raise a number of questions. Should the dishes be done once a day, or should everyone do their own? Should everyone wait for each other at the dinner table, or should you begin eating straight away? Should you take one big portion of food, or just a little at a time with the risk that you would leave the table hungry?[22]

In those places where these conflicts were managed, the communes were quite successful and long-lived, but the utopian ideal of total community mostly yielded to the day-to-day practical problems of living together.

Interestingly, the view the rest of society held of the communes was much more positive than the communes' members believed themselves. Their experiments were not perceived with *petit bourgeois* contempt, but rather with sympathetic interest, even in the right-wing media. The collectivists were described as "sympathetically humane" (*menneskekærlig*) and their experiments as "a possibility to find out how to get along with other people." Even the tabloid weekly *Billed Bladet*—seen as a symbol of bourgeois stupidity—ran a feature on their own experimental group family.[23] This shows the very conciliatory and tolerant atmosphere on the side of the general public toward most of the leftist scene in the late 1960s. Though there was a feeling in the communes of being discriminated against, and undoubtedly with some justification, Danish society was on the whole tolerant, even more so than other societies at the time. The explanation for this might be sought in the general consensual political culture of the northern societies,[24] or in the fact that left-wing ideas had, by the end of the 1960s, achieved hegemony in the cultural field and thus set large parts of the agenda of the time.[25] The fact remains that many of the leftist and countercultural activities benefited from support from official institutions rather than being oppressed by "the system."

Another form of institution appeared when *Studentersamfundet*, the forum of the Copenhagen leftist students, went bankrupt in 1968, and the freak and "square" student left went their separate ways. The more traditionally oriented Marxist groups formed *Studentersamfundet af*

1968 (Student Society of 1968), while anarchists and the more existentially inclined members formed an organization with the telling name The New Society (*Det Ny Samfund*). The New Society soon became the organizing center of the Copenhagen countercultural scene. It was organized on anarchist principles of non-hierarchical assemblies, which decided to form various "action groups" to coordinate different projects. Many of its founding members saw the experiments with spontaneous, basis democracy as a main purpose of the organization. They wanted to get beyond the locked structures of traditional political organizations and form a new form of dynamic, participatory democracy. In practice, however, the loose structure meant that strong, charismatic personalities could wield large power over the assemblies, unrestrained by formal structures and procedures. They could thus form an informal oligarchy in a very dynamic organization, where their ideas were easily realized. In the late 1960s, the scene was indeed characterized by such enthusiastic leaders, who would start a number of exciting projects and initiatives. Though basis democracy in practice worked far from its egalitarian ideals, it was a very effective vehicle for fast and effective realization of the leaders' plans. Members of the New Society had a large influence on the early Copenhagen student revolt especially in terms of experimenting with new forms of basis democracy and participation.[26] They also managed to influence other parts of the left, such as the circle around *Politisk Revy* and the leftist *Venstresocialisterne* (VS, Socialist Party), which at the end of the 1960s formed the rallying point of the Danish New Left. On the scene itself, the most important initiatives of the New Society were the "Project House" in central Copenhagen and the "Thy Camp" in Northern Jutland.

The Project House was an example of the tolerance and good will that counterculture experiments often experienced from official institutions. It was a joint venture between the New Society, Klub 27, and a number of cultural organizations. However, it had financial backing from the state and the city of Copenhagen. The idea was to make a giant "Culture-center without culture snobbism ('*kulturfims*')"[27]: 4,000 square meters of cinema, bookstore, café, theater, workshops, and a publishing company. The physical setting was three eighteenth-century warehouses in the city center called *Huset* (house), just a few minutes from the parliament building. While the old venues, *Galleri 101* and *Klub 27*, closed, *Huset* became the new refuge for the hippie scene. However, the ambitions combined with the open character and the loose leadership of the place soon turned it into something like a hostel for the bottom of the drug scene. As disillusion hit the scene by the early 1970s, *Huset* closed down as the last bastion of the dreams of the 1960s.

The largest project of the New Society, however, was the Thy Camp, which came about in the summer of 1970. The New Society had bought a large piece of land in the scarcely populated region of Thy in Northwest Jutland. Though clearly inspired by Woodstock, it was not a festival in the strict sense of the word. There was little official planning except the basic logistic tasks; instead, people were encouraged to spontaneously create the setting and the activities from scratch: "One of the ideas about it all is exactly that everybody is part of creating the camp. *The place is ours.*"[28] Each should freely be allowed to build a shed or raise a tent on the premises, without being responsible to anyone. In this way, the camp should form a temporary experiment to prove that a new and different society was possible. The experiences should then be used to change the old society from within, so that the example of the camp would spread like rings in the water.[29]

Quantitatively, the camp became a huge success with 25,000 participants: anarchists, artists, musicians, religious people, small traders, and drug dealers. However, a situation where all these different parts of the scene were forming a tightly knit community was bound to intensify the already present tensions.

The discrepancy between the rhetoric of openness and the exclusive tendencies of the community soon came to the surface in the establishment of several small groups and communities, which were far from always being on a good footing. Thus, groups with colorful names like the Corner-Rats, the Meadow Pissers, and the Silent Majority had vicious arguments amongst one another.

Also, the area of commerce was an issue of conflict. On the one hand, private initiative and entrepreneurship were welcomed as "activating," while, on the other hand, capitalist profit-making was criticized for reproducing the structures of the outside society: "It has to be in everyone's interest, also the traders, that we experiment ourselves away from the system that we have agreed to fight—at least until we arrived up here."[30]

The relationship to the surrounding society posed a third problem. The Thy region is quite isolated, traditionalist, and religious, and the locals did not receive the newcomers with unmixed joy. The camp newspaper *Folkets Avis* (People's Daily) printed several threatening letters about how the camp inhabitants should have their hair cut, needed a good beating, or even should be castrated. At the other extreme, the camp suffered from the many visitors who came out of pure curiosity and acted as if they were visiting a zoo. The nudity in the camp was no doubt a temptation to some. These tensions grew into physical confrontation as some inhabitants occupied the local church under the slogan "All power to the people." The local people reacted very strongly to the takeover of their church and the occupiers had to leave the premises and the angry crowd under police protection. Such confrontations, of course, badly affected the camp's self-image. One of the attractions of its remote location was the feeling of authenticity, away from plastic consumer culture. The animosity from the "authentic" locals (the "people") was hard to explain, because these were the ones who in theory were closest to the ideals of the scene:

> Maybe we fled [the church] from an unconscious feeling that the fishermen who still possess spontaneity also have fantasy, for this reason we should not fight against them, because they in reality through their attitude, if not through their way of life, show solidarity with us.[31]

The idealized image of the true people and the nostalgic longing for the simple and uncorrupted countryside thus collided with reality, and had to be explained away by some underlying, hidden bond between the camp hippies and their neighbors. The immediate experience, however, was one of alienation from the surrounding society.

Little by little, the feeling of alienation spread within the camp itself. The high hopes of the New Society to create a model that would inspire people to a greater and broader change, rather exposed the limits of the experiments themselves. After the return to "normal life," most of the participants agreed that their expectations for a new and better society had been disappointed. One example of this was the expectation regarding bodily and sexual liberation. Some felt the nudity to be an embarrassing obligation, as, for instance, the Danish artist Peder Bundgaard remembers: "Did I enjoy waddling about completely naked, only wearing sunglasses and a beer? Bloody hell I didn't. ... I hated it."[32] Others were frustrated and confused by the gap between the promises of complete freedom and the reality of the camp:

> I did not feel too good all the time. Among other things because I am full of sexual inhibitions and frustrations and other kinds of shit that I had hoped to get beyond up in Thy. I think that it was trumpeted abroad all the time how bloody liberated and uninhibited we all were, but I have to admit that my mind was just as twisted when I got home, as when I went up there.[33]

Thus, the largest and most ambitious attempt to form a new society had exposed all the weaknesses, contradictions, and paradoxes of the counterculture. It was the beginning of the great disillusion.

Disillusion and Disintegration

The year 1970 marked the downfall of the utopian counterculture. The drug-related deaths of Jimi Hendrix and Janis Joplin shook the international scene and demonstrated the dark side of the drug culture. As the *New York Times* wrote:

> God, what a year this is turning out to be. The king and queen of the gloriously self-expressive music that came surging out of the late sixties are dead, the victims, directly or indirectly, of the very real physical excesses that were part of the world that surrounded them.[34]

In Germany, the anti-authoritarian student movement was dissolving and the German Left moved toward democratic centralism; the same had happened in France and in Italy after the student revolts.

In Denmark, *Superlove* wrote about "sad tendencies" to keep on repeating the same things, and the editors did not feel that they had the energy to continue the magazine.[35] There were no issues during the summer, and after three issues in the fall—one of them featuring a very skeptical article about the Thy Camp—the publication stopped for good. Other underground magazines also closed down in the course of 1970. Single events such as Thy or the death of Jimi Hendrix were only the most visible examples of the many individual experiences of people who recognized that the utopian dreams of the counterculture were turning into nightmare. The point had been reached where the "state of desire" was no longer sustainable.

The biggest and most devastating experience was the transformation of the drug scene from mind-broadening experiments to death, insanity, and addiction. Many of the early users of hallucinogens became caught in a permanent bad trip and haunted the scene in a perpetual state of psychosis. Others died in accidents caused by their hallucinations, where psychedelic play turned into deadly reality:

> He was on a trip and thought he was a fish. And all the stoned dudes laughed; of course, he was a fish.
> Fish thrive under water. Humans drown.[36]

Other drugs appeared on the street. From the beginning of the 1970s, morphine-based drugs such as heroin were taking over from LSD and amphetamine, with the result that problems of addiction, crime, and prostitution replaced the psychoses of the synthetic hallucinogens. In this process, drug use changed from being a progressive-intellectual habit for the resourceful to being a problem for the bottom of the social hierarchy. In 1971, three out of four drug addicts came from the lower social strata.

Simultaneously, the music scene changed from experimental to political rock. Except for a few groups, the music heroes of the 1960s either died or the bands dissolved. They gave way to a new generation of political musicians, who were not as much interested in artistic experiments as they were preoccupied with a precise and simple message. The Art Nouveau style of magazines and record covers vanished and woodcuts of rebellious workers and clenched fists took their place. Even where the political message was not in the foreground, the musical expression moved away from the electronic experiments and toward a more traditional style, often as a revival of folk music. Internationally, *Get Back* from 1970, the last track of the last Beatles album, was an example of this trend. In Denmark the early 1970s saw the birth of groups with telling names like *Røde Mor* (Red Mother) or *Agitpop*.

Also, the more organized institutions faced defeats in the 1970s. The main asset of the New Society, the Project House, was unable to cope with the social problems of the disintegrating scene. As mentioned above, the open structure of the Project House left it vulnerable to this kind of social pressure. It worked as long as the users were still strong and resourceful, but when these left the scene, only the weakest, often drug addicts, were left. Hence, the Project House turned into a homeless shelter rather than a center of creativity. By 1971, the management stepped down and gave the premises back to the city:

> We stepped down with a public declaration that we simply could not handle the social problems of the society and that we would give the House back to the society. Because it was scary to walk around among five to six hundred people, who were really on drugs and far out, who lay about in the cellar in the middle of the big city, it was like walking around in gas chambers.[37]

By this time, the countercultural scene hardly existed anymore. Many of the former prophets of a new era left the scene in disillusion and began searching for new utopias in scientific Marxism. Some retained the practices in daily life, such as communal living or hash smoking (rarely stronger substances). However, these were now void of any existential or political connotations, having been reduced to a subordinate, purely aesthetic part of leftist identity.

The few faithful believers in the ideas of the late 1960s were dispersed in small groups, which lived almost in reservations of their own. A very small number remained (and remains) in Thy, while a larger group occupied some abandoned army barracks in Copenhagen. These were mainly squatters, who had been expelled from other buildings by the police and people from the Project House. They founded the (later famous) Christiania as a "free city" consisting of the barracks and parts of the old fortification. The term "free city" clearly expressed the image of a refuge from the surrounding society, not an exemplary social experiment like the Thy Camp (although later, the experimental side became the official justification for the place). Others, again, left for the countryside, where they established themselves in old farmhouses. Especially in peripheral areas such as Southern Funen (this was a popular destination) property was cheap and available because of the urbanization patterns of the 1960s that had brought people from peripheral to metropolitan areas. In these reservations the ideas lived on, but they had lost the utopian drive of the late 1960s. There was little talk of a complete transformation of society; the level of ambition had sunk from societal change to individual self-fulfillment.

On the left, the old critique of the existential currents reemerged as the scene began to disintegrate, as after the Rolling Stones concert at Altamont, for instance, which had turned into an orgy of violence. The old skeptics took up the theme of the damage the irrational ideas had done to enlightened leftist thinking: "[The] Stones and similar groups will undoubtedly keep on selling people individualism, escapism, and contempt. In this way, they prevent those young who are in opposition to the system to get a clear, leftist attitude."[38] Other events in 1970 made way for traditional leftist attitudes and strategies. In September the World Bank held a meeting in Copenhagen, where demonstrations ended in violent clashes between demonstrators and police. At the same time, squatters were removed by force from occupied buildings and the student movement initiated a new campaign against university reform. These clashes, as well as international events such as the shootings at Kent State University, gave the impression that the slogan "make love not war" did not take into consideration the intrinsic violence of imperialism. Many felt that they needed a militant, revolutionary strategy rather than existential experiments.

At the same time, a wave of working-class militancy spread across Western Europe. In Copenhagen, the ship builders—the traditional core of working-class radicalism—went on strike, mainly inspired by communist shop stewards, as did a number of other workers. After a decade of peace on the labor market, this seemed to refute the ideas that the working-class had been integrated into capitalism, and that the youth as well as the students now were the true revolutionary force. Instead, the strikes led to a revival of ideological and aesthetic workerism on the extreme left and in the student movement. Though some of the praise of the proletariat retained elements of countercultural longing for the authentic in the form of the "real people," it was hardly compatible with the hedonist hippie ideals.

Many turned to Leninism as an alternative to spontaneous action and inefficient basis democracy. In the frustration over the meager result of free and unplanned action, Lenin seemed to give a tempting alternative with order, discipline, and strategic planning. His centennial anniversary in April 1970 was not only celebrated by the communists and Maoists, but also by large parts of the New Left, who saw him as the main inspiration for the struggles to come. Where Leninism before had been associated with dogmatism and Stalinism, it was now rehabilitated, while the countercultural ideas were scorned, as in the following poem from the front page of the Copenhagen student magazine *Q*:

> She is called Else and he writes her from Copenhagen
> He writes that he is "high" and that God is great
> He writes that he is going hiking in Nepal
> And that the modern ESP-research is proving that
> The Tibetan chronicles were right
> I love you, he writes
>
> After two weeks she writes back
> She writes that EEC is an attack of monopoly capitalism
> On the working class
> And that the fight against testing in the schools continue
> She writes that she doesn't love him
> And asks what the hell he is doing in Nepal.[39]

The concrete struggle against state monopoly capitalism became more important than mysticism and self-fulfillment. Spontaneity and sensitivity were discarded as petit bourgeois; the true revolutionary kept his head and did not succumb to individual feelings. Rational, intellectual analysis of capitalism would provide the scientifically right strategy for the revolutionary struggle.

Thus, the left turned back to the language and ideology of the Comintern, re-enacting the battles of the 1920s and 1930s by copying the factions and restaging the arguments of Leninism, Stalinism, or Trotskyism in a farce-like game of petty politics.

The Fragility of Freedom

The period of the freak left was thus hectic, but short. Despite of its high visibility and enthusiasm, it disintegrated within months after having reached its zenith in the summer of 1970 with the Thy Camp. This disintegration, remarkably, happened as a collapse or implosion rather than a defeat in the face of pressure from other left-wing groups or from commercial capitalism. Moreover, it happened more or less simultaneously in all Western countries; during the 1970s, most of the global hippie community ceased to exist—except in the aforementioned ghettos. The keepers of the Comintern tradition now set the agenda, be it in the form of custodian Maoism, revived Leninism, or unconditional allegiance to the Soviet Union.

This process of disintegration mainly points at the internal paradoxes of the milieu. The specific fragility of the countercultural scene came from the mixture of high expectations and the resistance to forming stable forms of organization. The "state of desire" required a constant dynamic of satisfaction and new needs, which did not have ways of coping with setbacks and disappointments. Thus unfulfilled desires, like the promise of liberation in the Thy Camp, could not be substituted. There was no political or organizational structure to channel the frustration into other kinds of activity; the freedom of spontaneity had no safety net in a formalized structure to carry the ideas through crises. Instead, frustration led to disillusion. A pure taste-community might survive individual disappointments, but the high ambitions intrinsic to the explicit utopian element made the scene extraordinarily vulnerable. It did not, like other taste-communities, fade away or simply go out of fashion; its passing was received as a traumatic ruin of the hopes for a better world.

In this light, the attraction of the Leninist ideas of the Comintern tradition becomes more understandable. In contrast to spontaneous and expressive utopianism, Leninism gave no short-term promises of personal fulfillment, but a scientific foundation for the struggle. Nor did Leninism offer instant gratification. Instead, it appealed to personal sacrifices in a hard struggle. At the end, however, the promise of utopia was retained, but through heroic suffering rather than hedonism. This made the Comintern tradition much more resistant to setbacks and defeats, since these were inevitable in the great battle. It offered the organized vanguard party as a shelter during hard times, a formalized organization that could act as a custodian of revolutionary values. Thus, Leninist parties—Soviet communist, Maoist, or others—were ready to provide a new sense of meaning to those deprived of their utopian aspirations.

So, the circle from utopia to disillusion to a new utopian thinking was drawn. The long-haired hippies of the late 1960s were reborn as pure revolutionaries who exchanged individual fulfillment for self-sacrifice for the great cause, the tribal community for the vanguard party, and ultimately chose dogma over creativity.

Notes

1. Unfortunately, almost no non-Scandinavian literature exists on the subject; the main works are Klaus Rifbjerg, ed., *Den kulturradikale udfordring* (Copenhagen, 2001) and Bertil Nodin, ed., *Kulturradikalismen. Det moderna genombrottets andra fas* (Stockholm, 1993).
2. Duco van Weerlee, *Hvad er provo* (Copenhagen, 1966), translations provided by the author.
3. Luisa Passerini, *Autobiography of a Generation* (Hanover, NH, 1996).
4. This session was described in *Politisk Revy* 72 (1967), 6.
5. Ibid.
6. *Politisk Revy* 85 (1967), 5.
7. Ole Grünbaum, *Du skal ud* (Copenhagen, 1988), 51.
8. *Politisk Revy,* 82 (1967), 13.
9. Arthur Marwick, *The Sixties. Cultural Revolution in Britain, France, Italy, and the United States, c.1958–c.1974* (Oxford, 1998), 482.
10. Ebbe Reich, "Kosmos som forbrugsvare," in *Svampens tid* (Copenhagen, 1969), 90–91.
11. Luisa Passerini, "'Utopia' and Desire," in *Thesis Eleven* 68 (2002): 15.
12. The term is borrowed from Scott Lash, "Reflexivity and Its Doubles: Structures, Aesthetics, Community," in *Reflexive Modernization*, ed. Ulrich Beck, Anthony Giddens, and Scott Lash (Cambridge, 1994), 110–73.
13. *Superlove* 5 (1968), 8.
14. Marwick, *The Sixties,* 483.
15. Benedict Anderson, *Imagined Communities: Reflections on the Origin and Spread of Nationalism* (London and New York, 1991), 6.
16. *Superlove* 4 (1968), 2.
17. Peder Bundgaard, *Lykkens pamfil. Dansk rock i 60'erne* (Copenhagen, 1998), 158–59.
18. Lash, "Reflexivity and Its Doubles," 161.
19. Kokoo, *Kollektivet—en kogebog* (Copenhagen, 1969), 12.
20. Ibid., 94.
21. Søren K. Christensen and Tage S. Kristensen, *Kollektiver i Danmark* (Copenhagen, 1972), 182.
22. Niels O. Finnemann et al., *Livsstykker. Fem historier fra det nye venstres almanak* (Århus, 1979).
23. Kokoo, *Kollektivet,* 17–18; and *Politisk Revy* 119 (1969), 9-10.
24. For a discussion on this, see Henrik Kaare Nielsen, *Demokrati i bevægelse* (Århus, 1991), particularly 63–87.
25. Peter Madsen, "Kulturradikalismen og velfærdssamfundet," in *Den kulturradikale udfordring*, ed. Klaus Rifbjerg et al. (Copenhagen, 2001), 322–25.
26. Steven L.B. Jensen and Thomas E. Jørgensen, "Studenteroprøret i Danmark," in *Historisk Tidsskrift* 101/2 (2001): 435–69.
27. *Ekstra Bladet,* 21 November 1969, quoted in Bundgaard, *Lykkens pamfil,* 265.
28. Claus Clausen, *Frøstrup sommeren 1970* (Copenhagen, 1971); life in the camp was also recorded in the documentary movie *Skæve dage i Thy,* directed by Kjeld Amundsen (the 1974 version was renamed *Thy-lejren 1970*).
29. Clausen, *Frøstrup.*
30. Ibid.
31. Ibid.
32. Bundgaard, *Lykkens pamfil,* 304.
33. *Superlove* 36 (1970), 3.

34. Quoted in Ron Eyerman and Andrew Jamison, *Music and Social Movements. Mobilizing Traditions in the Twentieth Century* (Cambridge, 1998), 131.
35. *Superlove* 35 (1970), 2.
36. Bundgaard, *Lykkens pamfil*, 201.
37. Bente Hansen et al., *Dengang i 60'erne* (Copenhagen, 1978), 130.
38. *Politisk Revy* 154 (1970), 15.
39. *Q*, special EEC issue, September 1972, 1.

Chapter 16

Juvenile Left-wing Radicalism, Fringe Groups, and Anti-psychiatry in West Germany[1]

Franz-Werner Kersting

"If a cunning *Staatsschützer* [protector of the state, a member of an institution responsible for the security of the state and the defence of the constitution] had sought a means to paralyse the protest movement [in 1968], he would have been unable to find a way more efficient than the measures the movement inflicted upon itself: The 'Proletarian Turn,' the training courses, the Marx exegesis, the organizational debates, the foundation of parties. These were, despite the marches, the standstill of the movement, its ruin."[2]

The left-wing periodical *Kursbuch* voiced this critical and ironic opinion in a retrospective view published in 1985. Though this view can certainly be agreed with, it nevertheless blocks the insight that this product of the decaying protest movement of the 1960s again carried the traits of a *new* movement.[3] And again, this movement was predominantly a "youth movement."[4] During the transition from the 1960s to the 1970s there did indeed emerge a wide radical left organizational spectrum and youth scene "beyond the SPD" (Social Democratic Party of Germany) in West Germany.[5] This movement developed out of the mobilization, the conflicts, and the decay of the anti-authoritarian *Außerparlamentarische Opposition* (APO, extraparliamentary opposition) and its authoritative ideological pressure group, the *Sozialistischer Deutscher Studentenbund* (SDS, Socialist German Students Union), that dissolved officially in March 1970.[6] The revolutionary scene to the left of the Social Democrats consisted of a whole host of spiritual and social enlightenment groups, political parties, splinter groups, and numerous other projects. To a certain extent, all of them occupied again the "forbidden space" (Ulrich Klug)[7] left by the old *Kommunistische Partei Deutschlands* (KPD, Communist Party of Germany), illegal since 1956.

I apply the concept "left-wing radicalism" as an analytical category to examine this spectrum. It has to be noted, however, that the leftist anti-authoritarian push toward politicization and the *Utopieüberschuss* (surplus of utopian ideas and concepts)[8] of the late 1960s strongly influenced the new elite and the young generation on the whole. Politically, in conjunction with the lowering of the age required to vote from 21 to 18 years the SPD under Willy Brandt benefited most from this development.[9] Additionally, it has to be noted that the label "*linksradikal*" (leftist radical) played an important role within the temporary political culture of Germany as a derogatory slogan, often used synonymously with the terms "*verfassungsfeindlich*" (hostile towards the constitution), "*extremistisch*" (extremist), and "*terroristisch*" (terrorist).[10]

The revolutionary spectrum to the left of the Social Democrats was at the same time both red and colorful—proponents of the Old and the New Left, but also differing factions within these broader groups quarreled violently over the "correct" interpretation of the communist legacy and the adequate strategy the opposition movement should pursue. Here, the Soviet-Chinese antagonism marking and dividing the temporary communist world movement played a central role.

The following essay briefly introduces the revolutionary camp's most important networks, factions, and trends (I). In combination with a short examination of the main historical sources, it then develops guiding principles and perspectives for a historical approach to the phenomenon of left politicization and radicalization that the West German youth experienced during the so-called "red decade" from 1967 to 1977 (II).[11] Subsequently, these principles and perspectives will be studied more closely using two different examples (III and IV). Each example was chosen for a double aspect: they combine an examination of the possible prerequisites that enabled an individual to decide to make a commitment to the radical left, and a look at its development and results with a special emphasis on the important role "fringe groups" and "anti-psychiatry" played in the genesis and effects of this commitment.[12] Both case studies deal with young women who finally ended up as members of the West German terrorist group *Rote Armee Fraktion* (Red Army Faction/RAF): Ulrike Marie Meinhof (1934–76), cofounder of the RAF, who had criticized the conditions children, adolescents, and young adults had to endure in the homes of nationally organized youth welfare care during her former occupation as a journalist; and Margrit Schiller (born 1948), who came to the RAF from the anti-psychiatric *Sozialistisches Patien-*

tenkollektiv Heidelberg (Socialist Patients Collective Heidelberg/SPK). Finally, a short summary concludes this essay (V). In particular, the links between youth, feminism, and radicalism are taken into account.

I

Looking at West Germany's radical left during the 1970s, roughly five different factions can be discerned. This differentiation is strongly idealized, considering the almost countless number of smaller subfactions and splinter groups, changing connections between them, the dissolution and (re)foundation of some of them. The fluctuation among these groups is one of the reasons why reliable data regarding the total numbers, the composition, and the percentage of juvenile members is so hard to come by. An evaluation like this simply does not exist. It would have to compare the degree to which West German youth during the 1960s and 1970s was organized in radical left-wing groups with the membership and the supporters of other politically relevant groups, especially the association of young women and men with the radical Right *Nationaldemokratischen Partei Deutschlands* (National Democratic Party of Germany/NPD), the conservative *Christlich-Demokratische Union* (Christian Democratic Union/CDU), the liberal *Freie Demokratische Partei* (Free Democratic Party/FDP), the SPD, the labour unions, and their respective youth organizations and student associations.

The annual reports of the West German *Verfassungsschutz* (office for the defence of the constitution) are the most important source for a first overview over the radical left spectrum.[13] The numbers given there can at least suggest a general idea of the size of the radical left "mass movement."[14] However, the statistical data have to be clarified: if not only the membership in different organizations within the movement, but also the number and circulation of its publications shall be taken as an indicator of its importance. This raises the question what role the widespread foundation of the so-called "red bookshops" played in the radical left spectrum and the distribution of its ideas.

Firstly, the radical left movement consisted of the orthodox communist faction as represented by the *Deutsche Kommunistische Partei* (German Communist Party/DKP), established in 1968 and strongly oriented towards the GDR and Moscow.[15] The foundation of the DKP was practically equivalent to a reconstitution of the old KPD. But in the following years, a large number of the DKP members consisted of school and university students. In addition, there were the "mass organizations" of the party like the *Sozialistische Deutsche Arbeiterjugend* (Socialist German Workers Youth/SDAJ), the *Marxistische Studentenbund Spartacus* (Marxist Students Alliance Spartacus/MSB), and the children's organization *Junge Pioniere* (Young Pioneers). The DKP and its associated organizations had by far the largest following within the radical left. The party itself was able to quickly increase the number of its members from over 9,000 in 1968, its foundation year, to over 22,000 in 1969 and to nearly 40,000 in 1973. The growth continued during the following years (1976: over 42,000; 1981: nearly 49,000). The SDAJ comprised between 24,000 (1971) and 33,000 (1977) members, the MSB Spartacus counted between 1,000 and 5,800 followers during the same period and the Young Pioneers numbered about 6,000 in 1977.[16] Altogether, multiple memberships included, the DKP faction had, according to reports of the *Verfassungsschutz*, 83,000 followers in 1971, 117,000 in 1974, and 130,000 in 1977.[17]

Next to the DKP, the Marxist-Leninist (ML) groups, oriented toward China and Mao Tse-tung (and also toward Albania), comprised the second faction of the radical left spectrum. In Germany, these groups, who multiplied their following by ten between 1971 and the zenith of their success in 1977 (from 2,000 to well over 20,000 followers),[18] are also known as *K-Gruppen* (K-groups). The main organizations of this faction were the *Kommunistische Bund* (Communist Federation/KB)—also known by contemporaries as *KB Nord* (north), because of its strong anchorage and dominance in the city of Hamburg, the *Kommunistischer Bund Westdeutschland* (Communist Federation West Germany/KBW), the Maoist *Kommunistische Partei Deutschlands* (Communist Party of Germany/KPD), and the *Kommunistische Partei Deutschlands/Marxisten-Leninisten* (Communist Party Germany/Marxists-Leninists/KPD/ML).[19]

In number and social profile, the KBW represented the strongest Maoist core group of youthful system opponents: at the high point of its development in 1977, the organization counted about 6,000 "firmly organized" persons—about 2,600 cadres and nearly 3,400 members in its "mass organizations." Altogether, approximately 15,000 persons were at one time or other members of the KBW.[20] The KB also reached its statistical zenith in 1977, albeit with only 2,500 activists at most,[21] among them, for example, the current federal minister for the environment, Jürgen Trittin.[22] In contrast, the two Maoist parties that had only copied the *name* of the old KPD and its external form, apart from a few personal continuities at the level of the leadership cadres, were together not able to mobilize more than 1,500 members during the middle of the 1970s.[23] One youth organization in this second radical left field was, for example, the *Kommunistische Oberschülerverband* (Communist High School Students' Association/KOV).

Next to the Moscow-oriented and Maoist organizations, Trotskyist groups comprised a third, albeit very small segment of the radical left, with between 700 and 1,200 members at most during the 1970s.[24] The *Gruppe Internationale Marxisten* (Group of International Marxists/GIM) and the *Kommunistische Jugendorganisation Spartacus* (Communist Youth Organization Spartacus/KJO) should be mentioned as Trotskyist groups.[25] A precursor of the KJO was a group of West Berlin school and university students and apprentices centered around the periodical *Neuer Roter Turm* (New Red Tower). The young Trotskyist Peter Brandt, son of chancellor Willy Brandt, participated in this group.[26]

A fourth faction consisted of the undogmatic-anarchist youth, frequently called *Spontis*, who often had their roots in the squatter scene, the apprentice movement, and the alternative movement. They also regarded themselves as radical and revolutionary, but did not want to limit themselves within the narrow confines of an organizational and ideological cadre and party straitjacket. Current German Foreign Minister Joschka Fischer with his *Putzgruppe* (mopping group) in Frankfurt regarded himself as a member of the undogmatic left.[27] According to the *Verfassungsschutz*, their network numbered a maximum of 7,300 persons (including multiple memberships) in 1972 (1971: 2,850/1977: 5,700).[28]

Last but not least, the fifth segment of the radical left consisted of those activists that differed in one essential aspect from all other oppositional groups of the spectrum, despite ideological and mental concurrences: their willingness to practice the use of terrorist force, and live by the gun and underground, their everyday life of illegality, pursuit, and arrest, separated from their families.[29] The *Baader-Meinhof-Gruppe* (Baader-Meinhof Group) or RAF, which also called itself *Stadtguerilla* (City Guerrilla), became the most infamous West German terrorist organization of the 1970s. Other groups were the *Bewegung 2. Juni* (Movement 2 June), and the *Revolutionären Zellen* (Revolutionary Cells).[30]

II.

Meanwhile, in the Federal Republic of Germany historical research regarding the narrowly defined protest movement of the late 1960s, its journey from an "event to an object of historical science,"[31] has begun on a broad basis.[32] An examination of similar intensity, following analytical criteria and systematic, empirically based questions, is still missing with regard to the "red years" in the wake of the year 1968. As of now, the particular retrospective point of view the participants and their sympathizers maintain about the events of these years is still dominant, even though the participants have to share this rather subjective view with their contemporary observers, critics, and opponents.[33] This many-voiced choir is also responsible for the excited public debate that flared up in 2003 regarding the projected Berlin exhibition "*Mythos RAF*."[34] Nevertheless, the memories and interpretations of the contemporaries have a special value despite their lack of distance from the events; they can give access to the symptomatic mindsets and motives of historic persons, for the purpose of analytical research.

This is especially fruitful, if the left viewpoint coined by their own autobiography is productively combined with a scholarly perspective, as in the case of Gerd Koenen,[35] Wolfgang Kraushaar,[36] and Michael Steffen.[37] Examples of the recent fictional evaluation of these years, combined with autobiographic coloring, are the novels *Rot* by author Uwe Timm[38] and *Schritt für Schritt ins Paradies* by filmmaker Otmar Hitzelberger.[39] Finally, films are an important medium when dealing with the leftist radicalism of the 1970s.[40]

Besides autobiographic and filmic sources, a systematic sociohistorical examination of the radical left youth scene naturally has to consider and evaluate the records and files kept by national authorities and archives. However, probably even more important are the so-called "other" or "alternative" reports and publications kept outside of established archives, often originating from the (new) social movements of the 1960s and 1970s.[41] For example, the traditional International Institute for Social History in Amsterdam harbors the valuable *ID-Archiv*, originally established and based in Frankfurt. This archive comprises a collection vital for the analysis of the history of RAF terrorism, which developed out of the *Informationsdienst zur Verbreitung unterbliebener Nachrichten* (service for the distribution of withheld information).[42] The *Informationsdienst* was a weekly newspaper for the undogmatic and alternative left published from 1973 to 1981 in Frankfurt.

The *ID-Archiv* in Amsterdam also published the first guide in German detailing "free" archives. The *Reader der "anderen" Archive* (Reader of the "other" archives) appeared in 1990 and comprised a list of 278 institutions. Apart from West Germany (the country with the largest number of entries), institutions in the former GDR, Austria, Switzerland, Greece, and the Netherlands were represented.[43] An anthology of texts of the New Left followed the publication of the reader.[44] Nowadays, the left-wing *ID-Verlag*, which published an extensive compilation of RAF texts[45] is separated from the Amsterdam *ID-Archiv*.

The important potential alternative sources offer can also be illustrated by a local example: the historical memorial, research, and educational site *Villa ten Hompel* in Munster was kind enough to grant me access to new collection of documents it was able to purchase from an alternative left bookshop with a large second-hand department. The research produced a number of largely unknown contemporary local and regional youth and student periodicals. Even their titles are illuminating: *NOTWEHR!* (Self-Defence), *Peng. Zeitschrift für Rocker, Schüler, Studenten und andere* (Bang. Journal for Rockers, Students and Others), or: *PROJEKTil. anarchistisches magazin aus Münster* (PROJECTile. anarchist magazine from Munster).[46]

A historical examination dealing with the phenomenon of West German youth's left politicization and radicalization during the transition from the 1960s to the 1970s should at first take into account the evolution and practice of the youth's political commitment: In what way were these rooted in the events of 1967/68? Which aspects were already previously existent, and which driving forces were added later? How did this process connect political and ideological aspects with individual and cultural impulses? How was the inner structure of radical left groups and milieus organized? What was the individual and social "price" juvenile radicalism had to pay? Here, the victims of terror and militant actions come to mind, but also ideological pressure and the repression exerted by the cadres.[47]

On the other hand, the reactions of the adult generation, the "establishment" and its security agencies (police, state protection, justice), i.e. the "outside world," have to be considered, like the contemporary discourse about the aggravation of the penal code and the code of criminal procedure, the conflicts about the so-called *Berufsverbote*,[48] or the reactions to the *Buback-Nachruf* (Obituary to Buback): Using the pseudonym "Mescalero," an anonymous author, a member of the contemporary student "*Sponti*" group *Bewegung unabhängiger Frühling* (Independent Spring Movement/BUF), had on 27 April 1977 published an obituary in the *Göttinger Nachrichten*, the publication organ of the *Allgemeiner Studentenausschusses* (General Student committee/ASTA) at the University of Göttingen, in which he expressed his spontaneous reaction of "covert joy" when Supreme Federal Attorney Buback was murdered by an RAF commando on 7 April 1977.[49] The term "covert joy" led to a wave of "appeals for political action, accusations in the press and criminal investigations"[50] (with legal consequences for actual or supposed sympathizers of the obituary and the RAF), while other remarks the "Mescalero" made that were of a self-critical nature and disapproving of terrorism (like: "Our way to Socialism must not be paved with corpses"), were dismissed or simply not perceived.

Therefore, the role the state and its official policy played in this novel polarization and radicalization of the social climate has yet to be determined. Did not the sometimes excessive illiberal official reactions do their own kind of damage to democracy? How did leftist radicalism, society as a whole, and official policy interact with each other?[51] Was there a line of continuity from the "German Unrest" of around 1968 to the so-called "German Autumn" of 1977?[52] Last but not least, it remains to be asked where and how juvenile radicalism had a positive influence on West German culture and society (whether deliberately or unconsciously), despite the numerous societal fractures it caused.

In addition, the juvenile left-wing radicalism in West Germany has to be compared on an international scale: where can common ground be found, where are differences? And how important was the respective historical background? After all, contemporary leftist terror organizations like the RAF only emerged in countries with a determinedly fascist past: as with West Germany's RAF, there was also a Red Army in Japan, the *Sekigun*, which later split up into two wings: the *Nihon Sekigun* under the leadership of *Fusako Shi-genobu*, which operated mostly on an international scale, and the *Rengo Sekigun*, concentrated mainly on Japan.[53] Finally, the "Red Brigades," the *Brigate Rosse*, operated in Italy.[54]

This threefold "fascist echo" already noted by historical research,[55] has not yet been sufficiently explained.[56] Furthermore, the comparative international research of terrorism in West Germany, Japan, and Italy should be expanded and differentiated in order to take other radical left armed groups into view, like the American weathermen.[57] Finally, the personal contacts and mental connections between leftist (terror)organizations in different countries still have to be examined systematically.

III

The first case study examines the biography of the journalist and co-founder of the RAF, Ulrike Meinhof. An essay Meinhof wrote in 1968 for a "political anthology," titled "*Revolution gegen den Staat?*" (Revolution against the State?) and containing texts dealing with the extra-parliamentary protest movement,[58] provides a suitable starting point detailing her contemporary political views. The editor of the anthology, the journalist Hans Dollinger, had also won Renate Riemeck, Meinhof's long-time foster mother, as an author. Riemeck was a historian, a journalist, and a pacifist. After the Second World War she joined the SPD, then later became a co-founder of the *Deutsche Friedensunion* (German Peace Union/DFU) in 1960.[59] During the 1960s, Ulrike Meinhof, a member of the illegal KPD since 1959, became wellknown as columnist and—for a time—as editor-in-chief of the large and widespread left-wing student and public periodical *Konkret* (Hamburg) as well as through critical radio broadcasts and television features.[60] In part, both women shared a common biography, as already indicated, for Meinhof had grown up in a close relationship with Riemeck. For Meinhof, her foster mother's commitment in the antinuclear and peace movements of the 1950s had served as an example and as a role model[61] and she had also witnessed the fact, that Riemeck had been practically forced out of office as a university teacher through "anticommunist" animosities and disciplinary measures in 1960.[62]

For Dollinger's political anthology, Meinhof merely provided a short statement, while Riemeck contributed a more extensive and detailed article.[63] Both women shared the view that the German left had to, at least since the beginning of the "grand coalition" (of SPD and CDU) in 1966, promote a "critical consciousness" outside of the parliament for the possibility and necessity of structural social change.[64] Otherwise, society in West Germany would continue to persist "in a condition of prevented development,"[65] marked by alienation, class struggle, exploitation, inequality, and repression.[66] However, Meinhof and Riemeck differed with regard to the perspectives and means the left possessed to attain a change of the system. For Riemeck, it was still "an open question" whether the APO, which had assumed a radical counter-position against the existing social order, would yet be able to also make progress or at least implement improvements by influencing "the elected representatives in the parliament." Therefore, from her viewpoint the crucial changes could "not necessarily only be achieved by force."[67]

In contrast, Ulrike Meinhof assumed a position already clearly more radical:[68] "To speak of revolution means to be serious. To speak of revolution means to be finished with pacifism, with the asceticism of 'To-have-always-been-opposed-to the system,' with the excuse of 'To-have-always-said-it-between-the-lines,' with the pretty sorrow: What-else-could-one-have-done? A cue breaking a taboo, inasmuch as it justifies force, as it replaces *Weltanschauung* with the claim and the demand to change the world, as it sets obligation and reliability in place of tranquillity, and as it bars the way from a bad conscience into resignation." However, she adds, all "revolutionary talk of the intellectuals" would remain useless if its igniting spark does not spread to "quite some masses of people" to make them realize, "that their situation is intolerable, but not irreversible," that their "capacity to suffer is limited, but not their potential to resist." According to Meinhof, the revolutionary potential of the masses consisted of the "inconstant dockworkers," "the workers in the chemical industry threatened to be dismissed and replaced by machines," the "metalworkers turned into zombies by the monotony induced by mechanization," the "women living in master & dog relationships," the "teachers performing the Sisyphean task of educating full-day care children in half-day schools," the "physicians, nurses and social workers working in badly organized hospitals and homes," and, finally, the "youth suffering under their dependence camouflaged as being underage."

"The future of the German Left" would depend "on its ability to get this necessary and conceivable process of spreading awareness off the ground." The left's "contemporary revolutionary talk" would certainly constitute the "prerequisite to free themselves from internalised oppression and their own scruples, in order to be able to get to work." However, the question remained "open," whether the left would "get beyond this act of the self-liberation." Meinhof took a rather skeptical view and implied an alternative development, in which the "masses of people" in question would begin to see through the left intellectual "book"-discourse as "boring" and "uninteresting" and to carry out the "revolution without asking the [revolutionary] authors beforehand"!

With regard to her biography, this disillusioned and yet resolute political statement exactly mirrors Ulrike Meinhof's transitionary phase between her occupation as a journalist and her way into the terrorist underground of the RAF. At around the time that the text was written and published, Meinhof split up with her husband Klaus Rainer Röhl, co-founder and editor-in-chief of *Konkret*, privately at first and then also professionally, and moved to West Berlin. Here, she took part in the discussions (e.g. with Rudi Dutschke) and protest actions of the student movement. This change was connected with increasing doubts regarding the social effectiveness of her journalistic commitment as well as with a growing interest in direct (possibly also violent) forms of grass-roots work and resistance. Meinhof came into contact with Andreas Baader and Gudrun Ensslin, whose names were connected with these forms of action.

At the beginning of April 1968, Baader and Ensslin had committed an arson attack against a department store in Frankfurt to "set a signal against capitalism, the support of the US war in Vietnam and the *Konsumterror*"[69] (terror of consumption). Meinhof visited them in prison. However, in an article for *Konkret*, she argued against this act of arson: in the end, an action like this would be stabilizing for the system. The insurances would pay for the damages done; moreover, the risk that human lives could be jeopardized, would have to be taken into account. Nevertheless, she explicitly attested a progressive side to this act: "The progressive moment of the arson attack on the department store does not lie in the annihilation of goods, but in the fact that the deed constitutes a crime, in the breach of law."[70]

Meinhof was also interested in the so-called Hessian *Staffelberg-Revolte* against repressive conditions in the homes of closed welfare care education, co-organized (among others) by Baader and Ensslin as part of the left *Randgruppenstrategie* (fringe group strategy). Up into the 1960s, welfare care education was primarily concerned with the (pre-emptive) protection of society, and not with individual therapy, aid and integration. The juvenile clients, who predominantly came from a lower-class background, were subjected to a rigid system of internment, disciplinary measures, and punishment. The homes exerted punishments like shaving the head bare, isolation arrest, and beatings.[71] Ulrike Meinhof had already taken this fringe group under her wing in a 1965 radio broadcast.[72] In 1969 she not only prepared two additional radio broadcasts dealing with this subject,[73] but also the television film *Bambule. Fürsorge—Sorge für wen?* (Welfare care—Care for whom?).[74]

This first German television movie (still of interest today) dealing with the subject of the Berlin home for girls, *Eichenhof*, was scheduled for transmission on the channel ARD on 24 May 1970, but was dropped at short notice because Ulrike Meinhof was now wanted by the police. Ten days before, on 14 May she had been involved with the liberation of Andreas Baader by force from custody in West Berlin (together with the young Irene Goergens from Eichenhof) and subsequently went into hiding. During the last phase of shooting the film *Bambule*, Meinhof had again questioned the relevance and effect of this sort of journalistic involvement and partisanship: "An uprising in the home, the organisation of the youth themselves," would be "a thousand times more valuable than umpteen films." With her film, she'd merely produce "an aesthetic relation to the problems of this proletarian youth": "A TV play that messes around with the girls, that plays games with them, one may say: a crappy game."[76]

On 5 June 1970, under the heading "Building up the Red Army," the *Baader-Meinhof-Gruppe* published a statement dealing with the "*Baader-Befreiungs-Aktion*" (Baader-liberation-action) in the underground magazine *Agit 883*, which is regarded as the foundation document of the RAF. In perspective and language, it closely resembled Meinhof's statement "Revolutionary Talk": "Comrades of 883, it's pointless to want to explain the right things to the wrong people. We have done that long enough. We have to convey the action to the potential revolutionaries among the people. That is, to those who can understand the action immediately, because they themselves are prisoners. To those, who think nothing of the left's idle chatter, because it remained without consequences and actions. To those, who are fed up with it." Accordingly, the liberation action as the prelude to the foundation of the "Red Army" and its battle against "the swine of the system" and the "reign of the pigs," should precisely not be conveyed to the "petty bourgeois intellectuals" and the "left slimy gits," but rather to those "objectively left": "Find out where the homes are and the families with many children and the subproletariat and the proletarian women who only wait for the opportunity to smash the right face in. Those are the people that will take on the mantle of leadership."[77]

This proclamation once again illustrates the motto that led to the New Left's fringe group strategy (in theory, authoritatively determined by Herbert Marcuse[78]). In short, it read: "The lower the position within the social hierarchy, the more pronounced the interest in the revolution."[79] This dictum transferred the role of the revolutionary subject from the traditional working class to those social groups that lived on the lowest rung of the social ladder or on the edges of society. Especially the outcasts in the "totalitarian institutions"[80] of society (homes, prisons, etc.) were regarded as easy to mobilize. In a narrow sense, the fringe group strategy of the radical left failed miserably, but nonetheless, especially with regard to youth welfare, this strategy contributed decisively to the "public scandalization of the education in public homes."[81] This scandalization again was one of the driving forces for a process of reform of youth welfare care beginning during the transition from the 1960s to the 1970s that no longer favored the (preemptive) protection of society through rigid disciplining and confining measures, but rather called for and practiced a more liberal interaction with the "deviating behavior" of juveniles.[82]

IV

A similar process can also be observed in another backward and neglected field of the reconstruction of the West German welfare state since 1945—care for the mentally ill and handicapped. My second example, the *Sozialistische Patientenkollektiv Heidelberg* (Socialist Patients Collective Heidelberg/SPK) is closely connected to this field. Margrit Schiller, who later became an RAF terrorist, was a member of this group.[83]

The short-lived and violently disputed SPK Heidelberg emerged in February 1970 around the physician Wolfgang Huber; it comprised about 500 patients when it closed down in the summer of 1971. It became widely known far beyond the environs of Heidelberg. The collective developed out of Wolfgang Huber's out-patient department at the psychiatric clinic of the University of Heidelberg. Huber wanted to strengthen the position and the rights of the patients and to dismantle the old hierarchy in the relations between physician and client. Following conflicts with the directors of the clinic, Huber handed in his notice, and his department grew into the SPK Heidelberg, an independent entity in rooms outside of the clinic. For a short time, SPK members and sympathizers squatted in the staff rooms of the clinic management and university management. For a while, the SPK was tolerated as an institution of the university, but in late autumn of 1970 the administration of the university and the department for education and cultural affairs finally revoked this authorization. Henceforth, the collective permanently had to reckon with the possibility that it would have to close and would perhaps even be forcibly closed down. More and more, its members began to view themselves as an oppressed "fringe group."

In April 1971 the situation escalated, after a female patient of the SPK had committed suicide. Then, in June 1971, when unknown parties shot at a policeman in the small town of Wiesenbach near Heidelberg, flats and houses of SPK members were searched in the hunt for members of the RAF. Huber and other members of the SPK were arrested. Legal proceedings and sentences followed, for participation in a criminal association, the manufacture of explosive materials, and the forgery of documents. Eventually, more than a dozen young members of the SPK joined the armed struggle of the RAF, among them (along with Klaus Jünschke, Lutz Taufer, Hanna Krabbe, Siegfried Hausner, Elisabeth von Dyck et al.) Margrit Schiller, born in 1948, whose father was major in the *Militärischer Abschirmdienst* (Military Counterintelligence Service/MAD) of the army and whose mother was a teacher in a basic primary and secondary school and active in the Christian Democratic Union on a local scale.

Even before 1967/68, Margrit Schiller had begun her first steps toward emancipation, which were further accelerated by the student protests.[84] During this time of her life, between 1965 and 1970, the psychology student broke out from her parental home, the bourgeois way of life and sex morals, and from her ecclesiastical bonds, while simultaneously cultivating a critical attitude toward society. However, these changes did not yet tie together with a full politicization. During the zenith of the APO and the student movement, the 20-year-old student was more an interested observer than a participant. She had significant experiences for her development during an internship in a hospital, through temporarily joining a "Release," her first consumption of drugs, changing relationships, as well as by excessively listening to rock music.

Finally, in 1971, Margrit Schiller joined the RAF. These different stages of life are linked by the SPK, like a bridge between left politicization and radicalization. Schiller has described her experiences in the SPK in her autobiography as follows:

> "There was a Marx working group, a Hegel working group, a working group dealing with anti-psychiatry and one for the new left analysis of society. I registered immediately for one-on-one sessions, that were called "single agitation" in the SPK. During the sessions, I had at first a large need to speak about me, about my biography, my lack of assurances, my anxieties and my search for something different. Initially, I went to the

SPK several times a week exclusively for this reason. There, I realized that my loneliness and sadness and the many problems I had with myself were not my personal and inescapable fate. I started to become curious with regard to history and politics. In the SPK, there were books dealing with the Nazi crimes during the Second World War. I read them and could hardly sleep at night, struck with horror. After a few weeks, I felt at home in the SPK. I participated in several working groups, wrote leaflets with others, reproduced them on the little machine, felt well and worked with full energy. On the old record player, time and again we listened to the song *Macht kaputt, was euch kaputtmacht* of the group *Ton, Steine, Scherben* and sang along as loud as we could, because at that time the text expressed exactly how we felt. There was always something going on. Small or larger groups of people heatedly discussed the latest events, the situation in the world, books or personal questions. Protest actions or demonstrations were prepared.[85]

Margrit Schiller's memories not only illustrate once again the interaction of consumerism and hedonism with left politicization,[86] they can also serve to illuminate two additional aspects of the history of the SPK: the role played by anti-psychiatry and the significance of the National Socialist past.

Anti-psychiatry, as a flamboyant variant of the contemporary reform movement with regard to psychiatry, left its special mark on the practice and the effects of the SPK.[87] Among the proponents of the international anti-psychiatric debate of the 1960s and 1970s were the English psychiatrists Ronald Laing and David Cooper, the American psychiatrist Thomas Szasz, their Italian colleague Franco Basaglia, the American sociologist Erving Goffman, and, in part, Michel Foucault. In short, they refused to label psychic dysfunctions as a disease, but defined them as a consequence of social processes of rejection and discriminating exclusion from the allegedly "normal" and "healthy" majority of society. The old hierarchically structured mental hospitals were regarded as "totalitarian institutions" ensuring social control, stigmatization, and legal incapacitation similar to prison—and the medical doctors were to a certain extent seen as agents of this system. Accordingly, the young Germanist Tilman Fischer has used the following quotation as the title of his valuable study dealing with the position of Heinar Kipphardt's novel *März* (March)[88] in the context of the anti-psychiatry debate: "*Gesund ist, wer andere zermalmt.*" (He is healthy, who crushes others).[89]

The SPK modified and radicalized this position. Its motto read: "Turning illness into a weapon!" This slogan was also used as the title for a widespread agitation text introduced by the well-known philosopher Jean-Paul Sartre.[90] Illness was explained as a human reaction to the sickening social system of capitalism; and the patients themselves as self-aware revolutionary subjects who should now smash this system. In other words, "the recognition of the social backgrounds of illness" should be "transformed into revolutionary action"—even "conjuring the image of self-sacrifice, if need be, for the revolution: 'To come to life in this way, it must be risked.'"[91]

The Marx-oriented anti-psychiatrist concept and interpretation of the relations between illness and society therefore are an important medium of left sub- and countercultural radicalization. As a result, the anti-psychiatry movement simultaneously constituted one of the driving forces of the broad militant left discourse dealing with "repression" and "anti-repression" during the 1970s. The influence this subject exerted with regard to the contemporary left scene would be worth a study of its own.

David Cooper, for example, who also coined the term anti-psychiatry, was one of the speakers at the large TUNIX meeting of the *Spontis* on 27–29 September 1978 in West Berlin.[92] And the proclamation of another *Sponti* meeting in Frankfurt, announced as "Anti-Repression Congress," carried the headline, "We are calling the lunatics of Europe!"[93] Finally, however, the anti-psychiatric movement helped to create the contemporary social and political climate in Germany near the end of the 1960s, from which the reform movement to modernize and humanize the treatment of the psychically ill and mentally handicapped sprang.[94] In their interim report in 1973, the members of the central reform committee appointed by the Federal Government (*Psychiatrie-Enquete*) officially reported, "that very many mentally ill and handicapped patients had to live in the mental hospitals under miserable conditions, that can sometimes be only described as inhumane."[95]

The National Socialist past also played a central role in the specific West German SPK conflict. Members of the SPK went as far to compare themselves to the victims of the National Socialist "euthanasia" and genocide policies. Once again, according to their perception, a sick fascist society was on the verge of locking up or even liquidating patients and unwanted persons.[96] Medical doctors at the rival psychiatric clinic in Heidelberg were compared to the National Socialist "euthanasia" experts.

Theses accusations must have hit the Heidelberg psychiatrists Walter Ritter von Baeyer, Heinz Häfner, and Karl Peter Kisker[97] especially hard. During the 1950s and 1960s these three had already anticipated and introduced some of the most important steps of the later nationwide reformation of psychiatry: they had implemented the first exemplary transitional homes, day-care and night-care clinics, after-care clubs for the patients and even socio-psychiatric courses for the continued education of the nursing staff. In addition, they had also combined their professional commitment to reform their occupation with a self-critical meditation reflecting on the practice and the burden of the crimes their profession committed during the Third Reich. They were among the first to declare in public that the striking obstruction to reform of West German psychiatry (in international comparison) was not least a consequence of the devastations caused in the field of mental health care during the National Socialist regime and the war. As a result, they believed that West German society had a moral obligation towards the mentally ill and handicapped.[98]

Not surprisingly, these three psychiatrists suffered personal, almost "traumatic," wounds in the conflicts surrounding the SPK.[99] Their original liberal position was damaged and was replaced by a defensive attitude dismissing wholesale everything that was regarded as "Sixties" and "left-wing." This shock was shared with many others of the older so-called "skeptical generation"[100]—a circumstance that was once again significant for the social climate in which the debate and the conflict with the juvenile leftist radicalism took place.

V

A short résumé of the biographical examples and their incorporation into the political and social context of West Germany's "Red Decade 1967–77" must of necessity be ambivalent. The novel phenomenon of widespread leftist politicization and radicalization of young people developed, leading a few of them to terrorism. However, the body politic and society as a whole experienced a marked push toward democratization and liberalization, a push that simultaneously promoted respect for and implementation of human-, citizen-, and minority rights. There was a mutual overlay and permeation between both processes—with negative *and* positive results for the democratic civil society.

Two female biographies were the foci of this analysis. They underline the enormous effects the social changes of the 1960s and 1970s generally had—or at least could have—especially in relation to the biography and emancipation of women. With regard to the specific history of juvenile left-wing radicalism and its most extreme variant, the decision for armed struggle, murder, and illegality, these biographies confirm the impression, that the relatively high proportion of women as the possibly "most noticeable sociological feature of the terrorist groups"[101] should be of special interest to future historians dealing with the subject of terrorism.

Next to a closer attention to gender-specific aspects, the systematic differentiation of the radical left youth scene according to age categories constitutes a future challenge for historical research: there were parallels and transfers between the biographies of the older (exemplified by Meinhof) and the younger (Schiller) generations, but also differences in their particular biographical context and developments.

Notes

1. An initial version of this text was published under the title "Jugendliche und linker Radikalismus nach '1968,'" in *Politische Gewalt in der Moderne. Festschrift für Hans-Ulrich Thamer*, ed. Frank Becker, Thomas Großbölting, Armin Owzar, and Rudolf Schlögl (Munster, 2003), 323–36. I would like to thank Christoph Tiemann/Munster for translating the text into English.
2. Ruprecht-Karls Universität Heidelberg/Fachschaftskonferenz der Uni Heidelberg/ Fachschaft MathPhys, "'Aus der Krankheit eine Waffe machen!' Wo aus Psychiatrie-Patienten Revolutionäre werden sollten—das Sozialistische Patientenkollektiv SPK (1970/71)," *ruprecht*, no. 35, 16 May 1995; (http://mathphys.fsk.uni-heidelberg.de/ hopo/rupr1.htm)
3. See Gerd Koenen, *Das rote Jahrzehnt. Unsere kleine deutsche Kulturrevolution 1967–1977* (Köln, 2001), especially 17ff. Koenen's research is both stimulating and fundamental with regard to the subject. In addition, the early work of Gerd Langguth should be noted: Gerd Langguth, *Protestbewegung. Entwicklung—Niedergang—Renaissance. Die Neue Linke seit 1968* (Köln, 1983); also see Richard Stöss, ed., *Parteien-Handbuch. Die Parteien der Bundesrepublik Deutschland 1945–1980*, 2 vols. (Opladen, 1983–84). The manual includes articles detailing the parties and groups of the radical left. Published after the conclusion of this essay: Gerd Koenen, *Vesper, Ensslin, Baader. Urszenen des deutschen Terrorismus* (Köln, 2003).
4. Michael Steffen, *Geschichten vom Trüffelschwein. Politik und Organisation des Kommunistischen Bundes 1971 bis 1991* (Berlin, 2002), 26.
5. Detlef Siegfried, *An der Ostfront des Westblocks. Die westdeutschen, '68er' und die DDR*, unprinted manuscript (Copenhagen, 2001), 4.
6. See (simultaneously comparing Germany and the United States) Michael Schmidtke, "Reform, Revolte oder Revolution? Der Sozialistische Deutsche Studentenbund (SDS) und die Students for a Democratic Society (SDS) 1960–1970," in *1968— Vom Ereignis zum Gegenstand der Geschichtswissenschaft*, ed. Ingrid Gilcher-Holtey (Göttingen, 1998), 188–206.
7. Siegfried, *Ostfront*, 10.
8. Term coined by Friedhelm Boll and Bernd Faulenbach during the conference "Gesellschaftspolitik und Linke Szene. Forschungsperspektiven zu den 70er Jahren," of the *Institut für Sozialgeschichte e.V. Braunschweig-Bonn*, 22–24 November 2001 in Braunschweig.
9. See (with figures detailing the SPD's increase in voters, members, and students 1969ff.) Siegfried Heimann, "Die Sozialdemokratische Partei Deutschlands," in *Parteien-Handbuch*, ed. Richard Stöss, vol. 1, 2025–2216, here 2174ff. This context also saw the "euphoric emergence" of the "*Jungsozialisten*" in the SPD from 1969 (see ibid., 2161ff., quote: 2165). Also instructive: Peter Brandt, "Willy Brandt und die Jugendradikalisierung der späten sechziger Jahre—Anmerkungen eines Historikers und Zeitzeugen," in *Perspektiven aus den Exiljahren*, ed. Einhart Lorenz (Berlin, 2000), 79–97.
10. See Peter Frisch, *Extremistenbeschluss. Zur Frage der Beschäftigung von Extremisten im öffentlichen Dienst mit grundsätzlichen Erläuterungen, Argumentationskatalog, Darstel-*

lung extremistischer Gruppen und einer Sammlung einschlägiger Vorschriften, Urteile und Stellungnahmen (4th ed., Leverkusen, 1977); Klaus Riekenbrauk, "Die Verfassungsfeind-Bestimmung in den veröffentlichten Verfassungsschutzberichten des Bundes und der Länder. Ein Beitrag zum Verfassungsschutz neuer Art" (Ph.D. diss., University of Munster, 1986).

11. Koenen, *Jahrzehnt.*
12. The history of the fringe groups and the fringe group debate during the transitional period in West German society between the 1960s and the 1970s has lately been met with an increased scholarly interest. See Wilfried Rudloff, "Sozialstaat, Randgruppen und bundesrepublikanische Gesellschaft. Umbrüche und Entwicklungen in den sechziger und frühen siebziger Jahren," in *Psychiatriereform als Gesellschaftsreform. Die Hypothek des Nationalsozialismus und der Aufbruch der sechziger Jahre,* ed. Franz-Werner Kersting (Paderborn, 2003), 181–219; Julia Ubbelohde, "Der Umgang mit jugendlichen Normverstößen," in *Wandlungsprozesse in Westdeutschland. Belastung, Integration, Liberalisierung 1945–1980,* ed. Ulrich Herbert (Göttingen, 2002), 402–35; Markus Köster, "'Holt die Kinder aus den Heimen!'—Veränderungen im öffentlichen Umgang mit Jugendlichen in den 1960er Jahren am Beispiel der Heimerziehung," in *Die 1960er Jahre als Wendezeit der Bundesrepublik. Demokratisierung und gesellschaftlicher Aufbruch,* ed. Matthias Frese, Julia Paulus, and Karl Teppe (Paderborn, 2003), 667–81.
13. An initial systematic compilation of the figures provided by the *Verfassungsschutz,* in Langguth, *Protestbewegung,* 59ff.
14. Koenen, *Jahrzehnt,* 18.
15. See Siegfried Heimann, "Die Deutsche Kommunistische Partei," in *Parteien-Handbuch,* ed. Stöss, vol. 1, 901–81.
16. Figures provided in ibid., 973.
17. Figures based on Langguth, *Protestbewegung,* 57f.
18. Ibid.
19. See Jürgen Bacia, "Der Kommunistische Bund Westdeutschland," in *Parteien-Handbuch,* ed. Stöss, vol. 2, 1648–62; Bacia, "Die Kommunistische Partei Deutschlands [Maoisten]," in ibid., 1810–1830; Bacia, "Die Kommunistische Partei Deutschlands/Marxisten-Leninisten," in ibid., 1831–51; and, finally, Frank D. Karl, *Die K-Gruppen: Kommunistischer Bund Westdeutschland, Kommunistische Partei Deutschlands, Kommunistische Partei Deutschlands/Marxisten-Leninisten. Entwicklung-Ideologie—Programme* (Bonn-Bad Godesberg, 1976); Jörg Schröder, *Ideologischer Kampf vs. Regionale Hegemonie. Ein Beitrag zur Untersuchung der 'K-Gruppen'* (Freie Universität Berlin/Zentralinstitut für sozialwissenschaftliche Forschung, 1990); Steffen, *Trüffelschwein.*
20. According to Koenen, *Jahrzehnt,* 422ff.
21. See Steffen, *Trüffelschwein,* 175, 272.
22. See ibid., 236, 289, 310f.
23. See Bacia, "KPD/Maoisten," 1821, and also: Bacia, "KPD/ML," 1848.
24. According to Langguth, *Protestbewegung,* 57f.
25. See Peter Brandt and Rudolf Steinke, "Die Gruppe Internationale Marxisten," in *Parteien-Handbuch,* ed. Stöss, vol. 2, 1599–1647.
26. See Brandt, *Jugendradikalisierung,* 83f.; Koenen, *Jahrzehnt,* 278.
27. The jargon of the scene translated "*Putz*" as "*Proletarische Union für Terror und Zerstörung*" (Proletarian Union for Terror and Destruction). See Koenen, *Jahrzehnt,* 346. With regard to Fischer's radical leftist past see Wolfgang Kraushaar, *Fischer in Frankfurt. Karriere eines Außenseiters* (Hamburg, 2001), especially the chapters "Vom Außenseiter zum Außenminister," 19–37, and: "Der Frankfurter Häuserkampf," 38–79.

28. Figures according to Langguth, *Protestbewegung*, 57f. Next to the "undogmatic-anarchistic" left, they also include the remaining "other organizations of the New Left."

29. With regard to this essential distinguishing feature see especially Ulrike Edschmid, *Frau mit Waffe. Zwei Geschichten aus terroristischen Zeiten* (Frankfurt am Main, 2001), 54f., 126f.; Koenen, *Jahrzehnt*, 385ff.

30. "Pioneer works" of the historical examination of West German terrorism are: Bundesminister des Innern, ed., *Analysen zum Terrorismus*, 5 vols. (Opladen, 1981–84); Stefan Aust, *Der Baader Meinhof Komplex*, extended ed. (Hamburg, 1997; first published in 1985). Also see Aust, *Der Lockvogel. Die tödliche Geschichte eines V-Mannes zwischen Verfassungsschutz und Terrorismus* (Reinbek, 2002).

31. This programmatic title by Gilcher-Holtey, ed., *1968*, was based on: François Furet, *1789—vom Ereignis zum Gegenstand der Geschichtswissenschaft* (Frankfurt am Main, 1980; French original ed. 1978: *Penser la Révolution Française*).

32. See Klaus Weinhauer, "Zwischen Aufbruch und Revolte. Die 68er-Bewegungen und die Gesellschaft der Bundesrepublik der sechziger Jahre," *Neue Politische Literatur* 46 (2001): 412–32; Christoph Jünke, "Den Ursprung historisieren? Ein Literaturbericht zum 30. Jubiläum der Revolte von 1968," *1999. Zeitschrift für Sozialgeschichte des 20. und 21. Jahrhunderts* 16 (2001): 159–94; Detlef Siegfried, "Weite Räume, schneller Wandel. Neuere Literatur zur Sozial- und Kulturgeschichte der langen 60er Jahre in Westdeutschland," *Historische Literatur* 1 (2003): 7–34. See also Siegfried's essay in this volume; and finally: Franz-Werner Kersting, "Entzauberung des Mythos? Ausgangsbedingungen und Tendenzen einer gesellschaftsgeschichtlichen Standortbestimmung der westdeutschen '68er'-Bewegung," *Westfälische Forschungen* 48 (1998): 1–19.

33. For a short exemplary selection of the different perspectives see Oliver Tolmein, ed., *"RAF—Das war für uns Befreiung." Ein Gespräch mit Irmgard Möller über bewaffneten Kampf, Knast und die Linke* (2nd ed., Hamburg, 1997); Hans-Joachim Klein, *Rückkehr in die Menschlichkeit. Appell eines ausgestiegenen Terroristen* (Reinbek, 1986); Peter Brückner, *Ulrike Marie Meinhof und die deutschen Verhältnisse. Mit Texten von Ulrike Marie Meinhof, einem Vorwort von Ulrich K. Preuß und einem Nachwort von Klaus Wagenbach* (Berlin, 2001 [first published 1976]); Heinrich Hannover, *Die Republik vor Gericht 1954–1974. Erinnerungen eines unbequemen Rechtsanwalts* (Berlin, 1998); Hermann Lübbe, *Endstation Terror. Rückblick auf lange Märsche* (Stuttgart, 1978).

34. See e.g. Heribert Prantl, "Auf dem Grund der Republik. Warum Deutschland eine Ausstellung über die RAF braucht," *Süddeutsche Zeitung*, 24 July 2003; article "RAF war keine Art Bonnie and Clyde. Der Ausstellungsmacher Klaus Biesenbach verteidigt sein Projekt," ibid., 28 July 2003; Jens Jessen, "Mythos RAF," *Die Zeit*, 31 July 2003; Oliver Reinhard, "Der Staat als Zensor? Eine geplante Berliner Ausstellung über die RAF sorgt für Streit," *Sächsische Zeitung*, 14 August 2003.

35. See Koenen, *Jahrzehnt*.

36. See Kraushaar, *Fischer*; also Wolfgang Kraushaar, *1968 als Mythos, Chiffre und Zäsur* (Hamburg, 2000).

37. See Steffen, *Trüffelschwein*.

38. Uwe Timm, *Rot. Roman* (Köln, 2001); also see the contemporary novel: Uwe Timm, *Heißer Sommer* (Munich, 1974).

39. Otmar Hitzelberger, *Schritt für Schritt ins Paradies* (Frankfurt am Main, 2003).

40. With the history of the RAF as a notable focus. Better known examples include: *Die verlorene Ehre der Katharina Blum* (director: Volker Schlöndorff, Margarethe von Trotta/1975); *Deutschland im Herbst* (directed by a collective around Rainer Werner Fassbinder, Alexander Kluge et al./1977); *Die Bleierne Zeit* (Margarethe von

Trotta/1981); *Todesspiel* (Heinrich Breloer/1997); *Die Stille nach dem Schuss* (Volker Schlöndorff/1999); *Die innere Sicherheit* (Christian Petzold/2000); *Black Box BRD* (Andres Veiel/2001); *Baader* (Christopher Rot/2001); *Starbuck Holger Meins* (Gerd Conradt/2001); *Schleyer. Eine deutsche Geschichte* (Lutz Hachmeister/2003).

41. A brief overview over the secondary literature in: Franz-Werner Kersting, "Demokratisierung der Überlieferung? Die Archive sozialer Bewegungen," *Archivpflege in Westfalen und Lippe* 55 (2001): 7–10; also see: Thomas P. Becker and Ute Schröder, eds., *Die Studentenproteste der 60er Jahre. Archivführer-Chronik-Bibliographie* (Köln et al., 2000), especially 19ff.

42. See ID-Archiv at the International Institute for Social History Amsterdam, ed., *Projekt Gedächtnis. ID-Artikel zum Thema Gegenöffentlichkeit 1973–1981* (2nd ed., Amsterdam, 1990).

43. See ID-Archiv at the International Institute for Social History/Amsterdam, ed., *Reader der "anderen" Archive. Mit einem Beitrag von Rudolf de Jong* (Amsterdam, Berlin, 1990). A newly updated edition of this valuable work is currently in a preparatory stage. Also see Bernd Hüttner, *Archive sozialer Bewegungen. Eine Einführung mit Adressenverzeichnis*, 2nd ed. (Bremen, 2002).

44. See Redaktion *diskus*, ed., *Küss den Boden der Freiheit. Texte der Neuen Linken* (Berlin, Amsterdam, 1992). This publication followed: ID-Archiv s.a. Amsterdam, ed., *Die Früchte des Zorns. Texte und Materialien zur Geschichte der Revolutionären Zellen und der Roten Zora*, 2 vols. (2nd. ed., Berlin and Amsterdam, 1993).

45. See ID-Verlag, ed., *Rote Armee Fraktion, Texte und Materialien zur Geschichte der RAF* (Berlin, 1997).

46. Or even: *Neue Viehzucht. anarchistisches zentralorgan. deutschlands kleinste polemisierzeitung* (New livestock-breeding. anarchist central organ. germany's smallest polemical newspaper). See Historical Site Villa ten Hompel Münster, archive "Presse 022," no. 1–3; no. 20; no. 67; no. 11 (in the order mentioned); a brief "portrait" of *PROJEKTil* is already included in the valuable dissertation and bibliography of Bernd Drücke, *Zwischen Schreibtisch und Straßenschlacht? Anarchismus und libertäre Presse in Ost- und Westdeutschland* (Ulm, 1998), 298ff.

47. E.g. documented in: *Wir warn die stärkste der Partein... Erfahrungsberichte aus der Welt der K-Gruppen* (Berlin, 1977); Ute Kätzel, *Die 68erinnen. Porträt einer rebellischen Frauengeneration* (Berlin, 2002), here 116 (autobiography Susanne Schunter-Kleemann). Koenen, *Jahrzehnt*, 439, remarks (from his own KBW experience) the sometimes "inquisitional quality" of everyday life in the organizations and groups.

48. See note 10.

49. See *Göttinger Nachrichten*, 25 April 1977, 10–12. Meanwhile the "Mescalero" has revealed his identity as Klaus Hülbrock. See the extensive study: Stefan Spiller, "Linksterrorismus und bundesdeutsche Öffentlichkeit im Spiegel des 'Buback-Nachrufs' von 1977" (unpublished Master's degree study, University of Siegen, 2003).

50. Ibid., 95.

51. Important initial research dealing with these questions e.g. in: Anselm Doering-Manteuffel, "Freiheitliche demokratische Grundordnung und Gewaltdiskurs. Überlegungen zur 'streitbaren Demokratie' in der politischen Kultur der Bundesrepublik," in *Politische Gewalt*, ed. Becker et al., 269–284; Michael Sturm, "'Dazwischen gibt es nichts.' 'Bewaffneter Kampf' und Terrorismusbekämpfung in der Bundesrepublik am Beginn der 1970er Jahre," *SOWI. Das Journal für Geschichte, Politik, Wirtschaft und Kultur* 32, no. 2 (2003): 47–59. The following study should be regarded more critically: Oliver Tolmein, *Vom Deutschen Herbst zum 11. September. Die RAF, der Terrorismus und der Staat* (Hamburg, 2002); here e.g. the chapter "Die innerstaatliche Feinderklärung gegen die RAF," 77ff.

52. See Franz-Werner Kersting, "'Unruhediskurs.' Zeitgenössische Deutungen der 68er-Bewegung," in *Die 1960er Jahre*, ed. Frese, Paulus, and Teppe, 715–40.

53. The emergence of the *Sekigun* from the Japanese protest movement was documented impressively in the movie *Japan: Jahre des roten Terrors* by Michael Prazan (France 2001) (French-German broadcast on the channel "arte"). For an early German examination see Gebhard Hielscher, "Japans RAF und 'Zentralkernfraktion,'" in *Terrorismus. Gewalt mit politischem Motiv*, ed. Dieter Schröder (Munich, 1986), 169–79.

54. See e.g.: Mario Moretti, *Brigate Rosse. Eine italienische Geschichte. Mit einem Vorwort von Rossana Rossandra und Carlo Mosca* (Hamburg, 1996); Nanni Balestrini and Primo Moroni, *Die goldene Horde. Arbeiterautonomie, Jugendrevolte und bewaffneter Kampf in Italien* (Berlin et al., 2002); Carlo Feltrinelli, *Senior Service. Das Leben meines Vaters Giangiacomo Feltrinelli* (paperback ed.; Munich, 2003).

55. See e.g. Wolfgang Kraushaar, in conversation with Jörg Herrmann, "Die Aura der Gewalt. Die 'Rote Armee Fraktion' als Entmischungsprodukt der Studentenbewegung—Erinnerungen, Interpretationen, Hypothesen," in *Lettre International*, no. 52 (spring 2001): 7–16, here 16 (repr. in ibid., *Fischer*, 224–56).

56. This desideratum is also emphasized in Prazan's film (see note 53).

57. See the novel: Robert C. Moore Jr., *Weathermen* (New York, 1995; paperback 2001).

58. Hans Dollinger, ed., *Revolution gegen den Staat? Die außerparlamentarische Opposition—die neue Linke. Eine politische Anthologie* (Bern et. al., 1968).

59. See Renate Riemeck, *Ich bin ein Mensch für mich—Aus einem unbequemen Leben* (Stuttgart, 1992); Rolf Schönfeldt, "Die Deutsche Friedens-Union," in *Parteien-Handbuch*, ed. Stöss, vol. 1, 848–76, especially 849f.

60. See the compilations: Ulrike Meinhof, *Deutschland Deutschland unter anderm. Aufsätze und Polemiken* (Berlin, 1995); Meinhof, *Die Würde des Menschen ist antastbar. Aufsätze und Polemiken* (Berlin, 1995); Meinhof, *Dokumente einer Rebellion—10 Jahre "konkret"-Kolumnen* (Hamburg, 1972). The following biographical remarks are based on (if not explicitly noted): Aust, *Komplex*; Mario Krebs, *Ein Leben im Widerspruch* (Reinbek, 1988); Interview and Portrait "Renate Riemeck, Historikerin," in *Warum gerade sie. Begegnungen mit berühmten Frauen*, Alice Schwarzer (Frankfurt am Main, 1991), 255–68; Dieter Wunderlich, "Ulrike Meinhof. Moral und Terror," in *EigenSinnige Frauen. Zehn Porträts*, ibid. (Regensburg, 1999), 206–33. The newly published biography of Alois Prinz, *Lieber wütend als traurig. Die Lebensgeschichte der Ulrike Marie Meinhof* (Weinheim et al., 2003) largely confirms this picture.

61. Renate Riemeck was one of the authors of an antinuclear armament appeal to the unions signed by forty-four professors and titled "Appell an die Gewerkschaften gegen die atomare Aufrüstung der Bundeswehr," 26 February 1958. Also see: Wolfgang Kraushaar, *Die Protest-Chronik 1949–1959. Eine illustrierte Geschichte von Bewegung, Widerstand und Utopie*, 4 vols. (Hamburg, 1996), 3: 1804.

62. See Ulrike Meinhof's column, "Geschichten von Herrn Schütz," *Konkret*, no. 15 (1960).

63. See Ulrike Marie Meinhof, "Revolutionsgerede," in *Revolution*, ed. Dollinger, 208f.; Renate Riemeck, "Außerparlamentarische Opposition – heute," in ibid., 72–79.

64. Riemeck, "Außerparlamentarische Opposition," 73.

65. Ibid., 78.

66. See ibid., especially 72f.; Meinhof, "Revolutionsgerede," 208.

67. See Riemeck, "Opposition," 78.

68. Cit. and based on: Meinhof, "Revolutionsgerede," S. 208f. Prinz, *Lieber wütend*, 184, 186f., also worked with this notable but largely neglected text.

69. Wolfgang Kraushaar, *1968. Das Jahr, das alles verändert hat* (Munich and Zurich, 1998), 96. Student Thorwald Proll and actor Horst Söhnlein also participated in the arson attack.

70. See Meinhof, *Würde*, 153f.

71. See Köster, *Holt die Kinder*; Rudloff, *Sozialstaat*; Ubbelohde, *Umgang*.

72. See Ulrike Meinhof, "Heimkinder in der Bundesrepublik. Aufgehoben oder abgeschoben?," *Frankfurter Hefte. Zeitschrift für Kultur und Politik* 21 (1966): 616–26. Prinz, *Lieber wütend*, 140f. and 321, note 8, drew attention to this text.

73. Titles: *Guxhagen* (educational home for girls near Kassel) and *Jynette, Irene, Monika.* see Krebs, *Leben*, 119, 190, 279.

74. See Ulrike Marie Meinhof, *Bambule. Fürsorge—Sorge für wen?* (Berlin, 1994; first published in 1971). The paperback edition contains: U. Meinhof, "Vorbemerkungen," 7–12; the script of *Bambule* with pictures from the movie, 13–101; Klaus Wagenbach, "Nachwort," 103–10; Director Eberhard Itzenplitz, "Über die Filmarbeit mit Ulrike Meinhof," 111–35. Meinhof's *Bambule* would be worth a historical study of its own. Initial research can be found on the internet (www.spendierhosen.de/Home/Werke/Bambule): Manfred Haller, *Bambule—Fürsorge. Sorge für wen? Ein Fernsehspiel von Ulrike Meinhof, wiss. Hausarbeit im Rahmen eines Seminars "Pädagogische Hilfen für verhaltensauffällige Kinder und Jugendliche,"* (Heidelberg, 1999/2000). The photography book edited by Astrid Proll, *Hans und Grete/Die RAF 67–77* (Göttingen, 1998), 50ff., contains photographs from the "*Staffelberg-Projekt*" and shows Meinhof's work for *Guxhagen* and *Bambule*.

75. See Krebs, *Leben*, 215 ("wanted" poster).

76. In a letter to Dieter Waldmann, the director-general of the radio channel *Südwestfunk*, dated from 21 March 1970, here cit. (because of the exact date) from: Haller, *Bambule*, 8. Excerpts also in: Aust, *Komplex*, 102ff. and in: Prinz, *Lieber wütend*, 205. In contrast, Krebs, *Leben*, 192f., conveys the impression that Meinhof had "identified with 'Bambule' until the end and was convinced to continue her work in the area of TV plays."

77. Quote: ID-Verlag, ed., *Rote Armee Fraktion, Texte*, 24–26.

78. See especially: Herbert Marcuse, *Der eindimensionale Mensch. Studien zur Ideologie der fortgeschrittenen Industriegesellschaft* (Darmstadt and Neuwied, 1967).

79. Rose Ahlheim et al., *Gefesselte Jugend. Fürsorgeerziehung im Kapitalismus* (Frankfurt am Main, 1971), 108, cit. Köster, *Kinder*.

80. This topic became popular through the widespread reception of: Erving Goffman, *Asyle. Über die soziale Situation psychiatrischer Patienten und anderer Insassen* (Frankfurt am Main, 1972; first published in the United States 1961). Originally, the term was coined by the American sociologist Everett Hughes. See Tom Burns, *Erving Goffman* (London, New York, 1992), 142.

81. Ubbelohde, *Umgang*, 434.

82. Ibid., 417. With regard to this change of perspectives also see Köster, *Kinder*, and Rudloff, *Sozialstaat*.

83. As well as my own research, the following is based on: Cornelia Brink, "Radikale Psychiatriekritik in der Bundesrepublik. Zum Sozialistischen Patientenkollektiv in Heidelberg," in *Psychiatriereform*, ed. Kersting, 165–79; Brink, "(Anti-)Psychiatrie und Politik. Über das Sozialistische Patientenkollektiv Heidelberg," in *Die Phantasie an die Macht? 1968—Versuch einer Bilanz*, ed. Richard Faber and Erhard Stölting (Berlin and Vienna, 2002), 125–56; Margrit Schiller, *"Es war ein harter Kampf um meine Erinnerung." Ein Lebensbericht aus der RAF* (2nd ed. Hamburg, 2000); Ruprecht, *Krankheit*.

84. The following according to the memoirs of Schiller, *Kampf*, 20ff. (chapter "Aufbruch").

85. Ibid., 31f., 34 (chapter "Abschied vom bisherigen Leben").

86. See the contemporary study: Diethart Kerbs, ed., *Die hedonistische Linke. Beiträge zur Subkultur-Debatte* (Neuwied, 1970).

87. Tilman Fischer, *"Gesund ist, wer andere zermalmt." Heinar Kipphardts "März" im Kontext der Antipsychiatrie-Debatte* (Bielefeld, 1999), 97ff.; Heinz Häfner, *Das Rätsel Schizophrenie. Eine Krankheit wird entschlüsselt* (2nd ed., Munich, 2001), 71ff.

88. See Heinar Kipphardt, *März. Roman* (Munich, 1976). Before he wrote this novel, Kipphardt produced the television movie "Leben des schizophrenen Dichters Alexander März" (first broadcast on the channel *"Zweites Deutsches Fernsehen"*/ ZDF on 23 June 1975).

89. See note 87.

90. See *SPK—Aus der Krankheit eine Waffe machen. Eine Agitationsschrift des Sozialistischen Patientenkollektivs an der Universität Heidelberg. Mit einem Vorwort von Jean-Paul Sartre* (Munich, 1972).

91. See—summarizing—Brink, "Radikale Psychiatriekritik," 172f.

92. See Gerd Stein, ed., *Bohemien—Tramp—Sponti. Boheme und Alternativkultur. Kulturfiguren und Sozialcharaktere des 19. und 20. Jahrhunderts*, vol. 1 (Frankfurt am Main, 1981), 301.

93. Ibid., 292ff.

94. See Franz-Werner Kersting, "'1968' als psychiatriegeschichtliche Zäsur," in *Sozialpsychiatrie. Entwicklungen—Kontroversen—Perspektiven*, ed. Martin Wollschläger (Tübingen, 2001), 43–56; also see the papers in: Kersting, ed., *Psychiatrie-form.*

95. Sachverständigen-Kommission zur Erarbeitung der Enquete über die Lage der Psychiatrie in der BRD, *Zwischenbericht* (Bonn, 1973; Bundestagsdrucksache 7/1124), 23.

96. See Brink, "Psychiatriekritik," 173f., Ruprecht, *Krankheit*, 4f., and Margot Overath, *Drachenzähne. Gespräche, Dokumente und Recherchen aus der Wirklichkeit der Hochsicherheitsjustiz* (Hamburg, 1991), 82 (the memories of Klaus Jünschke).

97. Kisker had already left Heidelberg by the time of the SPK conflict. In 1966, he received the professorial chair for psychiatry at the newly founded Medical University in Hannover (as director of the department for clinical psychiatry).

98. See the memorandum: Heinz Häfner, Walter v. Baeyer, and Karl Peter Kisker, "Dringliche Reformen in der psychiatrischen Krankenversorgung der Bundesrepublik. Über die Notwendigkeit des Aufbaus sozialpsychiatrischer Einrichtungen (psychiatrischer Gemeindezentren)," *Helfen und Heilen. Diagnose und Therapie in der Rehabilitation*, no. 4 (1965): 118–125; Walter von Baeyer, "Die Bestätigung der NS-Ideologie in der Medizin unter besonderer Berücksichtigung der Euthanasie," in *Freie Universität Berlin, Universitätstage 1966: Nationalsozialismus und die deutsche Universität* (Berlin, 1966), 63–75.

99. See the memoirs of Walter Ritter von Baeyer, in *Psychiatrie in Selbstdarstellungen*, ed. Ludwig J. Pongratz (Bern, 1977), 9–34, here 29ff.

100. For a more extensive study, see Franz-Werner Kersting, "Helmut Schelskys 'Skeptische Generation' von 1957. Zur Publikations- und Wirkungsgeschichte eines Standardwerkes," *Vierteljahreshefte für Zeitgeschichte* 50 (2002): 465–95; Kersting, "Unruhediskurs."

101. According to Koenen, *Jahrzehnt*, 379.

Chapter 17

The End of Certainties: Drug Consumption and Youth Delinquency in West Germany

Klaus Weinhauer

During the summer of 1967, Fritz Bauer, a famous public prosecutor for a provincial court, inveighed against, as he put it "a West German nightmare," stating that "a ghost is making its rounds in West Germany—the ghost of rising youth delinquency."[1] In January of 1973, the news magazine *Der Spiegel* quoted the North Rhine-Westphalian minister of the interior Willi Weyer, who had said that juvenile delinquency[2] has "risen in an alarming way." Moreover, in the same article the magazine reported an "over-proportional rise in violent crime" committed by young people.[3] Looking for reasons why since the mid-1960s the threats of juvenile delinquency seem to have reached a new level, three aspects should be taken into consideration. First, police crime statistics should not be given too much attention, since these numbers are questionable.[4] Second, it seems promising not only to analyze the social historical facts but also to scrutinize the social perception of juvenile delinquency among politicians and police personnel as well as the media's perception; simultaneously, it should also be checked which offenses were at the center of public interest.[5] Third, it needs to be determined whether there were certain social "places" where juvenile delinquency could develop.

The debates about dangers of youth or youthfulness have a long history, which began in the late nineteenth century. The *Reichskriminalstatistik* (imperial crime statistics), established in 1882, demonstrated for the first time rising figures of convicted juveniles aged between 12 and

18.[6] It was mostly working-class youth that stood at the center of the more or less heated discussions. In the 1960s, however, it was not just working-class youth on which public concern was focused—but youth in general. Moreover, when at that time social science research was discovering youth culture(s)[7] there was a tendency virtually to equate youthfulness with social change. Thus, the changing patterns of consumption among youth gained public attention. When looking at the emergence and breakthrough of the consumer society in the 1960s, the words of the sociologist Trutz von Trotha should not be ignored, in which he underlined the "complementarity of youth and juvenile delinquency," since the model of youth simultaneously defines the model of juvenile delinquency and vice versa.[8] Ignoring for the moment the problems that are inherent in such a monolithically defined understanding of youth, which does not take into consideration differences in social stratum, class, age groups, and gender, von Trotha's argument remains important as it reminds us not to lose sight of the interaction of youth culture and its subcultural or countercultural opponents.[9]

As the crime statistics for the year 1974 of the Hamburg police forces demonstrate, nearly 60 percent of all crimes committed by juveniles under the age of 21 were thefts.[10] Among police personnel, politicians, and journalists, however, from the late 1960s, another offense stood at the center of their concern: drug consumption.[11] Starting during the mid-1960s, drug consumption took the shape that it still has today: it became an international youth problem—which, at least in the case of Germany, is still not well studied.[12] On the one hand, within youth culture, drugs were an expression of a revolt in lifestyle,[13] which can be characterized by self-realization, hedonism, and by the "attainment of new worlds of experiences."[14] On the other hand, debates about drugs figured prominently in a process of "normative self-assurance" made to combat the erosion of social norms and values.[15] According to the results of social science research, it is taken as a fact that drugs do not exist in themselves nor do they have any clear-cut effects. Drugs are social constructions.[16] As the American sociologist Howard Becker maintained in 1963, drug consumers have to learn the perception of drug effects. Moreover, drug legislation is influenced by this social construction of the drug problem.[17]

In Western European societies of the 1960s and 1970s, drug consumption figured prominently in the dramatization of juvenile delinquency. In this case it was not the "teenage consumer(s)" on which public attention focused but a kind of "marginalized" consumer who was at or moving toward the fringes of society.[18] As the well-developed research on England demonstrates, juvenile delinquency including drug consumption, however, should not be studied without referring to social stratum or class.[19] In England, roughly from 1964, the consumption of amphetamines in many big cities drew the attention of the press, politicians, and police personnel. Some years later, the same was true for hashish and LSD. In both cases, most of the consumers were white and of middle-class background.[20] About the same time, working-class youth subcultures began to attract public attention: at first the mods and the rockers and later the skinheads. Especially the clashes between mods and rockers and the social construction of folk-devils triggered moral panics, very well studied by Stan Cohen.[21] Skinheads and rockers tried to oppose the demise of traditional working-class culture by cultivating proletarian norms and values, which they thought were threatened. Often this was supported through group-based expressions of martial appearance and manners, underlined by physical violence.[22] Thus, there was a coexistence of middle-class based hedonistic lifestyle, on the one hand, and a short-time upsurge of a culture of rough, group-based proletarian expressions, which were articulated publicly in a provocative way, on the other hand.

This contribution analyzes whether similar developments can be found in West Germany. It focuses on social and on cultural-historical aspects of juvenile delinquency. First, I will analyze the emerging countercultural underground with its scenes and networks in some big cities in West Germany. Second, against this background the main emphasis of this essay will focus on drug consumption and on the social composition of drug consumers in the 1960s and 1970s. Third, in order to analyze a broad spectrum of juvenile delinquency, there will be a short section on the proletarian youth gangs of the "rockers" who, from the late 1960s until the early 1970s, were turned into folk-devils. Since the police plays not only an important role in fighting but also in the social construction of (juvenile) delinquency, there will be an analysis—as far as there are source materials—of how police personnel perceived these social problems.[23]

In general, for West German society, the 1960s was a decade of new departures, which did not start as late as "1968" but were already appearing at the beginning of this decade.[24] Changes in the norm and value systems—be they already visible or still under way—must be taken into consideration when delinquency and its social construction is studied. Moreover, roughly by the middle of the 1960s, the figures of the crime statistics (including juvenile delinquency) collected by the police showed a marked increase in the number of offenses. Simultaneously, public concern about crime grew stronger. This trend was supported by the fact that new television programs were established (for instance in March of 1964 and in October of 1967) which dealt with criminal cases.[25] At the same time, opinion polls were taken that demonstrated that from the mid-1960s onwards, there was a heightened search for security among West Germans;[26] round about 1967 crime became a main issue in the field of domestic concerns. Even now, however, it is not clear whether these television programs and opinion polls were expressions of fears about crime or whether they contributed to the increase of such fears.[27]

Threats of the Underground

Leaving the rising numbers of criminal offenses (as registered by the police) and the growing importance of crime for domestic concerns aside, during the mid-1960s juvenile delinquency transformed in two important ways: juvenile delinquency lost its traditional "place" and offenses were no longer exclusively committed by juveniles coming from the lower social stratums but also from those belonging to higher social classes. With regard to (juvenile) delinquency, for a long time the police were mostly concerned with the red-light and entertainment districts as well as the port areas of big cities. It was there that runaway youths found hiding-places when they had left their parental homes or reformatories. Moreover, large parts of the criminal underworld could be found in these precincts.[28]

From the mid-1960s, police, social workers, and politicians, however, had to face juveniles who were part of a complex—more or less countercultural—underground.[29] Political actions such as demonstrations, happenings, sit-ins etc. were only one part of these international networks, which were also structured by inner-city meeting points in the streets and in other public places. Communication in the underground networks was also centered around newspapers, music clubs, discotheques, and shops.[30] However, this underground was not exclusively concentrated in the traditional red-light or port districts but also in the city centers, in wealthy quarters as well as in the suburbs.[31] Moreover, it was not the underclass youth that constituted the core groups of the underground; instead, members of the middle and higher stratums of society dominated this new underground. Thus, the emergence of the underground meant a social as well as spatial expansion of delinquent milieux.

The underground networks—like the later student protests—were instrumental in changing the police's analysis of threats. From this time, there were so many patterns of social behavior exhibited by juveniles that the spectrum of normality (and of delinquency) could not be easily defined. With the spread of the international youth-cultural underground delinquency it made no sense to explain delinquency with the help of individual abnormal behavior. Moreover, it was not only the underground-youth that used the supplies of new consumer goods (clothes, beat-, rock-, and pop-music, drugs, motorcycles, etc.) to create their personal lifestyles. This also became increasingly true for "normal" young men and women.[32]

During the mid-1960s, the term society (*Gesellschaft*)[33] gained the upper hand vis-à-vis community (*Gemeinschaft*) when it came to describing and analyzing the social order in West Germany. Because of that and due to the discovery and the development of the underground, criminologists and police personnel were able to understand delinquency and criminality as a social problem, whereas, until the mid-1960s, it had been often ascribed to individual "animals."[34] As the criminologist Joachim Hellmer (University of Kiel) put it in 1966, the "strong increase" of juvenile delinquency had its "roots in society."[35]

During the mid-1960s, in West Germany the drop outs could be seen as the harbingers of the underground that developed in big cities like Munich, Frankfurt, Berlin, or Hamburg.[36] The drop outs, whose disposition (*Habitus*) and political directions differed from town to town, were predominantly 17- to 25-year-old males of middle-class background.[37] Often they hitchhiked to and from European cities, where there were certain meeting points: Covent Garden and "Finch's" in London, the pub "Dicke Wirtin" and the area around the *Gedächtniskirche* in West Berlin, the "Palette" in Hamburg, the street *Vestergade* and the pub "Nick" in Copenhagen.[38] The number of drop outs, however, bore no relation to the extent of the attention they received in the media, among politicians, and by the police. In September of 1966, the news magazine *Der Spiegel* underlined, "by far most Germans [had] never seen a dropout."[39]

By their mere presence, the drop outs were challenging widespread social norms and values. One of the "most important values" in West German society, that after hard work people had the right for "demonstrative consumption," was questioned.[40] Moreover, the work ethic, gender definitions, promiscuity, and norms of order as well as cleanliness stood at the center of these imagined social threats. As the sociologist Walter Hollstein put it in regard to the drop out's relationship to authority or authorities: "Without mocking [the authorities] directly [the drop out] mocks them nevertheless because he despises norms, values, and taboos." His hair is "long and insistently untidy, his beard is rough and not clipped by the hand of a barber." His "trunk never ever appears to be erected or straightened in a military way; he does not walk but strolls."[41] This was a pattern of behavior, that could already be found among the *Halbstarke* (a group of leather-clad young rowdies) of the late 1950s.[42] Especially the long hair of the drop outs "attacked the image of the masculine man; their untidiness was provoking bourgeois feelings of cleanliness; having no job and possessions they questioned the capitalist achievement-orientated society."[43]

An opinion poll taken by the Allensbach Institute in September 1967 disclosed that more than half of the interviewees were voting for compulsory measures to force the drop outs into regular work. Even within the more liberal-minded age group of the 16- to 29-year-olds, 45 percent supported this view.[44] When asked about the television program "*Herbst der Gammler*" (Autumn of the Drop outs), some people suggested putting the drop outs into workhouses. Others put forward the slogan "Off with his head" or underscored that Hitler would "have coped with these parasites in a different manner."[45] Thus, it comes as no surprise that in West Germany drop outs were often perceived as "riff-raff."[46] In the mid-1960s the contemporary work ethos, patterns of consumption, bourgeois virtues, and moral codes, as well as ideals of masculinity, were questioned by the drop outs. Moreover, all these imagined threats and uncertainties were further reinforced once the consumption of drugs spread.

Drug Consumption

The "Soft" Drug Scene

Until the first third of the 1960s, drug consumers, by and large, belonged to the health and medical professions such as doctors, pharmacists, or nurses. Moreover, some drug users were war veterans, who had been treated with morphine or had taken other stimulants, for instance amphetamines such as Pervitin.[47] However, according to West German police personnel in regard to drug offenses, in the years after 1968 "came the explosion."[48] As reflected in the statistics gathered by the West German police, the case was clear: in 1965, there were only 1,003 drug offenses registered, this number nearly doubled by 1968 to 1,891, and in 1970 more than 16,000 offenses had been registered.[49] After the Federal Drug Law (*Betäubungsmittelgesetz*) came into effect on 25 December 1971 and the crime statistics had been reformed, this upward trend continued, climbing as high as 62,395 offenses in the year 1980.[50]

Initially, drug consumption was spreading among the "better families," among high-school students, and among university students. By and large, the drugs consumed were "soft" drugs such as cannabis products (hashish and marijuana). Hallucinogenic substances like LSD and mescaline followed these cannabis products. Then came amphetamines such as Preludin or Captagon.[51] The climax of the so-called "drug wave" was reached in the early 1970s.[52] At the end of 1970, even the "smallest rural municipalities and district towns" had their drug scenes.[53]

In a representative survey by the EMNID-Institute in late 1969, three-quarters of the West German population were scared about the widespread consumption of drugs. Although alcohol was basically included in this term, the drugs that people meant were presumably hashish, marijuana, LSD, etc.[54] In the early 1970s, these attitudes did not become more liberal.[55] At the same time, drug consumers fell victim to public condemnation and stigmatization, with regard to the "bizarrely-dressed, long-haired addicts, people rashly sensed viciousness, something consciously criminal and abnormal."[56]

The police watched the rise of drug consumption with great apprehension. In its early phase, the dangers coming from drugs were attributed ethnical and even racial components. In the eyes of criminologists (especially from states of the former United States occupation zone), African-American US soldiers (as consumers and dealers) had imported the drug menace into Germany. The same was true of "guest workers."[57] Common interests and willingness given, a policeman stated, started "an infection resulted everywhere where there were points of contact between foreigners and Germans."[58] When drug consumption had become widespread, however, the blame could not simply be put on external influences. Nonetheless, a similar scenario reappeared in the early 1970s, when the police were trying to fight predominantly international drug traffic.[59] When drug consumption had developed into a "social problem,"[60] the police saw social norms and values, especially the work ethos, and the stability of the state and its economic order, threatened by the "mental disease" of drug consumption.[61] Some were even convinced that with the help of drugs the "will to crime" could be injected.[62] In the mid-1970s, drug scenes were sometimes seen as an "early phase of terrorism."[63]

As in the case of the drop outs in general, it was not the increasing numbers of drug consumers that caused widespread public attention; rather, the drug addicts' public appearance and their norms and values were what upset people. In contrast to the old "traditional" morphine consumers, the new drug youth of the 1960s did not hide in private places. Instead, collective drug consumption was celebrated in public spaces like the famous smoke-in in the West Berlin *Tiergarten* district. However, this was not merely a local but also an international manner of consuming drugs.[64] All this was possible because drug consumption was embedded into the networks of the underground. Roughly speaking, this underground consisted of different scenes: one scene centered more on political issues, and then there were the "soft" (hashish, marijuana) and the "hard" drug (heroin) scene. In this underground, a 1972 field study disclosed that until the latter third of the 1960s, there had been a "common consciousness of an extensive like-mindedness *despite* outer heterogeneity" supplied by "common basic positions *despite* different starting points and situations."[65]

Thus, from the mid- until the late-1960s, drug consumption was a collective activity among like-minded people.[66] The "ritual of the hashish community" was celebrated in the following manner. The joint was rolled in cigarette paper and held at an upright angle so that the contents would not crumble out of it. In order to prevent its cooling-off, the joint was embraced with both hands. After one or two individual drags, the joint was passed around. The circulating joint symbolized the sense of community, which should build the framework for each participant sharing with other participants their moods and feelings.[67] As Jakob Tanner defined it, this socially integrative and largely group-based drug consumption represented the central means to "experience and strengthen the sub-cultural cohesion."[68]

In West Berlin in 1967/68, the political activists of the "*Polit Szene*" and the "*Dope Szene*"[69]—the latter was not subdivided at that time—coexisted or even overlapped. This underground was concentrated in the city districts of Kreuzberg, Schöneberg, and parts of Tiergarten and Charlottenburg, in total an area of roughly sixty square kilometers with a high density of pubs and many big apartments.[70] Moreover, there was a "culture of people sharing apartments" (*Kultur der Wohngemein-schaften*)—only a few real communes existed at this time—some occupied houses and some run projects (for instance, cinemas, alternative youth clubs).[71] Also, there were left-wing playgroups (*Kinderläden*), drug support facilities (*Drogenhilfseinrichtungen*), publishing houses, and many district movements (*Stadtteilinitiativen*).[72] Within this underground, there existed a very high mobility. For a number of days, people would live in a shared apartment for a few days (*Wohngemeinschaft*), then switch to another or even sleep in public parks.[73]

Moreover, drug consumption and listening to rock music, often in underground pubs, were closely linked—not only in Germany. In retrospect, Inge Viett, a militant activist of the *Bewegung 2. Juni* (movement June 2nd), emphasized "shit and marijuana were part of our everyday life." Sometimes, LSD was consumed.[74] Till Meyer, also a militant activist of the *Bewegung 2. Juni* recalled the movement days similarly: "Lasting several hours, we listened, while consuming dope, to the music of Pink Floyd, Them or Deep Purple. We let ourselves stimulate by the Stones, Jimi Hendrix, Uriah Heep or Iron Butterfly."[75]

Drug consumption and drug traffic were not only suitable for testing one's entrepreneurial abilities but were also a means of supporting political ambitions. Until the early 1970s, many drug consumers were at the same time dealers and smugglers. Many middlemen showed an entrepreneurial spirit characterized by bourgeois ideals. They dreamt that later on they could start their own business with the money they had made in the drug trade.[76] The smaller dealers, however, imagined themselves more often as fighting for a revolutionary expansion of consciousness. Among the big dealers in Frankfurt in 1970, the spreading influence of the criminal underworld could be felt. At the same time complaints about the influence of "'down-and-out characters' 'conning' each other" *(von "'kaputten Typen,' die sich gegenseitig 'linkten'")* could be heard. During the 1970s, the increase of anti-drug law enforcement led to import, wholesale trade, and middlemen being cut off from each other. In 1978, the Berlin police department was sure to know that its opponents were mostly "foreign gangs."[77]

Police action against protesting students, and also pub raids, were instrumental in politicizing some members of the underground scenes.[78] Thus, in Berlin during the first half of 1969, the *Zentralrat der umherschweifenden Haschrebellen* (central council of roaming hash rebels) came into being. Its core members belonged to a commune in the Wieland Street—the so-called *Wielandkommune*—or had been part of the drop out scene.[79] Many political activists regarded drug consumption as a "useful tool" for political work. The leaflets of the *Zentralrat* referred positively to the consumption of drugs.[80] In the eyes of these "hash rebels," in particular the consumption of mind-expanding drugs was an "act of revolutionary disobedience."[81] In the latter part of 1970, 45 percent of the Frankfurt drug scene identified themselves with the model of the revolutionary, seeing drug consumption as a "revolutionary act."[82]

The early 1970s marked a multiple caesura in drug consumption and in its perception. From now on, more and more political activists declared themselves against the consumption of drugs.[83] The anti-drug congress initiated by the left journal *Konkret* in March of 1972 can be seen as the most visible expression of this transformation[84] that mirrored two developments, which have not yet been well researched. On the one hand, it can be seen as a change in norms and values of the political activists, which now changed from more hedonistic pleasure-oriented political style toward the more ascetic discipline of the emerging left-wing splinter groups—the more or less communist oriented "K-groups." Many of them followed the motto, "a true revolutionary could only be the one who with iron discipline succeeds in working for the revolution continuously."[85] This "puritanism" of such left-wing political groups was strongly criticized by members of the various drug scenes.[86] On the other hand, the disintegration of the underground was accompanied by a turning away from "soft" drugs (cannabis) and a turning to "hard" drugs (heroin).[87] At the same time, drug consumption lost the attraction of the particular and became integrated into every day life.[88]

All in all, the temporary homogeneity of the underground disintegrated during the late 1960s and the early 1970s. By the end of 1970, inside the drug scene of Frankfurt, there were hardly any "signs of the often cited solidarity." What was uniting these drug consumers, however, was a diffuse rejection of the state and its representatives.[89] Moreover, in Frankfurt, there was a trend for a "retreat out of society." Two-thirds of the members of this scene wanted to be left in peace.[90] They dreamt of a "life away from big city life" in farm communities.[91] The slang of the drug scene mirrored this depoliticization. Until the late 1960s *APO* had been relatively uniformly translated as *Ausserparlamentarische Opposition* (extraparliamentary opposition). But later, this interpretation competed with the abbreviation for *Apotheke* (Pharmacy), especially in connection with *APO-Bruch*, which stood for *Apothekeneinbruch*, i.e. a break-in into a pharmacy.[92] During the mid-1970s, inside the underground, the feeling of a "great frustration" was predominant.[93]

Even if, generally speaking, the political scenes and the drug scenes separated themselves from each other in the early 1970s, drug consumption still could give politicizing impulses. This was true in the case of the grass-roots self-help organization "Release," originally founded in London in 1967. Beginning in the latter part of 1970, in Hamburg and later in Berlin, members of the "Release" organization became politicized by the dogged and long-lasting negotiations with the local state authorities.[94] Moreover, in the *Sozialistische Patientenkollektiv* Heidelberg (SPK, socialist patients' collective), which existed from February 1970 until July 1971, drug consumption was still inseparable from political activities.[95]

Additionally, the consumption of drugs evolved out of the narrow political and drug scenes and became part of youth music culture. This link between delinquent and mainstream youth cultures can be demonstrated by the hashish experiences of a later heroin consumer. Reminiscing about a Deep Purple rock concert during the early 1970s, he remarked, "sometimes a pipe was passed. I took a drag, but basically I did not know what it was about. At one point, I got a circulatory collapse and then I realized that something had been in this pipe."[96] Thus, it is quite apparent that music pubs and rock concerts were still important places for drug consumption.[97] At any rate, in the pop culture of the late 1960s and early 1970s drugs and music built a close symbiosis. Many beat and rock bands had had drug experiences and admitted to them,[98]—it comes as no surprise that many rock lyrics were about drugs.[99]

The Heroin Scene

As we have seen, the long-haired hippie type of cannabis consumer was the main object of police and press perceptions of drug consumers of the late 1960s. From the early 1970s onwards, however, this picture changed. The heroin "junkie" became the folk-devil of this decade. What was neglected in these debates, however, was the existence of the socially integrated heroin consumers who lived a normal life without ever coming into contact with the police.[100] These heroin consumers were not the type of "either-or"-consumer dominating in the literature, who after he or she had tried heroin three or four times will inevitably become addicted. Because of a lack of sources, this essay must concentrate on those heroin consumers who came into contact with the police or other state agencies.

In the early 1970s, drug consumption (especially of heroin) spread among junior high school students and among students of vocational schools. In these years, in Germany's metropolitan cities the "soft" and the "hard" drug scenes finally separated from each other, even though there were still some overlapping networks based on personal contacts.[101] Thus, an independent "hard" drug scene came into being. Until 1972, in Hamburg as well as in Berlin, the consumption of heroin was not widespread. In the following year, however, a change became visible.[102] In general, when compared to hashish consumption, heroin consumption was more widespread among the lower stratums of society. In its early phase, politicized inmates of reformatories consumed in particular heroin.[103] From the mid-1970s, the heroin scenes were not concentrated in the inner cities but were also to be found in the suburbs. While soft drugs were at least sometimes consumed publicly or in pubs, heroin consumption was hidden in non-public places or in private apartments.[104] There were different ways of consuming heroin—not every heroin consumer injected the drug. In the early 1970s in Hamburg injecting heroin enjoyed a good reputation but this changed in the following years.[105] In North Rhine-Westphalia, a similar development occurred, when sniffing heroin through the nose became more widespread during the 1970s.[106]

Police statistics can give the impression that heroin consumption was expanding in the early 1970s. In 1970, in the whole of West Germany, the police had taken possession of as little as half a kilogram of heroin. Three years later, this amount reached roughly 15.5 kg and jumped to 167 kg in 1976.[107] At the same time, the number of dead drug consumers was increasing steadily from 29 in 1970 up to 623 in 1979[108]— a number that would not be reached again until the late 1980s.[109] Until the early 1970s, heroin from pharmacy break-ins was plentiful enough to meet the demands of the heroin market.[110] Later, the market became gradually more organized from above and became dominated by international gangs and wholesale dealers. If one follows police interpretations, mainly Turks and citizens from Arabian states dominated the drug trade—at least in West Berlin. Being used to think in strictly hierarchical categories, the Berlin police, however, emphasized that there were no "big bosses, leading big mafia-type organizations."[111]

Even if some authors paint a dark picture of the demise of the drug subculture in the early 1970s,[112] by no means all heroin consumers shared such an impression. The question why the consumption of heroin was held in high esteem can be answered when we look at how heroin consumers described the effects of the drug. Compared with the collectivity of the consumption of "soft" drugs, heroin consumption was individualized and scarcely group-based at all. Heroin consumers, especially during the initial phase, staged their first shootings individually. They either carried the syringe (their "gun") in black wooden boxes lined with fine red satin or—in a more masculine rough way—kept the syringes in the walls of their rooms.[113] Moreover, the first injection of the "stuff" was also a test of courage, an initiation rite, some kind of a "masochistical satisfaction."[114]

After an injection of heroin, the fixer became completely rapt and uninterested in his environment. This "total concentration on the state of euphoria, which was independent from external things and which could not be steered," signaled a state of special feeling of well-being. It was this state (the "flash") that heroin consumers were striving for.[115] Even from a critical perspective, the heroin-induced state of euphoria had an "anarchistic attraction of an exploding self-destruction" or was felt, as a heroin user recalled, like an "orgasm in each cell."[116] The heroin scene was characterized by a cult of youthfulness. There were no models of behavior for being or getting old since most members of the heroin scene accepted that they would die young. Thus, planning for a distant future was not necessary. Heroin users cultivated a "sweet-short-life-ideology." Therefore this drug could bee seen as an expression of the spirit of the 1970s, a decade that was called an "age of narcissism."[117]

About 1977/78, social cohesion inside the "hard" drug scene hardly existed anymore. It was the time when the ragged, emaciated, and aggressive "junkie-type" addict began to dominate the scene.[118] At that time, some heroin consumers were very young, aged between 12 and 16.[119] In order to get money for their drugs, many female junkies began to prostitute themselves, while male junkies often committed thefts and burglaries.[120] Simultaneously, heroin junkies came more and more from the lower social strata. In 1979 in Berlin, 75 percent of the members of the heroin scene had no higher educational qualifications than a junior high school diploma.[121] All in all, the late 1970s drug scene was more and more molded by a type of consumer willing to consume every drug, "without ever thinking about 'mind-expansion.' The main thing is and was ... that the drug 'rumbled,' that means closing [and] shielding from the outside world and its problems."[122]

Concerning drugs, the late 1970s witnessed two developments. On the one hand, there was a renaissance of cannabis. This resurgence was strongly influenced by the interaction of reggae music and the Jamaican Rasta-mythology. Looking at its influence on youth culture (hairstyle, clothing, music, shops) in the late 1970s, it becomes apparent that Jamaican culture played nearly the same role Indian culture had played in the late 1960s.[123] On the other hand, together with the punk music scene of 1977/78, drug consumption got new impulses. This time "speed" (amphetamines) and LSD were consumed. Hashish was frowned upon. It was considered a "hippie drug."[124]

Working-Class Youth Gangs: Rockers

Working-class-based delinquency did not disappear in the 1960s. It was in cities like Hamburg, Berlin, or Essen in 1968/69 where the press, in particular the *Bild-Zeitung*, turned the "rockers" into a public threat— into real folk-devils. The interest, the rockers earned from the police and from the press lasted until the early 1970s.[125] Rockers were seen as the tip of an iceberg of ever-increasing juvenile delinquency and violence.[126] Press reports gave the impression that anybody could become the victim of the violent acts of rockers—anywhere, anytime. These impressions were supported by other press reports about the increasing level of juvenile delinquency and violence.[127] Thus, the rockers' case was an example of the breakthrough the term violence enjoyed in these years.[128]

When the Hamburg police force checked their card files of 150 rockers in the year 1970,[129] it was discovered that most of them were born in 1950 or 1951. Four-fifths of them had been pupils of junior high schools (*Hauptschüler*), of which roughly 50 percent had not earned any qualification.[130] Another sample of 100 convicted rockers indicated nearly two-thirds were unskilled, many of them pursuing only odd jobs.[131] Like the members of the underground, rockers did not meet in the traditional delinquent areas of the red-light districts or in the city districts close to the ports. Instead, their pubs were spread all over the city.[132] Some rockers lived in high-rise concrete-laden residential districts such as the *Märkische Viertel* in West Berlin.[133]

The rockers reimported the long hair of the contemporary drop outs into their rough working-class outfit, wore black leather jeans and jackets, heavy boots and later also rode motorcycles. They gave their groups names like "Bloody Devils," "Hells Dogs," "Black Souls" or "Hells Angels."[134] The rockers showed off an aggressive pattern of masculinity with which they distinguished themselves from all actual social tendencies, which they considered would lead toward softness and femaleness. Therefore, they often attacked homosexuals and disliked "soft" hashish smokers.[135]

The rockers of the late 1960s, who resembled the *Halbstarke* of the late 1950s only in a limited sense, were a working-class component of contemporary youth delinquency in West Germany.[136] Their provocative appearance with their rough and aggressive masculinity was reinforced by their usage of Nazi symbols. On their jackets they displayed swastikas, skulls, and SS-runes. Furthermore, they wore steel helmets of the Nazi *Wehrmacht*. Thus—consciously or not—they tried to provoke their parents, the police, and German society as a whole with symbols of the Nazi past. Most of the rockers had tattoos on their bodies—often Nazi symbols and pop-cultural images like names of rock bands stood side by side. Nonetheless, police sources and sociological studies indicated that the rockers held no sympathies for a national socialist party or its ideology,[137] regardless of the fact that comradeship and trust enjoyed a high esteem among them.

In the early 1970s, the big gangs of rockers dissolved and only small groups were left. Simultaneously the clothing style of the rockers began to change toward a more civilian disposition: they wore leather vests, jackets with leather fringes, and jeans jackets with inscriptions. The Hamburg police approached this end of old certainties by "inventing" a new group of juvenile delinquents. They were "outwardly totally inconspicuous, in their group behavior and performance," however, they were "threateningly similar" to the rockers. Beginning in early 1972 this " *Tätertyp nach 'Rockerart*'" (a perpetrator-type quasi-rockeresque) was also labeled as "young violent offenders" (*Junge Gewalttäter*).[138]

This definition made it easy for the police to include young delinquent boys and girls who wore ordinary clothes. As a consequence, the numbers of "young violent offenders" skyrocketed from 563 in 1971 up to 1,909 in 1972.[139] This example underscores the close relationship between youth (culture) and youth delinquency since changes in the way of dressing led to this redefinition. On the one hand, "normal" youth copied the leather clothing style of the rockers (the clothing industry had made this style palatable to non-rockers). On the other hand, rockers apparently integrated new styles into their outfits. Even without rockers, the threat of juvenile delinquency could be maintained by this widening of the definition. Since the police decentralized the perspective on delinquency its threat seemed to be omnipresent with deep roots in the society. Even a friendly, normally dressed boy next door could turn into a "young violent offender."

Conclusion

In West Germany during the 1960s and the 1970s, there were two important changes in youth delinquency and in its perception. First, from the mid-1960s delinquent behavior was no longer concentrated in its traditional centers such as red-light or port districts of the cities. At the same time, delinquency was reaching broader strata of society. The establishment of the international countercultural underground networks, of which the drop outs were the first harbingers, played an important role for this development. The underground saw its golden age in the last third of the 1960s, when drug consumption spread into and within upper- and middle-class youth.

The early 1970s brought a second impulse for this end to certainty about the social location of delinquency. As the case of the rockers has shown, from now on it was impossible to ascribe delinquency predominantly to abnormal individuals or some "animals." From the early 1970s, delinquency had become an omnipresent phenomenon of everyday life; it was lurking everywhere, in every niche of society. At the same time, the inner-city heroin scenes began to dissociate into the suburbs as well as into privacy.[140] The social threats and fears about delinquency were intensified by a trend toward proletarization, since rockers and many heroin consumers were of working-class origin.

At the end of this contribution, I would like to come back to the importance of studying the relationship between youth culture(s) and its delinquent opponents, which is demonstrated, for example, by changes in the dress code of the rockers of the early 1970s. Moreover, it should be stressed here that the cult of youthfulness and the sweet-short-life-ideology of heroin consumers can be seen as forerunners of lifestyles which spread in the 1970s. Thus, by studying delinquency (and crime) it may be true that we lose some certainties but we might also gain some insights into future social life.

Notes

1. Fritz Bauer, "Zur Jugendkriminalität," *Neue Sammlung* 7 (1967): 459. According to the "*Polizeiliche Kriminalstatistik*" the numbers of juvenile offenders (14- to under 18-year-olds) and adolescents (18- to under 21-year-olds) increased from 156,287 (1963) to 185,293 (1966) and up to 225,827 (1970), see Bundeskriminalamt, ed., *Polizeiliche Kriminalstatistik 1966/1968/1970 Bundesrepublik Deutschland* (Wiesbaden, 1967/1969/1971).
2. The terms *crime* and *delinquency* are defined by Manfred Brusten, "Kriminalität und Delinquenz als soziales Problem," in *Handbuch Soziale Probleme,* ed. Günter Albrecht, Axel Grönemeyer, and Friedrich W. Stallberg (Opladen and Wiesbaden, 1999), 507–55.

3. *Der Spiegel* 26, 1 January 1973, 64.

4. Compare Werner Lehne, "Zu den Konstruktionsprinzipien der polizeilichen Kriminalstatistik am Beispiel der Jugendkriminalität," in *Stadt, Jugendkulturen und Kriminalität*, ed. Wilfried Breyvogel (Bonn, 1998), 153–71.

5. For pioneering studies, compare Stanley Cohen, *Folk Devils and Moral Panics: The Creation of Mods and Rockers* (London, 1973) and Stuart Hall et al., *Policing the Crisis: Mugging, the State and Law and Order* (London, 1978).

6. Compare Frank Kebbedies, *Ausser Kontrolle. Jugendkriminalität in der NS-Zeit und in der frühen Nachkriegszeit* (Essen, 2000), 29. Detlev Peukert, *Grenzen der Sozialdisziplinierung. Aufstieg und Krise der deutschen Jugendfürsorge 1878 bis 1932* (Cologne, 1986); in an international perspective the changes in the meaning of "youth" are discussed by Eric Hobsbawm, *Das Zeitalter der Extreme. Weltgeschichte des 20. Jahrhunderts* (Munich, 1994), 408ff.

7. Compare Detlef Siegfried, "Vom Teenager zur Pop-Revolution. Politisierungstendenzen in der westdeutschen Jugendkultur 1959 bis 1968," in *Dynamische Zeiten. Die 60er Jahre in den beiden deutschen Gesellschaften*, ed. Axel Schildt, Detlef Siegfried, and Karl Christian Lammers (Hamburg, 2000), 588; for an overview compare Uwe Sander and Ralf Vollbrecht, eds., *Jugend im 20. Jahrhundert. Sichtweisen—Orientierungen—Risiken* (Neuwied and Berlin, 2000).

8. Trutz von Trotha, "Zur Entstehung von Jugend," *Kölner Zeitschrift für Soziologie und Sozialpsychologie* 34 (1982): 262.

9. For the debates on subcultures, scenes, and countercultures, compare Ken Gelder and Sarah Thornton, eds., *The Subcultures Reader* (London and New York, 1997); for the stimulating British discussions, compare John Muncie, *Youth and Crime. A Critical Introduction* (London, 1999).

10. Compare Gerhard Mäckelburg and Hans-Jürgen Wolter, *Jugendkriminalität in Hamburg 1963–1974* (Hamburg, 1975), 20.

11. In this essay, the term *drugs* includes cannabis products (hashish and marijuana), opiates (morphine and heroin), cocaine, LSD, mescaline, amphetamines, and barbiturates. Alcohol is not included. Problems of definition are discussed in René Renggli and Jakob Tanner, *Das Drogenproblem. Geschichte, Erfahrungen, Therapiekonzepte* (Berlin et al., 1994), 10–15.

12. There is one stimulating local study by Robert Stephens, "The Drug Wave. Youth and the State in Hamburg, Germany 1945–1975," (Ph.D. dissertation, University of Texas at Austin, 2001). Compare also Arthur Marwick, *The Sixties. Cultural Revolution in Britain, France, Italy and the United States c.1958–c.1974* (Oxford, 1998), 78, 480–496; Jakob Tanner, "'The Times They Are A-Changin.' Zur subkulturellen Dynamik der 68er Bewegungen," in *1968. Vom Ereignis zum Gegenstand der Seschichts-wissenschaft*, ed. Ingrid Gilcher-Holtey (Göttingen, 1998), 207–23.

13. Compare Christoph Klessmann, "1968—Studentenrevolte oder Kulturrevolution?" in *Revolution in Deutschland? 1789–1989*, ed. Manfred Hettling (Göttingen, 1991), 90-105; Klessmann calls it a "*Lebensstilrevolution*" (lifestyle-revolution), ibid., 99; compare also Axel Schildt, "Vor der Revolte: Die sechziger Jahre," *Aus Politik und Zeitgeschichte* 22–23 (2001): 13.

14. Jakob Tanner, "Cannabis und Opium," in *Genussmittel. Eine Kulturgeschichte*, ed. Thomas Hengartner and Christoph Maria Merki (Frankfurt am Main and Leipzig, 2001), quote on 245.

15. Jakob Tanner, "Rauschgiftgefahr und Revolutionstrauma. Drogenkonsum und Betäubungsmittelgesetzgebung in der Schweiz der 1920er Jahre," in *Schweiz im Wandel. Studien zur neueren Gesellschaftsgeschichte*, ed. Sebastian Brändli et al. (Basel and Frankfurt am Main, 1990), 399.

16. The sociological research has been reviewed by Axel Grönemeyer, "Soziale Probleme, soziologische Theorie und moderne Gesellschaften," in *Handbuch Soziale Probleme*, ed. Albrecht, Grönemeyer, and Stallberg, 13–72.

17. Compare Howard Becker, *Außenseiter. Zur Soziologie abweichendem Verhaltens* (Frankfurt am Main, 1973, orig. published in 1963), in particular 36–70. For drug legislation in Germany and the Netherlands compare Sebastian Scheerer, *Die Genese der Betäubungsmittelgesetze in der Bundesrepublik Deutschland und in den Niederlanden* (Göttingen, 1982).

18. Mark Abrams, *The Teenage Consumer* (London, 1959); see also the analysis of Marwick, *The Sixties*, 41–45 and 58f.

19. Compare Scheerer, *Die Genese der Betäubungsmittelgesetze*, 94; for England, compare Muncie, *Youth and Crime*, in particular 160–92.

20. Max M. Glatt, *The Drug Scene in Great Britain. Journey into Loneliness* (London, 1967); Horace Freeland Judson, *Heroin Addiction in Britain* (New York and London, 1973); Philip Bean, *The Social Control of Drugs* (London, 1974); Jonathon Green, *All Dressed Up. The Sixties and the Counterculture* (London, 1999), 108–12 and 173–201.

21. Cohen, *Folk Devils and Moral Panics.*

22. Compare Cohen, *Folk Devils and Moral Panics;* Paul Willis, *Profane Culture* (London, 1978); John Clarke, "The Skinheads Magical Recovery of Community," in *Resistance Through Rituals. Youth Subcultures in Post-War Britain*, ed. Stuart Hall and Tony Jefferson (London, 1975); Geoff Mungham and Geoff Pearson, eds., *Working-Class Youth Culture* (London, 1976).

23. For London of the late 1960s, compare Jock Young, *The Drugtakers. The Social Meaning of Drug Use* (London, 1971).

24. The volume edited by Schildt, Siegfried, and Lammers, *Dynamische Zeiten* (2000) represents the state of research on the 1960s in Germany.

25. Eduard Zimmermann, *Das unsichtbare Netz. Rapport für Freunde und Feinde* (Munich, 1969), 11 and 45.

26. Compare Karl-Heinz Reuband, "Veränderungen in der Kriminalitätsfurcht der Bundesbürger 1965–1993. Eine Bestandsaufnahme," in *Kriminologische Opferforschung. Neue Perspektiven und Erkenntnisse*, ed. Günther Kaiser and Jörg Martin Jehle (Heidelberg, 1995), vol. 2; Klaus Weinhauer, *Schutzpolizei in der Bundesrepublik. Zwischen Bürgerkrieg und Innerer Sicherheit: Die turbulenten sechziger Jahre* (Paderborn, 2003), 249f. Compare as an opinion poll *Allensbacher Berichte*, no. 19 (August 1971). Using these kinds of material, one must take into consideration that the problems investigated are not expressions of social realities, however they may be defined, but are constructed by the polls themselves.

27. Compare Weinhauer, *Schutzpolizei in der Bundesrepublik*, 251–62.

28. Compare the descriptions of Wolfgang Werner, *Vom Waisenhaus ins Zuchthaus. Ein Sozialbericht* (Frankfurt am Main, 1969), 41–45; Rosamunde Pietsch, "Die Jugendschutztrupps," in *Grundlagen der Kriminalistik*, ed. Herbert Schäfer (Hamburg, 1965), vol. 1, 126; compare also Kurt Falck, "Der Jugendschutz in Hamburg-Mitte," in ibid., 161–73.

29. For the term "underground," compare Walter Hollstein, *Der Untergrund. Zur Soziologie jugendlicher Protestbewegungen* (Neuwied and Berlin, 1969), 24–27 and 106–42; *Der Spiegel* 21, 9 June 1969, 142–55; for an international overview compare Marwick, *The Sixties*, in particular 489–92.

30. Compare Wolfgang C. Müller and Peter Nimmermann, *In Jugendclubs und Tanzlokalen* (Munich, 1968); Margarete Andrae, Hans Georg Buchholz, and Lutz Rössner, "Jugend in Beat-Lokalen," *Deutsche Jugend* 17 (1969): 545–52; and Rolf Pausch,

"Diskotheken. Kommunikationsstrukturen als Widerspiegelung gesellschaftlicher Verhältnisse," in *Segmente der Unterhaltungsindustrie*, ed. Hanns-Werner Heister et al. (Frankfurt am Main, 1974), 196–214. The atmosphere in such meeting points of the different scenes is described by Klaus Gerdes and Christian von Wolffersdorff-Ehlert, *Drogenscene. Suche nach Gegenwart. Ergebnisse teilnehmender Beobachtung in der jugendlichen Drogensubkultur* (Stuttgart, 1974), 133f.

31. For a summary, see Arthur Kreuzer, *Drogen und Delinquenz. Eine jugendkriminologisch-empirische Untersuchung der Erscheinungsformen und Zusammenhänge* (Wiesbaden, 1975), 137–49.

32. For the term "bricolage," see Dick Hebdige, *Subculture. The Meaning of Style* (London and New York, 1979).

33. Paul Nolte, *Die Ordnung der deutschen Gesellschaft. Selbstentwurf und Selbstbeschreibung im 20. Jahrhundert* (Munich, 2000).

34. Helga Cremer-Schäfer and Heinz Steinert, *Straflust und Repression. Zur Kritik der populistischen Kriminologie* (Münster, 1998), 87.

35. Joachim Hellmer, *Jugendkriminalität in unserer Zeit* (Frankfurt am Main, 1966), 9.

36. See Dieter Claessens and Karin de Ahna, "Das Milieu der Westberliner 'scene' und die 'Bewegung 2. Juni'" in *Analysen zum Terrorismus*, ed. Bundesministerium des Innern (Opladen, 1982), vol. 3, 103–6; good contemporary impressions are provided by Margret Kosel, *Gammler, Beatniks, Provos. Die schleichende Revolution* (Frankfurt am Main, 1967).

37. Compare Hans-Georg Jaedicke, "Die Gammler. Adoleszenten- und Gesellschaftsproblem," in *Neue Sammlung* 8 (1968); 87.

38. Compare Walter Hollstein, *Die Gegengesellschaft. Alternative Lebensformen* (Reinbek, 1981), 29; Claessens and de Ahna, "Milieu," in *Analysen zum Terrorismus*, vol. 3, 104; Kosel, *Gammler, Beatniks, Provos*, 81–116.

39. *Der Spiegel* 19, 19 September 1966, 72.

40. "Keine Toleranz für Gammler," *Deutsche Jugend* 16 (1968): 93. For the meaning of consumption in West German society of the 1960s, compare Wolfgang Ruppert, "Zur Konsumwelt der 60er Jahre," in *Dynamische Zeiten*, ed. Schildt, Siegfried, and Lammers, 752–67; for an overview, compare Hannes Siegrist, Hartmut Kaelble, and Jürgen Kocka, eds., *Europäische Konsumgeschichte. Zur Gesellschafts- und Kulturgeschichte des Konsums (18. bis 20. Jahrhundert)* (Frankfurt am Main and New York, 1997).

41. Hollstein, *Der Untergrund*, 38. Also, compare *Der Spiegel* 19, 19 September 1966, 72.

42. Compare Kaspar Maase, *Bravo Amerika. Erkundungen zur Jugendkultur der Bundesrepublik in den fünfziger Jahren* (Hamburg, 1992), 118–20.

43. Hollstein, *Die Gegengesellschaft*, 12.

44. Compare *Allensbacher Berichte*, mid-July 1968, "Kein Platz für Gammler."

45. "Keine Toleranz für Gammler?," 93.

46. Ibid.

47. See Dieter Schenk, "Rauschgiftgefahren in der BRD?," in *Die Polizei* 59 (1968), 299–304.

48. "Bericht über eine Arbeitstagung des Polizei-Instituts in Hiltrup," *Kriminalistik* 25 (1971): 337.

49. Oskar Wenzky, "Bekämpfung der Rauschgiftkriminalität," *Kriminalistik* 26 (1972): 344. Compare Heinz-Günter Zimmermann, "Die Rauschgiftkriminalität im Spiegel der Polizeilichen Kriminalstatistik," in *Grundlagen der Kriminalistik*, ed. Herbert Schäfer (Hamburg, 1972), vol. 9, 239. In 1962, the police had taken possession of only 5.4 kg cannabis products (hashish and marijuana); in 1963, this increased to 38

kg; in 1968, to 381 kg; and in 1970, to 4,332 kg; in the same time period the quantity of LSD trips the police had taken possession of had increased from 10 (!) in 1967 to 178,925 in 1970.

50. Erich Strass, "Die Entwicklung der Rauschgiftkriminalität in der Bundesrepublik Deutschland," in *Polizeiliche Drogenbekämpfung*, ed. Bundeskriminalamt (Wiesbaden, 1981), 11.

51. Compare Josef Schenk, *Droge und Gesellschaft* (Berlin, 1975), 32f.

52. While in Hamburg in 1971, roughly 27 percent of students aged 14 years and older had experiences with drugs, in 1972, there were only 18 percent and in 1977, this quota dropped to 15 percent. See Karl-Heinz Reuband, "Zur Verbreitung illegaler Drogenerfahrung in der Bevölkerung der Bundesrepublik Deutschland—Versuche ihrer Messung im Rahmen der Umfrageforschung," in *Suchtgefahren* 32 (1986): 91; compare also Schenk, *Droge und Gesellschaft*, 28–32.

53. Walter K. Hausner, "Die Frankfurter Drogenscene. Beobachtungen bei jungen Drogenkonsumenten" (medical Ph.D. dissertation, Frankfurt am Main, 1972), 33.

54. *Emnid Informationen*, no. 2/3 (1970), 8–10. For good contemporary overviews, compare two articles in *Der Spiegel* 22, 10 November 1969, 76–102 and *Der Spiegel* 23, 10 August 1970, 38–56.

55. *Allensbacher Berichte*, no. 16 (1972), 6.

56. Wolfgang Schmidbauer and Jürgen vom Scheidt, *Handbuch der Rauschdrogen* (Frankfurt am Main, 1976), 158.

57. See Schenk, "Rauschgiftgefahren," 300. For much more differentiated study, compare Stephens, *Drug Wave*: in particular chapter 4. For racism in the late 1950s and early 1960s, compare Uta G. Poiger, *Jazz, Rock and Rebels. Cold War Politics and American Culture in a Divided Germany* (Berkeley and Los Angeles, 2000).

58. Schenk, "Rauschgiftgefahren," 300.

59. Compare note 110: Der Polizeipräsident in Berlin, *Der Rauschmittelmissbrauch in Berlin (West)* (Berlin, March 1980).

60. Günther Bauer, "Der gegenwärtige Rauschgiftmissbrauch aus der Sicht der kriminalistischen Praxis," in *Münchener Medizinische Wochenschrift* 112 (1970): 1562.

61. Herbert Schäfer, "Rauschgiftmissbrauch, Anarchismus und Terrorismus. Methoden der Selbstzerstörung," *Der Kriminalist* 6 (1978): 260.

62. Bauer, "Der gegenwärtige Rauschgiftmissbrauch," 1566 and 1568.

63. Schäfer, "Rauschgiftmissbrauch, Anarchismus und Terrorismus," 260. It remains an open question why the police did not address questions of gender and sexuality, which figured so prominently in public attention (especially in the media).

64. Michael 'Bommi' Baumann, *Wie alles anfing* (Munich, 1975), 50f. For England compare Green, *All Dressed Up*, 182f.; for the United States, David Farber, "The Toxicated State/Illegal Nation. Drugs in the Sixties Counterculture," in *Imagine Nation. The American Counterculture of the 1960s and '70s*, ed. Peter Braunstein and Michael William Doyle (New York and London, 2002), 17–40.

65. Gerdes and von Wolffersdorff-Ehlert, *Drogenscene*, 141 (emphasis in the original) and 365; see for the underground and its demise in London, Green, *All Dressed Up*, 113–27.

66. Horst Bieberstein, "Zur Situation der BTM-Kriminalität in Berlin," *Kriminalistik* 33 (1979): 251; compare also Peter Waldmann, *Phantastika im Untergrund* (Bonn, 1970), 28f.

67. Paul Schulz, *Drogenscene. Ursachen und Folgen* (Frankfurt am Main and New York, 1974), 49f.

68. Jakob Tanner, "Drogen und Drogenprohibition—historische und zeitgenössische Erfahrungen," in Rengli and Tanner, *Drogenproblem*, 119.

69. Baumann, *Wie alles anfing*, 33.
70. Claessens and de Ahna, "Milieu," 32–38; also, compare Ralf Reinders and Ronald Fritzsch, *Die Bewegung 2. Juni* (Berlin, 1995), in particular 11–26.
71. Claessens and de Ahna, "Milieu," 48.
72. Compare the descriptions in Till Meyer, *Staatsfeind. Erinnerungen* (Munich, 1998), 149f.; Gerd Koenen, *Das rote Jahrzehnt. Unsere kleine deutsche Kulturrevolution 1967–1977* (Cologne, 2001), 150–73.
73. In the summer of 1970, nearly one-fifth of the members of Frankfurt's local drug scene had no fixed abode, Hausner, *Frankfurter Drogenscene*, 34.
74. Inge Viett, *Nie war ich furchtloser. Autobiographie* (Hamburg, 1996), 76. A similar situation in Heidelberg is described by Margrit Schiller, *"Es war ein harter Kampf um meine Erinnerung." Ein Lebensbericht aus der RAF* (Hamburg, 1999), 27.
75. Meyer, *Staatsfeind*, 152. Examples from England can be found in Green, *All Dressed Up*.
76. For the following, compare Hausner, *Frankfurter Drogenscene*, 37 and 48.
77. Bieberstein, "Situation," 252.
78. For such police actions, compare Weinhauer, *Schutzpolizei*, 296–332; for pub raids, compare Reinders, Fritzsch, *Bewegung 2. Juni*, 22–27.
79. See Claessens and de Ahna, "Milieu," 106f.
80. See Baumann, *Wie alles anfing*, 51–54.
81. Meyer, *Staatsfeind*, quote on 151f.
82. Hausner, *Frankfurter Drogenscene*, 48.
83. Vgl. Jan Herha, "Erfahrungen mit Haschisch. Ergebnisse einer Befragung von 234 Konsumenten von Cannabis und anderen Drogen in Berlin (West) 1969/70" (medical Ph.D. dissertation, Berlin, 1973), 204; Claessens and de Ahna, "Milieu," 98f.; also Ronald Steckel, *Bewußtseinserweiternde Drogen. Ein Aufforderung zur Diskussion* (Berlin, 1969), quote on 116.
84. Compare the reader, *Konkret*, ed., *Sucht ist Flucht. Drogen- und Rauschmittelmissbrauch in der Bundesrepublik. Analysen, Berichte, Forderungen* (Hamburg, 1972).
85. Compare the critique of Herbert Stubenrauch, "Darf ein Linker LSD schlucken?," in *Spontan* (1973), quote on 48; and for the work of these political groups, compare Koenen, *Das rote Jahrzehnt*, 257–317 and 415–67. More critical about the everyday life of the political scene in Frankfurt is Ulrike Heider, *Keine Ruhe nach dem Sturm* (Hamburg, 2001).
86. Gerdes and von Wolfferdorff-Ehlert, *Drogenscene*, 187–91.
87. Tanner, "Drogen," 120. Compare also *Der Spiegel* 23, 10 August 1970, 38–56; Kreuzer, *Drogen*, 86.
88. Herbert Berger, Karl-Heinz Reuband, and Ulrike Widlitzek, *Wege in die Heroinabhängigkeit. Zur Entwicklung abweichender Karrieren* (Munich, 1980), 66.
89. Hausner, *Frankfurter Drogenscene*, 34.
90. Ibid., 63.
91. Ibid., 48.
92. Herha, *Erfahrungen*, 195.
93. Compare Gerdes and von Wolffersdorff-Ehlert, *Drogenscene*, quote on 83; also very impressive is Werner Gross, "Der Frust geht um," in *Spontan* (1976) 11, 8–11.
94. Compare the reports in Rolv Heuer et al., *Helft euch selbst. Der Release Report gegen die Sucht* (Reinbek, 1971).
95. On the SPK, see Butz Peters, *RAF. Terrorismus in Deutschland* (Munich, 1993), 101–3. Wanda von Baeyer-Katte, "Das Sozialistische Patientenkollektiv in Heidelberg," in *Analysen zum Terrorismus*, ed. Bundesministerium des Innern (Opladen, 1982), vol. 3, 183–316; also, compare Schiller, "Kampf," 26–39. See also Franz-Werner Kersting's contribution to this volume.

96. H. Peter Tossmann, *Haschisch-Abhängigkeit. Lebensgeschichten von Drogenkonsumenten* (Frankfurt am Main, 1987), 158.

97. For the early phase, compare Heinrich Heil, "Jugend und Marihuana," in *Grundlagen der Kriminalistik*, ed. Herbert Schäfer (Hamburg, 1965), vol. 1, 194–206; also Kreuzer, *Drogen*, 138.

98. For the terminology of music, compare Wolfgang Sandner, "Zur Definition von Pop-Rock-Beat," in *Musik und Bildung* 7 (1975): 266f.; Gotho von Irmer, "Popmusik und Rauschgift," in *Grundlagen der Kriminalistik*, ed. Schäfer (Hamburg, 1972), vol. 9, 161–77.

99. Green, *All Dressed Up*, 176f.; Tanner, "Times," 217f.

100. See J.U. Schlender and Charles D. Kaplan, "Die veränderte Heroin-Szene: Wissenschaftliches Konzept und resultierende politische Konsequenzen," *Kriminologisches Journal* 12 (1980): 35–45.

101. Kreuzer, *Drogen* (1975), 143–49.

102. See Herha, *Erfahrungen*, 199; Bieberstein, "Situation," 251; Stefan Aust, *Der Pirat. Die Drogenkarriere des Jan C.* (Munich, 1992), 91–96 and 136f. In Frankfurt in late 1970, an isolated fixer scene did not exist. Compare Hausner, *Frankfurter Drogenscene*, 34.

103. For the discussions, compare Berger, Reuband, and Widlitzek, *Wege*, 24–28; also *Der Spiegel* 22, 10 November 1969, 85; Gerdes and von Wolffersdorff-Ehlert, *Drogenscene*, 50f.

104. Wolfram Huncke, *Die Drogen-Jugend. Berichte, Analysen und Fakten über die Heroin-Abhängigkeit Jugendlicher* (Frankfurt am Main and Vienna, 1981), 81.

105. Kreuzer, "Aspekte," 100.

106. Berger, Reuband, and Widlitzek, *Wege*, 84, 88.

107. Günther Bauer, "Probleme der gewandelten Rauschgiftkriminalität," *Der Kriminalist* 4 (1978): 169; also Herbert Schäfer, "Der Rauschgiftmissbrauch aus (kriminal-) polizeilicher Sicht," *Die Polizei* 72 (1981): 109.

108. Strass, "Rauschgiftkriminalität," 15.

109. Arthur Kreuzer, *Jugend—Drogen—Kriminalität* (Neuwied, 1987), 15.

110. Kreuzer, "Kriminologische und kriminalpolitische Aspekte der Drogenproblematik. Erste Ergebnisse einer Erkundungsstudie," *Kriminalistik* 27 (1973): 100.

111. Der Polizeipräsident in Berlin, *Der Rauschmittelmissbrauch in Berlin (West)* (Berlin, March 1980), 15 and 21f.

112. Schulz, *Drogenscene*, 205.

113. For the following, see Berger, Reuband, and Widlitzek, *Wege*, 115 and 123.

114. Kreuzer, "Aspekte," 100.

115. Berger, Reuband, and Widlitzek, *Wege*, 81.

116. Heuer, *Helft euch selbst*, 45; Gerdes and von Wolffersdorff-Ehlert, *Drogenscene*, 269.

117. Christopher Lash, *Das Zeitalter des Narzissmus* (Hamburg, 1995, originally published in 1979).

118. Aust, *Pirat*, 178f.; Christiane F., *Christiane F.: Wir Kinder vom Bahnhof Zoo* (Hamburg, 1981), 197–202.

119. Christiane F., *Christiane F.*, 265f. It was controversial whether there was a general trend toward teenage heroin consumers, Huncke, *Die Drogen-Jugend*, 85.

120. Christiane F., *Christiane F.*, 272, Bieberstein; "Situation," 252f.

121. Huncke, *Die Drogen-Jugend*, 86.

122. Wolfgang Heckmann, Berlin's city official dealing with drug issues, commenting on this issue during the spring of 1981, cited in ibid., 199. Also, compare L. Barth et al., "Zur Entwicklung des Rauschmittelmissbrauchs in Berlin", in *Perspektiven der heutigen Psychiatrie*, ed. Helmut E. Ehrhardt (Frankfurt am Main, 1972), 174.

123. Compare Huncke, *Drogen-Jugend*, 94.

124. Jürgen Teipel, *Verschwende Deine Jugend. Ein Doku-Roman über den deutschen Punk* (Frankfurt am Main, 2001), 76f. For England, similar developments are reported by Jon Savage, *England's Dreamin. Anarchie, Sex Pistols, Punk Rock* (Berlin, 2001),175–77.

125. The state of research on the rockers is reviewed in Guenter Cremer, *Die Subkultur der Rocker. Erscheinungsform und Selbstdarstellung* (Pfaffenweiler, 1992); for an analysis of the press in Essen, compare Clemens Adam, "Rocker in einer Grossstadt des Ruhrgebietes. Ein Beitrag zur Jugendsoziologie" (social science Ph.D. dissertation, University of Bochum, 1972), 57–69; for a paradigmatic opinion poll, compare Staatsarchiv der Freien und Hansestadt Hamburg, Behörde für Inneres [Federal archive of the secretary for domestic affairs of the city of Hamburg, No. 824], *Infas Hamburg Report* (Bad Godesberg, 1974).

126. Adam, "Rocker," 62f.

127. *Der Spiegel* 26, 1 January 1973, 8, 15 and 22; *Konkret* (1972), 13.

128. Compare Cremer-Schäfer, Steinert, *Straflust*, 99f. and 117–22.

129. Compare Willibald Piesch, "Sind die 'Rocker' noch ein Problem?," *Kriminalistik* 24 (1970): 361–62.

130. Ibid., 362.

131. Arthur Kreuzer, "Rocker-Gruppen-Kriminalität," *Monatsschrift für Kriminologie und Strafrechtsreform* 53 (1970): 348.

132. Titus Simon, "Straßen-Szenen," in *Straße und Straßenkultur. Interdisziplinäre Beobachtungen eines öffentlichen Sozialraumes in der fortgeschrittenen Moderne*, ed. Hans-Jürgen Hohm (Konstanz, 1997), 270.

133. Peter Homann, "Marmor, Stein—Pflastersteine. Polit-Rocker in Westberlin," in *Konkret* (1969): 2, 12–15.

134. Compare Hans Jürgen Wolter, "Phänomene und Behandlung des Rockertums," *Kriminalistik* 27 (1973): 293.

135. Compare Kreuzer, "Rocker-Gruppen-Kriminalität," 339 and 352.

136. For literature on *Halbstarke*, compare Poiger, *Jazz*.

137. Compare the pictures and drawings in Kreuzer, "Rocker-Gruppen-Kriminalität," 351f.; also Wolter, "Phänomene," 289–95. For the political ideology of the rockers, compare Cremer, *Subkultur*, 179f.

138. Wolter, "Phänomene," 294.

139. Willibald Piesch, "Kriminalität junger Gewalttäter (Rocker) 1968–1973," *Kriminalistik* 29 (1975): 12.

140. It must still be analyzed how far this translocation was a reaction against police persecution.

Select Bibliography

Adam, Clemens. "Rocker in einer Grossstadt des Ruhrgebietes. Ein Beitrag zur Jugendsoziologie." Ph.D. dissertation, Bochum, 1972.

Anshelm, Jonas. *Mellan frälsning och domesdag. Om kärnkraftens politiska idéhistoria i Sverige 1945–1999.* Stockholm and Stehag, 2000.

Barnard, Stephen. *On the Radio. Music Radio in Britain.* Milton Keynes, 1989.

Brink, Cornelia. "Radikale Psychiatriekritik in der Bundesrepublik. Zum Sozialistischen Patientenkollektiv in Heidelberg." In *Psychiatriereform,* ed. Franz-Werner Kersting, 165–79. Münster, 2003.

Bundgaard, Peder. *Lykkens pamfil. Dansk rock i 60'erne.* Copenhagen, 1998.

Carter, Erica. *How German is She? Postwar West German Reconstruction and the Consuming Woman.* Ann Arbor, 1997.

Coleman, James S. *The Adolescent Society: The Social Life of Teenagers and its Impact on Education.* Glencoe, New York, 1961.

Confino, Alon and Rudy Koshar. "Regimes of Consumer Culture: New Narratives in Twentieth-Century German History." *German History* 19 (2001): 135–61.

Cremer, Guenter. *Die Subkultur der Rocker. Erscheinungsform und Selbstdarstellung.* Pfaffenweiler, 1992.

Cummings, Tony. "The Northern Discos." In *Rock File 3,* ed. Charlie Gillett and Simon Frith, 23–36. St. Albans, 1975.

Dreyfus-Armand, Geneviève et al., eds. *Les Années 68. Le temps de la contestation.* Brussels, 2000.

Dussel, Konrad. *Deutsche Rundfunkgeschichte.* 2nd ed. Konstanz, 2004.

Eberly, Philip K. *Music in the Air: America's Changing Tastes in Popular Music, 1920–80.* New York, 1982.

Eyerman, Ron and Andrew Jamison. *Music and Social Movements. Mobilizing Traditions in the Twentieth Century.* Cambridge, 1998.

F., Christiane. *Christiane F.: Wir Kinder vom Bahnhof Zoo.* Hamburg, 1981.

Farber, David. "The Toxicated State/Illegal Nation. Drugs in the Sixties Counterculture." In *Imagine Nation. The American Counterculture of the 1960s and 1970s*, ed. Peter Braunstein and Michael William Doyle, 17–40. New York and London, 2002.

Fink, Carole, Philipp Gassert and Detlef Junker, eds. *1968. The World Transformed.* Washington D.C., Cambridge, 1998.

Flügge, Sibylla. "1968 und die Frauen—Ein Blick in die Beziehungskiste." In *Gender und soziale Praxis*, ed. Margit Göttert and Karin Walser. Königstein, Taunus, 2002.

Foucault, Michel. *Politics, Philosophy, Culture: Interviews and Other Writings, 1977–1984.* New York, 1988.

Fourier, Charles. *L'Ordre subversif: trois textes sur la civilisation.* Paris, 1972.

Frank, Thomas. *The Conquest of Cool. Business Culture, Counter Culture, and the Rise of Hip Consumerism.* Chicago, 1997.

Frese, Matthias, Julia Paulus, and Karl Teppe, eds. *Die 1960er Jahre als Wendezeit der Bundesrepublik. Demokratisierung und gesellschaftlicher Aufbruch.* Paderborn, 2003.

Frith, Simon, *The Sociology of Rock.* London, 1978.

Frith, Simon and Andrew Goodwin, eds. *On Record: Rock, Pop and the Written Word.* London, 1980.

Frykman, Jonas. *Dansbaneeländet. Ungdomen, populärkulturen och opinionen.* Stockholm, 1988.

Gerdes, Klaus and Christian von Wolffersdorff-Ehlert. *Drogenscene. Suche nach Gegenwart. Ergebnisse teilnehmender Beobachtung in der jugendlichen Drogensubkultur.* Stuttgart, 1974.

Gilcher-Holtey, Ingrid, ed. *1968—Vom Ereignis zum Gegenstand der Geschichtswissenschaft.* Göttingen, 1998.

Greene, Jonathon. *All Dressed Up. The Sixties and the Counterculture.* London, 1999.

Hall, Stuart and Tony Jefferson, eds. *Resistance Through Rituals: Youth Subculture in Post-war Britain.* London, 1976.

Harris, Paul. *Broadcasting from the High Seas: The History of Offshore Radio in Europe 1958–1976.* Edinburgh, 1977.

Hebdige, Dick. *Subculture: The Meaning of Style.* London, 1979.

Henke, James, ed. with Parke Puterbaugh. *I Want to Take You Higher: The Psychedelic Era 1965-1969.* San Francisco, 1997.

Herbert, Ulrich, ed. *Wandlungsprozesse in Westdeutschland. Belastung, Integration, Liberalisierung 1945–1980.* Göttingen, 2002.

Herzog, Dagmar. "Antifaschistische Körper. Studentenbewegung, sexuelle Revolution und antiautoritäre Kindererziehung." In *Nachkrieg in Deutschland*, ed. Klaus Naumann, 521–51. Hamburg, 2001.

Hobsbawm, Eric. *The Age of Extremes: The Short Twentieth Century, 1914–1991.* London, 1994.

Hocquenghem, Guy. *Homosexual Desire.* Tr. Daniella Dangoor, intro. Michael Moon, preface (1978) by Jeffrey Weeks. Durham, NC, 1993.

Inglehart, Ronald. *The Silent Revolution. Changing Values and Political Styles among Western Publics.* Princeton, 1977.

Jamison, Andrew et al. *The Making of the New Environmental Consciousness. A Comparative Study of the Environmental Movements in Sweden, Denmark and the Netherlands.* Edinburgh, 1990.

Jensen, Steven L.B. and Thomas E. Jørgensen. "Studenteroprøret i Danmark." *Historisk Tidsskrift* [Copenhagen] 101 (2001): 435–70.

Josefsson, Sven.-O. *Året var 1968. Universitetskris och studentrevolt i Stockholm och Lund.* Gothenburg, 1996.

Juchler, Ingo. *Die Studentenbewegungen in den Vereinigten Staaten und der Bundesrepublik der sechziger Jahre: Eine Untersuchung hinsichtlich ihrer Beeinflussung durch Befreiungsbewegungen und -theorien aus der Dritten Welt.* Berlin, 1996.

Katsiaficas, George. *The Imagination of the New Left. A Global Analysis of 1968.* Boston, 1987.

Kersting, Franz-Werner, ed. *Psychiatriereform als Gesellschaftsreform. Die Hypothek des Nationalsozialismus und der Aufbruch der sechziger Jahre.* Paderborn, 2003.

Koenen, Gerd. *Das rote Jahrzehnt. Unsere kleine deutsche Kulturrevolution 1967–1977.* Cologne, 2001.

Kraushaar, Wolfgang, ed. *Frankfurter Schule und Studentenbewegung: Von der Flaschenpost zum Molotowcocktail 1946–1995,* 3 vols. Hamburg, 1998.

Kreuzer, Arthur. *Drogen und Delinquenz. Eine jugendkriminologisch-empirische Untersuchung der Erscheinungsformen und Zusammenhänge.* Wiesbaden, 1975.

Kroes, Rob. *If You've Seen One, You've Seen the Mall—Europeans and American Mass Culture.* Urbana, 1996.

Kroes, Rob, Robert W. Rydell and Doeko F.J. Bosscher, eds. *Cultural Transmissions and Receptions. American Mass Culture in Europe.* Amsterdam, 1993.

Kursawe, Stefan. *Vom Leitmedium zum Begleitmedium. Die Radioprogramme des Hessischen Rundfunks 1960–1980.* Cologne, 2004.

Langguth, Gerd. *Protestbewegung. Entwicklung—Niedergang—Renaissance. Die Neue Linke seit 1968.* Köln, 1983.

Lapassade, Georges and René Schérer. *Le Corps interdit: essais sur l'éducation négative.* Paris, 1976.

Laprouge, Benoît and Jean-Luc Pinard-Legry. *L'Enfant et le pédérastie.* Paris, 1980.

Lüdtke, Alf, Inge Marßolek, and Adelheid von Saldern, eds., *Amerikanisierung: Traum und Alptraum im Deutschland des 20. Jahrhunderts.* Stuttgart, 1996.

Luger, Kurt. *Die konsumierte Rebellion—Geschichte der Jugendkultur 1945–1990.* Vienna and St Johann, 1991.

Maase, Kaspar. *BRAVO Amerika: Erkundungen zur Jugendkultur der Bundesrepublik in den fünfziger Jahren.* Hamburg, 1992.

Martel, Frédéric. *The Pink and the Black: Homosexuals in France since 1968.* Tr. Jane Marie Todd. Stanford, 1999.

Martinov, Niels. *Ungdomsoprøret i Danmark. Et portræt af årene, der rystede musikken, billedkunsten, teatret, litteraturen, filmen og familien.* Copenhagen, 2000.

Marwick, Arthur. *The Sixties: Cultural Revolution in Britain, France, Italy, and the United States* c.1958–c.1974. Oxford, 1998.

Milestone, Katie. "Love Factory: the Sites, Practices and Media Relationships of Northern Soul." In *The Clubcultures Reader: Readings in Popular Cultural Studies,* ed. Steve Redhead with Derek Wynne and Justin O'Connor, 152–67. Oxford, 1997.

Muncie, John. *Youth and Crime. A Critical Introduction.* London, 1999.

Nelson, Elisabeth. *The British Counter-Culture 1966–73: A Study of the Underground Press.* New York, 1989.

Nichols, Richard. *Radio Luxembourg. The Station of the Stars.* London, 1983.

Nielsen, Henrik Kaare. *Demokrati i bevægelse.* Århus, 1991.

Nolte, Paul. *Die Ordnung der deutschen Gesellschaft: Selbstentwurf und Selbstbeschreibung im 20. Jahrhundert.* Munich, 2000.

Nordentoft, Johannes and Søren H. Rasmussen. *Kampagnen mod Atomvåben og Vietnambevægelsen 1960–72.* Odense, 1991.

Nowell, David. *Too Darn Soulful: The Story of Northern Soul.* London, 1999.

Nylén, Leif. *Den öppna konsten. Happenings, instrumental teater, konkret poesi och andra gränsöverskridningar i det svenska 60-talet.* Stockholm, 1998.

O'Dell, Tom. *Culture Unbound. Americanization and Everyday Life in Sweden.* Lund, 1997.

Ohlsson, Lars B. *Bilder av den "hotfulla ungdomen." Om ungdomsproblem och om fastställandet och upprätthållandet av samhällets moraliska gränser.* Lund, 1997.

Osgerby, Bill. *Youth in Britain since 1945.* Oxford, 1998.

Östberg, Kjell. *1968 när allting var i rörelse. Sextiotalsradikaliseringen och de sociala Rörelserna.* Stockholm, 2002.

Palladino, Grace. *Teenagers: An American History.* New York, 1996.

Pflieger, Klaus. *Die Rote Armee Fraktion—RAF.* Baden-Baden, 2004.

Poiger, Uta G. *Jazz, Rock, and Rebels. Cold War Politics and American Culture in a Divided Germany.* Berkeley, Los Angeles, and London, 2000.

Robinson, Deanna C., Elizabeth B. Buck, and Marlene Cuthbert. *Music at the Margins. Popular Music and Global Cultural Diversity.* Newbury Park, 1991.

Rochefort, Christiane. *Les Enfants d'abord.* Paris, 1976.

Rosenberg, Bernard and David Manning White, eds. *Mass Culture Revisited.* New York, 1971.

Ross, Kristin. *Fast Cars, Clean Bodies. Decolonization and the Reordering of French Culture.* Cambridge, MA, 1995.

Salomon, Kim. *Rebeller i takt med tiden. FNL-rörelsen och 60-talets politiska ritualer.* Stockholm, 1996.

Schérer, René. *Emile perverti, ou des rapports entre l'éducation et la sexualité.* Paris, 1974.

Schildt, Axel. *Moderne Zeiten: Freizeit, Massenmedien und 'Zeitgeist' in der Bundesrepublik der 50er Jahre.* Hamburg, 1995.

Schildt, Axel, Detlef Siegfried, and Karl Christian Lammers, eds. *Dynamische Zeiten. Die 60er Jahre in den beiden deutschen Gesellschaften.* Hamburg, 2000.

Schissler, Hanna, ed. *The Miracle Years: A Cultural History of West Germany, 1949–1968.* Princeton, NJ, 2001.

Schmidt, Gunter, ed. *Kinder der sexuellen Revolution. Kontinuität und Wandel studentischer Sexualität.* Gießen, 2000.

Sebbar, Leïla. *Le Pédophilie et la maman (L'amour des enfants).* Paris, 1980.

Siegfried, Detlef. "Modkultur, kulturindustri og venstrefløjen i Vesttyskland 1958–1973," *Den Jyske Historiker,* 101 (June 2003): 68–94.

———"Vom Teenager zur Pop-Revolution. Politisierungstendenzen in der westdeutschen Jugendkultur 1959 bis 1968." In *Dynamische Zeiten,* ed. Schildt, Siegfried, and Lammers, 582–623.

Siegrist, Hannes, Hartmut Kaelble, and Jürgen Kocka, eds. *Europäische Konsumgeschichte. Zur Gesellschafts- und Kulturgeschichte des Konsums (18. bis 20. Jahrhundert).* Frankfurt am Main and New York, 1997.

Staupe, Gisela and Lisa Vieth, eds. *Die Pille: Von der Lust und von der Liebe.* Berlin, 1996.

Stephens, Robert. "The Drug Wave. Youth and the State in Hamburg, Germany 1945–1975." Ph.D. dissertation, University of Texas at Austin, 2001.

Suominen, Tapani. *"Verre en Quislings hird." Metaforiska kamper i den offentliga debatten kring 1960- och 1970-talens student- och ungdomsradikalism i Norge, Finland och Västtyskland.* Helsinki, 1996.

Tanner, Jakob. "'The Times They Are A-Changin.' Zur subkulturellen Dynamik der 68er Bewegungen." In *1968. Vom Ereignis zum Gegenstand,* ed. Ingrid Gilcher-Holtey, 207–223. Göttingen, 1998.

———— "Cannabis und Opium." In *Genussmittel. Eine Kulturgeschichte,* ed. Thomas Hengartner and Christoph Maria Merki, 195–227. Frankfurt am Main and Leipzig, 2001.

Thomas, Nick. *Protest Movements in 1960s West Germany. A Social History of Dissent and Democracy.* Oxford and New York, 2003.

Thornton, Sarah. *Club Cultures: Music, Media and Subcultural Capital.* Oxford and Cambridge, 1995.

Trois milliards de pervers: grande encylopédie des homosexualités, Special Issue of *Recherches* 12 (March 1973).

Trommler, Frank and Elliot Shore, eds. *The German-American Encounter: Conflict and Cooperation between Two Cultures, 1800–2000.* New York, 2001.

Wala, Michael and Ursula Lehmkuhl, eds. *Technologie und Kultur: Europas Blick auf Amerika vom 18. bis zum 20. Jahrhundert.* Cologne, 2000.

Weeks, Jeffrey. *Sexuality and Its Discontents: Meanings, Myths, and Modern Sexualities.* London, 1985.

Weinhauer, Klaus. *Schutzpolizei in der Bundesrepublik. Zwischen Bürgerkrieg und Innerer Sicherheit: Die turbulenten sechziger Jahre.* Paderborn, 2003.

Wicke, Peter. *Von Mozart zu Madonna. Eine Kulturgeschichte der Popmusik.* Frankfurt am Main 2001.

Wiggershaus, Rolf. *The Frankfurt School: Its History, Theories and Political Significance.* Trans. Michael Robertson. Cambridge, 1994.

Wir warn die stärkste der Partein. Erfahrungsberichte aus der Welt der K-Gruppen. Berlin, 1977.

Young, Jock. *The Drugtakers. The Social Meaning of Drug Use.* London, 1971.

Zinnecker, Jürgen. *Jugendkultur 1940–1985.* Opladen, 1987.

Notes on Contributors

Julian Bourg is Assistant Professor of History at Bucknell University. He is editor of *After the Deluge: New Perspectives on the Intellectual and Cultural History of Postwar France* (2004), and author of *Forbidden to Forbid: May 1968 and the Turn to Ethics in Contemporary France* (forthcoming). He is currently working on the late Foucault.

Barry M. Doyle is a Reader in History, University of Teesside, Middlesbrough, UK. He specializes in twentieth-century British history, particularly urban politics, popular culture, and cinema. He has published numerous articles including "The Changing Functions of Urban Government: Councillors, Officials and Pressure Groups, 1835–1950," in *The Cambridge Urban History of Britain: Volume 3*, ed. M.J. Daunton (2000), 287–313 and "The Geography of Cinema Going in Great Britain, 1934–94: A Comment," *Historical Journal of Film, Radio, and Television* 22: 4 (March 2003).

Konrad Dussel is Professor of Contemporary History at the University of Mannheim. He is mainly working on media and cultural history and the history of Southwestern Germany in the nineteenth and twentieth centuries. He is the author of *Deutsche Tagespresse im 19. und 20. Jahrhundert* (2004) and *Deutsche Rundfunkgeschichte* (2nd vol., 2004).

Thomas Etzemüller is Associate Professor of Contemporary History at the University of Oldenburg and has specialized in German and Swedish history in the twentieth century, cultural history, discourse analysis, as well as in the theory and history of historiography. His latest publications include *Sozialgeschichte als politische Geschichte. Werner Conze und* *die Neuorientierung der westdeutschen Geschichtswissenschaft nach 1945* (2001) and *Ein "Riß" in der Geschichte? Gesellschaftlicher Umbruch und 68er-Bewegungen in Deutschland und Schweden* (2005).

Dagmar Herzog is the recipient of awards from the Ford Foundation, the American Council of Learned Societies, the Social Science Research Council, and the Andrew W. Mellon Foundation. She has taught at Harvard and Michigan State Universities and will be joining the faculty of the City University of New York-Graduate Center in 2005. Her major publications include *Intimacy and Exclusion: Religious Politics in Pre-Revolutionary Baden* (1996), *Sexuality and German Fascism* (2004), and *Sex after Fascism: Memory and Morality in Twentieth-Century Germany* (2005).

Steven L.B. Jensen received his MA in History from the University of Copenhagen. Afterwards he took his MSc in Second World War Studies at the University of Edinburgh and currently works as Program Officer at UNAIDS in Geneva. He is the editor of *Genocide: Cases, Comparisons, and Contemporary Debates* (2003). Along with Thomas Ekman Jørgensen he is preparing a book on the *Student Revolt in Denmark 1968* (expected in late 2005).

Thomas Ekman Jørgensen received his PhD in History from the European University Institute in Florence for a dissertation on the Left in Denmark and Sweden in the postwar period. His publications include *West European Communism after Stalinism* (EUI Working Paper 2002/4, with Maud Bracke) and *Studenteroprøret i Danmark 1968* ("The Student Revolt in Denmark 1968"—forthcoming, with Steven L.B. Jensen). Current research interests are totalitarian movements and political behavior/identity.

Franz-Werner Kersting is Research Associate at the Westfälisches Institut für Regionalgeschichte in Münster and Professor of Modern and Contemporary History at the University of Münster. His areas of research include the history of youth, psychiatry, urban and rural societies as well as the history of West Germany and international relations. Among his recent publications are *Psychiatriereform als Gesellschaftsreform. Die Hypothek des Nationalsozialismus und der Aufbruch der sechziger Jahre* (ed., 2003) and "Helmut Schelskys 'Skeptische Generation' von 1957. Zur Publikations- und Wirkungsgeschichte eines Standardwerkes," *Vierteljahrshefte für Zeitgeschichte* 50 (2002).

Rob Kroes is Professor and Chair of the American Studies program at the University of Amsterdam. His research interests are in transatlantic relations in the cultural, social, and political spheres. Among his recent publications are: *If You've Seen One, You've Seen the Mall—Europeans and American Mass Culture* (1996); *Them and Us—Questions of Citizenship in a Globalizing World* (2000), and with R.W. Rydell: *The Americanization of the World?* (forthcoming)

Arthur Marwick is Emeritus Professor of History at the Open University, UK. His research refers particularly to the following groups of topics: the cultural revolution of the long sixties, total war and social and cultural change, history of human beauty, purposes and methods of history. He is the author of *The Sixties: Cultural Revolution in Britain, France, Italy, and the United States, c.1958–c.1974* (1998), and *A History of Human Beauty* (2004).

Wilfried Mausbach is an Assistant Professor of History at the University of Heidelberg and a Research Fellow of the Volkswagen Foundation. He is the author of *Zwischen Morgenthau und Marshall: Das wirtschaftspolitische Deutschlandkonzept der USA 1944–1947* (1996), co-editor of *America, the Vietnam War, and the World. Comparative and International Perspectives* (2003), and an adjunct editor of *The United States and Germany in the Era of the Cold War, 1945–1990. A Handbook*, 2 vols. (2004). He is currently working on a book about Germany and the Vietnam War.

Henrik Kaare Nielsen is Associate Professor at the Institute for Aesthetic Studies, Aarhus University, Denmark. His work deals with topics such as theory of modernity, theory of modern culture, democracy, and social movements. His major publications include *Kultur og modernitet* (1993) and *Kritisk teori og samtidsanalyse* (2001).

Uta G. Poiger is Associate Professor of History and Adjunct Associate Professor of Women's Studies at the University of Washington, Seattle. She is the author of *Jazz, Rock, and Rebels: Cold War Politics and American Culture in a Divided Germany* (2000), and co-editor of *Transactions, Transgressions, Transformations: American Culture in Western Europe and Japan* (2000). Current projects include studies on the modern girl in Germany from the 1920s to the 1950s, and on the politics of consumption and international relations in twentieth-century Germany.

Axel Schildt is Professor of Modern History at the University of Hamburg and Director of the Forschungsstelle für Zeitgeschichte in Hamburg. He is the author of *Moderne Zeiten. Freizeit, Massenmedien und Zeitgeist in der Bundesrepublik der 50er Jahre* (1995) and a co-editor of *Modernisierung im Wiederaufbau. Die westdeutsche Gesellschaft der 50er Jahre* (1998) and *Dynamische Zeiten. Die 60er Jahre in den beiden deutschen Gesellschaften* (2nd ed., 2003).

Detlef Siegfried is Associate Professor of Modern German History at the University of Copenhagen and Research Fellow at the Forschungsstelle für Zeitgeschichte in Hamburg. His major publications include *Der Fliegerblick. Intellektuelle, Radikalismus und Flugzeugproduktion bei Junkers 1914 bis 1934* (2001) and, as co-editor, *Dynamische Zeiten. Die 60er Jahre in den beiden deutschen Gesellschaften* (2nd ed., 2003). He is currently writing a book on consumption and politics in the West German 1960s.

Klaus Weinhauer is a Research Fellow at the University of Bielefeld. He is currently working on a comparative study of juvenile drug consumption in West Berlin and London in the 1960s and 1970s. Among his recent publications are *Schutzpolizei in der Bundesrepublik. Zwischen Bürgerkrieg und Innerer Sicherheit: Die turbulenten sechziger Jahre* (2003) and "Terrorismus in der Bundesrepublik der 1970er Jahre: Aspekte einer Sozial- und Kulturgeschichte der Inneren Sicherheit," *Archiv für Sozialgeschichte* 44 (2004).

Peter Wicke is Professor of Theory and History of Popular Music at the Humboldt University of Berlin, where he also directs the Center of Popular Music, and Adjunct Research Professor at the Carleton University of Ottawa. His research interests are in theoretical, historical, and political aspects of popular music. Among his recent publications are *Music and Cultural Theory* (1997, with J. Shepherd); *Von Mozart zu Madonna. Eine Kulturgeschichte der Popmusik* (2001), and *Handbuch der Musik im 20. Jahrhundert, vol. 8: Rock und Popmusik* (2001).

Index

Lightning Source UK Ltd.
Milton Keynes UK
UKOW03f1325031113

220305UK00001B/3/A